EXPLORATIONS IN THE HISTORY OF SOUTH ASIA

SOUTH ASIA INSTITUTE, NEW DELHI BRANCH
HEIDELBERG UNIVERSITY
SOUTH ASIAN STUDIES NO. XXXVI

Explorations in the History of South Asia

Essays in Honour of Dietmar Rothermund

Edited by

GEORG BERKEMER   TILMAN FRASCH
HERMANN KULKE   JÜRGEN LÜTT

MANOHAR
2001

First published 2001

ISBN 81-7304-377-9

Published by
Ajay Kumar Jain for
Manohar Publishers & Distributors
4753/23 Ansari Road, Daryaganj
New Delhi 110002

Printed at
Rajkamal Electric Press
B 35/9 GT Karnal Road Indl. Area
Delhi 110033

Contents

The Man and His Work

State, Court and Religion in Pre-modern Contexts

India's Colonial Experience

Preface

Already seven years ago, when he celebrated both his sixtieth birthday and the twenty-fifth anniversary of his holding the Chair of South Asian History at the South Asia Institute of Heidelberg University (SAI), Dietmar Rothermund thought it the proper occasion to take stock of his life's work, thus following the Indian tradition of *śaṣṭipūrti* and. But his colleagues at the Institute as well as his students soon experienced that in the seven years to follow he did not simply look back on his many achievements. He rather entered upon a number of new ventures. Untiringly, he pursues his teaching and research duties, takes part in the academic bodies at the Institute and the Faculty, besides being member of several international institutions which are dedicated to South Asia-related research or European-South Asian dialogue.

His friends, colleagues and pupils who now, at the eve of his final retirement, dedicate a Felicitation Volume to him. Too late to adorn the birthday it was intended for, but still in the full awareness that none of the academic *rites de passage* will lead Dietmar Rothermund to enter upon the existence of a *vanaprastha* – forest-dweller – and not even dare to think of a *sannyasin*-Rothermund. But it is their desire to express with this Felicitation Volume their deep-felt gratitude, personal reverence and appreciation for his merits in the field of South Asian History, a subject he established as an academic discipline for the first time in Germany when he became a full professor in 1968.

In a time when globalization of knowledge on the one hand and expense-cuttings in academic research pose new challenges to this discipline, the Felicitation Volume is also meant to display Dietmar Rothermund's ponderous contribution to the field of South Asian History in Germany and his efforts to bring it into cooperation beyond national or disciplinary boundaries. In doing so, the importance of academic research in South Asian History becomes more than obvious. Dietmar Rothermund was among the founding-fathers of the "European Conference of Modern South Asian Studies", the 16th meeting of which will take place in Edinburgh in September 2000. These conferences, which perhaps has become Europe's foremost contribution in the field of Modern South Asian research, emerged from a successful symposium organised by Dietmar Rothermund in Bad Herrenalb (Black Forest) in 1966. In 1972, he became Speaker of the German Research Council's new Special Research Programme 16 "South Asia". In 1980, he initiated the meeting of those scholars working on extra-European History on the eve of the German History Congress (Deutscher Historikertag); besides he coordinates the attempt to make panels on extra-European History a regular part of the Historikertag. In trying to strengthen the position of extra-European History in academic research and school curricula, he started editing the Yearbook of Extra-European History *Periplus* (since 1991). Not confining research to the academic field alone, he introduced the "Heidelberger Südasien-Gespräche" as a platform for communication between the South Asia Institute's academic staff and representatives from Germany's politics, business and public administration. Since 1988, he is member of the "Network on the History of European Expansion" sponsored by the European Science Foundation, and between 1991 and 1998, he again acted as Speaker of the German Research Foundation's new Special Research Project "Transformationen der europäischen Expansion vom 15. bis zum 18. Jahrhundert" (Transformations in the course of European expansion between the 15th and the 18th century). In 1996, he was elected chairman of the "European Association of South Asian Studies" (EUROSAS).

Despite the many administrative activities, of which, in fact, only a small selection could be mentioned here, research and teaching stood in the middle of his academic activities. More than 30 dissertations and about 45 monographs give ample witness to that. Two main themes can be detected in his writings: Initially, he concentrated on political history such as the Indian National Congress (*Die politische Willensbildung in Indien, 1900–1960*, 1965; *Phases of Indian Nationalism*, 1970) and its key figure M. K. Gandhi (*Mahatma Gandhi*, 1989; rev. ed. 1997). Building upon that, he focussed on Indian economic history in the 19th and 20th centuries (*Government, Landlord and Peasant*, 1978; *Indian Economy under British Rule*, 1983; *An Economic History of India*, 1988). In the field of economic history, the question of the impact of the Great Depression on India and other colonies soon formed a new object of research (*Die Peripherie in der Weltwirtschaftskrise*, 1982; *India in the Great Depression*, 1992; *The Global Impact of the Great Depression*, 1996). His research on Indian history culminated in two books, the *Geschichte Indiens* (together with Hermann Kulke) which saw two German (1982, 1998) and three English editions (1986, 1990, 1998) besides an Italian translation (1991), and the comprehensive *Indien: Kultur, Politik, Wirtschaft, Umwelt. Ein Handbuch* (1996). In passing it may be added that in 1994, when the publication board of the "Kürschners Deutscher Gelehrtenkalender" for the first time compiled a version on CD-ROM and therefore allowed to include a list of publications, already at that time the space available was insufficient for a full list of Dietmar Rothermund's writings.

It is hard to imagine what a real retirement of Dietmar Rothermund in January 2001 will look like. For the years to come, the editors and contributors of this Felicitation Volume therefore prefer to wish him a persisting academic productivity besides good health and luck.

Georg Berkemer
Tilman Frasch
Hermann Kulke
Jürgen Lütt

A Bibliography of the Works of Dietmar Rothermund

Compiled by Georg Berkemer and Margret Frenz

1. Monographs

1961

The Layman's Progress. Religious and Political Experience in Colonial Pennsylvania, 1740–1770, Philadelphia.

1964

Studien zur Entwicklung in Süd- und Ostasien: Neue Folge, Frankfurt/Main/Berlin (Schriften des Instituts für Asienkunde in Hamburg 16).

1965

Die politische Willensbildung in Indien 1900–1960, Wiesbaden (Schriftenreihe des Südasien-Instituts der Universität Heidelberg 1).

1967

Der Freiheitskampf Indiens, 2. Auflage, Stuttgart (Quellen- und Arbeitshefte zur Geschichte und Gemeinschaftskunde 4251).

1968

Indien und die Sowjetunion, Tübingen (Forschungsberichte und Untersuchungen zur Zeitgeschichte 23).

1970

The Phases of Indian Nationalism and Other Essays, Bombay.

1976

Grundzüge der indischen Geschichte, Darmstadt.

1978

Europa und Asien im Zeitalter des Merkantilismus, Darmstadt (Erträge der Forschung 80).

Government, Landlord, and Peasant in India. Agrarian Relations under British Rule, 1865–1935, Wiesbaden (Schriftenreihe des Südasien-Instituts der Universität Heidelberg 25).

1979

Fünfmal Indien, München (3rd rev. ed. München 1990).

1980

Indien, Photos: Ursula und Willi Dolder, Text: Dietmar Rothermund, Luzern (2nd ed. Frankfurt am Main 1995).

1981

Asian Trade and European Expansion in the Age of Mercantilism, New Delhi.

1982

Geschichte Indiens (together with Hermann Kulke), Stuttgart (2nd ed. München 1998).

India, Photographs by Ursula and Willi Dolder, Text by Dietmar Rothermund, London.

Indische Geschichte vom Altertum bis zur Gegenwart: Literaturbericht über neuere Veröffentlichungen (together with Hermann Kulke et al., München (*Historische Zeitschrift*, Sonderheft 10).

1983

The Indian Economy Under British Rule and Other Essays, New Delhi.

1984

Gebrauchsanweisung für Indien, München.

1985

Indiens wirtschaftliche Entwicklung: Von der Kolonialherrschaft bis zur Gegenwart, Paderborn.

1986

A History of India (together with Hermann Kulke), London/Sidney/Totowa.

The German Intellectual Quest for India, New Delhi.

1988

An Economic History of India. From Pre-colonial Times to 1986. London/New York/New Delhi (2nd ed. 1993).

Buchers Indien: Tempel und Legenden, Photos: Jenner Zimmermann, Text: Dietmar Rothermund, München.

1989

Indische Geschichte in Grundzügen, Darmstadt. (1st ed.: *Grundzüge der indischen Geschichte*, Darmstadt 1976).

Mahatma Gandhi. Der Revolutionär der Gewaltlosigkeit. Eine politische Biographie, München 1989. München (2nd ed.: *Mahatma Gandhi. Eine politische Biographie*, München 1997).

1991

Mahatma Gandhi: An Essay in Political Biography, New Delhi (Perspectives in History 5; 2nd ed. 1998).

Storia dell'India (together with Hermann Kulke), trsl. M. Cristiani, Milano.

1992

Die Welt in der Wirtschaftskrise, 1929–1939, Münster etc. (Periplus-Texte 1).

India in the Great Depression, 1929–1939, New Delhi (Perspectives in History 6).

1993

An Economic History of India. From Pre-colonial Times to 1991. London (1st ed. 1988).

Staat und Gesellschaft in Indien, Mannheim etc. (Meyers Forum 15).

994

Geschichte als Prozess und Aussage: Eine Einführung in Theorien des historischen Wandels und der Geschichtsschreibung, München.

996

The Global Impact of the Great Depression, 1929–1939, London/New York.

997

History of India (together with Hermann Kulke), London/New York (1st ed. London/Sydney 1986).

Mahatma Gandhi. Eine politische Biographie, München (Beck'sche Reihe 1218; 1st ed.: *Mahatma Gandhi. Der Revolutionär der Gewaltlosigkeit. Eine politische Biographie*, München 1989).

1998

Delhi, 15. August 1947. Das Ende kolonialer Herrschaft, München (20 Tage im 20. Jahrhundert).

Geschichte Indiens. München (2nd ed.)

Mahatma Gandhi: An Essay in Political Biography, New Delhi (Perspectives in History 5; 1st ed. 1991).

2. Edited Works

1961

Rabindaranath Tagore in Germany: A Cross-Section of Contemporary Reports, New Delhi.

1973

South Asia Institute: The First Decade, 1962–1972 (together with A. K. Ray), Heidelberg (Bulletin of the South Asia Institute of Heidelberg University 1973).

1969

Mahatma Gandhi 1869–1969 (together with Eberhard Jäckel et al.), Bonn.

1975

Islam in Southern Asia: A Survey of Current Research, Wiesbaden 1975 (Beiträge zur Südasien-Forschung 16).

1978

Zamindars, Mines and Peasants: Studies in the History of an Indian Coalfield and Its Rural Hinterland (together with D. C. Wadhwa), New Delhi (South Asian Studies 9a and Dhanbad Research Project 1).

1980

Urban Growth and Rural Stagnation (together with Erhard Kropp and Gunther Dienemann), New Delhi (South Asian Studies 9b; Dhanbad Research Project 2).

1983

Die Peripherie in der Weltwirtschaftskrise: Afrika, Asien und Lateinamerika 1929–1939, Paderborn (Sammlung Schoeningh zur Geschichte und Gegenwart).

1984

South Asia Institute: The Second Decade (together with Siegfried Schwertner), Heidelberg (Bulletin of the South Asia Institute of Heidelberg University 1983/84).

1985

Regionale Tradition in Südasien (together with Hermann Kulke), Stuttgart (Beiträge zur Südasien-Forschung 104).

1986

Education and the Integration of Ethnic Minorities. Papers presented at a workshop held at Bad Homburg, Germany, 3.–6.6.1984 (together with John Simon), London/New York (A Publication of the International Centre for Ethnic Studies).

1990

Erste Heidelberger Südasiengespräche, Stuttgart (Beiträge zur Südasien-Forschung 135).

1991

Emporia, Commodities and Entrepreneurs in Asian Maritime Trade, C. 1400–1750 (together with Roderich Ptak), Stuttgart (Beiträge zur Südasien-Forschung 141).

Periplus 1991. Jahrbuch für außereuropäische Geschichte 1 (in cooperation with Willi Paul Adams et al.), Münster.

Regional Disparities in India: Rural and Industrial Dimensions (together with Suranjit K. Saha), New Delhi (Proceedings of the 10th European Conference on Modern South Asia Studies 2).

1992

Nationalstaat und Sprachkonflikte in Süd- und Südostasien (together with Dagmar Hellmann-Rajanayagam), Stuttgart (Beiträge zur Südasien-Forschung 149).

Periplus 1992. Jahrbuch für außereuropäische Geschichte 2 (in cooperation with Willi Paul Adams et al.), Münster.

1993

Periplus 1993. Jahrbuch für außereuropäische Geschichte 3 (in cooperation with Willi Paul Adams et al.), Münster.

South Asia Institute: The Third Decade (together with Siegfried Schwertner), Heidelberg (Bulletin of the South Asia Institute of Heidelberg University 1985/92).

1994

Indien: Kultur, Politik, Wirtschaft, Umwelt. Ein Handbuch, München.

Periplus 1994. Jahrbuch für außereuropäische Geschichte 4 (in cooperation with Willi Paul Adams et al.), Münster.

1995

Our Laws, Their Lands: Land Use in Modern Colonial Societies (together with Jap de Moor), Münster (Periplus Parerga 2).

Periplus 1995. Jahrbuch für außereuropäische Geschichte 5 (in cooperation with Willi Paul Adams et al.), Münster.

1996

Liberalising India. Progress and Problems, New Delhi (South Asian Studies 29).

Periplus 1996. Jahrbuch für außereuropäische Geschichte 6 (in cooperation with Willi Paul Adams et al.), Münster.

1997

Legitimacy and Conflict in South Asia (together with Subrata K. Mitra), New Delhi.

Periplus 1997. Jahrbuch für außereuropäische Geschichte 7 (in cooperation with Willi Paul Adams et al.), Münster.

1998

Periplus 1998. Jahrbuch für außereuropäische Geschichte 8 (in cooperation with Willi Paul Adams et al.), Münster.

1999

Aneignung und Selbstbehauptung. Antworten auf die europäische Expansion. Munich.

Periplus 1999. Jahrbuch für außereuropäische Geschichte 9 (in cooperation with Willi Paul Adams et al.), Münster.

3. Articles

1959

"Political Factions and the Great Awakening," *Pennsylvania History* 24, p. 4ff.

1960

"The German Problem of Colonial Pennsylvania," *Pennsylvania Magazine of History and Biography*, 84, p. 1ff.

"The Punjab Press and Non-Cooperation in 1920," *Indian History Congress. Proceedings of the 23rd Session*, Aligarh, p. 39–47.

1961

"Reform and Repression, 1907–1910," *Indian History Congress. Proceedings of the 24th Session*, Delhi 1961, p. 127–139

1962

"Bewegung und Verfassung. Eine Untersuchung der politischen Willensbildung in Indien, 1900–1950," *Vierteljahreshefte für Zeitgeschichte* 10, p. 126–48.

"Constitutional Reforms versus National Agitation in India, 1900–1950," *Journal of Asian Studies* 21, p. 505–22.

1963

"Lee Kuan Yew, der Gegenspieler in Singapur," *Indo-Asia* 5, p. 326–30.

"Nationenbildung in Indien," *Vierteljahreshefte für Zeitgeschichte* 11, p. 392–403.

1964

"Indonesien und die Weltpolitik," *Studien zur Entwicklung in Süd- und Ostasien*, Neue Folge Pt. 3., Frankfurt am Main (Schriften des Instituts für Asienkunde in Hamburg 16), p. 1–28.

1965

"Die Rolle der westlichen Bildungsschicht in den politischen Massenbewegungen in Indien im 20. Jahrhundert," *XIIe Congrés International des Sciences Historiques*, Rapport II, p. 163–76.

"Friedrich Schlegel and the Wisdom of India," in: Heimo Rau (ed.), *South Asian Studies*, New Delhi (Max Müller Bhavan Publications 2), p. 1–18.

"Three Systems of Higher Education: India, Germany, U.S.A," *Yearbook of the Max Müller Bhavan*, New Delhi, p. 17–36.

1966

"Die historische Analyse des Bodenrechts als eine Grundlage für das Verständnis gegenwärtiger Agrarstrukturprobleme, dargestellt am Beispiel Indiens," in: *Jahrbuch des Südasien-Instituts der Universität Heidelberg*, 1966, p. 149–66.

"Nehru and Early Indian Socialism," in: S. N. Mukherjee (ed.), *South Asian Affairs II. The Movements for National Freedom in India*, Oxford (St. Anthony's Papers 18), p. 98–111.

1967

"Geschichtswissenschaft und Entwicklungspolitik," *Vierteljahreshefte für Zeitgeschichte* 15, p. 325–40.

"The Bengal Tenancy Act of 1885 and its Impact on Legislation in other Provinces," *Bengal Past and Present* 86, p. 90–105.

1968

"Emancipation or Re-Integration. The Politics of Gopal Krishna Gokhale and Herbert Hope Risley," in: D. A. Low (ed.), *Soundings in Modern South Asian History*, London, p. 131–58.

"Indien im wechselnden Urteil der Sowjetunion," *Außenpolitik* 19, p. 437–46.

"Indien und die Sowjetunion. Handelsbeziehungen und Entwicklungshilfe," *Indo-Asia* 2, p. 247–60.

"Süd- und Südostasien," *Internationale Politik* 1962, p. 335–68.

"Südasien-Zentren an amerikanischen Universitäten," *Indo-Asia* 10, p. 174–82.

1969

"Chinas Einfluß in den Randgebieten Südasiens," *Internationale Politik* 1963, p. 401–5.

"Die begrenzte Neuorientierung Pakistans in der internationalen Politik," *Internationale Politik* 1963, p. 417–22.

"Die Grenzkonflikte Indiens und ihre Folgen für die Bündnisfreiheit," *Internationale Politik* 1963, p. 405–16.

"Gandhi als Phänomen der indischen Politik," in: *Aus Politik und Zeitgeschichte. Beilage zur Wochenzeitung "Das Parlament"* 10, p. 3–13.

"Gandhi als schöpferischer Politiker," in: Dietmar Rothermund et al. (eds.), *Mahatma Gandhi 1869–1969*, Bonn, p. 7–14.

"Government, Landlord and Tenant in India, 1875–1900," *Indian Economic and Social History Review* 6, p. 351–67.

"India and the Soviet Union," *Annals of the American Academy of Political and Social Sciences* 386, p. 78–88.

1970

"Bewegung und Verfassung. Eine Untersuchung der politischen Willensbildung in Indien, 1900–1950," in: Rudolf von Albertini (ed.), *Moderne Kolonialgeschichte*, Köln, p. 365–88.

"Constitutional Reforms versus National Agitation in India, 1900–1950," in: Dietmar Rothermund (ed.), *The Phases of Indian Nationalism and Other Essays*, Bombay, p. 116–43.

"Die historische Analyse des Bodenrechts als eine Grundlage für das Verständnis gegenwärtiger Agrarstrukturprobleme dargestellt am Beispiel Indiens," in: Rudolf von Albertini (ed.), *Moderne Kolonialgeschichte*, Köln, p. 293–309.

"Emancipation or Re-Integration. The Politics of Gopal Krishna Gokhale and Herbert Risley," in: Dietmar Rothermund (ed.), *The Phases of Indian Nationalism and Other Essays*, Bombay, p. 26–56.

"Ideologie und Machtkämpfe in Asien," *Internationale Politik* 1964–1965, p. 4–20.

"Impediments to 'Development from Below' in India's Economic History," *Asian and African Studies* 6, p. 47–73.

"Impediments to 'Development from Below' in India's Economic History," in: Dietmar Rothermund (ed.), *The Phases of Indian Nationalism and Other Essays*, Bombay, p. 221–48.

"Impediments to 'Development from Below' in India's Economic History," in: Martin Rudner (ed.), *Society and Development in Asia*, Jerusalem, p. 47–73.

"India's Silver Currency. An Aspect of the Monetary Policy of British Imperialism," *Indian Economic and Social History Review* 7, p. 351–67.

"India's Silver Currency. An Aspect of the Monetary Policy of British Imperialism," in: Dietmar Rothermund (ed.), *The Phases of Indian Nationalism and Other Essays*, Bombay, p. 249–66.

"Nehru and Early Indian Socialism," in: Dietmar Rothermund (ed.), *The Phases of Indian Nationalism and Other Essays*, Bombay, p. 65–80.

"Political Factions and the Great Awakening," in: D. B. Rutman (ed.), *The Great Awakening*, New York.

"Reform and Repression, 1907–1910," in: Dietmar Rothermund (ed.), *The Phases of Indian Nationalism and Other Essays*, Bombay, p. 83–92.

"The Bengal Tenancy Act of 1885 and its Impact on Legislation in other Provinces," in: Dietmar Rothermund (ed.), *The Phases of Indian Nationalism and Other Essays*, Bombay, p. 197–217.

"The Punjab Press and Non-Cooperation in 1920," in: Dietmar Rothermund (ed.), *The Phases of Indian Nationalism and Other Essays*, Bombay, p. 93–103.

"The Role of the Western Educated Elite in Political Mass Movements in India in the 20th Century," in: Dietmar Rothermund (ed.), *The Phases of Indian Nationalism and Other Essays*, Bombay, p. 144–62.

"Traditionalism and Socialism in Vivekananda's Thought," *Quest* 67, p. 34–8.

"Traditionalism and Socialism in Vivekananda's Thought," in: Dietmar Rothermund (ed.), *The Phases of Indian Nationalism and Other Essays*, Bombay, p. 57–64.

1971

"Süd- und Südostasien," *Internationale Politik* 58–60, p. 787–842.

"The Record of Rights in British India," *Indian Economic and Social History Review* 8, p. 443–61.

1972

"Marginalität und Elite in Entwicklungsländern," *Die Dritte Welt* 1, p. 15–22.

1973

"Freedom of Contract and the Problem of Land Alienation in British India," *South Asia* 3, p. 57–78.

"Impediments to 'Development from Below' in India's Economic History," in: Kulturabteilung der Deutschen Botschaft New Delhi (ed.), *German Scholars on India*, New Delhi (Contributions to Indian Studies 1), p. 245–67.

"Max Müller and India's Quest for a National Past," in: Heimo Rau (ed.), *F. Max Müller: 150th Birth Anniversary*, Bombay (Dialogue 1972/73), p. 53–62.

1974

"Nationalismus und Staatsbildung in Indien," in: Theodor Schieder (ed.), *Staatsgründungen und Nationalitätsprinzip*, München (Studien zur Geschichte des neunzehnten Jahrhunderts 7), p. 153–60.

"Probleme der deutsch-indischen Kulturbeziehungen," *Indo-Asia* 16, p. 26–35.

"Akkulturation und Herrschaft in Indien," *Zeitschrift für Kulturaustausch* 24(4), p. 42–6.

1975

"Indiens Verhältnis zu seiner Geschichte," *Indo-Asia* 17, p. 41–50.

"Regionale Schwerpunkte in der indischen Geschichte," *Indo-Asia* 17, p. 249–60.

1976

"Gebundene Gesellschaft: Soziale Schichtung und Emanzipation in Indien," in: U. Engelhardt (ed.), *Soziale Bewegung und politische Verfassung*, Stuttgart, p. 394–414.

"Koloniales Erbe und Wirtschaftsentwicklung in Indien," *Indo-Asia* 18, p. 140–6.

"The Land Revenue Problem in British India," *Bengal Past and Present* 97, p. 210–26.

1977

"A Survey of Rural Migration and Land Reclamation in British India, 1885," *Journal of Peasant Studies* 4, p. 230–42.

1978

"Europe and Asia in the Age of Mercantilism," *Yearbook of the Max Müller Bhavan 1978*, New Delhi, p. 87–96.

"Nationalismus und sozialer Wandel in der Dritten Welt – 12 Thesen," in: Otto Dann (ed.), *Nationalismus und sozialer Wandel*, Hamburg, p. 187–208.

"Recent Work on Indian History in the Federal Republic of Germany," *Yearbook of the Max Müller Bhavan 1978*, New Delhi, p. 81–6.

"Tenancy Legislation for Chota Nagpur: The Emphasis on Executive Protection," in: Dietmar Rothermund and D. C. Wadhwa (eds.), *Zamindars, Mines and Peasants: Studies in the History of an Indian Coalfield and Its Rural Hinterland*, New Delhi (South Asian Studies 9a; Dhanbad Research Project 1), p. 69–83.

"The Coalfield: An Enclave in a Backward Region," in: Dietmar Rothermund and D. C. Wadhwa (eds.), *Zamindars, Mines and Peasants: Studies in the History of an Indian Coalfield and Its Rural Hinterland*, New Delhi (South Asian Studies 9a; Dhanbad Research Project 1), p. 1–20.

1979

"Traditionalism and National Solidarity in India," in: R. J. Moore (ed.), *Tradition and Politics in South Asia*, New Delhi, p. 191–7.

1980

"Epilogue: Urban Growth and Rural Stagnation," in: Dietmar Rothermund, Erhard Kropp, Gunther Dienemann (eds.), *Urban Growth and Rural Stagnation*, New Delhi (South Asian Studies 9b; Dhanbad Research Project 2), p. 453–63.

"The Great Depression and British Financial Policy in India, 1929–1934," *The Indian Economic and Social History Review* 17.

1981

"British Foreign Trade Policy in India during the Great Depression, 1929–1939," *Indian Economic and Social History Review* 18, p. 349–76.

"Indiens Zukunft," *Indo-Asia* 23, p. 7–17.

"Pakistan's Relations with India and Afghanistan," *Journal of South Asian and Middle Eastern Studies* 5, p. 23–32.

1982

"Die Dimensionen der Armut: Indien und der Lebensqualitätsindex," in: Norbert Wagner and Hans Christoph Rieger (eds.), *Grundbedürfnisse als Gegenstand der Entwicklungspolitik: Interdisziplinäre Aspekte der Grundbedarfsstrategie*, Wiesbaden, p. 163–74.

"Einführungserklärung für die Arbeitsgemeinschaft Außereuropäische Geschichte im Verband der Historiker Deutschlands," *Wissenschaftsbörse Entwicklungspolitik* 82, p. 11–12.

"Pakistans Beziehungen zu Indien und Afghanistan," *Vierteljahresberichte: Probleme der Entwicklungsländer* 87, p. 29–36.

"Probleme der nationalen Integration in Südasien," in: H. A. Winkler (ed.), *Nationalismus in der Welt von heute*, Göttingen, p. 140–56.

1983

"A Survey of Rural Migration and Land Reclamation in British India, 1885," in: Dietmar Rothermund (ed.), *The Indian Economy under British Rule and Other Essays*, New Delhi, p. 54–72.

"British Foreign Trade Policy in India during the Great Depression, 1929–1939," in: Dietmar Rothermund (ed.), *The Indian Economy under British Rule and Other Essays*, New Delhi, p. 175–208.

"Chinas verspätete Krise: 1933–1935," in: Dietmar Rothermund (ed.), *Die Peripherie in der Weltwirtschaftskrise: Afrika, Asien und Lateinamerika 1929–1939*, Paderborn (Sammlung Schöningh zur Geschichte und Gegenwart 143), p. 226–44.

"Die Anfänge der indischen Wirtschaftsplanung im Zweiten Weltkrieg," in: P. Halblützel et al. (ed.), *Dritte Welt: Historische Prägung und politische Herausforderung*. Festschrift für Rudolf von Albertini zum 60. Geburtstag, Wiesbaden (Beiträge zur Kolonial- und Überseegeschichte 24), p. 81–93.

"Die Interferenz von Agrarpreissturz und Freiheitskampf in Indien," in: Dietmar Rothermund (ed.), *Die Peripherie in der Weltwirtschaftskrise: Afrika, Asien und Lateinamerika 1929–1939*, Paderborn (Sammlung Schöningh zur Geschichte und Gegenwart 143), p. 128–43.

"Social Structure and Emancipation in India," in: Rothermund, Dietmar (ed.), *The Indian Economy under British Rule and Other Essays*, New Delhi, p. 23–41.

"The Great Depression and British Financial Policy in India, 1929–1934," in: Dietmar Rothermund (ed.), *The Indian Economy under British Rule and Other Essays*, New Delhi, p. 152–74.

"The Land Revenue Problem in British India," in: Dietmar Rothermund (ed.), *The Indian Economy under British Rule and Other Essays*, New Delhi, p. 92–113.

"The Record of Rights in British India," in: Dietmar Rothermund (ed.), *The Indian Economy under British Rule and Other Essays*, New Delhi, p. 73–91.

"Weltgefälle und Wirtschaftskrise," in: Dietmar Rothermund (ed.), *Die Peripherie in der Weltwirtschaftskrise: Afrika, Asien und Lateinamerika 1929–1939*, Paderborn (Sammlung Schöningh zur Geschichte und Gegenwart 143), p. 14–35.

1984

"History as a Social Process and as a Social Science," in: Ravinder Kumar (ed.), *Philosophical Theory and Social Reality*, New Delhi, p. 79–98.

"Indien 2000," *Asien* 10, p. 22–38.

"Nord-Süd Dialog und Entwicklungshilfe: Indiens Wirtschaft in der Welt der Gegenwart," in: Institut für wissenschaftliche Zusammenarbeit mit Entwicklungsländern (ed.) *Indien: Probleme eines Schwellenlandes*, Tübingen (Reihe Länderseminare), p. 8–27.

"Wilhelm Hahn und das Südasien-Institut," in: H. Reutlinger and G. G. Wolf (eds.), *Kreuzwege. Festschrift für Kultusminister a. D. Prof. D. Dr. Wilhelm Hahn zum 75. Geburtstag*, Heidelberg, p. 179–82.

1985

"Pfeffer, Silber, Seide. Europas Weg nach China," in: G. Sievernich et al. (eds), *Europa und die Kaiser von China*, Frankfurt am Main, p. 38–57.

"The German Intellectual Quest for India," in: *1960–1985. 25 Years Deutscher Akademischer Austauschdienst (DAAD) in New Delhi*, p. 5–16.

"Regionale Differenzierung in Indien: Britische Herrschaft, Freiheitskampf und Föderalismus," in: Hermann Kulke and Dietmar Rothermund (eds.), *Regionale Tradition in Südasien*, Stuttgart, p. 205–18.

"Region, regionale Tradition und Regionalismus in Südasien: Versuch einer Einführung in die Thematik" (together with Hermann Kulke), in: Hermann Kulke and Dietmar Rothermund (eds.), *Regionale Tradition in Südasien*, Stuttgart, p. ix–xxiv.

"Indien 1985: Eine innenpolitische Bilanz," *Aus Politik und Zeitgeschichte. Beilage zur Wochenzeitung "Das Parlament"* 10, p. 3–12.

1986

"Lala Lajpat Rai and Indian Nationalism," *Maharshi Dayanand University Research Journal* 1, p. 65–78.

"The Legacy of the British-Indian in Independent India," in: Wolfgang Mommsen and Jürgen Osterhammel (eds.), *Imperialism and After*, London, p. 139–59.

1987

"25 Jahre Südasien-Institut," *Ruperto Carola* 39, p. 73–4.

"Anfänge und Beweggründe der europäischen Expansion nach Übersee 1450–1650," *Geschichte, Politik und ihre Didaktik* 15, p. 5–12.

"Die Entwicklung Indiens seit 1947," *Ruperto Carola* 39, p. 68–72.

"India's Economic Development: 1947–1987," in: Klaus Voll et al. (eds.), *Focus India: Prospects for Development*, Bonn (Vierteljahresbericht, Forschungsinstitut der Friedrich-Ebert-Stiftung 110), p. 359–63.

"Interdisciplinary Asian Area Studies Needed," in: *Interdisciplinary Science Review* 12, p. 6–8.

"Introduction: The Fate of the Portuguese in Asia," in: Roderich Ptak (ed.), *Portuguese Asia. Aspects in History and Economic History, 16th and 17th Century*, Wiesbaden (Beiträge zur Südasienforschung 117), p. v–viii.

1988

"Problems of India's Arrested Growth under British Rule," in: Clive Dewey (ed.), *Arrested Development in India*, Delhi, p. 3–11.

"The Philosophical Context of the Development of German Indology," *Indological Studies and South Asia Bibliography*, Calcutta (National Library Conferences 3), p. 117–30.

1989

"Der Traditionalismus als Forschungsgegenstand für Historiker und Orientalisten," *Saeculum* 40, p. 142–8.

"Regionale Disparitäten in Indien," in: Werner Draguhn (ed.), *Indien in den 90er Jahren*, Hamburg (Mitteilungen des Instituts für Asienkunde 175), p. 31–43.

1990

"A Vulnerable Economy: India in the Great Depression, 1929–1939," in: S. Bose (ed.), *South Asia and World Capitalism*, Delhi, p. 305–24.

"Economic and Social Indicators of Regional Disparities in India," in: Dietmar Rothermund and S. K. Saha. (eds.), *Regional Disparities in India. Rural and Industrial Dimensions*, New Delhi, p. 1–12.

"Indien 1990: Bestandsaufnahme und Zukunftsperspektiven," *Asien* 35, p. 5–12.

"Indien 1990: Strukturprobleme und Entwicklungstendenzen," in: Dietmar Rothermund (ed.), *Erste Heidelberger Südasiengespräche*, Stuttgart (Beiträge zur Südasienforschung 135), p. 13–16.

"Rabindranath Tagore in Darmstadt, 10. bis 14. Juni 1921," in: Edmund Weber (ed.), *Indien in Deutschland*, Frankfurt am Main etc., p. 11–18.

1991

"Asian Emporia and European Bridgeheads," in: Dietmar Rothermund and Roderich Ptak (eds.), *Emporia, Commodities and Entrepreneurs in Asian Maritime Trade, c. 1400–1750*, Stuttgart (Beiträge zur Südasienforschung 141), p. 3–8.

"Asiatische Emporien und europäische Brückenköpfe," *Periplus* 1, p. 1–6.

"Economic and Social Indicators of Regional Disparities in India," in: Dietmar Rothermund (ed.), *Regional Disparities in India: Rural and Industrial Dimensions*, p. 1–11.

"Problems of Parliamentarism in India," *Asien* 39, p. 21–31.

"Wenn ich ein Tscheche wäre." in: Heidi Bonet-von der Thüsen (ed.), *Denkanstöße '91. Ein Lesebuch aus Philosophie, Natur- und Humanwissenschaften*, München (Serie Piper 1171), p. 85–8.

1992

"Geschichte als Fragment. Konvergente Verursachung, disparate Wirkungen und beziehungslose Zeitgenossenschaft," in: H. D. Ebbinghaus and G. Vollmer (eds.), *Denken unterwegs*, Stuttgart, p. 93–104.

"Staat und Gesellschaft in Indien nach der Erlangung der Unabhängigkeit," in: E. Gormsen and A. Timm (eds.), *Zivilgesellschaft und Staat in der Dritten Welt*, Mainz (Interdisziplinärer Arbeitskreis Dritte Welt, Veröffentlichungen 6), p. 105–14.

"Staat und Gesellschaft in Indien," in: Jürgen Elvert and Michael Salewski (eds.), *Staatenbildung in Übersee*, Stuttgart (Historische Mitteilungen Beiheft 2), p. 125–36.

"Town and Country in India," in: J. Johansen, E. Petersen, H. Stevnsborg (eds.), *Clashes of Cultures. Essays in Honour of Niels Steensgaard*, Odense, p. 273–83.

1993

"Dokument zum Thema: Koçibeys Denkschrift über den Verfall des Osmanischen Reiches," *Periplus* 1993, p. 61–8.

"German Tamilology: Foreword," in: C. S. Mohanavelu, *German Tamilology: German Contributions to Tamil Language, Literature and Culture During the Period 1706–1945*, Madras, p. vi–vii.

"Nationale und regionale Geschichtsschreibung in Indien," *Periplus* 1993, p. 75–83.

"Vasco da Gama und der Weg nach Calicut," in: Christof Dipper and Martin Vogt (eds.), *Ringvorlesung: Entdeckungen und frühe Kolonien*, Darmstadt (Technische Hochschule Darmstadt, Schriftenreihe Wissenschaft und Technik 63), p. 187–209.

"Zerstörung der Moschee von Ayodhya – Indiens Schicksalsstunde?" *Geographische Rundschau* 45 (11), November 1993, p. 626–30.

1994

"Gandhi's Concepts of Individual Conduct and Social Life," *Indian Horizons* 43, p. 179–84 (Special Issue: Gandhi 125 Years, ed. by B. R. Nanda).

"Indien," in: Dieter Nohlen and Frank Nuscheler (eds.), *Handbuch der Dritten Welt*, Band 7: *Südasien und Südostasien*, 3. Aufl., Bonn, p. 205–43.

"Land-Revenue Law and Land Records in British India," in: Jap de Moor and Dietmar Rothermund (eds.), *Our Laws, Their Lands*, Münster, p. 120–33.

1995

"Das Bevölkerungswachstum," in: Dietmar Rothermund (ed.), *Indien: Kultur, Geschichte, Politik, Wirtschaft, Umwelt*, München, p. 59–65.

"Das Bildungswesen," in: Dietmar Rothermund (ed.), *Indien: Kultur, Geschichte, Politik, Wirtschaft, Umwelt*, München, p. 339–48.

"Die deutsch-indischen Beziehungen," in: Dietmar Rothermund (ed.), *Indien: Kultur, Geschichte, Politik, Wirtschaft, Umwelt*, München, p. 472–82.

"Die Industrialisierung Indiens im 19. und 20. Jahrhundert," in: Peter Feldbauer et al. (eds.), *Industrialisierung: Entwicklungsprozesse in Afrika, Asien und Lateinamerika*, Frankfurt am Main/Wien (Beiträge zur Historischen Sozialkunde Beiheft 6/1995), p. 101–16.

"Die Stadien der wirtschaftlichen Entwicklung," in: Dietmar Rothermund (ed.), *Indien: Kultur, Geschichte, Politik, Wirtschaft, Umwelt*, München, p. 485–501.

"Die Stellung der Frau in der Gesellschaft" (together with Chitra Rothermund), in: Dietmar Rothermund (ed.), *Indien: Kultur, Geschichte, Politik, Wirtschaft, Umwelt*, München, p. 134–9.

"Epochen der indischen Geschichte," in: Dietmar Rothermund (ed.), *Indien: Kultur, Geschichte, Politik, Wirtschaft, Umwelt*, München, p. 77–100.

"Genossenschaften, Gewerkschaften und Verbände," in: Dietmar Rothermund (ed.), *Indien: Kultur, Geschichte, Politik, Wirtschaft, Umwelt*, München, p. 537–49.

"Indien als asiatische Großmacht," *Internationale Politik* 50 (5), Mai 1995, p. 47–52.

"Indien: Von der Planwirtschaft zur Liberalisierung," in: Wolfram Fischer (ed.), *Lebensstandard und Wirtschaftssysteme*, Frankfurt am Main (Veröffentlichungen der DG Bank 20), p. 501-42.

"Parlamentarische Demokratie und Föderalismus," in: Dietmar Rothermund (ed.), *Indien: Kultur, Geschichte, Politik, Wirtschaft, Umwelt*, München, p. 389–408.

"Regionale Diskrepanzen," in: Dietmar Rothermund (ed.), *Indien: Kultur, Geschichte, Politik, Wirtschaft, Umwelt*, München, p. 66–73.

"Sri Lanka – Geschichte und Gegenwart," in: Georg Berkemer and Tilman Frasch (eds.), *Sri Lanka: Fünfte Heidelberger Südasiengespräche*, Stuttgart (Beiträge zur Südasienforschung 171), p. 1–6.

"Staat und Markt in Indien 1757–1995," in: Helga Breuninger and Rolf Peter Sieferle (eds.), *Markt und Macht in der Geschichte*, Stuttgart, p. 177–205.

1996

"Indien am Scheideweg," *Blätter für Deutsche und Internationale Politik* 8, p. 945–52.

"Wirtschaftsgesinnung im Hinduismus," *Geographische Rundschau* 48, p. 352–7.

"Liberalisierung in Indien," *Ruperto Carola* 3, p. 16–22.

1997

"Conflict as a Challenge to Legitimacy: A Historical Perspective," in: Subrata K. Mitra and Dietmar Rothermund (eds.), *Legitimacy and Conflict in South Asia*, New Delhi, p. 7–16.

"Deutschland und Südasien – Partnerschaft in Gegenwart und Zukunft," in: Georg Berkemer and Tilman Frasch (eds.), *Die Deutsche Zusammenarbeit mit Südasien. Sechste Heidelberger Südasiengespräche*, Stuttgart 1997 (Beiträge zur Südasienforschung 176), p. 9–14.

"Historische Aspekte der Ernährungssicherung in Indien," in: Hans-Georg Bohle et al. (eds.), *Ernährungssicherung in Südasien. Siebte Heidelberger Südasiengespräche*, Stuttgart 1997 (Beiträge zur Südasienforschung 178), p. 31–6.

"Indiens Rolle in der globalen Politik," in: Erich Reiter (ed.), *Österreichisches Jahrbuch für internationale Sicherheitspolitik 1997*, Graz/Wien/Köln, p. 359–73.

"Konstruktionen nationaler Solidarität in Asien. Universalismus und Traditionalismus," in: M. Brocker and Heino Nau (eds.), *Ethnozentrismus. Möglichkeiten und Grenzen des interkulturellen Dialogs*, Darmstadt, p. 170–90.

"Nationalism and the Reconstruction of Traditions in Asia," in: Sri Kuhnt-Saptowedo et al. (eds.), *Nationalism and Cultural Revival in Southeast Asia: Perspectives from the Centre and the Region*, Wiesbaden, p. 13–28.

"Indiens Wachstum in einem halben Jahrhundert," *Indien in der Gegenwart* 2 (1–2), p. 163–71.

1998

"Aussenpolitik und Entwicklungsstrategien in Indien und Bangladesh," in: *Jahrbuch für Internationale Politik 1995–96*, München, p. 239–46.

"Die Macht der Geschichte," in: *Der Bürger im Staat* 48,1 (Themenheft "Indien"), ed. by Landeszentrale für politische Bildung Stuttgart, p. 15–19.

"Gandhis Begegnung mit der Gewalt," in: Rolf-Peter Sieferle and Helga Breuninger (eds.), *Kulturen der Gewalt. Ritualisierung und Symbolisierung von Gewalt in der Geschichte*, Frankfurt/New York, p. 241–52.

"The Fall-out of a New Political Regime in India," in: *Asien* 68, 2, p. 5–20.

"Der Seeweg nach Indien," in: *Periplus. Jahrbuch für außereuropäische Geschichte* 8, Münster, p. 1–8.

"Geschichte von unten: Die 'subaltern studies' in Indien," in: *Jahrbuch für die Geschichte Lateinamerikas* 35, p. 301–18.

"Globalgeschichte, Weltgeschichte, Universalgeschichte," in: *Beiträge zur Historischen Sozialkunde*, Sondernummer 1998, S. 4–10.

"Indiens Arbeiterklasse als Forschungsgegenstand in der DDR," in: Wolf-Hagen Krauth and Ralf Wolz (eds.), *Wissenschaft und Wiedervereinigung. Asien- und Afrikawissenschaften im Umbruch*, Berlin, p. 363–72.

"Mahatma Gandhi's Ethics," in: Jaroslav Vacek and Jan Dvorak (eds.), *Trends in Indian Studies. Proceedings of the ESIS*. Prague, p. 151–58.

"Von den Moguln zu den Briten – Indien von 1526 bis 1857," in: *Brockhaus. Die Weltgeschichte*, vol. 4: *Wege in die Moderne* (*1650–1850*), Leipzig/Mannheim, p. 484–99.

1999

"Das Attentat auf Mahatma Gandhi," in: Roland Aegerter (ed.), *Politische Attentate des 20. Jahrhunderts*, Zurich, p. 125–39.

"The Changing Pattern of British Trade in Indian Textiles, 1701–1757," in: Sushil Chaudhury and Michel Morineau (eds.), *Merchants, Companies and Trade. Europe and Asia in the Early Modern Era*, Cambridge, p. 276–86 .

"Europa und Indien" in: Werner Weidenfeld (ed.), *Europa-Handbuch*, Gütersloh, p. 741–9.

"Indiens Wirtschaftspolitik im Zeitalter der Globalisierung," in: *Geographische Rundschau*, 51,3, p. 90–5.

"Regionale Disparitäten in Indien," in: Werner Draguhn (ed.), *Indien 1999*, Hamburg, p. 273–87.

"Der Strukturwandel des britischen Kolonialstaates in Indien, 1757–1947,"in: Wolfgang Reinhard (ed.), *Verstaatlichung der Welt?*, Munich, p. 69–86.

German Indology – From Roth to Rothermund
As I Observed It

C. S. Mohanavelu

"Wie man gräbt, so quillt im Sand der Brunnen;
Wie man übt, so quillt die Erkenntniß"*

German interactions with India is a vast and a deep-rooted phenomenon, spreading over a lengthy period, from the arrival of the first German in India[1] named Heinrich Roth (1620–1668), till the times of Prof. Rothermund, in honour of whom, this Festschrift is prepared. Hundreds of Germans contributed to these Indo-German interactions and as it is beyond my academic ability to deal with the contributions of all those Germans, I take up certain aspects of a few Germans, the so-called German Tamilologists, whose works I had dealt with at the doctoral level study.[2] In this article, I have tried to compare and contrast certain incidents, which took place in the careers of a few German Protestant missionaries, with those of Prof. Rothermund. As this article is not for any research journal and as it is meant to be a part of the felicitation, I may be permitted to state, with a tinge of sentimentalism, certain aspects, which flourish in my memory.

The first German Lutheran missionary Bartholomäus Ziegenbalg (1682–1719), who landed in Tranquebar on 9th July 1706,[3] like others in Europe, had the wrong idea, that the Tamil people were barbarous, "who burn their widows and marry a boy and a girl even before they knew anything of marriage. …"[4] But soon after moving in with the natives, he found good enough reasons to change this wrong notion. In one of his first letters to Europe, Ziegenbalg, with the view to change this wrong idea, wrote thus:

> Die meisten Christen in Europa sind wohl der Meinung, daß die Malabarischen Heiden ein recht barbarisches Volk seien, – aber das kommt daher, daß die Europäer, welche unter den Malabaren gewesen sind, ihre Sprache nicht recht verstanden, noch ihre Bücher gelesen, son-

* Karl Graul, *Der Kural des Tiruvalluver*, Leipzig 1856, p. 60.

1 Valentina Stache-Rosen, *German Indologists*, New Delhi 1981, p. 1.

2 C. S. Mohanavelu, *German Tamilology*, Madras 1993, p. 221.

3 Arno Lehmann, *Es begann in Tranquebar*, Berlin 1956, p. 28.

4 Benjamin Schultze, *Madras Stadt*, Halle 1750, p. 88–90.

dern ihre Schlüsse nach dem äußerlichen Schein gemacht haben: gleichwie ich von mir selbst gestehen muss, daß ich mir anfangs, als ich zu diesen Heiden kam, nicht einbilden konnte, daß ihre Sprache eine recht regelmäßige Sprache, oder ihr Leben ein bürgerlich eingerichtetes Menschen-Leben sei, sondern mir allerhand falsche Vorstellungen machte über ihr Thun und Lassen, als ob unter ihnen weder ein bürgerliches Gesetz noch ein Moralgesetz sei – aber sobald ich mir nur einige Kenntnis von ihrer Sprache erworben hatte und mit ihnen von allerhand Dingen reden konnte, wurde ich nach und nach von jener Einbildung frei, und fing an eine bessere Meinung von ihnen zu fassen; und als ich endlich vollkommen im Stande war, ihre eigenen Bücher zu lesen, so bemerkte ich, daß die Malabaren dieselben philosophischen Disciplinen, welche die Gelehrten in Europa behandeln, auch ganz ordentlich auf ihre Weise vortragen, und daß sie ein ordentlich geschriebenes Gesetz haben, worin alle theologische Gegenstände behandelt und bewiesen werden. Hierüber **verwunderte** ich mich recht sehr und bekam große Lust von ihrem Heidenthum und ihren eigenen Schriften gründlich unterrichtet zu werden. […][5]

But the Danish Crown and especially Prof. August Hermann Francke (1663–1727) considered all these notes of Ziegenbalg as "… heathen non-sense" and said that "the missionaries were sent to exterminate heathenism in India and not to spread the heathen non-sense all over Europe."[6] Ziegenbalg thus gained the wrath of his patron King Frederick IV (1699–1730) and of his godfather Professor Francke for having said the truth about the Tamil culture. Also he was summoned to appear before the Danish King to give explanation for this "cultural fact-finding". Knowing the threat and consequent punishment, Ziegenbalg hastily prepared a native convert to be taken with him as a sample of the Tamil society, to be shown to the Europeans. It was the custom in those days to select a pupil leader, whom the teacher liked the most and who would be very affectionate and loyal to his teacher. A native boy, named Malaiappan, was this kind of a pupil to Ziegenbalg. To prove his regard and love to his Guru, the following incident may be perused:[7]

Once Ziegenbalg visited the famous Vishnu temple city Thirupathy, to preach against idol worship among the natives. Knowing this, some jealous Brahmins, unable to tolerate Ziegenbalg's service to promote Christianity, decided to kill him. At about 4 o'clock in the early mor-

5 J. F. Fenger, *Geschichte der Trankabarschen Mission*, Grimma 1845, p. 22. Translation: "Most Christians in Europe suppose the Malabarians to be a very barbarous people, but this arises from the Europeans who have been amongst them not understanding their language, so that they have not been able to read their books, but have drawn their conclusions from outward appearances. I must acknowledge that when I first came amongst them I could not imagine that their language had proper rules, or that their life had the laws of civil order, and took up all sorts of false ideas on their actions as if they had neither a civil nor a moral law, - but as soon as I had gained a little acquaintance with their language and could talk to them on various subjects, I began to have a much better opinion of them and when at last I was able to read their own books I found that the Malabarians discussed the same philosophical subjects as the Savants of Europe, and that they had a regular written law, wherein all theological subjects were treated of and demonstrated. This **surprised me extremely,** and I was delighted to be thoroughly instructed in their heathenism from their own writings. […]"

6 Arno Lehmann, *Es begann in Tranquebar*, p. 56.

7 *Life of B. Ziegenbalg*, (author not known) 2nd ed., Tranquebar, 1893, p. 25. Also cf. Erich Beyreuther, *Bartholomäus Ziegenbalg*, Madras 1956, p. 55.

ning, they entered the inn where Ziegenbalg stayed and were about to strangulate him to death. Malaiappan, who expected that some danger would befall his Guru, kept awake the whole night and shouted when the Brahmins came near his teacher and thus saved Ziegenbalg.

There is no wonder that Ziegenbalg reposed faith and confidence in Malaiappan. Also did Ziegenbalg teach Malaiappan German language and made preparations to take him to Copenhagen. According to a diary dated 8th October 1714, a sum of 100 Rix Dollars had been set apart for Malaiappan's expenses in Europe.[8] On 26th October 1714 a Danish ship left Madras with missionaries Ziegenbalg and Jordan with an unusual co-passenger, Peter Malaiappan. This ship reached Bergen in Norway on 1st June 1715. Ziegenbalg met there his royal patron, King Frederick IV. The King granted an audience to this Tamil scholar guest and Malaiappan delivered a speech in **German language** in front of the King and his officers. Malaiappan should have possessed a very good command of the German language to deliver this historical "**well-sounding**" German speech.[9] This happened on 26th July 1715. History does not record such a parallel, wherein, any scholar, other than a Tamilian, of having been elevated to such a high academic eminence, nearly 300 years ago.

I wish to compare this with Prof. Rothermund's attempt to sponsor me during 1986, for a 3 months DAAD fellowship, to visit Heidelberg and Martin-Luther universities. Both Malaiappan and I visited Germany on a DAAD grant; for me it was the Deutscher Akademischer Austauschdienst (German Academic Exchange Service) and for Malaiappan, it was the Dänischer Akademischer Austauschdienst (Danish Academic Exchange Service)!

Now, let me compare the academic achievements of the Professor with those of a few German Tamilologists. Professor Rothermund's many dissertation supervisions from Baloch to Stadler,[10] the post-doctoral habilitation supervisions of Kulke, Lütt, Schwerin,[11] publications of research monographs from the *Layman's Progress*[12] to *India in the Great Depression*,[13] text

[8] Microfilm No. TM 2, Missions-Diarium, UTC Archives, Bangalore.

[9] Erich Beyreuther, *Bartholomäus Ziegenbalg*, p. 65.

[10] Inayatullah Baloch, *The Problem of "Greater Baluchistan": A Study of Baluch Nationalism*, Stuttgart 1987; Hans-Peter Stadler, *Gandhi und Nehru – Die Politik des kleinsten gemeinsamen Nenners*, forthcoming.

[11] Hermann Kulke, *Jagannatha-Kult und Gajapati-Königtum: ein Beitrag zur Geschichte religiöser Legitimation hinduistischer Herrschaft*, Wiesbaden 1979; Jürgen Lütt, *Religion und Politik in Indien: Pandit Malaviyas Vermittlerrolle im politischen Hinduismus des frühen 20. Jahrhunderts*, Habilitation Thesis, Heidelberg 1979; Kerrin Gräfin Schwerin, *Indirekte Herrschaft und Reformpolitik im indischen Fürstenstaat Hyderabad: 1853–1911*, Wiesbaden 1980.

[12] *The Layman's Progress. Religious and Political Experience in Colonial Pennsylvania, 1740–1770*, Philadelphia 1961.

[13] *India in the Great Depression, 1929–1939*, New Delhi 1992.

books from *Der Freiheitskampf Indiens*[14] to *Staat und Gesellschaft in Indien*,[15] certain general books such as *5mal Indien*,[16] *Mahatma Gandhi*,[17] besides his individual and co-editorship of volumes like *Rabindranath Tagore in Germany*,[18] *Regionale Tradition in Südasien*,[19] *Erste Heidelberger Südasiengespräche*,[20] *Emporia Commodities and Entrepreneurs in Asian Maritime Trade*,[21] *Nationalstaat und Sprachkonflikte in Süd-und Südostasien*[22] and more than 100 articles on Indo-German relations, international relations etc. reveal his unquenchable academic thirst. This kind of academic accomplishment reminds me of the works of Ziegenbalg, Graul and Schomerus. Ziegenbalg's *Kleinere Schriften*,[23] *Bibliotheca Malabarica*,[24] *Grammatica Damulica*,[25] *Malabarisches Heidenthum*,[26] Graul's *Reise nach Ostindien*,[27] *Der Kural des Thiruvalluver*,[28] *An Outline of Tamil Grammar*[29] and Schomerus' *Die Hymnen des Manikka-Vasaga*,[30] *Sivaitische Heiligenlegenden*,[31] *Politik und Religion in Indien*,[32] *Buddha und Christus*[33] etc. remind me of Professor's above-said works. A striking contrast is that the total quantum of the works done by these three German Tamilologists, had been done by the Professor alone! Professor's hard works, like those of Ziegenbalg, earned him international reputation. In 1986, the Asiatic Society in Calcutta, awarded him the Bi-centenary Gold Medal and in 1988, he was elected Fellow of the Royal Historical Society in London. This reminds me of how Ziegenbalg was honoured with the title "Provost" and also was honoured with a meeting with

14 *Der Freiheitskampf Indiens*, Stuttgart 1966.

15 *Staat und Gesellschaft in Indien*, Mannheim 1993.

16 *5mal Indien*, München 1979 (3rd rev. ed. 1990).

17 *Mahatma Gandhi, der Revolutionär der Gewaltlosigkeit: eine politische Biographie*, München 1989.

18 *Rabindranath Tagore in Germany: a Cross-Section of Contemporary Reports*, New Delhi 1961.

19 *Regionale Tradition in Südasien*, Stuttgart 1985 (ed. with H. Kulke).

20 *Erste Heidelberger Südasiengespräche*, Stuttgart 1990.

21 *Emporia, Commodities and Entrepreneurs in Asian Maritime Trade, c. 1400–1750*, Stuttgart 1991 (with R. Ptak).

22 *Nationalstaat und Sprachkonflikte in Süd-und Südostasien*, Stuttgart 1992 (with D. Hellmann-Rajanayagam).

23 B. Ziegenbalg, *Kleinere Schriften*, Amsterdam 1930.

24 W. Germann, "Ziegenbalgs Bibliotheca Malabarica," *Missionsnachrichten der Ostindischen Missionsanstalt zu Halle*, Jahrgang 32, Nos. 1 u. 2, Halle 1880, p. 1–20 and 62–94.

25 B. Ziegenbalg, *Grammatica Damulica*, Halle 1716.

26 W. Caland (ed.), *Ziegenbalgs Malabarisches Heidenthum*, Amsterdam 1926.

27 Karl Graul, *Reise nach Ostindien über Palästina und Ägypten*, 5 Bände, Leipzig 1854–56.

28 Karl Graul, *Der Kural des Thiruvalluver*, Leipzig 1856.

29 Charles Graul, *An Outline of Tamil Grammar*, Osnabrück 1969.

30 H. W. Schomerus, *Die Hymnen des Manikka-Vasaga*, Jena 1923.

31 H. W. Schomerus, *Sivaitische Heiligenlegenden: Periya Purana und Tiruvatavurar Purana*, Jena 1925

32 H. W. Schomerus, *Politik und Religion in Indien*, Leipzig 1928.

33 H. W. Schomerus, *Buddha und Christus*, Halle 1931.

King George I which "meant much in a time […] when George I seldom opened his royal purse for the mission."[34]

And now, coming to the express purpose of this article, I wish to state the following: The sun's white light is a composite one, it can be split into its constituent colours viz. violet, indigo, blue, green, yellow, orange and red. So also can German Indology be split into its various branches of Indology. Detailed researches will reveal, that German Indology can be split into German Tamilology, German Telugology, German Malayalamology, German Sanscritology etc. The German effects in these branches of Indology are already prevalent and in certain branches, this effect, or better-said, the German participation and mutual interactions had been more prevalent and conspicuous. The most influenced field of German Indology is the German Tamilology. That is, the participation in and contributions to the language, literature and culture of the people of Tamil Nadu, by the German Protestant missionaries, are more prominent than any of their similar activities in other Indian language areas. In short, German Indology had its firm origin *only* in German Tamilology and only here, in Tamilaham, German Indology was lit so ably and diligently by the first German missionary Ziegenbalg 300 years ago and this torch of Indo-Germanic academic, cultural and religious interactions was kept on glowing by his successors. But later on, there had been a loss of balance on the German side, for, the later German Indologists, as Prof. Arno Lehmann points out, thought that Indian literature meant only Sanskrit literature and unfortunately shifted their fields of interest to north India, the Buddhist India, the Vedic India or the so-called Sanskrit India. I appeal to the present day German Indologists, to cast their academic attention more to Tamilology, not only because Tamil Nadu served as the first labour field of German interests in India; but also the founding efforts of the Germans, are quite significant, both in terms of quality and quantity. Proof: Personal diaries, letters exchanges, historical accounts, zoological and botanical observations, meteorological observations, calendar, topographical notes, grant notices, diverse curiosities etc., all pertaining to the activities of the German missionaries in Tamil Nadu alone, form the major portion of the whole collection in the Francke's Archives in Halle an der Saale. Multitudes of scholars, belonging to various branches of science, will find this archives a treasure of original source materials, provided by those diligent German missionaries, nearly 300 years ago. "The heaps and heaps of yet unconsulted documents", as Prof. Arno Lehmann rightly said, "are to be likened to a green pasture and **many a doctorate** could be earned by working on them."[35]

[34] Erich Beyreuther, *Bartholomäus Ziegenbalg*, p. 68.

[35] Arno Lehmann, "German Tamil Studies," *Wissenschaftliche Zeitschrift der Universität Halle* 17, 1968, Heft 6, p. 140.

Last, but not the least, may I request Prof. Rothermund to cast his attention henceforth for the development of the Tamilo-German researches, based on the original source information found in the Francke's archives, regarding the activities of the German missionaries from Ziegenbalg to Schomerus, in the fields of Tamil language, literature, culture and medicine. This kind of inter-disciplinary researches, I believe, can be carried out with the cooperation of and interactions with subject experts in the related fields. German researchers, I hope, will find it comparatively easier to read and decipher the thousands of the diaries, travel accounts, station registers etc. written by those German missionaries in Frakturschrift. Except Dagmar Hellmann-Rajanayagam[36] as far as I know, no one else had been guided by the Professor, at the doctoral level, in the field of Tamilology. That is, a very small and a rather insignificant part of his research supervision had been devoted to Tamil study. I still believe that there are quite a few significant but very much discarded interactions of the pioneer German missionaries and their efforts to expose the exploitations of the down-trodden by the upper caste. While conducting religious disputations with the Brahmins, Ziegenbalg came to know of certain unjust customs and practices, imposed on the down-trodden. He noted down many such blind faiths, which were thrust on the down-trodden, during the early 18th century and they had been published in 1719 itself as a book.[37] A few such observations are given here for perusal. When Ziegenbalg was informed that the Brahmins had divine laws, he said thus:

> [...] Bramans indeed, do boast, that they have a Law written by God himself; in which his Will and Pleasure, in Relation to Mens Salvation, is clearly manifested; but in this they are great Impostors abusing the credulous Ignorance of the People; for they never can produce any such Law, and submit it to the impartial Perusal of learned Men. [...][38]

When some Brahmins claimed that they were the descendants of the God Brahma, Ziegenbalg asked them thus:

> [...] Why, said I, does not every Creature beget his like? And how comes it that you are born Mortal Priests; and not Immortal Gods, if descended from this Family of the Great God Biruma? He had four Heads, and you have but one only; and are in nothing unlike the rest of the Malabarians, [...][39]

When the Brahmins claimed that they conducted themselves according to the Divine Laws, Ziegenbalg exposed them thus:

36 Dagmar Hellmann-Rajanayagam, *Tamil: Sprache als politisches Symbol; politische Literatur in der Tamilsprache in den Jahren 1945 bis 1967*, Wiesbaden 1984.

37 B. Ziegenbalg, *Thirty Four Conferences between the Danish Missionaries and the Malabarian Bramans (or Heathen Priests) in the East Indies, concerning the truth of the Christian religion*. London 1719 (Translated out of High Dutch by J. Thomas Philipps).

38 *Ibid.*, p. 83.

39 *Ibid.*, p. 110.

You are always speaking of your Law, which you call God's Word but I am inclined to believe, said I, you have no such Law among you: For if you have any such Law, why don't you produce it; I never found hitherto any Braman, that could upon his own Experience affirm, that he ever saw this Law; but says, that such another Great Braman has it in his Possession; and if you address this great Braman, he refers you to some other Braman greater than himself; and so none of you can ever produce this Imaginary Law. [...][40]

Ziegenbalg wrote more about all the "pious frauds"[41] of the Brahmins of his times thus:

Besides, they are the greatest Impostors in the World: Their Talent lies in inventing new Fables every Day, and making them pass for incomprehensible Mysteries among the Vulgar, One of their Cheats is to persuade the People, that their Idols eat like Men: And to the end they may be plentifully provided with good Cheer, they make them of a Gigantick Figure, and to be sure, with a prodigious Paunch. [...][42]

An aspect of sharp contrast, in this context is, that Ziegenbalg did not fail to note the Dravidian monotheism, in which icon worship and imaginary Divine Laws were conspicuously absent. He praised Dravidian religion thus:[43]

[...] Especially in the Writings of Diruwalluwer and Tschiwawakkium; both which Authors have written incomparably well of the Absurdities of the Pagod-worship, of your gross Idolatry, [...]

Also, it goes to the credit of Ziegenbalg, to have educated the natives, including the Brahmins, about the dire need for the Europeans, to eat flesh of animals. We will hear from Ziegenbalg himself, as to how he explained this aspect:

[...] Dahero als wir vor wenig Monat in Nagapatnam waren und in eines Naikken Hausze unter einer groszen Anzahl Heiden von diesen und jenen Materien discourireten, so wurffen die Bramaner und andere uns Christen, sonderlich das Fleisch-eszen lebendiger Thiere vor, als eine Sache, die alles boese machete, was noch gutes an uns zu finden waere. [...] Weil sie nun Gott uns zur Speise gegeben, so koennten wir sie mit gutem Gewiszen zu unser Speise gebrauchen, zumal weil in Europa zur Winterzeit kein grün Kraut noch einige endere feldfrüchte wüchsen, da denn das fleisch-Eszen aller lebendiger Thiere es ersetzen müsze.[44]

Like this, there are many more personal observations of a few other Germans of the 18th century, especially of Benjamine Schultze, which need thorough investigation. Thus it may be noted that besides religious labours, the Germans interacted with the heterogeneous native Tamil society in socio-economic, cultural, linguistic and religious fields also. When the other five European powers, viz. the Portuguese, the Dutch, the Danes, the French and the British fought with each other for commercial and political supremacy in India, the Germans took deep

40 *Ibid.*, p. 138.

41 *Ibid.*, p. 132.

42 *Ibid.*, p. iv.

43 *Ibid.*, p. 82.

44 W. Caland, *Ziegenbalgs Malabarisches Heidenthum*, p. 201.

interest in the multifaceted aspects of the Tamil society, 300 years ago. Unfortunately much of them have not been brought to light. Now that the Professor has three more years of university teaching service, (in Germany, the retiring age is 68) I request him to devote his research attention to Tamilology and guide Ph. D. level German researchers in this field. Even after his retirement, he may bestow his attention to Tamilology so as to revive and continue the Tamilo-German researches, from where his fellow Germans, from Ziegenbalg to Arno Lehmann had left in Tamil Nadu, several decades ago! I sincerely hope that this request will get his serious consideration and affectionately yearn that the Professor be bestowed with the best health as he becomes an octogenarian, nonagenarian and a centenarian!

German Expertise in India?
Early Forest Management on the Malabar Coast, 1792–1805

Michael Mann

I

In 1991 the area of land officially designated as forest in the Union of India amounted to almost 20 per cent of the country's surface area. This implied an increase in forest area since 1987 when only around 17 per cent of the land was covered with forest. But the level of forest cover had actually declined annually by 45,000 square kilometres.[1] India's forest is of wide ranging composition and density. Only 12 per cent of the total surface area consists of 'dense forest', meaning more than 40 per cent ground cover.[2] This striking statistical unreliability has a long tradition in India, since the East India Company's officers on the Malabar Coast sought to assess not only its agricultural capacity but also the profitability of the region's teak forests. When Police Officer Joseph Watson became the first "Conservator of Forests" in India in 1806, Palghat's and Nilgiri's first incomplete and highly superficial forest reports and maps had just appeared.[3] The maps were to change little in the ensuing decades. Even though Dietrich Brandis introduced sustainable forest management in 1856 it is clear that only an incomplete systematic assessment exists of the actual level of forest to this day.

Research has until now paid scant attention to the field of early forestry in India. To a greater or lesser extent, forest policy only began with Governor General Lord Dalhousie's famous minute on forest management and the appointment of Dietrich Brandis as Inspector

1 Government of India, *The Forest Report 1991*. Forest Survey of India, Ministry of Environment and Forests, Dehra Dun, p. 7–10.

2 Norbert Stegbauer, *Wie indischen Ureinwohnern ihr Wald genommen wurde – Die Geschichte kolonialer Forstpolitik und ihre Folgen*, Saarbrücken 1995 (ASA-Studien No. 28), p. 83.

3 Forest management after 1806 under the monopoly of the East India Company is discussed at length in Michael Mann, *Flottenbau und Forstbetrieb in Indien 1794–1823* (transl. *Shipbuilding and Forestry in India*), Stuttgart 1996, p. 64–79 and p. 107–32.

General of Forests.[4] On the whole, forest policy is subsumed under agrarian policy. For a long time research followed the British administration which had introduced this classification and which had from the start subordinated the Conservator of Forests to the Collector of Revenues. This has a long tradition in the history of land use in Europe which was now applied on the Indian subcontinent. Even the more recent work in ecological history still makes this distinction.[5] The history of land use in India under colonial rule was until recently defined by agrarian history and its industrial and social consequences. Only at the end of the 1980s did this one sided approach to research find any opposition.[6]

But even the latest contributions to "forest history" only touch upon the subject. Hardly any work really deals with the actual use of forests, be it local use such as cattle herding or gathering, or the timber trade of local businesses.[7] The Himalayan forests are a rare exception, having awoken the attention not only of the British, but of the Mughals before them. There, local resistance to any erosion of rights was notorious.[8] The Malabar Coast's forests only get a brief mention in connection with local shipbuilding and construction for Arab customers.[9] Following their expansion in the Indian Ocean the Portuguese had their ships refitted or wholly built in Malabar teak.[10] This can be taken as proof of an advanced shipbuilding industry and organised timber trade. In Malabar itself there seems to have been some forest industry with the local population and its rulers replanting some types of trees.[11]

The state monopoly introduced in British India in 1806 is mentioned here and there, but is otherwise ignored.[12] Only Richard Tucker's study examines the East India Company's early

4 *Vide* Herbert Hesmer, *Leben und Werk von Dietrich Brandis 1824–1907. Begründer der tropischen Forstwirtschaft, Förderer der forstlichen Entwicklung in den USA, Botaniker und Ökologe*, Opladen 1975 (Abhandlungen der Rheinisch-Westfälischen Akademie der Wissenschaften, Band 58).

5 Madhav Gadgil and Ramachandra Guha, *This Fissured Land. An ecological History of India*, Delhi 1992, p. 191–2.

6 Madhav Gadgil and Ramachandra Guha, "State Forestry and Social Conflict in British India," *Past and Present* 123, 1989, p. 141–77.

7 Sumit Guha, "Forest Polities and Agrarian Empires: The Khandesh Bhils, c. 1700–1850," *Indian Economic and Social History Review* 33, 1996, p. 133–53 and Sivaramakrishnan, "British Imperium and Forested Zones of Anomaly in Bengal, 1767–1833," *IESHR* 33, 1996, p. 243–82.

8 Ramachandra Guha, *The Unquiet Woods. Ecological Change and Peasant Resistance in the Himalaya*, Delhi 1991.

9 Ralph Davis, *The Rise of the English Shipping Industry in the 17th and 18th Centuries*, London 1962, p. 257–337.

10 Charles Boxer, *The Carreira da India. Ships, Men, Cargoes, Voyages, O centro de Estudos Historicos Ultramarinos e as Comemoracoes Henriquinas*, Lisboa 1961, p. 37–8.

11 Board's Collections 89/1843, To the Honble Court of Directors, London, Bombay Castle, 10th October 1800, para. 35 and *ibid.*, Letter from the 13th June 1799, para. 27.

12 Ramachandra Guha, "An early Environmental Debate. The Making of the 1878 Forest Act," *Indian Economic and Social History Review* 27, 1990, p. 65–84. Most descriptions of early forest management and the state monopoly of 1806 refer to Berthold Ribbentrop, *Forestry in British India*, New Delhi 1989 (1st ed. 1900), p. 68–9.

forest policy in India. Even so, his reflections only begin with 1823, when the Bombay Government recognised teak and other wood as private property in two *talukas* in Thana District following abolition of the state monopoly.[13] Regional studies of forest policy in the first half of the 19th century are not available.[14] Jacques Pouchepadass recently tried to provide an overview of the Western Ghats' ecological history, including in one chapter "The progress of deforestation until the beginning of modern forestry". But an anticipated general paucity of sources on the history of British India in the 18th and first half of the 19th centuries seems to be the cause of the gaps in research. Explicit reference is made to the shortfall.[15] As Richard Grove found out, there were attempts before 1806 to bring a form of forest management into being on the Malabar Coast. Yet one must ask whether this was really a case of "German expertise" and to what extent the British demand for construction timber made systematic forest management necessary.[16]

II

Scientific record keeping in India began with the East India Company's territorial annexations. Cartography was of central significance, since it was important to the British to have the borders of their possessions exactly defined. Against this background the demarcation of clear borders also meant the simultaneous transformation of the East India Company from a trading company to a modern, absolutist state from the Western mould.[17] Only this way, so contemporary European conviction would have it, was an efficient state administration with secure revenues possible. Surveyor-General James Rennell recorded the British possessions in Bengal after 1763. In the mid 1770s his "Bengal Atlas" and "Map of Hindustan" were the first maps to

13 Richard Tucker, "Forest Management and Imperial Politics, Thana District, Bombay, 1823–1887," *Indian Economic and Social History Review* 16, 1979, p. 273–300.

14 Mahesh Rangarajan, *Fencing the Forest; Conservation and Ecological Change in India's Central Provinces, 1860–1914*, Delhi 1996.

15 Jacques Pouchepadass, "The Ecological History of the Central Western Ghats in the Modern Period. A Preliminary Survey," in: W. L. Werner (ed.), *Aspects of Ecological Problems and Environmental Awareness in South Asia*, Delhi 1995, p. 105–31.

16 Richard H. Grove, *Green Imperialism. Colonial Expansion, Tropical Island Edens and the Origins of Environmentalism, 1600–1860*, Cambridge 1995, p. 395.

17 Ainslee T. Embree, "Frontiers into Boundaries. The Evolution of the Modern State," in: Ainslee T. Embree and Mark Juergensmeyer, *Imagining India. Essays on Indian History*, Delhi 1989, p. 69–78. See also R. Prabhakar and Madhav Gadgil, "Maps as Markers of Ecological Change: A Case Study of the Nilgiri Hills of South India," in: D. Arnold and R. Guha (eds.), *Nature, Culture, Imperialism. Essays on the Environmental History of South Asia*, Delhi 1996, p. 152–84.

deliver the British their incalculable advantage in further strategic and military planning.[18] Furthermore, following the appalling famine in Bengal in 1770–71, a botanical garden founded in Calcutta was charged with investigating the introduction and distribution of new food crops. In 1786 Lieutenant-Colonel Robert Kyd made the first firm proposals to the Board of Revenue.[19]

The earliest European involvement in forest management in India was in 1792 when the Bengal-Bombay-Joint-Commission was encouraged to report on the economic and fiscal capacity of the areas of the Malabar Coast annexed after the war against Maisur.[20] The outbreak of the revolutionary wars in Europe in 1793 and a growing famine in the British Isles the following year drove the Westminster Government to action in domestic and foreign policy. On the one hand it considered how to assure the domestic population's food supply via the colonial possessions, including British India. On the other it was important to find a wharf for the Royal Navy outside England which was both secure and had access to delivery of sufficient timber. The 'wooden wall' remained axiomatic to British defence policy.

The timber shortage in England had reached catastrophic proportions. In 1772 London dockyard owners and the admiralty imposed a ban on the East India Company building big ships, unless its gross tonnage lay under 45,000 tons.[21] In 1791 the Royal Navy's buyer, Thomas Nickols, alerted the admiralty to the threatening lack of timber for shipbuilding. A Parliamentary Committee confirmed the situation without taking specific action.[22] The trading company took the precaution of having more ships built in India which were used in "country trade".[23] Calcutta developed into a wharf for ships of low to moderate tonnage, that is, up to 500 tons, whilst Bombay and Calicut built large, high quality ships of 1000 tons and more.[24]

Employees of the East India Company combed all the countries on the rim of the Indian Ocean for their teak supplies. Michael Symes' mission at the Court of Ava (Burma) in 1795 was not least of all to try and secure timber deliveries and maintain a dockyard. The Resident in Rangoon, Hiram Cox, made the Calcutta administration aware that with keen timber prices and

18 Zaheer Baber, *The Science of Empire. Scientific Knowledge, Civilization, and Colonial Rule in India*, New York 1996, p. 140–6.

19 *Ibid.*, p. 165–70 and Richard H. Grove, *Green Imperialism*, p. 336–40.

20 *Reports of a Joint Commission from Bengal and Bombay, Appointed to Inspect into the State and Condition of the Province of Malabar, in the Years 1792 and 1793*, (reprint Madras 1862), Instructions for the Commission mentioned in a letter from the Governor General dated 16th November 1792. The Commissioners were empowered to guarantee free trade except in pepper.

21 Richard G. Albion, *Forests and Sea Power. The Timber Problem of the Royal Navy 1652–1862*, Cambridge, Mass. 1926 (Harvard Economic Studies 29), p. 95–8.

22 R. A. Wadia, *The Bombay Dockyard and the Wadia Master Builder*, Bombay 1957, p. 17.

23 C. Northcote Parkinson, *Trade in the Eastern Seas, 1793–1813*, London 1966, p. 331.

24 William Kirk, "Shipbuilding in Southern Asia Ports, 1800–1820," *The Mariner's Mirror* 29 (4), 1953, p. 267 and 273.

modern English sawmills, construction costs could undercut even those at Hugli.[25] When in the same year Alexander Mackonochie suggested erecting a sawmill on the Malabar Coast in a letter to the chairman of the Board of Control, Henry Dundas, and simultaneously start up an extensive timber trade, the British government's interest seemed to have been awoken.[26]

Following the successful campaign against Tipu Sultan of Mysore in 1798–99 the East India Company controlled the entire Malabar Coast. In 1796 it had already annexed Cochin from the Dutch. The Bengal-Bombay-Joint-Commission's report in 1793 gave a temporary overview of the industrial, administrative and fiscal situation. The report only briefly mentioned forestry and the timber trade. Major Dow provided the basic information. The forests in the districts of Velatre and Ernaad did not belong to the state, but were privately owned. Duty was also levied from local Nayars according to the tree trunks' girths. Some Nayars leased their rights to Mappila traders, who controlled the entire timber trade. In any case, according to Major Dow, this had more or less come to a halt since the last war with Tipu Sultan, under whose rule the timber trade seems to have been organised by the state, since Tipu Sultan employed animals and forestry workers and remunerated the forest's owners per felled *candy* (about 10 imperial cubic feet).[27]

The Supervisor, Mr Farmer submitted a similar report. Most forests were private property. Tipu Sultan had, according to custom, paid two *fanam* for each felled tree of ten inches diameter. Farmer speaks vaguely of a monopoly which enabled the price of ship timbers to double after 1785.[28] The report further stated that Tipu Sultan had received 4000 *candies* annually, an amount which the East India Company needed for its wharf in Bombay. Eight to ten elephants were needed to work the forests. Basically the legal situation seems to have been unclear. On the one hand Mr Farmer wanted to establish the timber trade with unspecified local people, but the rajas' royalty constrained this. He wanted to abolish this system he considered oppressive as soon as possible. On the other hand he did mention a particular contractor who was willing to organise the whole trade in return for felling licences.[29]

Generally the local princes seem to have distributed felling licences to traders, to whom it was then left to organise the actual task. The Raja of Travancore granted the right to fell timber to "farmers". The timber traders for their part contacted the farmers and paid a fixed sum per tree felled. Responsibility for overseeing the forest lay with the farmers or the landowners.[30]

25 *Ibid.*, p. 272–3.

26 Letter dated 3rd June 1795 to Henry Dundas, quoted in R. A. Wadia, *The Bombay Dockyard*, p. 188.

27 *Reports of a Joint Commission*, para. 445, p. 260.

28 *Ibid.*, para. 447, p. 261.

29 *Ibid.*, para. 448, p. 262.

30 Board's Collections 221/4818, From the Political Resident in Travancore with Enclosure, G. A. Hughes, 17th December 1806.

The felling itself was generally carried out by the local population. Sometimes clans or groups of families specialised in forestry work. In the appendix of the report to the Joint Commission the Bombay Government decreed a ban on felling teak below 21 inches in circumference.[31]

The Bengal administration nevertheless directed Mr Farmer to leave the trade completely free and open and to levy only a duty of two rupees per *candy* as soon as the logs were transported to the coast. The government in Bombay thought this to be the best way of making a large profit out of the local timber trade.[32] But there was a desire to impose limitations "in view to which, there are Gentlemen who have already signified their wishes to the Supervisor, and through him to us, to undertake, at a great expense, to themselves, the erection of saw-mills, on a scientific construction, which, as far as depends on us, we have in concurrence with Mr Farmer expressed our approbation of the idea, as having an immediate tendency to promote the trade, in a manner the most convenient to all the docks, and other seaports in India."[33] If the Joint Commission was explicitly urged to clarify the legal position, it made heavy weather of it as far as rights to forests and their products were concerned. Just who had exploited the forest and who could register which rights remained a mystery to the British officers. Instead, they stayed with the private British business interests and supported Alexander Mackonochie's initiative.[34]

In 1795, with Mackonochie back in England, Leadenhall Street took this up. In his letter Mackonochie had alerted the Court of Directors to the superior quality of the teak that could be competitively obtained on the Malabar Coast. He calculated annual savings to the Company of almost £400,000. In London ship construction costs worked out at £17 per ton, whilst in Bombay they were only £13–14 per ton. In Baipur, south of Calicut Mackonochie wanted to establish a sawmill, for which he needed two mechanics in addition to the machines.[35] A year later he returned to India with authorisation and credit of £10,000. He closed a contract with Bombay to deliver 7000 *candies* annually. The administration there granted the business credit of a further 10,000 Rupees. The contract was to run initially for ten years. The Company looked after transport of the machines and recruited both the mechanics. So as to avoid suspicion of a hidden timber monopoly, the general and open nature of the trade was stressed.[36]

But success was elusive. A mere six months later Mackonochie had to go to the Company for state help, asking it to take over purchase of the working elephants, to buy the plot for the

31 Berthold Ribbentrop, *Forestry in British India*, New Delhi 1989 (reprint, 1st ed. 1900), p. 10.

32 *Reports of a Joint Commission*, para. 449, p. 262.

33 *Ibid.*, p. 262–3.

34 It is not quite correct to talk about a "syndicate", as Richard Grove suggests in his *Green Imperialism*, p. 392.

35 Home Misc. Series, vol. 210, p. 1–10.

36 Board's Collections 39/965, Revenue Department, Extract of Court's Public Letter to Bombay, dated 28th April 1795, para. 27–9. Reply to Mackonochie's letter dated 13th January 1794.

sawmill, and to a large extent look after transporting the timber.[37] The Company, however, did not take up this suggestion. In 1798 the whole business was on the verge of collapse. Although Mackonochie could claim some success in timber delivery, he had to close down the Baipur project for the time being after the death of both his mechanics. Only the following year, after London had sent out two new mechanics, could business start up again. Leadenhall Street told Bombay Castle that Mackonochie was to be granted enough time to build up his business. Even so, the Court of Directors made it known that the whole project would be reconsidered and if necessary shelved, in the case of delays or the contract being broken.[38]

Alexander Mackonochie's timber business was reliant on teamwork with local timber merchants. He acquired felling rights on good terms from the Zamorin of Calicut.[39] But Baipur still suffered from a chronic timber shortage. After the 1799 annexation the Court of Directors considered decreeing a monopoly of all hardwoods on the Malabar Coast. But the Bombay Government contested this. In its view the whole timber trade ought to be in private hands.[40] At that point, the Company had neither the means nor the possibility of directing forest management and the associated timber trade itself. Yet the technical capabilities of the Indian wood merchants were soon exhausted. The consequences of deforestation in preceding decades compelled the local merchants to push on into uneconomic and barely accessible areas to reach the desired trees. Their transportation was then correspondingly difficult, driving up the final price.[41]

The annexation of the entire Malabar Coast in 1799 gave the British an unobstructed line of attack on all its natural resources. In London the war against Tipu Sultan had been sharply criticised for its immense cost.[42] A Bengal-Bombay-Joint-Commission set up the same year ceased work after a few months having achieved nothing. Malabar's administrative inclusion in the Madras Presidency had rendered the commission obsolete.[43] To placate the disbanded Court of Directors, Governor General Richard Wellesley appointed the botanist Francis Buchanan, whose scientific knowledge had already served the Company on Michael Symes' mission to Burma, to compile a report on the newly acquired territories. Buchanan set off on the 24th January

37 Board's Collections 39/965, Extract Bombay Public Consultation, the 16th October 1796, Letter from Mr A. Mackonochie.

38 Bombay Despatches 1788–99, vol. 19 (Record Department), Revenue 19th March 1799, para. 29, p. 266–9.

39 Board's Collections 89/1843, Proceedings relative to Saw Mills at Beypore, para. 13.

40 R. Wadia, *The Bombay Dockyard*, p. 217.

41 Board's Collections 89/1843, Proceedings relative to Saw Mills, para. 38.

42 *Vide* for example Jacques Pouchepadass, "British Attitudes Towards Shifting Cultivation in Colonial South India: A Case Study of South Canara District 1800–1920," in: Arnold/Guha, *Nature Culture, Imperialism*, p. 123–51.

43 E. P. Stebbing, *The Forests of India*, vol. 1, London 1921, p. 63 and Board's Collections 89/1843, To the Honble Court of Directors, Bombay Castle, 10th October 1800, para. 35.

ary 1800, bound for Mysore, Coorg, Malabar and Canara, instructed "to investigate into the state of Agriculture, Arts and Commerce in the fertile and valuable Dominions acquired in the recent and former War from the late Sultaun of Mysore for the purpose of obtaining such insight into the real state of the Country as may be productive of future improvement and advantage."[44]

Buchanan had to compile a favourable report for Wellesley, which he duly did. The Court of Directors was so impressed it ordered that it be printed. The information on timber stocks and forest management was nevertheless sparse. Furthermore, most of it seemed to be second hand.[45] If the East India Company really wanted to get to know the country it needed more detailed information, which it was not going to receive from a purely summary report.[46] Methods were also needed which went beyond simply organising the timber trade. These included registering the number of trees and setting quotas for felling. But the legal situation also had to be clarified. The urgent need for such a systematic survey became ever more obvious.

It was Alexander Mackonochie who unstintingly pressed the Bombay Government to further 'state' measures. Since the local timber merchants were unreliable sources, the Company had to acquire its own overview of the timber resources and the logistics of the trade. Only thus could a long term future be secured for shipbuilding in Bombay.[47] The matter gained new momentum when in 1802 a letter arrived from London in which the Directors informed the Bombay Government that the British Government planned to have a teak ship of the line and a frigate built in Bombay annually. Plans were to be drafted appropriately. At the same time all obtainable timber was to be stocked in Bombay. The Company's shipbuilding programme was not to be compromised, this was especially true for the large ships of over 1000 tons.[48] The demand came also that Bombay declare its per ton building costs.[49]

44 Home Misc. Series 256, Extract of Bengal Public Consultations, 24th February 1800.

45 For a critical analysis of Buchanan's work *vide* M. Vicziany, "Imperialism, Botany and Statistics in early Nineteenth Century India. The Surveys of Francis Buchanan (1762–1829)," *Modern Asian Studies* 20, 1986, p. 653–4 and 659–60.

46 *Vide* the study by C. A. Bayly, *Empire and Information. Intelligence Gathering and Social Communication in India, 1780–1870*, Cambridge 1996, p. 56–141.

47 Board's Collections 182/3474, Appointment of a Committee for the Survey of the Forests in Malabar and Canara, Bombay 18th March 1801.

48 *Ibid.*, Our Governor in Council at Bombay, London 5th May 1802.

49 Parliamentary Papers, vol. 10, 1805, no. 220 and no. 40. In Bombay the price was £21/22 per ton, whilst in London it was £35.

III

What had happened? The East India Company's leasing system, through which it had put together its annual Indian fleet, had become too expensive. The Committee of Managing Owners, composed of the ships' husbands and the ships' captains, more or less dictated the freight rates. Pressure on this cartel from independent businesses had also increased. The 1796 reform sought to remedy this. Late in 1798 a member of the Court of Directors, David Scott, proposed permitting Indian-built ships to trade into London. He met with fierce opposition.[50] In October 1798, Governor General Richard Wellesley permitted exports on Indian-built ships against the advice of the Court of Directors. The main argument was the lower freight cost. Henry Dundas secretly gave this measure his blessing.[51] In fact, Indian-built ships had been docking in London for several years to unload food supplies. There were twenty two of them between June and August 1800 alone.[52] So when the Bombay Marine's frigate, the *Cornwallis*, appeared on the Thames and the Admiralty was so impressed by her quality that it immediately bought her, a cry of horror went through London's wharf owners and shipbuilders.[53]

Letters of protest from concerned shipbuilders were received by Parliament. There were fears for contracts and jobs. Henry Dundas thought it best to establish the combined value of all ships built in the British Empire and did not allow himself to join the general unfounded alarm.[54] A flurry of correspondence took place between the Court of Directors and the Board of Control. The directors set up a special committee of enquiry. But the Board of Control and the British government would not accept a compromise.[55] The Admiralty also imposed its plan and announced in 1802 that it was considering building two warships. But first it wanted to collate information about shipbuilding in Bombay. Philip Dundas, Henry Dundas' nephew was sent there in 1804 to take stock. Following the Governor of Bombay Jonathan Duncan's report, which was also favourable, the Admiralty decided to go ahead with the experiment.[56]

The much heralded report on Malabar's timber stocks was a long time coming. A first statement appeared in 1804. This stressed above all the immense teak forests. But before they

[50] C. H. Philips, *The East India Company 1784–1834*, Manchester 1961, p. 80–96.

[51] *Ibid.*, p. 107–8.

[52] R. Wadia, *The Bombay Dockyard*, p. 178–9.

[53] *Ibid.*, p. 185.

[54] *Ibid.*, p. 175.

[55] *Reports and Papers on the Impolicy of employing Indian built Ships in the Trade of the East India Company and of admitting them to British Registry* (London 1809, publ. by the Court of Directors), nos. 1–10, *passim*.

[56] A letter from Lord Viscount Melville to the Right Honourable Spencer Percival on the subject of naval timber, 22nd June 1810, p. 39–40.

could be used the undergrowth and small trees would have to be burned.[57] Robert Anderson, Superintendent of the Marine and his successor Philip Dundas in Bombay then demanded a comprehensive report on the forests and the possibilities for timber trade on the Malabar Coast.[58] The administration's inertia is hard to fathom. Finally, in April of the same year, Governor Jonathan Duncan introduced Henry Dundas to a man who had caused a stir with a memorandum written at the Governor's request, Baron Franz von Wrede, or Francis Wrede, who had been resident on the Malabar Coast since the mid 1790s and knew the country well.[59]

Franz von Wrede was born in Heidelberg in 1762 to a family of civil servants respected in the Palatine Electorate (Kurpfalz) in south west Germany.[60] His father, Ferdinand Wrede, or Wreden, as the name was sometimes spelled, had a university education in law and philosophy.[61] Ferdinand Wrede was court counsellor at the prince-bishopric of Speyer, then privy counsellor at Heidelberg Town Hall where he became state clerk from 1746 until his death. These posts required legal, administrative and fiscal knowledge.[62] In his role as state clerk Ferdinand Wrede was particularly involved in inter regional road building and local mining. This also included forest management.[63] As was usual at the time, his eldest son Franz Joseph (baptised 3rd June 1750) was groomed to step into his father's shoes, the post being regarded as a sinecure. In 1793 Franz Joseph took over his deceased father's position.

The Wreden family's elevation to the nobility followed an application to the electoral prince in 1790–1, resulting in their name being changed to "von Wrede".[64] Franz von Wrede seems to have spent a period in Frankfurt; there were at least bills in his name to be paid there.[65] In common with all his brothers, Franz Wrede studied philosophy, but does not seem to have taken his final exams.[66] Whether Franz Wrede gained an understanding of forest development

57 Board's Collections vol. 182/3473, Letter from the Commercial Resident in Malabar, with Enclosure, Phaulghaut 10th October 1804, Alexander Bell.

58 *Ibid.*, Letter from the Superintendent of the Marine, Robert Anderson, Bombay 11th January 1805.

59 Home Misc. Series 341, Governor Jon. Duncan to Lord Melville, introducing Baron de Wrede, Bombay 17th April 1805 and Home Misc. Series 341, The Baroness De Wrede to Lord Melville, Heidelberg 6th August 1806.

60 Katholisches Kirchenbuchamt Heidelberg, Taufregister. Franciscus Christopherus Mathias Josephus Wreden was baptised on the 10th May 1762.

61 Oskar Fürst von Wrede, "Zur Geschichte der Heidelberger Familie Wrede," *Neues Archiv für die Geschichte der Stadt Heidelberg und der Kurpfalz* 13, 1928, p. 458–65.

62 *Ibid.*, p. 468–9.

63 *Ibid.*, p. 470–1.

64 *Ibid.*, p. 474.

65 Maximilian Huffschmid, "Goethes Heidelberger Freundin Helene Dorothea Delph und ihre Angehörigen," *Neues Archiv für die Geschichte der Stadt Heidelberg und der Kurpfalz* 11, 1926, p. 267.

66 Gustav Toepke, *Die Matrikel der Universität Heidelberg, Band IV*, Heidelberg 1903, p. 297, Nr. 85. Franciscus Josephus Wreden was enrolled with 37 other students as "*logicus*" on the 5th December 1777, which means that he joined a preliminary university class (Universität Heidelberg, Universitätsarchiv).

and management from his family home and father's profession can only be a matter of speculation. The Palatine Electorate forest survey began at the instigation of Elector Karl Theodor in 1767. In the following years outstanding maps appeared, covering the whole state. Here too, it was the strategic, administrative and fiscal demands of the absolutist state which helped modern science to gain recognition and serve the state. Employees of Heidelberg University and the newly founded Academy of Science in Mannheim made a fundamental contribution to this work.[67]

Franz Wrede left Heidelberg as a young man and signed up on a Dutch or Danish East Indiaman in Hamburg.[68] One can assume his age to be around twenty at this time. At some stage he must have gone ashore in Cochin. There he rose to the position of Council Chairman.[69] Other sources have him as president of the Law Council in Cochin.[70] The family had no news of him for years and only learnt of Franz's career in Cochin coincidentally.[71] Conversely, Franz can only have learned by post of his family's new-found aristocracy. It was probably in India, too, that he married his wealthy wife, Anna Helena Daimichen.[72] No other information exists in Germany about Franz Wrede's life. The Wrede family obviously attached great importance to an education appropriate to their station. All Franz Wrede's brothers went into public service.[73] Franz himself seems to have had another plan for his life even if it was also in public service that he pursued his career in Cochin.

Let us return to Franz von Wrede's memorandum written early in 1805.[74] It dealt systematically with the pressing problems. To begin with von Wrede lamented the fact that in spite of over thirteen years of rule, the East India Company on the Malabar Coast had represented large areas of the country as blank spaces on the map. Although the Bengal-Bombay-Joint-Commission had stressed the importance of the teak forests for both trade and revenue purposes, there had been no further assessment of the situation. But this was all the more urgent, since so much

[67] Erich Bauer, "Rheinland-pfälzische Wälder in historischen Karten," *Wald und Holz im Wandel der Zeit*, Trier 1986, p. 49–52.

[68] J. Heilmann, *Feldmarschall Fürst Wrede*, Leipzig 1881, p. 3–4.

[69] Katholisches Kirchenbuchamt Heidelberg, Sterberegister. "[...] *quondam Praesidens Consilium Cochin in India orientalis*."

[70] Generallandesarchiv Karlsruhe, Verlassenschaft Franz von Wrede (72 v. Wrede 21), Lit. W. No. 19 Pupillaria. Auszug Kurbadischen Hofraths = Protokolls/Senats, d. d. Mannheim den 18ten Jun. 1806.

[71] J. Heilmann, *Feldmarschall Fürst Wrede*, p. 4.

[72] Oskar Fürst von Wrede, *Zur Geschichte der Heidelberger Familie Wrede*, p. 479–80.

[73] *Ibid.*, Stammtafel, after p. 480. The youngest son Carl Philipp von Wrede became the well known Field Marshall of the Bavarian Army, who successfully fought the important battle against the French army at Hanau on the 28th of October 1813.

[74] This memorandum has been edited by the present author in his *Flottenbau und Forstbetrieb in Indien 1794–1823*, p. 171–95. All quotations refer to the draft in the Board's Collections vol. 182/3474 (1805–1806), No. 11, Extract Bombay Consultations, 26th Feb. 1805.

was riding on it for the motherland.[75] Alexander Mackonochie's wind driven saw mill project was heavily criticised. Not only because a large sum of money was put into the venture, which had thus far shown no return, but because contrary to advance notices, there was in fact less timber available in Baipur, and at higher prices.[76]

Wrede urgently pressed for the long demanded survey. Without it all planning was fantasy and pure speculation. It could well be that given the conditions it could not be completed with the requested precision, but the British Government, after the fanfare of "inexhaustible naval resources", did expect an appropriate report if the East India Company did not want to face allegations of out and out carelessness. The survey was to be compiled by an expedition. Accompanied by an Engineer Corps, a doctor was also to take part in the reconnaissance and keep a diary of all his observations. Wrede attached particular value to drawing up maps in which the limit of the first elevations and hills were to be marked. Similarly, the limits of the living and planting areas were to be shown, as was jungle and the prevalence of teak and other large trees. In marking the course of rivers, their navigability and possibilities for floating timber were to be noted. Alexander Mackonochie, being familiar with the area, was to lead the expedition.[77]

To avoid future mistakes, Wrede referred back to earlier developments. Again, Mackonochie came in for strong criticism. Wrede categorically rejected transferring technology as long as the necessary number of operatives, technicians and supply of spare parts were not assured. A steam powered saw mill was just as unrealistic as the construction of wagon ways. Wrede based his position on the difference in development between two cultures in different climates, which made the introduction of technical innovations not only difficult, but in many cases quite impossible.[78] Wrede seems to have been prompted less by early racialist thinking than by the conviction that technology developed in Europe just could not be applied in the tropics. He was not able to think as far as modifying and adapting it.

The output of construction timber had dropped alarmingly to only 400 *candies* from 30,000. But as long as the question of forest ownership was not clarified there could not be any improvement here. If local chiefs or other individuals could come up with proof of private ownership of forest, the British-Indian state had to recognise it. All unmarked and unenclosed areas of forest were transferred into the East India Company's private ownership, that is, they became state property. This had worked in the same way under Tipu Sultan. The rajas of Travancore and Cochin operated similarly. Remaining claims on public forests were compen-

[75] *Ibid.*, para. 1–2, 7.

[76] *Ibid.*, para. 3–6.

[77] *Ibid.*, para. 11–20.

[78] *Ibid.*, para. 27–41.

sated by the Company with an annual pension. This did not mean there was a state monopoly, since private forest ownership was guaranteed, as was private timber trade.[79]

Without the concomitant privileges no private individual would enter the timber trade. Only the Musa family, which already controlled the pepper trade on the Malabar Coast to a large extent, and a few other individuals had, according to Wrede, sufficient capacity and capital to take over the timber trade on a large scale. But Wrede warned the Company against such perks, since past experience had shown that sooner or later such contractors ended up deciding all the conditions.[80] The Dutch, he felt, had had the most positive experience of forest management in their Indian possessions by leaving it exclusively in the hands of the Verenigde Oostindische Compagnie. A cooperative relationship with local workers was secured by the prospect of long term employment and regular pay.[81] Generally, however, access to the state's forests was to be controlled, if not prevented.[82]

Lastly, Franz von Wrede demanded that forests on the Malabar Coast be managed on the European model. All forests contributing to the long term yield were to be protected. Secondly, measures were necessary to ensure all the timber needed did in fact become available. Thirdly, the price of timber had to come down. This required exact knowledge of the quality and quantity of the trees in the forests, to help fix annual felling quotas. Furthermore, the forests' protection had to be actively pursued and replanting programmes carried through. Damage to the forest floor caused by felling and timber damage in transport was to be avoided. The heart of the plan was the establishment of a forest authority responsible for both the forest and the timber trade. An Inspector of Forests would lead the authority. Two foresters under him would oversee the work on site. Additionally there were carpenters, lumberjacks, porters and elephants. As second in command Wrede envisaged an active, well educated and competent man. He recommended Alexander Mackonochie for the post. Wrede saw one of the forester posts best occupied by Franz Missley from Munich, who served in the 84th King's Regiment. The more Europeans became familiar with forest management, the better.[83]

Detailed costings were contained in an appendix. The whole affair naturally had to be viable for the colonial state. The resulting fall in timber prices curtailed the venture's success. After a few years of experimentation there were thoughts of expanding the 'establishment', as Wrede called the forestry authority with its limited timber trade. For the Malabar Coast he had metal processing in mind, the quality of which at least matched, if not exceeded that in Sweden

[79] *Ibid.*, para. 42–9.
[80] *Ibid.*, para. 52–7.
[81] *Ibid.*, para. 87–90.
[82] *Ibid.*, para. 62.
[83] *Ibid.*, para. 64–78.

or Norway. In the long term Wrede envisaged a fully self sufficient shipbuilding operation in Bombay and Cochin.[84]

IV

Franz von Wrede obviously had precise ideas about efficient forestry and timber trade. Nevertheless, the memorandum does not bear the markings of a thorough knowledge of contemporary German forestry. It lacks more nuanced aspects of forest management and plantation. Wrede's memorandum can therefore only be seen as an early attempt to apply the basic principles of European forestry on the Malabar Coast. More careful scrutiny reveals its failings, which are demonstrable in several places. After far-reaching clarification of the legal claims, remaining local rights were to be financially compensated. Early forest ordinances in the German states of Franconia and Hesse, confirm these attempts to enforce rulers' claims and to also put common forests under state control.[85] This in turn involved limiting access to forests for the local population. Prevention was sought not only of uncontrolled felling, but also of secondary usage such as cattle herding and gathering leaf mould and mulch for fertiliser.[86] Yet for all his proposals, Wrede forgot the painstaking work which precedes the settlement of claims; the demarcation of borders.[87] Wrede does not seem to have had an inkling of the decades of daily grind which such a job entails.[88] Thus unperturbed he called for such delineation to be carried out.

Forest management was to be put in the hands of the state. Clearance work, transport and replanting would be done under Company overseers who would have fixed incomes under Wrede's plan. Only the lumberjacks would be local people under long term contract. Here too, there are hints of contemporary German forestry, where foresters monitored the woods and oversaw the felling.[89] Wages went from being financed locally through rates to state remuneration.[90] In Europe too, foresters and lumberjacks were employed by official forest authorities.

84 *Ibid.*, para. 102–5, 110.

85 Winfried Schenk, *Waldnutzung, Waldzustand und regionale Entwicklung in vorindustrieller Zeit im mittleren Deutschland. Historisch-Geographische Beiträge zur Erforschung von Kulturlandschaften in Mainfranken und Nordhessen*, Stuttgart 1996 (Erdkundliches Wissen, Heft 117), p. 59.

86 Verordnung für den dem Hochstift Speyer eigentümlich zugehörigen Böhnwald von 1782, Art. I, 2. Abschnitt, p. iii, in: Franz Müllenkampf, *Sammlung der Forstbestimmungen verschiedener Länder*, Mainz 1791.

87 "Ueber das Forstwesen vom 14. bis 17. Jahrhundert," *Zeitschrift für die Geschichte des Oberrheins* 2, 1851, p. 14–33.

88 *Vide* Hans Hausrath, *Forstgeschichte der rechtsrheinischen Theile des ehemaligen Bisthums Speyer*, Berlin 1898, p. 18–24.

89 "Die Wald-, Holz- und Forstordnung für die K. K. österreichischen Vorlande von 1787," in: F. Müllenkampf, *Sammlung der Forstbestimmungen verschiedener Länder*, p. 127.

90 W. Schenk, *Waldnutzung, Waldzustand und regionale Entwicklung*, p. 84.

Some lived in separate forest settlements.[91] Wrede also thought about moving forest workers to the teak forests, but there lacked the necessary integration in an administrative apparatus such as had established itself in the Palatine Electorate over the course of a century.[92] This included, for example, the policing role undertaken by the head foresters, as well as the submission of regular reports on the condition of the forest.[93]

The German Empire's varying regional forest regulations during the 17th and 18th centuries were by no means sophisticated works sharing some arcane unifying purpose. It was basically a matter of increasing revenue in the context of absolutist state fiscal management. This was promoted by finance-led forest management, headed by men often with university education and broad knowledge, but lacking any practically based experience.[94] Forests were therefore viewed in terms of financial profitability. In many parts of the German Empire the foresters' attention was focussed on the level of oak trees. These were a benchmark of the forest's condition, good or bad.[95] On the Malabar Coast the same point of view saw teak trees as the forest's only lucrative and economically useful product. For the Europeans other uses for the forest simply did not exist. In Wrede's memorandum this is already abundantly clear. The late 18th century forest regulations were the first to be extensively considered and developed. During the first half of the 19th century they came into general use.[96] A few 'progressive thinking' contemporaries lamented the absence of more scientific forestry.[97] It is worth noting here that historical consideration of forestry, apart from the purely Eurocentric point of view, couples the development of forests with advances in forestry and its science. Forests in the preindustrial age seen from an 'advanced' perspective register only as run down and badly managed woodlands, not as 'forest'.[98] Only 'sustainable forest management', those magic words of modern forestry, turns woodlands into valuable forests.

Wrede lay emphasis on sustainable management to maintain the long term level of trees. This requirement was also made in German 18th century forest regulations. But the replanted trees were often in a pitiful state. Some of the regulations were not enforced until after 1800.[99]

[91] Karl Hasel, *Forstgeschichte. Ein Grundriß für Studium und Praxis*, Hamburg und Berlin 1985, p. 177–9.

[92] Hans Hausrath, "Zur Geschichte der kurpfälzischen Forstorganisation," *Forstwissenschaftliches Centralblatt* 52, NF 29, 1908, p. 449–59 and p. 516–30.

[93] H. Hausrath, *Forstgeschichte der rechtsrheinischen Theile des ehemaligen Bisthums Speyer*, p. 24–32.

[94] K. Hasel, *Forstgeschichte*, p. 138–9.

[95] W. Schenk, *Waldnutzung, Waldzustand und regionale Entwicklung*, p. 101–3 and 154–7.

[96] *Ibid.*, p. 54–5.

[97] Georg Ludwig Hartig, *Grundsätze der Forst-Direction*, Hadamar 1803. The book suggests an elaborated form of forest management, as is supposed to have been practised in the German dukedom of Hesse-Nassau. *Vide* especially the Hartig's own efforts to educate young foresters at the "Forst-Lehr-Institut in Dillenburg", p. 301–5. For a brief account on Hartig *vide* K. Hasel, *Forstgeschichte*, p. 230–2.

[98] W. Schenk, *Waldnutzung, Waldzustand und regionale Entwicklung*, p. 39.

[99] *Ibid.*, p. 101–7 and 127.

To manage a forest on the Malabar Coast with any success at all, its care had to be in the hands of trained foresters. Where possible the carpenters would also be Europeans. Wrede seems to have had immense trust in the capabilities of the German forest industry. It certainly was one of the most modern in Europe.[100]

Local Indian influences do not seem to have had any part to play. Wrede's will records his possession of a memorandum on Malabar by the famous Dutchman Hendrik van Reede tot Drakestein, Governor of Cochin (1670–77), and of a Dutch description of the Malabar Coast and its hinterland, but neither of these affected the content of his own memorandum.[101] Similarly little of local traditional forest use found its way into the memorandum.[102] Thus Franz von Wrede produced a document based on general European principles of forestry, enriched by his experiences in Cochin and adapted it to local conditions in so far as insisting on employing local people, or rather bringing people in from Colombo (Sri Lanka). Local science and knowledge had no place in his writing.

Franz von Wrede probably left India in 1805 and returned to Germany. He may have been ill, since he died in Heidelberg on 2nd June 1806.[103] His wife had the will read the following day.[104] Wrede's widow was very clearly in financial difficulties. On 6th August that year she wrote to Lord Melville (Henry Dundas) offering to sell various books and writings from her husband's legacy.[105] The widow's position did at the very least improve after 1814 when her brother in law Carl Philipp von Wrede was made a prince by the Bavarian King, receiving with his title the residence of Gut Ellingen near Nuremberg.[106]

One anecdote recounts that the von Wredes when leaving India put their entire fortune on one shipload. The ship was then scuppered by the French. Baroness von Wrede had her nephew Karl Theodor von Wrede successfully pursue her compensation claim through the courts. Her award was apparently then used to build up the famous Ellinger stud.[107]

100 K. Hasel, *Forstgeschichte*, p. 219–28.

101 Home Misc. Series 341, The Baroness de Wrede to Lord Melville, Heidelberg 6th August 1806. In her letter widow von Wrede offered several books on various Indian subjects (Malabar grammars, history books on Maisur and Malabar, Natural History books etc.) from the inheritance to the East India Company. Lord Melville's secretary was not able to take action and passed the letter on to Grenville. There the trail goes dead. For the biographical background of Hendrik van Reede, whose father was a chief forester, and his botanical work *vide* R. Gove, *Green imperialism*, p. 84–6.

102 *Vide* Vandana Shiva, *Das Geschlecht des Lebens. Frauen, Ökologie und Dritte Welt*, Nördlingen 1989, p. 69–73, (orig. title *Staying alive. Women, ecology and survival in India*).

103 Katholisches Kirchenbuchamt Heidelberg, Sterberegister.

104 Generallandesarchiv Karlsruhe, Lit. W. No. 19. Pupillaria, 3. Juni 1806 – 18. Juli 1806.

105 Home Misc. Series 341, The Baroness De Wrede to Lord Melville, Heidelberg 6th August 1806; cp. n. 101.

106 J. Heilmann, *Feldmarschall Fürst Wrede*, p. 384.

107 Oskar Fürst von Wrede, *Zur Geschichte der Heidelberger Familie Wrede*, p. 480 and J. Heilmann, *Feldmarschall Fürst Wrede*, p. 489.

V

The Wrede memorandum was soon forgotten. Even though various surveys of Malabar's forests were prepared between 1806 and 1810, they remained piecemeal affairs.[108] State monopoly was the first result of attempts to organise forest management. It covered not only the state forests seen as Crown property, but every type of tree designated by the "Conservator of Forests", Captain Joseph Watson.[109] Additionally, the head forester received "plenary powers", granting him jurisdictional functions in the forests as well as supervisory ones. Captain Watson also appropriated a degree of executive power over the following years, leading to serious disagreements with the authorities in Bombay and Madras. The more than unsatisfactory timber trade and the clearly recognisable deficiencies in forest management resulted in the dissolution of the Bombay Forest Department in 1823, its function being transferred to the Revenue Department.[110]

The first attempt to introduce contemporary European forestry in Malabar failed. Wrede had rejected any form of general state monopoly and insisted upon guaranteeing use of the forests for private enterprise. In this he lagged behind forestry regulations as they existed in individual German states. There, the local princes sought to extend their sphere of influence to common and private forests. The East India Company's state monopoly extended far beyond sensible use of the forest and was only concerned with maximising timber production. Even fiscal interests were secondary. This behaviour alone, between 1806 and 1823 exemplifies the colonial state's purely exploitative nature. Since its staff were not capable of organising forest management, it soon had to fall back on licensing the local timber traders mentioned earlier; the Musa family.

The negative consequences of which Wrede had warned were soon reality. Following orders from London, the frustrated Bombay Government soon gave up the whole business with the exception of shipbuilding for the Royal Navy in Bombay, albeit on a smaller scale. In one sense the recognition of private forest in Thana District in 1823 represents a new start in British-Indian forestry. German expertise did stand behind Franz von Wrede's memorandum, even if we know little as to how he gathered it. The need for timber to build the Royal Navy's ships in Bombay certainly did not lead to the establishment of the proposed, albeit incomplete

108 M. Mann, *Flottenbau und Forstbetrieb*, p. 64–79.

109 Board's Collections 221/4818, President's Minute, 7th November 1806, and *Ibid.*, To William Taylor Money, Translate of a Proclamation issued by Thomas Warden Esqr., Principal Collector of Malabar, dated the 5th Dec. 1806.

110 M. Mann, *Flottenbau und Forstbetrieb*, p. 107–32.

state forestry management. Only construction of the Indian railways and their immense demand for sleepers led to the introduction of sustainable forest management and the development of adequate forest administration, again, with the help of German expertise.

India's Road to Berlin and Bonn – From War to Relations

Johannes H. Voigt

As part of the British Empire, British-India had been pulled automatically and unasked into the war with Germany from 1939 to 1945.[1] About two millions of Indian soldiers were fighting in the British-Indian Army on the side of the Allies, whereas tens of thousands of Indian nationals overseas had volunteered to side with the Axis Powers in Europe and Southeast Asia, finally taken prisoners of war by their own compatriots or the Western Allies. On account of her enormous war effort and sacrifices, British-India was amongst the few nations selected and invited to establish a Military Mission in Berlin attached to the four occupation powers' Allied Control Council.[2] While the German Reich had had Consulates in British-India before the war, there had been no British-Indian counterpart in Germany. Thus, a mission stationed in Germany meant for British-India to break new ground in her international relations.

1. Connections in Military Guise

After extensive deliberations, the British-Indian Government decided by early October 1945 to establish a Military Mission of two to three officers at Berlin.[3] In order "to compete with he Russians", the mission had a military title, with the result that some of the representatives were

[1] On India's participation in the war see Johannes H. Voigt, *India in the Second World War*, New Delhi 1987. Translated from the German version *Indien im Zweiten Weltkrieg*, Stuttgart 1978.

[2] D. M. Cleary (India Office) to Viscount Hood (Foreign Office), (London) 7.6.1945, India Office Library (abbr. I. O. Lib.), L/P & S/12/4552.

[3] Olaf Caroe to Cleary, New Delhi 9.7.1945, Government of India, External Affairs Department to Secretary of State. Tel., No. 8669, 8.10.1945, recd. 10.50 hrs; notice without signature, Col G. S., B. G. S., 30.10.1945, *ibid.*

political officers in the guise of military officers.[4] The major tasks of the Mission envisaged were

(1) to observe the military, political, economic and industrial situation and developments in Germany as they affected India's interests;
(2) to fulfil consular duties in the mission's capacity as "forerunner" of a possible future diplomatic representation;
(3) to coordinate the activities of various organisations entrusted to search for and protect Indian nationals, especially former members of the Indian Legion of the Wehrmacht still at large in Europe.[5]

Whereas the British military authorities were sure that the establishment of a Military Mission would be of value for the special tasks of a future peace conference, the Mission, even at the outset, was looked upon more in the nature of a diplomatic embassy than as a military unit.[6] Therefore, one of the chief objects in establishing the Indian Mission in Berlin was to "show the flag", and another, to be present in Germany once the Military Government were succeeded by a civilian.[7]

An initial problem was to find proper personnel to staff the Mission. The application by Henry Wolfgang Blanck, Sub Lieutenant of the Royal Indian Navy for the post of chief administrative officer seemed to be the key to solve the information problems of the new mission at Berlin: Blanck was a born German of Jewish descent, speaking the Berlin dialect, having left his country on account of the Nazis' racial policy, joining the Royal Indian Navy as an engineer and, while on leave, visiting his devastated birth-place by the end of 1945.[8] Unfortunately, the offer was turned down, the reasons alluded to in a reply from the Indian Naval Headquarters to the Admiralty: His junior position – he had completed only one year of service in the Royal Indian Navy – and his German birth were considered a security risk.[9]

Major Warren was put in charge of all consular functions, to be succeeded by Captain Francis in October 1947.[10] A much wanted Indian economic expert for questions of reparations was

4 Unsigned Notice, India Office, 30.10.1945, *ibid.*

5 Major MacAlston to Lt.-General Sir John Swayne, General Headquarters, B. G. S., War Office, India Office, 31.12.1945, I. O. Lib., L/WS/1/1582.

6 E. P. Donaldson (India Office, War Staff) to Lieut.-Col. R. R. Burnett (Joint Secretary, External Affairs Department, Government of India), London 28.12.1945; Major-General D. Stuart to Chief of the General Staff, Gen. Headquarters, India, Berlin 1.4.1946 I. O. Lib., L/WS/1/1582 and 737.

7 Donaldson to Burnett, 28.11.1945.

8 Major MacAlston to Brigadier J. R. Reynolds (India Office, War Staff), Berlin 2.1.1946. *Ibid.*

9 Major N. George to Major MacAlston, London 14.1.1946; Naval Headquarters India to Admiralty London, 27.1.1946, *ibid.*

10 Memorandum "Civilian Consular Officer for the Indian Military Mission, Berlin," (New Delhi) 1.12.1947, National Archives of India (abbrev. NAI), External Affairs and Commonwealth Relations Ministry (abbrev. Ext. Aff.), E II Branch, File No. 41 (2)-E II/47.

P. C. Chaudhuri, I. C. S., who acted as British India's representative in the Inter-Allied Reparation Agency (IARA).[11] India, a member of this Agency, had been allotted 2.9% of German reparations.[12] The Military Mission was to look after India's interests in this field.[13] Besides the wish for material compensation, there was a great Indian demand for technical and scientific know how. A first party of 18 German technicians left Cologne for India on 25th January 1949 accompanied by an officer of the Military Mission, and by early 1950 more than 100 technicians had been recruited by the Mission from Western Germany.[14]

The first Head of the Mission was Major-General D. Stuart, reporting the arrival at his post to Field Marshal Auchinleck on 25th February 1946.[15] By early 1947, the staff of the Mission consisted of its Chief, a Deputy Chief in the rank of a Colonel, two Staff Officers and some Warrent Officers.[16] As the task of the Mission was not anymore of a preponderantly military nature, a "civilianisation" was wanted. This was quite in line with India's post independence policy. A civilian official, Khub Chand, I. C. S., hitherto Deputy Secretary in the Ministry of Defence, was appointed Head of the Mission to take charge of the post in early 1948.[17] In order not to be denigrated as a civilian amidst the crowd of numerous Allied officers of the Military Missions, he was given the local rank of a major general. Knowing that he did not feel comfortable in a uniform, he was assured that he was practically a chargé d'affaires, almost as much as an ambassador!

[11] Inter-Allied Reparation Agency, *First Report of the Secretary General for the Year 1946*, n.p. p. 58. His alternate was S. A. Maybury-Lewis, and substitutes were K. V. Ramaswamy and G. A. Ahmed, *ibid*. See also Indian Military Mission, *Monthly Report* No. 1, 2.4.1946, I. O. Lib., L/WS/1/1593.

[12] Indian Military Mission, *Monthly Report* No. 2, 2.4.1946 and No. 7, 1.9.1946, *ibid*. According to the Inter Allied Reparation Agency's Secretary General's Report for the Year 1947 (Brussels 1948), India was to receive 3.09% of Industrial Capital Equipment and merchant Shipping Allocations as at 31.12.1947 (Annex xi, p. 67). British India's division and independence caused the Agency to divide the British-Indian share between the two successor states India and Pakistan. Of category A (German assets abroad) India was allotted 1.65%, Pakistan 0.35%, and of category B (industrial equipment and merchant ships confiscated in Germany) India 2.39% and Pakistan 0.51% (Inter Allied Reparation Agency, *Report 1948*, Brussels 1949, p. 21). For plants allocated of category B, see p. 68. By the end of 1949, India had received of category A reparations goods valued at 2.95% of reparations allotted to all countries. *Ibid*., p. 97; they were estimated to be at a value of about 20 million Reichsmark (based on values of the year 1938; Inter-Allied Reparation Agency, *Report of the Secretary General for the Year 1949*, Brussels 1950, Annex xv, p. 111). On categories and criticism of accounting procedure by the IARA see G. W. Harmssen (ed.), *Am Abend der Demontage. Sechs Jahre Reparationspolitik*, Bremen 1951, p. 21.

[13] Maj.-General Stuart to High Commissioner for India (India House, London), Berlin 25.2.1946, I. O. Lib., L/WS/1/1582.

[14] Fortnightly Report No. 42, 1.2.1949, NAI, Ext. Aff., File No. 51 (2)-R&I/49; Tel. Hicomind, London to Foreign, New Delhi, 13.3.1950, *ibid*, Eur. II Branch File No. 5 (115)-Eur. II/49.

[15] Maj.-Gen. Stuart to Field Marshal Auchinleck, Berlin 25.2.1946, I. O. Lib., L/WS/1/1582.

[16] P. N. Krishnaswamy, Dep. Sec., Ext. Aff. Min. to R. P. Sarathy, Min. of Finance, (New Delhi) 28.1.1948, NAI, Ext. Aff., Eur. II Branch, File No. 41 (2)-Eur. II/47.

[17] *Ibid*.

2. Wanted Legs: Two or Three?

When the Federal Republic of Germany was founded in 1949, followed shortly by the creation of the German Democratic Republic, the Indian Military Mission did not close its gates, but shifted the centre of its activities from Berlin to Bonn, where the head of the Mission was accredited to the Allied High Commission, comprising the High Commissioners of the United States, France and Great Britain. Khub Chand pleaded to his government, not to abandon Berlin as a seat of the Mission:

> India enjoys a peculiar position. We belong to the Commonwealth but take more or less an independent line in foreign policy, dictated solely by our own interests and the wider interests of world peace. We must, therefore, maintain our link, as long as possible, with both parties, even if your representative must sacrifice the luxury of working in a fixed abode. We must avoid effusive support to any party and accept the inconvenient but unavoidable situation of working as a Military Mission with the Russians, as members of a quadripartite set-up, while putting in more than occasional appearance in lounge-suits in Bonn.[18]

As long as the Four Power Control Commission existed, Khub Chand held, India should fly its new flag next to that of Australia and of many other countries.

And, despite India's far greater interests in Western Germany, he stuck to his advice of maintaining a leg in both camps, when the Allied High Commission at Bonn invited India to have a representative accredited to them. Abandoning Berlin would incur the Soviet reproach that they were stooges of American imperialism; and refusing to go to Bonn would mean the loss of American good-will. Therefore, a liaison officer should be posted at Bonn. In the fluent situation of Germany during late summer 1949 Khub Chand surmised that India might need a third leg with an East German government.[19] He advised caution: India should "avoid being too obtrusive" by going to Bonn, admitting though that "all our commercial and other interests lie almost wholly in Western Germany".

In order to promote its interests by normalising relations with Germany, the Indian Government had to take a decision in order not to miss the bus set in motion by the creation of the two German states and the increasing economic recovery:

> German sentiment strongly desires return to the comity of nations […]. We have close trade and cultural relations with Germany, particularly the part now under control of the German Federal Government, and we must not run counter the declared wishes of the German people. This is the time to make Germany a friend. Her recovery is so rapid and she is destined to play

18 Khub Chand to K. P. S. Menon, Berlin 7.7.1949, Secret. NAI, Ext. Aff., Eur. II Branch File No. 5 (42)-Eur. II/49.

19 The same to the same, Tel. Berlin 4.8.1949 and Berlin 9.9.1949, *ibid.*

a leading rôle in world affairs within ten or fifteen years that she can afford to neglect us if we do not treat her well.[20]

On 29th November 1949 Nehru as Prime Minister and Minister for External Affairs informed the Allied High Commission at Bonn that Major-General Khub Chand had been appointed Head of the Indian Mission to the Allied High Commission in the Federal Republic of Germany.[21] In the circumstances, normalising relations meant to take two steps: Firstly, to terminate the state of war, and secondly, to establish diplomatic relations. The second point demanded another decision: with whom were relations to be established – with West-Germany alone or also with East-Germany? The matter was complicated by the fact that each of the two German governments claimed to represent the entire country.[22]

No doubt, there was an Indian tendency to recognise both states if need be and if India's neutrality had to be assured in the cold war, in the words of S. K. Banerji:

> Our policy of neutrality between the two blocs should really mean that when necessary, we should be prepared to give equal recognition to the Democratic Government of Eastern Germany as well, as there is no fundamental difference in the nature of the two Administrations – both equally the creatures of Occupation Authorities to whom they are subservient. In the case of Western Germany, however, we had received an invitation to accredit a representative to the Allied High Commission.[23]

The British were informed accordingly. It seemed essential for India to maintain an uninvolved position in an increasingly spoilt international atmosphere due to the cold war. It was necessary to move with great caution in the German political field full of booby traps, as explained to the British High Commission in India:

> We do not propose to take any action towards the recognition of the East German Government until we are invited to recognise it and to exchange diplomatic representatives. It is certainly not our intention ever to recognise that Government as the Government of Germany. Whether, consistent with our policy elsewhere, it may be necessary for us to recognise it as the Government of Eastern Germany is a matter to which we shall give further consideration when the time comes.[24]

The decision to have the Head of the Military Mission at Berlin also accredited to the Allied High Commission at Bonn, had important consequences: Firstly, it could not be undone without offending the Western Powers and the West-German Government, and secondly, it

20 C. S. Jha (Joint Secretary, External Affairs Ministry) to Khub Chand, New Delhi 1.12.1949, NAI, File No. 5 (115)-Eur. II/49.

21 Jawahar Lal (Nehru) to Chairman, Allied High Commission for Germany, Bonn, (New Delhi) 29.11.1949, *ibid.*

22 S. K. Banerji, Memorandum, (New Delhi) 9.11.1949, NAI, Ext. Aff., File No. 5 (115)-Eur. II/49.

23 S. K. Banerji, Memorandum, 9.11.1949, *ibid.*

24 K. P. S. Menon to Frank K. Roberts (Deputy High Commissioner for the U. K.), New Delhi 16.11.1949, *ibid.*

might necessitate the recognition also of the East-German Government. K. P. S. Menon, Secretary of External Affairs, regarded the accreditation to the Allied High Commission an illogical step, which should not be followed by another one:

> We do not want to commit a further illogicality by recognising the West German Government and refusing to recognise the Government of East Germany. We may be able to postpone, but not to refuse recognition to the East German Government if they approach us.[25]

These considerations were connected with the decision to terminate the state of war, although they did not affect it directly, as such a step would relate to the whole of Germany, i. e. to the East as well.

3. How to Terminate the State of War

Four years after the war, when the Allied Control Commission was practically defunct, the Allied Control Council having handed over a great deal of their powers to the West-German Government, and the Soviets taking their own course by establishing another German state within their fold, the question of terminating the state of war was raised in the West.

Having many trading contacts with West German firms reestablished, India was faced with the question whether to follow a Western initiative, take the step at the same time or go ahead singly. The timing of the step was important mainly from a symbolic point of view, indicating friendship and interests. For newly independent India, there was one most important consideration, viz. to give a public and international sign that in her foreign policy decisions she cared for none of the Western Powers' interests and actions. In the circumstances, a step soon after that of the Western Powers was bound to create the false impression that India were still under the spell of Britain and her Allies.[26] By now, the Indian Government had a number of reasons not to go along with the Western Powers, apart from the public effect of taking an independent line: Firstly, these had developed their relations with Germany without consulting India, not even in their decision on reparations, depriving India of the full share once admitted to her. Secondly, they had decided that (West) Germany be rearmed.[27]

On the other hand, India's economic relations with Germany were not of a size to influence the general trend of developments, as Khub Chand noticed, and therefore, India "had no option but to acquiesce in the policy of the Allied High Commission or the Soviet Control Commission, as the case may be".[28] India, though ready to terminate the state of war, should not push

[25] K. P. S. Menon, Notes, 12.11.1949, *ibid.*

[26] U. S. Bajpai, Memorandum, 6.3.1950, *ibid.*

[27] B. F. H. B. Tyabji, Memorandum, 21.12.1950, NAI, Ext. Aff., File No. 5 (128)-Eur. II/49.

[28] Khub Chand to C. S. Jha, Berlin 5.1.1950, NAI, Ext. Aff., File No. 5 (115)-Eur. II/49.

the matter, even if pressed by the British, but take her own course of action without haste, as Khub Chand reasoned:

(1) India agrees, in principle, that the state of war with Germany be terminated;
(2) India does not propose to take precipitate action and would appreciate being kept in touch with developments, particularly the legal implications of the termination of the state of war;
(3) termination of the state of war is a matter of unilateral action on the part of the various Allied Governments and that, so far as India is concerned, a notification in the Gazette of India to the effect that the state of war between India and Germany declared on 3rd September 1939, is ended would be deemed sufficient;
(4) no question arises, as a result of the notification, of the recognition of any particular Government of the whole of Germany since the main thing is the notification in the Gazette of India, its communication to other parties being purely ancillary.[29]

This course was taken, as the British were informed.[30] The very fact that a coordinated Western action was dependent on the time-consuming legislative process in the USA, expected to be completed not before the middle of 1951, gave the Government of India sufficient leeway to terminate the state of war well ahead of the Western Powers. On 1st October 1950, Bajpai arrived at the conclusion: "Prima facie, there is much to be said for our formally bringing the state of war between India and Germany to an end without delay," adding that this was a step favoured at the top: "I have spoken to the Prime Minister who agrees."[31]

Therefore, all that was needed before the executive could act was a check by legal experts of the Ministry of Law whether any constitutional problems were involved. As the jurists could not discover any reason for objection, the way was clear for a decision. By 19th December 1950, the Government had decided, informing the Western Powers that India would terminate the state of war with Germany on 1st January 1951.[32] The British were not at all pleased with it, as Tyabji of the Indian External Affairs Ministry learnt: "They felt that in a matter of such 'psychological' significance as the termination of the state of war with Germany, the allied countries should march in step."[33]

On 1st January 1951, the *Gazette of India*, No. 1, carried the brief statement drafted by Tyabji, that India terminated the state of war with Germany. Why the date of the beginning of

29 Khub Chand to K. P. S. Menon, Berlin 5.1.1950, *ibid.*

30 Gundevia to F. K. Roberts, New Delhi 27.3.1950, NAI, Ext. Aff., File No. 5 (128)-Eur. II/49.

31 U. S. Bajpai, Memorandum, 1.10.1950, Bajpai's signature is followed by that of K. P. S. Menon, taking notice of the statement, *ibid.*

32 Minister for External Affairs (Jawaharlal Nehru) to High Commissioner of the U. K. and the Ambassadors of the USA and France in India, New Delhi 19.12.1950. *ibid.*

33 B. F. H. B. Tyabji, Memorandum, 21.12.1950, *ibid.*

the war was shifted from 3rd September to 30th September 1939, and that of the end of actual hostilities from 7th May to 5th June 1945, will probably forever remain a secret of the Indian bureaucratic machine![34]

Former dates, however, were less significant than the fact of India's early step – preceded only by that of Bolivia –, which was highly appreciated by the German public as a sign of friendship, as Prem Krishen, successor of Khub Chand, reported: India's action "generated a tremendous fund of goodwill amongst the German people".[35] Federal Chancellor Konrad Adenauer thanked India for her decision as a token for starting closer relations to new and independent India.[36]

4. Diplomats to the Fore

Once the state of war had been terminated and the victors ready to receive the vanquished back in the "comity of nations", diplomatic relations were a *conditio sine qua non.* Due to the accreditation of India's military representative at the Allied High Commission at Bonn, the question was not, which Germany they were to be established with – both German governments claimed to represent the whole of it – but how to deal with the Eastern state. Already in mid-September 1950, i. e. three months before the state of war had been terminated, the Indian military representative had invited the Federal Government to (re)open an economic and consular office in India. The delegation under A. H. van Scherpenberg visiting the subcontinent a few weeks later was to collect information and establish contacts with official India.[37] They encountered a self-confident Prime Minister Jawaharlal Nehru, stating that India was the leading power in Asia, rejecting the idea to join any of the power groups in the world, but prepared to build up her own power group of the old and new states of Southeast Asia![38]

Because of her uncommitted position internationally, India could not and did not view divided Germany in the same way as the Western Powers did, as Bajpai explained: "In our case, the difference between our interests in Western and Eastern Germany is not so wide, and politically we regard neither of the two governments as representative of all Germany."[39] Yet,

34 The last date may be explained by the fact that on 5.6.1945, the four occupation powers of Germany announced their take-over of the government in Germany.

35 Prem Krishen to Tyabji, Berlin 12.1.1951, *ibid.*

36 Adenauer to Prem Krishen, 9.1.1951, *ibid.*

37 Scherpenberg to Dr. Korth, Dienststelle für Auswärtige Angelegenheiten, Torquay 4.11.1950, Auswärtiges Amt (abbr. AA), Pol. Arch., Abt. IIIb, Bd. 1/205–00/29.

38 Scherpenberg, Aufzeichnung, Unterhaltungen mit leitenden Persönlichkeiten in Indien. With letter by Fricke to Consulate General, London, attached, 13.11.1950, *ibid.*

39 U. S. Bajpai, Memorandum, 16.10.1950, NAI, File No. 5 (128)-Eur. II/49.

not theoretical considerations were to decide the issue, but hitherto developed connections and material interests. Prem Krishen, Head of the Indian Mission, advised that India recognise the government at Bonn forthwith, and not that of East Berlin, as India's entire trade and all other relations were centred on Western Germany. The Indian Mission needed merely to be re-accredited at Bonn and re-named into "Indian Legation".

The concept of "one Germany", at that time still paid lip-service to in East Berlin, was adopted by India to justify her action to recognise but one government, viz. that in Bonn. Defending their decision in Parliament, the Indian Government stated in 1952, and ever since repeatedly, that they wished for the unification of Germany, and therefore did not intend to recognise the government of Eastern Germany as well. If they did so, it would mean to accept Germany's division as final.[40]

Once the decision in favour of Bonn had been made and convincingly justified, morally and materially, the course was free to establish diplomatic relations. The Head of the Indian Mission, Prem Krishen, informed Federal Chancellor Adenauer on 8th March 1951 of India's intention, stating: "I am happy that India has been the first country with which Germany has entered into an agreement in this regard as she was in the matter of formal termination of the state of war with Germany."[41]

Already a year before, on 15th March 1950, i. e. more than eight months before the state of war was to be terminated, the Indian Government had signalled to its Military Mission its preparedness that it would welcome "a Consular cum Commercial Representation of the German Federal Government in Bombay!" On second thoughts, however, the Military Mission was informed that there were no objections to the appointment of a German commercial representative in Bombay, but "we cannot agree to his exercising consular functions", the reason being India's attitude taken in the case of Japan, viz. that India could not agree to "full consular representation in advance of the conclusion of a peace treaty".[42] Khub Chand's reference to the Western Powers' proposed step of inviting German consular representation in their capitals did not help to change the Indian Government's attitude, nor did so the information that Chancellor Adenauer gave active consideration to such representation in countries like India, Australia and Brazil, where it was hoped to find stable markets to compensate for Germany's loss of the Eastern European trade.[43]

40 Memorandum on position of India to the German question and the GDR, (Berlin) 20.5.1955, AA, Pol. Arch. Ministerium für Auswärtige Angelegenheiten (abbrev. MfAA), A 13905.

41 P. Krishen to Adenauer, Berlin 8.3.1951, AA, Pol. Arch., Abt. 2. 210–01/29.

42 Foreign [Office], New Delhi, to [Military Mission of] India, Berlin, Tel., New Delhi 15.3.1950 and 17.3. 1950, NAI, Ext. Aff., Eur. II, Branch File No. 5 (115)-Eur. II/1949.

43 Khub Chand to K. P. S. Menon, Tel. 11.3.1950 and K. P. S. Menon to Khub Chand, Tel. 17.3.1950, *ibid.*

A full-fledged consulate general in Bombay was not established for another year, the appointment of Franz V. Mendelssohn as the first German Consul General there, being agreed to by the Federal Cabinet on 13th March 1951.[44]

It took once more another year to arrive at full diplomatic representation. The Federal Government sent its first ambassador to India by the middle of April 1952.[45] Professor Dr. Ernst Wilhelm Meyer was appointed the Federal Republic's ambassador in India, reporting on his first meeting with Prime Minister Nehru on 15th April and on handing over his credentials to the Indian President a week later.[46] India carried on for a while with their Military Mission's representative Prem Krishen, having, according to his predecessor, one leg in Berlin and as a chargé d'affaires a growing one at Bonn, before he was succeeded in the same year by the first purely diplomatic appointment of Subimal Dutt as India's Ambassador to the Federal Republic of Germany.

Little is known about reactions to India's decision in East Berlin. Yet it is hardly surprising that the GDR also made a bid for diplomatic relations with India. Nehru told ambassador Meyer at their first meeting, that there had been a very delicate situation when it was suggested that India also establish diplomatic relations with the German Government of the Soviet Zone.[47] The suggestion is most likely to have come from the Soviet Union. The Government in East Berlin followed it up by its ambassador in China, who in a meeting with the Indian ambassador at Peking argued that his Government had developed from a movement for freedom by the German people and therefore had formed the first independent German Government, whereas the West German Government had been shaped by the Bonn constitution originating from the Western Powers' statute of occupation. Therefore, the Bonn Government were not an expression of the German people's free will.[48] The Indian reaction was this:

(1) India stressed her sentiments of friendship to the German people, being sorry that the division of Germany made it impossible to establish relations with the whole of Germany.

(2) India was extremely interested in economic and trade relations with Western Germany.

[44] Ursula Hüllbüsch (ed.), *Die Kabinettsprotokolle der Bundesregierung*. Band 4, 1951, Boppard 1988, p. 223. Compare Wilhelm Haas, *Beitrag zur Geschichte der Entstehung des Auswärtigen Dienstes der Bundesrepublik Deutschland*, Bremen 1969, p. 52f.

[45] Meyer's appointment was agreed to by the Federal Cabinet on 20th May 1952 (Kai von Jena (ed.), *Die Kabinettsprotokolle der Bundesregierung*, Band 5, 1952, Boppard 1989, p. 339).

[46] Ernst Wilhelm Meyer to Auswärtiges Amt, New Delhi 15.4.1952 and 3.11.1952, AA, Pol. Arch. Abt. III b, 210–02/29, Bd. 1.

[47] Id. to Auswärtiges Amt, New Delhi 15.4.1952, *ibid*.

[48] Grüttner, Memorandum, 24.10.1954, AA, Pol. Arch., MfAA, A 10024.

(3) India maintained already a diplomatic mission at Bonn and is therefore not in a position to exchange diplomatic representatives with the GDR, as this would result in diplomatic complications.

(4) India stressed furthermore that the existence of a diplomatic mission at Bonn did not imply a recognition of the ideological or political attitude of the Bonn Government; it simply served to maintain existing economic relations.[49]

This explanation of India's "one-sided" recognition was repeated in the Indian Parliament on 13th October 1952.[50]

It may be concluded that India's termination of the state of war with Germany and the establishment of diplomatic relations with the Federal Republic were not just the result of an automatism developing from the creation of an Indian Military Mission in Berlin and its subsequent attachment to the Western Powers' High Commission at Bonn. They were the result of steps taken with contemplation and circumspection, firstly because of India's economic interests predominantly centred on the Federal Republic and secondly because of a moral inhibition to do anything that promoted the division of Germany. India decided to differ from the West, especially from Britain, but she did not do so at the cost of her ties with the larger part of Germany, but rather by strengthening them.

49 Ackermann, Memorandum, Berlin 5.11.1951, and MfAA, *Die Beziehungen zwischen der Deutschen Demokratischen Republik und der Republik Indien*, Berlin 1.10.1956, *Ibid.*, MfAA, A 15517 and A 14907.

50 MfAA, *Die Beziehungen zwischen der Deutschen Demokratischen Republik und der Republik Indien*, 1.10. 1956.

Wang Dayuan on Kerala

Roderich Ptak

Wang Dayuan's famous *Daoyi zhilüe* (now *DYZL*) was first introduced to European Orientalists in the last century. But it was only in 1915 that this source became widely known in the West through a long article by W. W. Rockhill. Rockhill translated about two thirds of the Chinese text into English. At around the same time there appeared an annotated version of the text with notes in Japanese. The philological explanations in this edition, prepared by Fujita Toyohashi, differ in many aspects from the ones furnished in the partial English version, but the latter has become the standard work on the *DYZL* and till today is considered as such.[1] Historians, anthropologists and geographers dealing with late medieval Southeast Asia, South Asia, and the Indian Ocean have frequently made use of Rockhill's long article, accepting most of his comments and identifications of place names as being correct and authoritative. Indeed, many authors have considered Rockhill's presentation of the *DYZL* as one of the key works to our knowledge of 14th century maritime Asia.

There can be no doubt that the *DYZL*, together with Ibn Battuta's account and the reports by Odorico de Pordenone and Marco Polo, form an important set of sources for the history of medieval Asian trade, comparable in importance to the books of Tomé Pires and Duarte Barbosa for the early 15th century. It is equally true, however, that all these works contain many descriptions which remain difficult to explain. When the Chinese scholar Su Jiqing published a new Chinese edition of the *DYZL* in 1981 (his own preface dates to 1965!), with copious comments and modern indexes, it became obvious that many of the identifications offered by Rock-

W. W. Rockhill, "Notes on the Relations and Trade of China with the Eastern Archipelago and the Coasts of the Indian Ocean during the Fourteenth Century," *T'oung Pao* 15, 1914, p. 419–47, and 16, 1915, p. 61–159, 236–71, 374–92, 435–67, 604–24 (references here to no. 16); *Daoyi zhilüe jiaozhu*, ed. by Fujita Toyohasi, series Xuetang congke, no. 10, n. p., Shangyu Lo shi, 1915. An earlier annotated version, entirely in Chinese – *Daoyi zhilüe guangzheng*, ed. by Shen Zengzhi, series Guoxue huikan, no. 4, Shanghai 1912 – is much inferior to Fujita's text and can be ignored here. Some segments of Rockhill's translations are also found in K. A. Nilakanta Sastri (ed.), *Foreign Notices of South India from Megasthenes to Ma Huan*, Madras 1939.

hill had to be reconsidered.[2] Sinologists are now increasingly referring to the Su edition but scholars of other disciplines who are not familiar with the Chinese language continue to rely on the old English text by Rockhill. Since this text has become obsolete in many respects, as Su has demonstrated, a new fully-annotated translation is urgently needed but, so far, no one has taken up this challenge. The present notes are intended as a small contribution to this end by examining the descriptions of places in Kerala found in Wang Dayuan's account. This is to be done in the form of new translations based on the Su edition.

A few introductory remarks are necessary before I can embark on the translations. First, the routes Wang Dayuan took during his voyages remain a matter for debate. This concerns his travels in Africa, as I have shown elsewhere, and certainly also his voyages in Indonesia.[3] In the case of Southwest India, major complications are unlikely to arise. A ship sailing from China to the Malabar coast would depart from Quanzhou or Guangzhou and eventually enter the Strait of Malacca. From there it followed the eastern shore of Sumatra up to the area near Bandar Aceh. Then it crossed the Bay of Bengal until Sri Lanka came in sight. Having reached this island, it could either turn north, to the Coromandel area, or sail into the Gulf of Mannar and then to Kerala. Alternatively it could proceed directly from Cape Comorin to the Gulf or the Arabian peninsula via the Maldive and Laccadive Islands. Other ways of approaching Southwest India were more complicated and took more time. They involved sailing along the coasts of Tenasserim, Arakan, Bengal, Coromandel, and Sri Lanka, or going through the Andaman and Nicobar groups, preferably through the Ten Degree Channel, in the direction of Sri Lanka. Given these "standard" possibilities, we may surmise that Wang Dayuan approached South India by one or two of these routes, seeing various places on either side of the Indian peninsula. What we do not know is whether he also travelled over land, for example from the area around Nagapatnam to the area south of Adam's Bridge, or through the hinterland of some Kerala ports.

Second, as I have demonstrated elsewhere, the *DYZL* reports many valuable *facts*, but at the same time it also follows a highly formalised arrangement and presents certain details from a biased viewpoint. A careful reader will easily detect Daoist and Confucian elements in this book and he will immediately doubt whether all details mirror the "real" world in an adequate way. To what degree these descriptions are "distorted", is of course difficult to say.[4] Wang Dayuan claims to have seen all ninety-nine places he describes but it is quite likely that he only

[2] *Daoyi zhilüe jiaoshi*, ed. by Su Jiqing, series Zhongwai jiaotong shiji congkan, Beijing. Zhonghua shuju, 1981.

[3] R. Ptak, "Glosses on Wang Dayuan's Daoyi zhilüe," in: Claudine Salmon (ed.), *Récits de voyages asiatiques: genres, mentalités, conception de l'espace. Actes du colloque EFEO-EHESS de décembre 1994*, series Etudes thématiques 5, Paris 1996, p. 127–41.

[4] R. Ptak, "Images of Maritime Asia in Two Yuan Texts: *Daoyi zhilüe* and *Yiyu zhi*," *Journal of Sung-Yuan Studies* 25, 1995, p. 47–75.

visited some of them. In spite of these doubts, it is important to note that for some locations, for example in eastern Indonesia, the earliest descriptions are found in his book. Our knowledge about certain islands such as the Moluccas or Timor thus goes back to Wang Dayuan.

Third, the *DYZL* carries several prefaces, one being written in the twelfth lunar month of the ninth year under the Zhizheng emperor (early 1350), one in the tenth and one in the eleventh year of that reign (1350 and 1351). There is also a short postscript by Wang Dayuan. Conventionally, the date of the *DYZL* is given as 1349/50 because the lunar year associated with the earliest preface began already in 1349. Information gathered for the compilation of this book, however, was certainly collected several years prior to that date. Su Jiqing thinks that Wang Dayuan put out to sea twice, from 1330 to 1334, and from 1337 to 1339.[5] Not all scholars agree with these dates but, by and large, it makes sense to assume that Wang sailed the Asian seas in the 1320ies or 1330ies and that his notes refer to this period.

Fourth, Su Jiqing based his annotated edition on the *Siku quanshu* version of the *DYZL* but also consulted three additional texts. He indicates all different readings. Most textual differences are restricted to variant orthographs of certain characters. Only in rare cases does this involve different meanings. Some of these differences can also be detected by comparing Su's text with the old English translation by Rockhill which is based on the *Zhifuzhai congshu* collection. In the translations which follow below, orthographic variants are not considered; the English version is strictly based on the Su edition. It has to be added that the original text of the *DYZL* is no longer extant. Su attempted to reconstruct its history through the Yuan and Ming dynasties but the picture one can obtain by consulting old library catalogues is meagre. The text, as it is now, in either version, probably goes back to some Ming copyist who also seems to have changed the original title from *Daoyi zhi* to *Daoyi zhilüe*.[6]

Finally, there are two fairly recent collections of Chinese descriptions of South Asia. Both works quote from those parts of Su Jiqing's text which deal with India, Sri Lanka, and the Maldives.[7] The proposed identifications of geographical names are more or less the same as the ones given by Su Jiqing. There is also a large body of special works on Song, Yuan and early Ming relations to India and on Chinese ceramics found on both the Malabar and Coromandel coasts but these works are of little relevance to the present study.[8]

5 For these dates, see Su's preface, *DYZL*, p. 10–11.

6 For the history of the text, see Su's preface, *DYZL*, p. 11–14.

7 Geng Yinzeng, *Hanwen Nanya shiliao xue*, Beijing, Beijing daxue chubanshe, 1991, p. 281–9; *Zhongguo zaiji zhong Nanya shiliao huibian*, ed. by Beijing daxue Nanya yanjiusuo, 2 Vols., Shanghai, Shanghai guji chubanshe, 1994, II, p. 749–817.

8 Many studies appeared in the Chinese journal *Nanya yanjiu*. Other surveys are: A. A. Bokshchanin, "Sino-Indian Relations from Ancient Times to the Sixteenth Century," in: S. L. Tikhvinsky and L. S. Perelomov (eds.), *China and Her Neighbours: From Ancient Times to the Middle Ages*, Moscow 1981, p. 130–4; Karashima Noboru, "Trade Relations Between South India and China during the 13th and 14th Centuries," *Journal of East-West Maritime Relations* 1, 1989, p. 59–81, and Yang Qinzhang, "Yuandai Quanzhou yu Nan Yindu

Translations

The *DYZL* contains descriptions of five places which have been identified with locations in Kerala: (1) Bandali (Pandalayini, north of Calicut); (2) Xiali (Alwaye, about thirty kilometres north of Cochin); (3) Dabadan (between Cannanore and Tellichery); (4) Xiao Ju'nan (Quilon); and (5) Gulifo (Calicut)

I
Bandali

[This] place is near the countries of Guiqu and Bosi. The mountains are steep and of piled-up rocks. The fields are barren and crops are sparse. The climate is rather hot, excessive rains [may] cause [great] damage.

The customs are strange. There are evil spirits who come close to the houses at night, wailing like human beings, keeping this up until the fifth watch [in the early morning] when the wailing stops. On the following day the chief must send out men on horseback, beating a gong to drive them away until no more trace of them can be seen. Thereafter a [small] shrine is erected on the rocks and a sacrifice is offered. If [this is] not [done], men and beasts become ill, and the country will be stricken by calamities. Men and women dress up the hair in chignons and wrap around them a Wulun cotton cloth. They do not use needles nor do they spin threads.

They boil seawater to obtain salt. The place produces turquoise, *yakut* stones, *tula* cotton stuffs, raw cotton, and mica. The goods used in trade [with them include] such things as satin of various colours, blue and white porcelain, iron-ware, and coloured beads.

Translator's Comments:

Bandali has been equated with a number of places: Pondicherry, some site in the Persian Gulf, Pedir on northern Sumatra, etc.; see, for example, Chen Jiarong, Xie Fang and Lu Jinling, *Gudai Nanhai diming huishi*, Beijing, Zhonghua shuju, 1986, p. 636, and *DYZL*, p. 254–6 n. 1. It is, however, the same place as Fandalayi'na, Fandali'na, or Bintuolanna; for these Chinese names, see Song Lian et al., *Yuan shi*, 15 Vols., Beijing, Zhonghua shuju, 1976, VIII, j. 94, p. 2402; the so-called Mao Kun map in Mao Yuanyi (compil.), *Wu bei zhi*, Tai-

guanxi xinzheng," in: *Zhongguo yu haishang sichou zhi lu* (*China and the Maritime Silk Route*), ed. by Quanzhou International Seminar on China and the Maritime Routes of the Silk Roads Organization Committee, Fuzhou, Fujian renmin chubanshe, 1991, p. 194–207.

bei: Huashi, 1984, j. 240, 20a; Chen Dazhen, *Dade Nanhai zhi canben*, Guangzhou, Guangzhou shi difangzhi yanjiusuo, 1986, p. 38; J. V. G. Mills (tr.), *Ma Huan: Ying-yai sheng-lan. 'The Overall Survey of the Ocean's Shores' [1433]*, Cambridge 1970, p. 192, 295 (Hakluyt Society Extra Series 42); and again Chen Jiarong et al., p. 679, 690, 776. All Chinese name versions stand for Pandalayini (Pandalayini-Kollam), a town north of Calicut. Pandalayini was called Fandaraina (Fandarina, etc.) in Arabic works; see, for example, G. R. Tibbetts, *Arab Navigation in the Indian Ocean Before the Coming of the Portuguese. Being a Translation of Kitab* ..., London 1981, p. 457 (Oriental Translation Fund, new series 42); Rockhill, "Notes", p. 463; Henri Yule (tr. and notes) and Henri Cordier (revisions), *The Travels of Marco Polo*, 2 Vols., New York 1993 (repr.), II, especially p. 391 n. 5, and Cordier's *Addenda* (included in vol. 2), p. 119–20.

Guiqu and Bosi: Su Jiqing proposes to equate Guiqu with Kottakal (about five kilometres south of Badagara), and Bosi with Mayyazhi (or Mahé, the former French possession near Tellicherry). He also draws attention to the fact that an initial *m* was frequently changed to *b* or *p* in Chinese transliterations of foreign names. See *DYZL*, p. 256 n. 2.

Evil spirits: it is unclear whether Wang Dayuan refers to one spirit or several spirits. Nor is it clear whether shrines were habitually erected, or whether the incidence reported should be understood to refer to a single event. Su Jiqing, *DYZL*, p. 256 n. 3, thought there might be a relation between this story and Cugnali Island, also called Sacrifice Rock by Western geographers, an island known for its religious sites.

Wulun cloth: Wulun *bu*. This expression frequently occurs in Wang Dayuan's book. Su Jiqing, following a note in an early essay by Gustav Schlegel (in *T'oung Pao* 12, p. 376), thinks it denotes a cotton fabric produced in and exported from Wulun, possibly Porong on eastern Java. See *DYZL*, p. 109 n. 5, p. 164–5 n. 10. It is strange, however, that people living on the Malabar coast should wear textiles produced in Indonesia.

Turquoise: *dianzi*.

Yakut stones: *yahushi*; one of many possible Chinese versions for Arabic and Persian *yakut* (*yaqut*, etc.), a term used for various kinds of precious stones, such as rubies, sapphires, etc. See, for example, J. V. G. Mills (tr.) and R. Ptak (ed.), *Hsing-ch'a sheng-lan. The Overall Survey of the Star Raft by Fei Hsin*, Wiesbaden 1996 (South China and Maritime Asia 4), p. 47, n. 72.

Tula cotton cloth: *douluomian*; often used for cotton fabrics from West Asia. For this term, see, for example, Friedrich Hirth and W. W. Rockhill (tr.), *Chau Ju-kua: His Work on the Chinese and Arab Trade in the Twelfth and Thirteenth Centuries, entitled Chu-fan chṁ*, Taipei: Ch'eng-wen Publishing Co. 1970 (repr.), p. 219; Paul Pelliot, *Notes on Marco Polo. Ouvrage posthume*, 3 Vols., Paris 1959–1973, I, p. 430–3, 477; Haraprasad Ray, *Trade and*

Diplomacy in India-China Relations: A Study of Bengal during the Fifteenth Century, New Delhi 1993, p. 90.

Mica: *qingmengshi*; Su Jiqing thinks this term is phonetically related to a Tibetian word (*mandzira*).

II
Xiali

[This] country is between Quilon and Calicut and is also called "Small Port". [Its] mountains are vast, the plateaus are level, and it [covers] an area of several thousand *li*. The dwellings of the people are scattered. There is enough for [every] family, [though] the fields are not too good. Farmers [rely on their own] physical strength to till [the ground]. The climate is warm.

The customs are pure, but [the people] are hot-headed, and whenever they go about they must carry bows, arrows and shields to protect themselves. Men and women cut the hair short and wrap Liu cottons around themselves.

The place produces pepper and [in this] it is superior to all other countries; [its plants] are so numerous that they cannot be counted. The pepper plants cover the hills, creeping [over them] like wistarias; they bloom in winter and bear fruit in summer. People gather [the fruits] and expose them in the sun until they are dry. Their flavour is bitter. For the most part gatherers do not mind [this], but if the smell becomes too offensive, they may get relief by using a decoction of *chuanxiong*. The pepper in other foreign [countries] is all the surplus product flowing out of this country.

Translator's Comments:

Fujita Toyohashi thought Xiali referred to Calicut but this is not possible because Wang Dayuan has another name for that port (see below). Rockhill, "Notes", p. 453, equated Xiali with Hili, i. e., with the kingdom of Eli described by Marco Polo. This name survived in Mount Delly (Ras Haili, and other forms), the first Indian land sighted by Vasco da Gama in 1498 (see, for example, Yule and Cordier, *The Travels of Marco Polo*, II, p. 385–8). Mount Delly, however, was north of Calicut, and not between Calicut and Quilon as our texts states. To solve the puzzle, Su Jiqing (*DYZL*, p. 268–9 n. 1) proposed to identify Xiali with Alwaye, a small village approximately thirty-five kilometres north of Cochin. – The area around Cochin was famous for its production of pepper. As Cochin only became important in the second half of the 14th century, Alwaye may still have been a leading pepper port in the days of Wang Dayuan. Early 16th century sources also refer to Alwaye, but by then, this place had clearly declined in importance. See, for example, K. S. Mathew, *Portuguese Trade with India in the Sixteenth Century*, New Delhi 1983, p. 6, 57, 141. – Su Jiqing thought that an identical Chinese name (Xiali), as mentioned by Fei Xin in the early 15th century, should refer to Alleppey (see J. V. G. Mills and R. Ptak, *Hsing-ch'a sheng-lan*, p. 65 n. 164).

"Small Port": a name, or a descriptive element? Su Jiqing thinks this expression refers to the mouth of the Periyar River; Alwaye lies on the shore of this river. The size of the land is debatable. What does Wang Dayuan mean – the territory, the mountains, the riverine system?

"Liu cottons": Liu *bu*. Elsewhere Wang Dayuan mentions Nanliu cloths (see under Dabadan, below). He also describes the Maldives which he calls Beiliu and he refers to Maldivian dried fish as Liu *yu* (*DYZL*, p. 264, and below, under Quilon). The syllable *liu* is phonetically derived from *dvipa*, "island". The Maldives were known as a producer of various cloths. See, for example, R. Ptak, "The Maldive and Laccadive Islands (Liu-shan) in Ming Records," *Journal of the American Oriental Society* 107 (4), 1987, p. 607–8, n. 15 (plus sources there).

Chuanxiong: usually identified with *xiongqiong*; *Conioselinum univitatum* and *Conioselinum vaginatum* (hemlock parsley). See, for example, Kong Qinglai et al. (eds.), *Zhiwuxue da cidian*, Shanghai: Shangwu yinshuguan 1933 (rev. ed.), p. 132; Joseph Needham et al., *Science and Civilisation in China*. vol. 6: *Biology and Biological Technology*. Part 1: *Botany*, Cambridge 1986, p. 256, 334–5.

"flowing out": for *liubo*.

III

Dabadan

[This] country is behind the Western Ocean and is called Qiaopoling. It commands a view extending several hundred *li*. The fields are level and there are rich harvests [because] seasonal rains soak [the soil] with [water]. In recent years a dense clump of rice more than one *zhang* in height and with forty-eight stalks was [found] growing in the fields. [Each stalk] had hundred and thirty grains with a length of circa one half *cun*. The people of the country jokingly called it "the king of stalks". They removed it to the headman's house, and it did not wither for more than one year. Afterwards the spikes fell off. They had a colour like gold. People applied the ashes of areca-nuts to them so that they would not be spoiled by insects. [The spikes] are still preserved in that country; from time to time they are exposed to the sun [because] they are treated as treasures.

The climate is hot, the customs are pure. Men and women cut their hair short and wear Nanliu cloths.

They boil seawater to obtain salt. The place produces cotton and jack-fruits. The goods used in trade [with them include] such things as southern silks, iron bars, purple coloured cosmetic powder, wooden combs, and white sugar.

Translator's Comments:

Fujita Toyohashi suggested that Dabadan be located somewhere on the Indian west coast. Rockhill, "Notes", p. 67, thought it was perhaps identical with Budfattan, a name found in Arabic works. Su Jiqing, *DYZL*, p. 281 n. 1, proposed to relate Dabadan to Ibn Battuta's Dahfattan, a place somewhere between Tellicherry and Cannanore. This name survived in Dharmapatam Island. For the latter see, for example, Tibbetts, *Arab Navigation*, p. 457. Karashima, "Trade Relations," p. 62–3, 65–7, thinks the topographical features given by Wang Dayuan point to a location in Ma'bar. He suggested Periyapatnam where Chinese potsherds were discovered. One reason for this suggestion is that *periya* means "big", i. e., *da*; "Big *patnam*" would thus give Dabadan. Chinese authors, however, have accepted Su's proposal (see, for example, Chen Jiarong et al., *Gudan Nanhai*, p. 139); therefore, the description was included in this brief study.

Qiaopoling or Quepoling: Su Jiqing, *DYZL*, p. 281 n. 3, thinks this name should be derived phonetically from Maina*koparv*ata, a Malabari name for the Western Ghats. Although his explanation may not sound very convincing, so far no better solution has been found.

"Commands …": this follows Karashima, "Trade Relations". I am not certain whether this is correct but have no better translation to offer.

"In recent years …": one *zhang* was circa one metre; half a *cun* was about 1.5 centimetres.

Nanliu cloths: Nanliu *bu*; probably the same as Liu *bu*, "Liu cloths" (see above, under Xiali), i. e., textiles from the Maldives. The difference between Beiliu and Nanliu – *nan* versus *bei*, or north versus south – may imply a geographical distinction between the northern atolls and the southern atolls of the Maldives, or between the Laccadives and Maldives (?), or it may be purely accidental.

Jack-fruits: *poluomi*, the fruit of *Artocapus integrifolia*. See, for example, Isaac H. Burkill, *A Dictionary of the Economic Products of the Malay Peninsula, with Contributions by William Birtwistle et al.*, 2 Vols. London and Oxford: On Behalf of the Government of the Straits Settlements and Federated Malay States, At the University Press, 1935, I, p. 254;

Paul Wheatley, "Geographical Notes on Some Commodities Involved in Sung Maritime Trade," *Journal of the Malayan Branch of the Royal Asiatic Society* 32.2, 1959, p. 76.

"Southern silks": *nansi*, a coarse thread manufactured in southern China. Wang Dayuan uses another expression, *nanbeisi*, literally "southern and northern silks" (Rockhill's translation), on various occasions. In the index to Su Jiqing's text, the expression *nansi* is put in the same category as *nanbeisi*, but no explanation is given.

"Purple coloured cosmetic powder": *zifen*, a product derived from the *Basella rubra*, used for dying, painting, and cosmetics. Most likely Wang Dayuan applied the name to some similar substance available on the market of Dabadan, and not necessarily to *Basella rubra*.

IV
Xiao Ju'nan

[This] land is near Dulanjiao. Its soil is black and [very] suited for cereals and wheat. [But] the people are careless about tilling [the fields] and each year they rely on the rice of Wudie for their subsistence. [Sometimes these merchant vessels] arrive late [due to] the direction of winds – [i. e.], after the departure of the horse ships [from Hormuz] – and cannot take on a full cargo. If the winds are contrary, they will not be able to cross the Lamuri Ocean, and they have to avoid the dangers from the submerged rocks near Colombo. So they pass the winter in this place and wait until the eighth or ninth month of the following year, when the horse ships return. [Then] they sail back to Calicut for trade.

The customs and the garments of men and women are the same as those in Calicut. They have village rulers but no chief ruler.

The place produces pepper, coconuts, areca-nuts, and dried fish. The goods used in trade [with them include] gold and silver, porcelain articles decorated in blue and white, cottons from Badan, satin of all colours, and iron-ware.

Translator's Comments:

Xiao Ju'nan, there can be no doubt, is Quilon (Kollam, Coilam, etc.; various Chinese names). Fei Xin copied this segment almost word for word, but changed the name of the place from Xiao Ju'nan to Da Ju'nan. He has a separate chapter on Xiao Ju'nan. Da Ju'nan may have stood for Attingal, a village in Kerala, but Kayankulum was also suggested. See J. V. G. Mills and R. Ptak, *Hsing-ch'a sheng-lan*, p. 65–6, 97–8.

Dulanjiao: Tellicherry, or Chirayankil (near Attingal)? See *DYZL*, p. 324 n. 2, and Chen Jiarong et al., *Gudai Nanhai*, p. 646.

Wudie: various identifications were proposed, for example Ussa (Pegu), Orissa, etc. The *DYZL* also describes a place called Da Wudie. This place was linked to Africa and other areas, including, once again, Orissa. See *DYZL*, p. 339–42, 375–8; J. V. G. Mills and R. Ptak, *Hsing-ch'a sheng-lan*, p. 98 n. 83.

Horses came by ship from Hormuz; see the chapter on Hormuz in *DYZL*, p. 364, where the horse ships are briefly described. Horses were also brought from Hormuz to Calicut, as mentioned below. For further details, see R. Ptak, "Pferde auf See: Ein vergessener Aspekt des maritimen chinesischen Handels im frühen 15. Jahrhundert," *Journal of the Economic and Social History of the Orient* 34, 1991, especially p. 204–5, and sources there.

"Sometimes …" till the end of the paragraph: This seems to imply, the horse ships had bought up all the goods available in Quilon; therefore the merchants of Wudie waited for the next season, wintering in Quilon. Thereafter they sailed northwards to meet the horse ships in Calicut. The term *hui* (here "sail back") may be wrong because Wudie was in the Bay of Bengal area and Calicut was north of Quilon. Alternatively, "Calicut" may be wrong. Perhaps the Wudie vessels wintered near Sri Lanka ("this place" is ambiguous) and "sailed back" from there to Quilon. Fei Xin changed this difficult-to-interpret passage: "When merchant vessels arrive late [due to] the direction of winds, the billows will be dashing on the beach. Then [the ships] cannot take on full cargoes, [and this is] because they do not dare to anchor [there]." See J. V. G. Mills and R. Ptak, *Hsing-ch'a sheng-lan*, p. 98. An earlier reference to the voyage from China to Quilon is found in the *Lingwai daida* (preface 1178): "Die Schiffe, die von Kanton kommen, erreichen nach 40 Tagen Lamuri (Lan-li), wo sie den Winter über liegenbleiben. Erst im folgenden Jahr laufen sie wieder aus. Die Seeschiffe treffen dann erstmals nach etwa einem Monat [in Quilon] ein." See Almut Netolitzky, *Das Ling-wai tai-ta von Chou Ch'ü-fei. Eine Landeskunde Südchinas aus dem 12. Jahrhundert*, Wiesbaden 1977, p. 40. Could it be that Wang Dayuan had in mind this passage when he wrote down his Quilon chapter?

Lamuri Ocean: various Chinese names; the sea extending from northwestern Sumatra to the Nicobar Islands and Sri Lanka. The name is related to Lambri and other forms. See, for example, J. V. G. Mills and R. Ptak, *Hsing-ch'a sheng-lan*, p. 60 n. 141, and sources indicated there.

"Submerged rocks": *lugushi*. Su Jiqing, *DYZL*, p. 91–2 n. 3, thinks this was possibly derived from a Malay expression referring to coral reefs. Here, most likely the Little Basses reef and the Great Basses reef near Sri Lanka.

"Dried fish": Liu *yu*; elsewhere *yu gan*, or *hailiu yu*. See *DYZL*, p. 264 and p. 266 n. 6; J. V. G. Mills, *Ma Huan*, p. 150. *Hailiu* probably was the phonetical equivalent of the Maldivian syllables *kalu*. Liu by itself stood for the Maldives. The above compounds were used to designate the *Thynnus tunnina*, exported from these islands to various places of the Arabian Sea. More in R. Ptak, "China, Portugal und der Malediven-Handel vom frühen 15. bis zum frühen 16. Jahrhundert. Einige Bemerkungen zur Wirtschaftsgeschichte Südasiens," in R. Ptak (ed.), *Portuguese Asia: Aspects in History and Economic History* (*Sixteenth and Seventeenth Centuries*), Stuttgart 1987, p. 138, and "The Maldive and Laccadive Islands," p. 677 (plus sources in n. 14 there).

"Cottons from Badan": either from Dabadan (above) or Shalibadan (possbily Nagapatnam; see, for example, *DYZL*, p. 272–4; Chen Jiarong et al., *Gudai Nanhai*, p. 457).

V
Calicut

[This place] is an important traffic junction of the high seas. It is near Sri Lanka and is also the [principal] port of all the foreigners of the Western Ocean. The mountains [near Calicut] stretch from east to west, the fields are barren and [only] suitable for growing wheat. Every year they rely on rice shipments from Wudie.

They cede the path to each other and will not pick up things dropped on the street; the customs approach those of antiquity [in honesty]. Their laws [honour what is] respectful. Should anyone steal an ox, the chief verifies the number of oxen, and the rightful owner seizes the property of the offender, the latter being put to death. The government area is in the remote hills, the place where trading is carried on is the sea-shore.

The place produces pepper, second best to that of Xiali. The people all have public storehouses to keep it. Each *bahar* [is equivalent to] 375 catties [in weight]. As customs they collect two tenths. Next [in importance are] *kajang* leaves, *pisang* cloths, rose-water, jack-fruits, and *assia catechu* syrup. Their corals, pearls, frankincense and other goods all come from Hormuz and Rum. The goods exported are the same as from Quilon.

They breed fine horses which come from the extreme West; hence, they are taken to this country by ship. Each horse, when sold, will fetch an enormous sum of gold, as high as forty thousand. If [prices are too low], foreigners [trading there] will consider the country to be impoverished.

'ranslator's Comments:

On Calicut in Wang Dayuan's times, see, for example, references in Geneviève Bouchon, "Un microcosme: Calicut au 16e siècle," in Denys Lombard and Jean Aubin (eds.), *Marchands et hommes d'affaires asiatiques dans l'Océan Indien et la Mer de Chine, 13e–20e siècles*,

Paris 1988, p. 57; Su Chung-jen, "Chinese Knowledge of Calicut during the 14th and 15th Centuries," in: *Proceedings of the First International Congress Seminar of Tamil Studies*, vol. 1, Kuala Lumpur 1968, p. 521–3; R. Ptak, "Ein mustergültiges Barbarenland? Kalikut nach chinesischen Quellen der Yuan- und Ming-Zeit," in: Denys Lombard und R. Ptak (eds.), *Asia maritima. Images et réalité, Bilder und Wirklichkeit, 1200–1800*, Wiesbaden 1994, p. 91.

Western Ocean: the northern sections of the Indian Ocean in Wang Dayuan's perception of the Asian seas. For Asia's oceans in Yuan geography, see, for example, R. Ptak, "From Quanzhou to the Sulu Zone and Beyond: Questions Related to the Early Fourteenth Century," paper prepared for a conference on Quanzhou, Leiden, September 1997.

"Stretch out from east to west", for *heng*. Parts of the Western Ghats near Calicut are indeed structured that way.

"They cede the path ...": This must be related to caste regulations. The second part of the sentence is an expression found in some Chinese classics; it usually indicates strict laws and good government. For a discussion, see R. Ptak, "Ein mustergültiges Barbarenland?" p. 91; also see J. V. G. Mills and R. Ptak, *Hsing-ch'a sheng-lan*, p. 67, 68.

"The chief verifies the number of oxen": this follows Rockhill, "Notes," p. 454, but may be wrong. Perhaps the Chinese text contains an error here. On oxen in Southwest India, also see, for example, Yule and Cordier, *The Travels of Marco Polo*, II, p. 341, 365. For another translation (based on Fujita Toyohashi's comments in *Daoyi zhilüe jiaozhu*, 95a–96a), see Su Chung-jen, "Chinese Knowledge," p. 521–2: "(If a person) steals a cow, the chief will impose on him (a fine of gold equal in weight to) the head of the cow. Nevertheless, the loser (of the cow) would rather see the offender suffer confiscation of all the property and death (as a felon)." The "chief" may or may not be the Zamorin.

Pepper: whether "inferior to" refers to quality (as translated here), or the quantity of production (as translated by Su Chung-jen), is open.

Kajang leaves: various ways of writing; used for matting; see, for example, J. V. G. Mills, *Ma Huan*, p. 80 and n. 3 there.

Pisang cloths: made of banana fibres. According to Su Jiqing, *DYZL*, p. 329 n. 9, *pisang* is Malay for *xiongjiao*.

Cassia catechu syrup: *haier'cha*, mainly used in medicine. More details in *DYZL*, p. 317 n. 6.

Coral: *shanhu*. In old texts this term refers to red corals from the Mediterranean. Later it was also used for black *Antipatharia* and other corals. In China red coral was used in medicine, for decorative purposes, and various arts and crafts. See, for example, Liu Xinru, *Ancient India and Ancient China. Trade and Religious Exchanges, AD 1–600*, Delhi 1988, p. 54–7;

R. Ptak, "Notes on the Word *shan-hu* and Chinese Coral Imports from Maritime Asia, c. 1250–1600," *Archipel* 39, 1990, especially p. 71.

Hormuz: the text has Ganli which is probably a mistake for Ganmaili, i. e., Hormuz; see *DYZL*, p. 364–9. However, Su Jiqing, *DYZL*, p. 329–30 n. 12, thinks that Ganli represented Kalhat, a port along the Oman coast. Also see Hirth and Rockhill, *Chau Ju-kua*, p. 117, 122 n. 12. More, for example, in Chen Jiarong et al., *Gudai Nanhai*, p. 252. – Some authors took Ganli and Ganmaili for the Comoro Islands; this is wrong.

Rum: Folang, a transcription of the Persian name for the eastern Mediterranean and Europe in a broader sense. Various Chinese ways of writing.

"Enormous sum of gold" paid for horses: literally "hundred(s) to thousand(s)"; two text versions read "four thousand" instead of "forty thousand".

Chinese Characters: Authors, Other Names, Expressions

Badan 八丹
Bandali 班達里
Beiliu 北溜
Bintuolanna 賓陀蘭納
Bosi 波思
Chen Dazhen 陳大震
Chen Jiarong 陳佳榮
chuanxiong 川芎
cun 寸
da 大
Da Ju'nan 大咀喃
Da Wudie 大烏爹
Dabadan 大八丹
Daoyi zhilüe 島夷誌略
dianzi 甸子
douluomian 兜羅綿
Dulanjiao 都攔礁
Fandalayi'na 梵答剌亦納
Fandali'na 番答里納
Fei Xin 費信
Folang 佛朗
Fujita Toyohashi 藤田豐八
Ganli 甘理
Ganmaili 甘埋里
Geng Yinzeng 耿引曾
Guiqu 鬼屈
Gulifo 古里佛
haier'cha 孩兒茶
hailiu yu 海溜魚
heng 横
hui 回
li 里
liu 溜
Liu *bu* 溜布
Liu *yu* 溜魚
liubo 流波
Lu Junling 陸峻嶺
lugushi 鹵股石
Mao Kun 茅坤
Mao Yuanyi 茅元儀
Nanliu 南溜
Nanliu *bu* 南溜布
nanbeisi 南北絲
nansi 南絲
poluomi 婆羅蜜
Qiaopoling (Quepoling) 雀婆嶺
qingmengshi 青蒙石
Quanzhou 泉州
Shalibadan 沙里八丹
shanhu 珊瑚
Shen Zengzhi 沈曾植
Song Lian 宋濂
Su Jiqing 蘇繼廎
Wang Dayuan 汪大淵
Wudie 烏爹
Wulun 巫崙
Wulun *bu* 巫崙布
Xiali 下里
Xiao Ju'nan 小咀喃
Xie Fang 謝方
xiongjiao 芎蕉
xiongqiong 芎藭
yahushi 鴉忽石
Yang Qinzhang 楊欽章
yu gan 魚乾
zhang 丈
Zhizheng 至正
zifen 紫粉

The Indian Merchant and the Indian Ocean 1500–1800

Ashin Das Gupta

Indian merchants are known to have visited the major ports of the Indian Ocean at the time of Vasco da Gama and during the three after-centuries. There is a problem about 'Indian merchants'. This general description becomes meaningful only abroad i. e. outside India. But within this label there are different kinds of people interested in different kinds of things. Thus we may have a Gujarati, a Tamil or a Bengali merchant who are all equally Indian. Similarly there can be a difference between shore-based merchants and shipping merchants, e. g., a baniya and a Gujarati Muslim. They may both come from the same city and go to the same place. But while the Muslim is a shipowner, the baniya is a settler. Such differences also existed between communities. Thus it has been argued that right from the time of Vasco da Gama, the Portuguese allied themselves with the Syrian Christians of Malabar and against the Mappillas of the same coast.[1]

So to have Indian merchants trading in the Indian Ocean is not enough. We must know from more specific details about them. Similarly the time is also very important. Indian merchants had different fortunes at diferent times. When the Portuguese first came, they were 'well established' in all the major ports. This may have been the case even for the 14th century when the Portuguese were not there. The Portuguese impact changed much in the Indian Ocean without changing the fundamentals of trade. The Indians soon learned what Moreland used to call the 'Rules of the Game'. They began to avoid Portuguese war ships wherever possible and cutivate the unofficial Portuguese in whatever way they could. The Portuguese themselves began to emphasise the private interest specially in the eastern Indian Ocean.

These rivalries between private and official interest took on a new form with the Dutch in the 17th century. The Dutch East India Company itself operated in the Indian Ocean trade and it

[1] For an early account of Vasco da Gama's first voyage, see S. Subrahmanyam, *The Career and Legend of Vasco da Gama*, Cambridge 1997. Subrahmanyam follows the anonymous diary of the first voyage, faithfully.

would not permit its own employees to join this commerce. It now appears entirely possible that the 17th century specially in its second half saw Indian trade at its peak.[2] Unfortunately we do not know the history of several Indian ports of the time to be confident about this verdict we think likely.

This prosperous structure broke down in the 18th century. There was a diversion of the major trading effort from India to Western Asia into one from India to China.[3] In other words, the trade in the Indian Ocean instead of going West began to go East. Moreover this century also saw the elimination of the large shipping merchants of India and their ships. Indian trade remained but from now on this trade was carried only in small vessels.[4] The major trade of the Indian Ocean was left to the Europeans while the Indians withdrew into the trade of roadsteads. This coastal trade was becoming important for some time and now in the 18th century coastal trade became important indeed. This was a trade of low value in bulky commodities like grain, salt, cowries. The European organisation stood aloof from this trade of small ports and bulky goods. They profited from this time onwards from the advancement of the technology as for example the discovery of the longitude.[5] This is why it became possible to speak off a division of the Indian Ocean into two – one the high trade of the Ocean and the other, coastal trade.

At the beginning of the 16th century the Portuguese of course did not see these things. But they noticed that Indian trade was well established in the Indian Ocean. In the West, Indian merchants were prominent at Aden, at the mouth of the Red Sea – Hormuz which commanded the Persian Gulf and they were also prominent in East African ports down to Sofala.[6] In the east they made Malakka their main centre. As Malakka commanded the narrow stretch of water which led from the Indian Ocean to the China Sea, the location was most convenient for international trade. In this sense the 16th century was very much a time of the trading euphoria. It appears certain that Aden had long been established and with Hormuz and Malakka we can confidently go back over the 15th century. The Portuguese impact was greatest in the west. They captured Hormuz (1517) and dominated eastern Africa excluding Arab traders. Their headquarters at Goa was also in the western Indian Ocean. Portuguese warships commanded the sea lanes in the West and Asian merchants usually would take a Portuguese *cartaz* whether

[2] This position had been strongly argued recently by S. Arasaratnam. I have tried to indicate some of his contentions in "S. Arasaratnam and the Bay of Bengal: A Note," *The Calcutta Historical Journal* 18 (2), 1995.

[3] This classic position is outlined by Holden Furber in his *John Company at Work*, Harvard 1948, and has been much commented upon ever since.

[4] I have indicated this position in "India and Indian Ocean in the Eighteenth Century," in: A. Dasgupta and M. N. Pearson (eds.), *India and the Indian Ocean 1500–1800*, Calcutta 1987.

[5] For a recent statement of the new navigational science see: J. E. D. Williams, *From Sails to Satellites – The Origin and Development of Navigational Science*, Oxford 1992, specially Chapter 5: "A Political History of the Longitude," p. 75–84.

[6] A recent admirable statement is in S. Subrahmanyam, *Portuguese Empire in Asia 1500–1700*, London 1993.

they liked it or not. The Portuguese spirit was superior to anything they encountered as was shown in their defence of Cochin and Diu. Portuguese navigation was certainly better than the Asian, and Portuguese navigators were welcome on board in Asian vessels. But even in the west Portuguese supremacy was not absolute. The gap at the Red Sea remained as Aden never became Portuguese. It appears very likely that Indian merchants specially from Gujarat and Malabar did not obey Portuguese rules. Another level of reality seems to have characterised many of the dealings in the Indian Ocean. Indian merchants freely bribed Portuguese officials and had their way. The Portuguese official policy became somewhat irrelevant.

From this time onwards it is possible to see some distinctions between the shipping lines in the Indian Ocean. There were ports which were opposed to the Portuguese like Calicut and Aden. There were ports which were neutral like Cambay or Dabhol. These ports would welcome Portuguese trade but not their arms settlement and of course there were ports which were completely dominated by the Portuguese, for example, Lower Chaul and Porto Novo. These were the ports of the Portuguese line and they had their armed settlements in these. Apart from the ports, commercial routes came to be different on the ocean. We know about the new line of spice trade from Sumatra to the Red Sea via the Maldives.[7] Gujarati vessels dominated this line and it is possible that the Mappillas of the Kerala coast quarrelled with the Portuguese about this trade. All in all the Indian Ocean in the 16th century split between Portuguese lines and lines which were not Portuguese. This was a distinction which would endure for three centuries.

One of the major reasons for it of course was the much discussed violence of the Portuguese. All over the ocean, the Portuguese would attack ships not carrying their own *cartaz*. But we must remember that the sea was vast and the ships small and slow. So no domination of this kind could be absolute.[8] But allowing for all that there were, nevertheless, embarassing incidents. These made for the peculiar dichotomy among the Portuguese: the dichotomy between official and private trade. There were many Portuguese who did not act to uphold the official policy, but acted in their own private interests. Such men included the Portuguese householders (*cassados*), priests, soldiers and sailors. For the most part they traded but they were to be found as navigators on Indian ships or artillery experts in Indian armies. Sometimes they would throw off such Christianity as they had and embraced Islam. This proved difficult to rectify. In any event, the private Portuguese were settled at many ports where the official force was absent like Cambay. Eventually in the later 16th century the eastern Indian Ocean was more private than official whereas, the west was more official than private.

7 For a meticulous compilation of evidence see Genevieve Bouchon, *Mamale de Cannanore*, Paris 1975.

8 See my paper "Moreland hypothesis," in: K. S. Mathew (ed.), *Mariners, Merchants and Oceans*, New Delhi 1995.

As the Portuguese divided themselves into official and private, Indian merchants appeared to have developed or strengthened their trade to the Red Sea. This story can only be told in bare outlines. As the Ottomans captured Aden, the Hejaj was ruled by the Sharifian family and the controlling power over the holy cities first belonged to the Mameluks and was then taken over by Ottoman Turkey in the second decade of the 16th century.[9] The Ottomans from this time onwards had the responsibility of protecting the Hajj – a responsibility they assumed gladly and very seriously. Two major caravans were organised every year for the Hajj pilgrims – one from Aleppo, the other from Cairo. Apart from the pilgrims who were numerous in these caravans, there were merchants who came every year to seek profit. Round about this time we have the development of coffee trade. Coffee which was grown originally in east Africa came to be grown in the Yemen. Coffee was frowned upon by religions including some of the rulers of Turkey, but it proved very popular in the Turkish empire. So a great deal of money came every year for coffee and a great deal of money came for various people living in the Holy cities of Mecca and Medina. The Indian banias settled in large numbers in the Yemen and, although under some civil disadvantages, they dominated the economic life of the area.[10] Yemen was organised as one state under the Zaidi Imams who had their capital at Sana. Mocha at the mouth of the Red Sea rose to replace Aden as a major port of the area. The Sharifian family controlled the navigation between Jedda and Cairo. Indian muslims were not allowed to go further than Jedda from which it was convenient to visit Mecca. All this seems to have led to a great increase in Indian trade to the Red Sea.[11]

This importance of the Red Sea was manifold. There was the undoubted fact of an Islamic zeal for the pilgrimage. The major force from India was the Mughal Empire but the Deccan Sultanates of Ahmadnagar, Bijapur and Golconda were also strongly attracted towards West Asia. We know that the Deccan Sultanates sent their capital ships to the Red Sea.[12] The Mughal Empire began to show an interest in the 1570s when Gujarat and Bengal were included in that Empire. But the major thrust of the Mughals came under Shah Jahan who had built up the carrying fleet for the Red Sea. We know that the English and the Dutch, in the early years of the 17th century were sending their ships to the Persian Gulf carrying freight goods. Shah Jahan expanded his fleet towards the middle of the 17th century and competition in the trade of freight

[9] See Suraiya Faroqhi, *Pilgrims and Sultans*, London 1994. Mrs. Faroqhi has worked exclusively from the Ottoman Archives.

[10] I have indicated the position of the baniya in Yemen in my article "Gujarati Merchants and the Red Sea Trade," now available in: A, Das Gupta, *Merchants of Martime India 1500–1800*, Aldershot 1994.

[11] The Indian thrust in the area from Mughals is dealt with by N. R. Faroqi, *Mughal-Ottoman Relations*, Delhi 1989.

[12] See my article "Indian Merchants and the Western Indian Ocean: the Early Seventeenth Century," in: A. Das Gupta, *Merchants of Maritime India, 1500–1800*, Aldershot 1994.

goods was joined with the north Europeans.[13] Therefore official trade of different kinds were competing with each other in the west by the 17th century.

The early 17th century has overwhelmingly been seen as a time of challenge by the north Europeans to the Portuguese. But from the point of view of the Indian merchants it must have been quite different. This was a time of the fall of the Konkan ports and the rise of the independent merchants of Surat. Unfortunately we know very little about the Konkan coast and all we can say definitely is that lower Chaul and Dabhol ceased to be an important centre of maritime trade in these years.[14] We can also say that Surat terminated whatever arrangements it had with Dabhol and struck out on its own. This was the rise of the independent merchants of that city. The Mughal fleet under Aurangzeb was a very different proposition from that under Shah Jahan. Aurangzeb was not interested in trade and the capital ships of the Mughal fleet came gradually to be the property of the merchants. These merchants were free in two important senses. For one thing, they did not have any alliance with any European powers and secondly they were not dependent upon the Mughal Emperor for their trade.

In the second half of the 17th century all these developments must have come together for the Indian merchants, so that Indian export trade appears to have reached a peak at this time. Masulipatnam and its merchants proved to be a great source of strength in this development. Indian trade to Southeast Asia showed no diminution. The West Asian trade was markedly strengthened while the coastal trade was growing. On top of all these a new demand for Indian textiles from northern Europe was added by the English and the Dutch. This development in Indian trade has been much commented upon by S. Arasaratnam. Previously, W. H. Moreland has described this development as perhaps a displacement by north Europeans of the Portuguese trade. The difference between Moreland's time and ours lies in the discovery of Indian trade and the Indian Ocean. Moreland was very careful about prominent European ports, but he knew nothing of ports where Europeans did not go. Arasaratnam is in the vanguard of the historians who are looking for this new departure.[15] Unfortunately it is till now far from complete.

In the 18th century the picture changed sharply again. The large shipowners on the Indian side gradually went out of business. One major reason for this commercial failure was the political collapse of the Indian order. Whatever that may be, in the later 18th century Indian capital ships were no longer plying in the Indian Ocean. Indian maritime trade now withdrew to ports like Nagore and Porto Novo of the southern Coromandel coast. These were the ports of the Chulia merchants who had important connections with the small kingdoms of southern Coro-

13 See N. R. Faroqi, *Mughal-Ottoman Relations*, Delhi 1989.

14 I have touched upon this problem in my article "Indian Merchants and the Western Indian Ocean: the Early Seventeenth Century," in: A. Das Gupta, *Merchants of Maritime India*.

15 For a brief discussion of these prints see my "S. Arasaratnam and the Bay of Bengal" and "Moreland Hypothesis" in: A. Das Gupta, *Merchants of Maritime India*.

mandel and with those of Southeast Asia.[16] They repeated on a small scale the domination of India's great merchants. But they do not appear to have been great themselves. On the other side of the Indian Ocean those Indians who could make a deal with Oman carried on a trade to east Africa, principally Zanzibar. But both the trades to the Southeast Asia and east Africa were to small ports. These was the nature of the new Indian trade which generally abandoned the trade of the high seas. Europeans, specially British merchants, took complete command of the trade of the major ports and managed it from the new British Indian ports of Calcutta, Bombay and Madras. These were the replacements of traditional ports like Hughli, Surat or Masulipatnam. The new technology of the 19th century also came exclusively to the assistance of the European shipowners. From this time onwards there were two very different kinds of shipping. On the Indian Ocean, the fleet of Hindustan from Surat gradually disappeared and the Calcutta fleet of British merchants grew. This decline and rise sum up the history of the 18th century.

But one thing did not change: a large number of pedlars were to be found on every sailing ship in the Indian Ocean. Now just as there is no denying the existence of the pedlars, similarly we know there were enough substantial merchants who were in the Indian Ocean trade as well. The majority of the historians do not like the label 'pedlar' particularly when it is applied to the substantial merchants. If we argue that the nature of the Asian market was such that it produced a peddling mentality, we seem to come out of one difficulty only to face another. The argument is that the Asian market was small and unpredictable at every port on the Indian Ocean. This is why even a substantial merchant was obliged to behave like a pedlar and get rid of his stocks as soon as possible. This argument assumes that we know the nature of the Asian market, which may not be true. The notion of the Asian market has been influenced by the market of Mocha. Recently this has been challenged and we are obliged to discuss the Asian market from the other areas.[17] This task is still pending.

[16] It is difficult to substantiate in detail any statement about the Chulia merchants. But see Susan Bayly, *Saints, Goddesses and Kings*, Cambridge 1992, for the close connection of the Chulias with India's principalities and Anne Bulley, *Free Mariner*, London 1992, for the connection with the south east.

[17] For the beginning of what I consider an important discussion see H. W. van Santen, "Trade Between Mughal India and the Middle East, and Mughal Monetary Policy," in: K. R. Haellquist (ed.) *Asian Trade Routes*, Copenhagen 1991.

India in the Indian Ocean Trading Network on the Eve of the Europeans' Arrival in the Asian Seas

Om Prakash

Among the historic consequences of the discovery by the Portuguese at the end of the 15th century of the all-water route to the East Indies via the Cape of Good Hope was the overcoming of the transport technology barrier to the growth of trade between Asia and Europe. The volume of this trade was no longer subject to the capacity constraint imposed by the availability of pack animals and river boats in the Middle East. Also, it was only after the discovery of the Cape route that the procurement of Asian goods as well as their transportation to Europe was organised by the Europeans themselves, who had travelled to the East in any number for the first time. What kind of trading network did the Portuguese find in operation on their arrival in the Indian Ocean? This paper analyses the central elements of this network from the vantage point of India, which was at the centre of the Portuguese – and later of the other Europeans' trading activities in Asia.

An analysis of the structure and the mechanics of the early modern Indian Ocean trade, alternatively referred to as Asian trade, ought perhaps to start with a recognition of the simple fact that this trade transgressed the boundaries of both the Indian Ocean as well as those of Asia. While in the east, it intruded prominently into the South China Sea, in the west, it embraced maritime trade with East Africa. Traditionally, the great arc of Asian trade included the Persian Gulf and the Red Sea in the northwest. The principal natural divisions of this huge area were the Arabian Sea, the Bay of Bengal and the South China Sea. Within each of these zones, there were important blocks of ports across which a large amount of trade had traditionally been carried on. The western or the Arabian Sea zone included ports in the Persian Gulf, the Red Sea, those on the East African coast and on the west coast of India. The Bay of Bengal network included ports in Sri Lanka, the Coromandel coast, Bengal, Burma, Thailand, Malaya and Acheh in Sumatra. Ports such as Canton and Zaiton in the South China Sea had extensive contacts both with the Indonesian ports as well as with ports in the straits of Malacca. Within each of these zones, there were also clearly identifiable sub-zones. To take an example, in the west, the ports of Aden, Hormuz, Cambay and Calicut formed one such sub-zone, while those of Kilwa, Mogadishu, Aden and Jiddah constituted another. Needless to emphasise, in terms of the ability of different constituents of a given zone to put important tradeable goods on the market, for which there was adequate demand elsewhere in the zone, there was a very definitive basis for trade within each of the zones. Such a basis also existed to an important degree across zones leading to the creation of significant long-distance trade flows in the Indian Ocean and beyond. By far the longest distance was covered by the route that connected Aden to Canton traversing a very large part of the total area covered by the great arc of Asian trade. There is evidence to suggest that this route was in regular use at least from the 7th century on. The principal group which had initiated trade on the route was the Persian merchants who had, however, been supplanted by and large by Arab merchants since about the 9th century on. The principal stops on the way were either Cambay or Calicut on the Indian west coast and a port such as Palembang in Sumatra. It would seem that sometime during the 12th century, Chinese junks also began operating on this route. There is evidence that the Chinese merchants established commercial contacts with places such as Sri Lanka, Quilon on the Malabar coast and with Hormuz in the Persian Gulf. The Chinese participation in trade on this route would appear to have reached important levels by the early years of the 15th century. Between 1404 and 1433, a series of seven commercial-cum-naval expeditions were dispatched from China under the command of Admiral Cheng Ho. The first of these expeditions is believed to have consisted of as many as 62 ships and 28,000 men. The fourth voyage is reported to have reached Hormuz and Aden, while those that followed claimed to have touched even the East African ports of Mogadishu and Malindi. But in 1433, the Chinese authorities abruptly withdrew from these ventures and, indeed, there is no record of these long distance voyages having ever been resumed. The precise circumstances behind this development are not quite clear but it would seem that the depredation of pirates infesting the South China Sea and the criticism that the profit earned from these voyages was not sufficiently attractive contributed to the decision of the Chinese authorities. In the meantime, the Arabs had also gradually pulled out of this long-distance route.

Whatever the reasons behind the Chinese and the Arab withdrawal from long-distance trade, it signalled a basic alteration in the organisational structure of Asian trade. The new structure was based on the segmentation of the great arc of Asian trade into the three divisions mentioned earlier – the Arabian Sea, the Bay of Bengal and the South China Sea. The ports of Cambay or Calicut and Malacca (founded at the beginning of the 15th century), which had until then served essentially as victualling and stopping points on the long route between West Asia and China, now became terminal ports. The role of these ports in providing a reasonably assured market in the goods brought in, as well as in making available those sought after by the visiting ships, besides offering facilities such as anchorage, warehousing and banking cannot be overemphasised. In the course of the 15th century, Malacca became a truly major centre of international exchange and a meeting point of traders from the east and the west. Allegedly, as many as 84 languages were spoken at this port. Also, each of the four major communities of merchants resident in and operating from Malacca – the Gujaratis, other 'western' merchants mainly from India and Burma, the merchants from Southeast Asia up to and including the Philippines, and finally the East Asians including the Chinese, the Japanese and the Okinawans – were allowed to have *shahbandars* of their own who managed the affairs of their communities autonomously of the local authorities.

India played a central role in this structure of Asian trade. In part, this indeed was a function of the mid-way location of the subcontinent between West Asia on the one hand and Southeast and East Asia on the other. But perhaps even more important was the subcontinent's capacity to put on the market a wide range of tradeable goods at highly competitive prices. These included agricultural goods, both food items such as rice, sugar and oil as well as raw materials such as cotton and indigo. While the bulk of the trade in these goods was coastal, the high seas trade component was by no means insignificant. The real strength of the subcontinent, however, lay in the provision of large quantities of manufactured goods, the most important amongst which was textiles of various kinds. While these included high value varieties such as the legendary Dhaka muslins and the Gujarat silk embroideries, the really important component for the Asian market was the coarse cotton varieties manufactured primarily on the Coromandel coast and in Gujarat. There was a large scale demand for these varieties both in the eastern markets of Indonesia, Malaya, Thailand and Burma as well as in the markets of the Red Sea, the Persian Gulf and East Africa. While it is impossible to determine precisely what proportion of total domestic demand for mass consumption textiles in these societies was met by imports from India, the available evidence would seem to point in the direction of this not being altogether insignificant. India's capacity to manufacture these textiles in large quantities and put them on the market at highly competitive terms made it in some sense the 'industrial' hub of the region surrounded by West Asia on one side and Southeast Asia on the other.

This circumstance also determined to a large extent the nature of India's demand for imports from the rest of Asia. This demand consisted essentially either of consumption goods which were not produced domestically for soil, climatic or other reasons, or of minerals and metals of various kinds whose domestic supply was either nil or substantially below the total demand. In the first category were items such as fine spices like cloves, nutmeg and mace from Indonesia, and horses and rose water from West Asia. The second category included rubies and other precious stones from Burma, as well as metals – both precious and non-precious. By far the most important non-precious metal imported was tin from Malaya. Precious metals, mainly silver, were imported overwhelmingly from West Asia. It was for this reason that from the 16th century onward, the port of Mocha was repeatedly referred to as the "treasure-chest" of the Mughal empire. It is really immaterial for our purposes whether the imported precious metals are treated as a commodity import or as a means of settling the adverse balance of trade that the concerned trading partner of the subcontinent had with it. The important point to emphasise is that by virtue of her relatively more advanced structure of manufacturing production and her capacity to provide large quantities of a basic manufactured consumption good such as inexpensive cotton textiles at highly competitive terms, India significantly enhanced the basis of trade in the Asian continent. She not only provided the textiles and, on a more modest scale, the food grains and the provisions in great demand in the neighbouring societies but also provided an important outlet for their specialised agricultural, mineral and other products. Trade satisfied different kinds of consumption needs for India as compared with her numerous trading partners in the Indian Ocean region. This by itself provided an excellent basis for a significant and growing level of trade. It is really in this sense that the critically important role of India in the structure of early modern Asian trade needs to be assessed.

The key position of India in the structure of Asian trade was also reflected in the important role of the Gujarati and other Indian trading groups in the actual conduct of this trade. This role, if anything, was strengthened in the course of the 15th century which, as we have seen above, witnessed the fragmentation of Asian trade into well defined segments. The participation of the Arab merchants got more and more confined to the trade between West Asia and the west coast of India. This left the trade between the west and the east coasts of India on the one hand, and the eastern Indian Ocean region on the other, almost exclusively in Indian hands – the Gujaratis more than any one else, but also the Chettis, the Chulias and other groups from the Coromandel coast, besides the Oriyas and the Bengalis. The participation of the Chinese merchants was now restricted by and large to controlling the trade between China and Malacca, while the Indonesian and the Malay merchants hardly seem to have ventured beyond the inter-island and the port to port trade in the Malay-Indonesian region. In sum, Indian merchants from different regions of the country constituted an important trading group operating in the Ocean.

From the vantage point of India, the two principal segments of maritime Asian trade were the western Indian Ocean and the Bay of Bengal. In the west, the link through the Red Sea and the Persian Gulf extended overland to the southern coast of the Mediterranean. The Bay of Bengal littoral extended through the straits of Malacca to the South China Sea going all the way to Japan. In the west, the area of operation of the Indian merchants stopped at the Red Sea and the Persian Gulf ports, while in the east it extended as far as Malacca. While there were clear-cut and by and large autonomous areas of operation and linkage in each of these two broad segments and there is a certain amount of merit in analysing each of these separately, it must be recognised that there was a considerable amount of interdependence and interaction across the two segments and that neither of the two should be regarded as a fully autonomous and self-contained system. One only needs to refer to the large volume of direct trade between Gujarat and Indonesia to realise the significance of this caution. This was equally true at the level of coastal trade as well, and one only has to remind oneself of the regular trade links in the 15th century between the ports of Bengal on the one hand and those of the west coast – both in Malabar and Gujarat – on the other.

In both the Arabian Sea and the Bay of Bengal, a considerable amount of trade was carried on both on the high seas as well as on the coastal trade circuits. The coastal circuits were often dominated by trade in agricultural products such as food grains and other bulk goods, and were usually characterised by the use of relatively small craft which would ordinarily not be useable on the high seas runs. Also, in comparison to the high seas connections, the role of the monsoon winds was comparatively limited in determining the rhythm of trade on the coastal circuits.

1. The West Coast

The west coast of India could conveniently be conceived of as consisting of four distinct segments divided roughly at the ports of Chaul, Karwar and Cannanore. To the north of Chaul lay the Gujarat coast, from Chaul to Karwar was the Konkan coast, south of Karwar until Mt. Eli immediately to the north of the port of Cannanore the Kanara coast, and to its south the Malabar coast. During the 15th century, the ports of Cambay in Gujarat and Calicut in Malabar were the two major international ports on the west coast of India, and between themselves handled a considerable amount of re-export trade. Gujarat was a major trading area in the subcontinent and the Gujaratis – mostly Muslims but also including Hindu traders – had traditionally been a dominant group amongst the Indian mercantile communities. Over the course of the 15th century, the trading activities of this group increased to a point where it emerged probably as the largest of all the groups engaged in trade in the Indian Ocean. This development would seem to be related to the cessation of the long distance trade between west Asia and China, and the rise of segmented Asian trade. The most important of the new ports to emerge during the 15th century was Malacca to which the Gujarati merchants shifted their trade from the Javanese and the Sumatran ports on which they used to concentrate until then in their eastern trade. The growth of Malacca continued in the second half of the 15th century, and so did the Gujarati share in the trade of the port. According to Tomé Pires, writing at a somewhat later date, about a thousand Gujarati merchants travelled each year to Malacca together with 4,000–5,000 sailors. It is true that the ships that left Cambay for Malacca each year included many owned and operated by Arab, Persian, Turkish, and other merchants from West Asia, but all these groups together were overshadowed by the Gujaratis who controlled the bulk of the trade on the route. The goods that the Malacca bound ships leaving Cambay carried were, in part, coloured woollen clothes and glassware from the Mediterranean, and items such as rosewater, opium, indigo and silver from west Asia. But a large part of the cargo would seem to have consisted of textiles manufactured in Gujarat – mainly of coarse cotton, though more expensive varieties including those manufactured from fine quality cotton and silk also seem to have figured in the list. The cargo obtained in exchange at Malacca included Chinese goods such as silk and porcelain, Indonesian spices such as pepper, cloves, nutmeg and mace, besides woods and aromatics, and precious and non-precious metals such as Malayan tin. In addition to Malacca, the Gujarati ships from Cambay called at ports such as Acheh, Kedah, Tenasserim/Mergui and Pegu. The goods carried to these ports were broadly similar to those carried to Malacca: the goods brought back were largely of local origin, rather than cosmopolitan as in the case of Malacca.

There was also a large amount of coastal trade carried on between Cambay and other smaller ports of Gujarat on the one hand, and ports on the Konkan, Kanara and the Malabar coasts to the south, and those in Bengal on the other. The principal commodity procured in the Konkan ports of Chaul and Dabhol was textiles, while the main item procured in Kanara and Malabar was pepper. A certain amount of rice was also procured in Kanara. At Calicut, limited quantities of Chinese and Indonesian goods were also picked up. Bengal provided food grains and provisions such as sugar, butter and oil in addition, of course, to textiles of different varieties.

A part of the large conglomerate of goods brought to Cambay was obviously destined for consumption in Gujarat, as well as the large north Indian hinterland supplied by it. But a good proportion would seem to have been re-exported mainly to West Asia, the most important ports in the region at this time being Aden and Jiddah. The other important constituent of the cargo to West Asia was textiles manufactured in Gujarat. These were predominantly those manufactured from coarse cotton and intended for mass consumption, though superior varieties manufactured from fine cotton and silk also figured in the list. The route from Cambay to Aden would seem to have been dominated by the Arab, Persian and other West Asian merchants, though the Gujarati merchants also operated on this route in an important way.

The Indonesian spices and other items imported from Cambay into Aden and other West Asian ports found their way in significant quantities in addition to the markets of West Asia to Europe via the Mediterranean. The two routes used for the purpose were those via the Red Sea and the Persian Gulf. While the Red Sea route terminated at the Egyptian port of Alexandria on the southern coast of the Mediterranean and involved only a small stretch of overland transportation, the Persian Gulf route made use of the Tigris or the Euphrates rivers and a fair amount of caravan transportation across Iraq and the Syrian desert. Important among the Mediterranean destination ports on this route were Tripoli (of Syria) and Beirut. This traffic was handled exclusively by the west Asian merchants. At the Mediterranean ports, the goods were procured mainly by the merchants from Venice and Genoa. While both the Red Sea and the Persian Gulf routes had been in use since antiquity, the relative amount of traffic on either at any given point in time depended partly on political circumstances. While during the 8th and the 9th centuries, the Persian Gulf route was the dominant one, the decline of the Abbasid Caliphate and the rise of the Fatimids in Egypt tilted the balance from the 11th century onward significantly in favour of the Red Sea route. This was also the period which witnessed a significant expansion in the volume of Euro-Asian trade. Evidence from the end of the 14th and the early years of the 15th century suggests that volume-wise the Alexandria trade was considerably larger – nearly double on an average – than the one via Beirut. However, since the latter handled the expensive spices much more, the difference between the two ports was much smaller in terms of value.[1]

Another direction in which the cargo arriving at Aden – particularly the coarse cotton textiles from Gujarat – moved was southwards to the East African ports of Mogadishu, Malindi and Kilwa through the agency of the West Asian merchants. There was also a certain amount of direct trade between Cambay and the East African ports carried on by the Gujarati merchants, but the extent of this trade was perhaps quite small.

On the southwest coast, the main ports in Konkan were Chaul and Dabhol. The principal orientation of these ports was towards West Asia, though the merchants of Dabhol are also known to have gone on to Bengal to join the fleet to Malacca. The volume of the latter traffic would, however, seem to have been quite small. The ports on the Kanara coast included Mirjan, Honawar, Bhatkal, Barkur, Basrur, Mangalore and Kumbla. Bhatkal was the principal port, the others being relatively minor and catering only to the coastal trade. Bhatkal was oriented exclusively to the west with connections to the Persian Gulf and the Red Sea. The principal exports from the port were white rice, sugar, iron, textiles, ginger and pepper, while the imports included copper, gold and horses from Arabia and Persia. The non-Islamic components of the trading community operating from the region consisted of Jains and the Saraswats, while the Muslims, who seem to have constituted the dominant group, included both the Navayat Muslims who claimed origins in Persia, as well as the so-called *pardesi* Muslim merchants, who were temporary residents in the area and came from the Arabian peninsula, Cairo, Turkey, Iraq and Persia.

1 C. H. H. Wake, "The Changing Pattern of Europe's Pepper and Spice Imports, c. 1400–1700," *The Journal of European Economic History* 8, 1979, p. 364–9.

The principal port on the Malabar coast was Calicut followed by smaller ports such as Cannanore, Cochin and Quilon. The principal orientation of the high seas trade from the coast was westward with the Red Sea and the Persian Gulf, though a fair amount of trade was also carried on with the eastern littoral of the Bay of Bengal and with Malacca. The coastal connections stretched both northwards up to Gujarat as well as around the Cape with Sri Lanka, and via Coromandel as far north as Bengal. The principal exports from the coast were pepper, other spices such as ginger and cardamon, textiles, coconut and its ancillary products. The principal imports from West Asia were gold, silver and horses and from the east spices and aromatics. The *pardesi* merchants dominated the trade to the west, while the coastal trade and the high seas trade to the east was controlled by the local Mappila merchants.

2. The East Coast

The two principal trading regions on the east coast of India were the Coromandel coast and Bengal. The Coromandel coast is conventionally defined to include the stretch between Point Godavari and the island of Mannar, south of which lies the Fishery coast. To the north of Point Godavari is the Gingelly coast which is sometimes also included in the Coromandel coast. For our purposes, Bengal would be defined to include the Orissa ports of Pipli and Balasore. There was a fair amount of coastal trade between the ports of the two regions dominated, it would seem, by the merchants of Bengal. At the beginning of the 16th century, the principal Coromandel port was Pulicat linked via Tirupati and Penukonda to the imperial city of Vijayanagar to the northwest. The port next in importance was that of Nagapattinam in south Coromandel, which also had two minor ports at Kunjimedu and Naguru. The northern Coromandel port of Masulipatnam was of little consequence at this time. In Bengal, by far the most important port was Chittagong which was linked to the capital city of Gaur. Satgaon was next in importance until about 1580 when due to the silting up of the waterway on which it was situated, it was succeeded by Hugli. Pipli and Balasore in Orissa were the other important ports in the region.

The high seas trade from Pulicat was basically in two directions: to Mergui and the ports of the Irrawaddy delta in southern Burma on the one hand, and to Malacca and ports further east in the archipelago on the other. While the trade with Mergui was marginal, that with Pegu and lower Burma, in particular the ports of Martaban and Cosmin was more substantial. The principal exports from Pulicat consisted of textiles produced all over the Coromandel coast and red yarn from the Krishna delta. The imports into Coromandel included items such as gold, rubies, timber, tin, ivory and copper. In 1516, Antonio Dinis, sometime Portuguese factor at Martaban, reported that on an average four or five ships were engaged each year in the trade between Cosmin and Coromandel. The link to Malacca was perhaps even more important. Until its capture by the Portuguese in 1511, the annual traffic to the port from Coromandel usually consisted of one big ship and as many as five smaller ships. The average annual value of the textiles cargo imported into Malacca from Pulicat in the early years of the 16th century has been put at 175,000 cruzados. There usually was also an annual ship to Pidie in northern Sumatra, as well as traffic from Pasai to Coromandel. The principal items imported into Pulicat included Indonesian spices, various kinds of woods, Chinese silk and other goods, gold and non-precious metals such as tin, copper, quicksilver and vermilion. A major trading group at Pulicat was that of Muslims, a few of Arab origin, but mainly members of the Muslim communities of coastal south-eastern India, known as Chulias in parts of Southeast Asia and Marakkayars on Coromandel. The trading community also included Telugu speaking Chettis of the Balija and Komatti communities as well as Armenians. At the Malacca end, the mercantile community consisted largely of the so-called *keling* merchants of Tamil and Telugu origin led by people like Nina Chatu and Nina Suryadev. The sultan of Malacca himself is also known to have participated in this branch of commerce.

In addition to the high seas trade carried on from Pulicat and other Coromandel ports, there was also a fair amount of coastal trade carried on with the Bengal ports in the north, the Sri Lankan and other ports in the south, and with ports on the Malabar coast. The precise position at the beginning of the 16th century remains somewhat obscure for the available data pertain mainly to the sixteenth and the early 17th centuries. The changes, if any, over the intervening period, however, do not appear to have been particularly marked, except in the matter of the growing role of Masulipatnam through the 16th century in the coastal, as in the high seas, network. The available information suggests that there was regular trade between Bengal and Coromandel based on the import into ports such as Masulipatnam of rice, gram, wheat, long pepper, opium, clarified butter and Bihar saltpetre by an annual coastal fleet from Bengal. In the late sixteenth and early 17th century, the number of vessels in the fleet was between thirty and forty. While the ships from Bengal usually returned from north Coromandel itself, those from the Gingelly coast went further south to supply central Coromandel as far as Pulicat and Sao Tomé. The Coromandel cargo carried back to Bengal was raw cotton, tobacco, iron and crucible steel and some textiles, but the profit seems to have been made largely on the outward journey. The pattern of coastal trade originating in southern Coromandel, however, was quite different. The ports of the Kaveri delta were all rice exporters, but this trade was directed southwards rather than towards the deficit pockets to the north. Nagapattinam supplied rice to the west coast of Sri Lanka, Jaffna and on a more limited scale, to southern Malabar in addition to Acheh, on which route rice was used mainly as a ballast item. The principal items brought back from Sri Lanka were areca, cinnamon, timber and elephants. It is somewhat intriguing that the sources do not mention any coastal contacts between the Coromandel ports on the one hand and the Kanara, Konkan and the Gujarat ports on the other.[2]

As far as Bengal was concerned, in addition to the coastal trade with south-eastern India, the major commercial links extended to the eastern littoral of the Bay of Bengal and Malacca, to Sri Lanka, the Maldives, and Malabar and finally to the Gujarat, the Red Sea and the Persian Gulf complex. The eastward trade was dominated by the trade to Malacca. According to Meilink-Roelofsz, five to six ships sailed on an average each year in the early part of the 16th century from Bengal to Malacca and ports such as Pasai and Pidie. Most of these were rather small vessels but they did include one or two larger ones whose cargoes may have been worth as much as 80,000–90,000 *cruzados*. The exports from Bengal included textiles, rice, sugar and conserves, while the imports were a variegated lot. These included Borneo camphor, Moluccan spices, pepper, sandalwood, Chinese porcelain and silk, precious metals – perhaps mainly silver –, as well as base metals such as copper, tin, lead and mercury. The connection with Burma was mainly through the ports at Martaban, Dagon and Cosmin. According to the 1516 testimony of Dinis, four to five Bengal ships visited Cosmin each year carrying mainly textiles which were exchanged primarily against silver made into rings or small hoops.

The exports to Sri Lanka, the Maldives and the Malabar coast were again mainly textiles and foodstuffs, including large quantities of rice. Indeed, besides Kanara, Bengal was the principal rice surplus area in the entire region and areas such as the Maldives depended mainly on Bengal for their rice requirements. The principal item brought back by the Bengal vessels were cinnamon and areca from Sri Lanka, *cauris* used extensively in Bengal both for ornamental purposes as well as in the form of low denomination currency from the Maldives, and pepper, of which again Bengal was an important consumer, from Malabar. The trade to Gujarat was carried on primarily through Cambay, while the trips to Mocha in the Red Sea were often made after a stop over at the Maldives. The principal goods carried were textiles, sugar and long pepper, while the principal item brought back from Mocha was silver. The evidence regarding the Persian Gulf connection is, however, somewhat ambiguous.

The accounts of Tomé Pires and Barbosa also enable one to decipher the principal components of the mercantile community operating from Bengal. The indigenous merchants of Bengal are described as "merchants with great fortunes" and were an important constituent of the trading community. But a large part of the trade would seem to have been controlled either by merchants based at the partner ports or by foreign merchant groups settled in the Bengal ports. Thus the trade with Malacca was dominated by the *keling* merchants settled there. The pepper trade with Pasai and Pidie was carried on by Persian merchants settled at the Port of Chitta-

2 Sanjay Subrahmanyam, *The Political Economy of Commerce. Southern India 1500–1650*, Cambridge 1990, p. 50–3, 93–8.

gong. This last mentioned group would seem to have also dominated the trade to the middle and the western Indian Ocean ports, though the traders on these routes also included Turks, Arabs, Rumis, Abyssinians and merchants from Chaul, Dabhol and Goa.[3]

To sum up, around the time the Europeans' participation in the maritime trade of India started at the beginning of the 16th century, India occupied a position of key importance in the structure of Indian Ocean trade. Of the three principal segments of this trade, the western Indian Ocean, the Bay of Bengal and the South China Sea, the first two were dominated by India. This domination was accounted for by India's mid-way location only in part. Perhaps more important was her capacity to put on the market a wide range of tradeable goods – particularly manufactured goods, the most important amongst which was coarse cotton textiles – at highly competitive prices. In the process, she helped expand the basis of trade in the region. This was a structure of trade in which the Europeans – of whom the Portuguese were the first – had no problem in finding a niche for themselves.

[3] Sanjay Subrahmanyam, "Notes on the Sixteenth Century Bengal Trade," *The Indian Economic and Social History Review* 24, No. 3, 1987, p. 265–89.

Historiography in Early Medieval India*

Hermann Kulke

The German medievalist Herbert Grundmann commented on the chronicles of early medieval Germany: "For the historian these rhymed chronicles have too little 'source value', for the literary historian too little literary value, but contemporaries appreciated them and drew from them their idea of history."[1] This estimate seems to apply to most works of early Indian historiography, too, which once have been termed as the problem child of history and the step child of Indology.[2]

The problems concerning the idea of history and historiography in India and in particular the reasons for their allegedly rudimentary development have often been raised. Among the great civilisations of Asia and Europe, India seems to be the only culture without a pronounced tradition of indigenous historiography which took the decisive step beyond a mythological and legendary idea of history and advanced to an understanding of history which submitted itself to the rational and critical search for truth of historical events. This peculiarity of the Indian culture appears to be particularly striking if one looks at the geographical location of India between the Arab-Persian world and China, two cultures with an extremely well-developed historiography,[3] or if one considers the vast amount of literature which otherwise India produced during the last three millennia in nearly all spheres of knowledge. Al-Biruni, the great scholar

* Revised inaugural lecture at the Faculty of Philosophy and History, Heidelberg University, 29th June, 1977 ("Geschichtsschreibung und Geschichtsbild im hinduistischen Mittelalter," *Saeculum,* 30, 1979, p. 100–12).

1 H. Grundmann, *Geschichtsschreibung im Mittelalter,* Göttingen 1965, p. 11; see also G. M. Spiegel, "Genealogy: Form and Function in Medieval Historical Narrative," *History and Theory* 22, 1983, p. 43–53 and *idem*, "Political Utility in Medieval Historiography. A Sketch," *History and Theory* 14, 1975, p. 318–25.

2 H. Bechert, "Zum Ursprung der Geschichtsschreibung im indischen Kulturbereich," *Nachrichten der Akademie der Wissenschaften in Göttingen*, Phil.-Hist. Kl., 1969, no. 2, p. 35–58.

3 See e. g. the volumes of the series *Historical Writings on the Peoples of Asia,* published by the London School of Oriental and African Studies: W. G. Beasley and E. G. Pulleyblank (eds.), *Historians of China and Japan,* London 1961, and B. Lewis and P. M. Holt (eds.), *Historians of the Middle East,* London 1962.

who had spent several years in western India in the beginning of the 11th century AD, and even learnt Sanskrit, is often called as witness as he complained about the lack of historical consciousness of the Indians: "Unfortunately the Hindus do not pay much attention to the historical order of things, they are very careless in relating the chronological succession of their kings, and when they are pressed for information and are at a loss, not knowing what to say, they invariably take to tale-telling."[4]

The lack of historical writing in Indian tradition is often explained by the dominating cyclical world view of Indian philosophy which is thought to have brought about the weakening of any interest in historical events – however epochal they might have been – in view of their eternal recurrence.[5] Neither the innumerable inscriptions of India which have been scientifically edited in several series since more than hundred years nor, for example, the discovery of Kauṭilya's famous *Arthaśāstra* at the beginning of our century have changed this negative judgement on India's relations with its history. From this text we know that, besides its numerous philosophical schools, India possessed since the 3rd century B. C. a compendium of highly rational political ideas (often compared with Machiavelli's "*Il Principe*"), which emphasized that princes must be instructed in the various fields of *itihāsa* or "history".[6] About seventy years ago Hermann Goetz challenged this almost dogmatic view of his time about India's alleged lack of historical writing: "In science there exist sometimes certain theories which arose from insufficient knowledge of the subject at the beginning of research and which remain ineradicable in spite of contradictory evidence gathered subsequently. One of these misunderstandings is the view that Indians possessed no real historiography and also no interest in history."[7] On the basis of a fairly large list of early medieval Indian chronicles which were known till 1924 he

4 This is perhaps the most frequently quoted "proof" for the lack of historical awareness in medieval India. *Alberuni's India*, trans. by E. C. Sachau, London 1910, vol. 2, p. 10.

5 See particularly U. Schneider, "Indisches Denken und sein Verhältnis zur Geschichte," *Saeculum* 9, 1958, p. 156–62, and K. Quecke, "Der indische Geist und die Geschichte," *Saeculum* 1, 1950, p. 362–79. See also D. Rothermund, "Indiens Verhältnis zu seiner Geschichte," *Indo-Asia*, 17, 1975, p. 41–50, and K. Löwith, *Weltgeschichte und Heilsgeschehen. Die theologischen Voraussetzungen der Geschichtsphilosophie,* Stuttgart 1953, p. 14ff. Romila Thapar, however, rightly pointed out that "the Hindu cycle concept is essentially a cosmological concept. It did not prevent the recording of the past in a form considered socially relevant and necessary to the present and the future". R. Thapar, "The Tradition of Historical Writing in Early India," in: *idem, Ancient Indian Social History. Some Interpretations*, New Delhi 1972, p. 287. For a critique of the assumption that the cyclic concept was a major cause of India's lack of historical writing see also B. Stein, "Early Indian Historiography: A Conspiracy Hypothesis," *Indian Economic and Social History Review* 6, 1969, p. 41–59.

6 "During the first part of the day, he should undergo training in the arts of (using) elephants, horses, chariots and weapons. In the later part, (he should engage) in listening to Itihāsa. The Purāṇas, Itivṛtta, Ākhyāyika, Udāharaṇa, Dharmaśāstra and Arthaśāstra, – these constitute Itihāsa", *The Kauṭilya Arthaśāstra, Part II. An English Translation* by R. P. Kangle, Bombay 1963, I.5.12–14.

7 Hermann Goetz, "Die Stellung der indischen Chroniken im Rahmen der indischen Geschichte," *Zeitschrift für Buddhismus* 6, 1924, p. 139–59.

came to the conclusion that apparently there was no lack of historical interest and writing but that instead one has "to assume an almost total destruction of the old chronicles."

In a more recently published article on the origin of historiography in South Asia it has been pointed out that Goetz' hope of the discovery of further historical literature has not been fulfilled. Thus, for example, the discovery of the extensive Gilgit and Turfan manuscripts of Indian texts in Central Asia yielded no further indication of the existence of Indian historical writing.[8] Therefore, it appears to be still nearly unanimously accepted,[9] that the Buddhist chronicles of Sri Lanka which were composed since about the 4th century AD.[10] and the *Rājataraṅgiṇī* chronicle of Kashmir which Kalhaṇa wrote in the 12th century have to be regarded as the only genuine historiographical works of pre-Islamic South Asia. An important question, however, which so far has not yet been answered is, whether – as it is often presumed – these works from Sri Lanka and Kashmir, after all marginal areas of India, are exceptions to the rule of India's alleged antipathy to history or whether they represent the final, though rare, products of a fairly well-developed Indian tradition of historical writing.

We may begin our discussion on these problems with a rather detailed reference to the Kashmir chronicle and its sources.[11] The *Rājataraṅgiṇī* or "Stream of Kings" was compiled in 1148/49 by the Brahmin Kalhaṇa at the same time when Germany's great medieval chronicle was written by a priest at Regensburg soon after 1147 and in which the history of the world was narrated from Caesar up to the contemporary times in a "fabulous, legendary and mythical manner"[12] in over 17,000 verses. In the *Rājataraṅgiṇī*, Kalhaṇa described in about 8,000 double verses in excellent Sanskrit the history of Kashmir. The first three books of the chronicle deal with the early period up to the 7th century AD. For the earliest portions, Kalhaṇa adopted the traditional mythological-legendary traditions. In the following three books, he described the story of Kashmir from the 7th to the early 11th century, for which he could rely at least partly on historical sources. The last two books take the history through the 11th to the early 12th centuries, of which Kalhaṇa himself was partly a witness. This last section is very reliable and detailed and comprises more than half of the entire chronicle.

8 Bechert, "Zum Ursprung der Geschichtsschreibung," p. 39ff.

9 See e. g. C. H. Philips in the introduction to the volume edited by himself, *Historians of India, Pakistan and Ceylon,* London 1961, p. 5, and Bechert, "Zum Ursprung der Geschichtsschreibung," p. 40.

10 Bechert regards the "early, so-called Singhalese-Buddhist nationalism" as the guiding line and major impulse for historiography in Ceylon, "Zum Ursprung der Geschichtsschreibung," p. 58.

11 M. A. Stein, *Kalhaṇa's Rājataraṅgiṇī. A Chronicle of the Kings of Kaśmīr. Text and Translation,* Bombay 1892 and Westminster 1900 (reprint Delhi 1960, 1961). See also B. Kölver, *Textkritische und philologische Untersuchungen zur Rājataraṅgiṇī des Kalhaṇa,* Wiesbaden 1971. For a most recent attempt to apply the narrative discourse to an analysis of the *Rājataraṅgiṇī*, see Christiane Schnellenbach, *Geschichte als 'Gegengeschichte'? Historiographie in Kalhaṇas Rājataraṅgiṇī,* Marburg 1996.

12 Grundmann, *Geschichtsschreibung im Mittelalter*, p. 10.

Kalhana wrote not as historian, but designated himself expressively as poet (*kavi*) whose task it was to "reveal to all men" past events by means of his divine intuition (I.4–5). But he also stated in the introduction, that he regarded it as his task to act like a judge and to keep himself "free from love and hatred in relating the facts of the past" (I.7). And, moreover, he assured his readers to compose a connected poem from the many scattered and unconnected narratives (*prabandha*) about earlier kings of Kashmir (I.9–10) and to arrange properly the fluctuating data of earlier chronicles with regard to the time and place of former kings (I.21).

Kalhaṇa, a son of a deposed minister, himself no more in the service of the ruling king of Kashmir, revealed thus indeed a remarkably critical historical awareness. But his main personal concern seems to have been rather moral and political. From the listener of his chronicle he expected a "sentiment of resignation (*śānta rasa*) which is to rule supreme in this work" (I.23), when confronted with the brief and fateful life of men entangled in their actions. We may assume that this attitude was in fact the basic approach of Kalhaṇa's educated contemporaries towards their own history. His own political ideas can be perceived from statements which he usually put in the mouth of counsellors of former kings in a textbook-like manner. After a century of disturbances he warned the kings of Kashmir against rebellious landlords (*ḍāmara*, IV.344ff) and bureaucrats (*kāyastha*). Particularly harsh is his judgement of the latter, against whose thirst for power the king should protect his people. According to Kalhaṇa, they are plagues for the people rapidly destroying everybody. "The crab kills its father, and the white ant destroys her mother, but the ungrateful Kāyastha when he has become powerful destroys everything" (VIII.89).

From a historiographical point of view it is of greatest importance that Kalhaṇa enumerated in the introductory verses of his work an impressive large number of different sources for writing his chronicle (I.11–18).[13] According to his own claim he critically used "eleven works of former scholars containing the chronicles of king" (I.14).[14] He criticised the "List of Kings" (*nṛpāvali*) of the poet Kṣemendra in which, according to Kalhaṇa, not a single part is free from mistakes (I.13). Furthermore he complains about the incompleteness of an abbreviated version of the royal chronicles of Kashmir by a poet Suvrata (I.11) and mentions another "List of Kings" of Kashmir (*pārthivāvalī*) by the Brahmin Helārāja of about 12,000 double verses, which was thus half longer than his own *Rājataraṅgiṇī*. In addition, Kalhaṇa used also the Nīlapurāṇa, a compendium of mythological-legendary traditions. In order to check the information given in these various chronicles and legendary texts, he visited temples for consulting

[13] Kölver investigates in detail the sources used by Kalhaṇa (Kölver, *Textkritische und philologische Untersuchungen*, p. 2–9).

[14] *Pūrvasūrigranthā rājakathāśrayāḥ*, I.14. – Kölver, *Textkritische und philologische Untersuchungen*, p. 3ff, regards these "books of earlier scholars", as biographies of rulers (*carita*) rather than chronicles or genealogies.

their founding inscriptions (*pratiṣṭhāśāsana*) engraved on their walls. He had further recourse to royal charters of land donations (*vāstuśāsana*) and to copper plate inscriptions (*paṭṭa*) for the sake of their long dynastic eulogies (*praśasti*) of the royal donors. Various hints in his chronicle allow us to assume that he used also coins as a source for his historical writing (e. g. VII. 926).

The significance of Kalhaṇa's chronicle therefore lies not only in its account of Kashmir's history, particularly for the 11th and early 12th centuries. Its more general value for early medieval historiography rests on the unique insight which his work provides us into contemporary historiographical sources of an Indian region. In Kashmir there existed obviously a large number of extensive genealogies as well as dynastic chronicles and an abbreviated popular version of them. Furthermore Kalhaṇa had at his disposal innumerable temple and copper-plate inscriptions as well as coins as historical sources. Even if Kalhaṇa's chronicle itself may be unique in early medieval historiography of India, similar sources which he used for compiling his chronicle may have also existed in other regions of India. Already in much earlier times we have references for the existence of a well-organised information and archives system in north India. From Kauṭilya's *Arthaśāstra* we know e. g. that from the village level upwards government officials (*gopa*) were entrusted with a detailed recording of important details regarding the number of residents of every house, their caste, professions and income etc., which were in turn checked by spies of the central government.[15] In the 7th century AD the Chinese pilgrim Xuanzang (Hsiuen-tsang) confirmed in his travel report on India the existence of provincial offices which were responsible for keeping records of all important events in their provinces.[16] Since such reports and daily records of transactions were written almost exclusively on palm leaves, the assumption of a more or less complete destruction may particularly apply to this category of archive material of India. Kept at the centres of power, they were exposed to all sorts of political upheavals. Even undestroyed palm-leaf archives, which were lying forgotten as a result of dynastic changes and were not copied again from time to time, fell inevitable victims to the humid climate or the notorious ants. Only in the dry deserts of Central Asia palm-leaf manuscripts were preserved for more than a thousand years.

On the other hand, as far as royal genealogies were concerned, things were at least somewhat more favourable. In some cases these genealogies were drawn up and handed down by specific castes whose origins go back to pre-Christian centuries. According to a text of the early

15 *Arthaśāstra*, II.35.

16 *Buddhist Records of the Western World*, translated by S. Beal, London 1906, p. 78. The existence of archives is also evident from numerous documents of land donations. For example, in the copper-plates of Bengal of the 5th and early 6th centuries AD the administrators of the district record offices (*pustapāla*) are explicitly mentioned. In the case of land donations they had to check in their registers the state of ownership of the concerned land and also to supervise the making of the copper-plates from which they preserved copies in their registers (see e. g. *Epigraphia Indica* 20, p. 64, and 23, p. 157ff).

centuries AD, their task was "to preserve the genealogies of gods, *ṛshis* (sages) and most glorious kings, and the traditions of great men".[17] These genealogies, mostly called *vaṃśāvalīs* or *vaṃśānucaritas* ("dynastic books"), were the inheritable possessions of royal genealogists and of bards, and, in case of danger, could be protected by them more easily than royal archives.

The "royal genealogies" (*rājavaṃśānucarita*) of the early dynasties of north and parts of central India are preserved in numerous Purāṇas. The part of the Purāṇas which is most important for historiography is the "History of the royal dynasties" (*rājavaṃśānucarita*). As early as 1913 Pargiter has ascertained that their different variants in the Purāṇas go back to an original text.[18] It must have been composed in the early decades of the 4th century AD, since it ends with the early conquests of the Gupta kings who finally founded their empire under Chandragupta I in 320 AD. Since Pargiter's publications, further research on early Indian history revealed that these royal genealogies of about twenty dynasties between the 6th century B. C. and the early 4th century AD are in considerable agreement with other historical sources.[19] What is important in these early royal genealogies is the fact that they cover the whole of northern India and parts of central India and their dynasties for nearly one millennium. These Purāṇic genealogies are by far the most intensively researched texts of early Indian historical writing.

However, to my knowledge an interesting question still remains unanswered: why did the early royal genealogies of the Purāṇas break off at the very moment when north India was united again by a great dynasty after several centuries of political fragmentation. To my mind it is likely that this sudden break in the *writing* of history was a direct consequence of the Brahmanical cyclic *conception* of history. For centuries northwestern and parts of northern India, the Āryavarta and heartland of Brahmanical learning, had been under foreign rule of mainly central Asian dynasties. In Indian literature they were usually called *Yavanas* after the Graeco-Bactrians in northwestern India in the 2nd century B. C. Many of these foreign rulers adopted Buddhism which ignored the Hindu caste system and world order, and thus the dominating role of the Brahmins, too. The rule of these cosmopolitan foreign dynasties thus corresponded exactly to the evils of the Kaliyuga and confirmed the Brahmanic world view and cyclic idea of history of the ever worsening ages. The Brahmin compiler of the early Purāṇic genealogies therefore concluded his work with an apocalyptic description of the evils of the last age of the world:

17 *Vāyu Purāṇa*, quoted from R. C. Majumdar, "Ideas of History in Sanskrit Literature," in: C. H. Philips, *Historians of India, Pakistan and Ceylon*, p. 15.

18 F. E. Pargiter, *The Purāṇa Text of the Dynasties of the Kali Age,* 1913 (reprint, Varanasi 1962); *idem*, *Ancient Indian Historical Tradition,* London 1922 (reprint Delhi 1962); W. Kirfel, *Das Purāṇa Pañcalakṣana. Versuch einer Textgeschichte*, Leiden 1927.

19 More recent attempts to defend the historicity of the Purāṇic genealogies are R. M. Smith, *Dates and Dynasties in Earliest India*, Delhi 1973, and in particular H. von Stietencron, "Die purāṇischen Genealogien und das Datum Buddhas," in: H. Bechert (ed.), *The Dating of the Historical Buddha,* pt. 2, Göttingen 1992, p. 148–81. R. Thapar discussed the Purāṇic genealogies in several papers in a broader context of social history of lineages and early state formation in northern India: *Ancient Indian Social History* (see fn. 5).

> There will be Yavanas here by reason of religious feeling *or* ambition *or* plunder; they will not be kings solemnly anointed, but will follow evil customs by reason of the corruption of the age. Massacring women and children and killing one another, kings will enjoy the earth at the end of the Kali age. Kings of continual upstart races, falling as soon as they arise, will exist in succession through fate. They will be destitute of righteousness, affection, *and* wealth. Mingled with them *will be* Ārya and Mleccha folk everywhere: they prevail in turn; the population will perish.[20]

This apocalyptic depiction of the Kaliyuga was written most likely at the time when Chandragupta, the founder of the Gupta dynasty, had re-established Hindu kingship by his performance of the grand brahmanical horse sacrifice and when his son Samudragupta undertook his unique campaign across north and eastern India and thus founded, within a few decades, the classical empire of ancient India. The success of the Gupta emperors as well as their promotion of Hindu institutions thus directly contradicted the apocalyptic world view of the present Kali age, as depicted in the Purāṇic genealogies. To my mind it was this contradiction between the old Brahmanical cyclic idea of history of the ever-worsening ages and the glorious contemporary history of the early Gupta emperors which brought about the discontinuance of the early royal genealogies of the Purāṇas.

It is even possible that the compiler of the Purāṇic royal genealogies intentionally ended his lists of dynasties with his drastic depiction of the evils of the Kaliyuga in order to warn future kings of the fateful recurrence of these evils. Although this assumption is based purely on conjecture we know a similar case from Sri Lanka's "Great Chronicle", the *Mahāvaṃsa.* In the early 6th century AD, Mahānāma, its author, concluded his chronicle which is essentially the chronicle of his Mahāvihāra at Anuradhapura with a detailed description of the wicked deeds of the Sri Lankan king Mahāsena (334–62 AD). During his rule the orthodox Theravāda Buddhist Mahāvihāra was destroyed by "heretic" Mahāyāna Buddhist monks of the neighbouring Abhayagiri monastery, the arch-rival of the Mahāvihāra. Hitherto it has been generally assumed that this abrupt end of the *Mahāvaṃsa* chronicle was caused by the destruction of the chronicles of the Mahāvihāra during Mahāsena's rule.[21] But from the later *Cūlavaṃsa* we know that the historiographical tradition of the Mahāvihāra did not end with Mahāsena's rule. Therefore it has been pointed out elsewhere that there is a great probability that Mahānāma purposely ended his chronicle with Mahāsena's misdeeds in order to warn Sri Lanka's future kings not to deviate from the orthodox Theravāda teaching of the Mahāvihāra.[22]

20 Pargiter, *The Purāṇa Text*, p. 74 (Italics added by Pargiter).

21 W. Geiger, *The Dīpavaṃsa and the Mahāvaṃsa and their Historical Development in Ceylon*, Colombo 1908, p. 71.

22 H. Kulke, "Sectarian Politics and Historiography in Early Sri Lanka," in: U. Everding (ed.), *Wilhelm Geiger and the Study of Sri Lanka*, Colombo n. d. (1999), p. 112–35.

Whatever may have caused the discontinuance of the early Purāṇic royal genealogies with their decisive negative perception of the past, the classical age of the Gupta dynasty witnessed a definite change of the world view and idea of history. The medium of a radically new historical writing were the great Sanskrit poems which experienced a unique flowering under the rule of the imperial Guptas. In the Mahākāvya poetry the conception of the cyclical world order of continuous political decline receded in favour of the projection of the mythical golden age into the present age. In these epics, the rule of great kings and thus also of the great Gupta emperors was equated with the Golden Age and its mythological rulers. This new world view found its clearest expression in the works of Kālidāsa, India's *mahākavi* or "great poet", who may have lived around 400 AD at the Gupta court during Chandragupta's II rule. In his epic poem *Raghuvaṃśa*, Raghu, the mythical ancestor of the Rāma, performs a "conquest of the world" (*digvijaya*) the description of which resembles in many details the successful conquests of Chandragupta's father, Samudragupta. The *Vikramorvaśī* may have eulogised Chandragupta II who seems to have been equated with the great legendary king Vikramāditya and the poem *Kumārasambhava* likewise might have been an allusion to the then crown prince Kumāragupta.[23] Kālidāsa thus transformed contemporary history into the mythological events of the glorious past. This, however, was by no means an expression of world-denial.[24] It was instead a complete affirmation of the happy conditions of the Gupta empire. Through his epic poems Kālidāsa was endeavouring to give a glorious and almost cosmic dimension and legitimation to the Gupta rulers. This transformation of historical events by literary means into a mythical past and the legitimisation of contemporary rulers by means of divine and epic prototypes has, in my opinion, strongly influenced the idea of history and the concepts of historiography during early medieval India. Kings were now no more the executors of an inexorable law of the early cyclical conception of history. On the contrary, many of them explicitly claimed, for instance, to be "free from any impurity of the Kali age" or even to be "the destroyer of the manifold strength of the Kali age".[25] They manifested themselves as divine heroes and gods on the earth, to whom was granted the privilege of perpetuating, indeed of eternalising, through their power the state of the perfect, mythical golden age.[26] Kālidāsa's conception of history was not com-

[23] A. B. Keith, *A History of Sanskrit Literature,* London 1920, p. 80f.

[24] D. Rothermund, "Indiens Verhältnis zu seiner Geschichte," p. 41, terms this type of historiography as romantic in contrast to the mythical-cyclic and the teleological historical writing.

[25] N. N. Vasu, "Copper-plate Inscription of Narasimha-deva II of Orissa, dated 1217 Śaka," *J. of the Asiatic Society of Bengal* 65, 1896, p. 265; K. V. Subrahmanya Aiyar, "Kanya Kumari Inscription of Virarajendra-Chola," in: *idem, Travancore Archaeological Series*, vol. 3.1, Trivandrum 1921, p. 87–158 (157).

[26] In his Allahabad inscription Samudragupta is praised as "a god, dwelling on the earth" (*Corpus Inscriptionum Indicarum*, vol. 3, p. 8, line 28). In a clear refutation of the cyclic world view, it is stated in the *Arthaśāstra* (I.3), that the world will never perish but progress if the king upholds dharma.

pletely new in India, but it exerted an enormous influence on the courtly culture of the successor states, for which the Gupta empire and its poets remained for centuries the great model.[27]

The disintegration of the north Indian Gupta empire and the emergence of regional kingdoms throughout the Indian subcontinent with their distinct modes of state formation and social organisation marked the end of the classical era and the beginning of early medieval India.[28] It witnessed the emergence of two new forms of historical writing, the royal *carita* biographies and the long *praśasti* eulogies of the royal copper-plate inscriptions. The royal caritas praised the great "deeds" (*carita*) of a king. On the one side, they continued the *mahākāvya* tradition which aimed at the fulfilment of poetic rules rather than the detailed description of historical events. But, on the other side, early medieval *carita* biographies pertain – in contrast to Kālidāsa's *mahākāvyas* – directly to historical rulers although their historical deeds are alluded to in most cases only metaphorically. These *carita* biographies are genuine pieces of narrative historical writing if one does not restrict their historiographical value to the mere detection of historical facts.[29]

The oldest royal vita known to us is the *Harṣacarita*, the "Deeds of Harṣa", by the famous poet Bāṇa. It is a eulogy of king Harṣa who succeeded at the beginning of the 7th century to set up for one generation a successor state of the Guptas empire, even though it was limited to north India. After a century of political fragmentation which followed the disintegration of the Gupta empire and the Hun invasion in northwestern India, the work of Bāṇa was an appropriate glorification of the deeds of king Harṣa. He is, of course, not depicted as a ruler of the Kali age but equated with the rulers of the First or Golden Age (*prathamakṛta-yuga*) and his life-story is praised as a second *Mahābhārata*. The *Harṣacarita* contains also detailed information about Harsa's rise to power and the struggle with Śaśāṅka, the king of Bengal, whereas other events are indicated only metaphorically. Thus the conquest of Nepal by Harṣa is alluded to only by stating that the supreme god now allows taxes to be raised by Harṣa in the hitherto invincible Himālaya mountains.[30]

It was only around 1100 that we come again across several important biographies of rulers of different regional kingdoms of India, out of which only the *Vikramāṅkadevacarita* and *Rāmacarita*, the biographies of the Chalukyan king Vikramāditya VI (1076–1126) of western

27 Aihole inscription of Pulakeśin II of AD 634/635. Its author Ravikirti compares himself explicitly with Kālidāsa (*Epigraphia Indica* 6, p. 7).

28 B. D. Chattopadhyaya, *The Making of Early Medieval India*, New Delhi 1994; R. S. Sharma, *Indian Feudalism, c. 300–1200*, Calcutta 1965; H. Kulke, "The Early and the Imperial Kingdom: A Processural Model of Integrative State Formation in Early Medieval India," in: *idem* (ed.), *The State in India 1000–1700,* New Delhi 1995, p. 233–62.

29 V. Pathak, *Ancient Historians of India. A Study of Historical Biographies,* London 1966 and C. Prabha, *Historical Mahākāvyas in Sanskrit* (*Eleventh to Fifteenth Centuries AD*), New Delhi 1976.

30 *The Harshacarita of Bāṇadaṭṭa*, ed. by P. V. Kane, Bombay 1918; text p. 40, notes p. 179.

India and of king Rāmapāla (c. 1077–c. 1119) of Bengal, may be mentioned here. Although these texts contain important historical information, their authors, too, felt themselves indebted more to poetic principles than to painstaking descriptions of historical events. Like Kalhaṇa, the author of the almost contemporary chronicle of Kashmir, Bilhaṇa, the author of the *carita* of king Vikramāditya, regarded himself as a poet to whom was given the privilege of preserving the fame of the kings through the charms of his poetry.[31] He accused critics of his poetic ethos of sparing no pains in finding mistakes, thereby ignoring the beauty of his poetry which is ambrosia for the ears. He therefore compared his critics with camels looking merely at the thorns when they enter a pleasure garden (I.29).[32]

The historical *carita* literature reached its climax in the *Rāmacarita* of the poet Sandhyākara Nandin.[33] It narrates the deeds of king Rāmapāla, who restored the power of the Pāla dynasty around 1100. Its historical information is quite dependable, but it is couched in a particular manner, typical of Brahmin Sanskrit scholarship. By virtue of the ambiguity of the Sanskrit words and compounds, the verses of the four chapters of this biography have a double meaning.[34] According to one way of reading, the deeds of the mythical hero Rāma are praised, while in another way of reading those of the historical king Rāmapāla are narrated. In a line of the final chapter the poet stated explicitly that the poem praises the heroic deeds of the two Rāmas, of the divine Raghu dynasty and of the king of Bengal.[35] He refers to his poem therefore as the *Rāmāyaṇa* of the Kali age and calls himself, after the legendary author of the *Rāmāyaṇa* epic, Valmiki. The *Rāmacarita* therefore provides an excellent example for early medieval idea of history, which conceives great historical events neither as expressions of a cyclic or a linear-teleological development but as the renewal of the eternally present mythical age.

The second major historiographical contribution of the early medieval India are the great eulogistic (*praśasti*) genealogies of the numberless inscriptions, particularly those of the great copper-plate inscriptions. Earlier inscriptions, e. g. of Aśoka (3rd cent. B. C.), Khāravela (1st cent. B. C.) and Rudradāman (2nd cent. AD), narrate exclusively the great achievements of these

[31] *The Vikramāṅkadevacarita of Bilhaṇa*, I.26, ed. by G. Bühler, Bombay 1895; Engl. translation by S. C. Banerji and A. K. Gupta, *Bilhaṇa's Vikramāṅkadevacaritam. Glimpses of the History of the Chalukyas of Kalyana*, Calcutta 1965.

[32] The *Vikramāṅkadevacarita* is an excellent example for the nature of the *carita* literature to conceal all unpleasant facts while glorifying the ruler. Although Bilhaṇa narrates that the gods created the Chāḷukya dynasty and Vikramāditya in order to ward off the enemies of religion (*dharma-druha*), he did not mention even by a single word the preceding devastating annual inroads of Mahmud of Ghazni in the years 1000 to 1027. This is all the more striking as Bilhaṇa mentions his own visit to Somanātha (XVIII.97), the most famous temple of northwestern India which Mahmud had destroyed in 1025 and in the defence of which thousands of Hindus were killed.

[33] *Rāmacaritam of Sandhyākara Ṇandin*, rev. ed. and transl. by R. G. Basak, Calcutta 1969.

[34] The fifth book is on "Fame of the Poet" (*kavipraśasti*).

[35] The connection between the "two Rāmas" gives an opportunity to the poet to praise King Rāmapāla as "new incarnation of God Nārāyaṇa" (*abhinava nārāyana avatāra,* V. 5).

individual rulers without mentioning any genealogical links or mythological ancestors. It was greatly to the credit of the Gupta rulers to have inserted short dynastic genealogies into their inscriptions. It began with Samudragupta's famous Allahabad inscription which mentions just in one short phrase the names and titles of his three ancestors. This short genealogy was stepwise extended by his successors Chandragupta II and Kumāragupta who added each the names of their deceased father to this genealogy.

But it was only during the early Middle Ages that these short dynastic lists grew to full-fledged eulogistic genealogies and became a most essential part of the inscriptions.[36] These inscriptions usually contain two distinct portions, viz. the royal *praśasti* and the actual deed of the gift. The *praśasti*s praise in great detail the greatness and beauty of the ruling king and of his forefathers. Only rarely they allude in highly eloquent Sanskrit to their historic accomplishments but usually mention their regnal years. The size of the royal copper-plate charters (*rāja-śāsana*) were particularly impressive under the imperial Cōḷas in the 11th century. Their greatest ruler Rājendra (1014–43) issued the biggest set so far discovered. It consists of 55 plates with altogether 2,539 lines and weighs about 98 kg. About one quarter of the inscription is the *praśasti* of Rājendra and his royal ancestors, the "rest" contains the deed of gift and the list of altogether 1,073 donees.[37] The temple inscriptions of Rājendra and his father Rājarāja which cover nearly the whole basement of his monumental Rājarājeśvara temple at Tānjavur are equally impressive.[38] A particular interesting case of a royal *praśasti* in a temple inscription is the Kanyā Kumārī inscription of Vīrarājendra, Rājendra's youngest son. It is engraved on six pillars in a temple near the southernmost point of India. Out of its 444 lines 419 lines, written in excellent Sanskrit, narrate the royal *praśasti* of Vīrarājendra and his ancestors. Only 25 lines, written in Tamil, comprise the royal deed.[39] This inscription shows that the royal *praśasti* eulogy in fact became the most important part of early medieval inscriptions.[40] Burton Stein therefore certainly was right when he observed that "the Chola inscriptions are intended rather obviously to distribute to all inhabited places the standardised message of a great kingship".[41]

To my knowledge none of the standard works on Indian historical writing includes these long royal *praśasti*s into their discourse on Indian historiography although more recently some

36 See also G. Berkemer, "Aspekte des Zeitdenkens in den Inschriften des vormodernen Indien," in: K. E. Müller and J. Rüsen (eds.), *Historische Sinnbildung*, Reinbek 1997, p. 277–95.

37 D. C. Sircar, *Indian Epigraphy*, Delhi 1965, p. 124.

38 E. Hultzsch and V. Venkayya, *Tamil Inscriptions of Rājarāja, Rājendrachōla, and others in the Rājarājeśvara Temple at Tanjavur,* Madras 1891–1916 (*South Indian Inscriptions*, vol. 2, 1–4).

39 Kanyā Kumārī Inscription of Virarājendra (see above, fn. 25).

40 Similar cases are known from other kingdoms, too. Thus, for instance, a copper-plate inscription of the Narasiṃhadeva II of Orissa consisted of 206 lines, out of which 176 lines are the eulogistic genealogy of the Gaṅga rulers up to Narasiṃha II. The actual deed is dealt with in only 30 lines (see above, fn. 25).

41 B. Stein, "The Segmentary State in South Indian History," in: R. G. Fox (ed.), *Realm and Region in Traditional India,* New Delhi 1977, p. 17.

aspects of these "epigraphical genealogies" have been studied. G. Spencer, for instance, analysed the Cōḷa genealogies and stressed the political validation function of their mythological section against subordinate rulers as it "traces the 'decent' of the reigning king in a double sense, both ancestrally and cosmologically".[42] So far it seems to have escaped the notice of historians that the heyday of these royal *praśasti*s of early medieval copper-plates and temple inscriptions coincided more or less exactly with the 8th to 11th centuries, the period when no important literary *carita* poems so far have been discovered. During these centuries the inscriptional *praśasti* genealogies appear to have replaced the great *carita* poems and to have taken over their important socio-political functions. In fact, during this period the long *praśasti*s have become veritable *carita* poems, the longest of which being not much shorter than e. g. the above-mentioned *Rāmacarita*. The reason why Bāṇa's great example, the *Harṣacarita*, apparently found no imitation for several centuries appears to be quite obvious. Royal *carita* poems remained court literature whose impact on the wider state society remained, most likely, rather restricted. The dynastic *praśasti*s of the inscriptions, however, were issued again and again by great rulers and distributed the message of their own greatness and of their dynasties to various parts of their kingdom, thus multiplying the socio-political impact of literary historiography. One may even go a step further and come to the hypothetical conclusion that the literary *carita* poems re-entered the historiographical scene in the 12th century when the inscriptional *praśasti*s have become too long and the copper-plate sets too bulky.

Till recently the *Rājataraṅgiṇī* dominated the historiographical discourse of early medieval India. It was regarded as India's unique piece of early medieval historical writing rather than as an outstanding example of a larger historiographical tradition. The royal *carita* biographies were, if at all, only partly accepted as pieces of genuine historical writing as their authors regarded themselves and wrote their works not as historians but as Sanskrit poets. The important royal *praśasti*s of India's innumerable inscriptions were treated even less favourably as they were obviously not regarded as historical writing. The result of this rather negative assessment of India's (and in particular of early medieval India's) historiographical heritage are the well-known statements about India's lack of historical consciousness.

Even though the hope of discovering new chronicles which Hermann Goetz once had raised was disappointed, our estimation of India's historical writing is changing considerably in recent times. This development is caused mainly by an epistemological change. It is no longer the so-called historicity of a text which defines its "historiographical value" but its functions within its broader socio-political contexts and its significance to the narrative discourse. These new studies meanwhile produced important contributions, particularly in the fields of ethnic conscious-

[42] G. Spencer, "Heirs Apparent: Fiction and Function in Chola Mythical Genealogies," *Indian Economic and Social History Review* 21, 1984, p. 415–32 (425).

ness or identity[43] and ethnohistory.[44] An important "by-product" of all these studies is their focus on regional and local chronicles of late medieval India which usually are written in regional languages. But although none of these late medieval chronicles have yet been dealt with explicitly in more general studies on Indian historiography it has become clear by now that our conventional perception of India's – and in particular early medieval India's – alleged lack of historical interest is a question of epistemology rather than a lack of historical writing.

[43] See for instance the special issue ed. by H. L. Seneviratne, "Identity, Consciousness and the Past: The South Asian Scene," *Social Analysis, Journal of Cultural and Social Practice* 25, 1989, and in particular V. Narayana Rao and D. Shulman, "History, Biography and Poetry at the Tanjavur Nayaka Court," in: Seneviratne, "Identity, Consciousness," p. 115–30; H. Kulke, "Historiography and Regional Identity. Some Considerations on Late Medieval Chronicles of South Asia" (unpublished manuscript).

[44] N. B. Dirks, *The Hollow Crown: Ethnohistory of an Indian Kingdom,* Cambridge 1987; G. Berkemer, "The Chronicle of a Little Kingdom. Some Reflections on the *Tekkali-tālūkā Jamīṃdārla Vaṃśavali,*" in: B. Kölver (ed.), *Law, State and Administration in Classical India,* Munich 1997, p. 65–95; B. Schnepel, *Die Dschungelkönige. Ethnohistorische Aspekte von Politik und Ritual in Orissa*, Stuttgart 1998.

The Buddhist Connection: Sinhalese-Burmese Intercourse in the Middle Ages*

Tilman Frasch

1. Introduction

In many – if not most – cases, progress in historical research is achieved by way of short steps when newly found sources supply additional information or the old ones are read again with new questions in mind. The new evidence thus acquired can be compared to a piece of mosaic that doesn't make a full picture, but the picture a piece fuller. This paper intends to be such a short step that will not completely revise our knowledge of the Sinhalese-Burmese relations, but enlarge it by one aspect, namely their intensity. It is my aim to show that the exchange especially in the field of religion has been much more intensive than it had looked like up to now. This intensity, as borne out e. g. by the frequency of travels or the variety of purposes, becomes even more remarkable if viewed against the few things both societies had in common apart from their affinity to Theravāda Buddhism. One may even argue that the Burmese-Sinhalese connection, itself being a part of a wider Buddhist network within the Bay of Bengal (and beyond, as far as Indonesia and China), never ranked much behind each country's relation with India despite India's (especially Bodhgaya's) great attraction to Buddhist pilgrims from near and wide and despite the great impact Pala art had on Buddhist art abroad. This may partly reflect the dramatic change of the political situation in northern India at the turn of the 11th–12th century, when the Muslim invaders put a final blow on Indian Buddhism and its culture. That Theravāda Buddhism thereafter continued to flourish only outside India

* Originally doing research on this topic in preparation of my thesis (*Pagan. Stadt und Staat*, Stuttgart 1996), I presented an earlier version of this paper at the Postgraduate Institute of Pali and Buddhist Studies, Colombo (in connection with the Goethe-Institute, Colombo) in September 1995. In the meantime, my intention at that time to have the whole Bay of Bengal covered has been materialised: "A Buddhist Network in the Bay of Bengal: Relations between Bodhgaya, Burma and Sri Lanka, c. 300–1300," in: Claude Guillot et al. (eds.), *From the Mediterranean to the China Sea: Miscellaneous Notes*, Wiesbaden 1998, p. 69–92.

must have contributed to bolster the East-West alliance. Before looking into purposes and components of the connection, I'll first have a glance at the nautical prerequisites on which Buddhist travellers were depending.

2. Nautical Prerequisites

Even though research on the ancient and medieval sea links and trading networks of the Indian Ocean has been booming for more than a decade now, it is still difficult to come across data relating to Burma for the simple reason that the Burmese never established themselves as a seafaring nation and never paid much attention to foreign trade.[1] Moreover, Burma was not touched by the main shipping route (now sometimes called the "silk road of the sea") that linked the Middle East with India, Southeast Asia and China.[2] The following thoughts are therefore not more than a tentative approach, at least as far as Burma is concerned.[3] Pagan was an up-country state that virtually looked down upon Lower Burma: the latter was a "foreign" area that had to be conquered (*nuiṅ-ṅaṃ*), and afterwards one didn't pay much attention to the affairs there – this is basically the Upper Burman perspective as represented by the Pagan inscriptions. Nevertheless, occasionally some Lower Burman place names appear in the inscriptions. Among them, Tala seems to have been the most prominent place, serving as an administrative outpost as well as a kind of royal lodge for some kings on their pleasure trips.[4] *Henbuiw* also appears in relatively early inscriptions; it should be placed in the vicinity of Rangoon. Bassein (*Kusumi*) and Martaban (*Muttama*) are both known from Sinhalese sources only. There are now references concerning wharfs or ship-building, but it should be kept in mind that

[1] Even if the situation may have slightly different in Lower Burma which was more exposed to foreign interest, the only notable exception may have been the short period between 1554 and 1634 when the kings of Taungoo used the conquered town of Pegu as their capital, see Victor Lieberman, "The Transfer of the Burmese Capital from Pegu to Ava," *Journal of the Royal Asiatic Society* 1988, p. 64–83.

[2] Cp. e. g. the conference volume *Sri Lanka and the Silk Road of the Sea*, ed. by S. Bandaranayake et al., Colombo 1990, or the *Studies in Silk Road Coins and Culture* (*Ikuo Hirayama Felicititation Volume*), ed. by Katsumi Tanabe et al., Kamakura 1997, which also includes an article on Sri Lanka.

[3] Sinhalese ports are considerably better investigated. Apart from the emporia along the island's southern coast, Mahatittha (the modern Mantai) served as an important port during the Anuradhapura period (c. 200 B. C. to 950 AD), see e. g. B. J. Perera, "Foreign Trade and Commerce in Ancient Ceylon," *The Ceylon Historical Journal* 1 (2), 1952, p. 109–19 (for ports in general); Vasant Shinde, "Mantai. An Important Settlement in North-West Sri Lanka," *East and West* 37, 1987, p. 327–36; Petr Charvat, "External Contacts of Sri Lanka in the 1st Millennium (Archeological Evidence from Mantai)," *Archív Orientalní* 61, 1993, p. 13–29. Moreover, Persian sources of the 10th century mention the construction of ocean-going vessels there, see Marek Meißner, *Die Welt der 7 Meere. Auf den Spuren arabischer Kaufleute und Piraten*, Weimar/Leipzig 1987, p. 95ff. A summary on this topic by C. W. Nicholas, "The Sinhalese Naval Power," *University of Ceylon Review* 16, 1958, p. 78–92.

[4] Cp. Frasch, *Pagan*, p. 74–6.

Burma has always been famous for its teak wood so there is still a possibility for it not reported in the inscriptions.

Coming to the traders, two groups deserve special attention. First there are Arabian merchants whose presence in the Bay of Bengal had strongly increased since the 9th century. They left their footprints in Sri Lanka through coins and artefacts and they are reported from the coastal strip of Arakan,[5] but so far no traces have been found at Pagan or from the Pagan period. The second group are the South Indian merchants who had organised themselves into guilds and maintained a strong trading network all around the Bay of Bengal, usually centred round their temples.[6] Tamil inscriptions have been found in Takuapa (Lower Thailand),[7] Sumatra[8] and even in Quanzhou (South China).[9] As far as Burma and Ceylon are concerned, a good number of references show the activities of these Tamil trading associations. At Pagan, their business centred around the Nat-hlaung-kyaung-temple which is in fact a Vishnu temple.[10] The founding date of the temple is not known, but a new porch was added to it in the course of the 13th century by a member of the *nānādeśi* merchant guild.[11] Sri Lanka, being an immediate neighbour to South India and moreover having experienced Cōḷa rule for almost a century (c. 980–1070 AD), offers much richer material referring to Tamil traders.[12] The number of references for the *nānādeśi*s, e. g., is only second to the one from South India. Apart from their entrepôts along the coast, the *nānādeśi*s had been assigned special quarters at both Anuradha-

[5] U Ba Shin, "Coming of Islam to Burma down to 1700 AD," *Bulletin of the Burma Historical Commission* 3, 1963, p. 1–20. U Ba Shin suggests that they came to Arakan on the land route, though most of the evidence he presents comes from the post-13th century periods.

[6] For a general overview, see Meera Abraham, *Two Medieval Merchant Guilds of South India*, Delhi 1988. For an overview of the role the Cōḷas played in the politico-economic struggles for supremacy in the Bay of Bengal, see Hermann Kulke, "Der asiatische Seehandel im 11. Jahrhundert," *Periplus* 1, 1991, p. 7–24.

[7] K. A. Nilakanta Sastri, "Takuapa and its Tamil Inscription," *Journal of the Malayan Branch of the Royal Asiatic Society* 22 (1), 1949, p. 25–30. J. J. Boeles, "A Note on Tamil Relations with South Thailand and the Identification of Tacola," *Proceedings of the First International Conference Seminar of Tamil Studies*, vol. 1, Kuala Lumpur 1966, p. 53–7.

[8] E. Edwards McKinnon, "Mediaeval Tamil Involvement in Northern Sumatra, c. 11–c. 14 (The Gold and Resin Trade)," *Journal of the Malayan Branch of the Royal Asiatic Society* 69 (1), 1996, p. 85–99.

[9] T. N. Subrahmaniam, "A Tamil Colony in Mediaeval China," in: R. Nagaswamy (ed.), *South Indian Studies*, Madras 1978, p. 68–73.

[10] For a description, see Nihar Ranjan Ray, "The Nat-hlaung-kyaung Temple and its Gods," *Indian Antiquary* 61, 1932, p. 175–200.

[11] *Epigraphia Indica* 7, 1902, p. 197–8. The foundation of the temple is commonly attributed to the reign of King Anawrahta, that is mid-11th century, cp. Paul Strachan, *Pagan. Art and Architecture of Old Burma,* Whiting Bay 1991, p. 39–41.

[12] For summaries, see K. Indrapala, "South Indian Mercantile Communities in Ceylon, c. 950–1250," *The Ceylon Journal of Historical and Social Studies* 1 (2), 1971, p. 101–13, and S. Pathmanathan, "The Nagaram of the Nanadesis in Sri Lanka, circa AD 1000–1300," *The Sri Lanka Journal of the Humanities* 10, 1984, p. 122–63.

pura and Polonnaruwa. These areas appear to have been specially demarcated market places within which the corporation had the right to collect taxes.[13]

Finally, it will be interesting to have a look at the trading routes which also allows an approximate calculation of the time needed for crossing the Bay of Bengal because distance and time were linked as long as one did not miss the season. The wind systems divided the year into two parts: The eastward journey profited from the Southwest Monsoon (starting in April), while the Northeast Monsoon was prefered for the return voyage. As said above, Lower Burma was not touched by the two major shipping routes that lead through the Bay of Bengal.[14] The northern route connected Sri Lanka and South India with Bengal, while the eastern one lead to Sumatra and Malaya, touching the southern tip of the Nicobar islands. This route was taken by most of the Buddhist monks who went to China from (or via) Sri Lanka.[15] In the 6th century, the Chinese monk Fa-hsien travelled in 14 days from Tamralipti (in Bengal) to Ceylon. When crossing the Bay to Java, the ship went into a storm which blew it astray, so the journey took him almost four months.[16] The 11th century Arab geographer Al Idrisi (who, however, drew his information from earlier Greek and Roman sources) stated that the journey from *Serendip* to *Lankablus* (the Nicobar Islands ?) took ten days. From there to the island of *Jalus* (Barus, Sumatra) two days and further to *Kala* (Kelantan ?) another six days were needed.[17]

Besides the main routes, at least casual direct links between Sri Lanka and Burma seem to have existed. Thus I-tsing reports that his fellow-monk Wu-hing arrived at "Harikela which is the eastern limit of Eastern India and of Jambudvipa".[18] Likewise, the list of ports conquered by king Rājendra Cōḷa I during his sea expedition against Śrī Vijaya (modern Palembang) in 1025 AD suggests that Pupphalama (identified as Martaban) was part of the trading network along the Malayan west coast.[19] Almost 400 years later in 1419, some monks from Chiang Mai were

13 Slab Inscription marked D/8 of Queen Lilavati, *Epigraphia Zeylanica* 1, no. 14, p. 176–82. Cp. S. Pathmanathan, "The Bronce Seal of the Nanadesis from Hambantota," in: K. M. de Silva et al. (eds.), *Asian Panorama. Essays in Asian History Past and Present*, Delhi 1990, p. 139–50.

14 Cp. the map in Kirti N. Chaudhuri, *Trade and Civilization in the Indian Ocean*, Cambridge 1985, p. 130.

15 W. Pachow, "The Voyage of Buddhist Missions to South-East Asia and the Far East," *University of Ceylon Review* 18 (3–4), 1960, p. 195–212.

16 James Legge (ed./trsl.), *A Record of Buddhistic Kingdoms*, Oxford 1886 (repr. New York 1965), p. 100 and p. 111–13.

17 Al-Sharif Al-Idrisi, *India and the Neighbouring Territories*, trsl. by S. Maqbul Ahmad, Leiden 1960, p. 32–4. This statement seems to be more reliable than the one from the Mahavamsa which says that King Tissa's envoys managed to reach Tamralipti from Ceylon in only seven days (Mv. 11. 23–4).

18 Edouard Chavannes, *Mémoire composé a l'époque de la grande dynastie T'ang sur les Religieux Eminents ... par I-tsing*, Paris 1894, p. 144–5. Wu-hing had arrived at Ceylon via Śrī Vijaya, Malayu (15 days), Kedah (15 days) and Nagapattana (30 days). The journey to Harikela lasted approx. one month.

19 K. A. Nilakanta Sastri, *The Colas*, Madras (2nd ed.) 1955, p. 211–13. Direct intercourse between Burma and South India is also demonstrated by the Cōḷa lady who was sent to Pagan during the reign of King Kyanzittha (1084–1112 AD): *Epigraphia Birmanica* 1, ed. Charles Duroiselle, Rangoon 1921, p. 165.

sent to Sri Lanka for study. They embarked on a merchant vessel (presumably at Martaban) which needed four months for the passage.[20] Another century later, the European traveller Varthema crossed the Bay in opposite direction from Pulicat (near Madras) to the coast of Tenasserim. Perhaps due to favourite winds, he was able to disembark after only 14 days of travelling.[21] In between, king Dhammaceti's well-documented reform of the *saṅgha* at Pegu took place which began with a mission to Sri Lanka. 22 monks and their disciples left the town on two ships in the month on Māgha (around Jan.-Feb.) of the year 1475 AD. While one ship reached Kalambu harbour (presumably Colombo) after 24 days, the second vessel met "adverse winds" that blew it to Valligami (mod. Weligama). Having been on sea for almost six weeks, the monks had to walk for five days before they arrived at Kotte, the then capital of Sri Lanka. Things happened the other way round on the return journey: This time, the monks who started from Weligama were lucky enough to finish the journey within two weeks, whereas the other ship was wrecked in the Palk Straits, forcing the monks to proceed to Nagapattinam in order to find a new carrier. One groups of monks came across a merchant of near-by Navutapattinam who "annually sent two ships for trading purposes to Ramaññadesa". Calling at Bassein first, the ships arrived at Pegu in 1477 after three and five weeks of travelling respectively. Another group of monks had in the meantime proceeded to Komalapattana where they stayed until 1479. The returned to Pegu via Cape Negrais and Bassein in altogether eight weeks.[22] What may be learnt from these itineries is that merchant vessels of various origin were readily available for Buddhist monks who wanted to cross the Bay of Bengal and that they would reach their destination usually within a short time, unless a natural calamity caused unintended delay. With these few remarks on the technical side of the passage as background information, I will now consider the religious connection between Sri Lanka and Burma in greater detail.

3. The Buddhist Connection: Our Present Knowledge

Generally speaking, the relations between Burma and Ceylon, both political and religious, during the Pagan- and Polonnaruva-periods (c. 1000–1300 AD) were good, with one exception.[23] King Anawrahta (or Aniruddha, reigned c. 1044–c. 1078 AD), for instance, is said to

[20] Sao Sāimön Maṅgrai, *The Paḍaeng Chronicle and the Jengtung State Chronicle Translated*, Ann Arbor 1981, p. 49.

[21] Ludovico de Varthema, *Reisen im Orient*, trsl. by Folker Reichert, Sigmaringen 1996, p. 197. Reichert, in his well-argued introduction, hints at Varthema's tight time frame which could hardly have enabled him to travel personally. Therefore, the time span stated has to be taken with care.

[22] Taw Sein Ko (ed./trsl.), "A Preliminary Study of the Kalyani Inscriptions of King Dhammacheti, 1476 A. D.," *Indian Antiquary* 22, 1893, p. 41–6.

[23] For several aspects and a general estimation, see W. M. Sirisena, *Sri Lanka and Southeast Asia*, Leiden 1978 (espec. p. 58–81); C. E. Godakumbura, "Relations between Burma and Ceylon," *Journal of the Burma Re-*

have supported king Vijaya Bāhu I (reigned 1059–1114) in his struggle against the Cōḷas by sending men and goods.[24] When reorganising his state, Vijaya Bāhu I needed help from the Burmese again, as there were not enough fully ordained monks left on the island to carry out a valid ordination.[25] It is possible, however, that these were Sinhalese monks who had fled to Burma and now returned to their place of origin.[26] The exception mentioned was the 1165 sea raid on Lower Burma sent by king Parakkama Bāhu I for which economic (trade in elephants), diplomatic (treatment of ambassadors) and strategic (alliance between Ceylon and Cambodia) reasons were given.[27] It has been claimed that this expedition even advanced up to Pagan where it caused an interregnum as the Burmese king fell in defence of his capital;[28] but recent research has refuted this theory.[29] A peace treaty immediately after the expedition and a handwritten letter from Vijaya Bāhu II to the Burmese king[30] show that the relations returned to normality at the end of the 12th century.

In the field of religion, relations had developed well, too. In both countries, Buddhism of the Theravāda school dominated, so it was only natural that monks were trying to get into contact, hold disputations and common recitations or explain each other their writings and teachings. Seemingly, Ceylon was more attractive, not only because it had a longer Buddhist tradition,[31] but also because it possessed two of Gautama's bodily relics, the collar-bone and the

search Society 49 (2), 1966, p. 145–62; Sirima Wickremasinghe, "Ceylon's Relation with Southeast Asia," *Ceylon Journal of Historical and Social Studies* 3 (1), 1960, p. 38–58; U Bo Kay, "Relations between Ceylon and Burma in the 11th Century AD," in: U Ba Shin and H. Griswold (eds.), *Essays Offered to G. H. Luce*, vol. 1, New York/Ancona 1968, p. 93–5.

24 *Cūlavaṃsa* 58.8. This sentence is, as Wickremasinghe has rightly observed ("Ceylon's Relation," p. 41), somewhat cryptic because it has no obvious connection with the following verses 58.9–10.

25 *Cūlavaṃsa* 60.4–9. This is confirmed by the almost contemporary Velaikkāra-inscription from Polonnaruva (*Epigraphia Zeylanica* 2, no. 40, p. 242–55). Cp. U Bo Kay, Relations.

26 This theory has been favoured especially by Sinhalese scholars. It was first presented by Senarat Paranavitana in the *University of Ceylon, History of Ceylon*, vol. 1 (2), p. 564, and repeated by Godakumbura (Relations, p. 148–9). Additional support was given by Sirisena (*Sri Lanka and Southeast Asia*, p. 62–3) based on an improved reading of the manuscript of the *Nikāyasaṁgrahaya*, a 14th century Buddhist history.

27 *Cūlavaṃsa* 76.1–68. It is confirmed by the Devanagala-Rock-inscription, according to which king Parakkama Bāhu rewarded one of the victorious officers with a land grant (*Epigraphia Zeylanica* 3, no. 34, p. 312–25).

28 The main advocate of the interregnum-theory was G. H. Luce, e. g. in his "Economic Life of the Early Burman," *Journal of the Burma Research Society* 30 (3), 1940, p. 293–335, and still in his *Old Burma – Early Pagan* (*OBEP*), vol. 1, New York 1969, p. 117–25. It was echoed by U Than Tun in his thesis "History of Religion in Burma, AD 1000–1300," *Journal of the Burma Research Society* 61, 1978, p. 12.

29 Michael Aung-Thwin, "The Problem of Ceylonese-Burmese Relations in the 12th Century and the Question of an Interregnum at Pagan," *Journal of the Siam Society* 64 (1), 1976, p. 53–74; Frasch, *Pagan*, p. 105–6.

30 *Cūlavaṃsa* 76.75 (treaty) and *Cūlavaṃsa* 80.6 (letter).

31 While it is generally accepted that Buddha's teachings reached Ceylon during the reign of king Aśoka (3rd cent. BC) through the hands of the king's own son Mahinda, it is still difficult to proof that it reached to Lower Burma at the same time. Burmese tradition links *Suvaṇṇabhūmi*, where Aśoka had sent the monks Sona and Uttara to, with *Sudhammapura* or Thaton in Lower Burma. This identification is recorded for the

tooth. When king Anawrahta of Pagan wanted to have it, the latter one miraculously duplicated in order to be enshrined at Pagan.[32] This king is also said to have replaced the canon he had captured in Lower Burma[33] by the one he had obtained from Ceylon.[34] The next important event was the pilgrimage of the monk Uttarajīva to Ceylon in 1170 AD,[35] taking the grammar *Saddanīti* with him.[36] Perhaps written in or around 1154 AD,[37] the book reached Ceylon more or less "fresh from the press". When Uttarajīva's pupil Chapaṭa returned to Pagan ten years later, he again carried a good number of Sinhalese works with him.[38] At Pagan, he took part in a purification of the *saṅgha* which founded the Sinhalese fraternity there.[39] King Narapatisithu who supported this fraternity reported few years later that he enshrined four out of the 30 relics the Sinhalese king had sent to him in his pentagonal Dhammayazika- (Dhammarājika-)Stupa.[40] Finally, there was – among other evidence for contacts between monks[41] – another purification of the *saṅgha* at Pagan which took place in the year 1248 AD.[42] We do not know much about the result of this reform: Not being mentioned in the Burmese chronicles, our main source, a contemporary inscription, is partly illegible. Luce's suggestion that the reform introduced the

first time in the Kalyāṇī-inscription of the year 1476–9 AD (trsl. Taw Sein Ko, "Kalyani Inscription," p. 11f). from where it was quoted in the chronicles (U Kala, *Great Chronicle*, vol. 1, p. 254–6; *The Glass Palace Chronicle of the Kings of Burma*, trsl. by G. H. Luce and U Pe Maung Tin, Rangoon (repr.) 1962, p. 142–7). In 1955, the Austrian indologist Erich Frauwallner also tried to prove it: "Die ceylonesischen Chroniken und die erste buddhistische Mission nach Hinterindien," in: *Actes du IVe Congrès International des Sciences Anthropologiques et Ethnologiques*, vol. 2, Vienna 1955, p. 192–7. In spite of Frauwallner's study, this view has not become fully acknowledged in Burma, cp. Sao Sāimön Maṅgrai, "Did Sona and Uttara come to Lower Burma?" *Journal of the Burma Research Society* 59, 1976, p. 155–64.

32 *Glass Palace Chronicle*, p. 88–91.

33 *Ibid.*, p. 78–9.

34 Luce, *OBEP* 1, p. 40.

35 Kalyani-inscription, p. 17; U Kala, p. 253–4. The *Glass Palace Chronicle* alters the date to 1180 (p. 142).

36 Cp. Mabel Bode, *The Pāli Literature of Burma*, London 1909 (repr. Rangoon 1965), p. 16–7. The grammar has been edited by Helmer Smith, *La grammaire Palie d'Aggavaṃsa*, 5 Vols., Lund 1928–65.

37 Bode, *Pāli Literature*, p. 16. In a recent paper from Burma, however, it was suggested that the grammar was written only in the first half of the 13th century: U Tin Lwin, "The Saddanīti," in: *In Honour of Mingun Sayadaw's 80th Birthday*, Rangoon 1991, p. 117–26.

38 See Bode, *Pāli Literature*, p. 17–8.

39 Kalyani-inscription, p. 32f; *Glass Palace Chronicle*, p. 144.

40 *Inscriptions of Burma*, pl. 19, l. 24–6 (AD 1198). For its edition and translation, see G. H. Luce and U Pe Maung Tin, "Inscriptions of Burma, Edited and Translated," *Bulletin of the Burma Historical Commission* 3, 1963, p. 118–42, and U Tin Htway, "The First Burmese Royal Inscription," in: Wolfgang Voigt (ed.), *Vorträge des 18. Deutschen Orientalistentages*, Wiesbaden 1974, p. 679–89.

41 Perhaps at the beginning of the 13th century, a Sinhalese monk wrote a letter to a fellow-monk at Pagan: "Mānāvulu Sandesaya," ed. and trsl. by Lionel D. Barnett, *Journal of the Royal Asiatic Society* 1905, p. 265–83. Though usually this edition is quoted from, it is inferior to the one by Herbert Günther, "Der Mahānāgakula-Sandeśa," *Wiener Zeitschrift für die Kunde des Morgenlandes* 49, 1942, p. 257–81.

42 *Inscriptions of Burma*, Pl. 302, a Pāli inscription from the area around of the Dhammayazika-stupa. For some remarks on it, see G. H. Luce and U Tin Htway, "A 15th Century Inscription and Library at Pagan," in: O. H. de A. Wijesekera (ed.), *Malalasekara Commemoration Volume*, Colombo 1976, p. 205–6.

position of a chief monk (*saṅgharāja*) in the way it had been established by king Parakkama Bāhu I or II[43] cannot be substantiated with the inscription: the reading is clearly "[...] *ca rājagurussa* [...]" and not "[...] *ca saṅgharājassa* [...]"[44] But as long as the reading of the inscription remains incomplete, the question of the 1248-purification has to be left undecided.

King Māgha's invasion of Sri Lanka seems to have brought an end to the close relation between Ceylon and Burma, at least there are hardly any more references in the Sinhalese sources. Likewise, the decline of Pagan as a political centre and the fragmentation of the Burmese empire in the 14th and 15th centuries impeded contacts and prevented monks from travelling. Only at the close of the 15th century, when king Dhammaceti of Pegu invited monks from Ceylon to perform his purification of the *saṅgha*, the knots of the Buddhist network were tied again. We may thus sum up the information collected from the Sinhalese inscriptions as well as the chronicles from Burma and Sri Lanka that during the 12th and 13th centuries, intercourse between Burma and Ceylon existed in the fields of politics and religion, though of a more or less sporadic nature. It rested on mutuality, although Ceylon may have been dominant on the religious side, supplying Pagan with relics, scriptures and the "pure" Buddhism. I will now add some aspects to this picture from Burmese epigraphy.

4. Gleanings from Pagan Epigraphy

The picture drawn here deserves correction insofar as the Sinhalese religious dominance cannot be seen that clearly on closer view. Burmese monks did not simply copy the teachings and institutional structures of the Sinhalese order. This can be illustrated best with the position of the head-monk or *saṅgharāja* as described above. In Ceylon, it might have existed from the time of Parakkama Bāhu I or Parakkama Bāhu II latest, whereas in Burma, it doesn't appear in connection with the purifications of either king Narapatisithu (around 1181) or Kyazwa (1248). The only Pagan period record comes from the year 1261 AD, when a certain Saṅgharājapaṇḍit made some donations, but here it appears more like a personal name than like a formal title.[45] It was only at the close of the 13th century and especially during the 14th centuries[46] that the term *saṅgharāja* came into a more frequent usage – actually too numerous to denote single chief

43 Cp. Wilhelm Geiger, *The Culture of Ceylon in Mediaeval Times*, Göttingen (repr.) 1986, p. 185; R. A. L. H. Gunawardana, *Robe and Plough*, Tucson 1979, p. 333. It should be noted, however, that none of the Sinhalese chronicles use the term in their reports of the purifications by Parakkama Bāhu I (*Cūlavaṃsa* 73.12–22 and 78.1–27) and Parakkama Bāhu II (*Cūlavaṃsa* 84.7–10). Neither it is used in the Galvihara-inscription (*Epigraphia Zeylanica* 2, no. 41, p. 255–83) which twice calls Mahākassapa the "chief" or "chairman" (*pramukha*) of the council.

44 *Inscriptions of Burma*, Pl. 302, l. 25.

45 *Inscriptions of Burma*, Pl. 201b, l. 2.

46 *Inscriptions of Burma*, Pl. 503, l. 1 (1330 AD); *Ibid.*, Pl. 588, l. 18 (1345 AD); List 481, l. 33 (1332 A. D.).

monks of the order, so they should be seen as monastery-elders or abbots. Therefore, the idea that a *saṅgharāja* as the sole head of the order existed at Pagan is of little plausibility.[47]

The few references for travelling monks we have come across in the chronicles are considerably increased when we look at the Pagan inscriptions. In Old Burmese, the term *siṅhuil-rok*, which refers to monks who had "arrived at/from Ceylon"occurs quite frequently all through the 13th century.[48] In most of the cases, it cannot be decided whether the monks in question were Sinhalese or Burmese. The only instance where a suggestion seems plausible comes from a recently discovered inscription according to which "Sīlavisuddhi, preceptor of king Siri Dhammāsoka" was staying at Pagan in the year 1228.[49] Although kings from Pagan alluded to the Maurya king[50] who can be regarded as the classical ideal of Buddhist kingship[51] by imitating his acts, it is not known that any of them ever bore the name or title Asoka. Very likely, it was the Sinhalese prince Dhammāsoka – a child who ruled around 1208/09 AD for few months – whose preceptor was mentioned in the inscription. Pagan will have been a safe place in the troubled times during the reign of the usurper Māgha in early 13th century Ceylon.[52] The inscription comes from the Tāmanī-complex (some miles south of the city walls, close to the village of Myinkaba) which is linked to Ceylon through the monk Tāmalinda, the name-patron of the monastery. Tāmalinda had come to Pagan as a companion of Chapaṭa, he took part in the purification of the *saṅgha* that introduced the Sinhalese fraternity at Pagan[53] and became the leader of one of the three separate groups after the split of the Sinhalese *nikāya*.[54] The importance of the Tāmalinda- (or Tāmanī-)complex for the relations between Ceylon and

47 Differently Michael Aung-Thwin, *Pagan. The Origin of Modern Burma*, Honolulu 1985, p. 138–40, who even claimed a *mahāsaṅgharāja*.

48 *Inscriptions of Burma*, Pl. 87, l. 13 (1235 AD); *Ibid.*, Pl. 103, l. 18 (1238 AD); *Ibid.*, Pl. 223a, l. 13 (? 1238 AD); *Ibid.*, Pl. 265, l. 20 (1278 AD); List 415, l. 30. Cp. the "Theingoyauk" of the *Glass Palace Chronicle*, p. 144. It has to be left open, whether Burmese monks who "arrived at Ceylon" and returned or Sinhalese monks who "arrived from Ceylon" are meant, as the Burmese suffix is missing. In the chronicles, "Theingo-yauk" seems to mean the latter.

49 *Rhe:-hoṅ: Mranmā Kyokcā-myā:* (Old Burmese Inscriptions, *OBI*), vol. 1, ed. by U Aung Thaw, Rangoon 1974, p. 202, l. 10–1.

50 See, e. g., Kyanzittha's Shwesandaw-inscription, *Epigraphia Birmanica* 2, pt. 1, no. VIII (p. 164): "there-after, the great building which king Dharmāśoka built, […] he built anew, finer than before". Another repair of the Mahābodhi-temple at Bodhgaya in the way king Aśoka had done is mentioned in the Burmese inscrip-tion from Bodhgaya (*Inscriptions of Burma*, Pl. 299, 1295–98 AD).

51 The most detailed study on this problem was done by Stanley Tambiah, *World Conqueror and World Renouncer*, Cambridge 1976, espec. ch. 5. A more recent study arguing slightly different comes from Robert Lingat, *Royautés Bouddhiques. Aśoka et la fonction royale à Ceylan*, Paris 1989.

52 From the strictly arithmetical point of view, it also might have been the teacher of a *mahārājādhirāja* Srī Dhammāśoka who reigned in 1167 AD (*Śaka* 1089) at Ban Map Makham (Menam-basin, Central Thailand), see George Coedès, "Nouvelles données epigraphiques sur l'histoire de l'Indochine centrale," *Journal Asiati-que* 246 (2), 1958, p. 132–6.

53 Kalyani-inscription, p. 29.

54 *Ibid.*, p. 31; *Glass Palace Chronicle*, p. 146–7.

Burma is further illustrated by inscriptions which mention monks from Ceylon: the monastery's cadastral register has one *siṅghuil-rok*,[55] and another inscription from the southern fringe of the complex reports the name of a "noble thera from Ceylon" (*skhiṅ siṅghuiṅ*) as Buddharaṁsī.[56] The Tāmanī-complex was, as these inscriptions suggest, one of the main stays of the Sinhalese *nikāya* at Pagan.

Unfortunately, it is not possible to give similar particulars on the other two monks of the Sinhalese *nikāya*, Ānanda and Sīvali. The meagre information we possess concerning Sīvali intimates that he was dwelling in the vicinity of Salin, one of Pagan's "satellite cities" downriver.[57] Further south, at Myingun, we hear of the "sister of the Sinhalese monk", and seemingly there was another monastery with Sinhalese monks.[58] The role of Ānanda was acknowledged by one Pagan donor who stated that he, "having appeared in the lineage of Mahinda and scrupulously guarding his conformity therewith, he came from the city Laṅka to that known as Arimaddana (= Pagan) and purified the supreme religion of the Conqueror".[59] There is an Ānanda-monastery at Pagan in which he could have lived; its precise location, however, is not known.[60]

The intensity of intercourse can finally be shown from literary works which the monks took along with them as Chapaṭa did on his return from Ceylon. Likewise, his companions Sīvalī, Ānanda and Tāmalinda had "their famous books on religious topics sent abroad".[61] Some of these "books" (rather manuscripts) reached the opposite side of the Bay of Bengal in a very short period after their completion. In addition to the already mentioned grammar *Saddanīti*, one can point at two more examples. Around 1112–1114 AD, prince Rājakumār, son of king Kyanzittha (1084–c. 1113/4 AD), built the "great variegated cave-pagoda (Kubyaukkyi) at Myinkaba whose walls were embellished with paintings taken from Buddhist scriptures, canon-

[55] *Inscriptions of Burma*, Pl. 265, l. 20 (1278 AD). Again, the meaning is not certain: the reading "*sinkhuil-rok Dīpaṅkarā dhāt-tāuw puiw-so-khā-nhuik*" means either "when (the monk) Dīpaṅkarā brought the relics from Ceylon" or "when (the monk) from Ceylon brought the relics of Dīpaṅkarā". Perhaps the former should be preferred.

[56] *Inscriptions of Burma*, Pl. 373b, l. 9, 18, 19 (1233 AD).

[57] List 116, which is only preserved as a copy, mentions a Sīvali-monastery there under the date 1185 AD. Inscriptions of Burma, Pl. 261, l. 16, has a *skhiṅ* Sīvali, but with the date being 1279 AD, his identity is not certain. It should be noted that he originally stayed together with Tāmalinda according to the Kalyāṇī-inscription, p. 31 (*Glass Palace Chronicle*, p. 146).

[58] *Inscriptions of Burma*, Pl. 223a, l. 12 (? 1268 AD). Line 8, if emendated correctly, reads (*siṅ*)*khuiw-saṅ aluṁ*, that is "all the monks from Sīhala". OBI (vol. 3, p. 46) reads in the same line the name Sivali, however, the correct reading is Sīlavi(suddhi).

[59] *Inscriptions of Burma*, Pl. 226, l. 1–6. Translation from Luce, *OBEP* 1, p. 127.

[60] *Inscriptions of Burma*, Pl. 212, l. 18 (1260 AD).

[61] U Kala, *Great Chronicle*, p. 256. The translation of the *Glass Palace Chronicle* ("... published their books abroad ...", p. 146) can be misunderstood.

ical as well as non-canonical.[62] Among other episodes taken from the Sinhalese chronicle *Mahāvaṁsa* (and its continuation *Cūlavaṁsa*) one finds two pictures with glosses reading "This is when king Vijayabāhudev ...". While the name of the king can be read with certainty, the rest of the glosses is illegible or lost.[63] We do not know when the biography of the king was included in the chronicle, but even if it happened in the early years after his ascension, it took only 30 or utmost 40 years until the "updated" version had reached to Pagan. I even dare to suggest that the continuation of the chronicle can only have been taken up after Vijaya Bāhu had proved himself as an important ruler, that is after driving the Tamil invaders out of the new capital Polonnaruwa in the 1070s. This would shorten the period for transmission to perhaps less than 30 years. The other example comes from a newly found inscription of the year 1236 AD.[64] Here, among other works that were given to the monk Mahādhammarājapaṇḍit, we come across the two chronicles *Dhā(t)uvaṅ* and *(Dāthā)vaṅ*.[65] Whereas there are many *Dhātuvaṁsas* (dealing with the Budda's hair (*kesa*), collar bone (*laḷāta*) etc.) extant, we can be pretty certain that the "Chronicle of the Tooth Relic" was written under the auspices of queen Līlāvatī who administered the throne of Ceylon three times between 1197 and 1211 AD. If Geiger's assumption that it was written in 1211 AD[66] is correct, the chronicle was transmitted to Pagan in less than 25 years.

My final example to illustrate the close connection between the two Buddhist states refers to the field of art and architecture. After repelling the Cōḷa conquerors from the island, King Vijayabāhu I decided to move the capital from Anuradhapura to Polonnaruva. There another sacred area was established to the immediate north of the citadel, assembling several religious buildings on a terrace. The most important of them, of course, were the two temples of the Tooth Relic and the big circular relic stupa (called Vatadage), but in the Northeastern and Southwestern corners are two buildings of similar interest were constructed. The former one, the Satmahal Prasada, seems to have been copied from late Khmer and Northern Thai stupas, whereas the latter one, the Thuparama, has many features that can be found in Pagan temples right from their beginning: a small porch leading into an almost square sanctum, a flat roof built over vaults and embellished by small square towers on both flanks, and finally a second

62 These are edited and described by G. H. Luce/U Ba Shin, "Pagan Myinkaba Kubyauk-gyi-Temple of Rājakumār (1113 AD) and the Old Mon Writings on its Wall," *Bulletin of the Burma Historical Commission* 2, 1961, p. 277–416. A summary in Luce, *OBEP* 1, p. 373–83.

63 Luce (*OBEP* 1, p. 382) suggested the emendation "This is when king Vijayabāhudev (received the paritta ?) which cannot be found in the chronicle. The king's name first occurs in ch. 58. 1 of the Cūlavaṁsa.

64 OBI 1, p. 289–90, l. 14–15.

65 Having checked the rubbing in the office of the Arch. Dept., Rangoon, I think that the reading of OBI ("*mahāvaṅ*") should be improved.

66 Wilhelm Geiger, *Dīpavaṁsa und Mahāvaṁsa und die geschichtliche Überlieferung in Ceylon*, Leipzig 1905, p. 88–9.

storey accessible by a narrow staircase within the southern wall of the porch.[67] Unfortunately, we have no other information regarding any of the two buildings and especially no dates. On the whole, however, one gets the impression as if an attempt has been made to create a kind of miniature Buddhist cosmos by assembling at Polonnaruva the typical religious buildings of the important centres of Theravāda Buddhism. In the reverse direction, the many monks who came to Pagan brought with them their own aesthetic values which were integrated in Pagan architecture. Noteworthy are the hemispherical (rather than bell-shaped) domes and square *āmalakā*s of stupas which are quite frequent at Pagan. In general, these stupas are now classified as "Sinhalese".[68]

5. Summary

The relations between Sri Lanka and Burma which were an important part of the Buddhist network in the Bay of Bengal, can be regarded as relatively well known, as most of the sources, Sinhalese inscriptions, Sinhalese and Burmese chronicles, have been made full use of since long. In this paper, an attempt has been made to add a new aspect, viz. the intensity of the exchange, by scrutinising the Burmese inscriptions which have been more or less neglected up to now on the one hand, and on the other by checking some of the already used sources afresh. In doing so, two main insights were to be gained: Quite a considerable number of monks who had been to or who had originally come from Sri Lanka lived at Pagan and other important religious places of the Burmese kingdom. These monks had moved partly for political reasons, leaving behind them a war-torn island, and partly for religious studies. At least two monasteries at Pagan served as their regular dwelling; but taking into account that the inscriptions never produce a full picture, there may have been more. As the communication of people always means the transfer of knowledge, too, the monks brought with them their ideas and interpretations of Buddhism, usually in a written form. These books (or rather manuscripts) and scriptures played an important role in the intercourse, and with many monks travelling, the time between the completion of a manuscript at one place and its manifestation at the other was generally very short, at least if seen against the background of mediaeval traffic. Commuting monks, close contact and quick exchange, if accepted in the way it is presented here, had an

67 It should be noted that Sinhalese scholars tend to regard the Thuparama as a typical Sinhalese temple, hinting on the one hand at the Anuradhapura prototypes and on the other at the other temples at Polonnaruva with vaults (Tivanka temple and Lankatilaka temple), see Senarat Paranavitana, "The Art and Architecture of the Polonnaruva Period," in: S. D. Saparamadu (ed.), *The Polonnaruva Period*, Dehiwala 1955, p. 77–101 (= *Ceylon Historical Journal*, 4). However, I can see no direct link that would suggest an "evolution" between buildings at Anuradhapura and Polonnaruva, nor does the existence of other vaulted temples – which are of a later date than the Thuparama in all likeliness – seem to be convincing for their indigenousness.

68 Cp. Pierre Pichard, *Inventory of the Monuments at Pagan*, vol. 1, Paris/Gartmore 1995, nos. 167, 187, 190.

effect upon the preservation of the Theravāda Buddhist canon, too, as destruction occurring in times of political turmoil – the Cōḷas in Sri Lanka, the Mongol invasion of Pagan – became repairable more easily.[69] The intercourse between the two countries partly died down in the course of the 14th century (though it was never fully abandoned), but the availability of texts became once more important in the course of the 18th and 19th centuries, when the Buddhist *saṅghas* of Burma and Sri Lanka were trying to find self-assurance *vis-à-vis* the challenge proposed by Christianity and colonialism. In Sri Lanka, it seems that even the famous Buddhist chronicles had to be re-imported from Burma.[70] Research on this problem of a cross-cultural tradition of Buddhist texts has only begun,[71] but we may expect that it will produce further evidence for the intensive exchange and cooperation between the Buddhist communities of Burma and Sri Lanka.

[69] This view has already been expressed by Vincent Panditha, "Buddhism during the Polonnaruva Period," S. D. Saparamadu (ed.), *The Polonnaruva Period*, Dehiwala 1955, p. 126, though with much stress on the superiority of the Sinhalese tradition.

[70] As Hermann Oldenberg (ed./trsl.), *The Dīpavaṃsa. An Ancient Buddhist Historical Record*, London 1879, p. 10–11, has shown, all his Sinhalese manuscripts of this chronicle are derived from a Burmese archaetype.

[71] Cp. especially the works of Oskar von Hinüber, "Notes on the Pāli Tradition in Burma," *Nachrichten der Akademie der Wissenschaften in Göttingen, Phil.-Hist. Klasse*, 1983, pt. 3, p. 64–83, and *idem*, "Die Sprachgeschichte des Pāli im Spiegel der südostasiatischen Handschriftenüberlieferung," *Abhandlungen der Geistes- und Sozialwissenschaftlichen Klasse der Akademie der Wissenschaften und der Literatur in Mainz*, 1988, pt. 8, Mainz 1988.

Between Villages and Cities: Linkages of Trade in India (c. 600–1300 AD)

Ranabir Chakravarti

I

Recent perspectives (roughly since the 1950s) of early Indian history give a distinct impression that the period from c. 600 to 1300 AD witnessed significant changes in political, socio-economic and cultural (including creative activities in literature and art) conditions. The changes are considered so significant that the centuries preceding c. 600 AD are portrayed as having witnessed a different kind of formation(s). There is considerable divergence of scholarly opinions on the perceptions of these changes and the causes and impacts these changes brought about. This is indicated by the various labels by which the seven centuries are designated in different genres of historical researches. The particular chronological segment is variously called post-Gupta, late ancient, late classical, early medieval and proto-medieval. The changes are sought to be located in the emergence and crystallization of regional features and tendencies in dispersed areas of the subcontinent. The rise of many regional powers and the endemic hostilities among them caught the imaginations of scholars presenting conventional accounts of dynastic history which is featured by the absence of a paramount political power either in north India, or the Deccan or the far south. In the conventional historiography little emphasis is placed on the issue whether these centuries were associated with appreciable changes in socio-economic and cultural situations. The other genre of historical research – best represented by Marxist historiography – highlights and explains the processes of fragmentation and parcellisation of sovereignty which is linked up with the rise of *sāmanta*s (vassals), languishing trade, marginal use of coins and widespread urban decay. In other words, this position situates significant changes outside dynastic shifts; the perceptions of a large number of Marxist historians in this context may be appreciated by what could be termed as 'decline syndrome'. Departures from these two dominant historiographical standpoints have been attempted by some scholars designated as the 'non-aligned' historians. The last mentioned ones seek to explain the changes during these crucial seven centuries, neither by the yardstick of the oscillation between centralization and decentralization of polity, nor by the logic of a crisis or decline. The crystallization of regional features, in the estimation of the third group of scholars, was an outcome of local level formations, a development from within, rather than the breakdown of an earlier socio-economic and political order. An epicentric position is ruled out by these scholars for the appreciation of these local and regional formations.[1]

Local level formations appear to have been generated by an unprecedented expansion of agriculture from AD 600 to 1300 mainly with the practice of creating *agrahāras* (*agrahāram-atisṛṣṭam*), i. e. the grant of land to a brāhmaṇa or brāhmaṇas or to religious establishments (Brahmanical temples and *maṭhas*, Buddhist *vihāras* and Jaina monasteries) by the issuance of copper-plate charters under the instruction of the local and/or the apex of politico-administrative authority. With this practice of granting land mostly in non-arable tracts were inseparably associated the penetration of the complex *jāti-varṇa* system into the relatively less differentiated tribal society and the gradual absorption of tribal deities within the Brahmanical *bhakti* cults. These developments from within are suggested to have ushered in monarchical system into areas hitherto experiencing pre-state polities; these were also conducive to the emergence of local and supra-local centres of trade. The spread of agriculture, the formation of local and

[1] Differing and divergent perceptions of the period from AD 600–1300 have resulted in debates which have indeed enriched Indian historiography. Burton Stein considered these debates as among the "stunning developments" of Indian historiography. See Burton Stein, "A Decade of Historical Efflorescence," *South Asia Research* 10 (2), 1990, p. 124–38. Niharranjan Ray, "Medieval Factors in Indian History," Presidential Address, in: *Proceedings of Indian History Congress*, 1967 (Patiala session), locates significant changes and the beginnings of regional features in Indian society and cultural life from 4th century AD onwards. The Marxist perspectives of these centuries revolve around the concept of Indian feudalism. Vide in this context D. D. Kosambi, *An Introduction to the Study of Indian History*, Bombay, 1956; R. S. Sharma, *Indian Feudalism*, Delhi, 1980; B. N. S. Yadava, *Society and Culture in North India during the Twelfth Century*, Allahabad, 1973; D. N. Jha (ed.), *Feudal Social Formations in Early India*, Delhi, 1987. For a critique of the 'decline syndrome' in the historiography of Indian feudalism see B. D. Chattopadhyaya, *The Making of Early Medieval India*, Delhi, 1994 (Chattopadhyaya has elaborated on the 'decline syndrom' in a recently delivered, but unpublished, lecture in the Department of History, University of Calcutta). Also see R. Champakalakshmi, "The State and Economy in South India: 400–1300," and B. D. Chattopadhaya, "The State and Economy in North India: Fourth Century to Twelfth Century," in: Romila Thapar (ed.), *Recent Perspectives of Early Indian History*, Bombay, 1995, p. 266–307 and 308–46. The discussions on the formation of local and regional powers in different parts of India as an outcome of 'integrative polity' are available in Hermann Kulke (ed.), *The State in India 1000–1700*, Delhi, 1993. A recent statement has also been made by Ranabir Chakravarti, "Politics and Society in India 300–1000 AD," in: K. Satchidananda Murty (ed.), *Project on the History of Indian Science, Philosophy and Culture*, vol. 2 (to be published). A large number of historians designate this period as 'early medieval', suggesting thereby that this phase is to be located between the 'early historical' or 'ancient' and the 'medieval' phases of Indian history. Romila Thapar, "The Tyranny of Labels," *Social Scientist* 24 (9/10), p. 3–23 analyses the problems of the naming of different chronological segments. Kesavan Veluthat, "Into the 'Medieval' – And Out of It," Presidential Address, Medieval India section, *Proceedings of Indian History Congress*, Bangalore session, 1997 strongly argues against clinging to the European tripartite division of historical studies (ancient, medieval and modern) in the context of the study of non-European (including Indian) history.

regional polities and the development of local level exchange centres resulted in the emergence of urban centres in disparate regions of the subcontinent.[2] The significant point is that in the above scenario the village is not seen as an isolated or as undifferentiated type;[3] on the other hand, the image of trade and urban development certainly suggests the existence of different types and categories of non-rural settlements.

The above historiographical overview now may take us to the examination of a crucial issue of trade in the light of the possibilities of local level formations during the 600–1300 AD phase. A major problem of the understanding of early Indian trade lies in the indiscriminate use of a blanket term like 'trader' or 'merchant' to denote any type of purveyors of commodities. Both textual and epigraphic accounts, on the other hand, show a clear awareness of the authors of these texts of the different levels and types of merchants: e. g. *vaidehaka*/*vanik* (a petty trader), *bañjāra* (itinerant merchant or pedlar), *sārthavāha* (caravan trader), *śreṣṭhi* (a very rich merchant, also an investor of wealth in commerce), *rājaśreṣṭhi* (royal merchant), *nauvittaka* (ship-owning merchant) etc. That these terms referred to specific types of traders is unmistakable.[4] Similarly, the much-used generic expression 'trade centre' tends to blur the distinctiveness of diverse of types of centres of exchange that existed during the period under review. Another steady notion is to describe an impressive urban area where trade thrived and to trace villages (adjacent to and distant from the urban centre) which served as the rural hinterland of a city. This simple two-tier arrangement rarely accommodates the scope of looking for the existence of intermediate areas or centres providing the vital linkages between urban settlements and their rural surroundings. To this problem the present essay is devoted.

It largely focuses on three types of exchange centres known as *maṇḍapikā*, *peṭha*/*peṇṭhā* (variously called *piṇṭhā* and *peṃtā*) and *nagaram*. The three terms occur in literature (both normative and creative) and inscriptions alike respectively in the contexts of north India, the Deccan and the far south. No less significant is the fact that these terms are seldom encountered in sources prior to 6th century AD.[5] The regular appearance of these terms to denote centres of commerce in sources datable to the period of our review urges us to situate them in the context of the seven centuries under discussion. It should be pointed out that the evidence at our dis-

[2] See Chattopadhyaya, *The Making of Early Medieval India*; also *ibid.*, "The State and Economy in North India". D. C. Sircar, *Indian Epigraphy*, Delhi 1965 provides lengthy discussions on creations of revenue-free settlements of different types.

[3] B. D. Chattopadhyaya, *Aspects of Rural Settlements and Rural Society in Early Medieval India*, Calcutta 1990; the much cherished notion that Indian villages were self-sufficient and closed and hence bereft of changes and linkages is strongly questioned nowadays.

[4] Ranabir Chakravarti, "Merchants of Konkan," *Indian Economic and Social History Review* 23, 1986, p. 208–15; Ranabir Chakravarti, "Merchants and Other Donors at Ancient Bandhogarh," *South Asian Studies* 11, 1995, p. 33–42.

[5] An overview of the situation prior to the 6th century AD is presented by Ranabir Chakravarti (ed.), *Trade in Early India*, especially the Introduction (forthcoming).

posal is not only very sketchy, but also not even directly related to trade. The inscriptions are mostly land grant records offering glimpses of commercial activities almost in the form of incidental notices; they often speak of transfer of revenue (including levies on commodities) to deities and temples. Literary texts either lay down certain socio-religious and political norms which may or may not relate to existing practices, or may offer stereotyped images of trade and traders. Moreover, it is nearly impossible to come across any quantifiable data on trade, traders and centres of trade from these sources which provide us with what Udovitch calls 'qualitative' information.[6]

II

A survey of *maṇḍapikā*s is presented in this section on the basis of north Indian inscriptions and textual gleanings. The term *maṇḍapikā* literally stands for a covered hall. The sources would, however, rarely portray them as halls or covered structures, but mostly as centres of exchange. This is best shown by the regular references to merchants and diverse commodities in the descriptions of *maṇḍapikā*s. A further and in fact clearer proof of their being centres of exchange is seen in the expression *śulkamaṇḍapikā*, i. e. *maṇḍapikā* which were also centres of collection of tolls and customs. It is not therefore difficult to suggest that *maṇḍapikā*s often combined commercial activities with administrative functions. The term *maṇḍapikā* survives in the modern Hindi word *maṇḍi* which still denotes a centre of trade, especially trade in bulk commodities and grains. It is rather strange that the earliest possible reference to *maṇḍapikā* comes not from north India, but from the Deccan. An early Pallava record of 4th century from Andhra Pradesh speaks of an officer *māṇḍavika*, i. e. in charge of a *maṇḍapikā*.[7] This is a stray reference to *maṇḍapikā* which began to appear in inscriptions quite regularly from the 8th century AD.

A *maṇḍapikā* figures in an 8th century AD inscription from Kangra in Himachal Pradesh. Two brothers of a merchant family constructed a Śiva temple at Kirāgrāma (modern Kangra) and donated in favour of the deity two oil mills (*tailotpīḍanayantra*) and 6 *dramma*s (silver coin) out of the daily (*pratyaham*) collection at the *maṇḍapikā* of Kirāgrāma.[8] Although the settlement is not described as a town or city (*pura/nagara*) and is called a *grāma*, non-agricultural activities there can logically be assumed on the basis of the references to its oil mills and

[6] L. Udovitch, "Commercial Techniques in Early Medieval Islamic Trade," in: D. S. Richards (ed.), *Islam and the Trade of Asia*, Oxford 1970, p. 37–62.

[7] D. C. Sircar, *Select Inscriptions Bearing on Indian History and Civilisation*, vol. 1, Calcutta, 1965, p. 461–6 (4th century AD).

[8] *Epigraphia Indica* 1, 1892, inscription no. 16, p. 112–18.

the *maṇḍapikā*. The *maṇḍapikā* must have functioned as a toll-taking centre also. The daily collection of tolls at the *maṇḍapikā* of Kirāgrāma further points to its character as a centre of regular trade, distinct from an exchange centre of periodic nature (like a seasonal fair or weekly centre of exchange). The epigraphic account leaves an impression that this *maṇḍapikā* was located in a settlement which was perhaps neither an agricultural tract nor a full-fledged city, but something intermediate between the two.

In the 10th century Sīyāḍūnī (= present Siyadoni near modern Gwalior in Madhya Pradesh) was a thriving urban centre within the Gurjara-Pratihāra realm. Inscriptions, ranging in date from 907 to 968,[9] enlighten us on the streets (*rathyā*), exchange centres (*haṭṭa*), professional quarters or shops or workshops (*vīthi*) of distillers (*kallapāla*), braziers (*kāṃsyakāra*) and oil-men (*tailika*). The presence of high ranking functionaries of the Gurjara-Pratihāra kingdom amply shows that it was also a politico-administrative centre. That it was a brisk centre of trade is demonstrated beyond doubt by the presence of merchants, the most prominent among whom was one salt-dealer (*nemakavaṇija*) named Nāgaka whose father Caṇḍuka too was a *nemaka-vaṇija*. Inscriptions also categorically mentioned it as a *pattanamaṇḍapikā* or an exchange centre located within an urban (*pattana*) site. The *maṇḍapikā* at Siyadoni is differentiated from a *haṭṭa* (a market) located within the *pattana*; it is also distinctly different in size and complexity than the one standing at Kirāgrāma. Merchants at this *pattanamaṇḍapikā* are praised for having made donations both in kind and cash to different deities, enshrined in several temples. There is a clear impression of regular commercial transactions on daily basis at Sīyāḍūnī, since daily collections at the *maṇḍapikā* are explicitly recorded. The collection of cess on liquors and oil mills, voluntarily paid by merchants and professional groups at the *maṇḍapikā*, is further endorsed by a *pañcakula*, literally a body of five. The *pañcakula* probably stands for a town-council consisting of representatives of important socio-economic groups in a city. The Sīyāḍūnī inscription points to the possibility of trade in liquors, edible oil and diverse crafts products; we have already indicated that transactions in these items had revenue-yielding potentials.

Another *pattanamaṇḍapikā* stood near present day Jabbalpur in Madhya Pradesh, as is known from the Bilhari inscription of 975 AD.[10] It was included within the realm of the Kalacuris, an important regional power of central India. That the centre of trade at Bilhari was located within an urban space is evident from its designation as a *pattanamaṇḍapikā*. The principal purport of the inscription is to record donations of various cess on commercial items in favour of the deity Nohaleśvara. There is little doubt that these commodities were brought to the *maṇḍapikā* at Bilhari for commercial exchanges. In the list of items of trade figure local and

[9] *Epigraphia Indica* 1, inscription no. 21, p. 162–79; Chattopadhyaya, *The Making of Early Medieval India*, p. 130–54 for an in-depth analysis of epigraphic data to understand the urban character of Siyadoni.

[10] V. V. Mirashi, *Inscriptions of the Kalachuri-Chedi Era*, in two parts, being the volume IV of the *Corpus Inscriptionum Indicarum*, Ootacamund 1955, p. 215–23.

daily necessity products like green vegetable and aubergines (*śākavārttāku*), products of oil mills (i. e. edible oil), dried ginger and liquor. Along with these items are enlisted salt (*lavaṇa*), betel (*pūga*), black pepper (*marīca*) which are probably bulk items but unlikely to have been locally available. The betel and the black pepper could have reached the *maṇḍapikā* respectively from Karnataka and Malabar, possibly via overland communications. Significantly enough, elephants and horses also figure in the list of commodities transacted at the *maṇḍapikā* of Bilhari. While the elephant could have been locally procured from the central Indian forest tracts, the horse must have been brought from a more distant source. On the sale of each elephant was imposed a levy of four *paura* coins and on the sale of each horse the levy of two *paura* coins. It is somewhat unusual that the levy on the sale of a horse at the *maṇḍapikā* of Bilhari is lesser than that on an elephant, though the horse was generally a more expensive means of communication and warfare.[11] What can hardly escape one's notice is the range of commodities available at Bilhari; there converged in Bilhari daily necessities, staples, locally available crafts and agricultural products, bulk items brought from afar and more expensive commodities like the elephant and the horse. The fact that levies and cesses on these items were mostly collected in cash, points to the circulation of coins of different types and denominations at this centre of trade. It is also interesting to note that a charge of one *paura* coin was fixed for issuing a couple of *yuga*s per day. The term *yuga* has been explained as "a voucher, authorizing the owner to exhibit his article in the market place everyday".[12] The administration at Bilhari was thus entitled to collect a cash payment from merchants in return of allowing merchants to use the space of the market place to display their respective products. In other words, the authorities used to let out space of the marketplace to merchants. The brisk trade at the *pattana-maṇḍapikā* of Bilhari can hardly be lost sight of.

Attention now be turned to two *maṇḍapikā*s in more or less contemporary Rajasthan. In the Bayana inscription from Bharatpur, dated 955 AD, are recorded the *maṇḍapikā*s of Śrīpatha and Vusavaṭa.[13] Both the *maṇḍapikā*s appear to have been noted for trade in horses, as the local queen donated in favour of a Viṣṇu temple the sum of three *dramma*s and one *dramma*, to be levied on the sale of per horse respectively at Śrīpatha and Vusavaṭa. The reason for the impo-

[11] Chitrarekha Gupta, "Horse Trade in North India: Some Reflections on Socio-Economic Life," *Journal of Ancient Indian History* 14, 1983/84, p. 186–206. A horse-fair (*ghotaka-yatra*) is known from Pṛthudaka, modern Pehoa, Karnal district, Haryana, from a 10th century inscription. The importance of war horses and their demand among rulers is discussed by Ranabir Chakravarti, "Horse Trade and Piracy at Tana (= Thana, Maharashtra): Gleanings from Marco Polo," *Journal of the Economic and Social History of the Orient* 33, 1991, p. 189–208; Ranabir Chakravarti, "Trade in Horse in Early Medieval Bengal: A Note," *Journal of the Economic and Social History of the Orient* 17, 1999 (forthcoming).

[12] Mirashi, *Inscriptions of the Kalachuri-Chedi Era*, p. 223, footnote 6.

[13] *Epigraphia Indica* 22, inscription no. 20, p. 120ff.

sition of different rates of levies on the sale of horses at two *maṇḍapikās* was not specified in the record.

This would now take us to a survey of *maṇḍapikā*s in western India (mainly Rajasthan and Gujarat) where *maṇḍapikās* seem to have proliferated from 1000 AD onwards. At a *maṇḍapikā*, according to an inscription of 1017 AD from Shergadh in Rajasthan,[14] were present a number of *śreṣṭhi*s who were also members or representatives of a local body. This body approved of the donation of a cess (*ādāya*) of ¾ *tolā* of ghee by three merchants Narasiṃha, Govṛṣa and Thirāditya in favour of the deity Bhaṭṭāraka Śrī Nagnaka. The close association of the *maṇḍapikā* with merchants is clearly borne out by the record.

B. D. Chattopadhyaya's excellent study of about two dozens of similar epigraphic records brings to limelight the emergence of a number of *maṇḍapikā*s and *haṭṭa*s as rural and local level centres of exchange in Rajasthan during the period from the 7th to the 12th century.[15] The inscriptions tend to distinguish *haṭṭa*s, identifiable generally with village level centres of exchange, from *maṇḍapikā*s which probably were supra-local in character. This image is well driven home by the epigraphic information regarding Naḍḍula. The combined testimony of three inscriptions of 1114, 1155 and 1161 AD[16] may suggest that Naḍḍula (present Nadole in Rajasthan) was a village, probably located at the centre of twelve villages (*Naḍḍulapratibaddhadvādaśagrāmah*). The geographical position of Naḍḍulagrāma was particularly conducive to its emergence as a nodal point in the cluster of twelve rural settlements. Naḍḍula, originally a *grāma*, transformed into a *maṇḍapikā*, as it could develop into a centre of exchange of local agricultural products grown in surrounding twelve villages. Like other *maṇḍapikā*s, the *maṇḍapikā* at Naḍḍula also yielded tolls and customs in cash. The inscription of 1114 speaks of the levy of six *dramma*s from there. The information regarding the daily collection of one *rūpaka* (silver coin) underlines that transactions were undertaken at this centre on an everyday basis and not on a periodic or seasonal basis. Naḍḍula is described as a *talapāḍa-śulka-maṇḍapikā*, implying thereby that it yielded tolls and customs and was located in a land, fully assessed for revenue (*talapāḍa*).[17] Naḍḍula became a well known centre of exchange for agricultural products and daily necessities. The emergence of Naḍḍula from a village to a trade centre of supra-local nature with the capacity to yield tolls and customs (*śulka*) seems to have been well appreciated by the local Chahamana rulers; Naḍḍula then became a *pura* or town and was turned into the political centre of the Chahamanas.

[14] *Epigraphia Indica* 23, inscription no. 20B, p. 437–41.

[15] Chattopadhyaya, *The Making of Early Medieval India*, p. 89–120.

[16] Dasaratha Sharma, *Early Chauhan Dynasties*, Delhi 1959, p. 181–2; also *Indian Antiquary* 11, 1883, p. 20ff; *Epigraphia Indica* 9, p. 63ff.

[17] D. C. Sircar, *Indian Epigraphical Glossary*, Delhi 1966, p. 333.

Another *śulkamaṇḍapikā* stood at Salakhanapuri in 12th century Rajasthan.[18] The basic purport of the inscription is to record the usual transfer of a part of the cesses levied on commodities brought to the *maṇḍapikā* at Salakhanapuri. But more significant is the diversity of items being transacted at Salakhanapuri. There were madder (*mañjiṣṭha*), silk yarn (*paṭṭasūtra*), coral (*pravālaka*), camphor (*karpūra*), *kasturi* (fragrance), asafoetida (*hiṅgu*), *kuṃkuma*, incense (*agaru*), *mālapatra*, *jaiphala*, *jaitrī*, cloth (*kāpaḍa*), pepper (*marīca*), date (*kharjjura*). The *maṇḍapikā* in question experienced transaction of both daily necessities and precious materials.

The proliferation of *maṇḍapikā*s in the coastal regions of Kathiawad during the 12th and 13th centuries is borne out by the existence of two such *maṇḍapikā*s at Maṅgalapura (modern Mangrol)[19] and at Somanātha, a famous Śaiva sacred centre.[20] Both are mentioned in inscriptions. The inscription from Mangrol, dated 1144 AD, not only speaks of the *maṇḍapikā* thereof, but also suggests that commodities were brought to this *maṇḍapikā* on the backs of *balivardda* (pack oxen), *rāsabha* (donkeys) and *uṣṭra* (camels). The last mentioned animal must have been particularly useful as the carriers of merchants and their merchandise in the arid zones of western India. Somanātha, apart from being a celebrated centre of Śaiva religion, also offered an outlet to the sea, because it was situated at the confluence of the river Sarasvatī and the Arabian Sea (*Sarasvatīsāgarasamprayogavibhūṣita*). It is no wonder that Somanātha was called a *paṭṭana* or a port-town in the inscription 1287 (variously called Somanāthapaṭṭana, Somesvarapaṭṭana and Devapaṭṭana). It was probably integrated to the coastal trade network along the Gujarat-Kathiawad coast and could have functioned as some sort of a feeder port for Cambay (Stambhapura or Stambhatīrtha in Sanskrit sources and Kanbaya of the Arabic and Persian texts), the premier port of Gujarat. It is not difficult to speak of Somanātha's long-distance overseas network too, as to this port came the ship-owner (*nakhuda*) Nuruddin Firuz from the famous Persian Gulf port of Hormuz in 1264.[21] The graphic description of the layout of the town of Somanātha in the 13th century leaves little room for doubt about the existence there of a storehouse (*koṣṭhāgara*), offering warehousing facilities and a *maṇḍapikā* where transactions took place and which also yielded tolls and customs on the movement of commodities. The commodities enlisted in the inscription of 1287 are mainly agricultural products and bulk items. Recent researches inform us about the linkages of this littoral area with regions of the interior.[22] Somanātha, although an immensely important religious and cultural centre of 13th century

[18] *Indian Antiquary* 6, 1877, p. 202ff.

[19] Chattopadhyaya, *The Making of Early Medieval India*, p. 109.

[20] "The Cintra Prasasti of the Reign of Śaraṅgadeva," *Epigraphia Indica* 1, p. 272–87.

[21] Ranabir Chakravarti, "Nakhudas and Nauvittakas: Ship Owning Merchants in the Ports of Western Coast of India 1000–1500," presented to the South Asia Seminar, St. Antony's College, Oxford (to be published).

[22] V. K. Jain, *Trade and Traders in Western India 1000–1300*, Delhi 1989.

Gujarat, was not the premier city of Gujarat. It was not the apex city, but was marked by significant linkages with other ports and the rural hinterland as well. It is in this context that the significance of Somanātha having a *maṇḍapikā* within its urban space is to be appreciated.

The *maṇḍapikā*s in north India were not undifferentiated. Some of them were located in an urban space and therefore, were considered as *paṭṭanamaṇḍapikā*s. The *Lekhapaddhati*, probably assignable to 13th–14th centuries, speaks of a *mahamandapika* which must suggest that some *maṇḍapikās* were much larger than other 'ordinary' *maṇḍapikās*.[23] The *Lekhapaddhati*, which deals with the preparation of models of official documents, is generally located in the political and material conditions in the-then Gujarat. The proliferation of *maṇḍapikā*s reached such a state that the *Lekhapaddhati* speaks of an administrative department concerning *maṇḍapikā*s (*maṇḍapikā-karaṇa*). The concerns of the administration in Gujarat about *maṇḍapikā*s are represented by the appointment of an officer-in-charge of a *maṇḍapikā* and he is designated as a *māṇḍavi*. The text expectedly has a thrust on the toll-yielding potentials of the *maṇḍapikā* (*maṇḍapikādāna*). There were not only cess collectors (*pathakīya*s), but tax inspectors (*uparihiṇḍiyas*) too. There is a recommendation to levy taxes on the ingress and egress (*āgamanigamadānam*) of foreign merchants (*vacchivitta*s). There is an extremely interesting suggestion in the text that a small present (*vikarapadāni*) could be accepted by toll collectors. Does it not convey the message that some bribes were accepted by customs officers in Gujarat from merchants assembling at *maṇḍapikās*? The *Lekhapaddhati*, however, strongly recommends that the itinerant merchants and foreign traders should be received with honour (*manapurasarah*) and should not be disturbed by demanding excessive taxes (*kimapyadhikadānam*). It is not unlikely that the toll-yielding potentials of the *maṇḍapikā* could have led to rapaciousness of the revenue collectors and that could have been counter-productive in the long run. That is why such a caution is uttered and the appointment of a tax inspector (*uparihiṇḍiya*) – distinct from a toll collector - is recommended.

The commercial activities at *maṇḍapikā* listed above cannot but point to their distinctiveness from seasonal or periodic fairs (*yātrās*) and weekly or bi-weekly village exchange centres (*haṭṭa*s or *haṭṭikā*s, i. e. modern *hāt*s). The role of the *maṇḍapikā* as a supra-local centre of trade and as providing crucial linkages between the rural markets (*haṭṭa*s) and large urban centres and ports (*pura*s, *nagara*s and *paṭṭana*s) can, therefore, hardly be overemphasised. It is interesting to find that *maṇḍapikā*s are rarely seen in the records from near contemporary eastern India, especially the Bengal and Bihar. This however should not lead us to assume the absence of middle-category trade centres from this region. Linkages of local and supra-local trade were available through centres with different designations. A probe into this is presented below.

[23] C. D. Dalal/G. K. Shrigondekar (eds.), *The Lekhapaddhati*, Baroda 1925, p. 54–5.

A copper-plate, dated to 971 AD , was discovered from Madanpur near Sabhar, lying close to modern Dhaka in Bangladesh.[24] It recorded the customary grant of a revenue-free plot to a *brāhmaṇa* by king Śrīcandra (c. 925–75 AD). What demands our close scrutiny is the location and name of the place recorded in the charter. The donated plot was located at Vaṅgasāgara-saṃbhāṇḍāriyaka in Yola-maṇḍala. The rather unusual toponym Vaṅgasāgara-saṃbhāṇḍāriyaka denoted neither a village nor a town. The content and context of the charter would suggest that the donated area was located close to Sabhar, which is a noted archaeological site on the banks of the river Banshi. The very name Sabhar, according to N. K. Bhattasali, was originally derived from *saṃbhāra* or merchandise.[25] The term *saṃbhāṇḍāriyaka* should logically suggest the availability of warehousing facility (*samyak* = proper; *bhāṇḍāra* = warehousing, storage) at that place. It would be logical to infer that Sabhar, situated on the banks of a navigable river in the active Bengal delta, was a local trade centre which functioned as a stockade. Of immense significance is the name Vaṅgasāgara, prefixed to *saṃbhāṇḍāriyaka*. Vaṅgasāgara stands for the *sagara* or sea of Vaṅga, i. e. in other words, it denotes the present Bay of Bengal. *Vaṅgasāgara-saṃbhāṇḍāriyaka* itself was not situated on the coast and was not called a port (*velākula* or *paṭṭana*). But as a local and riverine trade centre in the central part of the Ganga delta it certainly was linked to Vaṅgasāgara and the littoral tracts of Bangladesh, through the inland riverine network. The premier port in Bengal from the 9th–10th centuries onwards was Samandar or Sudkawan, identified with present day Chittagong region. The deltaic region provided ample scope of riverine communications between the coast and the interior and paved the way for the emergence of local level riverine trade centre like the one that stood at Sabhar. That riverine trade was vital to Sabhar can be established on the basis of the presence of officers like *nauvāṭaka* and *arddha-nauvāṭaka* (senior and junior officers watching riverine fleets) at the time of the grant of land at *Vaṅgasāgara-saṃbhāṇḍāriyaka*.[26]

[24] The plate was originally edited by R. G. Basak, *Epigraphia Indica* 28, p. 51–8. Basak dated it to the regnal year 44 of Sricandra, i. e. 969. An improved reading of the plate by D. C. Sircar shows that it was issued in the 46th regnal year of Sricandra; see *Epigraphia Indica* 28, p. 337–9.

[25] N. K. Bhattasali suggested this in course of his editing the Ghughrahati copper plate; see *Epigraphia Indica* 18, p. 74–86.

[26] For an elaborate discussion on this riverine port linked up with major ports in the south-eastern littorals of present Bangladesh, see Ranabir Chakravarti, "Vangasagara-sambhandariyaka: A Riverine Port of Early Medieval Bengal," in: Debala Mitra (ed.), *Explorations in the Art and Archaeology of South Asia. Essays Dedicated to N. G. Majumdar*, Calcutta 1996, p. 557–72. Neither Basak nor Sircar offered any explanation of the term Vaṅgasāgara-saṃbhāṇḍāriyaka. The mention of *nauvāṭaka* and *arddhanauvāṭaka* in the list officers addressed at the time of the grant is also unique in the inscriptions of Bengal. The paper also brings into focus another inland riverine port of Bengal, namely Devaparvata (near Mainamati in the Comilla region, Bangladesh) which was situated on the river Ksiroda (= present Khirnai) and was approachable from all four sides (*sarvatobhadra*). Devaparvata is mentioned as a inland riverine port town and also as a politico-administrative centre in the Kailan copper plate of Sridharanarata (c. 675 AD), the Asiatic Society copper plate of Bhavadeva (8th century) and the Paschimbhag copper plate of Śrīchandra (930 AD).

In the deltaic area of present West Bengal in India was ruling a petty local ruler, named Śrīmad-Ḍommanapāla. He was a vassal (*mahāmaṇḍaleśvara*) under the Sena rulers of Bengal, but was de facto an independent ruler in the Sunderban area, as he issued a land grant without at all referring to his overlords, the Senas. This copper-plate (dated 1196 AD),[27] recording the grant of land to a brāhmaṇa, was issued from a place Dvārahāṭaka. Dvārahāṭaka stood on the eastern bank (*pūrvakhāṭikā*), obviously of the river Ganga. The plate itself was discovered from Rakshasakhadi in the 24 Parganas (South) district of West Bengal; the find spot lies only 12 miles due east of the famous centre of pilgrimage, Gangasagara, located at the confluence of the Ganga and the Bay of Bengal. The point to take note of is the association of Dvārahāṭaka with the river Ganga and its proximity to the sea as well. The very name Dvārahāṭaka can be explained as a *hāṭaka* or *haṭṭaka* (i. e. a local level trade centre) located at the *dvāra* or gate. The *dvāra* or gate certainly refers to it as an opening to or as an outlet to the sea. The likely assumption is that Dvārahāṭaka was another local level trade centre with facilities of inland riverine movements and also linked to an opening to the sea. At the close of the 12th century it was important enough to be chosen as an administrative centre for the issuance of a copper-plate charter.

A hitherto unknown type of settlement began to appear in the late Sena records of the late 12th and early 13th century. This is *caturaka*. So far four such *caturaka*s, distinct from a village and an urban centre, figure in Sena records. These are Betaḍḍa-caturaka, Urā-caturaka, Nava-saṃgraha-caturaka and Lauhaṇḍa-caturaka.[28] The *caturaka*s are not categorically mentioned as trade centres, but they appear to have designated an administrative tier between villages below and a *maṇḍala* above them. Once again, one cannot but be impressed by their intermediate position between individual villages and an upper stratum of administration in the late phase of the Sena rule. What is particularly significant is the almost invariable association of the *caturaka*s with the course of the Ganga. While Betaḍḍa-*caturaka* was situated on the western bank (*paścimakhāṭikā*) with the Ganga as its eastern landmark (*pūrve Jāhnavī*), the three other *caturaka*s were in the Vaṅga region to the east of the Ganga. The term *caturaka* has an obvious connection with the number four (*catuḥ*) and could have been associated with a place (neither a village nor a town) where converged roads from different directions. In other words, the *caturaka* could have functioned as a node in the same manner as performed by a *maṇḍapikā* in contemporary north India. A case in point is Betaḍḍa-caturaka, identified with Betor, at present a suburb of the town of Howrah on the Ganga. According to the Govindapur copper plate of

27 *Epigraphia Indica* 30, p. 43–5; this is an improved study of the copper plate by D. C. Sircar. The plate was originally edited by R. G. Basak.

28 Betadda-caturaka is mentioned in the Govindpur copper plate of Laksmanasena (1179–1206), regnal year 2; the three other *caturaka*s are mentioned in the Calcutta Sahitya Parishat copper plate of Visvarupasena (1206–22). Both the copper plates are available in N. G. Majumdar, *Inscriptions of Bengal*, vol. 3, Rajshahi 1929, p. 92–8 and 140–8.

Lakṣmanasena (regnal year 2, c. AD 1181), Betaḍḍa-caturaka had within it the donated village of Biḍḍāraśāsana and not far away from Betaḍḍa-caturaka stood a town, Dharmanagara. One has to remember here that the same Betore in the 16th century was vitally important for providing the crucial riverine connection up to the famous port of Saptagram, the *porto piccolo* of the Portuguese. Larger Portuguese ships could not go upstream; they anchored near Betore and between Betore and Saptagram regularly plied river crafts.[29] The preliminary indications of the potentials of Betaḍḍa-caturaka as a linkage in the inland riverine network in the western part of the Bengal delta are first noticed around the close of the 12th century; its mature phase did not fail to attract the attention of Portuguese ships in the 16th century.

III

*Maṇḍapikā*s and *caturaka*s are conspicuous by their absence from contemporary Deccan to which we would now like to focus our attention. In the Deccan, embracing the modern states of Maharashtra, Karnataka, Andhra Pradesh and the southern part of Madhya Pradesh, can be seen numerous centres of supra-local trade with name-endings like *peṭh*, *peṭta*, *peṭṭai* etc. The antiquity of these words can be pushed back to much remote times, as the following pages would show.

It is interesting to note that the term *peṭha* in the sense of a centre of supra-village administration figured as early as 529 and 533 in two copper plates from the Bundelkhand region in central India.[30] These two copper plates inform us about grants of land in favour of goddess Piṣṭapurikā. The donated areas were located in three villages, Opānigrāma, Vyāghrapallikā and Kācharapallikā, all of them being included within Maṇināgapeṭha. Maṇināgapeṭha formed a part of the eighteen forest chiefdoms within the kingdom of Ḍābhala *(aṣṭādaśāṭavīrājyābhyantara Ḍābhalarājyāntargata)*. That the said *peṭha* stood above a collection of individual villages cannot be missed. Such grants of land in forest tracts must have resulted in the subsequent expansion of agriculture and the spurt of rural settlements. The *peṭha* as an administrative unit seems to have consisted of a few villages. As an administrative tier above individual villages, Maṇināgapeṭha was witness to the presence of several high ranking functionaries, e. g. the *amātya* (minister or important royal officer), the *sandhivigrahika* (the officer in charge of war and peace), the *dūṭaka* (royal envoy or messenger) and *lekhaka* (scribe). The *peṭha* thus provided linkages between individual villages and the upper tiers of administration. The area in

[29] L. S. S. O'Malley, *Gazetteer of Bengal, Howrah and Hooghly Districts*.

[30] J. F. Fleet, *Inscriptions of the Imperial Guptas, Corpus Inscriptionum Indiacarum*, vol. 3, Calcutta 1882, p. 115ff for the inscription of 529 and p. 135–9 for the inscription of 533. The two records belong respectively to the reigns of Samksobha and Śarbanātha.

question also saw the activities of craftsmen (*kārus*) and merchants (*vaṇik*). Maṇināgapeṭha thus combined administrative functions with that of a crafts and trade centre.

In the second half of the 6th century, the locality level administrative system in the Maitraka kingdom of Valabhī in Kathiawad was also conversant with *peṭha* as a supra-local unit of administration. In 571–72 AD land grants referred to the donated villages and its linkages with upper tiers of administration like *peṭha*, *sthalī* and *viṣaya*.[31] While *peṭha* was an unit above villages and the *viṣaya* stood for a district, *sthalī* was another tier between a *peṭha* and a *viṣaya*. Placed above individual villages the *peṭha* was conducive to providing linkages between villages and the upper tiers of administration.

It is true that the *peṭha* makes its earliest appearance not in the Deccan but in central and western India. The *peṭha* as an administrative unit is not encountered before the 6th century, implying thereby that significant, albeit slow, changes in the social, economic and political organisations at the locality level were in the offing around that time. The so far known earliest occurrence of *peṭha* in the context of the Deccan is seen in an inscription from Satara district, Maharashtra. This copper-plate charter, palaeographically assignable to the 7th century, records the grant of the village of Undivāṭikā belonging to the *peṭha* of Paṅgāraka (*peṭha-Paṅgārakiya*) in favour Dakṣina-Śiva.[32] At the time of this grant a high ranking officer, named Jayasiṃha and in charge of Harivatskoṭṭa, was also present. The grant was issued during the reign of an early Rāṣṭrakūṭa king Abhimanyu (of Mānapura and not belonging to the famous Rāṣṭrakūṭa house of Malkhed). Here once again we encounter the *peṭha* as an administrative unit standing above an individual village. That the *peṭha* was linked with higher tiers of administration is well driven home by the officer in charge of a *koṭṭa* or a fortified settlement. The *koṭa* was certainly not a village, but probably signified a non-rural politico-military centre.

That the *peṭha* was a centre of commerce, besides an administrative unit between individual villages and a district, is amply demonstrated by a graphic description of trade at a *penṭha* in the *Yaśastilakacampu* of Somadevasuri. Before delving into the literary images of the *penṭha*, a few words about the text itself will be in order. The *Yaśastilakacampu* is a prose romance often drawing upon Jaina morals and teachings. It would be futile to seek historical actualities in this genre of literature. Moreover, many tales of this text are set in north India. Yet they often have an important bearing on the Deccan. Somadevasuri explicitly states himself to be a contemporary of Kṛṣṇa III (939–67), the last great ruler of the Rāṣṭrakūṭa empire, the most formidable regional power in the Deccan (c. 754–974). His remarkable awareness of the political situation in the Deccan is best illustrated by his mentioning the fact the text was composed

[31] *Indian Antiquary* 15, 1886, p. 187–8; according to the copper plate the village Vaṭagrāma, situated in Dīpnakapeṭha which was a part of Bilvakhātasthalī, was donated.

[32] *Epigraphia Indica* 8, p. 163–6. Pangara is identified with Pagara, 4 miles from Panchmarhi, Satara district, Maharashtra.

in 959 AD when the victorious Rāṣṭrakūṭa ruler was residing not in his capital Mānyakheṭa but in Meḍupattyam or Melpadi in the North Arcot district within the Coḷa realm. His first-hand knowledge of the conditions in the Deccan is also seen in the excellent pen-picture of a cow-pen (*go-śālā*) in Karahāṭaka or present Karhad (Satara district, Maharashtra). All these endow this work of Somadevasuri with a Deccanese flavour.[33]

The account of a *peṇṭha* (probably hyper-Sanskritised form of *peṭha*) is found in a tale which goes to demonstrates the outcome of theft (*steyaphala*). The narrative centres around a cunning brāhmaṇa minister named Śrībhūti who established the *peṇṭhasthana*. The *peṇṭha* was divided into many well laid out chambers (*vibhaktānekāpavarakaracanaśālinī*); it had also large storage areas for merchandise (*mahābhāṇḍavāhinī*) and was provided drinking places (*prapā*), feeding houses (*sattra*), assembly hall with seats (*sabhāsanātha*) and streets or shops (*vīthi*). Merchants from different directions and quarters flocked at the *peṇṭha* (*nānādigdeśopasarpanayūjāṃ vaṇijām*). Covering an area of a couple of miles (*gorutpramāṇa*) the *peṇṭha* was marked by ditches (*kulyāḥ*), rampart (*vapra*), fortification (*prākāra*) and a moat (*parikhā*). The description highlights the impressive size of the trade centre where excellent items were stored in boxes which were watched over by adequate number of guards (*bhāṇḍanārambhodbhātabharīrapeṭakapakṣarakṣāsāram*). The most important point to establish the character of this *peṇṭha* as a centre of trade is its epithet *puṭabhedinī*.[34] The term *puṭabhedana* or *putabhedinī* literally denotes a place where lids of boxes (of merchandise) were broken (i. e. opened). It would therefore refer to a stockade with warehousing or storage facility,[35] a point which is highlighted in the account of the *peṇṭhāsthāna* in the *Yaśastilakacampu*. Śrībhuti, according to this text, let out spaces to merchants for storage, display and sale of their commodities and established the system of collecting tolls, shares and rent at a moderate rate (*praśāntaśulkabhāgahāravyavahāramacikarat*).

A similar type of trade centre, but with a slightly different designation *piṇṭhā*, figures in another work of Somadevasuri. Somadevasuri is also credited with composing a theoretical treatise on polity, named *Nītivakyāmṛta*, which closely follows the model of the *Arthaśāstra*, albeit in an abridged form. In this text Somadevasuri explains *piṇṭhā* as a *paṇyapūṭabhedinī*, which is obviously the same as *puṭabhedana*. The *piṇṭhā* is considered as a trade centre which generates tolls and customs (*śulkasthāna*). The *peṇṭha* or *piṇṭhā* of Somadevasuri, more or less

33 Sivadatta/K. P. Parab (eds.), *Yasastilakacampu of Somadevasuri*, Bombay 1901. The Rāṣṭrakūṭa ruler's presence in the Toṇḍaimandalam area of the Coḷa kingdom is explained by Kṛṣṇa III's major military success against the Cola king Parāntaka I (907–55) in the battle of Takkolam in 949 AD. See in this context G. Yazdani (ed.), *Early History of the Deccan*, 2 Vols., London 1960, esp. the ch. on the Rāṣṭrakūṭas by A. S. Altekar.

34 The description of the *peṇṭhasthāna* is found in the *Yaśastilakacampu*, book VII, section 27.

35 Ranabir Chakravarti, "The Putabhedana as a Centre of Trade in Early India," *South Asian Studies* 12, 1996, p. 33–9.

the same as a *peṭha*, thus combines trade and administrative functions. The *Nītivakyāmṛta* lays down that the *piṇṭhā*, if judiciously and righteously maintained, would be a wish-fulfilling cow for the ruler (*nyāyena rakṣitā puṭabhedinī piṇṭhā rajñaṃ kāmadhenu*).[36] This, in other words, points to the considerable revenue-bearing potential of this trade centre and that is why Somadevasuri highlights its importance to the ruler. A major difference between the accounts of the two texts of Somadevasuri lies in that the *peṇṭhā* in the*Yaśastilakacampu* was owned by the minister himself, while in the *Nītivākyāmṛtam* it is viewed as being under the jurisdiction of the king.

The possibilities of commercial transactions at the *peṇṭha/piṇṭhā* are therefore beyond any doubt. By placing it in the category of *puṭabhedana*, the author clearly underlines the regularity of trade there; the literary image of trade is far from that of a periodic nature.[37] It is quite different from weekly rural market places and seasonal fairs. Somadevasuri, however, does not call it a city or town (*nagara/pura*). In fact, his recommendation on *piṇṭhā* in the *Nītivākyāmṛtam* figures in the *Janapadasamuddeśa* (concerning country side) section and not in the *Durgasamuddeśa* (concerning fortified urban settlement) section.

In the inscriptions of the Kakatiyas of Warangal, the most formidable regional power in Eastern Deccan during the 13th and 14th centuries, we come across *peṃṭa*s, which are certainly the same as *peṇṭhā* and *piṇṭhā* of Somadevasuri. Inscriptions speak of different types of trade centres like *aḍḍa*, *santhe* and *pemta*. These terms and their relation *vis-à-vis* the *peṃṭa/peṇṭhā* require a careful scrutiny. The word *aḍḍa* is the same as *haṭṭa* in Sanskrit, generally denoting a village-level market centre. Such a marketplace in rural areas usually took place on a particular day or days of a week. The term *santhe* stands for a fair, which could have been organised during a particular season or on the occasion of some festivities. It closely corresponds to what is called *yatra*[38] in north Indian sources. The trade at *santhe* could also be earmarked for a certain day of the week; that is why, terms like a Wednesday-fair (Budhavāra-santhe), Saturday-fair (Śaṇivāra-santhe) are commonly met with in inscriptions of the Deccan from c. 1000 AD onwards. The point to take note of is that our sources clearly distinguished *santhe*s and *aḍḍa*s from *peṃṭa*s (i. e. *peṇṭhā* or *peṭha*).[39] The principal distinctiveness of the *peṃṭa/peṇṭhā* lies in their being a centre of regular and daily transactions, *vis-à-vis* the periodic nature of exchanges taking place in *santhe*s and *aḍḍa*s. Moreover, while references to *aḍḍa*s are mostly

36 S. L. Sastri (ed./trsl.), *Nitivakyamrtam of Somadevasuri*, Varanasi 1976; see 19.21.

37 It is difficult to agree with both K. K. Handiqui, *Yasastilaka and Indian Culture*, Sholapur 1949, p. 119–20, and Jain, *Trade and Traders in Western India*, that the *pentha* was a fair or an exchange centre of periodic/ seasonal nature.

38 See fn. 11.

39 A. Appadorai, *Economic Conditions in Southern India 1000–1500*, vol. 1, Madras 1936; G. R. Kuppuswamy, *Economic Conditions in Karnataka 973–1336*, Dharwad 1979.

associated with individual villages, the *peṃṭa* is generally located at a nodal point of a supra-local character.

This helps us appreciate the description of a *peṃṭa*, according to a Kakatiya record, being located in a very large village. Such a village in all likelihood was little different from Naḍḍula in Rajasthan which, because of its being a node among twelve surrounding villages, transformed from a village to a *maṇḍapikā*. The *peṃṭa* in the Kakatiya records yielded *peṃṭasunka*. *Śunka* is the same as *śulka* or tolls and customs. We may recall that Somadevasuri was fully aware of a *penṭha* being a *puṭabhedana* and a *śulkasthāna* as well. Such *peṃṭaśunka*s were often collected by *mānyagaṃḍaru* tax farmers. These general comments on *peṃṭa*s in Kakatiya inscriptions help us take a close look at two specific instances.

During the time of Ganapati (1199–1261), the most powerful ruler of this family, a few *peṃṭa*s were located in Warangal. The Warangal fort inscription of Ganapati (1249) speaks of three such *peṃṭa*s. Āku-peṃṭa was noted for the presence of the Sasirbaru group of merchants who dealt in betel leaves, coconuts, mangoes and tamarind. The second one was known as Nuvula-peṃṭa and there the Sasirbaru group of merchants and the Svadeśī-Paradeśī group of traders participated in the transactions of wheat, paddy, gram, millet and edible oil. Trade in salt took place at the third one, Uppu-peṃṭa (*uppu* = salt). The inscription conveys the message that the *peṃṭa*s were marked by transactions in bulk commodities and daily necessities, including agricultural products.

About six decades later, another *peṃṭa* figures in the Koccherlakota inscription of 1310 AD. In this *peṃṭa* there were thatched sheds (*paṃkas*) where merchants could keep their merchandise temporarily against the payment of a rent in cash (1 *gadyanaka*). Commodities stored in *paṃka*s could be displayed at the time of transactions at the market yard; this required the merchant to pay another *gadyanaka* coin. In other words, the Kākatīya administration levied separate charges for letting out spaces in the storage area and also for the market-yard where items were taken from sheds. Further, there were also shops (*aṃgāḍis*) where the presence of the Bacchus and Kommati merchant groups have been noted. A levy, called *aṃgāḍi-mudrā-suṃka*, was imposed for registering articles which were to be taken into *aṃgāḍi*s or shops, probably from the thatched storage spaces (*paṃkas*).[40] One cannot fail to note the close correspondence between the 10th century textual account of a *penṭha* and the epigraphic images of the *peṃṭa* in the Kākatīya realm. The features of the *penṭha* nar in the narratives of Somadevasuri seem to have matured in the 12th and 13th centuries.

40 The references to *peṃṭa*s and *peṃṭaśunka*s in Kakatiya inscriptions are mainly drawn from P. V. Parabrahma Sastry, *The Kakatiyas of Warangal*, Hyderabad 1978, p. 449ff.

IV

The far south, located to the south of the river Krishna, seems to offer another regional type of locality level trade centre. Neither the *maṇḍapikā* nor the *peṇṭhā* appears in the inscriptions of the Pallavas and the Colas (especially those of the Coḷas, the most formidable regional power in the far south from c. 985 to 1150).[41] The far south presents a scenario of inland commerce in which a new centre, *nagaram* – rarely appearing before the 8th century – gains considerable prominence. Our understanding of the *nagaram* as a locality level centre is enriched by the in-depth empirical research of Hall.[42] The wealth of data from profuse number of Coḷa inscriptions is effectively utilised by Hall to argue his case. He has enlisted as many as 93 *nagarams*, widely distributed over different parts of the extensive Cola realm. The *nagaram* of the far south is not the same as Sanskrit *nagara* or city. Instead, the *nagaram*, in his estimation, is both an administrative centre and at the same time the commercial centre of a *nāḍu*. Drawing largely from the quantifiable epigraphic data presented by Subbarayalu and also the theoretical perspectives of a segmented polity, formulated by Burton Stein, Hall views the *nāḍu* as an autonomous locality level unit.[43] The *nāḍu* stands above and incorporates several villages. Thus the *āḍdu* is perceived as an agglomeration of several villages. The role of the *nāḍu* in the integration of the agrarian order in the Coḷa realm, which like other regions of India also experienced expansion of sedentary agricultural settlements, is particularly stressed by Stein who argues for a brāhmaṇa-peasant voluntary alliance that consolidated the organization of *nāḍu*.

The *nagaram* is clearly distinguished in the Coḷa records from a *brahmadeya* (villages granted to brāhmaṇas) and an *ūr* (a village with non-brāhmaṇa residents). *Nāḍus* with their

41 For a general overview of the political organization and economic conditions in the Coḷa empire, vide K. A. Nilakanta Sastri, *The Colas*, Madras 1955.

42 K. R. Hall, *Trade and Statecraft in the Age of the Colas*, Delhi 1980; our foregoing study of the *nagarams* in the Cola inscriptions is largely based on Hall.

43 Y. Subbarayalu, *Political Geography of the Cola Country*, Thanjavur 1973; Burton Stein, *Peasant State and Society in Medieval South India*, Delhi 1980. Stein based himself heavily on the study of the numerical distribution of *nāḍus* made by Subbarayalu. Stein attempts to provide an alternative to the conventional historiography of the Coḷa state which is considered to have combined two dissimilar systems, the centralised almost Byzantine monarchy of the Colas and the local-self bodies at the rural and locality levels. Stein and his followers consider the *nāḍus* as the peasant macro region and the real foci of the Coḷa state, which was not marked by political integration. The Coḷa ruler's effective political control is assumed to have been limited only to the core area of the Coḷas who had little bureaucratic organization, neither a standing army nor a sound resource base. Borrowing from the African model of the Alur society (A. Southall, *The Alur Society*, Cambridge 1956), Stein proposed that the Coḷa state consisted of a loose assemblage of segments. Coḷa political control would fade, according to him, as one went from the core area of the Coḷa state to the intermediate and peripheral areas. The Coḷa polity is therefore seen by him as a segmented polity, opposed to a centralized state system.

nāṭṭar assemblies are considered the real foci of the Coḷa political organization. The autonomy of the *nāḍu* became so pronounced and effective that it could, according to Stein, check the penetration of the Coḷa monarchy into the locality level. Firmly entrenched in the idea of the autonomy of the *nāḍu*, Hall further incorporates the model of Skinner to understand the hierarchy of market places in China. This has led him to consider the *nagaram* as the administrative centre and also the commercial centre of the *nāḍu*. The principal point of interest here is the image of the *nagaram* as a supra-village level market centre.

The *nagaram* as a market place appears to have within its space a bazaar (*kaḍai*), permanent shops (*aṃgāḍi*) and even stables and stalls for elephants and horses. The members of the *nagaram* assembly were entrusted with the collection of levies from shops (*aṃgāḍikuli/aṃgāḍippaṭṭam*) and bazaars (*kaḍaippaṭṭam*). An inscription from Tanjavur, the very core area of the Coḷas, informs that the local *nagaram* assembly levied taxes on flowers, dry crops, areca nuts, betel leaves, saffron, ginger, sugarcane, salt and goldsmith's produce sold at the *nagaram*. Liḳe the *maṇḍapikā*s and *peṇṭha*s, the *nagaram* in south India is also noted for the impressive range and commodities transacted at this supra-local trade centre. Information is available in the Coḷa inscriptions about the inspection of commodities entering the *nagaram*'s market place, supervision by clerks (*karaṇam*), regulation of weights and measures and fine imposed on adulteration. Strongly clinging to the notion of the autonomy of both the *nāḍu* and the *nagaram*, Hall argues that the *nagaram* had an effective organization of merchants and precluded the easy penetration of non-local and itinerant merchants into the marketplace of the *nagaram*. He therefore, postulates a *nāḍu-nagaram* collaboration with a view to exercising control over their locality and hindering the access of itinerant and foreign traders into rural areas included within the *nāḍu*.

There are other dimensions of the *nagaram* as a supra-local centre of trade. Besides the intra-*nāḍu* exchanges, Hall upholds the possibilities also of the inter-*nāḍu* trade. The interlinkages among different *nagaram*s in different *nāḍu*s, as proposed by Hall, could pave the way for the horizontal spread of trade. Above the *nagaram*s were placed ports (*paṭṭinam/pattanam*), located in or near the sea-coast and larger market places at extensive urban centres (*erivīra-paṭṭinam/mānagaram*). These ports and urban market places occupied the highest tier in the hierarchy of markets in the far south under the Colas. The exchange centres in individual villages can be conveniently placed in the basic and lowest tier of this structure. The *nagaram*, according to Hall, thus performed the crucial role of the intermediate stage between the rural markets deep in the interior villages and the celebrated urban markets and ports at the top. At the *nagaram* converged agricultural produces and bulk items from the adjacent rural hinterland; the nagaram also helped the supply of local produces and manufactured items to ports and more important (and larger as well) urban markets. From these larger markets precious commodities like gold and goods and services could have reached the middle tier of the *nagaram*, which would help some of those commodities reach the smallest and farthest exchange centres in villages in the interior. The *nagaram*, according to Hall, serves a series of local villages by providing them with a vital linkage with the upper levels of a market hierarchy. The role of the *nagaram* as a middle-tier centre of trade, offering commercial linkages between distant rural hinterlands and large urban markets and ports, is highlighted to such a degree by Hall that he strongly argues for the existence of one *nagaram* per *nāḍu* in the Cola kingdom.[44]

The insistence of Hall on the 1:1 ratio of the *nāḍu vis-à-vis* the *nagaram* in the Coḷa realm, however, has been sharply criticised. It has been rightly pointed out that Subbarayalu's study reveals the existence of 112 *nāḍu*s (excluding 114 *naduvil-nadu*s, which would give a total of 226) in Coḷamaṇḍalam itself, the very core area of the Coḷa kingdom. The present districts of Tiruchirappalli, Pudukottai and Tanjavur embracing Coḷamaṇḍalam area, have yielded 9, 6 and 24 epigraphic references to *nagaram*s respectively. Thus the total number of *nagaram*s is a mere 39 against the recorded existence of 112 *nāḍu*s (if not 226) in Coḷamaṇḍalam. If the assumed ratio of 1:1 for the *nāḍu* and its *nagaram* does not hold water even in the very core area of the Coḷa state, doubts have been raised about its applicability in the intermediate areas like Toṇḍaimaṇḍalam and Pāṇḍimaṇḍalam and peripheral zones like Koṅgumaṇḍalam in the Cola realm.[45] In fact the formulation of the segmented nature of the Coḷa polity, the pivotal feature of which is the 'autonomous' *nāḍu*, has been effectively debated on empirical and conceptual grounds.[46] The important role of the non-local and itinerant merchants in the development of local and supra-local trade in the far south has been ably highlighted in recent literature.[47] That would once again raise some reservations about Hall's portrayal of the *nagaram* as an effective check against the infiltration of non-local merchants in the *nāḍu*-level trade. In spite of several limitations in the perspectives, methods and conclusions of Hall, his presentation of rich epigraphic materials on trade in the Cola time has certainly established the *nagaram*s as centres of

[44] Hall, *Trade and Statecraft*, is influenced in his formulation of the hierarchical structure of the market centres in the Coḷa kingdom by G. William Skinner, *Marketing and Social Structure in Rural China*, Ann Arbor 1974.

[45] B. D. Chattopadhyaya's review of Hall's book *Indian Historical Review* 10, 1984, p. 186–9.

[46] Hermann Kulke (ed.), *The State in India*, Editor's Introduction and the annot. bibliography; B. D. Chattopadhyaya, "Political Processes and Structures of Polity in Early Medieval India: Problems of Perspective," Presidential Address, Indian History Congress, section I, 1983 (Burdwan session), incorporated also in Kulke (ed.), *The State in India*; R. Chamapakalakshmi, "Peasant State and Society in Medieval South India: A Review Article," *Indian Economic and Social History Review* 18, 1981, p. 411–26; H. Kulke, "Fragmentation and Segmentation versus Integration? Reflections on the Concepts of Indian Feudalism and Segmentary State in Indian History," *Studies in History* 4, 1982, p. 237–64; R. S. Sharma, "The Segmentary State and Indian Experience," *Indian Historical Review* 16, 1990, p. 80–108; Kesavan Veluthat, *Political Structure of Early Mediedval South India*, Delhi 1993.

[47] Meera Abraham, *Two Medieval Merchant Guilds of South India*, Delhi 1988; R. Champakalakshmi, *Trade, Ideology and Urbanization in South India 300 BC to AD 1300*, Delhi 1996.

supra-local trade, as vantage nodes providing opportunities of intra-*nāḍu* and inter-*nāḍu* trade and as middle tier centres of exchange linking rural market places with *mānagarams*, *erivīra-paṭṭinams* and *paṭṭinams*.

V

The foregoing pages attempt to examine the possibilities and the nature of the linkages of trade, spanning over seven centuries. The *maṇḍapikā*, the *caturaka*, the *peṇṭhā/peṭha* and the *nagaram* as nodes of commerce have distinct regional features. This is seen in their respective zones of spatial distributions. It is true that the *nagaram* as a middle category centre of exchange did not continue to figure prominently in sources after the 15th century. In fact the *peṭh*, which is still commonly seen as a name-ending to many inland trade centres in the Deccan, is also encountered in the Tamil area. The *peṇṭhā* assumes the form of *veṇṭhā* in several inscriptions of the Vijayanagar empire.[48] A Vijayanagar inscription of the 15th century speaks of a *samṭe-peṭe*,[49] showing that the centre of exchange was a combination of a *santhe* (fair) and *peṭha* (regular market). In other words, the term may suggest the gradual transformation of a *santhe* into a *peṭha*; or it might also suggest that the centre was in the stage of transition from *santhe* to *peṭe*. Another Vijayanagar inscription of 1554 from Holalkere Taluq in Karnataka records the restoration of an old *peṭha* and remission from taxes for merchants who would settle down in the revived trade centre.[50] The process continues even in the late 18th century Coromandel. A recent study enlightens us how new *peṭhs* like Nyenda Petta (100 miles from Madras; receiving cotton from the hinterland and then sending the same to ports in the Nellore district), Lalapet (60 miles from Madras; receiving cotton yarns which was distributed through Lalapet to all coastal weaving centres) and more significantly Walajahpet (68 miles from Madras, founded by Rayoji, minister of Nawab Muhammad Ali Walajah; one of the busiest of marts which was initially exempted by Rayoji from taxes to induce merchants of neighbouring *peṭhas* to flock at Walajahpet) were instrumental in providing the crucial linkages between the Coromandel coast and its hinterland.[51] A more or less similar pattern is also discernible in the continuous spread, development and proliferation of *maṇḍis* in north India during the early modern times, espe-

48 The term *veṇṭha* occurs in two inscriptions from Harihara, respectively of 1354 AD (*Journal of the Bombay Branch of the Royal Asiatic Society* 12, 1884, p. 347) and 1538 AD (*Indian Antiquary* 4, 1875, p. 331).

49 *Annual Report of Indian Epigraphy*, 1918–19, inscription no. 223 of 1918.

50 B. Lewis Rice (ed.), *Epigraphia Carnatica* 11, 1903, Holalkere Taluq, p. 131–2; inscription no. 112.

51 Bhaswati Bhattacharyya, "The Hinterland and the Coast: The Pattern of Interaction in Coromandel in the Late Eighteenth Century," in: Rudrangshu Mukherjee/Lakshmi Subrahmanyam (eds.), *Politics and Trade in the Indian Ocean World, Essays in Honour of Ashin Das Gupta*, Delhi 1998, p. 19–51.

cially the 18th century. North India also witnessed the emergence of *qasbas* to prominence as commercial suburbs of large urban centres.[52]

One may venture here to suggest that the centuries after 1300 probably mark the phase of maturity and consolidation of the middle category centres of trade both in north India and the trans-Vindhyan India, where the beginnings of the process are located around 600 AD. The *maṇḍapikā*, the *peṇṭhā* and the *nagaram* were certainly rooted to their respective regions and endowed with regional features. Their emergence cannot be explained in terms of a crisis in 'early medieval' society, economy and polity. On the other hand, their significance is to be appreciated in terms of local formations. All such centres were largely facilitated by the remarkable expansion of agriculture, the resultant availability of exchangeable grains and cash crops and the emergence of local and regional powers which could exploit their local-level resource bases. Another common feature of these centres can be seen in the transactions in daily necessities and agricultural products. In spite of their pronounced regional features, the *maṇḍapikā*, the *peṇṭhā* and the *nagaram* appear to have shared certain common traits spanning across regions and centuries. They were situated at important points where breaking the bulk was possible; this is especially conveyed by the epithet *puṭabhedana* or *paṇyapuṭabhedinī* associated with *peṇṭhasthāna* in Somadevasuri's works. Some of these supra-local centres also assumed urban features. In the study of urbanization of pre-modern India scholarly attention is perhaps excessively focussed on very large cities, premier ports towns and politico-administrative headquarters – which Braudel labelled as "Sun cities". He also underlined the fact the urban centres often form hierarchies and the tip of the urban pyramid, however significant, does not always throw light on other tiers of the urban hierarchy.[53] It is to address this issue that the present exercise has been made.

52 B. R. Grover, "An Integrated Pattern of Commercial Life in the Rural Society of North India during the late Seventeenth and early Eighteenth Centuries," in Sanjay Subrahmanyam (ed.), *Money and the Market in India 1100–1700*, Delhi 1994, p. 219–53.

53 Fernand Braudel, *The Structures of Everyday Life* (trsl. by S. Reynolds), London 1982, p. 482–3.

Political Systems and Political Structure of Medieval South India*

Georg Berkemer

In Indian history, times of relatively stable social conditions with a steady flow of cultural and political changes can be separated from times of rapid development. For South India, such a period of slow change can be observed before 1323 AD , the year in which the Delhi Sultanate finally overthrew the Kākaṭīya empire and with it the entire well established order of early medieval South Indian Hindu kingdoms, and again after 1580, the time of an expanding economy and stable state finances during the Golkonda Sultanate under Muhammad Quli Qutb Shah. Between these two dates, a phase transition from one political structure to another had occurred.

1. Terminological and theoretical considerations

This paper is strongly influenced by Weberian sociology and synergetics.[1] "System" is therefore understood as a relational term and refers to networks of observable political, religious, symbolic etc. relations between historical persons and groups. Individuals and groups within a network are simultaneously integrated into various systems of social action, out of which in the present context only their political activities will be considered.

South Indian political systems were historical phenomena and subject to change on a day to day basis through political actions. Since no political system in history was ever completely segregated from its cultural and social environment, the shifts of alliances, conquests, extinc-

* Christoph Antweiler, Christian Guksch and Hermann Kulke were kind enough to spend time reading earlier versions of this paper and offer suggestions and criticisms. I would like to express my gratitude to them for their time and effort.

1 Hermann Haken, "Synergetics," *Naturwissenschaften* 67, 1980, p. 121–8.

tions of ruling families and the integrations of upstart adventurers or tribal[2] chiefs made for an overlap of the system's boundaries[3] and caused fluctuations in peripheral areas which resulted in further rapid changes of state territories, even in times of relatively stable political conditions. From the core area to the periphery of any state the influence of the central authority decreased thus leading to an equilibrium of power in the border regions between two systems. In the context of South Indian history, the decision, whether a system should be treated as an independent (but never closed) unit or as a sub-system of a larger one depends on the particular historical situation.[4]

Several systems share a structure. The term "structure" refers to categories which describe the ideal type or the abstract notion of a system. A structure is a system of "emic" categories. The structure provides modes of communication through different channels like kinship ties, trade, symbolic acts, warfare, art, architecture, diplomatic relations, espionage, etc.[5]

While data for describing a political system can be collected by observation and historical research, the structural features behind the systemic changes are inferred from abstraction and theoretical reasoning. A political unit such as a state will be treated as a system in relation to its segments or sub-systems. But as soon as one considers the political situation of South India at any given time in its totality, this larger system includes the states as sub-systems. In this way a hierarchy of systems can be constructed where each system contains a number of sub-systems which are themselves smaller replicas of the total system, thus resulting in a structure of scale invariance,[6] thus causing self-similarity of different levels.

[2] The terms "tribe" and "tribal" are used here in an "indological" sense which differs from that of cultural evolutionism. In India, any non-Hindu stateless society is called a tribe.

[3] A boundary is to be understood as a geographical area at the periphery of a state rather than as a demarcation line, even though some rivers or mountains are traditional border marks of certain states or cultural regions.

[4] If not indicated otherwise, the term "system" refers to independent polities, i. e., to states whose rulers do not acknowledge a suzerain power in their historical records. Otherwise a state is treated as a sub-system of a higher order system, i. e., as a segment of a larger political unit. For the rulers of a political sub-system the term "little king" has been introduced. Cf. Nicholas Dirks "The Structure and Meaning of Political Relations in a South Indian Little Kingdom," *Contributions to Indian Sociology* (N. S.) 13, 1979, p. 169–206 and id. "The Pasts of a *Pālaiyakārar*: The Ethnohistory of a South Indian Little King," *Journal of Asian Studies* 41, 1982, p. 655–83.

[5] Bernard S. Cohn and McKim Marriott, "Networks and Centers in the Integration of Indian Civilization," *Journal of Social Research* 1, 1958, p. 1–19.

[6] For a discussion of mathematical self-similarity see Benoît Mandelbrot, *The Fractal Geometry of Nature*, San Francisco 1982, ch. 1.3 and 4 and Hartmut Jürgens et al., "Fraktale – eine neue Sprache für komplexe Strukturen," *Spektrum der Wissenschaft*, September 1989, p. 52–64. Jürgens description of this phenomenon is: "If one analyzes these structures at different magnitudes, one encounters again and again the same basic elements," (*ibid*, p. 52). While the structure of the segmentary state is self-similar, and actors in a segmentary state are aware of this. Christoph Antweiler pointed out to me that self-similarity in the case of South Indian political systems is due to a strong bias on continuity between micro- and macro-entities in the classical Indian conception of cosmos.

2. Political structures, polythetic classes and the segmentary state

Early South Indian political systems influenced each other's evolution by feedback processes which kept them at an approximately equal level of development. Therefore, the analysis of the structure of a single political system is meaningful because systems in a network develop in a process of co-evolution.[7] If this premise is taken seriously, speaking of a political system's structure can only imply the same as speaking of the structure of medieval South Indian states as a polythetic class[8] at a given time, provided they are all at the same evolutionary level, i. e. in the same phase between two phase transitions.

Objects in polythetic classes do not have all constituent properties of the class in common, and, speaking in terms of quantities, the value of some elements may be zero. In such cases an element may structurally be present (e. g. unconsciously as disproportions between political institutions or consciously as known deviations from a theoretical ideal), but not manifest in a historical context. But there is a set of rules that enables transformations from the properties of one object to another. Such a structure contains two types of information: Information which is useful for analysing phenomena on the systemic level of individual objects within a polythetic class, and more abstract information about how one object's set of properties changes to describe another object, i. e., structural information about the polythetic class as a whole.

If one made quantitative statements about any one of the constituent elements of each political system in the network, a relative measure of integrative power could be achieved. Integrative power is the ability of a central administration to monopolise or at least dominate the channels of control over economic essentials such as labour-force and surplus or the ideological context in which political action takes place.

A thorough study of serial data from historical sources can give insights in the efficiency of an administration.[9] If one compares institutions that determine the durability of a political system, such as, for example, the internal administration, the departmental setup at the centre, the

[7] The term is meant to refer here to evolutionary processes which both a system and its environment are subjected to. In the present context, a system's environment is understood to be made up of similar political systems which influence the development of any system collectively as a cluster of states. Even though the evolutionary processes of the different systems influence each other, they are not meant to be simultaneous in all respects. Especially, the ways how their respective sub-systems evolve, may not be determined by relationships between systems on the higher level.

[8] The term "classification" refers to "the ordering or arrangement of objects into groups or sets on the basis of their relationships". Robert Sokal defines such sets of objects recognised as a polythetic class as "objects that share a large proportion of their properties but do not necessarily agree in any one property" (R. Sokal, "Classification: Purposes, Principles, Progress, Prospects," *Science* 185, 1974, p. 1117).

[9] Noboru Karashima, *South Indian History and Society*, Delhi 1984.

control over land, the ways how essential information is managed, corruption kept under control, officers paid, the quality of the army, the amount of regular state income, the external relations, etc., a relative measure of integrative power could be stated.

Whether a state becomes dominant over or subordinate to its neighbours sharing the same political structure is determined not only by ecological preconditions such as the area of arable land under the control of the centre or the way how borders can be protected, but also by internal feedback process within the socio-cultural sphere: A cause as well as a result of the amount of integrative power in a state system can be is, at the level of political and social institutions, the way routine tasks are managed. Successful organisation keeps the bureaucratic élite free to work out solutions for more complex situations. Max Weber calls this process "Veralltäglichung" (Routinisation). Examples of such effective ways to deal with problems are the cases of two well-known dynasties: the Eastern Gaṅgas of Orissa and the Cōḷas of Tamil Nadu.[10]

a) System and structure in medieval South India: segmentary versus patrimonial state

The majority of historians working on medieval South India classify the pre-colonial political systems under one or more of the following three theoretical concepts: feudalism, segmentary state,[11] or patrimonialism.[12] The models of the segmentary state and the patrimonial state are both applied to "late medieval India" (roughly the centuries between 1300 and 1600). Scholars

[10] Hermann Kulke, *Jagannatha-Kult and Gajapati-Königtum. Ein Beitrag zur Geschichte religiöser Legitimation hinduistischer Herrscher*, Wiesbaden 1979 and id., *Kings and Cults: State Formation and Legitimation in India and Southeast Asia*. New Delhi 1993; Burton Stein, *Peasant State and Society in Medieval South India*, Delhi 1980.

[11] The segmentary model can be summarised thus: 1) The political and religious institutions are combined into a single social complex. 2) There exists only a limited recognition of the centre's territorial sovereignty among the peripheral smaller political systems. This recognition is continually decreasing from centre to periphery. Thus, the central power apparatus coexists with half-autonomous peripheral administrations. 3) The division into a central authority and half-autonomous peripheral administrations is repeated within the peripheral segments, thus forming a pyramidal system of political alliances. 4) The centre does not claim any monopoly of state power and state income. However, it is first in the hierarchy of gift exchange and has the right to grant honours, emblems, titles and land to lesser rulers. Even though the central ruler is regarded as the owner of all land, he is expected to share the land with groups of equal rank. 5) The half-autonomous smaller centres at the periphery of the system act independently of each other, i. e. they pursue alliances and conflicts of their own. Such relations cannot be controlled by the centre through legalistic or military actions, but influenced through acts of symbolic and ritual nature. 6) In times of weakness in the institutions of the central authority, there will always be attempt at the periphery to establish a new centre in a fertile region somewhere outside of the old core area.

[12] Burton Stein refers to Stephen Blake's "The Patrimonial-Bureaucratic Empire of the Mughals" (*Journal of Asian Studies* 39, 1979, p. 77–94), while defining the following attributes as essential for the patrimonial structure: "(1) a ruler claiming special, divine authority which was (2) highly personalistic and (3) enforced, or rendered powerful, by a standing army (4) directed by an administration of royal household servants without (5) distinguishing between military and civil functions." (B. Stein, "Vijayanagara and the Transition to Patrimonial Systems," in: A. L. Dallapiccola and S. Zingel-Avé Lallemant (eds.), *Vijayanagara: City and Empire*, vol. 1., Wiesbaden 1985, p. 75).

who approach the demarcation line between the era of segmentary states and the age of the patrimonial states from the direction of ancient history and work themselves with the flow of time towards the late middle ages, tend to include these centuries into the era of the segmentary state, whereas those who look back in time from the history of the Great Mughals, the paradigmatic patrimonial state of India,[13] are inclined to find here the predecessors of their own field of study.[14] Moreover, the demarcation line is very often drawn between Hindu states, which are regarded as less centralised, less successful and therefore more segmented than the Muslim patrimonial or even "sultanistic"[15] regimes which succeeded them in most parts of India.

My hypothesis is that the segmentary state and the patrimonial state models describe structures of political systems at two different levels of cultural evolution. The levels are distinct from each other by the means employed to integrate the sub-systems into the state. The distinction between them will be illustrated by an example taken from medieval South India. These states emerged out of earlier chiefdoms and tribal societies in the first half of the first millennium AD and developed a distinct structure of internal sub-systems and specific external relationships with each other. After a period of relative stability and growth, the structure became over-strained by internal factors like expensive military activities of the political élite and finally underwent a phase transition in which a new pattern of inter-state relations (a new structure), were set up under the influence of outside forces.

b) The segmentary state structure in South India

The indigenous Dravidian civilisation of the Cankam age (1st century BC to 4th century AD) in Tamil Nadu can best be characterised as a structure of complex chiefdoms.[16] The three classical "tribes" of the Cankam age, the Cōḷas, Pāṇḍyas and Cēras were already mentioned in the oldest written documents found in South India, the inscriptions of the North Indian Maurya king Aśoka (268–233 BC)[17] and thus play a dominant role in the Tamil literary sources of the Cankam age. Distribution of power was organised along kinship ties, surplus production and the

[13] S. Blake, *The Patrimonial-Bureaucratic Empire of the Mughals*; Peter Hardy, "Islamischer Patrimonialismus: Die Mogulherrschaft," in: W. Schluchter (ed.), *Max Webers Sicht des Islams*, Frankfurt, 1987, p. 190–216.

[14] For South India, the Golkonda Sultanate is taken here as the paradigmatic patrimonial state. This sultanate is clearly less spectacular in its outer appearance, but has the same structural features as the Mughal empire.

[15] The terminology of this paper is, except for the concept of the segmentary state, Weberian. Max Weber defines "sultanism" in his *Economy and Society* as an extreme form of the patrimonial regime where rulership is an almost complete personal monopoly of the absolute ruler.

[16] Robert Carneiro, "The Chiefdom – Precursor of the State," in: G. D. Jones and R. R. Kautz (eds.), *The Transition to Statehood in the New World*, Cambridge 1981, p. 37–79.

[17] E. Hultzsch (ed.), *Corpus Inscriptionum Indicarum*, vol. 1: *Inscriptions of Aśoka*, Oxford 1925, p. 51, 70, 83.

support of artisan groups through military leaders is known from contemporaneous texts.[18] Excavations prove classical Greek and Roman sources: along the South Indian shores Roman emporia incorporated the traders of the Cankam chiefdoms into the network of international long distance trade.[19] This early age of South Indian civilisation was brought to an end by the Kalabhras, a tribe from the interior of Tamil who occupied the costal regions for a short time around 450 AD. These events coincide with or even trigger the first phase transition from chiefdom to segmentary state of the political structure which thus became integrated into the all Indian great tradition.

As a result, a new political structure emerged which was more influenced by the Great Tradition of North India than any political system in the South had been before. For the first time, the ruling élites of South India designed their mode of rulership along the lines of the North Indian canonical scriptures. South India becomes massively influenced by the culture of the northern Brahminic religion and the "heretic" movements such as Buddhism and Jainism. This new phase saw first a triad of kingdoms, partly under the old Cankam age names: the Cōḷas, Pāṇḍyas and the Pallava dynasty were the leading powers, and later, from 871 onwards, dominated the rise of the Cōḷa dynasty to hegemony in Tamil Nadu.

The segmentary state model, deveoped first by A. Southall[20] has been proposed by Burton Stein to describe the prototypical South Indian kingdom of the Cōḷas (871–1279).[21] When Stein applied this model to the South Indian state in Tamil Nadu, he implicitly performed a polythetic transformation which allowed him to abstract from typically "African" features of Southall's model for the Alur of Uganda and use comparable South Indian features instead. Stein's model contains an implicit set of rules that make such a transformation possible.[22]

If the inner logic of an old political structure fails to cope with new political and social conditions, the structure as a whole is being replaced by a better adapted and more stable one in a phase transition. The political systems of the old structure either become more complex, i. e.

[18] K. A. Nilakanta Sastri, *The Colas*, Madras 1955 (2nd ed.); N. Subrahmanian, *Śaṅgam Polity: The Administration and Social Life of the Śaṅgam Tamils*, Madras 1966.

[19] Clarence Maloney, "The Beginnings of Civilization in South India," *Journal of Asian Studies* 29, 1969, p. 603–16; id., "Archaeology in South India: Accomplishments and Prospects," in: B. Stein (ed.), *Essays on South India*, Honolulu 1975, p. 1–40.

[20] Aidan Southall, *Alur Society: A Study in Process and Types of Domination*, Cambridge 1956.

[21] Southall employed this model to explain the political system of the Alur society in Uganda and the former Belgian Congo (Zaire), a rather small and not very complex segmentary state. Later he defined the segmentary state as "one in which the spheres of ritual suzerainty and political sovereignty do not coincide. The former extends widely towards a flexible, changing periphery. The latter is confined to the central, core domain" (A. Southall, "The Segmentary State in Africa and Asia," *Comparative Studies in Society and History* 30, 1987, p. 52–82).

[22] On the other hand, his model does not allow the polythetic transformation as in Fig. 3 between a state in Tamil Nadu and the East Indian Orissa, nor is it useful for a transformation from an early state to a later empire, as will be shown below.

they add a new level of organisation to the already existing means of control, which enables them to deal more successfully with the new requirements. If this adaptation fails, a system collapses.[23]

The South Indian segmentary structure of the early middle ages thus evolved into a patrimonial structure through an intermediary period of structural change in the late middle ages, in which new parameters became dominant features in the surviving or newly established political systems. Erstwhile dominant parameters either disappeared together with the social groups who made their living on them, or became incorporated into the new structure at intermediate levels of integration.[24] The consequence for a political system undergoing this process is inevitably an absorption into the newly established systems which in the time of the phase transition may already be part of a newly developed structure.

In the network of South Indian states all states are managed by kings and state officials according to the same principles of political action. The emic political theory under which the whole network operates, forms a part of a common structure of social categories. In such a network, each node stands for one state and all states have a set of properties or elements in common.

I shall take here an emic point of view in the tradition of Indian *nītiśāstra* and *arthaśāstra* (the doctrine of state craft). By applying the traditional Hindu theory of the *saptāṅgas* or seven constituent elements of the state,[25] the sub-systems may be reduced to seven characteristics, and seven dimensions can be handled if this model should ever be tried out in practice.

The seven constituent elements of the state are identical in their internal setup (i. e. structurally), and polythetic transformations can be performed in this seven-dimensional space, if the

23 Examples of state systems which fail to adapt to new conditions and as a result collapse are given in *The Collapse of Ancient States and Civilizations*. Of special interest is the contribution by Bennet Bronson who analyses the "Role of Barbarians in the Fall of States" and his discussion of North Indian states (B. Bronson, "The Role of Barbarians in the Fall of States," in: Norman Yoffee and George L. Cowgill (eds.), *The Collapse of Ancient States and Civilizations*, Tucson 1988, p. 208–10). Contrary to the South Indian case, these northern states were never able to defend themselves successfully over a long period of time against invading groups from outside their own cultural sphere. The model presented here for South India draws also from my adaptation of Manfred Eigen's model of the hypercycle (M. Eigen and Peter Schuster, *The Hypercycle – a Principle of Natural Self-Organization*, Heidelberg/New York 1979) into cultural evolution, but I do not claim to be the first person working on this approach. The method requires the assumption that systems such as macromolecules and political systems have certain common structural features: all are open systems in a steady state condition. They utilise energy and raw materials from their environment and process them according to a specific set of information. In this way they produce replications of themselves at various levels of organisation.

24 Consider as an example the highly influential role of Buddhism and Jainism at the courts of South India in the early medieval times. Both religions disappeared altogether during the Vijayanagara period (14th to 16th century) when a revival of popular Hinduism as a reaction to Islam became the politically dominant doctrine.

25 The saptāṅgas are: king (*svāmin*), minister (*amātya*), country (*janapada*), fortified city (*durgā*), treasury (*kośa*), army (*daṇḍa*), ally (*mitra*). (*Arthaśāstra* 6.1.1; ed. and transl. by R. P. Kangle, vol. 2, Bombay 1969, p. 314).

attributes of each *aṅga* (element) is seen either as a simple quantity, or is defined as composed of sub-systems and has therefore itself the properties of a polythetic class.

Stein has made use of the segmentary state model for the analysis of the internal structure of a much more complex political system than the Alur, and in a completely different historical context: the case of the Cōḷa kingdom. Stein, as well as Southall, categorises the structure of a political system as a segmentary state, if the system has a dominant, but not all-powerful core area, and a hierarchically ordered élite that is based on symbolic and ritual sovereignty. This élite does not possess sufficient material means to use mere military force for keeping the centrifugal tendencies within the segmentary state under control.[26]

Stein has introduced his model for the first time in the paper "The State and the Agrarian Order in Medieval South India: A Historiographical Critique".[27] In it he criticised K. A. Nilakanta Sastri[28] and his epigones, who use a model of the early medieval South Indian state that was influenced by the type of the bureaucratic empire predominantly displaying features of a monolithic block. Nilakanta Sastri has called this type of state "byzantine". Stein developed his own ideas on the segmentary state model in a paper of 1977, and then used it for an in-depth study of the Cōḷa state in his opus magnum *Peasant State and Society*.[29] The segmentary state model can be used to describe all early medieval states of the South Asian peninsula as well as South East Asia, as far as they were influenced by the Hindu theory of the state. This idea of the ideal state and the righteous king, as it is laid down already in the age of the North Indian Maurya empire (320–185 BC) in treatises on statecraft like Kauṭilya's *Arthaśāstra* (c. 320 BC) and the classical law-texts (the *Dharmaśāstras*), was propagated from approximately 400 AD onwards by Brahmin priests from North India who thus supplied the necessary theoretical superstructure for new political and religious developments. The simultaneous existence of two independent cultures on the Indian subcontinent, the classical North Indian culture of the post-Maurya times and the Gupta empire (320–510 AD), and the already mentioned Cankam culture of the extreme south was replaced by a new pattern of statehood that encompassed for the first time all of Hindu India and the Indianised states of Southeast Asia in the second half of the first millennium AD.

[26] Still, there remains the threat from those groups called the "tribals" in traditional Indian anthropology. Groups who are integrated into the overall pattern of social and political action on the margins of Hindu society, who know very well how a state is run, but prefer to stay outside. These groups who live in ecologically unfavourable places like arid highlands and hill jungles could never been kept under control by any of the pre-modern states of India, not even the Mughal empire.

[27] B. Stein, "The State and the Agrarian Order in Medieval South India: A Historiographical Critique," in: B. Stein (ed.), *Essays on South India*, Honolulu 1975, p. 64–91.

[28] K. A. Nilakanta Sastri, *The Cholas*; id., *A History of South India from Prehistoric Times to the Fall of Vijayanagara*, Madras 1975 (4th ed.).

[29] B. Stein, *Peasant State and Society in Mediaeval South India,* Delhi 1980.

Even though the network of relationships between the polities of south India in the first millennium AD varied considerably throughout the region, the "theory" of how a state should be built and run was accepted by all participants of the political, established local and imperial élites as well as immigrants and upstart tribal chiefs. They all shared a common language of symbolic and ritual communication centred around pilgrimage shrines, state temples, and the person of the king, and the aim was not to destroy the structure, but to establish one's own lineage or dynasty as favourably as possible within the overall pattern. This attempt has been vividly described by N. Dirks for the Kallars and Maravars of Tamil Nadu, who became dominant land owning castes in a certain region by associating themselves with the rulers of the time.[30]

The political ideology of this structure reflects North Indian imperial traditions. The old, probably Iranian notion of true kingship as being the authority over lesser kings who are again kings over kings, and so on, was brought to India more than a millennium before the Cōḷas used it to create a new cosmos of political symbols. It was first introduced as a foreign concept to North India, where Greek and Central Asian rulers (c. 200 BC–300 AD) styled themselves kings of kings in their respective languages. With the general movement of the Brahminic culture to the south, this notion of kingship became known there and was finally utilised by the dominant South Indian powers. There, it culminated in the days of the Cōḷa imperial expansion under the two most powerful Cōḷa rulers, Rājarāja I (985–1014) and Rājendra I (1014–1047).

Recently, other authors have added some new ideas to Stein's segmentary state model which developed into a paradigm beyond his original intentions. Stein has used the model predominantly in a descriptive way, thus demonstrating the inner logic of the Cōḷa state in an ethnohistorical way.[31] The new contributions were made to overcome the lack of flexibility of Stein's original model and attempted to explain structural change that occurred in the Cōḷa kingdom at c. 1000 AD (see below). One important point the critics stress is the one-sided view "from above" and "from within" the power structure. Dirks says:

> The segmentary state model is neither sufficiently well calibrated to index changes in political or social relations, … nor is it culturally sensitive enough to identify the differences between East Africa and India, or even more particularly between north and south India.[32]

N. Dirks, *The Pasts of a Pāḷaiyakārar*; id., *The Hollow Crown. Ethnohistory of an Indian Kingdom,* Cambridge 1987.

B. Stein, "The State and the Agrarian Order in Medieval South India: A Historiographical Critique," in: B. Stein (ed.), *Essays on South India*, Honolulu 1975, p. 64–91.

N. Dirks, "Political Authority and Change in Early South Indian History," *Indian Economic and Social History Review* 13, 1976, p. 126; the last half of Dirk's remark deserves some critical remarks. Instead of only trying again and again to find differences between North and South India, it seems to me more useful to work towards a comparative approach within a yet to be formulated structural framework which can explain the social structures of both macro-regions. If this endeavour proves that a theory of South Asian segmentary cultural institutions is possible, a large step towards a general theory of early political systems in large cul-

Moreover, the model is still too much oriented towards the geographical conditions of Tamil Nadu with its fertile pockets of wet soil separated by stretches of barren land to be generally accepted. Attempts by J. Biller and the author to utilise the model for Orissa could not overcome this strong Tamil Nadu bias.[33] A similar approach, which includes aspects of Orissa's historical geography has been used by H. Kulke, where the distinction between core areas (*Kerngebiete*) and extended areas of influence (*erweiterter Herrschaftsbereich*) has been made. The map of Orissa in Kulke shows the nuclear areas of regional dynasties and the interactions that result from the extensions of their territories.[34]

Others use the segmentary state model in a wider sense and employ it to analyse all South Indian states during the times of the Cōḷas and later, thus taking into account that the state of the Cōḷas itself acted as a stimulus for the internal organisation of other polities in the region, such as the Gaṅga empire, the Cāḷukya state and smaller principalities in the coastal plains of Andhra and Tamil Nadu.[35]

Dirks' abstraction of Stein's segmentary state model reminds in its horizontal components[36] of the already mentioned Kauṭilyan model of the *sāmanta-cakra*. The *Arthaśāstra* of Kauṭilya is a work that has to be treated as an analytical approach as well as a historical source. Even though Kauṭilya stresses the function of the state's military and administrative institutions and the glory of the righteous warrior-king, which can be explained by the intention of the author to write a kind of manual for the ancient Indian crown-prince, the overall picture of variable and flexible foreign policy of the rulers and their military, ritual and administrative institutions make this model a paradigm not only for ancient India, but for the medieval Hindu kingdoms as well. Furthermore, the classical Kauṭilyan model of the *sāmanta-cakra* is together with

tural regions would be achieved. This could even lead to a general theory of political systems which encompasses African as well as South Asian and South East Asian segmentary states. One could begin this project by working out a comparative analysis of the pre-Aryan south Indian Cankam-chiefdoms, Alur Society, and the South Indian segmentary system of the early Cōḷas. At a first glance, this looks like an evolutionary sequence through several phase transitions, leading from complex chiefdoms towards highly integrated but not centralised states.

33 Jürgen Biller, *Zur Entstehung von Herrschaft and Staat. Das Beispiel des indischen Regionalreiches von Orissa*, Freiburg 1986; Georg Berkemer, *Little Kingdoms in Kaliṅga*, Stuttgart 1993; id. "The Chronicle of a Little Kingdom: Some Remarks on the Tekkali-tāḷūkā Jamīṃdārla Vaṃśāvali," in: B. Kölver (ed.), *The State, the Law and Society in Classical India*, Munich 1997, p. 65–95.

34 H. Kulke, *Jagannath-Kult*, and the articles in the volume *Kings and Cults*.

35 Cf. N. Dirks, "Structure and Meaning of Political Relations in a South Indian Little Kingdom," *Indian Economic and Social History Review* 13, 1979, p. 125ff; id., "The Pasts of a Pāḷaiyakārar: the Ethnohistory of a South Indian Little King," *Journal of Asian Studies* 41, 1982, p. 655ff; id., *The Hollow Crown*; James Heitzman, "State Formation in South India, 850–1280," *Indian Economic and Social History Review* 24, 1980, p. 35–61; id., "Temple Urbanism in Medieval South India," *Journal of Asian Studies* 46, 1987, p. 791–826.

36 "Horizontal" refers to relations between components on the same level of the segmentary system. From an outside point of view they can be regarded as approximately equal in their symbolic and ritual relations among each other and approximately equally inferior in their relations with the centre. "Vertical" implies hierarchical relationships between higher and lower components.

Dirks' abstraction of the segmentary state model and Bernard Cohn's work on political systems in eighteenth-century North India[37] the only one known to the author which in its horizontal components is applicable to all levels of the political and ritual hierarchy with the same heuristic value.[38] Dirks stresses the holistic aspect of the segmentary state model. After combining Dirks' with Rudolph's ideas, the resulting model of the structure of south Indian political and ritual systems is a multi-level self-similar system as described above. Thus the model transcends the descriptive approach of ethnohistory, and leads the way towards a comparative theory of complex social systems in India of regional or even subcontinental significance.

As an analytical and therefore comparative, rather than merely descriptive concept, the model of the segmentary state seems to me the most successful attempt so far to illustrate the structure behind historical events in the time of the Cōḷa kingdom from the early formative phase to the extension of the Cōla kingdom beyond Tamil Nadu. The Cōḷa state was based on well established local institutions and corporations of cultivators, merchants and land-owning Brahmins (*nāḍus*) which were able to function independently of state control, but were the major support of the early Cōḷa rulers.

The great Cōḷa kings Rājarāja I and Rājendra I were the first rulers of a South Indian segmentary state who were able to lead successful military campaigns not only against the core areas of the neighbouring segmentary states, but found themselves capable of launching long range attacks. Even though these did not result in, and were probably not planṇed as, continual occupations, raids like the campaign to the north as far as the Ganges river (the "Conquest of the Gaṅga" of 1022 AD) and the naval operations across the Bay of Bengal into Southeast Asia (1025 AD) displayed a kind of organisational know-how and a concentration of military power in the hand of the central ruler, which were superior to what earlier South Indian kingdoms were able to muster. Territories in closer range, such as Sri Lanka, the Maldives and Laccadives and the large alluvial plains of the Krishna-Godavari delta in Andhra Pradesh, became temporarily incorporated into the segmentary system. Military success and the enlargement of the empire were reflected in the manifold symbolic features of new state temples in the old capital Tanjore and the new one, Gaṅgaikoṇḍacōḷapuram (the "City of the Cōḷa who conquered the Ganges"). These temples were the largest built in India so far and represented not only the centre of the Cōḷa political system which encompassed almost all of South India, but, as a

[37] Bernard S. Cohn, *An Anthropologist Among the Historians and Other Essays*, Delhi 1987, p. 483.

[38] "Units in such a system are replications of each other" (Susanne H. Rudolph, "Presidential Address: State Formation in Asia – Prolegomenon to a Comparative Study," *Journal of Asian Studies* 46, 1987, p. 739). Rudolph recognises reduplication in Stein's segmentary state model and also in Tambiah's "Galactic Polity" model (Stanley Tambiah, *World Conquerer and World Renouncer: A Study of Buddhism and Polity in Thailand Against a Historical Background*, Cambridge 1976) of Thai society and interprets it as a kind of counter approach against the notion of Oriental Despotism. But similar to Stein, Rudolph keeps the point of view from above, the perspective from the centre of the empire.

symbolic extension of the segmentary state beyond its own sphere of direct influence they also signified the centre of the world of man.

A distinction is made here between the sphere of power, i. e. the territory under direct control of a segmentary lord and the sphere of influence. Both are connected in a "tax – tribute – plunder continuum".[39] In Weberian terminology, the tax pole of the continuum is called the "patrimonially extended household", the core area where direct rulership is executed. The ruler's officials or family members collect regular tax payments from the subjects. Next follows the area of direct influence, where the central ruler can intervene into the core areas of lesser rulers by using his own (e. g. symbolic, political or military) means. From this zone, more or less regular tributes come to the capital, and symbolic gifts are returned. Peripheral are the territories of those rulers who can be "pacified" only with the aid of allies or subordinates. Material goods from this zone are collected by mere force through plunder. Influence in such territories is most effectively executed in an indirect way through intermediaries or through merely symbolic acts, since any direct intervention needs support from the allies who require symbolic or material compensation. A central ruler may even weaken himself through such military campaigns by causing internal disruptures in his own segmentary state, if he "over-expands" the state.

Such attempts to transgress the structural limits of the segmentary state can be observed not only in the architectural symbolism of the state temples. In the time of the greatest extension of the Cōḷa segmentary state, the tendency to over-expand the inner core area of the kingdom, i. e. the territory under direct administration by members of the central ruler's household, and to annex formerly independent segments into the segment of the central power became evident. Areas around the core domain of the Cōḷa empire were now managed by relatives of the king and not by little kings. In this way the Cōḷa king was able to extend the material basis of his personal power beyond that of a ruler of an earlier segmentary state.[40] Formerly small corporate bodies (*nāḍus*) became larger and had to allow closer control by the central ruler. Here, a trend towards a patrimonial structure becomes perceptible within the most centralised part of the segmentary state of the Cōḷas. Similar tendencies can be observed in the core areas of other large segmentary states of South India. As a general rule it can be assumed that occupation of territory was easier than the administration of newly conquered territory. The larger the peripheral areas became, the more of the surplus production from the core domain had to be invested by the centre into institutions which could keep rebellious peripheral rulers under control. Efficiency of tax collection and administration, enlargement of areas under cultivation and increase of military power could only be achieved within the limited area under direct

39 George Spencer, "The Politics of Plunder: The Cholas in Eleventh-Century Ceylon," *Journal of Asian Studies* 35, 1975, p. 405–19.

40 J. Heitzman, *Temple Urbanism*.

control of the centre and only to an extent which was limited by the role of the king as a mediator among conflicting interest groups and their traditional rights and privileges. The segmentary model explains very well why the Cōḷa state began to disintegrate as soon as the centre incorporated too much of peripheral territory into the core domain without being able to increase the effectiveness of its central institutions, such as the ritual and political bureaucracies and the military. But at last, the kingdom failed to overcome its "constitutional" weaknesses; the amount of labor that had to be invested in the centre to create sufficient means of control of the periphery[41] could not be increased at the same speed as the peripheral areas grew. The "politics of plunder"[42] undertaken to support the centre's need for redistributable goods with raids into neighbouring territory outside of the own segmentary state supported both the élites of the core area of centre and the rulers at the periphery. This strategy could even prove counterproductive. The stronger the centre already was, the more it could claim from the booty, but if the centre was already weak, the raids were more advantageous for the peripheral systems. Eventually, the centre would loose control over the peripheral eras.

The successful Cōḷa type of rulership was a model for other leading regional and imperial dynasties of peninsular India, such as the imperial Gaṅgas of Orissa (1031–1435), the Hoysaḷas of Karnataka (c. 1006–1343), and the successors of the Cōḷas, the Pāṇḍyas of Tamil Nadu (1216–1323), the Kākaṭīyas of Warangal (1040–1323) and other smaller dynasties in the Krishna-Godavari region of coastal Andhra Pradesh, who became independent powers in the 13th century when the Cōḷa empire lost control over its peripheral regions. All these dynasties displayed their power through grandiose temple architecture and extended their own patrimonial dominions into the areas of formerly independent lords. Even though the overall structure of these state systems remains clearly at the level of the segmentary state, new internal developments towards the concentration of state power in the central domain become visible within these systems.

c) The Phase Transition

The raids of the Delhi Sultanate into the Deccan became a serious threat to the Hindu powers after 1300 AD. In 1323, Sultan Muhammad Tughluq (1320–1351) finally succeeded to defeat and oust the Kākaṭīya king Pratāparudra (1289–1323). This incident, as well as the contemporaneous downfall of the Hoysaḷa rulers of Karnataka brought the well calibrated South Indian

41 Attempts to counteract the centrifugal forces were made (e. g. irrigation, foundation of cities, increase of trade) and military outposts were created to support central authority.

42 The term has been coined by George Spencer in "The Politics of Plunder ...".

system of political alliances, ritual obligations and flow of goods to an abrupt halt.[43] Inscriptional sources, giving us information about this time,[44] describe the disastrous effects in vivid words and do not forget to mention that legitimate authority ceased to exist.

As an interpretation of these accounts it can be said that the accepted ideological structure underlying the interactions of all co-sharers of the political institutions before the disruptive events was not able to compensate the consequences of the catastrophe any more. After a time of political chaos, new alliances between surviving noble families who had served under the Kākaṭīyas and Hoysaḷas established a new political order. In Andhra, an alliance of local rulers and previous leaders (*nāyakas*) of the Kākaṭīya army was founded. They organised their resistance under the leadership of Prōlaya Nāyaka. Weakened by wars at its western frontiers, the Delhi Sultanate had to withdraw its troops to a line north of the Godavari river in 1336.[45] Several of these victorious Nāyakas became the founders of new dynasties and retained their independent domains until the end of the 14th century.

Meanwhile, a new central power had emerged at Vijayanagara in Karnataka (c. 1346). This state soon united the whole of South India in a political system that contained patrimonial elements of administration mainly in the military sector, even though it kept alive the ideology of the segmentary state in the ideal of military confederacy. Around 1400 AD a new constellation of political powers had emerged that combined various unstable sultanates in the north of the Deccan with two Hindu states, Vijayanagara and the Orissan kingdom.

The activities of the new Hindu rulers, whether emperor or little king, were aimed at the reestablishment of the old system of segmentary states. Thus, structural self-similarity is one of the characteristic features reflected in the new forms of literary sources that ensued as a reaction to the traumatic events. Normative writings such as the temple chronicles (*sthala māhātmyas*) were produced to collect the dynastic and ritual knowledge of the temple priests and scribes as a source of information useful in the re-establishment of the religious cults and the legitimation of the new secular protectors.

In a contribution to the history of Bengal, S. Bhattacharya shows that the very loosely knit segmentary states of Bengal had no chance to defend themselves against the invasions of the centrally organised Moslem armies as early as 1199. The political system there was overthrown so quickly that they could not develop any centralised institution that could muster successful resistance against the invaders.[46]

43 The only large political system that survived the tumultuous 14th century, however weakened, was the empire of the Gaṅgas of Orissa.

44 For a list of the most important sources see N. Ramesan, "Epigrapy, Sanskrit and Telugu," in: H. K. Sherwani and P. M. Joshi (eds.), *History of Medieval Deccan (1295–1724)*, vol. 2, Hyderabad 1974, p. 345–59.

45 K. A. Nilakanta Sastri, *History of South India*, p. 236.

46 Swapna Bhattacharya, *Landschenkungen und staatliche Entwicklung im frühmittelalterlichen Bengalen (5. bis 13. Jh. n. Chr.)*, Stuttgart 1985, p. 121.

In contrast, this structural weakness of the central secular authority in Orissa was compensated for by orientating the population towards the regional deity, Jagannāth of Puri, who was made the state deity. The rulers of Orissa, the Gaṅga and Sūryavaṃśa kings who claimed to rule under the protection of the deity as his viceroys (*rāutta*), were able to centralise their administration and organise successful resistance against their enemies for centuries (until 1568). The relatively centralised structure of the Gajapati empire was created by making use of the integrative power of the cult at Puri for the purposes of the state, which did not fall apart even though the kingdom fell prey to more than one Muslim and Vijayanagara invasion.

Both the Gajapatis of Orissa and the Vijayanagara rulers claimed a monopoly of political authority. However, they did not demand this monopoly as sovereign rulers of a secular state, but as the deputies of the state deity, whose absolute power they claimed to enforce. The king is the first and most exalted steward of the deities' realm. In this function, he also claims authority over all those who are devotees of the god.[47] Here we see a hybrid structure in which elements of the segmentary state are combined with those of the patrimonial state.

The idea of sharing as a means of political authority had been abandoned in political institutions and transcended into the relationship of state deity and king. They are co-sharers in units of the realm and in the devotion of their subjects. While the notion of sharing being removed out of the daily requirements of a state administration into the sphere of divine or semi-divine beings, segmentation is evident only at lower political levels. Thus the structure of the state looks centralised from the top of the political hierarchy and from the capital, but segmented from below and from the periphery, where each step towards a strong centre may still be seen as a loss of sovereignty. There are the same or new local ruling families who continue to issue their inscriptional charters as co-sharers of the realm, and whose political actions even in the 18th century are still those of a segmentary élite.

Patrimonial features in late medieval Hindu states during the period of phase transition are visible for instance in the way how new dynasties come to power. While the context of the segmentary structure allowed new ruling families the foundation of new capitals, in the transitional phase and later, coups d'état at the old dynasty's capital that can be enacted at lesser cost, occur in Vijayanagara and in Cuttack, the capital of the Gaṅgas and the Sūryavaṃśa Gajapatis, as well as in Muslim states. Kapilendra, the first Sūryavaṃśi ruler (1436–1467), had been an officer under the last Gaṅga king, at whose death he proclaimed himself king. Here a patrimo-

[47] Precondition for this development was the increased awareness by the subjects of political developments in their cultural region beyond one's own local concerns and a growing sense of regional identity. Symbolic figures of the cultural regions that emerged from c. 1400 onwards, were the state deity (*rāṣṭradevatā*), the king and, on a subregional level, the local ruler (*nāyaka*) and his local guardian deity (*iṣṭadevatā*). For details see H. Kulke, "Die frühmittelalterlichen Regionalreiche: Ihre Struktur und Rolle im Prozeß staatlicher Entwicklung Indiens," in: H. Kulke and D. Rothermund (eds.), *Regionale Tradition in Südasien*, Stuttgart 1985, p. 104.

nial model of dynastic change becomes dominant that enabled strong persons to gain power without bringing the governmental institutions of the state to a complete halt. The new ruler could also replace functionaries of the old regime with his own followers at a reduced risk, i. e. without inevitably causing a civil war in their home districts.

As a consequence of such new order parameters, well established dynasties of little kings disappeared completely. The structural affinity of the new Hindu polities to patrimonial systems can be further corroborated by a look at the Golkonda Sultanate, a patrimonial state of the 16th and 17th centuries, where the administrative system was completely in the hand of state functionaries who could be employed and dismissed in the same way as contemporary European ministers, military officers and other state functionaries.[48]

If 1323 is a landmark indicating the beginning of structural change in the political systems of South India, the year 1589 can be taken as its end: In 1589, the new capital of Golkonda, Hyderabad, was founded without any fortification, a symbolic act that clearly expressed the new political stability in that state. Such a degree of political stability had not been seen in South India for at least 300 years.

3. Conclusion

I have tried to show that a clear typological distinction between segmentary Hindu states and centralised Moslem regimes in medieval and early modern South India cannot be made. The external threat caused by the invading Muslim armies to South Indian Hindu dynasties induced a transition towards a patrimonial political structure which was similar to the already existing one of North India. The most important difference between the old segmentary structure of the year 1000 AD and the new structure of the year 1600 AD lies in the way how local institutions were incorporated into the central state. The ideal that a state can be organised differently than in the classical segmentary way was developed indigenously during the times of the great Cōla kings and further advanced in the successor states of the Cōḷas. This slow development was then accelerated by the Muslim invaders and thus became the new dominant order in the time of the phase transition which was largely the time of the Vijayanagara empire. This transition is therefore to a large extent an indigenous development.

This paper is meant as a contribution to a comparative theory which stresses the processual characteristics of states during the period of their formation as well as other phases of their

48 "The Persian, Deccani, and Afghan nobles formed a pool of administrators which could be drawn upon by the king or the chief minister for both civil and military posts at the centre – or, indeed, for service anywhere in the kingdom," (John F. Richards, "The Seventeenth Century Concentration of State Power at Hyderabad," *Journal of the Pakistan Historical Society* 23, 1975, p. 5).

existence. A theory is in the present context meant to be a system of statements which fulfill the criteria for "integral comparison": The point of integral rather than parallel comparison is to formulate generalisations that allow me, working on North Indian states, to understand their particularity by comparing them to the Chinese state under the Tang, Song, or Ming, each with its different strategies for sustaining empire.[49]

[49] S. Rudolph, *State Formation in Asia* ..., p. 731.

Religious Dignitaries in the Court Protocol of Jaipur (Mid-Eighteenth to Early Nineteenth Century)

Monika Horstmann

This paper attempts to study an aspect of the relations which the Kachavāhā court of Jaipur (eastern Rajasthan) entertained with the representatives of three religious institutions, namely, the custodians (*adhikārīs*) of the temple of Govinddevjī; the militant Rāmānandīs attached to the lineage to which belonged Bālānand, who was the most prominent Rāmānandī soldier-ascetic of the second half of the 18th century; and the Dādūpanthīs.[1] Not only did these groups interact with the court but also, to a varying degree, with each other. The three groups differ in several aspects, a major one being that two of them were militant while one, that of Govinddevjī, was not. The focus is on the court protocol applying to these three groups. The period under review spans less than a century, namely, roughly the years from 1750 to 1840.

All the three institutions wielded power, either religious or both religious and military. Although there exists a vast stock of archival material, no comprehensive history of the role of religious institutions in the Kachavāhā state has been produced so far and no more than a fraction of the relevant documents has been studied. The extant sectarian historiography often refers faithfully to documents, but is naturally inclined to exalt the role of the writer's own religious group.[2]

This study of the court protocol, undertaken against the backdrop of the political and, to some extent, the institutional history of the three groups, aims at exploring the differential treatment given to them by the court and thus, from this limited perspective, linking them by

[1] This paper is based on research conducted in Bikaner and Naraina, Rajasthan, in 1988 and 1991. I am grateful to the Deutsche Forschungsgemeinschaft for funding my archival studies.
I have used of the following abbreviations:
DK: *Dastūr komvār,* for which see p. 145
DPP: *Dādū paṃth paricay*, for which see fn. 2.
Unless preceded by "V. S.", the dates given follow the Christian era. V. S. is Vikrama-Samvat of 58 B. C.

[2] A rather convoluted but rich account of the Dādūpanth is Sv. Nārāyaṇdās. *Śrī Dādū paṃth paricay.* 3 Vols. Jaipur, n.d. [V. S. 2035–36], henceforth abridged as DDP.

comparison. Moreover, the paper also aims at highlighting the importance of one special type of papers from among the many categories of administrative records of the Jaipur court. Like that of several other pre-colonial modern states, Jaipur excelled in a brilliant administrative machinery which was not thwarted by the political turbulence which affected Jaipur as much as the other states which emerged as successor powers to the Mughals. Stewart Gordon, while focussing on the Marāṭhās, speaks of the historic facts which, during the past two or three decades, have changed our view of the Indian history of the 18th century. While the British drew an image of that period as having sunk into chaos, the study of the archives of the various states reveals an entirely different picture.

> What did not fit this [the British – MH] image, however, was the huge archive at Pune, filed with millions of documents of an enormously sophisticated revenue administration. As I and other scholars began to examine these materials, we understood why the British colonial administration had closed this archive to all historical researchers. Here was no evidence of 'chaos' or 'decay', but a vibrant administration recording the minute details of rural and urban life and committed to agricultural development. A similar process of discovery has taken place at every archive of regional successor states of the eighteenth century, ...[3]

The accuracy of this remark leaves nothing to be added.

Historians have used the court protocol of Jaipur with great benefit as a source of information on individuals. However, this body of records speaks also a language distinctly its own in positioning individuals or representatives of institutions by the way in which they interact with the king and/or the court as the body representing him.

1. Historical background

In its forepart the period under review was for about a decade marked by Marāṭhā invasions into the Jaipur territory.[4] These and the ensuing battles were mainly caused by arrears of tribute which the Marāṭhās, but also the Mughals tried to secure from Jaipur. Mādhosiṅgh's (Mādhavsiṅgh) reign ended in 1768, in a turbulent period of war with the Jāṭs. His son and successor, Pṛthvīsiṅgh, was a minor when Mādhosiṅgh died, and he himself died in 1778 at the age of fifteen. The minority rule helped widen the interior rifts of the Jaipur state. Pratāpsiṅgh succeeded Pṛthvīsiṅgh at the age of thirteen. Right from the beginning of his reign Jaipur was immersed in external fights with the imperial forces, who sought to exact outstanding debts by coercion, and internal fights amongst the various factions at court. In the years 1786–87 Jaipur was again invaded by the Marāṭhās. In 1787 the Jaipur army encountered the Marāṭhās under

3 Stewart Gordon, *Marathas, Marauders, and State Formation in Eighteenth-Century India,* Delhi 1994, p. IX.

4 The following paragraph is based on Jadunath Sarkar, *Fall of the Mughal Empire,* vol. 2: Calcutta 1950, vol. 3: 3rd ed. Calcutta 1964.

Mahadjī Śinde at Lālsoṭ, and after that repeatedly between 1790 (Pāṭan) and 1800 (Malpurā). Pratāpsiṅgh died in 1803. By the end of the 18th century, negotiations with the British had commenced. These led to the conclusion of a treaty in 1803 and, finally, to the establishment of British Paramountcy over Rajputana in 1818. In the period between 1803 and 1835 the Jaipur State was further weakened by mutually inimical court factions. From 1835, when the infant Rāmsiṅgh II succeeded to the throne, to his attainment of maturity in 1851 Jaipur was ruled by a Council of Regency under the supervision of the British Political Agent.

While the temple of Govinddevjī and its custodians played a prominent ritual role, the militant Rāmānandīs and the Dādūpanthīs gained ascendance overwhelmingly due to the military contingents which they were able to provide to the Kachavāhā state as well as to neighbouring states. The image of the deity Śrī Govinddevjī, to whom the temple by that name is consecrated, and that of his consort had come to the Kachavāhā territory by the end of the 17th century.[5] Formerly they had resided in Vrindaban, in the temple by the same name. That temple had been built by Rājā Mānsiṅgh, the then ruler of Āmber, which was the predecessor of Jaipur as the capital of the Kachavāhās. He was a high-ranking noble at Akbar's court and was *sūbadār* of Kabul, Bihar and Bengal between 1585 and 1606. The deity Govinddevjī was connected with the first generation of the Caitanya or Gauḍīya *sampradāya,* more specifically with the line of Rūpa Gosvāmī. The temple of Mānsiṅgh, built with the support of Akbar, was a symbol of regnal power. Govinddevjī thus had been the object of enduring attachment of the Kachavāhā family. It was removed from Vrindaban to the dynastic territory, allegedly only because of turbulences caused by the aggressive stance which the Mughal power took against Hindu places of worship, but perhaps also in a more articulate symbolic assertion of Kachavāhā dynastic power. In 1739 Mahārāja Jaisiṅgh II (r. 1700–1743) installed Govinddevjī in the temple which forms part of the precincts of the City Palace, the centre of his new capital Jaipur.

The ascendance of Govinddevjī had not remained uncontested by other religious groups who enjoyed a special position in the Kachavāhā state. This is especially visible in the years before the consolidation of Govinddevjī as another deity of the state when the position of the Caitanyites as a religious group, who could rightfully claim orthodox legitimacy, was questioned by those competing groups. From these trials they arose triumphantly.[6]

A formidable contestant of the Caitanyites and thus of the rank of Govinddevjī had been the Rāmānandīs. In the period preceding that under review they had been represented by two lineages, that of Galtā and that of Raivāsā (Revāsā). The Rāmānandīs, who worship the divine

[5] For a comprehensive treatment of various aspects of the temple's history cp. Margaret Case (ed.), *Govindadeva: A Dialogue in Stone*, New Delhi 1996.

[6] Stuart Elkman, *Jīva Gosvāmin's* Tattvasandarbha: *A Study on the Philosophical and Sectarian Development of the Gauḍīya Vaiṣṇava Movement*, Delhi 1986, p. 25–50; Monika Horstmann, "Ein Kapitel nordindischer Religionspolitk: Jai Singh II. und die religiösen Orden," *Zeitschrift für Religionswissenschaft* 2 (1), 1994, p. 49–67.

couple Sītārām, had been connected with the Kachavāhā family since the 16th century. In the royal ritual they enjoy a prominent position because the dynasty claims descent from the mythical ancestor Ikṣvāku and is thus related to the lineage of Rāma. They pay allegiance to Sītārām as their family deity which is demonstrated conspicuously by the fact that the seal of the Mahārājas has borne the name of these deities ever since the seal's legend stopped expressing allegiance to the Mughal emperor. This change is found to have been made after the death of Emperor Bahādur Śāh (1712), at the latest by 1716.[7] Around 1730 the militant Rāmānandīs are documented in Jaipur as emerging as an armed force which caused concern to the political power.[8] When the contesting political powers were increasingly in need of soldiers, the militant Rāmānandīs consolidated their position. In the 1750s one Bālānand welded the Vaiṣṇava fighting ascetics into an organised military body. He was the sixth in an alleged spiritual genealogy, but in fact only the second in the actually traceable new lineage of Rāmānandīs, which had been established by his guru Virjānand (Vṛjānand), evident since around 1720. These Vaiṣṇava ascetics are called the *vairāgī*s or by the more general term, which applies to various groups of fighting ascetics, *nāgā*s. The Dādūpanthīs remained outside the pale of this organisation. The seat of Bālānand was a fort named Bālānand Pīṭh or Hanumān Gaḍhī, which is located inside the walled city of Jaipur near Cāndpol Gate and to the south of Nahargaṛh Fort. It was reportedly built in 1753.[9] Allegedly land to build this seat was given to Bālānand in exchange for land which was eventually allotted to Govinddevjī as the site for the deity's new temple.[10] In 1767 we find Bālānand engaged with a contingent of 20,000 *nāgā*s in the battles between the Jāṭs and the Marāṭhās from where he returned to Jaipur.[11] In 1786 he was made Jaipur's envoy to Mahadjī Śinde with whom he negotiated the conditions for a treaty with Jaipur. His impact on the politics of Jaipur is illustrated by the following passage:

> In the face of Sindhia's threat to overthrow the Kacchwa monarchy, the monk [Bālānand – MH] […] set out with the Dewal Khush-hali Ram Bohra […] to negotiate with the Maratha lord, outside Jaipur. On arrival near the Maratha camp, he was honoured by Sindhia personally kneeling down at his feet and laying down a gift of one hundred gold coins and receiving one necklace of pearls and four [d]oshalas, one for himself and the rest for his high officers, as a token of blessings. (*Ibrat*, A. S. b. II. 481)

7 Monika Horstmann, *In Favour of Govinddevjī: Historical Documents Relating to a Deity of Vrindaban and Eastern Rajasthan.* (Forthcoming,) "Introduction".

8 Monika Thiel-Horstmann, "Die Kriegermönche Rajasthans: Jaisingh II. und das Bālānand-Problem". *XXIV. Deutscher Orientalistentag ... 1988*, ed. by Werner Diem and Abdoldjavad Falaturi, Stuttgart 1990, p. 478–90. Cp. p. 486–7.

9 Ashim Kumar Roy, *History of the Jaipur City.* Delhi 1978, p. 191.

10 Keśavdatta, *Kīrti-sudhāsāgar.* Prayag 1944, p. 5. This pamphlet is undocumented and vague, but expresses popular sectarian opinion.

11 Jadunath Sarkar, *A History of Dasnami Sanyasis.* Daraganj, Allahabad, n. d., p. 177.

On the 10th [March 1786 – MH] commenced the negotiations in the course of which Sindhia's preposterous demand of three krores and forty lakhs of rupees as the arrears of tribute was whittled down to sixty three [*sic*!] lakhs (D. Y. 163). When, owing to Jaipur's inability to pay, Sindhia brandished his sword again, Bālānand returned to Jaipur; he brought back some money, stood personal security for two lakhs of rupees (D. Y. 165. H. P. 476) and finally led Sindhia out of the state.[12]

Jadunath Sarkar called Bālānand the spiritual guide of Mādhosiṅgh.[13] It remains doubtful if Bālānand had formally initiated him, for he is not called the king's *gurmahant mahārāj.* This designation is, however, appropriately applied to Bālānand's disciple and successor, Govindānand, who in V. S. 1839/AD 1783 initiated the young king Pratāpsiṅgh.[14] This detail apart, there can be no doubt as to the power which was wielded by Bālānand and Govindānand. As for Bālānand's relations with the Dādūpanthīs, the third group figuring in this paper, these managed to remain an independent organisation. One reason for this was that they did not belong to the Vaiṣṇava groups who practised iconic worship and who had been declared orthodox. Another reason was the resistence on the part of the Dādūpanthīs. Their sectarian history has it that at an unmentioned date Bālānand and his soldier-monks came to Narainā, the headquarters of the Dādūpanthīs, with the intention to lay siege to the seat, usurp it and converse the monks by force to Vaiṣṇavism. This plan was thwarted by the stiff resistance of the Dādūpanthīs.[15]

The balance in the relations of the three groups was thus anything but stable. While the Dādūpanthīs never gained any impact on the religious court ritual, the cult of Govinddevjī and the cult of Sītārām as represented by the Rāmānandīs had to be kept ritually balanced. The present situation, as it has prevailed from a time not precisely definable, has been comprehensively described by Clémentin-Ojha,[16]

> Ils (the custodians of Govinddevjī and the Rāmānandī priests of Sītārām – MH) entrent librement au palais et sont associés aux grandes cérémonies du royaume [...] Parmi les Rāmānujī-Rāmānandī, le responsable de Galta affirme sa préséance sur ses confrères de Raivasa et de Bālānada Pīṭha puisqu'en tant que chef spirituel du temple de Sītārām [...] il y supervise toutes les cérémonies rituelles. Son titre d'*ācārya* (les deux autres sont appelés mahant) traduit cette superiorité de statut. Mais tout ācārya qu'il soit, il doit parfois s'effacer devant l'*adhikārī* (shebait) de Govindadeva puisque, depuis Jai Singh II, Govindadeva a supplanté Sītārāma dans le cœur des souverains, et dans certaines cérémonies à la cour. Pour cette raison d'ailleurs, le statut du shebait de Govindadeva est également supérieur à celui des trois autres mahant Gauḍīya-vaiṣṇava de la ville. Aussi le soir du couronnement, devient-il le vishnouïte le plus en

12 *Ibid.*, p. 235–6.

13 *Ibid.*, p. 234.

14 The initiation is described in DK 31: 478–9.

15 DPP 1: 103–8.

16 Caṭherine Clémentin-Ojha. "*L'affaire des tilaka: Procès des vishnouïtes à Jaipur 1863–1867.*" Thèse d'habilitation, Ecole des Hautes Etudes en Sciences Sociales. Paris 1997 (manuscript), p. 57.

> vu du royaume: le nouveau Maharaja rend d'abord hommage à Govindadeva, puis aux déesses protectrices du territoire et du clan,[17] avant de se présenter au temple de Sītārāma [...] A la grande fête de Vijayā-daśamī, toutefois les Rāmānadī (Galta en tête) sont à l'honneur: le śālagrāma Sītārāma, porté sur un char, ouvrant la procession royale, ils ont la préséance sur tous les Gauḍīya-vaiṣṇava et sur leurs autres confrères vishnouïtes.

The ritual precedence given to Govinddevjī *vis-à-vis* the Dādūpanthīs, whose ritual weight was relatively marginal, is also reflected by a brief passage in DK (31: 542) which reports that in 1803 Jīvandās, the designated successor of the Dādūpanthī abbot-in-chief, and five of his monks visited the Govinddevjī temple, where the Mahārāja, Jagatsiṅgh, joined them and had the *darśan* of the deity. No similar face to face contest of religious rank is reported for the Bālānandīs.

The third group, the Dādūpanthīs, were founded around 1600. They are composed of several branches which are united under an abbot-in-chief, the *mahant* of Narainā. They, too, rose to special military importance around the middle of the 18th century.[18] From a not precisely known but probably early period of their existence there had also been soldier-ascetics among the Dādūpanthīs. These had made their presence felt since the first half of the 18th century. The headquarters of the Dādūpanth, Narainā, lies about 40 km to the southwest of Jaipur, but the Dādūpanth spread mainly over what is today Rajasthan, Haryana and the Panjab. Under Cainrām's predecessor Kṛṣṇadev the headquarters had been shifted to Mertā in Mārvāṛ, but under Cainrām, who re-established Narainā as their headquarters, the Dādūpanthīs drew closer to the Jaipur court. One Jogīdās, who was the disciple of the abbot of Narainā, figures as a focus of attention on the part of Jaipur's Mahārāja Mādhosiṅgh.[19] His place at Jaipur's Ruī kī maḍhī (maṇḍī), which became also known by the name of "Sahajrām's place", became the often frequented *caumāsā*[20] sojourn of the Dādūpanthī abbots-in-chief. Jogīdās and Sahajrām seem not to have been *nāgās*.[21] The increasing military impact of the Dādūpanthī *nāgā*s, however, must have contributed to the prestige of the abbots-in-chief, themselves never *nāgās*, and the entire community. Although factually dating much earlier, the official constitution of the Dādūpanthī militant ascetics took allegedly place in 1755.[22] As mentioned before, as an organisation they

17 The Kachavāhās thus worship four deities as attached to their dynasty, namely (1) Sītārām, (2) Govinddevjī, (3) the clan goddess Jamvā Mātājī, and (4) the territorial goddess Śilā Devī. Clémentin-Ojha, *L'affaire des tilaka*, p. 28, 38–9.

18 For the best comprehensive history see William G. Orr, *A Sixteenth-Century Indian Mystic* [*Dadu and His Followers*], London and Redhill 1947.

19 DK 32: 565–7, for the years 1753ff.

20 The period of the rainy season when the Dādūpanthī monks observe *stabilitas loci* with a lay or monk community, who invite them for this.

21 DPP 2: 122 identifies Sahajrām as a member of the Dādūpanthī lineage of Maskīn which stems from one of Dādū's sons but lost power at the centre of the Dādūpanth around 1693.

22 DPP 3: 32.

kept separate from the Vaiṣṇava *vairāgīs*. Like all other *nāgās* they, too, operated also outside of eastern Rajasthan. In Jaipur, Gaṅgārām established the lineage of the *jamāt* of Nivāī, to this day the most prestigious branch of Dādūpanthī *nāgās*, which, in its turn, split into several lineages. Gaṅgārām occurs in the Jaipur court protocol from V. S. 1825/AD 1768 toV. S. 1829/ AD 1772.[23]

Dādūpanthīs fought with distinction in the battle of Khāṭū (1779), by which the imperial forces tried to coerce Jaipur to pay its arrears of tribute. Gaṅgārām's disciple Maṅgaldās, who died in that battle, represents the Dādūpanth's paragon of heroism and loyalty. With or subsequent to, that battle the Dādūpanthīs emerged as a major military force. Around the time of the battle of Lālsoṭ (1787),[24] which added to the prestige of the Dādūpanthī *nāgās*, Maṅgaldās's disciple built the *havelī* of the Nivāī-*jamāt* at Jaipur (near Rāmgañj)[25] which reflects the *nāgās* intensified contact with the Jaipur court. In 1797 the Dādūpanthīs were made a regular contingent of the Jaipur army. They proved their loyalty to the court during the Mutiny of 1857, but thence, due to the political and military changes, turned quickly insignificant as a military factor.

In the present paper I have focused on the protocol which refers to the heads of the religious institutions, and that is, for the Dādūpanthīs, their abbots-in-chief, although the attention given to them by the court was largely determined by the military potential provided by the *nāgās*.

2. The court protocol

The court protocol of Jaipur is named the *Dastūr komvār* (DK), "Rules applying to the people". Comprising 32 volumes, these records were excerpted by the administration of Jaipur State from the loose leaf records (*taujīh*) and cover mainly the years 1718–1918.[26] Written in the chancery Ḍhūṇḍhārī of the Kachavāhā state, they record the relations of the court with its own subjects or with foreigners and are arranged by the names of individuals, including the names of deities. Under the names there are recorded in chronological order the instances of ceremonial intercourse. These instances are of basically two types. The first one represents the minutes of personal encounters between the king or his deputy/deputies and those individuals, while the

23 From 1768 his 700 *nāgās*, more than 20 horses and 5 camels are listed to have been sustained by the court which cost c. 3,000 rp. a month (DK 31: 492–5).

24 See p. 145.

25 W. Orr, *A Sixteenth-Century Mystic* ..., p. 202: 1787–88; Rāmprasād, the *mahant* of Nivāī: 1786 (personal communication, March 1985).

26 V. S. Bhatnagar, *Life and Times of Sawai Jai Singh, 1688–1743*, Delhi 1974, p. 351–2 for the period covered by DK and a brief description of its arrangement. The period of V. S. 1649 to 2000 is, however, given by Anonymous, *A Preliminary Guide to the Rajasthan State Archives*. Bikaner, n. d., p. 21.

second type records ceremonial gifts sent by the court to individuals without implying royal presence. The first type is complex in representing a combination of generally all the salient, subtle aspects of ceremonial exchange, whereas the second type of minutes records the date and item given, which may, but need not, include information on the occasion and the value of the item of gift. The first type of minutes is clearly of a more narrative kind and thus more immediately informative as one tries to find out about the differential treatment given to various individuals.

The minutes of personal encounters have a relatively fixed pattern which can be abstracted as follows:

Date, place, occasion
Persons involved
Modes of approach
Greeting
Accommodating the guest, modes of seating and sitting of host and guest, resp.
Gifts made by the king or his deputy; value of the gift recorded more often than not
Duration of stay/conversation
Reciprocating gifts
Modes of departure

The following quotation provides an example.[27]

Jugrāj Govindānandjī, disciple of Mahant Bālānandjī
V. S. 1839

On Monday, Śrāvaṇa b. 8, at Savāī Jaipur, His Majesty, mounted on horse, passed Jorāvarsiṅgh kau darvāzā and [entered] Jomharī kī bagīcī. Śrī Gurmahant Mahārāj Govindānandjī was on his way to Gāzī kā thānā. He sojourned in the *tibārā*[28] of Hīrānand Jomharī kī bagīcī. His Majesty approached, prostrated himself full-length and sat down on a *masnad* (throne cushion, throne). He gave his *bheṭ*[29] of two gold coins and one coconut to Śrī Gurmahant Mahārāj Govindānandjī. He stayed one and a half *gharī*s (= 36 minutes).[30] Then Mahant Mahārāj Govindānandjī and His Majesty set out from there. They mounted the howdahs of separate elephants. The Mahantjī's elephant was made to head [the cortege], His Majesty's elephant followed. This is how they

27 All translations are by the author.

28 A hall with three doors.

29 A complimentary gift; here: the present given to a religious person, which, if reciprocated, is reciprocated b *prasād*, a gift of grace.

30 A *gharī* is 24 minutes.

> went. Proceeding from parapet gate His Majesty talked for a while to the Mahantjī and then entered Sarah Dyoṛhī[31] (DK 31: 480–1)

a) Death and investiture of religious leaders

i) Custodians of Govinddevjī

In the period under review three investitures of *adhikārīs* took place. In 1781 Kisansaraṇ (Kṛṣṇaśaraṇ) was designated junior *gosvāmī* and successor of Gosvāmī Balrām. On this occasion the court sent him and his family gifts worth 240 rp. They consisted of a necklace (150 rp.), 1 shawl (*dusālo*) for Kisansaraṇ and a gold coin (*mohur, muhar*) and a coconut each for himself and Balrām's wife (80 rp.) (DK 5: 292–3).

Kisansaraṇ died in 1806. He was granted a funeral cortege of

> an elephant bearing the flag
> a horse bearing the drum (*naqāra*)
> a caparisoned horse
> an elephant with a howdah for the distribution of sweets
> a band of musicians "and other items".

In a torchlight procession Kisansaraṇ's body was taken by boat to the ghat in the vicinity of the Govinddevjī temple where it was cremated in the presence of Roḍārām Khavās, the king's closest confidant, the *dīvāns* and other courtiers. The ceremony would have required the presence of Mahārāja Jagatsiṅgh, who, however, at that time happened to be in Jodhpur (DK 5: 298). The king did, however, attend Kisansaraṇ's *mātamī*, the condolence ceremony which was often accompanied by the investiture of a successor to the office of the deceased person. Kisansaraṇ's successor, Rāmnārāyaṇ, whose investiture is not recorded, died in 1822 and was granted the same funeral cortege as his predecessor but for the horse bearing the drum missing which is probably due to a copying mistake, for his cremation is stated to have been performed "according to the rules", *muvāphik dastūr* (DK 5: 541–2), which were also observed in 1825, when Govindnārāyaṇ died. He had been adopted by Rāmnārayaṇ's widow which entitled him to succeed to the custodianship. On that occasion the king with his nobility, officers and retinue of other courtiers should have been present. However, as he was a minor, he was represented "according to the rules" by his sword, which was carried by the highest-ranking noble (DK 5: 326–7).

ii) Rāmānandī nāgās

Svāmī Bālānand succeeded to the abbotship in 1752, two days after the death of his predecessor Virjānand. This was commemorated by the court by a three-piece robe of honour, *siropāv,*

[31] The palace area.

which cost 97 rp. 12a. and was sent to Bālānand (DK 31: 669–70). His investiture was not attended by the king, Mādhosiṅgh, who sent him a horse with twelve items of caparison (no value mentioned).[32] Only about four months later the king and his nobles are recorded to have visited the new abbot. The king offered him ten gold coins and two coconuts, and in return Bālānand gave to each of the party a shawl (*dupaṭo*) and *prasād* after which the king had the *darśan* of the deity and departed for his palace (DK 31: 671). The standard *bheṭ* would consist of one gold coin and one coconut. Ten gold coins mark an extraordinary event, while the two coconuts were probably meant for the deity and for Bālānand.

Bālānand died in 1794. On that day the king, Pratāpsiṅgh, visited his place for the *mātamī* visit. Five days later there took place the investiture of Bālānand's successor Govindānand. He had been designated *jugrāj*, designated abbot,[33] fourteen years earlier and, a year after his designation, had given his *gurudīkṣā*, initiation, to Pratāpsiṅgh which had made him the king's *gurmahant.* The king applied the *mātamī ṭīkāṭ* to him, presented him with a five-piece robe of honour, put a pearl necklace round his neck and gave him an elephant-chain (?)[34] (DK 31: 490). A similar procedure was followed when Govindānand was succeeded by Gambhīrānand in 1805.[35]

iii) Dādūpanthīs

On the death of a Dādūpanthī abbot-in-chief and the investiture of his successor the court sent a *mātamī* gift of two woolen *thirmā*s with floral motifs,[36] 100 rp. and a horse, as is recorded for Svāmī Dalairām, who succeeded Jīvandās in 1820 (DK 31: 594). *Thirmā*s figure prominently in standard ceremonial gifts and they can also form part of sets of robes of honour. As for the Dādūpanthīs, if only one item of gifts was presented to a Dādūpanthī monk or abbot, it was a pair of *thirmā*s.

b) Festivals

The Mahārāja participated in the festivals of the family of Govinddevjī's custodians. Thus in 1783 Pratāṅsiṅgh attended those of Kisansaraṇ's wedding ceremonies which were performed at Jaipur. Accompanied by his nobles, officers and retinue of courtiers, he came on horseback. As he entered Kisansaraṇ's place, silk and satin cloth was spread on his entrance way. He sat on a *masnad* and watched the women's (*bhagataṇī*s', "woman devotees"') dance. He and his com-

32 Mārgaśiras ś. 13, V. S. 1809.

33 Also "heir apparent".

34 *Haṭhanī jyāt kī jaṃgīr.*

35 Cited from DK [31; p. not given] in "Nagar parikramā" of *Rājasthān patrikā*, 9th Oct. 1996.

36 Precious pileless cloth.

pany were treated to a festive meal. The visit lasted the long period of 2 hours (5 *gharīs*). When Kisansaran returned from the wedding ceremonies at his in-laws's, he was received by the *dīvāns* in the garden by the ghat[37] (DK 5: 283–4).

The king would also attend the *mātamī* ceremonies at the death of a *gosvāmī's* father as well as the weddings of his sons, daughters and nephews when he also made presents of money.

Among the seasonal festivals, two are mentioned in the regnal period of Pratāpsiṅgh. In 1782 the Rāmānandī *jugrāj* Govindānand presented the *rakṣābandhan* to him, and in 1801 the birthday of Kṛṣṇa was observed by a gift of 2 *thirmās* (41 rp.) to Govinddevjī's custodian Kisansaraṇ.[38] No private or seasonal festivals are mentioned in connection with the Dādūpanthīs.

c) Meeting a religious dignitary

The etiquette observed when paying a visit to or receiving a religious dignitary and when meeting him en route varied considerably so that the three types of encounters require separate treatment.

(1) Paying a visit to a religious dignitary, which included taking the *darśan* of the temple image and/or the dignitary had the following basic pattern:

The king (alone or with retinue) approaches on horseback and alights
He offers the dignitary his *bheṭ* (one or more than one gold coin and coconuts)
He takes the *darśan* of the temple image (if there is one)
In return he receives the dignitary's *prasād*, namely, a shawl and consecrated food
He mounts his horse (and rides back to his palace).[39]

The more elaborate descriptions of the king's visits to religious dignitaries add details of etiquette which concern the way in which the royal guest was received, seated and entertained. A visit of Mahārāja Pratāpsiṅgh to abbot Bālānand and his designated successor, Govindānand, in 1782 went as follows.[40] His Majesty betook himself to the Mahantjī in order to take his meal at his place. First, however, he took *darśan* of the image of Raghunāthjī (one of the deities of Hanumān Gaṛhī – MH). He made a *bheṭ* of one gold coin and one coconut. Then he went to Bālānandjī, who sat on a rug (*jājam*, a rug with floral motifs) in the courtyard of the threshold

[37] Probably the ghat in the vicinity of the Govinddevjī temple.

[38] DK 31: 482; DK 5: 297.

[39] Instances of this type of encounter are, for example, Mādhosiṅgh's visit to the Rāmānandī Bālānand (V. S. 1809; DK 31: 670–1) and Pṛthvīsiṅgh's and the crown-prince's visit to the Dādūpanthī Cainrām (V. S. 1832 and DK 31: 528).

[40] For the sake of brevity the following paraphrase omits the full titles of the persons referred to. For these cp. the passage quoted on p. 146.

of the upper-storey pavilion, where the king joined him. He made his full-length prostration, gave him a *bheṭ* of two gold coins and one coconut and stayed with him for 1 *ghaṛī*. Then he went to his *gurmahant* Govindānand. He was made to sit on a *masnad* in the upper mansion above the gateway of the temple. [...] Govindānandjī was sitting on his *gaddī* (mattress, seat), which had been arranged opposite the *masnad*. The king gave his *bheṭ* of one gold coin and one coconut. Govindānandjī gave him a shawl (*dupaṭo*) and *prasād*. His Majesty stayed with him for one *ghaṛī* and then betook himself to eat in the same place. He ate in the company of his nobles and retinue. After the meal he betook himself to Bālānandjī and stayed with him for a *ghaṛī*. Then he rode back to his palace (DK 31: 481).

In 1800 Pratāpsiṅgh went to see off the Dādūpanthī abbot-in-chief, Nirbhairām, who had spent his *caumāsā* in Jaipur. The king was again seated on a *masnad* opposite the abbot's *gaddī*. Nirbhairām received the *bheṭ* of one gold coin, one coconut, and two *thirmā*s (55 rp.) while remaining seated. He stood up to don the king with a shawl (*dusālo*) and to give him *prasād*. Then the king took leave and rode back to his palace (DK 31: 639).

(2) Receiving a religious dignitary, as reported for Govindānand's visit to Mahārāja Pratāpsiṅgh in 1783 (DK 31: 482–3). The Mahārāja received him standing. Govindānand was given a seat on top of two *gaddī*s, mattresses, cushions and presented with the obligatory cold coin and coconut. On another visit in 1788 Govindānand was accompanied by Himat (Himmat) Bahādur, the powerful leader of the *saṃnyāsī nāgās*.[41] Govindānand sat to the right of the king on two *gaddī*s, while Himat Bahādur was given a single one below Govindānand's (DK 31: 483–4). No visits are recorded either for the custodians of Govinddevjī or for the Dādūpanthīs.

(3) Meetings en route occurred often. Dignitaries would leave Jaipur and return; those resident elsewhere might spend some time in Jaipur, such as Dādūpanthīs during the *caumāsā* period. The custodians of Govinddevjī went to Vrindaban regularly. Especially right after their investiture a visit to Vrindaban seems to have been the established custom. Rāmānandīs and Dādūpanthīs were engaged in warfare and therefore very mobile. The general rule was that on their arrival the dignitaries would be received either by the Mahārāja or his deputies. The paraphernalia accorded to an arriving, passing or leaving dignitary and the vehicle and precedence he would enjoy were publicly visible and hence prominent distinguishing markers of rank.

(a) Govinddevjī

When Govinddevjī's custodian went to Vrindaban or elsewhere, he was seen off in the garden by the ghat of the temple. This was the task of the minister. At that time the same ex-

[41] Cp. Jadunath Sarkar, *A History of Dasnami* ..., *passim*.

change of ceremonial gifts took place as at the time of the king's visit to the custodian.[42] When a custodian returned, alone or in company, the same procedure was followed.[43]

(b) Rāmānandī *nāgās*

When in 1780 (Kārtika ś. 7, V. S. 1837) Bālānand was on his way to the Vinodīlāl temple near Cāndpol Gate,[44] Mahārāja Pratāpsiṅgh met him in the garden outside Cāndpol Gate and stayed with him for one *gharī*. When they prepared for proceeding to the Vinodīlāl temple, Bālānand was asked to mount the howdah of an elephant while the king followed him in his *nālkī*, a closed sedan-chair with an arched roof. At the temple the abbot alighted from the elephant, [both] took *darśan* of the deity. The king stayed there for two and a half *gharī*s and than returned to his palace on horseback (DK 31: 677–8). If both the king and the abbot were seated in elephant howdahs, the Mahārāja's elephant followed that of the abbot. On entering a temple, both would alight and mount a sedan-chair, the abbot a *pālkī*, and the king a *nālkī*, which followed the abbot's *pālkī*.[45]

(c) Dādūpanthīs

By the time of Nirbhairām, that is, in the regnal periods of Mahārājas Pratāpsiṅgh and Jagatsiṅgh, the abbot-in-chief had made it a habit to often spend his *caumāsā* in Jaipur. The following ceremonial reception had become the rule, as is, for example, reported for the year 1799, when he came with his designated successor (*adhikārī*) and retinue. The king's deputy, Rūpcand, who was Darogā of the Palace, met him outside the city at Ḍālān kau kuṇḍau, from where he was led to his sojourn via Motī Ḍuṅgrī. The cortege consisted of an elephant bearing the five-coloured flag,[46] an Arab horse and a horse bearing the *naqāra.*

A little more than a month later the crown-prince called upon Nirbhairām. The visit followed the pattern described earlier.[47] The crown-prince was seated on a *masnad* opposite the *gaddī,* on which the abbot was and remained sitting. The crown-prince's *bheṭ* consisted of two gold coins (one for Nirbhairām and one for his *adhikārī*) and a coconut, and the abbot returned this by a shawl (*dupaṭo*) and *prasād.* Then the crown-prince presented the young *adhikārī*, Jīvandās, on his nomination to that rank with [a pair of] woolen *thirmā*s (33 rp. 6 a.), after which the prince departed for his palace (DK 31: 638–9).

42 Reported, for example, for Kisanśaraṇ, 1783; DK 5: 284 (Jyeṣṭha b. 5, V. S. 1840).

43 Reported for Govindnārāyaṇ accompanied by his mother, 1833; DK 5: 329 (Āṣāḍha ś. 8, V. S. 1880). The usual *bheṭ* was also given to Govindnārāyaṇ's mother.

44 DK 31: 681 for the locality.

45 DK 31: 690–81 for V. S. 1846.

46 Both the Kachavāhās and the Dādūpanthīs have a five-coloured flag.

47 Cp. p. 149.

At the end of his *caumāsā* the abbot-in-chief would be bid farewell by the Mahārāja himself, who presented him with a *bheṭ* of gold coin, coconut and a pair of *thirmā*s (55 rp.).[48] During minority rule, the king would be represented by the cortege of nobles headed by the Minister bearing the royal sword, which was placed on the *masnad*.[49]

A rather unusual situation arose when in 1832 another farewell ceremony was due, and it was therefore commented in greater detail than any previous one. The meeting was between Dalairām, abbot-in-chief, and the minor, thirteen-year old Mahārāja Jaisiṅgh III. The record reflects the attention which was given to minute details which are otherwise not spelt out.

> In the *havelī* of Mahant Govinddās,[50] in the *tibārā* in the outer courtyard of the entrance gateway of the *havelī*, there was sitting the *mahant* on a *galīcā* (a rug with floral motifs). He did not pay obeisance to the Mahārājā, because according to the custom neither does the Mahārājā pay obeisance to him nor he to the Mahārājā. He (Jaisiṅgh – MH) stepped over to him and sat down on the same [*galīcā*]. He made a full-length prostration on which the *mahant* blessed him.

The account then records the usual exchange of *bheṭ* and *prasād* (DK 597–8).

3. Conclusion

The protocol was enacted before an audience and as such it confirms the public ranking of the actors involved.[51] The protocol follows rules which were worked out by the court.[52] Over and over again is it emphasised that a given procedure is in accordance with the prevailing rules. This, of course, does not mean that these rules were inflexible, but it clearly implies that departures from an established rule required careful consideration.

The relations as they are expressed by the protocol follow patterns or rather represent subtly adjustable configurations of elements. These are, however, no simple linear patterns of increment or decrement which would be indicative of rank, say, a horse more or less in the cortege of a dignitary. Linear indicators do exist, but used exclusively they would have been a poor tool and failed an important function of the protocol, namely, marking precedence *and at the same time* keeping the structural balance between different and asymmetrical relations. The pattern of the protocol is, therefore, variable and adjustable to the particular conditions which apply to

48 DK 31: 639 for V. S. 1857.

49 DK 31: 595–6 for V. S. 1880.

50 The Jaipur residence of the Dādūpanthī *mahant* of Rāmgaṛh where Dalairām spent his *caumāsā*.

51 Stewart Gordon, "Robes of Honour: A 'Transactional' Kingly Ceremony," *The Indian Economic and Social History Review* 33 (3), 1996, p. 225–42, draws attention to the presence of an audience as a distinguishing feature of the robe of honour ceremonies.

52 The procedures involved in this require further research.

a person. Thus, not to grant a funeral cortege can mark the deceased person's and/or his institution's hierarchical position, but it can also be in conformity with the deceased person's status in life other than the hierarchically defined one. For a monk, for example, a pompous funeral cortege would be easily inappropriate because during his lifetime he was, religiously speaking, no longer part of the world. Therefore, the protocol does not evolve from principles applicable independently of the individual conditions applying to the person concerned.

The nucleus of the protocol as it applied to the three groups of dignitaries is an act of exchange, namely *bheṭ* (gold coin, coconut, additional gifts), which was given by the king, against the religious dignitary's *prasād* (shawl and *prasād* proper). This exchange of "gift" against "gift of grace" is a precisely defined religious act. *Bheṭ* is given by a layman and *prasād* by a religious functionary, though not necessarily a monk. This nucleus implies a behaviour which, for the time of its enactment, relegates the king to an inferior position *vis-à-vis* the religious functionary. The king makes a full-length prostration, then stands up, while the religious dignitary remains seated until he, too, stands up to give the king his *prasād*. Giving the *prasād* in an upright position indicates respect for the king, for to ordinary people *prasād* may be given while being seated.

Consequently, that nucleus is found to be missing in events outside the binary structure of layman vs. religious functionary. In this respect the relationship between the king and the custodian of Govinddevjī is a telling example. As a religious dignitary, and exclusively in that function, the nuclear religious protocol is applicable to him. Beyond his strictly religious function, however, and as a *gṛhastha*, he enjoys a position which makes him eligible to socially mix with the king and his court, though it hardly needs to be emphasised that the impact of the office bears on his entire social standing. As a guest, the king takes part in the custodian's festivities, and in this respect the custodian enjoys the position of a noble. The Rāmānandī *nāgā*s and the Dādūpanthīs are, as far as the protocol goes, barred from this kind of social intercourse. The Dādūpanthīs are, however, granted a *caumāsā* cortege in which, though in less grand a configuration, symbols occur that also mark the funeral cortege of the custodian of Govinddevjī, namely, an elephant bearing the flag, a horse bearing the *naqārā*, and an Arab horse.

The funeral cortege for Govinddevjī's custodian and the *caumāsā* cortege for the Dādūpanthī abbot differ not only in size, but in another significant feature, namely, the presence or absence of the king himself. The investiture of a new custodian of Govinddevjī requires the presence of the king. Also in the case of the Rāmānandī *nāgā*s the king's presence is a noticeable feature. While he was absent when Bālānand succeeded to the abbotship, he attended the investiture of Govindānand, whose position of the king's *gurmahant*, however, constituted a special relationship with the king. Never, however, was the investiture of a Dādūpanthī abbot-in-chief attended by the king. The king's presence is an element of the protocol which is minutely recorded by the exact duration of the king's interlocution or sojourn with a person. The royal presence being so significant, it is never recorded if he is replaced by a deputy. Therefore, the duration of the king's sojourn is a supremely and uniquely relevant indicator of rank. Whereas his stay at the custodian's or the Rāmānandī *nāgā* abbot's was often extended,[53] it was normally brief in the case of Dādūpanthīs and lasted only around a quarter of an hour.[54]

The inferior rank displayed by the king while he offers *bheṭ* is neutralised immediately afterwards by the way the royal and religious interlocutors are seated. They sit opposite each other, face to face, the king on the *masnad* and the religious dignitary on his *gaddī*. Although the rank accorded to a distinguished religious dignitary in the presence of the king was displayed in an especially ostensible fashion in the case of the Rāmānandī *nāgā* abbot when the king would cede precedence to the abbot in making him ride on an elephant while following him in a *nālkī*, the king did, however, not cede his precedence to the abbot completely, for when following the abbot who rode in a *pālkī*, he would follow him in his royal *nālkī*. Never were the two conveyances exchanged. The distinction between the realm of the king and that of the religious functionary was never blurred.

From the data it seems conclusive that the rank accorded to Govinddevjī's custodian and the Rāmānandī *nāgā* abbot by far excelled that of the Dādūpanthī abbot-in-chief, a result actually foreseeable from other known historical facts. The relationship between Govinddevjī's custodian and the king is vital, for none can fulfil his function properly without the other. The custodian's investiture requires the presence of the king and the king's coronation the presence of the custodian.[55] The relationship between the king and the Rāmānandī *nāgā* abbot is different. The abbot is part of the ritual of the king's coronation, but his authority derives from the ritual function of the more ancient Rāmānandīs of Galtā, the caretakers of the *śālagrāma* worship.[56] The distinction that he received during the period under review was rather caused by the king's political and personal dependence on him, but had not been sanctioned by the established royal ritual.

Although the rank of the Dādūpanthīs was comparatively inferior, the protocol accorded to them stressed elements of their identity which to them were of unique importance. For the Dādūpanthīs the *caumāsā* of their abbot-in-chief is one of the two prominent festive and ritual occasions in the religious year of the group, the second one being the several-week long gathering (*melā*) of the Dādūpanth at the group's holy places which takes place in spring. It is during this gathering that the host of the current year's *caumāsā* is announced. Hosting the abbot dur-

[53] Cp. p. 150.

[54] See, for example, DK 31: 637 for V. S. 1844.

[55] Cp. p. 144, 147.

[56] Cp. p. 143, 144.

ing his *caumāsā* is the greatest honour a Dādūpanthī can attain. The court protocol inserted itself in this specific custom and accorded to the abbots-in-chief an ostensible, though, comparatively speaking, not a unique, cortege and two visits by the king, one some time after the abbot's arrival and the second one on his departure. Within the ritual value system of the Dādūpanthīs themselves, this meant great distinction and recognition of customs which were essential to them, whereas it would range less prominently in a comparative perspective.

Mahārājas of Jaipur and Religious Dignitaries[1]

Mahārājas of Jaipur	**Custodians of Govinddevjī**	**Rāmānandī nāgās**	**Dādūpanthīs**
Mādhosiṅgh I 1750–68	Kisansaraṇ 1788–1806	Bālānand 1752–94	Cainrām 1753–80
Pṛthvīsiṅgh 1768–78			
Pratāpsiṅgh 1778–1803		Govindānand 1794–1805	Nirbhairām 1780–1814
Jagatsiṅgh 1803–1818	Rāmnārāyaṇ 1807–22	Gambhīrānand 1805–1825	Jīvandās 1814–20
Jaisiṅgh III b. 1819–d. 1835 (minority rule)	Govindnārāyaṇ 1823–25		Dalairām 1820–40

[1] The spelling of names, which varies according to the sources, is in conformity with *Dastūr komvār*.

Iconographic Remarks on some Folios of the Oldest Illustrated Kṣemakarṇa Rāgamālā

Joachim Karl Bautze

Kṣemakarṇa worked for Rāja Rām Cand of Rewa in Madhya Pradesh and in 1570 AD compiled a theoretical text on a *rāgamālā* which is hence known as Kṣemakarṇa's Rāgamālā. Kṣemakarṇa's system basically consists of 84 imageries: There are 6 [male] *rāga*s, each with 5 [female] *rāgiṇī*s and eight *putra*s [sons]. Most of the illustrated *rāgamālā*s following Kṣemakarṇa's system of classification stem from the so-called Pahari area, where the probably oldest survivors do probably not predate the 1670s.

Though Kṣemakarṇa's system was not unknown by name earlier this century, the credit goes to Ernst Waldschmidt for having first analysed and published the relationship between Kṣemakarṇa's text and the Pahari *rāgamālā*s.[1] Waldschmidt rather unfortunately did not publish the complete text of Kṣemakarṇa's compilation. At times he just summarised an English translation of the respective *dhyāna* or iconographic text rather than quoting the original text in full. This he mostly did when the painting showed but little correspondence to Kṣemakarṇa's iconographic part of the text, which was quite often the case.[2]

The *rāgamālā* of which we want to introduce 8 paintings out of many more that we have seen is outstanding for a number of reasons:

(1) Until recently it was practically unknown.

(2) It predates all other *rāgamālā*s following Kṣemakarṇa's system.

[1] E. and R. L. Waldschmidt, *Musikinspirierte Miniaturen aus der Sammlung des Museums für Indische Kunst Berlin. Teil 1: Rāgamālā-Bilder aus dem westlichen Himalaya Gebiet*, Wiesbaden 1966; English edition: *Miniatures of Musical Inspiration in the Collection of the Berlin Museum of Indian Art. Part 1: Rāgamālā-Pictures from the Western Himālaya Promontory*, Wiesbaden 1967.

[2] E. and R. L. Waldschmidt, *Miniatures of Musical Inspiration*, p. 41: "It occurred but rarely that a closer relationship between the painting and the text was discernible" [all quotes from Waldschmidt's book follow the 1967 English edition].

(3) Each of its folios is inscribed with Kṣemakarṇa's iconographic text.[3]

(4) Its illustrations follow Kṣemakarṇa's text (*dhyānas*) more closely than any other known comparable *rāgamālā*.

(5) The artist cared but little for the visualisation of the source of voice or sound to which the music is compared in verses 98–109 of Kṣemakarṇa's text.

It is probably this *rāgamālā* which R. K. Tandan already mentioned in 1983: "[…] and at least one outstanding c. 1615 AD *rāgamālā* known to the author, and possibly from North Deccan, are also based on Kshemakarna's System".[4] Tandan in collaboration with Saryu Doshi published a note on this *rāgamālā* in a recent edition of *Marg*.[5] The mere fact that the Prince of Wales Museum of Western India in Bombay acquired and published at least one folio from this *rāgamālā*[6] and that the late Karl Khandalavala reportedly lectured on it in New York may account for the great importance of this highly attractive set.

The folios of this *rāgamālā* measure approximately between 22.2 and 22.6 cms x 30.1 cms (height precedes width as with all other mentioned measurements in this article).[7] The size of the paintings varies. Text and painting are not separated from each other, they both appear on the recto, the verso is generally uninscribed. The text is written in Nāgarī script. The *rāgamālā* is said to consist of altogether 86 folios, which were apparently still united when found "in a private collection near Udaipur".[8] The pagination of *rāgiṇī* Kauṅkaṇī seems to sustain this statement (see below).

The first folio of this *rāgamālā* naturally illustrates *rāga* Bhairava (fig. 1). It measures 14.0 x 21.0 cms and is numbered "1" in the lower right corner of the folio. The inscription is in three lines, it starts: "Śrī kṛṣṇāya namaḥ (reverence to Krishna), *rāgamālā* likhyate ([the] *rāgamālā* is described [thus])". What follows is precisely Kṣemakarṇa's iconographic description of this *rāga*, in the translation quoted by Waldschmidt: "Of white body, with a white dress, bearing the moon on his head, with a horn as a (wind-)instrument, a string of pearls put on, arisen from the lotus-like mouth of Śambhu (Śiva), his throat filled with (coloured by) poison, red-eyed is Bhairava. He carries the spear (trident), the skull(-bowl), has in both of his ears rings made of

[3] In most other illustrated *rāgamālās*, especially those from the Pahari-area, only the name of the illustration and the rank within the system are mentioned. The only other fully inscribed *rāgamālā* of uncertain origin (Deccan?) only quotes a certain number of Kṣemakarṇa's verses on several folios, cf. J. Bautze, *Lotosmond und Löwenritt. Indische Miniaturmalerei*, Stuttgart 1991, p. 123.

[4] R. K. Tandan, *Pahari Ragamalas*, Bangalore 1983, p. 46, fn. 5.

[5] R. K. Tandan and S. Doshi, "A Ragamala Series," *Marg* 34 (3), n. d. [1984], p. 96–8.

[6] Acc. no. 82. 3; cf. M. Chandra, *Indian Art*, Bombay 1987 (Fourth Revised Edition), Plate LII.

[7] The measurements given in R. K. Tandan and S. Doshi, "A Ragamala Series," p. 97 differ slightly.

[8] R. K. Tandan and S. Doshi, "A Ragamala Series," p. 97.

lotus and jewels, a (third) pupil, a mass of braided hair; in autumn he (this musical mode) is sung by the host of gods".[9] The text ends: "1 iti bhairava" ([this is] Bhairava, 1).

The artist has followed this description word by word. Shiva's body is white, the sickle of the moon hovers in front of his head, the horn ("śṛṅgavādya") can be seen in his left hand. It is a slightly curved black horn of some animal, perhaps some sort of deer, but certainly not from a buffalo as Waldschmidt suggested. Śiva has put on several strings of pearls in red and black. His neck is in fact coloured dark in accordance with the incident which gave Śiva the name of Nīlakaṇṭha ("the one with the blue throat"). His eyes are in fact red in the corners, he carries the trident with his left hand a bowl with his right. This bowl ("*kapāla*" in the text) should actually be made of a skull but resembles here more a pot or lota. His earring is made of a dried pistil of a lotus flower, the third eye on his forehead and the masses of hair on his head are quite evident. In addition to this description Śiva wears the skin of a tiger and a garland made of human skulls (*muṇḍamālā*). Śiva is placed against a lilac background between two trees and a stool (*caukī*) in front of him. The tree behind him is a mango-tree. His wooden sandals are red as are the blossoms of several flowers around him.

Fig. 2 introduces the "Velāvalī, the third *rāgiṇī* of Bhairava" as the third line of the description informs us (size of the painting, including the pinnacle on top of the building: 15.2 x 20.5 cms, German private collection). The preceding text quotes Kṣemakarṇa's stanza 15, which Waldschmidt summarises as "a woman whose eyes are darkened with lampblack and anointed with the oil of sesame, whose tip of the nose is adorned with a pearl, on whose forehead a beauty-mark is shining, who is of fair complexion and wears a bright garment, whose tress is decorated with *campaka* and *ketakī* blossoms, who holds a lump of betel (*vīṭikā*) in the hand, and exhales various fragrances".[10] The folio is accordingly numbered "4".

Certain passages of this stanza are hard to illustrate. The eyes of the women are generally coloured with lampblack ("*kajjala*" in the text) and the oil of sesame on her skin is also difficult to show. But the tip of her nose is indeed adorned with a pearl, more precisely two pearls. The "beauty-mark" on her forehead is probably a dot which cannot be seen in profile. The centrally seated lady is in fact of fair complexion. She wears a red bodice, a blue skirt and a transparent sari. The ornaments on the *pallū* of her sari are probably to be identified with the mentioned variety of flowers. She holds the betel-preparation in her left hand. She is set against a yellow backdrop and has a female servant standing behind her waving a *caurī*. The whole composition is framed by architectural devices.

Folio 25 of the set is shown here under fig. 3. It represents "Caṅdrakāsa, the fifth *putra* (son) of [rāga] Mālākośika" according to the last part of the superscription. The rest of the text

9 E. and R. L. Waldschmidt, *Miniatures of Musical Inspiration*, p. 108.

10 E. and R. L. Waldschmidt, *Miniatures of Musical Inspiration*, p. 193.

quotes verse no. 36 of Kṣemakarṇa's text: "Caṅdrakasa is as bright as camphor and [a particular kind of] jasmine,[11] he is speaking (as sweet as) nectar, with leaves of [a particular creeper] as necklace,[12] holding lotus-flowers in (one) hand and a [particular kind of] spear ["*kuṅta*" in the text] (in the other hand)".

The artist followed this description as closely as possible. The man set against a brown background wears three lotus flowers in his right hand. His left hand holds some kind of scythe, presumably the "*kuṅta*" in the text. The necklace made of the leaves of the particular creeper that is mentioned in the text is not indicated as such since the man wears necklaces of white pearls and presumably one necklace made of *rudrākṣasas*. The creeper behind him should thus be interpreted as the visual presence of that particular plant. The man is of a silver-like complexion and thus visualises the cooling brightness of camphor and a particular type of jasmine very well. The servant on the threshold of the building behind Caṅdrakāsa was introduced through the artistic freedom of the painter, he is not mentioned in the text. The same applies to the peacock on the crenellated wall. This folio, now in a private collection, measures 22.2 x 29.9 cms. The painted surface, including the spire to the left, covers an area of 16.1 x 18.5 cms.

Our 4th figure represents folio 30, "Tailaṅgī, the first *rāgiṇī* of *rāga* Hiṅdol" as the third line of the inscription says. The painting measures 17.2 x 20.2 (folio: 22.1 x 30.0) cms and is kept in a German private collection. The rest of the text quotes stanza 41 of Kṣemakarṇa's text, which, for the said reasons, is only very rudimentarily summarised by Waldschmidt. Tailaṅgī, according to Kṣemakarṇa's text, is together with women, wears a dress which shines like the moon, has large black eyes, round lips, the sweet voice of a *kokila*, wearing attractive ornaments, a flower garland on her head and is "fanned by the breeze arising from excellent chowries".[13] Most of the beauty-qualities of this *rāgiṇī* were not to be painted by the artist due to the difficulty in depicting them and due to their general description, since all beautiful women have wide dark eyes, round lips or a sweet voice while wearing attractive ornaments. All other parts of the stanza, however, were transformed into the picture: The seated woman is in the company of three standing women, she receives the mild wind caused by the "chowry" of the woman standing in front of her. As such, the artist of the present painting has followed the text more

11 "*Kuṅdopam*" in the text, not in S. C. Banerji, *Flora and Fauna in Sanskrit Literature*, Calcutta 1980, p. 53.

12 That the plant from which the leaves derive is a creeper is indicated by the word "*latā*" in the text. It is however not clear, which particular creeper was meant by Kṣemakarṇa. It is not to be found in S. C. Banerji, *Flora and Fauna*, and it is certainly not a "*suryalata*" as suggested by R. K. Tandan (cf. R. K. Tandan, *Pahari Rangamalas*, p. 77).

13 E. and R. L. Waldschmidt, *Miniatures of Musical Inspiration*, p. 181; we could not follow totally the translation given by R. K. Tandan (cf. Tandan, *Pahari Ragamalas*, p. 79).

closely than any of his colleagues in the Pahari area.[14] The women are placed against a red background, while the right third of the picture is occupied by a bed-room.

Fig. 5 is part of the same *rāga* family. It is "Caṅdrabiṃba, the third *putra* (son) of *rāga* Hiṅdola" as the text in the second line of the inscription informs us. It measures 16.6 cms (including the pinnacle of the building to the right) x 22.1 cms [German private collection]. It is numbered "36" in the lower left corner. Waldschmidt summarises the *dhyāna* as follows: "The *Dhyāna* (stanza 47) depicts Candrabimba as dressed in lotus-leaves, having a lotus in his hand, wearing a garland made of various kinds of blossoms round his neck, provided with lotus-like eyes and holding an axe [? *ṭakkā*]".[15] The "*ṭakkā*" proved to be the most important attribute in the hands of the *putra* Candrabimba. It is the big drum of which his left hand holds the white rope which keeps the drum in position on his back. The "*ṭakkā*" is hence not an axe as Waldschmidt cautiously suggested. The garland around the neck of the male figure is indeed made of various flowers as the different colours suggest. He holds a lotus in his right hand. Only his dress is not made of the petals of the lotus as is mentioned in the text. The woman in front of him seems to converse with him as the position of her left hand might indicate. Both figures are set against a red background with evenly distributed flowers. The whole composition is framed again by architectural devices which transform the red background with its flowers into a red, embroidered curtain, as is the case with folio 30.

Folio 51, our fig. 6, represents "Rāma, the third *putra* of [*rāga*] Dīpaka" as quoted from the third line of the partly cancelled inscription. The painting, presently in a German private collection, measures 13.1 x 20.8 cms. The second line and the beginning of the third line were translated and transcribed by Waldschmidt: "The Rāga Rāma who, himself (Rāma), is in the forepart whereas a friend is in the rear, holds a quiver, holds a bow; fled to the shadow (of trees), having lotus-like, wide eyes he speaks to his love".[16]

The artist again followed the stanza meticulously. Bow and arrows can be seen in the *putra*'s left hand, he shoulders a quiver full of arrows. The woman behind him is the "friend in the rear" whereas the woman in front of him is meant to be his "love" to whom he gives a preparation of betel. The bed in the left part of the painting seems to indicate what would be the consequence of the frolic of Rāma with his [female] friends as shown in this picture. Kṣemakarṇa only mentions the shadow in his text but no trees as suggested by Waldschmidt. The artist placed *putra* Rāma into the shade of a palace-like structure, studded with various kinds of flowering plants set against a background of bright yellow.

14 Cf. J. Bautze, *Lotosmond und Löwenritt*, p. 127ff.

15 E. and R. L. Waldschmidt, *Miniatures of Musical Inspiration*, p. 114.

16 E. and R. L. Waldschmidt, *Miniatures of Musical Inspiration*, p. 42; R. K. Tandan's translation is here not precise (Tandan, Pahari Ragamalas, p. 85).

Fig. 7 illustrates folio 57 of the set, "*rāga* Śrī" as stated by the last words of the superscription, which starts: "Here (follows the description of) the form of *rāga* Śrī". The folio measures 22.1 x 30.0 cms. The painted surface, including the spire above the room with the throne, measures 14.9 x 20.9 cms. The rest of the text quotes stanza 68 of Kṣemakarṇa's text, it "presents Śrī as fair skinned, with a white garment, rich jewellery, and of pleasant tender body. It is said that he originates from the navel of the earth and is sung by the great beings in the hot summer and again at the fall of the days in the cool season".[17]

The description of this *rāga* is comparatively general. The artist has visualised every part of the text possible. The man seated on the bed-like furniture is in fact of white complexion and he wears an almost transparent white *cākdār jāmā*. The throne in the left part of the painting together with the *caurī*-waving attendant behind the personified form of the *rāga* remind the scholar of near contemporary representations of this *rāga* in *rāgamālā*s following other iconographic systems.[18] The artist of this Kṣemakarṇa *rāgamālā* was hence certainly aware of the iconic tradition of other *rāgamālā*s outside Kṣemakarṇa's system.

The last illustration which we would like to introduce here is "Kauṅkaṇī, the fifth *rāgiṇī* of [*rāga*] Megha" as the third line of the superscription informs us (fig. 8). The painted area, inclusive of the pinnacle on top of the building in the right hand part of the composition, measures 14.5 x 18.9 cms. The other two lines quote stanza 89 of Kṣemakarṇa's text which says "that gay Kauṃkaṇī is sung by the people in the evening [...]; furthermore, she is visualised as of white complexion, wearing a many coloured dress and a bodice; her breasts and body – we are told – are smeared with kumkuma; she has a lotus-garland round her neck, has bracelets and anklets, has a pearl in her nose, and is chewing a betel-lump".[19]

Kauṅkaṇī, being fanned by a female servant behind her, is seated on a stool facing left while wringing her hands near her left knee. She wears a blue skirt, a yellow bodice and an orange-coloured sari. She is of fair complexion and has, in full accordance with the text, a garland of lotuses around her neck. Besides, she wears the ornaments mentioned in the *dhyāna*, including a nose-ring consisting of two pearls. The position of her hands and her slightly raised head may indicate her chewing of the pan preparation. The servant behind her as well as the servant arranging the bed in the right hand part of the picture are not mentioned in the text.

17 E. and R. L. Waldschmidt, *Miniatures of Musical Inspiration*, p. 176.

18 We would like to refer here to two examples (out of many more): 1) Sotheby's N. Y., [auction catalogue of] *The Carter Burden Collection of Indian Paintings*. Wednesday, March 27, 1991, New York, lot 6, coloured (dated 1605, Chawand). Here, Śrī holds a flower, reminiscent of the two lotusses held by Śrī in our fig. 7. 2) K. Khandalavala, M. Chandra, P. Chandra, *Miniature Painting. A Catalogue of the Exhibition of the Sri Motichand Khajanchi Collection Held by the Lalit Kala Akademi*, New Delhi 1960, fig. 113 (= Chhavī, *Chhavi Golden Jubilee Volume, Bhārat Kalā Bhavan 1920–1970*, Banaras 1971, col. Plate A, facing p. 160): the attendant waves a [typically Deccani] shawl, Śrī holds a lotus in his left hand (Deccani, late 16th century).

19 E. and R. L. Waldschmidt, *Miniatures of Musical Inspiration*, p. 139.

Of this *rāgamālā*, many more folios are known to exist, particularly in private collections in the United States and in Germany. Despite rather unscholarly speculation published recently, we have to accept the fact that it is of uncertain provenance. The paintings follow a style prevalent in large parts of northern India during the first quarter of the 17th century. The rather intense colours betray a strong Rājput influence, whereas the rendering of the dresses is typical Mughal. The set belongs to a rather refined "Subimperial" or "Popular" Mughal style. A more precise location of this *rāgamālā* in terms of style and origin has to be left to future research, when more illustrations of this beautiful set are available to scholars.

Figure 1

Figure 2

Figure 3

Figure 4

Figure 5

Figure 6

Figure 7

Figure 8

Professor Henry Green (1843–1854): Assessment of the Indian Economy of the Mid-Nineteenth Century

A. R. Kulkarni

The conquest of the Maratha territories in 1818 finally brought the entire subcontinent of India directly or indirectly under the sway of the East India Company, and at least for sometime the hostilities with the indigenous powers halted. But the conquest at the same time posed new problems before the Company, namely the management of these vast territories with limited human resources at their disposal and simultaneously raising revenues from its domain not only to meet the demands of administration of the Indian territories, but also to earn some surplus to pay dividends to the share-holders of the Company.

The conquest of India generated a good deal of discussion among the political thinkers, economists and administrators. The main issue before political thinkers was "whether or not the established modes of thought were well suited to the case of India and whether or not the new conceptual formulations should be devised for its circumstances".[1] To Adam Smith "the condition of India was an intellectual problem", and he was in a puzzle how to categorise this part of the world "as an example of an expanding, stationary or declining economy". He emphatically stated that "the government of an exclusive company of merchants is perhaps the worst of all governments for any country whatever".[2]

In India, the administrators were also debating whether the Ricardian economic theories would suit India or a philosophy of Bentham would help them to achieve the greatest happiness of the greater numbers. Professor Henry Green, a member of the Bombay Educational Service between 1843 and 1854 also participated in this debate. He was contemporary of Captain Goldsmid and Captain Wingate of the Bombay Revenues Settlement and Survey Department.

[1] For detailed discussion of this debate please refer to chapter 1 of William J. Barber, *British Economic Thought and India*, Oxford 1975.

[2] *Ibid*., p. 98.

Unfortunately his full biographical details are not available, but an attempt has been made in the following pages to present a brief account of his career in India with the help of the relevant Reports of the Bombay Education Board[3] and the collection of Wingate papers deposited in the archives of the Durham University, Durham, United Kingdom.

1. Indian Years of Green

Professor Henry Green of England, it seems, was born some time in the second decade of the 19th century. He reached Bombay on 15th March, 1843 to take up his assignment as Head Master of the Surat English School on a monthly salary of Rs. 300. He was kept at the Elphinstone Institution till the end of April, 1843 to examine the current educational system in India. The well-known Marathi grammarian, Dadoba Pandurang Tarkhadkar was his assistant at the Surat School which was established in 1842.

Green was in charge of the Surat School for more than six years. The Board of Education was entirely satisfied with his management of the School. The Report for the year 1849 expressly mentions that there was a great increase in the number of pupils, from 58 in 1843 to 292 when he left the school in August 1849.[4] E. Perry, the President of the Board gave an eloquent testimony to Mr. Green in April, 1849, for the services rendered by him to the Surat School.[5] He acquired good knowledge of Gujarati and wrote a book on astronomy called, *Khagol Vidya* in Gujarati in 1850 and *A Collection of English phrases with their idiomatic Goojarathi Equivalents* (1851).

His experiences as Head of the Surat School are quite revealing. He says that the teachers in his school discharged their duties in "mechanical manners", and lamented that

> We must probably wait for an almost entirely new race of teachers …, the present school masters, generally perhaps, neither believe nor understand much that they profess to teach, but go through it as a form which is to be complied with before they are entitled to draw their pay.[6]

[3] Its members were Mr. E. Perry, President John Warden, Jagannath Shankarshet, Framjee Cowasjee, Mahomed Ibrahim Muckbe and Mr. Stovell (Secretary).

[4] *Report of the Board of Education for the Year 1849*, published in 1851, vol. 8, p. 12–13, 27. (henceforth referred to as *RBE*).

[5] "The school, which of all others in the Mofassil, is by far a largest, is under a most energetic teacher and is a fair example of what zeal and healthy interests in the cause of education can produce." 15th April 1849, *RBE*; see also A. K. Priyalkar, *Rao Bahadur Dadoba Pandurang*, Bombay 1947, p. 151, 156, 157, 170, 173, 195 for the friendly relationship between H. Green, the Head Master and Dadoba Pandurang, the Assistant Master at Surat School. He refers to such instances as how he helped students, how they enjoyed the Holi festival at Baroda, and the 'Garba' dance of Gujarati women of Surat etc. Green was fond of classical Hindustani music and Marathi 'lavani', Indian food, playing chess etc.

[6] *RBE* for 1846 (1847), vol. 6, p. 4–5. Here he cites the case of a teacher who was in the habit of telling his pupils: "You must learn these things so that you may be able to give satisfactory answers to the superinten-

The Education Board had specially brought to the favourable notice of the Government the name of Mr. Green and recommended it for the Acting Principalship of the Elphinstone Institution, in the vacancy caused by the departure of Mr. Harkness, the Principal.[7] He was in Bombay hardly for two years (1849–51) and after performing "the arduous and most important duties of Principal of the Elphinstone Institution, he joined the Poona College as Acting Professor of English Literature, in 1851 under the stewardship of Principal, Major Thomas Candy".[8]

Professor Green resigned his job of the Company's Government after a distinguished career of nearly ten years to take up a position in the Parsi Benevolent School, Bombay, in 1853 as its Principal and served it for nearly two years. The Board of Education which had repeatedly brought to the notice of the Government, the services of Mr. Green to the cause of education, paid glowing tributes to him and expressed satisfaction that he would still continue as teacher after his resignation.[9]

While in Bombay he was the President of the Students' Literacy and Scientific Society in 1853–54. In that capacity he delivered three lectures to the Society in 1853 on political Economy with reference to Indian conditions for the students of the Students' Literacy and Scientific Society at Bombay.[10] In one of his lectures, he urges that the Indian capitalists should emulate the example of England which had achieved most of the marvels of modern industry which could be attributed to the order, discipline, the admirable division of labour, the concentration and the energy of the capitalist. The Indian capitalist is for the most part a mere usurer. He appeals to the youth of India that the training they receive in America or England, should be applied to set the peasantry in India to work more efficiently adding at once to their own wealth and that of the country generally.

In the course of his lectures, he also makes a reference to the often discussed issue of the Tribute of India, and observes:

> [Tribute] A cruel drain on India. But a small matter of England. But the Industrial prosperity of England was not due to this 'tribute'. England produces services and commodities one hundred million a year – which could be easily made 150 millions a year. This is due to their immense effectiveness of their industry.

dent when he comes, but God knows whether they are true or not".

7 *RBE* for 1849 (1851), vol. 8, p. 2, 12–13.

8 RBE for 1852, vol. 10, p. 22.

9 The remarks of the Board of Education in this respect are, "the educational department has lost a man of powerful intellect, of large experience, of unbounded energy and untiring zeal. It is a consolation however, to know that though Mr. Green's services are lost to us, they are not lost to the cause of education, for his new career as Principal of the Parsi Educational Institution, a large segment of the Native community have the full benefit of his talent and experience and we warmly congratulate the Parsis, on having obtained the services of so distinguished a man". *RBE* 1852–53, p. 30.

10 H. Green, *Three Lectures on Political Economy Bombay*, Printed at the Bombay Gazette Press 1853. See pages 45–6 for a discussion on Tribute.

He further says: "The 'tribute' then, although a terrible factor for India, is of no very great importance to England."

However, he confesses that England should have been magnanimous enough to remit a large portion of its 'tribute', to pay a part of the home charges out of its own taxes and thus increase the facility for the accumulation of capital in India; relying as it so well might, that all increase of prosperity in India would react on England in the way of commerce, and reflecting that, could India be made as flourishing as the United States of America; the trade with it would be as important and as profitable as that with the Americans. As regards the founding of colony in India as well as in America, he unhesitatingly says that the founders became prosperous themselves, and added to the prosperity of the mother country by affording it valuable market.[11]

He died unexpectedly on 4th August, 1854 in Bombay. His death was very much lamented both in Bombay and Pune. In the condolence meeting held in the Students' Scientific Society, Bombay, it was his humanitarian approach that was much emphasised besides his academic attainments and activities. It was pointed out that "one of his most amiable qualities – the interest which he always manifested in his social speculations for bettering those classes of society, who most require it, he was always the poor man's advocate". While mourning his death, the Society paid glowing tributes to their President and beloved friend. In another meeting of the Society, one of Green's pupils, Mr. Kaikhoshro Hormazji paid homage to his teacher in a paper which he presented to the Society, entitled "Memoir of the Indian Career of the Late Professor Green", which was later published in a book form in 1854.[12]

The leading Marathi newspaper, *Dnyan Prakash* while publishing the news of his unexpected death paid eloquent tributes to him on behalf of the scholars and students.[13] The scholars of Pune organised a meeting of the friends and admirers of Professor Green in which it was decided to publish a commemoration volume in honour of the late Professor to keep his memory alive. In this meeting, it was emphasised that Professor Green not only endeavoured to better the lot of the people as a servant of the Government, but he also could not forget them

11 "In him your society lost a warm friend and an able advocate of its most just claims, and one moreover who possessed a very extensive acquaintance with several departments of general Literature and of science". *Proceedings of the Students' Literacy and Scientific Society, Bombay, for the years 1854–55 and 1855–56*, p. 21–3. Kaikhoshro Hormazji, *The Indian career of Professor H. Green, Published at the expense of an Admirer of the late Professor*, Bombay Gazette Press, 1854. See also *RBE* 1855, p. 32.

12 *Dnyan Prakash* a leading Marathi newspaper, says: "He (Mr. Green) was formerly Professor in Poona College. He was a learned man and a sincere teacher and so even after two years of his departure from Pune, he was constantly remembered by his pupils and colleagues. He was a benefactor of Indians, and so his death will be mourned by them, but some Britishers in the heart of their hearts would not feel so sorry about his death." Free rendering of the Marathi passage published in Issue No. 60 of the year 6, of *Dnyan Prakash*, dated 10th August, 1854.

13 *Dnyan Prakash* dated 15th August, 1854.

during his leisure period. It was quite well-known to the people of Pune that he used to discuss with flawless and appropriate arguments the subjects of which he had deep knowledge either in the meetings at his residence, or in the class-room of the college or in the public meetings. His death was thus felt as an irreparable loss to the academics of Pune, and so it was felt that it was obligatory on their part to do something to perpetuate the memory of the dear departed soul.

This was proposed by Krishna Shastri Chiplonkar, Assistant Professor of Vernacular Language in Poona College and nick-named by his students as 'Brihaspati' – a know-all person. The proposal of Krishna Shastri was accepted and it was decided to raise contributions from Green's friends, admirers and citizens to execute this plan of a commemoration volume. This appeal was responded by some scholars by paying their share immediately and ninety rupees were collected on the spot.[14]

2. Green and Revenue Settlement

About Green's interest in the revenue settlement, Francis' *Report on Indapur Settlement* says: "Professor Green, a talented public servant, a special correspondent of the Bombay Gazette reviewed the whole history and progress of the Survey settlements from their first introduction."[15]

The Wingate papers preserved in the Oriental MSS Library, Durham University[16] contain about fourteen letters of Professor Green of which two were addressed to Wingate, one to Goldsmid and the addressee of the remaining two letters could not be traced, but most probably he was Wingate. All these letters were written from Pune. They illustrate a fine piece of intellectual dialogue between an academician and an administrator, on a very vital subject namely the new revenue settlement of the Government of Bombay Presidency.

An analysis of these letters suggest that Green was a follower of the Elphinstone tradition as far as political relationship was concerned and of John Stuart Mill, the contemporary liberal economist of Britain in matters of economic policy. He did not develop any antipathy towards the British Empire; in fact, he was an imperialist like Elphinstone, but at the same time had developed a sympathetic feeling towards the people of the Deccan. He writes to Wingate in 1851: "Our feeling the matter beyond the desire for the good of the people among whom my lot has been cast, and by whose industry I live – together with, perhaps, some patriotic pride in our

[14] *Dnyan Prakash*, year 6, issue 68, dated 31st August, 1854, p. 406, columns, 1 and 2.

[15] Selection from the Records of the Bombay Govt., No. CVII, New series papers relating to the revision of the *Assessment of the Indapoor Talooka in the Poona Collectorate*, Bombay 1868 (Selections from the records of the Bombay Government, No. CVII, Bombay 1868, referred to as *Francis' Report*).

[16] The Sudan Archives, Palace Green Section, University of Durham, Durham has six boxes of Wingate papers, donated by Sir Reginald Wingate who was the Governor General of Sudan for sixteen years.

great eastern Empire and a wish that our rule over it may be such as to reflect the most possible of credit upon us."[17]

Mr. Francis in his report mentions that captain Wingate was in regular correspondence with Green while he was preparing his report.[18] Green was afraid that his correspondence packed with a number of queries, might bore Wingate and he would stop replying them. He writes: "I fear this correspondence will tire you, but pray stop it when you find it growing too troublesome with my best thanks for the kindness with which you have answered all my queries."[19] He was so fond of Wingate that when he learned about his departure from India shortly he wrote: "I am very sorry to hear that your departure is so near. I do not know how you are to be replaced in India. I hear of no one on whom your mantle is likely to fall. Which I wonder will be the best man for me to persecute with questions after you go, as I have persecuted you."[20]

The influence of John Stuart Mill, the advocate of the Classical School, on Green is reflected in his writings on economic matters, particularly in his letters to Wingate. Like Mill he too was placed in two schools – the utilitarian and that of the Saint-Simon and Auguste Comte. Mill though he was not a complete convert to socialism, his writings opened the door for social reforms.[21] With reference to the growing feud that was emerging between labour and capital in Europe, Green says "that all political economy before Mill seems to have been written with too little sympathy for the masses – to have taken too much of the point of view of the capitalists, the government and the powerful classes generally". However he feels that some of the attempts of the workmen to become their own capitalists – to undertake themselves their own management and superintendence –, would succeed in the long run.[22]

When the Company conquered territories from the Peshwa, Mountstuart Elphinstone immediately addressed himself to the task of settlement of the rights and privileges of the sardars, the jagirdars, and others rather than improving the lot of the commonalty. The same policy continued in one way or other during the period of the Government of the Company along with its experiments in revenue settlement. Green believed that the British officials were more sympathetic towards the 'sinking and decaying aristocracy'. He writes that if Government intends to support the aristocracy, it could do so only by exacting more from the mass of the people to pay the aristocracy. He refers to the principle of political economy that an aristocracy cannot maintain any portion of the people, but is supported by them. He puts the question: "What services

17 Wingate-papers, 23rd Dec. 1851.

18 *Francis' Report*, para. 85.

19 Wingate-papers, 30th Dec., 1853.

20 *Ibid.*, 18th Sept., 1852.

21 C. Gide and C. Rist, *A History of the Economic Doctrines from the Time of the Physiocrats to the Present Day*, London 1923, p. 352, 367.

22 Wingate-papers, Sept. 1852.

does it render to the nation for the portion of nation's wealth that it consumes? And if at all there are any, they are over-stated."[23]

He was so much impressed by the writings of J. S. Mill that he induced two Marathi 'compilers' to render his *Principles of Political Economy* (1848) in Marathi to educate the people of Maratha country. While officiating as Principal of the Elphinstone Institution of Bombay, he agreed to act for a short-time as Secretary of the Deccan Vernacular Translation Society of Pune in the absence of Harkness. During his tenure a native offered to translate for the society Mrs. Marcet's popular book *Conversations* on political economy published in 1817. It was believed in Britain that the science of political Economy was already complete with the publication of Ricardo's *Principles*, and so these *Principles* are now 'truisms' which could be taught in elementary schools.[24] Mrs. Marcet's book gave expositions of political economy in the form of tales or conversations, meant for schoolchildren. To the translator of Mrs. Marcet's book, Green suggested an amendment that the work should be in a popular dialogue in imitation of Mrs. Marcet, but should otherwise be founded on Mill's *Principles*. He undertook to watch the progress of the work gratuitously and superintend it generally. He furnished the native translator and his co-author with a plan and asked him to send the parts of the translation from time to time as and when they were completed. He had also suggested to treat the Political Economy of India as something special and gave instructions to study carefully the "Report" itself and Capt. Wingate's two subsequent letters.[25] The compiler and his co-author mentioned here were Hari Keshavaji Pathare, Translator in the Sadar Adalat and Vishwanth Narayan Mandalik, First Normal scholar of the Elphinstone Institution. The title page mentions that it was compiled under the supervision of H. Green Professor of Literature in the Poona College, and was published from Bombay in 1854. It also mentions that it is a free translation of Mrs. Marcet's *Conversations* and Mill's *Principles*. The Marathi title of this book is *Deshvyavahar Vyavastha*.[26]

The second compiler mentioned in Green's letter was Krishna Shastri Chiplonkar, Assistant Professor of Vernacular Literature in the Poona College. He made a free translation of J. S. Mill's *Principles of Political Economy* in Marathi under the title *Artha Shastra Paribhasha* which was published from Poona College in 1855. This was done independently of Prof. Green, but he has, it seems, carried out his instruction of giving special treatment to Indian political economy, as the author makes references to Indian conditions whenever possible. For instance while discussing the laws determining the income from land, Chiplonkar compares the land tenures in England, Scotland with that of where the Mirasi tenure of peasant proprietorship

23 *Ibid.*, Oct. 1851.

24 C. Gide / C. Rist, *A History of Economic Doctrines*.

25 Wingate-papers, 23rd Nov., 1851.

26 D. K. Bedekar (ed.), *June Marathi Artha Shastriya Grantha (1843–1855)*, Pune 1969, p. 75.

prevailed, whereas in England and Scotland the capitalists used to hire land from the land-owners with a view to making profit out of it.[27] About these two Marathi books Green says: "(They are) in a state of great forwardness, each of which will contain in substance the same account of the Revenue Settlement."[28]

3. Economic Policy of the Company

Land being the major source of revenue of the State, the Company, in its formative period of administration, was preoccupied with the various problems of land. They had realised that the revenue administration was completely broken during the last phase of the Peshwa's government and normalcy could be restored only after winning the confidence of the ryots and at the same time raising the revenue of the State. For ensuring better returns from land, the first and foremost requirement was a survey and a settlement of revenue assessment with a view to raising agricultural production, which would not only meet the cost of administration but at the same time procure some profit to the Company by increasing the supply of raw materials, particularly cotton through experiments of producing better varieties of cotton by importing seeds and technology from abroad.

The early British administrators from the days of Elphinstone, Chaplin, and others, tried to combine the Ricardian theory of rent and the utilitarianism of Bentham for resolving the problem of land, particularly at the instance of James Mill who had joined the Company as Assistant Examiner of the Indian correspondence in 1819. The first experiments in survey and settlement were made in Indapur pargana in 1828 under the supervision of R. K. Pringle, Assistant Collector of Junnar. However, Pringle's experiment failed, according to Professor Green, partly from want of the requisite experience and skill in Mr. Pringle and his subordinates and partly from the unprincipled character of the native agents employed.[29]

Francis finds the cause of its entire failure in the faulty and dishonest manner in which the classification of the soil was carried out and the crop returns prepared.[30] Revision in the assessment was, therefore, necessary to quiet the restless peasantry and stop the exodus of people from Indapur region. This task of revision was entrusted to Goldsmid who was assisted by Wingate and Davidson and a new settlement was introduced shortly in Indapur. It was during this preparatory period that Wingate must have come into contact with Professor Green, per-

27 *Ibid.*, p. 366.

28 H. Green, *Three Lectures on Political Economy*.

29 H. Green, *The Deccan Ryots and their Land Tenure*, published in Poona, Sept. 1852, p. 7.

30 *Francis' Report*, para. 12.

haps the only Professor of Political Economy who was available to him for consultation and thus started the dialogue between the academician and the administrator.

Capt. Wingate came to India in 1831 to join the Engineer corps at Surat. In 1835 he was appointed to assist Mr. Goldsmid of the Civil Services in revising the assessment of the Poone Collectorate, and it was during this period he must have met Professor H. Green of the Poona College. Green's letter of Oct. 1851 addressed as 'Sir' seems to have been written to Wingate as its internal evidence suggests. The points made by him in this very letter are of vital importance and one notices the same trend of thought continued throughout the course of his correspondence with Wingate.

Green did not ask the Government to part with its hold on the land. He, however, maintained that the collection of the actual rent from land was not objectionable, but he thought it might give rise to the tyrannical and corrupt bureaucracy to which the management of land on the part of Government was entrusted. He accused the management as shamefully shortsighted and selfish, and that its exactions had affected the capital of the country – it was like killing the goose that laid the golden eggs. The system had discouraged frugality, industry and the spirit of enterprise and improvement.

To overcome this situation he strongly recommended not the sale of land, but a moderate assessment fixed for long terms with proprietary rights to the cultivator subject to the condition that this fixed rent might be paid, regularly. He further said that the accounts system should be simplified and there should be no inter-meddling of the officials both Native and European; the system should inculcate more independent and self-relying habits on the part of the ryots.

As regards the economic development of the region his contention was, if the capital was allowed to accumulate by moderate assessments fixed for long periods, the useful arts and trades would gradually improve and a commercial and manufacturing aristocracy, an inventive, enterprising and producing aristocracy in place of the idle debauched one would emerge. Earlier he had objected to the sympathetic attitude of the Government towards the aristocracy which was not rendering any service to the society, but had become a burden on it.

He maintained that all discussion on the causes of poverty was futile and the only remedy to eradicate it was a proper revenue settlement, which was in fact a foundation of all other remedies. This alone would lead to capital formation. He accused the Government that though it was aware of it, it was apathetic, careless and sluggish about it. The natives should be induced to be frugal and become their own capitalists rescuing themselves from their slavery to the Marwadis.

While summing up, he reiterated that the satisfactory settlement of land question, improving the productiveness of the native population by stimulating artisan ingenuity among them, and lastly diffusing useful ideas among them on social subjects was the major task of the Government. He also made a suggestion, knowing fully well that much attention would not be paid to it, that "the greatest exhibition of philanthropy which we could make in Hindustan would be the gradual and skilful introduction of great deal of local-self government". He also anticipated the possible objections to this suggestion from the Government side. The two probable objections according to him would be (I) extreme unfitness of the natives for it, and (II) natural alarms of the Government in resigning a fraction of its powers. As regards the second objection first (perhaps the first would be debatable) he said:

> The fear of the Government can be removed by grasping all central and imperial power and allowing district affairs to be managed by the people as Turkey was doing.[31]

Wingate was away in England between 1840 and 1842 and he returned in 1843 to take up his new job as Superintendent, Revenue Survey and Settlement of the Southern Maratha Country, which he held up to 1850. He was then promoted as Revenue Commissioner for the Bombay Presidency in 1851, which office he held till his retirement from the Civil Service in 1854. Captain Wingate in his Report on Ratnagiri Collectorate referred to the problem of population which was causing hardships to the people of Konkan. Green in his letter raised the point: "What are the social conditions under which population becomes unwilling to multiply till positive starvation is the only check on its numbers?" He argued that the problem of over-population in Ratnagiri Collectorate was due to under-supply of capital and a general low degree of productiveness. To face such problems emerging from overpopulation, a study of science of sociology, he thought would be useful in finding out some answers or give some clues to resolve them.[32]

By 1852, the Government had produced a good deal of material on revenue settlement of various parts of the Bombay Presidency. Green wrote a series of articles between June and August 1852 in the Bombay Gazette, "the spirited and ably conducted Journal" as he calls it, which were later published in book form in 1852 under the title *The Deccan Ryots and their Land Tenure*. Here he reminds the reader of the agitation of the Tenant Right League in Ireland and the rights which were voluntarily granted by the Bombay Presidency to its subjects. The Government placed at his disposal all its records and provided him every facility for elucidation of the subject.

Prof. Green, however, complimented the authors Goldsmid, Wingate and Davidson of the *Joint Report* providing New Settlement in these words: "We must admit that the extreme liberties of the settlement and the skill and care with which it has been conducted have been rewarded by the most entire success."[33] But at the same time he had raised four major questions

[31] Wingate-papers, Oct. 1851.

[32] Wingate-papers, Sept. 1852.

[33] H. Green, *The Deccan Ryots*, p. 80.

– (I) Has the new settlement followed by extension of cultivation and to what extent? If it has not what are the obstacles? (II) Whether there has been any corresponding increase in other branches of production of the home market? (III) What is the increase of exports from the districts where New Settlement was introduced? And lastly, (IV) what is the history of prices there since the introduction of the New Settlement?[34]

After examining throughly the new revenue arrangements, Prof. Green sums up its major results to which Captain Wingate makes certain suggestions to explain his points. He says: "The perfect fairness of your whole representation and your summing up agrees in the main with my own views, though considerably less favourable to the survey." He pointed out certain reservations to Green's suggestions and remarked: "Your conclusions seem to me to be as sound as the whole tone of your review is eminently fair and impartial."[35]

Mr. Francis in his report, briefly summarises the arguments of Green and comments:

> It is extremely difficult to form an estimate of the condition of any class of people merely from statistical and oral evidence unchecked by personal observations and Mr. Green was placed in this position, as I believe never had an opportunity of visiting the interior of any of the Deccan districts.[36]

Green pointed out that every where a lamentable amount of indebtedness and of a tharldom to moneylenders were most depressing in its effects on the ryots' energies. "But at the same time he expressed his satisfaction over the fast diminishing of indebtedness."[37] Wingate agreed with Green on this point. However, he drew his attention to a report published in the Bombay Gazette about the murder of a moneylender in the Sholapur Collectorate by some of the debtors, whose action was approved by the whole body of villagers. This state of things appeared quite appalling to Wingate, if it was viewed as a general result which our administration of Civil Justice has brought about between debtor and creditor in agricultural villages.[38]

Green in his letter of 1853 expressed his accord with the views of Wingate on the *sawkars* (moneylenders) and suggested the idea of a bank connected with the Government making advances at a moderate interest and collecting them by a simple process through the revenue department. He was aware of the probable objection from the judiciary to such a scheme. To overcome this problem he suggested that the lands of those who were hopelessly indebted should be thrown into the hands of the capitalists thereby making it difficult for the moneylender to recover his claims without himself becoming a landholder thus bringing the capitalists and the land together and forcing the imprudent peasant, who had brought himself with condi-

34 *Ibid*, p. 68–9.

35 *Francis' Report*, para. 85.

36 *Ibid*, paras. 80–7.

37 H. Green, *The Deccan Ryots*, p. 124.

38 *Francis' Report*, para. 85.

tion of helpless indebtedness, to descend from the rank of a proprietor and become a labourer for hire. He says further that the New Settlement might have made some progress in the state of cultivation in Dharwar and Sholapur region, but he emphatically maintains that the Poona country presents a picture of sombre character, though nobody denies the intrinsic excellence of the new settlement.[39] Green could make such a statement only on the basis of the reports from the Poona Collectorate in which it was strongly stated that the increased cultivation and revenue were both entirely normal and that there was in reality a decrease, both of acres cultivated, and, of course of rupees. This very positive statement by the collector of Poona in his official reports to Government greatly embarrassed Green.[40]

Green was very much impressed by the information on sugar trade which Wingate gave him with reference to the revenue settlement of Madras. He expressed his longing that something similar should spring up in the Deccan. He also sought explanation from him why prices at Indapur be 50% higher than in Poona.[41]

Unfortunately the entire set of letters could not be traced so far but if one could lay his hands on the letters from both the sides it would make an interesting study of the British attitudes towards revenue administration in particular and economic policy in general. In his letter of 1851 Prof. Green wrote to Wingate from Pune, that if he still entertained the same kind of intentions with respect to the enquiries, he would venture to trouble him with the remarks of some people, particularly of the *sardar*s and *jahagirdar*s, who thought that "screwing up a good high assessment was the only thing to keep the people industrious."[42] However he stated that he still maintained his notion, which he expressed in 1851, that India required moderate assessment, fixed for long periods with full proprietary rights subject to the sole condition that it should be paid.[43]

He had still not exhausted his queries. He wrote to Wingate in the same year about the success of his settlement. However, he expressed certain doubts about it. He writes:

> The great increase of cultivation has fed the farmer and his cattle better and has forced greatly supply of corn and other raw produce into the market; this produce has gone down in value, the non-agricultural part of the community not having anything like, in the same proportion, increased their supply of exchangeable commodities and services. This latter part of the population is also better fed then, but in a certain sense and to a certain extent, at the expense of the cultivator, part of whose increased industry and increased advantages are made over gratuitously, as it were to the rest of the community.

But he thought that this was the least desirable that had occurred.

39 *Ibid.*, para. 85; H. Green, *The Deccan Ryots*, p. 124.

40 Wingate-papers, Aug. 1852.

41 *Ibid.*, Dec. 1853.

42 Wingate-papers, 16th Nov., 1851.

43 *Ibid.*; comp. letters of Oct. 1851 and Nov. 1853.

Secondly, he claimed that the increase of agricultural industry has stimulated a proportionate increase in other branches of production and the signs of this were, although produce had fallen in prices, that other things had fallen equally.

Thirdly he said corn had not even fallen in price, the balance had been completely preserved; command over silver had increased, and there had been so much of ingenuity and enterprise among the people and such sufficient means of transit supplied to them that a due proportion of the increased industry of the country had been successfully devoted to supply of foreign demands and the obtaining of foreign commodities. He further remarked that the increase in food, and in general wealth and trade had given rise or would give rise to the emergence of a trading aristocracy. His conclusion was that the revival of industry which had followed the new assessment had conclusively proved that the previous rates were higher than the country could really bear. He wanted Wingate to answer the question: "What can it be that has brought about and still maintains, the fabulously low range of prices which this must indicate?"

His own reply to this question was the Tribute – i. e. interest, home establishment, pensions and savings of servants etc. – and the overwhelming competition of the manufactures, the drain of money, brought prices down, the competition drove the Indians from the general markets of the world and generally diminished its purchasing capacity of foreign goods particularly silver, and also greater demand for British goods disturbing the balance of trade – all these factors contributed to low prices.[44]

Professor Green always considered the *Joint Report* as the most important document which had yet appeared in connexion with the administration of the British Indian dependencies. He also discussed, in this respect, whether the principles of political economy could apply to India. When he asked the young scholars to translate Mrs. Marcet's *Conversations* and J. S. Mill's *Principles*, he specially told them to go carefully through this *Joint Report* and give a special treatment to Indian economy in their books.

While studying the economic situation in the Deccan, Green always used to verify the statement made by Wingate that a reduced assessment in the Deccan although ultimately certain to stimulate production is likely to produce a rise rather than a fall of prices or at least is unlikely to produce a rise rather than a fall of price – or at least unlikely to produce a fall. The reasons given by him in support of his statement were thoroughly examined by him in his elaborate letter of 15th Dec. 1851, written from Pune. He was, however thoroughly convinced that whatever might be the state of agriculture, industry or prices, the Government must lower its money rates on land. He was badly in need of tables of exports and imports and of authentic materials for a history of prices in the Deccan.[45]

44 *Ibid.*, 6th Dec., 1857.

45 H. Green, *The Deccan Ryots*, p. 7; *Francis' Report*, paras. 86–7.

The remaining brief letters are about his pamphlet or some clarifications, and therefore are of not much significance. If the entire correspondence between these two persons could be traced, it would certainly make an interesting study of the British revenue settlement of the Deccan in the first half of the 19th century.

Land Transfer in the Undivided Panjab 1865–1940: An Overview

Mufakharul M. Islam

Prior to the annexation of the province in 1847 and some years thereafter land transfer in the Panjab was rare except in the immediate neighbourhood of large towns. However, conditions changed with the individualisation of property rights in land, fixation and rigorous collection of land revenue in cash, introduction of a new legal-administrative system, increased market-orientated production in agriculture and monetisation of economic transactions. An active land market developed, and by the 1870s area transfers annually exceeded one hundred thousand acres. As the area alienated further increased it became a matter of concern to some members of colonial bureaucracy who warned that there was a political danger in the situation, given that a substantial part of the area sold and mortgaged was going to the professional moneylenders. If no remedial measures were taken, it was argued, the antagonism of the peasant proprietors would be directed against the government. Initially the government refused to take any remedial step, arguing that the facts were insufficient "to warrant interference by legislature to restrict the transfer of land".[1] But ultimately the opinion that land transfer posed a political problem and, therefore, the peasant proprietors should be given legislative protection prevailed and the colonial government passed the Punjab Alienation of Land Act in 1900.

The Act forbade (a) the sale of land by agriculturists to the members of the non-agriculturist tribes except under specific conditions, (b) the sale of land in execution of a decree and (c) the Bengal form of mortgage with a conditional sale clause.[2] Total sale and mortgage declined in the province with the enactment of the protective legislation (Table 1). But land transfer contin-

[1] Inderjit Sharma, *Land Revenue Administration of the Punjab 1849–1901*, New Delhi 1985, p. 177. For further details about the background of the legislative protection see, among others, P. U. M. van den Dungen, *The Punjab Tradition*, London 1972; Norman G. Barnier, *The Punjab Alienation of Land Bill of 1900*, Durham 1966.

[2] For details for the provisions of the Act see Om Prakash, *Agrarian Legislation in the Punjab*, vol. 1, Lahore 1940 and J. M. Douie, *Punjab Land Administration Manual*, Lahore 1931.

ued to draw attention, because, much against the prediction of many who opposed the Land Alienation Act, prices of land maintained an upward trend, the professional moneylenders were contravening the provisions of the Act to acquire land from the agriculturists and a section of the local press complained that the small and marginal farmers were being "swallowed up" by the bigger ones. The question of price rise figured particularly prominently in the discussion on the agrarian scene of the province both in the official and non-official circles. This essay is an attempt to present an overview of the problem of land transfer in the undivided Panjab, focussing attention on (a) trends in the volume of land transferred over time, (b) factors behind the appreciation in the price of land alienated and (c) on the question whether land transfer was creating the problem of landlessness.

I

Trends in land transfer through sale and mortgage have several features. Firstly, both sale and mortgage increased during the last three and a half decades of the 19th century (Table 1), but the rate of increase from the 1880s was not as sharp as it would otherwise appear. This is clear from the fact that a large number of transfer which was not recorded in the earlier years was included in the annual figures from 1883/84. Things improved very soon, but this practice meant that for some years the statistics on transfer were "unduly swollen".[3] This point deserves emphasis as it was supposedly this increase in land sales which tipped the scale in favour of the protective legislation. But overall, there is no denying the fact that land market developed on a significant scale, total alienation through mortgage and sell being of the order of 403 and 227 thousand acres per annum respectively during the period 1865/66–1899/00. As aptly pointed out by Himadri Banerjee, alienation was generally the result of two sets of circumstances: Zamindars had to sell, under pressure of debt, more lands than before and the purchasers considered it more worth while than before to purchase such lands.[4]

The contention that debt was the most important factor behind land alienation, at least in the early years of the development of land market, is borne out by the relevant statistics: during the period 1874/75–1884/85 debt accounted for 57% of the total mortgage and 81% of the total sales in the province.[5] Peasant indebtedness has been attributed to different factors by different commentators. According to Thorburn the causes of debt were (a) fluctuations in yields (b) losses of cattle (c) fragmentation of holdings and (d) the obligation under fixity principle to pay

[3] *Annual Report on the Land Revenue Administration of the Punjab* (henceforth *LRARP*) 1901/02, p. 25.

[4] Himadri Banerjee, *Agrarian Society of the Punjab 1849–1901*, New Delhi 1982, p. 118.

[5] *LRARP* of the relevant years.

land revenue even at times of crop failure.[6] The most important factor which led the purchasers to invest in land purchase was the reduction in land revenue rates in real terms through appreciation in agricultural prices.[7] In other words, in real terms revenue demand came to be assessed at rates lower than rent, thus creating private rent property which served to give commercial

Table 1
Statistics on Sale and Mortgage
(Annual average in 1,000 acres)

	Area sold		Price per acre		Area mortgaged		Cultivated area redeemed	Accumulated area under usufructuary mortgage
	Total	Cultivated	Total	Cultivated	Total	Cultivated		
1865–69	69	–	10	–	106	–	–	–
1870–73	85	–	15	–	175	–	–	–
1874–78	102	–	19	–	227	–	–	–
1879–82	168	–	18	–	299	–	–	–
1883–87	318	–	18	–	604	–	–	–
1888–92	338	164	26	–	554	382	–	–
1893–97	370	205	36	–	668	474	–	–
1898–00	399	219	42	–	604	433	–	–
1901–05	228	136	47	79	231	180	178	3358
1906–10	239	122	64	114	290	211	274	3300
1911–15	267	140	97	166	313	226	251	3239
1916–20	228	126	156	258	356	233	277	3131
1921–25	238	127	238	400	347	259	218	2925
1921–30	234	138	254	392	346	272	164	3214
1931–35	219	129	261	411	391	296	130	3735
1936–39	276	150	241	409	310	228	189	4147

Source: *Report on the Land Revenue Administration, Punjab* (annual). No Adjustment has been made for boundary changes. 1865 stands for 1865/66 and so on.

value to landholding (Table 3). Creation of private rent property also served as an incentive to the prospective mortgagees. But there was another incentive. Prior to the passage of the Land Alienation Act the Bengal form of mortgage with conditional sale clause (i. e. mortgage was to be transformed into sale if the debt was not repaid within the stipulated time) was in vogue in

6 *LRARP* of the relevant years.
7 Brij Narain, *Eighty Years of Punjab Food Prices, 1841–1920*, Lahore 1926.

the Panjab. Moneylenders, both agriculturists and non-agriculturists, were making use of this clause to acquire land.[8]

Secondly, the available statistics suggest that during the last decade of the 19th century sales (and mortgage) to the non-agriculturists was declining (Table 2). In other words, the Land Alienation Act was passed against a background in which the agriculturists were increasing their share of land purchase. Thirdly, data on the volume of sale and mortgage in the first half of the 20th century are not comparable with those of the late 19th century. This is because in 1901 several districts were separated from the Panjab to constitute the North-Western Frontier Province. In other words, while the statistics on land transfer in the pre-1901 period include data relating to the Frontier districts, those of the post-1901 period exclude the data relating to these districts. But it will be safe to suggest that the volume of land transfer both through sale and mortgage was lower in the years following the passage of the Land Alienation Act. This was primarily due to the sharp rise in the price of land as well as its mortgage value.[9] For this made it possible for the peasants to get a much larger loan by alienating (through sale or mortgage) a smaller plot of land. This is clear from the fact that the average cultivated area sold per transaction declined from 3.3 acres in 1900/01 to 2.6 acres in 1919/20.[10]

Trends in permanent alienation during the Great Depression (1929–36) reveal a significant aspect of the agrarian economy and society of the Panjab. With the slump in agricultural prices cash needs became more burdensome for all sections of the farmers, particularly those belonging to the middle and upper strata. This explains why in the face of falling prices the Panjab cultivators increased their production level through the extension of cultivation.[11] Increased production did not neutralise the impact of the slump in agricultural prices. This is evidenced by the large-scale distress sale of gold during the depression years. We can make some idea about the magnitude of such sale from the fact that only during the nine months from October 1933 to June 1934 gold worth Rs. 50.00 crores was sold.[12] But despite all these land sale in the Panjab did not increase, it slightly declined. On the other hand, appreciation in the price of land continued, though at a reduced rate (Table 1). This was in sharp contrast to the experience in the auction market in the colony districts where land prices showed a marked downturn. The experience in land mortgage was different in the sense that area mortgaged annually somewhat

[8] Some idea about the nature of the problem may be had from the fact that out of 742 families examined in details by Thorburn in 1876 only in 13 cases did a man once involved recovered his freedom. Cited by M. L. Darling, *Punjab Peasant in Prosperity and Debt*, London 1925, p. 228.

[9] Mortgage value per cultivated acre increased from Rs. 100/– in 1908/9–1910/11 to Rs. 258/– in 1942–43.

[10] H. Calvert, *Wealth and Welfare of the Punjab*, Lahore 1922, p. 109.

[11] M. M. Islam, "Punjab Agriculture During the Great Depression," *International Journal of Punjab Studies* 1 (1), p. 31–48.

[12] Total export of gold from India during this time was worth 200 crores of rupees. M. L. Darling, *Wisdom and Waste in the Punjab Village*, London 1934, p. 21.

increased. The adverse impact of the depression was felt in two other areas. Firstly, the value of mortgaged land per acre declined by about one-fourth (28%). Secondly, disparity between cultivated area mortgaged and redeemed in a year became more marked during these years. Such a trend obviously resulted in an increase in the accumulated area under usufructuary mortgage in the province by 800 thousand acres (Table 1). Like the distress sale of gold, this pattern in the field of land mortgage (i. e. continued practice of mortgaging land even though price fetched per acre and the prospect of immediate redemption was much less) leaves no doubt about the tendency of the Panjab landowners to resist permanent alienation of land even under the most difficult circumstances.

As about the distribution of land sold between the agriculturists and non-agriculturists, it has already been pointed out that the Land Alienation Act was passed against a background in which the share of the former (agriculturists) was increasing (Table 2). But the question whether they were acquiring land in net terms (area purchased exceeding area sold) can not be answered, for data on the volume of sales by the two classes are not available for the pre-1901 period. But what can we say for the expectation that in the post-1901 period the agriculturists as a group would not at least loose land to the non-agriculturists even if they did not gain from them? If we proceed on the basis of the published data the answer is that agriculturists gained more land than they sold to the other agriculturists, thus indicating that the non-agriculturists were losing (to the extent of 538 thousand acres during the period 1901–39) in net terms. But several considerations suggest that we should not draw any conclusion on the basis of these data. Firstly, it was regularly pointed out in the official publications that the non-agriculturists were contravening the Act by resorting to *benami* transactions.[13]

When the Unionist Party formed the provincial government the revenue officials of the province investigated 18,420 sales by the agriculturists (out of a total of 59,390 by them in 1937) and 9986 cases (i. e. 54%) were sent for review.[14] It is not known what percentage of these reviewed cases were found to represent *benami* purchase. But given the widespread perception among the contemporary observers about the incidence of such transactions, it may safely be assumed that *benami* purchase by the non-agriculturists constituted a significant part of the sale by agriculturists. Secondly, the Act of 1901 was contravened in several other ways – sale to non-agriculturists disguised as gift,[15] misdirection of a caste or a tribe,[16] collusion with *patwaris* to show their adverse possession in revenue records so that decree could be obtained

[13] *LRARP*, 1928/29, p. 29. See also *LRARP*, 1909/10, p. 14; *LRARP*, 1930/31, p. 28; *LRARP*, 1937/38, p. 40. I have dealt with this problem in greater detail in my "The Punjab Land Alienation Act and the Professional Moneylenders," *Modern Asian Studies* 29 (2), p. 271–92.

[14] *Report of the Alienation of Land Inquiry Committee, West Punjab*, Lahore 1949.

[15] *LRARP*, 1911/12, p. 14.

[16] *LRARP*, 1915/16, p. 13.

Table 2
Distribution of Sales & Mortgages
(Annual average in 1,000 acres)

	Sales to		Sales by		Mortgage by		Mortgage to	
	Agriculturists	Others	Agriculturists	Others	Agriculturists	Others	Agriculturists	Others
1874–78	61 (60)	41 (40)	–	–	–	–	90 (40)	137 (60)
1879–82	119 (72)	46 (28)	–	–	–	–	138 (61)	116 (39)
1882–87	223 (70)	95 (30)	–	–	–	–	347 (57)	262 (43)
1888–92	269 (69)	69 (21)	–	–	–	–	375 (68)	179 (32)
1893–97	300 (81)	70 (19)	–	–	–	–	475 (71)	193 (29)
1898–00	316 (79)	83 (21)	–	–	–	–	429 (71)	175 (29)
1901–05	149 (71)	60 (29)	150 (71)	61 (29)	190 (82)	41 (18)	162 (70)	69 (30)
1906–10	178 (74)	61 (26)	170 (71)	61 (29)	239 (83)	51 (18)	219 (76)	71 (24)
1911–15	216 (81)	51 (19)	188 (70)	79 (30)	265 (85)	48 (15)	237 (76)	76 (24)
1916–20	185 (81)	43 (19)	160 (70)	68 (30)	260 (73)	96 (27)	289 (81)	67 (19)
1921–25	187 (79)	51 (21)	173 (73)	65 (27)	294 (85)	53 (15)	270 (78)	77 (22)
1926–30	172 (74)	61 (26)	160 (68)	73 (32)	298 (86)	84 (14)	263 (76)	83 (24)
1931–35	154 (70)	66 (30)	147 (67)	73 (33)	328 (84)	63 (16)	250 (64)	140 (36)
1936–39	207 (75)	69 (25)	190 (69)	86 (31)	258 (83)	52 (17)	195 (63)	115 (37)

Source: Data for the period 1874–1900 are drawn from the *Report on the Land Revenue Administration, Punjab* (annual). Those for the subsequent years are based on data presented in statements XXVI and XXVII of this Report for 1939/40. Figures in the parenthesis represent shares in percentage terms. No adjustment has been made for boundary changes. 1874 stands for 1874/75 and so on.

and transfer entered.[17] A method adopted by the artisan caste to evade the Act of 1901 was to "return" at decennial census as belonging to "agricultural tribes".[18] Thirdly, there is a great deal of evidence to show that the government itself allowed permanent alienation to certain classes of non-agriculturists. Thus, in 1914/15 the Abbasi, Ansari, Kureshi and Sheikhs of Ambala, Sainis of Kangra, Syeds of Hoshiarpur, Mughals of Ferozepore and the Khombas of Gurdaspur were notified as members of agricultural tribes.[19] From the foregoing discussion it is clear that the officially published data do not reveal the exact position about purchase by non-agriculturists.

In one respect the pattern in land mortgage was the same as in land sale: the Land Alienation Act was passed at a time when the relative share of the non-agriculturists was on the decline. Once again, we cannot say whether they were gaining or losing in net terms, because

17 *LRARP*. 1931/32, p. 33.

18 H. C. Sharma, "Caste Mobility among the Artisan Castes of the Punjab," *Proceedings of the Punjab History Congress*, March 1971.

19 *LRARP*. 1914/15, p. 12–13.

the relevant data are not available for the pre-1901 period. But as far as the post-1901 period is concerned the picture is unambiguous: except during the quinquennium 1916–20 the agriculturists were losing in net terms, that is, as a group they were mortgaging out more land than they mortgaged in, the extent of loss being of the order of 1157 thousand acres during 1901–1939 (Table 2). The extent of loss peaked during the last eight years under review and stood at 637,000 acres. Slump in agricultural prices during these years with its adverse impact on loanable funds at the disposal of the agriculturist moneylenders must have contributed to such a pattern.

With regard to the trends in redemption of mortgaged land we face two problems. First, everywhere redemptions were of two kinds: real and technical.[20] Technical redemptions were those which were recorded by the *patwaris* in cases when the mortgagors incurred more debt on the security of the same land. For example, A mortgaged land to B for Rs. 200/–. He needed more money and therefore asked B to lend another amount of Rs. 50/–. The *patwari* would then record two items: (a) redemption of land for Rs. 200/– and mortgage of the same for Rs. 250/–. In case of real redemption the *patwari* would record only one as under (a). It is obvious that technical redemptions were made possible by the increase in the mortgage value of land. But no distinction was made between these two categories while reporting the data in the official publications. Secondly, while statistics on transfer were recorded every year, area encumbered with usufructuary mortgage of a village was attested every fourth year. This means that the area under usufructuary mortgage in the province as a whole in a certain year (T) actually represents the area of one quarter of villages of that year, one quarter in the previous year (T-1), one quarter in the year before previous year (T-2) and the rest one quarter two years before the current year (T-3).[21] There is no way we can overcome these problems. To proceed then on the basis of available statistics, we find that the accumulated area under usufructuary mortgage in the province as a whole slightly declined during the first five quinquennial periods of the current century, from 3.4 million acres during 1901/02–1905/06 to 2.9 million acres during 1921/22–1925/26. On the other hand, during the next 14 years the same increased by 1.1 million acres and, as mentioned earlier, the Depression years (1929/30–1936/37) witnessed an increase of about 800 thousand acres. This must have further increased the area under sharecropping tenancy. This possibility is suggested by the fact that there was a sudden spurt in the share of the moneylenders in the mortgage market.[22]

20 *LRARP*, 1901/02, p. 4.

21 *LRARP*, 1901/02, p. 23.

22 *Assessment Report* (henceforth *AR*) *of the Attock Tahsil of the Attock District*, 1925, p. 23; *Settlement Report* (henceforth, *SR*) *Hoshiarpur District 1901–1914*, p. 18.

II

In absolute terms land prices were not as high as it would otherwise appear from the officially published data (Table 1). This assumption is based on three considerations: (a) The Punjab Pre-Emption Act provided that agnates and agriculturists residing in a village had the first claim on land sold by a villager. This fear of preemption led the buyers to record a price which was higher than actually paid. (b) The price paid by non-agriculturists to agriculturists contained a substantial part of "fictitious price", because when an agriculturist sought permission of the Deputy commissioner to sell land to non-agriculturist the vendor had to prove that no member of an agricultural tribe had offered a 'fair' price for the land. This again created a situation in which price recorded would be higher than price actually paid.[23] (c) Sometimes 'fancy' prices were offered for lands surrounding village or town sites as these were used for the construction of houses.[24] But while making allowance for the consequent upward bias in the available statistics it must be admitted that land prices registered phenomenal increase. Price per acre of total area (cultivated and uncultivated) increased nearly thirteen-fold between 1874 and 1939 (Table 1) or at the rate of 4.92% per year[25] during the period 1891–1942. The rate of appreciation was particularly marked during 1906–10 to 1921–25. Data on the price per acre of cultivated area are not available for the pre-1897 period, but the pattern is similar.

Table 3

Per Capita Cultivated Land and Canal Irrigated Area (Figures in Thousands)

	Population	Cultivated Area	Canal Irrigated Area	Col. 3/Col. 2	Col. 4/Col. 2
1868	16250	20172	1373	1.24	6.8
1881	16939	23400	1950	1.38	8.3
1891	18653	26000	3016	1.39	11.6
1902	19943	27800	6001	1.39	21.6
1911	19579	28483	7227	1.45	25.4
1921	20685	29336	10274	1.42	35.0
1931	23581	30675	12984	1.30	42.3

Source: Hirashima Shigemochi, *The Structure of Disparity in Developing Agriculture*, Tokyo 1979, p. 26.

[23] *SR* Gujarat 1930, p. 13; *Punjab District Gazetteers* (henceforth *DG*) *Muzaffargarh District*, 1929, p. 136.

[24] *AR of the Gurshankar Tahsil of Hoshiarpur District, 1912/13*, p. 17–18; *LRARP*, 1934/35, p. 30.

[25] Hirashima Shigemochi, *The Structure of Disparity in Developing Agriculture. A Case Study of the Pakistan Punjab*, Tokyo 1974, p. 49.

Several scholars[26] have tried to analyse the factors behind the phenomenal rise in land prices in the Panjab province and Hirashima's attempt is the most comprehensive one. He is of the opinion that the moneylenders withdrew from the land market after the passage of the Land Alienation Act and this was due to the decline in the profitability of investment in land purchase, even below 12%, the rate of interest charged by co-operative societies (Table 4). Earlier the moneylenders were active in the land market because land purchase yielded a higher rate of annual return. The vacuum caused by the withdrawal of the moneylenders was filled in by the wealthy farmers and landlords. This was so despite the fact that trends in all-crop production (1.39% per year) and yield per acre (0.50% per year) fell for short of the annual rate (4.92%) of increase in land prices and a substantial part of the increased demand for land was absorbed by the extension of arable land during the British period (Table 3). The rich peasants and landlords remained active in the land market because (a) the members of the farming community had a higher propensity to hold or own land, (b) they had an investable surplus and, in the absence of alternative avenues of investment, the opportunity cost of such investment was zero or near zero and (c) the expected intangible future benefits such as prestige, power and security was large enough to justify investment in land at much lower return than interest rates.[27]

Table 4

Trends of Rent-land Price and Private Rent Property-land Price Ratios (Rs-acre)

	GR	GRx1/3	LR	PRP	PL	R_1 (%)	R_2 (%)
1891–1895	34.8	11.6	–	–	69	16.8	–
1896–1900	36.3	12.1	–	–	81	14.9	–
1901–1904	39.9	13.3	1.07	12.3	78	17.0	15.7
1905–1908	39.3	13.1	1.07	12.0	101	13.3	12.2
1909–1912	40.9	13.6	1.30	12.4	120	11.4	10.3
1913–1917	37.4	12.5	1.50	11.0	225	5.6	5.0
1918–1922	41.0	13.7	1.80	11.9	300	4.9	3.3
1923–1927	40.0	13.4	1.90	11.5	414	3.3	2.8
1928–1932	39.7	13.3	1.90	11.3	396	3.3	2.9
1933–1937	45.6	15.2	1.87	13.3	404	3.8	3.4
1938–1942	47.3	15.8	2.00	13.7	476	3.3	2.9

Source: Hirashima Shigemochi, *The Structure of Disparity in Developing Agriculture: A Case Study of the Pakistan Punjab* (Tokyo, 1974), Table 10; Hirashima presents annual data for the entire period.

Note: 1891 stands for 1891/92; Gr: Gross agricultural product per acre; LR: land revenue; Grx1/3: rent per acre; PRP: private rent property; R_1: rent/land price ratio; R_2: private rent property/land price ratio.

[26] *Ibid*; K. Mukerji, "Land Prices in the Punjab," in: M. K. Chaudhuri (ed.), *Trends of Socio-Economic Change in India*, Simla 1969, p. 529–46.

[27] Hirashima, *Structure of Disparity*, p. 45–53.

Hirashima is justified in suggesting that land was treated as a symbol of *izzat* or status and position in the society and that it was the most durable and secure of all the assets. But his exercise is inadequate in the sense that he confines his attention to one variable only, important though it is. Moreover, it needs to be explained, why, in the first place, land was treated as a symbol of *izzat*. Speaking generally, the decision to invest in land purchase is influenced by several other considerations which determine the *total* expected rate of return, and two most important of those are annual rate of return and capital gains.[28] This paper argues that the explanation for the sharp rise in land prices in the Panjab lies in the fact that the rate of capital gains was very high and the annual rate of return much higher than indicated by Hirashima's data. To these must be added yet another factor: relative abundance of investable surplus at the disposal of the agriculturists and non-agriculturists and the absence of better alternative avenues for the investment of the same.[29]

Hirashima defines the annual rate of return by expressing private rent property (rent minus revenue) as proportion of the price per acre of cultivated land. Further, he takes one-third of the gross produce of land as proxy value of rent. This mode of calculating the annual rate of return is relevant for the non-agriculturist buyers (and those buyers among the agriculturists who leased out their land on cash or kind rent), but not for those who cultivated the land themselves or partly with the help of hired labour.

For this latter group of buyers the annual rate of return should be estimated by expressing net produce (gross produce minus wages paid to hired labour, if any) as percentage of the price of land. This, in itself, implies that the rate of return was higher than indicated by Hirashima's data. But the same assumption is strengthened by the fact that yield per acre of different crops as worked out by the Agricultural Department was underestimated.[30] Secondly, the rate of decline in the annual returns in the years after 1906 should have been lower. This assumption is based on the fact that, as mentioned earlier, in absolute terms land price did not appreciate as much as indicated by the officially published data. Thus argued, annual rate of return must have been an important consideration behind investment in land purchase by the agriculturists, especially those who practised self-cultivation.

[28] S. R. Howlader, "Portfolio Selection and Demand for Assets in a Peasant Economy: A Theoretical Analysis," *Dhaka University Studies*, Part C, 7 (December 1987), p. 52–71.

[29] Given the high rate of interest paid by peasant borrowers the total expected rate of return was positive in the case of investment in moneylending. But capital gain in this latter case was zero and the risk of holding the asset in this form was high because of the uncertainty of getting the loan back from the borrowers. For further details see *ibid*.

[30] It was found that official Standard Yield of cotton during 1927/28–1931/32 was lower by 28.5%, whereas the actual yield of wheat was higher than official estimates by about ⅓. For details see *Report on the Marketing of Wheat in the Punjab*, Lahore 1940.

Expectation of a high rate of capital gains was another factor behind the sharp appreciation in land prices. The expected rate of capital gains was very high because there was a marked difference between the expected price of land when it would be sold and the price when land was purchased. Some idea about the magnitude of this difference may be had from the fact that, as already mentioned, price per acre increased thirteen times between the two quinquennial periods 1873/75–1878/79 and 1936/37–1939/40. This is not to suggest that appreciation at such phenomenal rates led to land speculation, people buying land with a view to selling it later at a profit.[31] On the contrary, under normal circumstances the buyers were extremely reluctant to permanently alienate their land. For, contrary to the impression usually given by historians, not much land was available for purchase in the province. Calvert has shown that during the 21 years (1896/97–1916/17) on an average 29 sales were taking place in a village and assuming that there were 2.5 million families in the province each family had, on the average, only one chance of buying a plot in 54 years.[32] This means that there was no assurance that if a plot of land was sold for a high profit, another plot would be available very soon and, even if available, would be as advantageously situated as the one sold or the price to be paid would be within the buyer's reach. However, the perspective buyers would also realise that land constituted such a valuable asset that it could be sold at any time at an enhanced price to raise funds to go abroad, buy or lease in more productive lands in the canal colonies or another plot more advantageously located, to purchase a bride or to start a business or to meet some unforeseen cash needs in connection with domestic consumption. Thus considered, the sharp appreciation in land price became, in itself, a factor behind further rise in price, for, it created a wide gap between the demand for purchase and supply of land for sale.

In this connection it would also be mentioned that the mortgage value of land was also increasing and this meant that an increasingly larger amount could be obtained by mortgaging the same or a smaller plot of land. Neeladri Bhattacharya's case studies on mortgages shed a flood of light on the subject.[33] In 1862 Mussalmal Bhage of Bother village in Rohtak district mortgaged 19 acres for Rs. 430/–. As more money was needed, the land was redeemed and mortgaged for Rs. 700/–. The old debt was paid off and the rest was spent on current requirements. Thus, in 13 years debt increased by 79 per cent and the mortgage value by 192 per cent. In the same village Tok Ram mortgaged 11 acres for Rs. 25/– in 1881. When, by 1888, the debt

[31] The Punjab Provincial Banking Enquire Committee was told "... no Zamindar buys land with the idea that it will appreciate in value and he will then sell." *Evidence* 1, p. 94. There is, however, a contradictory evidence which reports "in few villages there has been land speculation [...] The purchasers are in many cases men who have emigrated to Bombay, China or East Africa and returned full of money." *AR Attock Tahsil*, 1930, p. 21.

[32] For details see Calvert, *Wealth and Welfare*, p. 110.

[33] Neeladri Bhattacharya, "Lenders and Debtors: Punjab Countryside 1880–1940," *Studies in History* 1 (New Series), 1985, p. 305–42.

increased to Rs. 45/– he remortgaged it to another person for Rs. 45/–. The old debt was repaid, but within one year the debt increased to 49.00. Tok Ram redeemed his land again and mortgaged it to another person for Rs. 98.00. Thus, in eight years the debt increased by 136 per cent and the value of mortgage by 292 per cent. Such rates of increase in the mortgagee value of land may be taken as yet another evidence of capital gains which could be expected from land purchase.

The fact that surplus fund was relatively abundant in supply and there was no alternative avenues of its investment cannot be in doubt. But given the importance of this phenomenon some comments will be in order. First, let us take up the case of agricultural surplus. Per capita crop output was larger in the Panjab than in any or most other provinces. This is because the size a of holding and yield per acre was larger. The assumption about the latter, i. e. yield rates, is based on the fact that the proportion of irrigated area to total sown area was higher. What is more, given that the sown area continued to increase and the yield of certain crops registered on upward trend as a result of the introduction of high-yielding varieties of seeds[34] crop output increased faster than population growth. In other words, the per capita crop output was also increasing over time. This meant that the per capita quantum of agricultural produce sold in the market was getting increasingly larger in this province. In a situation where agricultural prices were also increasing, except during the Great Depression, this in turn meant rising per capita income. It is true that because of the wide disparity in the distribution of land the fruits of market-oriented production[35] were not equally shared by all sections of the agricultural classes. But the increase in per capita income meant that there was now an investable surplus especially at the disposal of the rich peasants and the landlords. Secondly, increased market-oriented production meant the expansion of trade in agricultural produce and moneylending business. This, in turn, brought into existence a class of merchants/moneylenders. Many of them were now in a position to compete for land. Moreover, a sizeable section among the members of other non-agricultural classes (including the village menials) earned a regular income from the cultivation of owned or mortgaged lands in the canal colonies and the older villages[36] and by working as tenants and/or agricultural labourers. Some of them earned an income from employment in government offices as petty officials or subordinate staff or as coolies employed for the

[34] Thus, in 1938/39 about half of the wheat area, 64% of the area under sugarcane and, in 1944/45, 70% of the cotton acreage were sown with these seeds. For wheat and sugarcane see *Report on the Operations of the Department of Agriculture, Punjab, 1938/39*, p. 71 and p. 77. For cotton see B. S. Kartar Singh, *A Text Book of Punjab Agriculture*, Lahore 1947, p. 437.

[35] Earnings from export of raw cotton from the province increased from Rs. 970,000.00 in 1891/92 to Rs. 97,450,000.00 in 1918/19. Export earnings from the export of grains and pulses increased from Rs. 50,040,000.00 to Rs. 24,370,000.00 during the same period.

[36] In 1910/11 the non-agriculturists owned 14% of the total cultivated area of the province, *LRARP*, 1910/11, Statement III.

construction of roads, railways and canals. Thirdly, a large number of Panjabis permanently or semi-permanently settled in other parts of India and in foreign countries. Moreover, at the beginning of 1914 there were over 103,000 Panjabis in the Indian Army and during world War I no less than 392,493 were recruited in the province. These two developments are important in the present context because every year there was a considerable flow of liquid funds from abroad and other parts of India. The annual average remittance during 1900/01–1917/18 amounted to Rs. 15.8 million.[37]

Overall, there was a considerable volume of liquid funds generated by increased economic activities which the Panjab experienced under British rule more than any or most other Indian provinces as well as by employment abroad or in other parts of India. In the absence of alternative avenues of investment the liquid funds would have, in any case, been invested in land purchase because it was the most durable and secure of all assets. But given the fact that such investment promised considerable annual return and a high rate of capital gains there was now an intense competition for land. The units of sale were normally small and this meant that even the marginal savers among the agricultural and non-agricultural classes could compete for land. The desire for land purchase was so intense that, as mentioned earlier, the non-agricultural classes contravened the provisions of the Land Alienation Act to acquire land from the agricultural classes. Anyway, while the demand for land thus increased its supply remained stable or even declined. The consequent gap between demand for land and its supply led to a high rate of appreciation in its price. This was despite the fact that part of the demand of the peasantry, landlords and urban professional classes was being met by the government through land grants and auction sales in the canal colonies. Incidentally, between 1885 and 1947 the canal-irrigated area in Panjab increased from under 3 million acres to around 14 million acres. The great bulk of this expansion took place in the canal colonies.[38]

III

Echoing the contention of the contemporary observers of the agrarian scene of the province Naved Hamid has argued that the development of a land market resulted in the dispossession of the peasantry. Consequently by the end of the colonial period a highly differentiated structure of peasantry had emerged in the Panjab with most of the peasantry in the categories of poor

[37] For details see Calvert, *Wealth and Welfare*, p. 163.

[38] Imran Ali, *Punjab Under Imperialism*, New Delhi 1989, p. 9–10.

peasants, landless share-cropper and agricultural labourer, and more than half the land in the hands of the landlord class.[39]

There is no denying the fact that with the passage of time during the British rule the distribution of ownership holdings was getting increasingly unequal (Table 5). But it seems that (a) at the time of the establishment of British rule the distribution of land was not as egalitarian as it is supposed, (b) increase in the number of agricultural labourers and the proportion of area cultivated by sharecroppers cannot be taken as an index of the extent of dispossession of the poorer section of the peasantry and (c) land sale by the poorer section of the peasantry was not the primary causative factor behind the process of differentiation.

Let us start with the first point (a) as mentioned above. For the earlier period of the British rule we do not have data comparable to those presented in Table 5. But there is evidence to suggest that even as early as in 1860 the agrarian structure of the Panjab was marked by a considerable degree of differentiation. Thus around that year 81 per cent of the landowners in the province paid less than Rs. 50/– in land revenue per head per annum, 9.29 per cent paid between Rs. 50/– and Rs. 100/– and another 9.64 per cent paid between Rs. 100/– and Rs. 5,000/–.

Table 5
Distribution of Land – 1924 and 1939

Size of holdings	% of holdings in each group		% of cultivated area in each group	
	1924 (a)	1939 (b)	1924 (a)	1939 (b)
(i) 0 to 1 acres	17.9	20.2	1.0	0.8
1 to 3 acres	25.9	28.6	4.4	5.2
3 to 5 acres	14.9	14.9	6.6	6.2
Proper peasants	58.7	63.7	12.0	12.2
(ii) 5 to 10 acres	18.0	16.9	15.1	13.1
10 to 15 acres	8.0	7.3	11.5	9.1
Middle peasants	26.0	24.2	26.6	22.2
(iii) 15 to 20 acres	4.3	3.6	8.4	7.2
20 to 25 acres	2.7	2.2	6.8	5.6
Rich peasants	7.0	5.8	15.2	12.8
(iv) 25 to 50 acres	4.8	3.9	20.4	14.8
50 a. above	3.3	2.4	25.7	38.0
Landlord class	8.1	6.3	46.1	52.8

Source: (a) H. Calaert, *Size and Distribution of Agricultural Holdings in the Punjab*, Lahore 1925, p. 17.
(b) B. S. Saini, *The Social and Economic History of the Punjab*, Delhi 1979, p. 184.

[39] Naved Hamid, "Dispossession and Differentiation of the Peasantry in the Punjab during the Colonial Rule," *Journal of Peasant* Studies 10, 1982, p. 52–72.

Such an evidence[40] clearly indicates that there was a considerable degree of inequality in the distribution of landownership at the commencement of foreign rule. With regard to the second point (b) the area operated on sharecropping terms increased from 1.2 million acres[41] in 1875/76 to 7.4 million acres in 1901/02. But up to 1899–1900 the extent of recorded sale stood at about 8.2 million acres. Area cultivated by sharecroppers increased by another 3.3 million acres up to 1931/32, and during the same period (1901/02–1931/32) another 8.3 million acres were sold. We have no data to indicate what portion of land sale represented such sale by small and middle peasants which was subsequently leased out on sharecropping terms. But in all probability the proportion was small. As a matter of fact if we proceed on the assumption (which is more likely to be a valid one) that the larger part of the accumulated area under usufructuary mortgage which stood at 3.6 million acres in 1931/32 and a certain part of the area sold was operated by sharecroppers, the total area transferred through sale and mortgage can not be said to have accounted for half of the area under sharecropping tenancy.

As about (c), dispossession of the poorer section of the peasantry through sale could have contributed to the differentiation among the rural population of the province in two years: (i) complete dispossession as a result of which proportion of landless people would increase and (ii) partial dispossession which would increase the preparation of the poor peasantry. As for (i) we do not have the kind of data on the basis of which it will be possible to generalise for the entire period of British rule or a larger part of it. All that we can asset is that there was always a substantial body of landless people and this section mostly consisted of village menials or *kamins*.[42] They were engaged in their caste-prescribed occupations which did not include agriculture (except as agricultural labourers and/or subtenants). In the absence of hard evidence it is not possible to say whether the number of landless people remained static over time or was declining or increasing. According to the findings of a survey conducted in the province over one-third (36.9%) of the vendors among the "members of the agricultural tribes" became landless[43] after sale during the quinquennium of 1922/23–1926/27. These data do serve to indicate how many among the previously landless people among the "agriculturists" and "non-agriculturists" acquired land during these sample years. But a section among the landless, especially

Sukhwant Singh, "Social Differentiation Among the Peasantry in the Punjab (1849–1901)," *Proceedings of the Punjab History Congress*, 1987, p. 12–47.

The figure on the proportion of sharecropped area in 1875/76 is arrived at as follows: On p. 530 of his work (*Wealth and Welfare*) Calvert mentions that in 1872/73 the cultivated area in Panjab stood at 18.8 million. For 1875/76 it is assumed to have been 19 million acres. Then on p. 87 the same author mentioned that 14% of the cultivated area was operated by tenants-at-will paying rent in cash and kind. Of the area thus operated 52% was cultivated on sharecropping terms. For the subsequent years statistics on sharecropping tenancy (and usufructuary mortgage) are drawn from *LRARP*.

For details see Himadri Banerjee, *Agrarian Society*, ch. 7.

C. P. K. Fazal, *A Note on the Sales of Land between Notified Agricultural Tribes in the Punjab During the Quinquennium 1922/23 to 1926/27*, Lahore 1931.

among the *kamins* was acquiring land through purchase. As a matter of fact the practice had started much earlier in the late 19th century.[44] It is true that the Punjab Alienation of Land Act imposed legal restrictions on the sale of land from the "members of agricultural tribes" to the non-agriculturists including the *kamins*. But there was no bar for the *kamins* to buy from the "non-agriculturists" vendors. The fact that a section among the *kamins* possessed the means to bid for land (which was available in small plots) is indicated by their persistent attempt to be recognised as "members of agricultural tribes" and in some cases their attempt was successful. However, it is unlikely that such purchasers outnumbered those agriculturist vendors who joined the rank of the landless. The situation could not have been different in the late 19th century. As mentioned earlier on, in all probability "distress sale" (of land) constituted a sizeable section of the total sales during these years. This implies that a large part of such vendors belonged to the category of small and marginal proprietors who became landless after sale. Again the probability is that such vendors exceeded the number of those who were earlier landless but now acquired land. Thus, it seems that there was a trend, though not quite pronounced, towards increasing landlessness in the province.

With regard to the question of increase in the proportion of poor peasants we have data relating to two points of time during the last two decades or so of the British rule. These data generated by the Punjab Board of Economic Inquiry indicate that, irrespective of the legal distinction between "agriculturists" and "non-agriculturists" the proportion of poor peasants increased from 58.7% in 1924 to 63.7% in 1939 (Table 5). Part of this increase is explained by a fall in proportion of the middle peasants. Does this represent the continuation of a trend which had set in earlier? In the absence of relevant data nothing definite can be said on this question. But it seems that even if there was such a trend it is unlikely to have been a pronounced one. Incidentally the decrease in the proportion of middle peasants that is indicated by the data in Table 5 took place during a period which witnessed a drastic slump in agricultural prices spreading over several years. Overall, partial or complete dispossession through land sale should have contributed to the growing inequality among the Panjab rural population, but this was by no means the primary factor.

As a matter of fact, the primary causative factor behind increased differentiation in the agrarian structure of the Panjab lay in the manner in which the British government disposed of lands in the canal colonies. It may be recalled in this connection that beginning from the 1880s the foreign government launched a massive canal building activities. Canal construction in the Panjab differed from similar works in other parts of India not only because the scale was much larger, but more fundamentally in the sense that the government had to launch a colonisation programme. For in the Panjab canals were built in areas which were practically deserts with

[44] *Census of India*, 1891, vol. 19, *The Punjab and Its Feudatories;* Himadri Banerjee, *Agrarian Society*, p. 184

little settled population. Thus, the government had to fulfill a dual role: construction of canals and the task of colonisation in the unclaimed lands (taken over as Crown Waste) commanded by them. Two aspects of the land grant policy pursued by the government in the colonisation programme need to be emphasised in the present context: (a) the size of grants and (b) the virtual exclusion of the landless section of the rural population, especially the *kamins* (or the village menials) from land grants. The size of the grants was always bigger than the average holding size in the province and in many cases these ran into several hundred – and in some cases several thousand – acres.[45] Thus, overall, the colony district had a larger concentration of such large holdings in which self-cultivation (i. e. cultivation without the help of hired labour on a substantial scale) was not going to be possible. Indeed many holdings were so large that if the grantees were to launch large-scale farming it would have been necessary to use labour-saving implements like tractors. But while other social groups (peasants, landlords, retired civil servants, lawyers, physicians, army personnel) received land grants, the government systematically decided against allotments to the landless rural population. Thus, the colonisation programme gave a powerful boost to the growth of a class of rich peasants and landlords, thereby increasing the differentiation in the rural society. This, in turn, meant a vast expansion of area cultivated by sharecroppers. For, instead of launching large scale farming with the help of hired labour, most of the grantees and auction purchasers resorted to the practice of leasing out the whole or larger part of their land to sharecroppers. This is quite clear from the preponderance of sharecropped area in the canal colony districts.[46]

However, a qualification needs to be added here. We have suggested that there could have been a certain increase in landlessness in the province. But this did not necessarily mean a worsening off in the economic condition of the landless people. Many small peasants who were forced to sell their land under pressure of debt or otherwise, and thus became landless, migrated to the canal colonies to take up employment as share-croppers and some even as agricultural labourers. Many others sold their land voluntarily for the same purpose. This meant a certain lowering in their social status, but they were now economically better off. For they were now in a position to cultivate a larger holding with greater yield per acre and security of harvest. Of course, the *kamins* constituted the largest group among the sharecroppers[47] and agricultural labourers[48] in the colony districts and for them this meant both a certain improvement in social status and economic conditions. Thus, though land sale may have slightly increased the number

45 Imran Ali, *Punjab Under Imperialism*.

46 This part of the discussion is based on my *Irrigation, Agriculture and the Raj; Punjab* 1887–1947, New Delhi 1997.

47 H. C. Sharma, "Caste Mobility among the Artisan Castes of the Punjab."

48 N. Bhattacharya, "Agricultural Labour and Production: Control and South-East Punjab, 1870–1940," in K. N. Raj et al. (eds.), *Essays on the Commercialization of Indian Agriculture*, Delhi 1986.

of the landless, effective landlessness in the province was drastically reduced by the expansion of sharecropping tenancies in the canal colonies.

To summarise, land transfer through sale and mortgage recorded considerable increase in the Panjab province during the last three and half decades of the 19th century and then, following the passage of the Land Alienation Act (1901), there was a certain decline. The rate of decline was more marked in the case of mortgage. Secondly, officially published statistics indicate that the objective of the Punjab Alienation of Land Act was being achieved, but there is a whole range of evidence to suggest that the non-agriculturists were contravening the provisions of this Act to acquire land from the "members of the agricultural tribes". Thirdly, the land price gradually increased from the last quarter of the 19th century and the rate of appreciation became very marked from 1915 onwards. At no stage was this increase matched by improvement in yield rates or product prices. But there was nothing paradoxical, feudal or semi-feudal about it, given that considerable surplus fund was available in the Panjab rural areas and its investment in land purchases yielded the highest rate of total return. Such a situation brings into sharp focus the significance of the fact that agricultural development (limited though it was) in the province under foreign rule was not matched by industrialisation efforts. Finally, the specific manner in which the foreign government disposed of lands in the canal colonies, but not land transfer, was the primary factor behind the rise of a class of rich peasants and big landlords and the vast expansion of sharecropping tenancy in the province.

Benoy Kumar Sarkar, 1887–1949: Political *Rishi* of Twentieth Century Bengal

Robert E. Frykenberg

"Whenever I find two persons trying to agree with each other," wrote Benoy Kumar Sarkar, "I feel inclined to suspect that there is a chance for some moral or spiritual injustice happening in the world."[1] With such words as these, at once arresting and evocative, one of the most energetic and insightful Bengal thinkers of the century captured and held his audiences. The boldness of Sarkar's contributions to social and political thought, his departures from traditional molds of thought, are the subject of this essay. Yet, these can hardly be appreciated without looking, in only briefly, at who and what he himself was.

I

Born at Malda, Bengal, in the year 1887, the son of Sudhanya Kumar Sarkar, he came from a *bhadralok* middle class family. He passed the entrance examination for the Malda Zilla School at age thirteen; and, in 1905, just seventeen, he stood first in the B. A. examination at Calcutta University, gaining double honours in English and History and being awarded of the 'Ishan Scholarship'. Calcutta, at that time, enjoyed academic preeminence over the whole of the then undivided Bengal Presidency, including Assam, Burma, Bihar and Orissa. The Government of India, ever on the look-out for promising young candidates for the I. C. S., offered him a further scholarship for higher studies in England.

But 1905 was a time of unprecedented political activism. Sarkar could not, and did not, escape its excitements. Lord Curzon's division of Bengal had caused a socio-political furor, and Sarkar had become an apologist for the nationalist agenda. He was later to recall:

[1] Benoy Kumar Sarkar, *The Political Philosophies Since 1905*, Madras 1928, p. 1–2.

> For the first time since the Mutiny, people of this country resolved to return a hit by a hit. Positivism got the upper hand of our spirituality and our traditional stoicism found a new "Taj-mahal" for its grave. New blood began to flow in the old veins and Bengal took the firm to resolve to boycott foreign goods, foreign dress, and to non-cooperate with the foreign rulers.[2]

It was during this twilight of the Raj, when old values were melting and new values were being moulded, that, at least initially, Benoy Kumar Sarkar put deeds before words. He declined both the proffered scholarship and the subsequent offer of a position as Deputy Magistrate. A much coveted prized post in the I. C. S. was exchanged for a place in the ranks of *swadeshi* revolutionaries.

Yet, despite full participation in the Anti-Bengal Partition Agitation, in the Swadeshi Boycott Movement, and in the first of the Gandhian Civil Disobedience (*Satyagraha*) campaign, Sarkar soon seems to have become disenchanted with the direction of nationalist activity. Forsaking the sword for the pen, he decided to leave active politics and turned instead to developing and exploring political thought. The broadening of his experiences both in India and in the world moderated his political passion, but deepened his insight and judgement. As a result, instead of becoming an official or a politician, he became a scholar and thinker. In 1907, he established the Malda Jayiya Shiksha Samity and then organised a district branch of National Council of Education there. Shortly after this, he joined the Bengal National College as an Honorary Professor of History and Economics – a school affiliated to Sri Aurobindo and the National Council of Education (the then embryonic swadeshi university) in Calcutta.

Between 1910 and 1914, Benoy Babu turned to the organisation of cultural societies and to the translation of local folklore into English and popular vernacular literature. Living almost like a "saint", wearing neither coat or shirt, and using only a simple "*chadar*", he moved barefooted in the streets. His activities now became too many to recount quickly. He wrote extensively in many languages: he was chosen to write one of the volumes of the *Sacred Books of the East* series; he sponsored the "Gambhira" folk movement in north Bengal; and he associated himself with Satish Mukherjee, founder of the Dawn Society.

It was at this time that Sarkar instituted and organised the program which eventually would take him abroad for ten years. Seventeen young scholars were sent abroad for higher education and technical training under the sponsorship of various local cultural societies. On the very eve of the outbreak of World War I, Benoy Sarkar, together with Shib Prasad Gupta of Varanasi, left India on a extended world tour. Intent on gaining a first-hand understanding of industry, education, literature, art, science, and social institutions everywhere, he visited Egypt, England, Scotland, Ireland, Hawaii, Japan, Manchuria, spent four years in the United States, and more years in central and southern Europe, not returning to India until 1925. During this eleven year

[2] *In Memorium, Benoy Sarkar: 1887–1949*, Calcutta, University Senate Hall, January 10, 1955, p. 1.

odyssey, he was invited to serve as a visiting professor in many universities – e. g. Columbia, Harvard, California, Iowa, Clark, Pittsburgh, Leipzig, Munich and Rome; and he addressed many learned societies – e. g. the Academy of France, the Royal Asiatic Society, and other academic fora.

All through these years of study, travel, and work abroad, Sarkar acted as an unofficial ambassador and spokesman for India. Moreover, because when lecturing in Europe he was able to speak the indigenous languages fluently, he became well-known and popular, receiving many titles and honours. But his most serious advanced study was done in Germany. There he became the first Indian ever to be awarded a decoration from Munich University, and also received a doctorate from Leipzig University. (He later received a doctorate *honoris causa* from University of Iran in 1937). In 1925, he was invited to teach a course in sociology at the University of Rome and in 1931 he presided over the International Population Congress in Rome, held under the auspices of the League of Nations. Sarkar crowned all of these many international achievements by marrying an Austrian whom he had met in Germany.[3]

It was during this middle period of his life, from 1917 until the early 1940s, that Benoy Sarkar made his most notable contributions as a theorist and philosopher. Greatly influenced by the weight of German scholarship – with its stress on meticulous investigation, verification and classification of research data – he became obsessed with the need for greater precision in academic discourse. Indeed, during the years prior to his return to India, he produced a series of books entitled *Bartaman Jagat* – thousands of pages of descriptive, highly informative findings written in Bengali.

In 1926, Sarkar joined the Economics Department of Calcutta University, as a senior lecturer of political philosophy, sociology, economic history and political economy. This position was held until 1947 when he was made head of the Department of Economics and Commerce. Specialising in post-graduate studies, with an emphasis on research, he demanded that each of his students learn at least one European language (beyond English) and learn it well. His seminars became well-known. The increasing mass of writings which flowed from his desk became famous, both in India and abroad. His students gained recognition in Europe and America for the quality of their work. The "new school" of thought in the social sciences which grew up

[3] *Ibid.*, p. 2–5.
Note: Much of the material included in this paper was gained through an interview with Dr. Richard L. Park (my Berkeley mentor and friend when I was his Research Assistant). Park was a long-standing personal friend of Benoy Sarkar.
**Note:* Benoy Sarkar had one child, Indira Sarkar, who took her Ph. D. from the Sorbonne. At one time, she was in Switzerland with her mother and worked for the Indian Foreign Service. Many of Mrs. Sarkar's relatives later moved to the United States.

around him became known as "Sarkarism". It is this systematic formulation of systematic ideas which we will now examine more closely.[4]

II

Benoy Sarkar rebelled against the idea that the East and West were or ever could really be different in any essential way. The notion that one civilisation was founded upon some deeper spirituality and the other on materialism repelled him, and he categorically rejected it. A positivist, he saw no reason for holding that any fundamental, or underlying, difference between or among peoples of the world might exist. In standing out against the "universally admitted conclusions of Max Muller and Kipling", he elaborated upon ideas which had been developed by Sir Brojendra Nath Seal, doing so with more comprehensive and detailed empirical and theoretical care. He went beyond the so-called "biogenetic" concept of races, according to which various "nationalisms" or "nationalities" make up the entire human race, asserting instead that whatever differences in culture, decorum or "spirit" might be noticeable in the patterns between the life of the East and West were differences principally due to "accidents" of history, to uneven developments in science and technology between different regions of the world.[5]

1. *Epistemology*: "Not truth [or Truth], but truths constitute the objective verdict of philosophy." Truth is multiple and not single; it is particular and personal rather than universal, concrete rather than abstract, relative to space and time rather than abstract or metaphysical. Knowledge is thus drawn from myriads of diversities within a matrix of philosophic complexity. Philosophical world views, or *Weltanschauungen,* as these are observed, must always be pluralistic and cannot possess singularity, even if "caught" or "held" for a short time. So seen, personality is to be perceived as essentially an ever-moving, dynamic quality, intrinsically differentiating organisms and possessing those certain "automatic" functions and mechanisms found in any a "transformer". So-called "new" truths are ever being differentiated, transformed, transvaluated into thought; and thought thence transformed into and within institutions.[6]

Political philosophy, for Sarkar, can be seen as a stream (or streams) of diverse cultural currents, rather than as a tightly organised rational system. He wanted to find out more about "tendencies" and "movements", not about "finished" products or ossified relics. He was interested in political thought, as manifested within functioning political institutions. Depending upon one's particular interpretation of political philosophy, the point at which "modernity"

4 *The Political Philosophies Since 1905*, p. 1–2.

5 *Ibid.*, p. 1.

6 *Ibid.*, p. 2–3.

might be considered to have begun varies considerably. Thus, for all that, ideas within the speculative world of today, embodying the political tradition from Machiavelli and Bodin to Rousseau and Hegel, are all artifactual and antiquarian. New problems in the makeup of personality, community or society, constitute the social data of the contemporary world. New truths, in turn, are ever generating new theories of knowledge. New values are always being differentiated. These must be oriented to new circumstances. This, Sarkar believed, is a natural process, in which "automatic" and "autonomous" political adjustments of, and within, both personality and society occur. Such political processes can be spelled out either in evolutionary or in revolutionary sequences. The process of understanding and communicating such tendencies of change, he held, is the "One Grand Message of speculation in politics".[7]

2. *Ethics*: Sarkar made a clear distinction between what might be called "discourse" or "propaganda" and information which strove to give "objective description". Generally speaking, for him, philosophy and science could be thought of as disciplines which were, in large measure, synonymous, and, hence, equal. But in politics or political discourse, such terms, as concepts, take on new meaning.

Political philosophy is that body of ideas, ideals, and theories which is developed, or held, by one man. Since it is thus the concern of one man, be he a thinker and philosopher or not, all political philosophy is essentially ethical, normative and propagandistic. Every person is a propagandist, or a moralist, regardless of his conscious realisation of this fact. Thus, for Sarkar, political philosophy, as "pure thought", is a contradiction of terms: by its nature political philosophy must be applied, dynamic, practical, or "goal-full". It must deal with the purposes and motivations of living actions undertaken by living agents. The basis of war, party politics, constitutionalism, and law-making are to be found in political philosophy as a branch of ethics.

Political science, on the other hand, he saw as a human enterprise which is essentially descriptive-historical, comparative and universal. It deals, in the main, with an objective presentation of all facts and view-points. Hence, it is the discipline by which tendencies and movements of society are identified and/or indicated. While the history of thought might give men various propagandas of politics, these doctrines, along with states and institutions in which they suffer or create, could be, and are still, subjected to critical examination and, thereby, reduced to a descriptive science of politics.[8]

3. *Logic*: Thought must be justified. Its development and existence is not accidental. Two preconditions are necessary for such development. Speculative complexities must be evoked; and this can only occur within a contextual atmosphere of doubt as to the soundness of the "established order" of existing institutions. Hope and challenge, rather than apathy, must be aroused.

[7] *Ibid.*, p. 1.

[8] *Ibid.*, p. 3.

There must be a minimum of expectancy and motivation. Thus seen, Sarkar sounds an ultimatum: the methods of skepticism are the bedrock underlying the rationale for the use of logic in systems of political thought.

But all such thought must be classified. Its communication necessitates precision, or its content will break down in transit. Sarkar divided thought arbitrarily into what he called "*category*" and "*substance*". *Category* is the class or form into which a thought is cast; it is a symbol, an item of internal mechanics or a structural item within a logical frame. *Substance* is the datum of material and descriptive content of thought; it represents the obvious and the real in man's experience – the record of stimulus and response of life within the world. As content is the meaning within a word, so is substance the value equivalence within a category. The same category may hold or indicate a number of different contents. On the other hand, the identity of one "life value" does not necessarily imply identity with another thought substance. Thus, for example, such categories as property, freedom, justice, good and beauty have different substances in different regions of the world and in different spans (epochs) of time; and, although some categories of political thought may happen to seem identical today with those of yesterday, there is no justification for considering them identical in the measurement of their actual values. Revolution in political philosophy occurs when altogether new, and utterly unknown, categories are brought into being and when new substances or new values are imparted to already well-known categories.[9]

4. *History*: In applying Sarkar's rationale to his interpretation of history, especially the history of ideas, we discover that he placed special significance in modern political philosophy. Traditional "Hindu" or Indian concepts of the state, property, law and international relations both were, and are, useful as categories in political philosophy. As such, they can be subjected to comparative analysis and systematisation against the theories of Machiavelli, Hobbes, or Rousseau. Sarkar, however, felt that conventional and traditional concepts could take on new "moral", "political" or "spiritual" values. He set 1905 as that pivotal point in a time, when "contemporary" political philosophy "began". Modern political philosophy he saw as dividing itself into three rationally well-marked stages: (1) the primitive beginnings indicating the time of gestation (1776–1870); (2) the recent developments tending to the establishment of characteristically modern ideologies (1870–1905); (3) contemporary phases (1905–). The test of the distinction between contemporary and previous political philosophies is that certain categories are absolutely new and other older categories have new substances. The distinction is to be seen objectively in the contrast between the political parties of today and yesterday. The American constitution and other more recent constitutions, and trends toward public finance, economic

[9] *Ibid.*, p. 4–6.

legislation, and the welfare state in our own times, he saw as quite distinct when compared with those previous to 1870.

"Young India", as Sarkar conceived it, has lagged behind in appropriating elements within the main currents of modern political philosophy. Generally speaking, that body of political speculation in India which had been expressed in Bengali, Hindi, Urdu or Indian-English, he felt, has represented only the kinds of thought that prevailed in "Euro-America" prior to 1870. The constitutional, legal, economic and international experiences of the Western world since 1870 had yet scarcely touched the fringe of higher intellectuals in India. India's nationalistic philosophy of politics, that which continues to furnish the chief "spiritual urge" in Indian public life and in its speculative idealism, has been confined only within certain circles of the "educated middle class"; and, as such, it could be with the substances of thought which lay behind the American Revolution (1776), from Montesquieu to Joseph Mazzini. The deepening and expanding strands of Western thought in India which have excited the interest of a few intellectuals in India, he saw more as novelties rather than as vital forces of social reconstruction.[10]

Within the web of modern political philosophy, Sarkar saw at least five forces as shaping, or as being woven within any ideological complex. These sets of ideas and ideals, as concepts, were: (1) sovereignty; (2) economic welfare; (3) international relations; (4) human development and societal evolution; and (5) mental and moral personality. In every new era, new constitutional and legal theories have arisen which have then influenced concepts of sovereignty. Though its significance has so often been overlooked, economics he saw as having come into its own as a basic factor in politics. Imperialistic internationalism became an economic, political and social fact of modern civilisation during the period 1870 to 1905; but only after 1905 did it acquire importance in theory – both in imperialistic and anti-imperialistic conceptualisations. The discipline of sociology, indeed the social background of political thought in all ages, had only recently exerted itself as an independent science and, consequently, had only recently influenced political thinking with perspectives from its own angles of vision. The impact and role of psychology upon politics could be seen as even more recent.

> Violence and revolution are not only the milieu for the turning of philosophies but they are often the embodied thoughts and applications of such philosophies. To such innate philosophy as category belong all economic legislation and constitution making. Tendencies in political thinking cannot be analyzed without proper orientation to wars, revolutions, laws and constitutions.[11]

For Sarkar, understanding of these five deeply formative kinds of forces, whether viewed as independent, interdependent or in conflict with one another, is a prerequisite for engaging in

[10] *Ibid.*, p. 9.

[11] *Ibid.*, p. 12.

the modern science of politics. The "web of political philosophy", he concluded, "is the joint-product of global cooperation in theory making".[12]

No good student of history or political science, Sarkar warned, should ignore the contributions of any particular nation. American thought, often ignored in the East because of its lack of strong metaphysical dosage, had much to teach the world. For clarifying intelligence, energising will, and engaging vital issues of life and duty, as well as confronting spiritual factors which aim at the rebuilding of mankind, he wrote:

> [...] the annals of political philosophy can point to some of the world`s greatest exemplars in the direct, realistic and perspicuous thoughts of Alexander Hamilton and Thomas Jefferson, Calhoun, and Lincoln, Woodrow Wilson and John Dewey.

While Americans might lack some of the finesse of French creative imagination or the depth and grasp of German genius, they were:

> [...] pragmatic and straight-forward thinkers in whom the ideas and ideals of liberty, democracy and national welfare have been broadening down from precedent to precedent.[13]

III

Having uncovered some of the foundations of the philosophic rationale and science constructed by Benoy Sarkar, we may now proceed to see how he applied his theoretical system – how he made use of his structured ideas to develop concepts of boundaries, states, and governments.

1. *Boundaries*: For Sarkar, it is sword which determines the boundary. The might of the sword is the only guarantee for the existence of the state. Culture may be borrowed, as also language, religion, race; but, in a very essential sense, the sword must be its own: "A swordless state is a contradiction of terms." More than that: One of the most profound vital urges in human life has ever consisted in the effort to make boundaries. The making and remaking of the frontiers is perhaps the greatest single item that has been pushing the world's history on a monumental scale since mankind began to live in groups.[14] Artifacts and landmarks in political evolution can be found in narratives of wars, in musty treaties and industrious making of new maps; but ultimately. it is the sword which decides. An unarmed region can be labelled in many ways – as "buffer", "sphere of influence", "mandate", "territory", "protectorate", "dependency", or given any number of other names. But, without the sword, a political low pressure area figures on a map only as a land of humanised servants, slaves, or subjects – ever to be counted within the

[12] *Ibid.*, p. 11–14.

[13] *Ibid.*, p. 13.

[14] Benoy Kumar Sarkar, *The Politics of Boundaries*, Calcutta 1926, p. 1.

category of second-class human beings. Such a country must ever remain peripheral, lying on the outskirts of civilisation until its own "sword" is found, stolen or developed to the point where it can win and gain respect, and other things, for itself.[15]

The compositions, territorial extents, and qualities of states, Sarkar saw, as being bounded by force. Such being the case, every treaty is provisional. Every boundary is temporary, fixed or challenged only by exercises of sheer power. Every frontier is conditional and provisional, until the next trial of arms comes along. All such arrangements are "temporary", codified only on "scraps of paper". But "gunpowder" must always be kept dry, ready for the next contingency, the next emergence of events.

> There is thus no mystical absoluteness or inalienability to the limits of a state. The 'scientific frontiers' may advance or recede with every generation according to the dynamics of inter-social existence. The only architect of the world's historical geography from epoch to epoch is the *shakti-yoga* or energism of man.[16]

States are born in blood and violence. Boundaries depend on blood and iron. They are forged upon the anvils of war, of treaties, and of tariffs.

For the political engineering of boundaries, size is no obstacle. Two people, or three hundred million, it does not matter. Assassins, pirates, robber-bands, guerrillas: each and every kind of social unit can constitute, or possess, the political essentials of statehood. There is nothing mystical about this.

> There is a state in posse [...] an embryonic nation [...] whenever and wherever the status quo of the powers that be is challenged by a group of armed human beings.[17]

A single revolutionary, in the most extreme form of this theory, exists as the nucleus of a state. The problem is nothing more than "giving sovereignty" – of "giving habitation a name". The practical statesman wishing to manufacture a state must have a variable combination of the necessary ingredients. There must be such constituent elements of mankind as can consent (or can be coerced, or made to consent) to the bringing of such a structure into existence, such resources as will afford lands, waters, mines, forests in sufficient disposition as to provide the power to force by arms in open war.

> The will to create a state and the ability to protect and develop it are the sole items in the methodology of statesmanship.[18]

This principle applies to "as much as the market will bear" – as much of the world, its territory and people, as can be organised into such an entity. Only two things prevent a One World government: the will and the resources to implement such will.

15 *Ibid.*, p. 13–14.

16 *Ibid.*, p. 14–15.

17 *Ibid.*, p. 16–18.

18 *Ibid.*, p. 23.

2. *States*: The state is not a natural organism. It is "a voluntary association, an artificial corporation, and institution consciously created or manufactured like the Standard Oil Company or Oxford University". It is one of many of the products of man's creative will and intelligence. It can be made and unmade. Its genesis, expansion, contraction and dissolution are all different "reactions [...] of a social group to the stimuli of its milieu". It is a mechanical conglomeration of domestic units, clan communities, socio-economic trusts, and partnerships. Nationality, as a form of socio-political formulation, is a very young historical phenomenon, and hence subject to much vague thinking. In theory, it represents the idea of "one language, one culture, one race, one people, one state". In practice, it is merely an abstract concept and, as such, has never been realized on earth.

> When by a fiat of human creativeness an artificial corporation is brought into being, homogeneity of interests is not necessarily a source of strength, nor is heterogeneity a special weakness.[19]

Political thinking is often muddled. It is muddled by not realising the discrepancy between wishful theorising and hard historical facts. J. G. Fichte, G. F. Hegel, F. Mazzini and J. S. Mill confused dogma with abstract idealism. With prescient insight, Sarkar asked: "Which of the new 'nation-states' of Europe, such as Jugoslavia, Czechoslovakia and Poland are not polyglot, and multi-racial? What will happen to Europe? Will it 'Balkanize'? What of the *irredenta* problems of the Germans and Italians and Greeks? These realities serve only to thwart the nation-state idea."[20]

History knows only of "states". Patriots, poets, and philosophers may dream or talk. They may evolve romantic soul-theories of nationality. But only diplomats, politicians, and soldiers *know* states. The empires of the great state-systems of world history, pragmatically speaking, have had the same basic characteristics and underlying ingredients as the tiniest of households. When thus reduced, the nation is denuded of its multifarious trappings; and the state alone can be seen in an attitude of stark reality, unburdened by those traditional auras of sanctity which become attached to the dignity of political institutions. No innate force compels or obliges any one race, one language, one religion or one culture to embody itself within a state-like structure as its sole and most characteristic expression.

Sovereignty and independence are limited as a matter of course. The state may come and go; but people do not disappear: they continue and may live to create new partnerships or states according to the needs of the hour. The state must be sought out in the will of the people; and its sole origin must be their will to *agree* to its formation. Agreement may be tacit or expressed, self-determined by a free corporation or forced upon a subject race. Voluntary agreement by

[19] *Ibid.*, p. 21.

[20] *Ibid.*, p. 5–11. C. f. B. K. Sarkar, *The Political Institutions and Theories of the Hindus*, Leipzig 1922.

subject races, "minorities", or *irredenta* is a legal fiction. (The same rule would also apply relations between labour and management in "collective bargaining".) A contract renders internal sovereignty automatically dependent on the whims and interests of the constituent partners and gives a conditional external sovereignty.[21]

Sovereignty is dependent on the conjuncture of international circumstances. National independence is the product of conflicts between neighbours; moreover, it cannot function unless or until accepted as such by neighbouring powers. This is a tacit contract regulating the external relations of states by mutual recognition.

> It is impossible that a nation should be able to acquire or preserve freedom or prestige solely on the strength of its own resources in national wealth and character [...] every people has to settle its policy and course of action by detailed study of the disposition of the world-forces (*vishwa-shakti*) and the situation of the political center of gravity at the time.[22]

> A country must seek its own interest. World-forces, including internationalism, are its tools. The same contract that brings a state into being [...] can also create a system of arbitration and international law. But in the last analysis, it is the few that make and rule the state for their own interest. Though formally run in the name of the one or though camouflaged to seem the institution of the many [...] it is always the *few* that really rule.[23]

3. *Governments*: Sarkar viewed what he called "demo-despotocracy" as the most fundamental reality of politics. This reality, of course, he felt, is a direct product of the twin creative agencies in the formation of a state, consent and force. Democracy and despotocracy are not in antithesis to each other, he claimed, but in reality supplement and complement each other. Neither is absolute; both are limited and conditional.

> Democracy is as stern, as eternal and as universal or ubiquitous a reality in societal organizations as despotocracy. The two polarities constitute a moral unit in inter-human relations and forms (Zwischen-menschliche Beziehungen und Gebilde) [...] Hobbes' *Leviathan* is then but a partial, one-sided, erroneous and misleading view of the human nature in politics. It is as inadequate and incomplete as Rousseau's *Contract* [sic!] *Social* which presents almost the exact opposite picture of inter-human relations.[24]

Democracy and Despotocracy cannot act separately; nor is there such a phenomenon as a completely despotic or democratic state. Thus Chamberlain was a despot who knew how to ignore Parliament, and Hitler was a democrat who knew how to heed the *vox populi*. The Leviathan has not yet been able to thoroughly sweep away the British constitution; nor have inher-

[21] Subodh Krishna Ghoshal, *Sarkarism: the Ideas and Ideals of Benoy Sarkar on Man and His Conquests*, Calcutta 1939, p. 31; B. K. Sarkar, *The Politics of Boundaries*, p. 14. Also see Sarkar's *Science of History and the Hope of Mankind*, London 1912.

[22] S. K. Ghoshal, *Sarkarism*, p. 30; B. K. Sarkar, *The Politics of Boundaries*, p. 14.

[23] *Ibid.*, p. 14.

[24] S. K. Ghoshal, *Sarkarism*, p. 35. "Demo-Despotocracy and Freedom," given at the first Indian Political Science Conference, Benares 1938.

ent or innate or underlying elements of '*social contract'* been entirely silenced within the inner foundations of totalitarian '*Staatsräson*'.

As applied to the administration of India, the principle of demo-despotocracy was found to be a process which was becoming even more apparent. The transfer of power to the Company was not accomplished exclusively by some simple or forced subjugation of an unwilling people by the will of a superior military strength of an invading "foreign" army. There has always been an element of free choice by which the peoples and princes of India, whose actions as exemplified by the *farmans* and *sanads* of the Mughal Emperor or other rulers, participated in the construction of their own political system (whatever its "chains may have been"). Thus seen, the peoples of India did not revolt against this transfer of power to the Company, nor did all princes join in enlisting the aid of the French against the British. For Sarkar, such events as the Wahabi movement, the Great Revolt of 1857, or the formation of the Indian National Congress in 1885 were but stages, markers within a process of social mobilization, part of a steadily increasing strength in the *vox populi* elements within a newly and truly "Indian" polity.[25]

So seen, it was important for the Indian National Congress to continue to adhere to this principle of government. In Sarkar's time, one could still hope that such a principle would clearly emerge as the *de facto* internal constitution for what was becoming, after all, the 'third corporate dynasty' of the Raj (although he himself never used these exact words). Congress had become, in Sarkar's view, virtually an *imperium in imperio.* But, not for a moment did he fail to see the corrupting the despotic tendencies which had always been dominant, even inherent, within the Indian political system. He wrote:

> The Congress High Command has during the entire course of its history comprised from time to time just a few individuals or families, both Hindu and Moslem. These individuals or families possess [...] the sinews of war, i. e. bullion.[26]

The antipathy of Sarkar for Gandhian policies became obviously more marked in his writings the older he became. The often mindless events related to so-called 'mass' actions in civil disobedience worried him. He saw in such events an underlying tendency toward corruption and despotism within the Congress machine, lubricated and powered as it was by the *dal-roti* of 'feudalistic zamindars', bankers, and industrialists (such as Birla). Indian politicians, no matter how sincerely patriotic, idealistic and self-sacrificing some of them may have been at the start, were coming, consciously or unconsciously, under the corruption and exploitation by the wealthy. Sarkar laid out the plans for a campaign against the corrupting despotism of the rich, the literate, the high born and the school-going classes.[27]

25 S. K. Ghoshal, *Sarkarism*, p. 36.

26 *Ibid.*, p. 37.

27 Cf. B. K. Sarkar, *Progress Planning: A Scheme of Emancipation on Five Fronts*. n. p., n. d.

VI

Sarkarism, as an intellectual and/or ideological system of thought, repudiated the notion that there could be any inherent difference in the ideals of the East and the West. Humanity is fundamentally one. India's troubles lie in its poverty, over-population and its caste structures. This problem is reflected in the politics of the land, though the solution must lie in a renewed assertion of positivism as demonstrated in socio-economic reform. The thesis that India can teach nothing but sublime speculations of an other worldly character – the psychology of the soul, the retreat from life struggles and the metaphysics of the infinite, as all notions of Asian quietism and non-resistance – was fiercely denounced as unable to stand up under historical criticism or scientific scrutiny.[28]

Only in the 17th and 18th centuries did the East commence to lag behind the West in technological science. Achievements of Hindus in the field of positive science, ever since the time the Vedas and down to 1600 (C. E.) had been noteworthy; however, thereafter, both Hindus and Muslims had been gripped by a peculiar pessimistic and apathetic mentality, a strange lack of imagination or initiative in materialistic or physical fields of science. They had refused to learn the scientific-cum-technological developments ushered in by the West. Neither Muslim nor Hindu culture was inherently at fault; rather, blame had to be laid squarely on short-comings in the character of the 17th and 18th century leadership within the Indian subcontinent.[29]

1. *Poverty*: Sarkar's prognosis for India's poverty contradicted the views of most economists in India and elsewhere. He did not follow Gandhi's castigation of modern industries; nor did he fall in with the 'statist' nostrums of socialist diehards. Indian poverty, he felt, has not been due to inequitable distribution of either income or wealth; nor has it been a consequence class exploitation. The poverty problem is a problem which has to be faced by almost the whole Indian people.

> Poverty in India is not so much a resultant of inequities in the distribution of wealth as of the dearth or want of creative occupation […] The Indian poverty problem is to be envisaged as a question of unemployment on a vast continental scale.[30]

[28] B. K. Sarkar, *Futurism of Young Asia*, Berlin 1922, p. 7.

[29] B. K. Sarkar, *Positive Background of Hindu Sociology*, Allahabad 1937, lectures delivered at the Second Indian Cultural Conference, Calcutta, 1937.

[30] Banesvar Dass, *The Social and Economic Ideas of Benoy Sarkar*, Calcutta 1940, p. 294. S. K. Ghoshal, *Sarkarism*, p. 38.

The task for the poverty doctors was to remedy this huge unemployment by creating myriads of jobs and careers, new opportunities and professions. This called for imaginative individual initiatives on a grand scale.

The medicine Sarkar prescribed for poverty was a massive growth in commercial development and industrialisation. Economic activities would have to grow in multiplicity and diversity, the production of wealth would have to increase in every field, so that the millions of people could scope for functioning and performing as industrial workers, office clerks, insurance agents, bank-managers, chemists and engineers. Governmental and popular pressure would be needed in order to compel factories and workshops, in their own interest, to open elementary and vocational schools, research institutes, and technical colleges. Only in this way would it be possible to meet increasing demands for trained personnel. Agriculture, relieved of the burden of maintaining the teeming millions of "village India", would have to adjust to problems of redistribution required by such a vast population by improved methods of crop production, backed by new systems of marketing, communication, and transport. Handicrafts, shedding their primitiveness, would have to become subsidiary industries, adapted to the needs of a new industrial age. Villages would then grow into municipalities, so that sanitary and cultural conditions have to be improved. Only then would the world begin to know, and to realise, that there is an India. Only then, when India makes its proper and proportionate impact upon the world, would the world begin to take India seriously.[31]

The biggest question confronting India, as Sarkar saw it, was that of finding a way to break the impetus of inertia. It would require immense capital and social will to initiate and sustain such a vast economic movement, and to preserve its momentum. India alone, by itself, would never be able to provide this. Large-scale loans and investments, in sufficient quantities, could only be found abroad. Here, a distinctive feature of Sarkarism, as a form of applied economics combined with economic statesmanship, was posited. India's leaders would have to generate and hold a single-minded and grand mission. They would need to approach the big bankers of the world and invite them to invest in Indian men and materials; moreover, these bankers would have to be made to see that the standards of living in Europe and the United States could be maintained, raised and/or sustained only insofar as there were also a simultaneous development in the industrially under-developed countries. Capital investors would have to find and generate wealth in India. India would have to attract and to compensate investment. Exploitation was not an evil which ideologues and theorists were always seeking to picture. Foreign capital, within limits and restrained, was not to be seen merely as a curse, but should be treated as a God-send. Indians would have to learn to admit that without the help from foreign sources

[31] B. K. Sarkar, *Economic Development,* vol. 1, Madras 1926, p. 392; S. K. Ghoshal, *Sarkarism*, p. 38–44; B. Dass, *Social and Economic Ideas*, p. 295–7.

India's economic and cultural poverty would only become more palpable, extensive and profound.[32]

Sarkar's theory of "stages of economic development" was somewhat similar to that of Friedrich List, but in stark opposition to the school of Sir Vithal Das Thackeray. The contribution of Sarkar to economic theory lay, and still lies, in the doctrine that

> […] whatever has happened in the economic sphere in Euro-America during the last half-century is bound also to happen more or less on similar and identical lines in Asia and, of course, India during the next generation or so.[33]

Although an exponent of 'capitalism', Sarkar also introduced Indian thinkers to neo-socialism and neo-capitalism by drawing attention to the benefits of labour economics and social insurance. Foundations of capitalistic morphology as found in the industrial achievements of the German *Sozialpolitik,* combined with England's "positive democracy" and "constructive socialism" can be credited with having influenced Sarkar's unique kinds of contributions to the *swadeshi* movement in Bengal.[34]

2. *Over-Population*: This problem was not seen as being peculiar to India. Over-population is not a numerical magnitude, as generally believed. The mere number of inhabitants per unit of area is no index of "optimum" over-population or under-population. Over-population is fundamentally an economic category and as such is difficult to demonstrate in a precise manner since economic categories, as a rule, are elastic and relative. Whenever and/or wherever there is poverty, low purchasing power and low standard of living, there is over-population. Every country, including rich countries, are liable to this danger; and many have always been beset by it. The stress of over-population is likely to grow apace with modernisation involving better health and lower mortality rates. When seen in this light, India's problem is no worse than that of any other country.

The international coefficients of vital statistics, as measured by the natural increments of birth, death and infant mortality, are objectively indifferent to considerations of climate, race, religion and politics.

> Under uniform conditions of temperature, altitude, isotherms, as well as physiognomy, social mores and legal institutions […] we discover an extensive diversity of birth and death rates; and on the other hand identical or neighboring coefficients are distributed over regions of the world marked by very diverse physico-physiographical and socio-cultural characteristics.[35]

---

32 B. Dass, *Social and Economic Ideas*, p. 297.

33 B. K. Sarkar, *Economic Development*, vol. 1, p. ix.

34 B. Dass, *Social and Economic Ideas*, p. 297–302; Cf. B. N. Sarkar, *Social Insurance Legislation and Statistics*, Calcutta 1936; B. K. Sarkar, *Ingrajer Janmabhumi*.

35 Ghoshal, *Sarkarism*, p. 22.

High birth rates are not exclusively Indian, oriental or "tropical", but may be seen as Euro-American as well. Only in recent times have the undesirable rates disappeared from the pioneering people of Euro-America. Demographic comrades are not necessarily bound by geographical, ethnological and sociological kinship. If India could enjoy more popular instruction and general sanitation, if India could use her finances for what other modern countries consider to be their first charges, it is likely that India could catch up to and go ahead of the world in the not distant future.[36]

3. *Caste*: The fundamental fact of caste is that it is both cultural and physical Castes are groups of human beings set apart for the production of mates and, as such, have been designed for the regulation of marriage. Caste, as 'birth' or '*jati*' should be studied as a form of eugenics, and certainly not as either economics or theology.

> A scientific treatment of the caste system [...] is tantamount to the history of marriages or blood relationships among the Hindus and of the changes in their eugenic ideas.[37]

Caste has been powerfully influenced by political and military history. Its study should be undertaken from a view of dynastic changes, military expeditions, subjugation of races, empire building and political disruption. It must be observed as the influence of warfare on social and economic conditions. When caste is thus seen as a branch of military history, it is found to possess vastly different values and meanings through different epochs of history, insofar that it would not be difficult to reveal its arbitrary claims as an antiquarian fiction.

Economic and cultural progress appears often to have been diverse from group to group; but progress really follows in a wake of racial ups and downs. Caste metabolism is as much a historical unreality in the domain of intelligence quotients as is race, monism and absolutism. Socio-economic solutions for the world can be instituted only after such artificial differences as caste, class struggle, Western materialism versus Eastern spiritualism, racial superiority and other blindly accepted credos are laid in the dust.

> Probably the most universally accepted postulate in the thought of Europe and America is that the occidental races are superior to the oriental [...] The whole world-culture of the previous 5000 years is assumed as but a preamble to the grand domination of the orient by the occident during the last few generations. But how does the same history appear to the oriental angle of vision? [...] it has been the historic role of Asia to be always the aggressor and Europe ever on the defensive. By the test of arms the superior races of the world have been Asians more often than Europeans.[38]

36 *Ibid.*, p. 22.

37 *Ibid.*, p. 20.

38 B. K. Sarkar, *Sociology of Race, Cultures and Human Progress*, Berlin 1939, p. 2.

Having made this point, Sarkar turned against all of the man-made eugenic barriers which have crystallised into economic and cultural stagnation. For him, men and women constitute basic items of commercial and civic existence. Progress can come only after the caste is gone.[39]

V

No further investigation or careful observation is required to discover that Benoy Sarkar was an extraordinary person, a thinker whose energy and vitality was remarkable – 'a man for all seasons' and times. For nearly half a century he was one of the dominant figures in research and scholarship on politics and education, not just in India but in world. He was been credited with having written more works and words than any other modern Indian scholar. Commencing as a somewhat radical partisan, his perspective broadened through the years, to such an extent that, in his last days, much of what he did was dissipated in gigantic works of systematising and classifying data. During this time his role as theorist and philosopher was slowly transformed into that of an encyclopedist, a gatherer of facts. At his death, Sarkar is said to have left several trunk loads of little scraps on which facts had been carefully jotted down.

To understand and appreciate Sarkar and his contribution to the social sciences, it is necessary to glance hastily at the spread of his activities during the last years of his life – years when he became increasingly dissatisfied and critical of Indian scholarship and politics. To promote technological education in India, he founded the Jaydavpur Engineering College. In collaboration with his friend, Dr. N. N. Law, he brought out an economic journal in Bengali. He was a consultant to some of the largest industrial firms and business houses in India. Commercial enterprises between Indians and foreign businessmen were formed, in some of which he was personally involved. Over a hundred research fellows were employed through his direct influence. He organised societies, fellowships, and associations in economics, demography, politics, literature and much more, insomuch that he was able to maintain an enormous range of contacts – with most of his students, associates and disciples. Of the other fields of work, of the sources of financial support, of the colloquiums, conferences and seminars for the interchange of interests and ideas which he organised: the list seems endless. His work was brought to a close when he succumbed from over-work after coming to the United States on some special projects in 1949. He suffered a heart attack after a lecture at George Washington University, in Washington, D. C.

[39] B. Dass, *Social and Economic Ideas*, p. 287f; c. f. B. K. Sarkar, *Greetings to Young India*, Calcutta 1927, p. 117–18.

Sarkar possessed an penetrating vision of society and its needs. He was starkly aware of India's miserable plight. In pursuance of his vision he poured out his energy as a man dedicated to a mission. His work was ended, as in a grand and final crescendo, when he tried to demonstrate the inter-responsibility of peoples and nations. In delivering over fifty lectures, down to his last month in the U. S., he expressed concern over the devaluation of currencies in the Sterling block and attempted raise American aid for Indian exchange students. Still, for all that, he seems to have had the joy and preoccupation of a child at play or of a man absorbed with his hobby. This is difficult to measure because his own personality appears to be hidden in his work. Yet one has the feeling that the regular Sunday morning discussions in Calcutta, which occurred on "Narain Laha's Verandah", were enjoyed as a form of constructive recreation, and that they were not without humour.

The syncretistic tendencies at work in India today are evidenced in the writings and influence of Benoy Sarkar. Being a positivist, profoundly influenced by German thought, with a profound respect for the methods of objective research, he was in a position to give new interpretation and direction to the traditional views of Hindu political theory. Such concepts as *maṇḍala-nyāya* (the "logic of spheres": relations between entities of relatively equal power, size or strength; as in international diplomacy and interstate conflict), *matsya-nyāya* (the "logic of fish": relations between entities of unequal size, strength and power), and *daṇḍa* ("the stick": coercive force or sanction) were reflected in a hard, earthbound and practical light. Sarkar tried to tear away the illusion that some peoples, that segments of mankind (e. g. humanity), could be fundamentally so different or that any epoch or region could necessarily be innately and exclusively more mystical or mechanical than another.

We have examined the personality, theory and science of an extremely unconventional, highly illuminating and exceedingly controversial figure. Perhaps the true image of the man has been blurred by near or farsightedness. Some misemphasis is certainly inevitable. The scope and purpose of this study necessitates an unhappy degree of selectivity. Thus, dimensions of the depth, breadth and surface, the proportions of life and thought, which could be examined are limited. But the fact that the qualities of the observer can be rubbed off onto the analysis, does not automatically nullify the value of the effort. The political science of Benoy Sarkar needs no vindication for it stands or falls on its own merits.

Bibliographic Note and Select List of References

No complete bibliography of the published articles, books, lectures, pamphlets, papers and other works of Benoy Sarkar has ever, as far as I know, been compiled. Many years ago, some bibliographical work was done by the advocates of *Sarkarism*. Much of Sarkar's thought, moreover, has been duplicated in encyclopaedic volumes or in later publications. This is somewhat confusing. Some of Sarkar's most classic works are to be found in the main libraries of major research universities in the West – such as California (Berkeley), Cambridge, Chicago, Columbia, Duke, Michigan, Oxford, Pennsylvania, Wisconsin (Madison), or SOAS. Over forty years ago, a large portion of Sarkar materials were made available to me from the private library of one of very my earliest mentors, Richard L. Park, when we were both at Berkeley. Presumably that collection is now at Berea College in Ohio where all of his library was sent before he died. Needless to say, I am greatly indebted to Park and to his friendship with Sarkar, whom he had met while he was on military service in Bengal during the World War II (1942–5).

a) Works about Benoy Kumar Sarkar

Dass, Banesvar, *The Social and Economic Ideas of Benoy Sarkar*, Calcutta 1939.

Ghoshal, Subodh Krishna, *Sarkarism – The Ideas and Ideals of Benoy Sarkar on Man and His Conquests*, Calcutta 1939.

Malakar, Dilip, *The Political and Sociological Publications and Lectures of Benoy Sarkar: 1926–49*, Calcutta 1949.

In Memoriam – Benoy Sarkar, Calcutta: University Senate Hall, Tuesday, January 10th, 1950.

b) Larger Works by Benoy Kumar Sarkar

The Science of History and the Hope of Mankind, London 1912.

The Positive Background of Hindu Sociology, Allahabad, vol. 1, 1914, 1922 [revised]; vol. 2 [revised], 1927. Reprint New York 1974 (Lectures given again at Second Indian Cultural Conference, Calcutta: 1937).

The Beginning of Hindu Culture as a World-Power, Shanghai 1916.

The Futurism of Young Asia, Berlin 1922.

The Political Institutions and Theories of the Hindus, Leipzig 1922.

The Politics of Boundaries, Calcutta 1926 (A work having to do with tendencies in international relations).

Greetings to Young India, Calcutta 1927

Economic Development: Studies in Applied Economics and World Economy, 2 volumes. Madras 1926; Calcutta 1932.

The Political Philosophies Since 1905, Madras 1928 (An outline of a course of lectures given at the Kashi Vidyapitha, Benares, in October 1927).

Demo-Despotocracy and Freedom, Benares, First Indian Political Science Conference, 1938.

The Sociology of Races, Cultures and Human Progress, Berlin 1939 (A revision of *Futurism* ..., with additional materials).

Hermann Schumacher und Indien, Eine Lebenserinnerung und eine Dankaussprache, Calcutta 1948.

Re-thinking Iran, Calcutta, Iran Society 1949 (Presidential address at annual general meeting of the Iran Society).

India's Epochs in World-Culture, Calcutta, Bharata-Kaumudi, *s. a.*

c) Some Sample Articles by Benoy Kumar Sarkar

"Dharmapala Through Bengali Eyes," *The Maha-Bodhi Journal* (September, 1948).

"The Re-making of Higher Studies in Economics, Commerce, Politics and Sociology for Dominion India," *Calcutta Review* (October, 1948).

"Gandhi, Non-Gandhi and Anti-Gandhi in the Pattern of Indian Ideologies," *Calcutta Review* (1948, Gandhi Number), reprinted by Calcutta University.

d) Pamphlets, Papers by Benoy Kumar Sarkar (articles, papers, etc.)

"The Asian Movement in India as an Inter-human Pattern" (January, 1947).

"Euro-America and India in Class Inequalities" (December, 1947).

"Cheap Money, Commercial Policy and Indo-Pakistan Economic Relations," (January, 1948).

"Some Economic Fundamentals of the Indian Dominion in World Economy," (January; June, 1948).

"Criminology in India" (March, 1948).

"Social Legislation in Housing and Health" (April, i948).

"Formless Bengal and the Fluid Bengali" (May, 1948).

"The Demobilization Economy of Dominion India," (1948 ?).

"Government's Anti-Inflationary Policy," (*s. a.*).

"Financial Data of Dominion India in Anglo-American Perspectives" (*s. a.*).

"Wanted Mrityunjayis or 'Death-Conquerors' for West Bengal" (*s. a.*).

"The Remaking of Public Health for West Bengal" (*s. a.*).

"The Role of Bengalis in the Remaking of Dominion India" (*s. a.*).

"The Parianization of the Aryan" (*s. a.*).

The Leadership of the Muslim Political Community in Madras, 1914–1918[*]

Kenneth McPherson

1. Introduction

Between 1914 and 1918, the political life of the Urdu- and Tamil-speaking Muslims of the Madras Presidency underwent profound changes. In 1914, political leadership of the community was provided by a small élite group of Urdu-speaking Muslims[1] – mostly landowning aristocrats and a few wealthy merchants – but by 1918 new groups had emerged to challenge the role and views of the old leadership.

By 1918, leadership of both the Urdu and Tamil Muslims was passing into the hands of various alliances of Western-educated Muslims and prominent merchants from the Urdu and Tamil groups. The most active alliance comprised men drawn from all these groups, united by a growing distrust of the British and a burgeoning sympathy for the objectives of Congress. Other alliances, comprising men from the same mix of backgrounds, were in contrast less enamoured of Congress, and were more firmly wedded to a conservative and constitutional view of political change.

It may be argued that 1918 is an odd point at which to end this study, but I have done so deliberately to underscore two major points. There is a need to recognise that the Muslims of British India cannot be treated as a homogenous group – in cultural, linguistic, economic or political terms – and that if we are to understand their history we need to recognise their diversity. Also, it needs to be noted that Muslim involvement with Congress movement was well underway before the emergence of Gandhi in 1918–19.

Developments amongst the Muslims of the Madras Presidency between 1914 and 1918, provide a microcosm of developments within the Muslim community India-wide.

* My thanks to Professor Peter Reeves for his incisive and constructive comments on drafts of this article.

1 Hereafter the Urdu-speaking Muslims and the Tamil-speaking Muslims are referred to as Urdu Muslims and Tamil Muslims.

2. Origins of the Community

In 1914 the Muslims of the southernmost political division of British India – the Madras Presidency – were divided amongst three main linguistic groups. Apart from the Malayalam-speakers concentrated on the Malabar Coast, the Urdu- and Tamil-speakers were the largest and most important Muslim groups in the Presidency: with about 1,100,000 Urdu Muslims and nearly 500,000 Tamil Muslims. Collectively Muslims comprised nearly 5% of the total population of the Presidency.

Most Tamil Muslims lived in the populous coastal rice-cropping districts to the south of Madras city, whilst Urdu Muslims formed approximately half the Muslim population in what are now the drier northern districts of Tamil Nadu including Madras city, and the eastern districts of modern Andhra Pradesh. The majority of Muslims living in Madras city were Urdu-speakers.

The earliest Muslim communities developed when Arab and Persian merchants settled in various places along the Gulf of Mannar and the Coromandel coast. They intermarried with Tamils and over the centuries the community grew in size through conversions. The Tamil Muslims were an integrated part of Tamil society, being separated from other Tamils by religion alone; their place in local society was not dictated by their religion but rather by their relationship with local power élites and their interaction with other groups in the Tamil social landscape.[2] From the 14th century there was also a steady expansion of Islam into central and southern India from the north. These Urdu- and Persian-speaking settlers congregated in garrison and administrative centres in the Deccan districts where they served Muslim and Hindu rulers as an administrative/military élite.

3. The Economic Background of Muslim Life in the Madras Presidency

With the exception of the Mappila Muslims of the Malabar Coast, few Muslims elsewhere in the Madras Presidency were engaged in agriculture. Most Tamil Muslims were traditionally coastal merchants and dealers in skins and hides. Until the establishment of British rule, Urdu Muslim economic life was underpinned by Muslim political authority. Most Urdu Muslims were urban dwellers; the majority were undoubtedly poor – petty artisans, shopkeepers, scholars and clerics – but a few prospered in government service and as merchants. With the estab-

2 S Bayly, *Saints, Goddesses and Kings. Muslims and Christians in South Indian Society, 1700–1900*, Cambridge 1989.

lishment of British rule in southern India in the late 18th century, processes of change began which all but eliminated the Urdu Muslim élite from political and administrative life, but introduced the Tamil Muslims into the mainstream of economic life in British India.

The new economic opportunities opened up to Tamil Muslims were related to their involvement in the land-based skin and hide trade where they interfaced with Urdu Muslim communities. Tamil Muslims found a niche in the modern leather industry as the main suppliers of raw hides and skins. This occupation brought them into increasingly intimate contact with their Urdu-speaking co-religionists in northern India, and exposed them to religious and cultural ideas and movements which were shaping Muslim attitudes elsewhere in the sub-continent.

Unlike the Tamil Muslims, the Urdu Muslims did not identify so closely with their non-Muslim neighbours. Whilst some lived in Tamil-speaking areas – where they remained aloof from their Tamil co-religionists whom they considered somewhat heterodox – most lived in the Telugu- and Kannada-speaking areas of the Presidency. British rule was as disastrous for many of the traditional Urdu Muslim élite in the Presidency as it was for their peers elsewhere in India. The new order cast the Urdu Muslims adrift in a world in which they had no immediate focus or purpose. Few members of the old Muslim élite adapted to the requirements of the new regime, and during the 19th century most slipped into poverty. Some entered the administration, but only at the lowest level. In the Madras Presidency the only aristocratic Muslim families to escape this fate were the descendants of the Nawabs of the Carnatic, headed by the Prince of Arcot, and the descendants of Tipu Sultan: all were stipendiaries of the government. Prestige within the community passed increasingly to the small number of families that had made a successful transition to commerce or had access to Western education. The mass of Urdu Muslims remained aloof from the new order. Most rejected the modern educational opportunities offered by the British and retreated into a world in which they clung desperately to the remnants of an older lifestyle. Much of the old élite had vanished and leadership was provided by a very small circle of families.

Whilst the Urdu Muslim community in the Madras Presidency as a whole suffered from the imposition of British rule, it is an irony that to the British the term "Muslim" was synonymous with "Urdu-speaking Muslims" rather than a more complex image which included other Muslim linguistic groups. The immediate result was that the British across India looked to prominent, particularly aristocratic, members of the Urdu Muslim community to act as intermediaries for the entire community – and to inform the British of Muslim opinion – until the political reforms of 1909 brought Muslims from other linguistic groups slowly into the formal political process. In the Madras Legislative Council between 1863 and 1909, for example, the nominated non-official Muslim members were British pensioners drawn from a very small pool of candidates descended from either Tipu Sultan or the Nawabs of the Carnatic. By the end of the

19th century, the spokesmen for the Urdu Muslims were drawn from three inter-related groups: the small mercantile élite of Madras city, the descendants of the Nawabs of the Carnatic (led by the Prince of Arcot) and of Tipu Sultan, and religious leaders.

Although Madras city was a powerful magnet which attracted immigrants from the *mofussil* it was not a colossus overshadowing all other urban centres in the Presidency. It was the largest and most cosmopolitan city in the Presidency, but in the Tamil *mofussil* there were other smaller, but thriving cities such as Madurai, Tiruchirapali, and Salem which were centres of vigorous business, educational and cultural life, and which generated their own mercantile and Western educated élites (both Hindu and Muslim), who considered themselves every bit as good as the sophisticated leaders of Indian society in Madras city. In addition to these flourishing centres of modern life there were also more ancient centres of Tamil Muslim settlement such as the small ports of Nagore and Nagapattinam. These towns were important Tamil Muslim religious centres and were home to wealthy Tamil Muslim merchant families with their own bases of local influence and power. In time, Madras city would become home in the late 19th and 20th centuries to wealthy Tamil Muslim merchant dynasties such as the family of Jamal Mahomed which made its fortune in the late 19th century from the skin and hide trade, but such families shared leadership of the Tamil Muslim community with other prominent merchants in the Tamil

The wide leadership base of the Tamil Muslims was not evident amongst the Urdu Muslims. Urdu Muslim leaders in Madras city had few peers in the *mofussil*, but also there were few similarities in lifestyle and aspirations between city and village. The city-*mofussil* divide between Urdu Muslims in the Presidency grew throughout the nineteenth and early 20th centuries. Madras city provided an environment in which Urdu Muslims could, albeit sometimes unwillingly, enter the modern world through the agency of trade, industry, government service and Western education. In the *mofussil*, however, Western influences were less pronounced. In this environment new educational and employment opportunities were rare. In small towns and villages scattered throughout the northern Tamil and Telugu *mofussil* traditional patterns of culture, education, trade and artisanal activity survived to set Muslims apart from their non-Muslim neighbours, and local leadership was provided by a petty bourgeoisie who viewed the modern world with suspicion and scorn.

Despite the obvious lack of unity within the various groups of Muslims in the Madras Presidency, they shared vital characteristics which made them susceptible to external influences which later helped arouse an encompassing self-consciousness. These shared characteristics were their common religion, their relatively high degree of literacy and their relatively high degree of urbanisation. Both these latter characteristics facilitated communication within and between the Urdu and Tamil Muslim groups, while the urban concentration of Muslims made organisation easier than if the community had been scattered uniformly throughout rural areas. There was also a bond of similar economic interest between the modern Urdu and Tamil Muslim élite by the early 20th century. Both were active in mercantile pursuits, though Tamil Muslims were generally more prosperous and more thoroughly imbued with a mercantile ethos.

4. The Road to Communal Rapprochement

As early as 1906, there is evidence of some dissatisfaction with British rule amongst leading Urdu Muslims in the Madras Presidency on the grounds of the depressed social and economic circumstances of most members of their community. Also, from 1906, Pan-Islamic sentiment added to growing discontent and increased feelings of insecurity and unease. Political concessions from the British – such as the creation of separate electorates under the Morley-Minto reforms in 1909 – did not silence Muslim complaints, in fact, quite the reverse, for such concessions reinforced group identity. The creation of an India-wide Muslim political bloc, with the foundation of the All-India Muslim League in 1906, reinforced bonds between the Urdu Muslims of north and south that the various religious and educational movements had been fostering since the late 19th century. The bloc may not have been united or a single, clearly-defined political entity, but it did facilitate the growth of an increasing identity of interests amongst Urdu-speaking Muslim leaders throughout India, based on commonly held grievances and aspirations.

Pan-Islamism also provided a bridge between Muslims in Madras city and the *mofussil*. It was a cause which united Muslims of all backgrounds because it was based on the concept of the universal community of Islam (the *umma*) which transcended sectarian and linguistic differences amongst Muslims. Thus in the Presidency, Pan-Islamism not only helped unite Urdu Muslims in a common cause, but it was also the first issue which began to break down the indifference of Urdu and Tamil Muslims to one another.

Apart from frustration engendered by local grievances, events elsewhere stimulated Urdu Muslim unrest. The annulment of the Bengal partition in 1911, the Tripolitanian and Balkan Wars between 1911 and 1913, and the Cawnpore Mosque affair of 1913 aroused considerable feeling within the Indian Muslim community. Urdu Muslims in the Presidency shared the excitement and resentment of Muslims elsewhere in India at these events. For some this alienation and resentment led them to take up the Pan Islamic cause with greater enthusiasm, and separated them further from their British rulers and Hindu compatriots. For others alienation and resentment encouraged a growing feeling of camaraderie with Congress, which some young Muslims saw as a vehicle for confronting the British. Tamil Muslims were less stirred by the problems of the Ottoman empire than their Urdu co-religionists, but they were not entirely unaffected by the spirit of Pan-Islamism.

Corresponding to the rise in antipathy towards the British was a slow development of a more accommodating and sympathetic attitude amongst some Urdu Muslims towards Congress. The Reforms of 1909 no doubt mitigated Muslim fears *vis-à-vis* the Hindus, particularly fear of outright political subjugation, and this growth of Muslim political confidence, combined with their growing sense of grievance toward the British, tended to draw Muslims closer to the Hindus and Congress. In 1913, the main English-language Muslim newspaper in southern India, the *Muhammadan*, noted that the recent troubles involving the Ottoman empire "have … tended towards the consolidation of Hindus and the Muslims".[3]

The lead towards conciliation in Madras was given by the Madras Presidency Muslim League, and the pro-League *Muhammadan* commented favourably upon the absence of "anarchist elements" in Congress and upon the conciliatory tone of its 1910 annual session.[4] In the same year, at the annual session of the All-India Muslim League in Nagpur, the speeches of the Madras League's delegation, and in particular of the young merchant, Yakub Hasan, kept strictly to non-communal problems of all-India concern. In the following year the provincial League was represented at the abortive Allahabad Conference when an attempt was made to reach an understanding with Congress. In 1911, and again in the following year, the *Muhammadan* spoke gratefully of the help that the Muslims in Madras city had received from Hindu sympathisers in their efforts to promote the Red Crescent Society and to organise public meetings in support of the Ottoman empire at the time of the Balkan Wars.[5]

Despite growing sympathy for Congress amongst some members of the Presidency League there is no evidence that between 1911 and 1914 it was intimately involved in developing the Congress-League *rapprochement*. Yakub Hasan and his supporters within the League were favouring such an accord, but there was no widespread agreement amongst Urdu Muslims on the desirability of a *rapprochement*.

Urdu Muslim opinion of Congress depended upon their attitude towards the British at particular times, for example at the time of the Balkan wars and the Cawnpore affair. But even at such times there was not always an unanimous swing of sentiment towards Congress, and vague fears of Hindu domination still persisted. Urdu Muslim leaders in Madras were divided in their objectives. The Pan-Islamists were orientated away from domestic concerns, and their cause aroused an emotional response that diverted loyalties and energy from the nationalist struggle. On the other hand leaders concerned with regional grievances and demands relating to

[3] *Muhammadan*, 14th August, Madras Native Newspaper Reports (hereafter MN) 1913.

[4] *Ibid.*, 23rd November, MN 1910.

[5] *Ibid.*, 5th January, 9th November, MN 1911; *Ibid.*, 14th October, MN 1912.

education and employment in government service were wary of a communal *rapprochement* because their grievances could only be resolved at the expense of other communities.

Despite the reservations of some Muslim leaders it is clear that the activities of certain prominent Urdu Madras Muslims contributed to the cause of a Congress-League understanding. For example, Nawab Syed Muhammed Bahadur,[6] was reconciled to the idea of a Madras League: he joined the League in 1910 and was one of their delegates to the 1910 annual session of the All-India Muslim League at Nagpur. He was elected President of the Southern Indian Muhammedan Educational Association for the year 1911–12. Furthermore in 1913, as President of the annual Congress session in Karachi, he argued strongly for communal unity, and, with Yakub Hasan, was prominent in the debates of the 1914 session of Congress held in Madras city. It was at this Congress session that the custom of appointing a Muslim as one of the General Secretaries to the All-India Congress Committee was initiated with the Nawab as the first incumbent of this office.[7]

In August 1914, Germany and Britain commenced hostilities, with the Ottoman empire joining with Germany in the following month. Between August and September, Madras Muslim newspapers voiced the belief that war between the Ottomans and Britain was impossible and exhorted Indian Muslims to give their full support to the Imperial Government. Even when the tragedy occurred, Muslims continued their protestations of loyalty and levelled bitter criticism at the Germans and Young Turks whom they blamed for dragging the innocent *Khalif* and peoples of the Ottoman empire into an unholy war. The All-India Muslim League cancelled its annual session as a gesture of loyalty to the King-Emperor, and it appeared that the British were succeeding in their desire to keep Muslims away from the "subversive" Congress. In Madras the government restricted the movements of the Honorary Ottoman consul, Khan Bahadur Abdul Aziz Badsha, causing him to protest that "I am a Muhammedan and a British subject and not a Turk".[8]

5. The Lucknow Pact

Once the initial shock of the outbreak of war had worn off there was a resurgence of interest, at least within the Madras Presidency Muslim League, in the question of communal *rapproche-*

6 A great grandson of Tipu Sultan; member of the Madras Legislative Council 1900–4 and the Imperial Legislative Council 1904–16; prominent local philanthropist; active in local community and Congress organisations from the 1890ies.

7 B. P. Sitaramayya, *History of the Indian National Congress*, n. p., Madras Congress Working Committee, 1935, p. 182.

8 Madras Presidency Government, Political Department (hereafter MP, Pol.), Confidential File, GO 640, 2/12/19.

ment. By early 1915 patriotic fervour had begun to wane, and Muslim newspapers were questioning press restrictions and suggesting that Indian loyalty warranted the post-war gift of *svaraj*. The most vociferous Madras Muslim critic of Britain's actions in India was the Urdu daily, the *Qaumi Report*, the leading Presidency Pan-Islamic newspaper. It was edited by Moulvi Abdul Majid Sharar, son of a Madras city *alim* and a keen supporter of the Pan-Islamist leaders, the Ali brothers. Under Sharar the *Qaumi Report* gave increasing support to Congress, particularly after the internment of the Ali brothers late in 1915.

In nationalist circles too, the initial surge of support for the war had begun to evaporate. Congress had approached the British for further constitutional reforms in return for support of the war effort, but the British response was disappointing and some prominent leaders in Congress began to cast about for means to bring more Muslims into the organisation. By broadening the base of Congress it was hoped that more pressure could be put on the British to make realistic political concessions.

In November 1915, the Madras representatives on the Council of the All-India Muslim League voted at Lucknow to accept the invitation of Congress, which had been delivered by Mohammad Ali Jinnah, to hold the annual session of the League in December 1915 concurrently with the Congress session in Bombay. Despite considerable opposition from conservative Muslims, who opposed both Jinnah and any co-operation with Congress, the invitation was accepted. Amongst the Madras Muslims at the session, Yakub Hasan, Nawab Syed Mahomed and Walji Lalji Sait (a prominent Madras city merchant) were appointed to the committee set up to consult with Congress on the reforms scheme. At Lucknow in 1916, the Madras League's delegation supported Jinnah's plea for a communal *rapprochement*. Undoubtedly, Yakub Hasan, who was both Secretary of the Presidency League and a member of the All-India Muslim League Council, played a critical role in this decision: he was the best known League member in Madras and as its Secretary he was the pivot of its organisation. More significantly, it was he, rather than the Prince of Arcot, who had the personal support of the merchant members of the Presidency League, with many of whom he had been involved in business ventures.

Other factors which increased Madras Muslims' susceptibility to Jinnah's blandishments, was the endorsement Jinnah received from the Aga Khan in 1915, the temporary eclipse suffered by the Pan-Islamic movement as a result of the internment of its leaders – the Ali brothers, Abul Kalam Azad and Zafar Ali Khan – in 1915, and the activities of the Home Rule League in the Presidency.

The support of the Aga Khan effectively neutralised pro-British and politically conservative Muslim opposition to a communal *rapprochement*, whilst the eclipse of the Pan-Islamic movement left the *rapprochement* as the only avenue available to Muslims to expend their aroused political energies and frustration with the British. The Madras Presidency was fortunate that, unlike, for instance, in the Panjab, communal relations had not been soured by the activities of organisations such as the anti-Muslim Arya Samaj.

The Home Rule League provided a bridge between Congress and sympathisers in the Muslim community who were wary of the apparent political extremism of Congress in the years immediately preceding the War. During the early years of World War I, Congress was seeking new political directions. On the outbreak of war the organisation was dominated by the Moderates who sought an orderly and constitutional progress towards self-government, in opposition to the Extremist faction which pressed its demands more urgently upon the British. The Extremists had been driven from Congress in 1908, but by 1915 had found a champion in Annie Besant, the charismatic English Theosophist who effected their re-entry into Congress.

Congress lacked clear leadership, and was dragged in a many directions by feuding factions. But Annie Besant had established the All-India Home Rule League outside Congress, and for a time it provided the more radical members of Congress with a model for future action. The League, at least in 1915 and 1916, worked assiduously to achieve a broader basis of popular support than Congress by establishing a national network of branches, and it laid the foundations for mass political action which was to be so successfully developed by Gandhi a few years later. In an attempt to win popular support across communal lines, the Home Rule League adopted the cause of the Ali brothers and communal *rapprochement*, and temporarily attracted the support of more radical Muslim spokesmen.

The League concentrated on winning the support of communal élites for a rapid and constitutional evolution towards independence by means of nation-wide agitation on a scale previously unknown in India. The League prefaced the emergence of mass popular involvement in politics developed by Gandhi from 1919, but it lacked Gandhi's radicalism which was to push the nationalist movement beyond boundaries Besant was prepared to cross. Besant's attachment to Theosophy limited her appeal to many Hindus and Muslims, whilst her essentially Western approach to politics in time lost her the support of more extremist nationalists who, like Gandhi, were moving towards a rejection of political activity within the Western constitutional framework.

In early 1915, Annie Besant gained the approval of Mazharul Haque and Wazir Hasan, two prominent north Indian Muslim leaders, for her proposed Home Rule League, and in the same year she attempted to win the active participation of Madras Muslims and Hindus in her organisation. In the Presidency she gained support from S. Kasturi Ranga Iyengar and his nephew A. Rangaswami Iyengar, who came from a Brahmin family with a long association with government and the legal profession and who were successively editors of *The Hindu*, the premier nationalist newspaper in the province. Her newspaper, *New India*, ran a series of articles on "Hindus and Mussalmans", lauding the cause of communal unity and blaming communal friction on the British.[9] *New India* also welcomed the decision of the council of the All-India Muslim League to hold the League's annual session in Bombay in December 1915 as "a distinct step towards common action".[10] To secure a wider basis of Muslim support Besant dropped her opposition to separate electorates in 1915 and in 1916, and made overtures to Mr Justice Rahim of the Madras High Court in a blatant attempt to win his approval for the Home Rule movement.[11]

Rahim's well known sympathy for the cause of Indian advancement recommended him to Annie Besant. As a member of the Public Service Commission in 1913, Rahim had dissented from the majority report and strongly recommended that Indians be given a larger share of responsibility in the Public Service. Also, in 1913, when passing judgement against Annie Besant's newspaper, *New India*, for contravening the Press Act he had intimated his disapproval of the scope and terms of the Act.[12] In December 1916, Rahim became President of the Young Men's Indian Association, organised by Annie Besant, but there does not appear to have been any other response on his part – or from the community in general – to her overtures which continued into 1917.

Despite the fact that by the terms of the Lucknow Pact the Madras Muslims, who formed barely 5% of the population, were conceded 15% of the elected seats at the provincial level, there was not unanimous support for the Pact within the community. It evoked no response from the Tamil Muslims, and was subject to some criticism from several Urdu Muslim newspapers. The pro-British *Jaridah-i-Rozgar*, the oldest Urdu daily in the Presidency and which was subsidised by the Nizam of Hyderabad, was critical of Jinnah and it argued that the differences between the Hindu and Muslim communities were unsurmountable: its circulation dropped rapidly from c. 1500 in 1914 to c. 300 in 1916! On the other hand the anti-British *Qaumi Report*, which initially supported the Pact after months of criticising plans for communal *rapprochement*, finally declared that "our [i. e. the Muslim] mode of living is entirely different and nowhere has there been any contact between the two communities": its circulation stood at c. 1000 in 1916.[13] The Pact was anathema to both newspapers, whose editors represented the extremes of the Muslim political spectrum in Madras. The *volte face* by the editor of the *Qaumi Report*, Abdul Majid Sharar, was due to a strong personal animosity towards Hasan, and to Sharar's belief that the Pact was a farce.[14] Sharar's relations with most Muslim leaders in Ma-

9 *New India*, 1915, 11th and 13th September.

10 *Ibid.*, 11th November.

11 *Ibid.*, 1916, 5th May; H. F. Owen, *The Leadership of the Indian National Movement 1914–20*, (PhD thesis, Australian National University, 1965), p. 160.

12 G. Natesan, *Indian Judges*, Madras 1932, p. 460–3.

13 See MN 1917.

14 *Qaumi Report*, 21st June, MN 1916; *Ibid.*, 22nd February, 18th March, 19th May, MN 1917.

dras were strained, and he was considered an *enfant terrible* whose outrageous swings of temper and opinion both tantalised and infuriated. His pessimism regarding the Pact was provoked by bickering between Muslim and Hindu politicians in northern India over the final details of the political representation of Muslims. Sharar turned away from Congress, and became a propagandist for a highly personal and religious brand of Pan-Islamism.

In the *mofussil* there was some criticism of the Pact as an instrument of Nawab Syed Muhammad Bahadur – regarded by some Urdu Muslims as a lackey of the Hindus.[15] Two other prominent Urdu Muslims supporters of the Pact did not suffer the same bitter criticism as the Nawab. Yakub Hasan was elected by Urdu Muslims to the provincial Council in July 1916, and Mir Asad Ali Khan won the Madras Muslim seat in the Imperial Legislative Council, at a time when the pro-Pact views of both these men were well known. Hasan and Asad Ali Khan's advocacy of separate electorates for Muslims "because they are an important part of the Indian nation and must have equal opportunities with the other component part to serve the motherland" apparently compensated adequately for their adherence to the Pact.[16]

Despite mixed feelings amongst Urdu Muslims over the Lucknow Pact, it was formally accepted by the Presidency League. Although this did not lead to any formal liaison between the Madras League and local nationalist organisations prior to the rise of the Khilafat movement in the early months of 1919, the meetings of the League's Executive Committee were held from January 1917 until April 1921 in the chambers of the Mahajana Sabha, a leading Congress organisation in Madras city.[17]

The tentative nature of the Congress-League understanding was due to two major factors: the restricted membership of the Presidency League, and the slow politicisation of the Tamil Muslims. Membership of the Presidency Muslim League was small and confined almost entirely to Madras city with no provisions in its constitution for *mofussil* branches. Between 1917–20 the number of members increased substantially but never exceeded 300, and until 1918 there were few Tamil Muslim members.

Apart from differences of language and culture between the two groups, the activities of Urdu Muslims in the period 1901–16 maintained the barriers between Urdu and Tamil Muslims. Neither the Educational Association nor the Presidency Muslim League displayed any interest in Tamil Muslims. Both organisations were Urdu Muslim-dominated, and they articulated their educational and employment grievances without reference to Tamil Muslim opinion.[18] Neither the Pan-Islamic movement nor the pursuit of communal *rapprochement* stirred the Tamil Muslims as they did the Urdu Muslims. *Rapprochement* with the Hindus, with

[15] C. Ramalinga Reddy to P. Kesava Pillai, 6th March 1917: Kesava Pillai Papers.

[16] Y. Hasan, *Hindu-Muslim Problem*, Madras 1917, p. 5.

[17] Madras Presidency Muslim League (hereafter the MPML), Minutes, 19th March 1917–28th August 1921.

[18] *Ibid.*, Minutes, 19th March 1917–27th April 1921.

whom they had long lived in harmony, was regarded as unnecessary, while the Turkish bias of the Pan-Islamic movement in its early stages found only limited support in a community which traditionally regarded the Arabian peninsula as its source of inspiration. They were more responsive to concerns for the safety of the *Khalif* and the Holy Places of Islam, but as yet these had only been peripheral to the main thrust of Muslim political agitation. The world view of Tamil Muslims was firmly rooted in southern India and Arabia, the world view of Urdu Muslims linked them to their co-religionists in northern India. The mélange of nationalism, Pan-Islamism and communalism which stirred the Urdu Muslims of British India during World War I, could strike a chord in the minds and hearts of the Urdu Muslims in the Madras Presidency, but meant little to Tamil Muslims, until threats were posed to the Holy Places of Islam in Arabia and the office of the *Khalif*, by the Arab revolt against the Ottomans in 1916.

6. Madras Muslims and the Reforms Proposals

In August 1917, Edwin Montagu, Secretary of State for India, announced a plan to increase Indian participation in the governing of India. This announcement and the visit of Montagu to India later in 1917 to gauge public opinion, caused considerable excitement throughout the subcontinent. Politically-conscious Indians were faced with the prospect of rapidly crystallising their objectives and building organisations to support these objectives if they wished to impress their opinions on Montagu.

In the Madras Presidency, the announcement split the membership of the Presidency Muslim League. After failing to reverse the League's support for the Pact, opponents of *rapprochement* seceded from the provincial League in November 1917, and formed a rival organisation, the Islamia League. The men behind this move were not fanatical communalists such as Sharar, the editor of the *Qaumi Report*, but were rather politically conservative men such as the Prince of Arcot and Ahmed Thambi Marakayyar MLC, who favoured constitutional evolution in co-operation with the British. Marakayyar was a prominent merchant-contractor from Nagapattinam, and was the first Tamil Muslim to be elected to the Madras Legislative Council where he held a seat from 1913–20. In addition, he was one of the few leading Tamil Muslims to be involved with Urdu Muslims in organisations such as the Southern Indian Muhammedan educational association.

The immediate cause of the rift was the submission of an address to Montagu by the Presidency League. The President of the organisation, the Prince of Arcot, objected to certain demands in the submission and alterations were made to comply with his objections. However, the League refused to delete a reference demanding the curtailment of the Viceroy's power of veto, and Arcot and many of his relatives resigned. But the reasons for secession went much deeper than the question of the submission. Arcot represented conservative Muslim opinion in Madras and had his counterparts elsewhere in India, especially in Bengal and the Panjab. In Bengal, a group of politically conservative Muslims, led by C. Hussain Cassim Ariff, Nawab Syed Ali Choudhury and Dr A. Suhrawardy defected from the pro-Pact provincial Muslim League to form the Indian Moslem Association, and in the Panjab the League under Mian Mohammed Shafi was disaffiliated by the All-India Muslim League for its opposition to the Lucknow Pact.[19] The term "conservative" Muslim covered a variety of biases within the community. They ranged from blatant communalists who rejected any form of co-operation with Hindus, to political conservatives, who both feared and opposed the aims of Congress in the belief that Indians, and in particular Muslims, were inadequately-equipped for any major step towards self-government.

In the Madras Presidency, Muslim conservatives rejected the provincial League and its submission to Montagu for several reasons. Many believed that Muslim representation under the terms of the Lucknow Pact was inadequate, but, more important still, most opposed the entire spirit of the Pact which was directed towards securing a rapid and substantial devolution of political power. One of their spokesmen, Ahmed Thambi Marakayyar MLC, wrote to Annie Besant's newspaper, the *New India*, that the differences between Muslims and Hindus were far from being solved with Muslims needing a long period of preparation to equip themselves adequately for even the most limited form of self-government. Without such preparation the conservatives believed the Muslims would be subject to Hindu domination.[20] The Islamia League prepared its own address to Montagu, and began strengthening links with like-minded Muslims elsewhere in India. The provincial government was sympathetic towards the Islamia League, and accepted its submission whilst rejecting that of a large, pro-nationalist, Muslim-dominated organisation, the Southern Indian Skin and Hide Merchants' Association. The links between Muslim political conservatives in northern and southern India were reinforced when Arcot and Marakayyar were elected respectively President and Vice-President of the All-India Muslim Conference at Calcutta in January 1918. The Conference was arranged by the Panjabi Muslim leader, Shafi, in an attempt to form a rival conservative Muslim political organisation to the All-India Muslim League. However, it did not survive beyond 1918.

Some of the defectors from the Presidency League, who formed the Islamia League and denounced the Presidency League's submission on November 30th 1917, had accepted the terms of that address as recently as November 8th. It is tempting to see the hand of the British administration behind this apparent *volte face*, but in fact many of Arcot's supporters had only grudgingly given their approval to the Presidency League's address at its meeting on the 8th,

19 *The Hindu*, 1917, 5th December; MPML, Minutes, 30th November 1917; Home Political (hereafter HPL), Deposit, January 1918, No. 2.

20 HPL, Deposit, March 1917, No. 26; *New India*, 1917, 3rd March.

and Muhammad Usman – a kinsman of Arcot and the main organiser of the Islamia League – left the meeting before a final vote was taken.[21] Although the defection of Arcot and his followers meant the loss of many of the Presidency Muslim League's office-bearers, the League was quick to recover. Yakub Hasan retained his post as Secretary, Mir Asad Ali Khan (member of the Imperial Legislative Council) was elected President, and C. Abdul Hakim, a prominent merchant and employer of Hasan, Vice-President.[22] All had been amongst the most energetic members of the League since 1908, and they and their followers were perfectly capable of filling positions that had in reality only been filled nominally by members of the Arcot clique. The defection of the conservatives gave full rein to the pro-*rapprochement* merchant members of the League, and proved the death blow to any notions of community leadership that may have been entertained by the predominantly aristocratic Arcot faction.

But to describe this breach in the community as simply a division between "conservatives" and "modernists" is too simplistic. The dispute contained an element of rivalry between an old pro-British clique and younger Muslims scornful of their ways. But it also represented the clear emergence of a new leadership drawn from the Urdu Muslim mercantile and professional élite. Initially at least this new leadership was united in their rejection of the old leadership, but it contained its own contradictions comprising wealthy merchants and rentiers in temporary alliance with artisans, petty merchants and local Muslim religious leaders. For the moment they were united against the old leadership and against the British, but it was a fragile unity soon to be tested as the nationalist movement became more radical.

Many of the new leaders of the Presidency Muslim League were also members of Congress, the Home Rule League, and local nationalist organisations such as the Mahajana Sabha. Following the departure of Arcot, contact between the Presidency League and the nationalists intensified particularly as the latter were busy organising protest meetings against the internment of the Ali brothers and other popular Muslim leaders in northern India, in an attempt to stimulate Muslim support for the communal *rapprochement*.[23] In August 1917, the espousal of the cause of the Ali brothers by the Home Rule League captured the interest of Muslims for a few months – at least in Madras city – and the British noted that "the Muhammedan community [is] being stirred up to an extent which has never been equalled for very many years".[24] But by the end of 1917, the attention of both the Muslims and Annie Besant was diverted from the Ali brothers by the reforms announcement and Montagu's visit. Concern for the Ali brothers

21 *The Hindu*, 1918, 24th November, 5th December; MPML, Minutes, 8th November and 13th December.

22 MPML, Minutes, 30th November 1917.

23 *The Hindu*, 1917, 3rd, 10th and 27th October; HPL, Deposit, August 1917, No. 3; *Ibid.*, November Nos. 6, 29–30; *Ibid.*, January 1918, No. 2.

24 HPL, Deposit, August 1917, No. 2; *Ibid.*, November 1917, Nos. 6, 29–30.

had been the only common bond between Muslims and Annie Besant, and once the attention of both shifted from the brothers, Muslim support for Annie Besant waned.[25]

The addresses presented to Montagu and the Viceroy, Lord Chelmsford, in December 1917 by the two major Muslim political organisations in the Presidency illustrated the two divergent strains of Muslim political sentiment. The address of the Presidency Muslim League stated its full and unqualified support for the Lucknow Pact, while that of the Islamia League decried any rapid devolution of power to provincial legislatures or curtailment of the Viceroy's power of veto, and urged the continuation of a strong, British-dominated centralised administration. The Islamia League was also firmly against the principle of ministerial responsibility to popularly-elected legislative chambers.[26] Some of the *ulema* of the Presidency supported the Islamia League, in active opposition to the growing nationalist sentiment in the community, reflecting similar divisions amongst Muslim religious leaders elsewhere in India. A group of *ulema*, styling themselves the "Ulema of Madras", told Montagu that "we does [*sic*] not want Home Rule", adding that they could find no sanction in any Holy Book for the Congress-League Pact.[27] They claimed that

> if the British Government were to make over the administration of India to the Hindu community (polytheists) as that community desires it is feared that many rights of Mussalmans would be destroyed [and that it] is contrary to the Sacred Law [for Muslims] to reside in a place where there is no security and which is hostile.

A similar address was presented by Dr Zyn ul-abidin, a prominent *unani* medical practitioner, ex-MLC and former Sheriff of Madras, on behalf of the Muthiapet Muslim Anjuman. Muhammad Usman was the organising force behind this ephemeral educational and religious organisation of *ulema* and used its office bearers to provide the first *ad hoc* committee of the Islamia League. In contrast to the views of these *ulema*, at least one prominent *alim*, Moulvi Mir Zynuddin of Vellore in North Arcot, who, like Dr Zyn ul-abidin, was a foundation member of the Southern Indian Muhammedan Educational Association, and was also President of the Southern Indian Skin and Hide Merchant's Association, remained an active supporter of the Lucknow Pact and the Presidency Muslim League after the formation of the Islamia League.[28]

The pro-Islamia League stand of some *ulema* reflected their hostility towards Hasan and other Muslim nationalist sympathisers as well as towards the Home Rule movement. Hasan had emerged as the leader of pro-*rapprochement* sentiment within the Muslim community by November 1917, and had set the Presidency League on a course parallelling that of the nationalist movement. His connections with Annie Besant, and his election to the Provincial Congress

[25] *Ibid.*, January 1918, Nos 1–2.

[26] Parliamentary Papers (Great Britain) (hereafter PP), 1918, vol. 18, Cd. 9178, 61, 62–3.

[27] E. Montagu, *An Indian Diary*, London 1930, p. 118.

[28] PP, 1918, vol. 18, Cd. 9178, 63; MPML, Minutes, 1917–21, *passim*.

Committee for 1918 in November 1917, may have appealed to the predominantly pro-*rapprochement* Urdu Muslim merchants of Madras city and the growing number of Western educated Muslims, but these connections only served to arouse further the suspicions of many conservative and traditionally-educated Muslims.

In October 1917, a group of *ulema* from Madras city issued a *fatwa* in Urdu condemning the Home Rule agitation, with individual *ulema* distributing pamphlets in support of the *fatwa*. Even the fanatical Pan-Islamist, Abdul Majid Sharar, who had been in the forefront of the agitation over the Ali brothers in co-operation with Hasan and Besant, condemned the Home Rule movement.[29] This apparently contradictory attitude can, in part, be explained by the strong communal bias of Sharar and to a fairly widespread belief among Muslims that the Hindu supporters of communal *rapprochement* were not sincere. Muslim attitudes towards both the Hindus and the British were confused and inchoate. The Hindus were not fully trusted, while the British were not completely distrusted. The local Muslim press was often critical of the British, but in general it remained wary of draconian press laws and remained sullenly loyalist throughout 1917–18.

The split between Hasan and some of the *ulema* was exacerbated in 1918 when he championed a Bill in the Madras Legislative Council for the voluntary registration of Muslim marriages and divorces. Presidency-wide agitation developed against the Bill, led by *ulema* and the Islamia League. With the aid of the *Mukhbir-i-Dakhan*, a Madras city Urdu-language weekly edited by a member of the Islamia League, the merchant Mohammed Abdul Qadir, they sought to arouse orthodox opposition to the proposed legislation.[30] The Bill aimed to produce some order in a situation rendered chaotic by lax *qazis*, who failed to register Muslim marriages and divorces. The fact that it entailed voluntary registration promised to make the bill fairly ineffective, but this did not prevent the Islamia League opposing the bill as a means of rallying orthodox Muslim opinion against Hasan. Despite the activities of its opponents, the Bill won the support of the reformist-orientated Southern Indian Muhammedan Educational Association, and members of the Presidency Muslim League were able to organise a meeting sympathetic to the *ulema*. Hasan's Bill caused dissension within the Islamia League: Ahmed Thambi Marakayyar MLC, one of the League's foundation members, opposed the Bill on the ground that it was too mild and should have provided for the compulsory registration of marriages and divorces! Opposition to the Bill was half-hearted and ill-organised, and its eventual enactment elicited little comment from the Muslim press.[31]

[29] HPL, Deposit, 1917, Nos 6 and 29; *Ibid.*, January 1918, No. 1.

[30] *Madras Legislative Council Debates* (hereafter *MLCD*), vol. 46, 13th August 1918, 43; MN 1917–18, *passim*.

[31] *The Hindu*, 1918, 3rd November, 3rd December.

Notwithstanding attacks by the Islamia League and its supporters amongst the *ulema*, the Presidency Muslim League drew closer to the nationalist movement. In December 1917, Sarojini Naidu, a leading member of Congress, spoke at the Presidency League's annual session, and later delivered an address on self-government to a Muslim meeting in Madras city. Also, a revival of agitation over the Ali brothers in 1918 led to a further upsurge of support for Hasan and other Muslim Leaguers who helped organise the agitation.[32]

Pan-Islamic sentiment and fears regarding the future of the Ottoman empire gathered momentum throughout 1917–18. This undermined the loyalist stand of opponents of the Presidency League. As early as January 1917, *ulema* from Aligarh, accompanied by translators, toured southern India stirring up the Tamil Muslims by declaring that the defeat of the Ottomans would mean the end of the *Khalif* and of Islam.[33] Until this period, the Tamil-speaking Muslims had not shown much interest in the Pan-Islamic cause, and were not concerned about the temporal aspects of the *Khalif's* authority. By identifying the fate of the temporal power of the *Khalif* with the fate of Islam, the *ulema* shrewdly manipulated the intense religious consciousness of the Tamil Muslims and now ensured a wide basis of support for the Pan-Islamic propaganda and the Khilafat movement.

In May 1917, the Pan-Islamic movement in Madras received a further boost when the all-India session of the *Nadwatul Ulema* was held in Madras city for the first time since 1901. The headquarters of this religious-educational association was in Lucknow, which by 1917 shared with Aligarh the honour of being one of the main centres of the Pan-Islamic movement in India. Justice Rahim was President of the Reception Committee, and leading Madras city Urdu Muslims gave the conference their support. The presence of many prominent north Indian Pan-Islamists at the session contributed towards keeping Madras Muslims abreast of developments and Muslim sentiment elsewhere in India. Even though the opinions expressed at this conference may not have directly aroused sympathy for Congress, they did serve the aims of the Lucknow Pact indirectly by weakening Muslim loyalty and attachment to the British.

7. Muslim Merchants, Leadership and the Communal Rapprochement

Support for the Presidency Muslim League spread rapidly amongst articulate Muslims in Madras city from both the Tamil and Urdu Muslims. Among the provincial League's major sympathisers between 1917 and 1919 were the Muslim members of two leading Presidency mercantile organisations, the Southern Indian Chamber of Commerce and the Southern Indian Skin and Hide Merchants' Association, led by Jamal Mahomed. Neither was a purely Muslim

32 MPML, Minutes, 20th December 1917; *The Hindu*, 1917, 21st December.

33 HPL, Deposit, March 1917, No. 26 and KW.

organisation, but the former had a large number of Muslim members and the latter was Muslim-dominated. The Chamber of Commerce had been founded in 1909 in the wake of the Minto-Morley Reforms, as a result of the growing realisation amongst many Indian merchants that "while the European commercial community had organisation to influence policy, the Indian commercial community lacked the power and instrument to express its views."[34] The Skin and Hide Merchants' Association, founded in 1917, was likewise established by Indian merchants to influence government policy.

The support of the Muslim members of the two trade organisations was due to increasing dissatisfaction with wartime restrictions on trade and industry implemented by the Government of India in 1916 and 1917, as well as with wartime increases in taxation.[35] The President of the Chamber of Commerce, P. Theagaraya Chettiar, who was not sympathetic to Congress and was prominent in the South Indian Liberal Federation – the precursor of the Justice Party which he was later to lead – temporarily broke with the Chamber over the presentation of an address to Montagu in 1917. However, he was later apparently reconciled to the Chamber of Commerce, although his political views did not prevail within the body, and it was "due mainly to the efforts of the Muslim members of the Southern Indian Chamber of Commerce that the Madras Presidency Muslim League resisted the reactionary efforts [of Arcot and Usman] within the Muslim League".[36]

Despite the antipathy of Chettiar towards Congress, the Muslim members of the Chamber of Commerce, led by its Vice-Presidents between 1909 and 1920 – Khuddas Badsha (member of the Presidency and All-India Muslim Leagues) and Govindoss Chathurbujadoss, a prominent merchant of Gujarati descent who was Vice-President of the Chamber between 1909 and 1936 – gave increasing support to the cause of communal *rapprochement*. Chathurbujadoss had long been a generous supporter of Muslim charitable and educational institutions. Government restrictions on trade and industry particularly affected the prosperity of Tamil Muslim traders and entrepreneurs. The restrictions were promulgated to conserve tanning materials and to build up stocks of raw hides and skins for military use. Although the Government bought up stocks of skins and hides held by the merchants, and diverted contracts to idle tanneries, their actions caused a drop in market prices for both raw and tanned skins and hides, and brought to an end the boom enjoyed by tanners and merchants in the first two years of the war. But the Skin and Hide Merchants' Association was a divided lobby. Its membership included both tanners and skin and hide merchants whose interests were to diverge over the next few years. The skin and hide merchants actively lobbied the government to lift export restrictions and duties intended to

[34] Southern Indian Chamber of Commerce *Golden Jubilee Souvenir 1902–52* (Madras, 1952), p. 2–3.

[35] MP, GO 729 (Ms), 19th September 1916.

[36] *The Hindu*, 1917, 24th November.

boost the Indian tanning industry, whilst the Europeans who owned the tanneries were more concerned to urge the government to maintain such restrictions and ease taxes on local materials needed in vegetable tanning processes![37] Tamil Muslim businessmen particularly resented the Government Orders of December 1916 and January 1917 prohibiting the tanning of skins and the export of raw hides and skins. In October 1917, they gave their support to the efforts of Yakub Hasan and Jamal Mahomed to form an association for skin and hide merchants to agitate for the removal of restrictions. Haji Moulvi Ziauddin, an *alim* and hide merchant from Vellore and member of the Presidency Muslim League, was elected the Association's first President. In January 1918, a deputation from the Association consisting of Ziauddin, Hasan, Mahomed and C. P. Ramaswamy Aiyar (editor of the nationalist newspaper, *The Hindu*, and a prominent member of Congress), presented a petition to the Viceroy and secured the relaxation of some of the export prohibitions.

Prior to this success, the Association attempted to present an address to Montagu, but the Government rejected its plea on the grounds that it had been submitted too late. This rejection, combined with the galling ease which the Islamia League obtained permission to present an address, further strained relations between Muslim merchants and the Government, particularly when it was remembered that prominent members of the Presidency Muslim League had joined with members of the Home Rule League to persuade the Government to reverse a similar decision regarding the non-Brahmin, pro-Congress Madras Presidency Association.[38]

The rise of animosity between the Government and an important section of the Muslim mercantile community was of vital significance for the future development of Muslim politics in the Madras Presidency. Not only did it lead to an increase in the membership of the Presidency Muslim League – from some 70 members in 1916 to approximately 200 in 1918 and 300 in 1920 – but it also marked the first occasion upon which any sizeable number of Tamil Muslims had joined with their Urdu co-religionists on a common political platform. Indeed, for the majority of such Tamil Muslims it was the first occasion on which they had participated in any form of overt political activity.[39]

As the Presidency Muslim League grew in strength and prestige between November 1917 and July 1918, when the Montagu-Chelmsford Reforms proposals were published, the Islamia League rapidly sank into obscurity. By 1919 it was a spent force, having urged the conservative Muslim viewpoint upon Montagu without success. It lost influence as the Muslim community became pre-occupied with grievances and demands that weakened its loyalty to the British. The Islamia League did not seek representation before the Parliamentary Joint Select Committee on

[37] Imperial Institute, *Indian Trade Inquiry Report on Hides and Skins*, Madras 1920, p. 87; *Mussalman*, 1920, 16th July.

[38] MPML, Minutes, 30th December 1917.

[39] *Ibid.*, Minutes, 19th March 1917–27th April 1921.

the reforms, in London in 1919, and appears to have been bereft of any effective leadership. Arcot had never been more than a figurehead within the organisation: inspiration for the movement lay with his kinsman Muhammad Usman, who by 1919 had abandoned the League, in preference for an alliance with the non-Brahmin Justice Party. Arcot played no decisive role in the activities of the Islamia League, and between December 1917, when he presented the Islamia League's address to Montagu, and his death in 1952, he stood aloof from the politics of the Muslim community and concentrated his energies on petitioning the British to increase the number of guns in his official salute and the size of his pension.

Not all of the members of the Islamia League followed in the footsteps of Arcot and Usman. Moulvi Zyn ul-abidin, a member of the Madras Legislative Council, 1913–16, returned briefly to the bosom of the community at the height of the Khilafat agitation in 1920, and then vanished into obscurity. Others, such as Ahmed Thambi Marakayyar, who was hailed in 1917 as one of the foremost leaders of the non-Brahmin movement, followed Usman into the reformed councils in 1920–21.[40] But men such as Marakayyar were restrained in their support of the alliance with the non-Brahmin Justice Party, preferring instead to retain some semblance of independence.

In contrast to Marakayyar, the other leading Tamil Muslim merchant, Jamal Mahomed, remained a supporter of the Congress-League *rapprochement*, although he retired temporarily from public life during the Non-Cooperation campaign in the early 1920s. In the 1930s he re-emerged as the leading spokesman for the community. Despite superficially different political paths, Marakayyar and Jamal Mahomed were typical of the new type of Muslim leadership which emerged in the Presidency during the war. They were not driven by the historical and cultural legacy of the Urdu Muslims and had little sympathy for their grievances. On the other hand, they had very particular economic grievances which provided an incentive for political activity. Entrée to formal political processes was through the system of separate electorates, but once elected, men such as Marakayyar were frequently more comfortable with politically moderate Hindus than they were with more radical Urdu Muslims. Caution was the watchword of this orthodox Muslim mercantile leadership, which sought to maintain links with a broad spectrum of political and social interests in the Presidency.

Within the Urdu Muslim community, leadership also passed to merchants. They carried a more complex cultural bag and baggage than their Tamil Muslim peers, but economic grievances and aspirations were incentives which provided them with common ground when they began to work with Tamil Muslim leaders such as Jamal Mahomed.

Even amongst more politically conservative Urdu Muslim merchants and professional men, the rejection of the Congress-League *rapprochement*, did not necessarily herald a move to-

[40] *Non-Brahmin*, 1st April 1917.

wards communal isolation. For example, the Urdu Muslims majority in the Islamia League, supported Usman in seeking an understanding with the Justice Party. The beginnings of this conservative Muslim-Justice Party alliance may be traced back to November 1917 when the Islamia League claimed "a fraternity of creed" with the South Indian Liberal Federation, the precursor of the Justice Party, which had Usman as its first Secretary and P. Theagaraya Chettiar (nominal President of the Southern Indian Chamber of Commerce) as President. This "fraternity of creed" was based upon non-Brahmin promises of special consideration of Muslim wishes concerning education and employment, and was strengthened by the antipathy and suspicion of both conservative Muslims and non-Brahmins towards the Brahmin-dominated Congress organisation in the Presidency, and the Lucknow Pact.[41] Both Usman and Chettiar were in favour of constitutional reform and ultimate independence, but they envisaged a slow and cautious devolution of power which would enable their respective communities to improve their educational and social positions *vis-à-vis* more dominant groups. They opposed any demand for a rapid devolution of political power, seeing it as the seal which would confirm the traditional dominance of Brahmins in southern India.

8. The Montagu-Chelmsford Reforms

The Montagu-Chelmsford Reforms proposals were well received by Muslims in the Presidency when published in July 1918, even though the concession for separate electorates was only grudgingly made. Muslim newspapers of different political persuasions – such as the loyalist *Jaridah-i-Rozgar* and the Pan-Islamist *Qaumi Report* – were quick to support the proposals.[42] Unlike many nationalists, who attacked and rejected them as insufficient later in 1918, most Muslims wished to accept the proposals as a platform from which the Muslim viewpoint could be voiced and the power of the administration curtailed. Hasan indicated his qualified approval of the proposals and, like other leading nationalists, stated that they would be even more acceptable once certain modifications had been made that would bring them in line with the terms of the Lucknow Pact.[43]

The enthusiastic reception of the reforms proposals by the Muslims vindicated the policies of the Presidency League and the pro-*rapprochement* activities of Hasan, and assured the League of its position as the premier provincial Muslim political organisation. But Hasan's willingness to accept the proposals led to a temporary decline in relations between the League and Congress. This decline, which developed in the last months of 1918, was exacerbated in

[41] *The Hindu*, 1917, 25th November; *MLCD*, vol. 15, 27 November 1924, p. 50.

[42] *Jaridah-i-Rozgar*, 29th July; *Qaumi Report*, 13th, 21st, 31st July, MN 1918.

[43] MP, GO 327 (Ms), 7th June 1919.

the early months of 1919 by the development of Gandhi's Rowlatt Act *satyagraha* which many Muslims opposed.

By late 1918, Gandhi was radically altering the political complexion of Congress. The moderates within Congress, who wished to follow a path of constitutional agitation, were side-lined by the advocates of more radical forms of protest, culminating in the Non-Cooperation program. Gandhi was fast moving towards total rejection of the Reforms to the discomfort of most Muslims and the Moderates within Congress. The difference of opinion between Hasan and Congress came to a head at the Special Session of Congress at Bombay in August 1918 where hostility towards the Reforms dominated discussions. Upon his return to Madras he, and other leading Muslim Leaguers, joined the Madras Liberal League formed by nationalists who were willing to work the Reforms.[44]

The decline in relations between the more extremist nationalists and the Madras Presidency Muslim League did not last long. By late 1919, closer relations were restored between Congress and the Presidency League. This reconciliation was prompted by the rising tide of Muslim discontent and apprehension, stimulated, ironically, by the activities of the Pan-Islamists at the 1918 session of the All-India Muslim League, regarding the fate of the Ottoman empire. The British delay in announcing the terms of the peace treaty with Turkey heightened Muslim anxiety, and stimulated Pan-Islamic sentiment in the Muslim press of Madras, led by the increasingly popular *Qaumi Report*.[45] Rumours of proposals to dismember the Ottoman empire widened the breach between the British and the Muslims. There was "a change from their early attitude of passive acquiescence to a later hope that the Government's hand might be forced."[46] Finally in 1920, the "alliance" between the Muslims and the British, which had been supported by many more conservative Muslims in their desire to gain support and protection from the Hindus, snapped. Stimulated by anxiety over the Khilafat and hostility towards the British, who were suspected of plotting the dismemberment of the Ottoman empire in the face of Indian Muslim opposition, Hasan and the Presidency Muslim League swung back towards Congress. Having dispensed with the external support of the British the Muslims "began to look for support in an organised development of the Pan-Islamic idea as an alternative to the British connexion", and they found this in the development of the Khilafat movement.[47]

Apart from instilling a unique unity into the community, the support of Congress for the movement swept away any lingering doubts about the desirability of a communal *rapprochement*. Ultimately this led to Muslims rejecting the Reforms proposals.

44 *First Annual Report of the Madras Liberal League*, Madras, 1918, p. 1, 4, 32.

45 *Qaumi Report*, April–October, MN 1919.

46 *India in 1920*, Delhi 1921, p. 78.

47 A. Toynbee, *The World After the Peace Conference*, London 1925, p. 78.

9. Conclusion

Between 1914 and 1918 the leadership of the Urdu and Tamil Muslims of the Madras Presidency passed into the hands of the merchant élite. This did not preface a monolithic outlook, rather it meant that common class and economic interests now provided a bridge for leaders from both groups to work with one another in defence of perceived Muslim interests. Until 1916, leading Tamil Muslims were largely absent from the political life of the Muslim community in the Presidency, but within two years they had become a powerful force in Muslim political activity across the political spectrum. The leadership role of the mercantile élite was never challenged after 1918, and men from this group were to shape the many and varied political alternatives the Urdu and Tamil Muslims pursued from 1918 to 1947.

By 1918 it is possible to discern a new type of leadership which – despite petty quarrels and factionalism – was united by common economic interests and driven by the realisation that to achieve their objectives the Muslims could not operate in political isolation from non-Muslims. Under the leadership of Urdu and Tamil Muslim merchants in the 1920s and 1930s, various Muslim factions would champion communal interests, but the leadership of these causes was always to keep a weather eye on the possibilities of cross-communal alliances be they with Congress, the Justice Party or the Liberal Party in southern India, until the development of an India-wide Muslim political movement under the leadership of Jinnah in the late 1930s.

Caste and Entrepreneurship in Colonial Andhra, South India, 1900–1947*

A. Satyanarayana

The main purpose of this paper is to discuss the social background of commercial and industrial entrepreneurs of colonial Andhra in terms of caste/community composition. It proposes to analyse the nature and character of entrepreneurial response to the growth of medium and large-scale industries at the regional level under colonial conditions. It also discusses the growth of modern industries and its impact on the emergence of entrepreneurship in Andhra during the pre-independence period.

Studies on the growth of modern capitalism and industrial entrepreneurship have indicated regional variations. It has been suggested that the traditional merchant groups belonging to the Marwari, Parsi, Gujarati communities etc. dominated the private commercial and industrial sectors in eastern and western India; while in southern India the Chettiars took a leading role in investments in trade, commerce and industry during the colonial period.[1] Yet the macro studies dealing with the growth of capitalism and capitalist class paid inadequate attention to certain important issues like:

(1) What was the inter-relationship between caste, capital and entrepreneurship as well as the role of caste system in the emergence of capitalist class?

* This article is a part of my research project on "Caste and Dominance in Andhra Pradesh". I am grateful to Prof. H. Yanagisawa, Institute of Oriental Culture, University of Tokyo, Japan and Prof. D. Rothermund, South Asia Institute, Heidelberg University, Germany for their help and encouragement in writing this paper. I am also thankful to the authorities of the Japan Foundation, Tokyo and the German Academic Exchange Service (DAAD), Bonn for providing financial assistance to my research project.

[1] A. I. Levkovsky, *Capitalism in India*, Bombay 1966; V. I. Pavlov, *The Indian Capitalist Class*, New Delhi 1964; A. K. Bagchi, *Private Investment in India, 1900–39*, Cambridge 1972; R. K. Ray, *Industrialization in India 1914–1947*, Delhi 1979. For regional studies: T. A. Timberg, *The Marwaris*, Delhi 1978; s. D. Tripathi (ed.), *Business Communities of India*, New Delhi 1978; D. Tripathi, *Business and Politics in India*, Delhi 1991.

(2) What were the different processes of evolution of industrial capital and entrepreneurship? and

(3) How did entrepreneurs belonging to the non-trading castes/communities emerge?

The multi-dimensionality of the formation of industrial capital and the evolution of modern capitalist class can be better understood on the basis of detailed micro-level studies. It may be pointed out that such regional studies will clarify some of the issues raised above and provide insights into the specific character and forms of the process of evolution of indigenous capitalism and capitalist class in the colonial context. Hence, this paper will highlight the changing nature of caste system and the disjunction between traditional occupation and modern entrepreneurial activities. It also questions, of course on the basis of empirical evidence at the regional level, the validity of certain assumptions of Max Weber that the Hindu caste system and the irrational doctrines of Hinduism are not conducive for the economic/technological transformation of India. He also asserted that the caste system which reduces occupational mobility and prevents innovation was not favourable for the emergence of a dynamic industrial capitalist class. He wrote:

> The core of the obstruction was rather imbedded in the spirit of the whole system [...] it must still be considered extremely unlikely that the modern organization of industrial capitalism would ever have *originated* on the basis of the caste system. A ritual law in which every change of occupation, every change in work technique may result in ritual degradation is certainly not capable of giving birth to economic and technical revolutions from within itself, or even of facilitating the first germination of capitalism in its midst.[2]

However, recent studies by some sociologists, economists, historians etc., have suggested that the dynamics of Indian social structure did allow certain adaptive strategies towards occupational mobility and modernisation.[3] Nafziger remarked: "Despite the powerful socio-religious sanctions given the caste system, there are several dynamic factors making fluidity and flexibility in occupational and caste structures possible."[4] Moreover, "modifications of the caste system and the modernisation of traditional occupational cultures have gone farther than Weber seems to have believed possible".[5]

In explaining about the entrepreneurial activity in some industries in Tamil Nadu Berna observed, "sociological factors, such as caste, attachment to traditional activities, and approval or disapproval of the social group to which a potential entrepreneur belongs are less important

[2] Max Weber, *The Religion of India*, Glencoe 1958, p. 112 (emphasis in original).

[3] See M. Singer (ed.), *Entrepreneurship and Modernization of Occupational Cultures in South Asia*, Durham 1973; Morris D. Morris, "Values as an Obstacle to Economic Growth in South Asia: An Historical Survey," *The Journal of Economic History* 27, 1967, p. 588–607.

[4] H. A. Gould, "The Adaptive Functions of Caste in Contemporary Indian Society," *Asian Survey* 3 (9), 1963, p. 429.

[5] E. W. Nafziger, *Class, Caste and Entrepreneurship*, Honolulu, 1978, p. 47.

than economic factors such as access to capital and possession of business experience and technical knowledge".[6] Baldwin's study indicated that, "in Indian industry, the caste system seemed to be considerably looser and more flexible than it often appears [...] Its novelty quaintness, and historical importance produce an exaggerated estimate of its present role in the cities, where disintegration may proceed rapidly."[7] Therefore, in this paper an attempt is made to explain certain aspects of convergence and divergence between caste system and class formation, viz., caste/class origins of entrepreneurs in modern Andhra.

The integration of Andhra's economy into the world market commenced since the late 19th century. It facilitated and accelerated commercialisation of agriculture in terms of the export of raw materials like cotton, oilseeds, tobacco, jute etc., and the import of manufactured goods from England such as cotton textiles, gunny bags and oil. Thus till about the depression years in the 1930s, Andhra's economy tended to primarily cater to the needs of export-oriented foreign trade. The growth of trade and commerce in agricultural commodities necessitated the establishment of agro-processing small-scale industries such as rice mills, cotton gins, jute presses, and groundnut decorticating factories. The total number of such industries, which came under the Factories Act increased from 11 in 1899 to 242 in 1920.[8] A brief over view of the nature of industrial growth in colonial Andhra during the 1930ies and 1940ies is presented below.

I

The *laissez faire* policy of the colonial state in India, till about the end of the first world war was meant to facilitate the flow of surplus from India to England. However, due to certain changed circumstances in the international economic order and domestic compulsions a shift was noted in its fiscal, monetary and industrial policies. *The Report of the Indian Industrial Commission* did provide the basis for the new industrial policies of post-1920 years. Thus the inter-war period did witness industrialisation in terms of the development of import-substitution consumer industries in India. The Telugu speaking districts of Madras Presidency[9] had also witnessed the rise and growth of several domestic-market oriented medium and large-scale industries. Among them the agro-based industries like rice mills, oil mills, cotton mills, tobacco

6 J. J. Berna, *Industries Entrepreneurship in Madras State*, Delhi 1960, p. 84.

7 Cited in E. W. Nafziger, *Class, Caste and Entrepreneurship*, p. 47.

8 For details see, A. Satyanarayana, *Andhra Peasants under British Rule, 1900–1940*, Delhi 1991, ch. 5.

9 They were Ganjam, Vizagapatam, East Godavari, West Godavari, Kistna, Guntur, Nellore, Bellary, Anantapur, Kurnool, Cuddapah and Chittoor. See O. H. K. Spate, *India and Pakistan: A General and Regional Geography*, London 1960, p. 689.

and sugar factories played a significant role. As the Andhra region was endowed with considerable natural and agro-economic resources, it offered vast scope for the growth of such industries. For instance, the growth of modern rice mills was possible because of the better irrigation and canal system of the delta districts like Kistna, Guntur, East and West Godavari. Landlords, rich peasants and local Komati merchants took active part in their growth. It has been found that by the end of 1940s rice mills, in numerical terms, accounted for more than half of the total industries in the coastal Andhra districts of Kistna, Guntur, East and West Godavari and Nellore.

The growth of major agro-industries in Andhra districts during the 1930s and 1940s marked an important turning point with regard to capital investment in industry. The depression years, which changed the terms of trade between agriculture and industry in favour of the latter brought about a significant shift of capital from agriculture and moneylending to industry.[10] The boom in investment in local industries was also encouraged by the changes in the industrial policy of the Madras government, viz., tariff protection to sugar and cotton textile industries and the post-war development plans with regard to oil mills and cement factories. Certain other factors like the availability of abundant raw materials also accelerated the growth of the agro-based industries. The growth of sugar industry in Andhra was sustained by increases in sugarcane area over time, particularly in localities where sugar mills sprung up or where there was a prospect of their establishment.

Coastal Andhra districts, especially Vizagapatam, East and West Godavari and Kistna were eminently suited for the development of sugar industry, as sugarcane was one of the important cash crops. Following the recommendations of the *Indian Sugar Committee* in 1920, the Madras government favourably considered the growth of sugarcane cultivation and sugar industry. But due to certain constraints like ryots preference for paddy cultivation, insufficiency of irrigation system, high costs of cane cultivation, widespread prevalence of *jaggery* making etc., the efforts of the government did not succeed. However the passing of the Sugar Industry (Protection) Act of 1932 together with the effects of world economic depression caused a sudden growth of sugar industries in the Andhra region. It was found that fall in the prices of paddy and other commercial crops led to the extension of cane cultivation. Area under sugarcane expanded in the vicinity of sugar factories. Between 1934 and 1937 a dozen new sugar industries were established in the whole of Madras Province, of which six were located in the Andhra districts. It is interesting to note that in the formation of sugar mills, landlords and rich peasantry played a significant role. Unlike in the United Provinces, most of the sugar factories

10 For a detailed discussion on various aspects of the world economic depression see D. Rothermund, *India in the Great Depression, 1929–39*, Delhi 1992; id., *The Global Impact of the Great Depression, 1929–39*, London 1997; C. J. Baker, *An Indian Rural Economy, 1880–1955*, Delhi 1984.

in Andhra were formed by the sugarcane growers associations and co-operative societies.[11] It can be said that the growth of sugar industry during the post-depression period was due to positive state intervention. By the end of colonial rule there were eight sugar mills in the Andhra districts with a daily crushing capacity of 5275 tons; they produced 20,744 tons of white sugar during 1948–49.[12]

The development of cotton textile mills in Andhra can be traced as far back as the 1870s. Three unsuccessful attempts were made by private capitalists to establish cotton mills in coastal Andhra between 1870 and 1920. A modest beginning was made in the mid-1920s by the weavers of Devanga/Padmasali caste and others to start cotton mills in East Godavari district; mainly for spinning cotton yarn for which there was a very great demand in the district, especially in the villages around the mills. Despite the fact that Coastal Andhra had many advantages for developing cotton mills such as adequate supply of raw material, fuel, water supply, labour and market, only two small mills were established before 1930. This was due to several factors like lack of interest among investors in joint-stock enterprises, preference for investment in trade and moneylending, indifference on the part of government to extend help and encouragement to local industries etc.[13]

However, the grant of protection, effects of depression and subsequent changes in government policies led to the development of large-scale cotton mills in Andhra districts. In fact, the provincial government had been frequently pressurised by the political leaders and business communities to extend help and encouragement in establishing more cotton mills particularly in the ceded districts. It has been suggested that Bellary, Kurnool and Anantapur districts fulfilled all the requirements for the successful working of a cotton textile mill, viz., proximity to raw cotton producing tracts, sufficient supply of labour and nearness to market. During the 1930s, many official and non-official committees also recommended the establishment of cotton mills in the cotton growing areas of the Andhra region as well as financial assistance by the provincial government to them. Consequently, private investment in cotton mills was encouraged by the government in terms of extending financial assistance, though limited, under the State Aid to Industries Act. The number of cotton mills in Andhra thus increased from two to five between 1924–46.[14] It should be noted that this was possible both due to changes in the policy of the government and the availability of private finance and enterprise.

11 For details see A. Satyanarayana, "The Evolution of Agricultural and Industrial Entrepreneurs in Coastal Andhra: A Study of Sugar Industry, 1932–1947," in: *A. P. Economy Association Conference Papers*, Srikakulam 1989, p. 38–56.

12 Andhra Chamber of Commerce, *Silver Jubilee Souvenir*, Madras 1953, p. 203.

13 A. Satyanarayana, "Industrialization in Colonial Andhra, 1914–47," p. 23–30 (Mimeograph).

14 Andhra Chamber of Commerce, *Silver Jubilee 1953*, p. 211.

Prior to the first world war a considerable quantity of groundnut produced in the Andhra districts was exported to foreign countries. It has been estimated that the quantity of such exports from Andhra ports increased from 60,000 tons to 2.06 lakh tons during the period 1925–26 to 1940–41.[15] Yet only a small percentage of the annual out turn of oilseeds was converted into oil within the province or region. Some enterprising merchants and rich peasants built small-scale oil pressing units to utilise the locally available raw material and cater to the growing market for oil. They proved to be moderately successful and obtained profits during the first quarter of the 20th century. But the economic depression of the 1930s caused dislocation of markets both for groundnut kernel and oil. It also caused a setback to the nascent oil crushing industry in Andhra. During the depression period and later there was a growing demand from merchants, peasants, and nationalist forces for the development of oil mills with state aid and encouragement. The effects of depression, dislocation of foreign markets, changing official attitude and the need to develop domestic market for industrial crops prompted limited state initiative and intervention in the development of oil industry in the province. The ceded districts seemed to provide immense opportunities for the growth of oil milling industry. In accordance with the changing official attitude, the Industries Department and its director had been advocating the installation of vegetable oil and hydrogenation factories in select districts in the province. It has been suggested that the development of oil mills would not only bring down the large exports of groundnut kernel, but also help meet the local requirements of vegetable *ghee* and fallow. In order to accelerate the growth of oil mills, the Madras government granted financial assistance to some private capitalists and encouraged others to float more mills. As a result, during the post-second world war period *vanaspati* and oil refining industries witnessed significant growth in Andhra.

II

From the discussion in the preceding pages it is clear that during the post-depression period Andhra districts witnessed a boom in investment in modern agro-industries, which produced mainly for the home market. To repeat, this was possible in the context of changing government policies and economic/political conditions. In fact, since the late 19th century expansion of commercial agriculture and trade provided immense opportunities for investments in the agro-processing industries. Elsewhere we have analysed the process of the formation of peasant bourgeoisie in Andhra and pointed out that it invested surplus capital mainly in land, money-

[15] A. Satyanarayana, "Industrialization in Colonial Andhra," p. 39–46.

lending, trade and small-scale processing industries.[16] The emergence and crystallisation of the rural rich belonging to the dominant peasant castes like the Kamma, Kapu, Reddi, Velama etc., played an important role in the formation of peasant capital.

Nevertheless, it was not until about the depression years that major agro-industries developed in Andhra. As Baker pointed out, "the depression [...] persuaded many of the rural wealthy to try and place their surplus funds in the town" and it also created "impetus for a shift of capital, entrepreneurship, and artisan skills from country to town."[17] This was also true of Andhra, as the table below indicates rapid growth of joint-stock companies and capital mainly in the 1930s and 1940s.[18]

In contrast to the earlier period, investment during the inter-war period primarily went into the manufacturing sector. The aggregate capital investment in the 1940ies in this sector in Andhra totalled Rs. 245.31 lakhs. What is significant to note is the fact that the industrial structure of Andhra, during the inter-war period, was characterised by its diversity; whereas in the pre-depression years the small-scale agro-processing industries were predominant, but the later period saw the emergence of major enterprises of various kinds. After the grant of protection local entrepreneurs took the lead in the development of agro-industries as well as others like cement, ceramics, chemicals and fruit canning which catered to the needs of the internal market. The participation of foreign capital in the industrialisation of Andhra was negligible; it mainly dominated the export-oriented industries like tobacco (Indian Leaf Tobacco Development Company) and Jute (Macleod). Besides the manufacturing industries, new investments by the local capitalists were also made in various other commercial/business ventures. An examination of the composition of the joint-stock capital in Andhra indicates that new concerns such as investment trusts, trading companies, film industry, and mica companies registered significant growth. Likewise, capital enterprises like electric supply companies were formed in almost all the important towns of Andhra in the 1930s. Electricity produced in the thermal power stations at Bezwada, Kakinada, Masulipatnam, Nellore etc., was supplied to many towns. The aggregate capital investment in the power supply companies in 1945 amounted to Rs. 29.57 lakhs.[19] Profits generated in trade,

Table 1
Joint-stock companies and capital mainly in the 1930s and 1940s

Years	No.	Rs in lakhs
1919–20	37	47.74
1924–25	69	89.88
1933–34	47	72.66
1938–39	90	116.60
1945–46	178	217.01
1947–48	260	415.05

16 A. Satyanarayana, "The Evolution of Agricultural and Industrial Entrepreneurs," p. 50–2.

17 C. J. Baker, *The Politics of South India*, Delhi 1976, p. 85.

18 *Report of the Joint Stock Companies in India* for the years shown in Table 1.

19 This is based on *Kothari Investors Encyclopaedia, 1946*.

commerce and commercial agriculture were channelled into such ventures as capital investment. Most of the investment in manufacturing industries was undertaken by merchants (who were actively involved in raw cotton and oilseeds trade), small and big landlords and substantial peasants (who made profits in commercial agriculture, rural credit, agrarian trade and processing industry). It seems that dislocation in export trade and decline in profit in moneylending compelled many of them to seek investment in industries and other commercial enterprises. It was not as if capital was "shy" in colonial Andhra to enter into the industrial sector, but because of the indifference of government and lack of adequate official assistance, at least till about the 1930s local capitalists confined themselves to more secure sources of profit, viz., moneylending and trade. But once new opportunities for industrial investment opened up, indigenous capital was increasingly channelled into manufacturing industries.

Therefore, we find the predominance of merchants and landlords in the establishment of large-scale industries in Andhra. It is generally admitted that merchants, being men in possession of capital and entrepreneur skills entered into the industrial sector, i. e., conversion of merchant capital into industrial capital. So in Andhra, merchants constituted the largest single occupational group which invested in industry. Studies on entrepreneurship in other parts of India[20] revealed a negligible number of entrepreneur drawn from agricultural background. It has been said that in most cases merchants first, then artisans and finally professionals have been the principal groups from which capitalists have emerged. But the findings of this study show that the agrarian classes were as prominent as the traditional merchants and professionals in industrial development in Andhra during the period under study. An examination of the available data on the socio-economic background of the Board of Directors of various industrial/ commercial concerns reveals that two groups, viz., the merchants and landlords dominated the manufacturing sector. Let us look at the typical example of the *Rayalaseema Cotton Mills*, Adoni, Bellary:

No. 1 Proposed Director is a Cotton Grower and owner of a Cotton Ginning Factory. He was a member of the Indian Central Cotton Committee from 1938 to 1940 and was also a Director of the East India Cotton Association, Bombay. He has experience of Company Management as the Chairman of The Rayalaseema Bank, Ltd., Bellary, Director of the Cuddapah Electric Supply Co., Ltd., and Prithvi Insurance Co., Ltd., Madras.

No. 2 Proposed Director is the Chairman and Director of Vauhini Pictures Ltd., Cuddapah Ceramics Ltd., Director, The Cuddapah Electric Supply Co., Ltd., and the Rayalaseema Bank, Ltd. He has been running a cotton hand-spinning and weaving centre at Tadpatri, Anantapur district very successfully. He is the owner of a Cotton Ginning and Pressing factory at Tadpatri.

20 See footnote 1.

He is the Managing Director of India Fruits Ltd., Kadiam and has considerable experience of Company management in several other companies.

No. 3 Proposed Director is the President of the Yemmiganur Weavers' Co-Operative Production and Sale Society, Ltd. This society is the largest Handloom Weavers' Society in South India having more than 1,000 looms under its management, and as such he has considerable experience in yarn and cloth business.

No. 4. Director is one of the biggest cotton growers of Bellary District.

No. 5. Proposed Director is a Cotton Merchant of over 25 years standing at Adoni.

No. 6. is one of the big Cotton and Yarn Merchants of Adoni. His family has been supplying Cotton to Mills for the last 30 years and more.

No. 7. is a Yarn Merchant and is the owner of a Cotton Ginning and Pressing Factory at Adoni.

Nos. 8, 9 and 10 are yarn, cotton and cloth merchants respectively. They and their families have been doing this business for more than 30 years.[21]

So, this company consisted of eight merchants and two Reddi landlords, including "one of the biggest cotton growers of Bellary District". This was also true of the *Bezwada Cotton Mill*; out of nine Directors, five were merchants and four were landlords. In another big cotton mill *The Hemalatha Textile Mills Ltd.*, Guntur, merchants were predominant.[22] Similarly, in the development of oil milling industry it was merchants and big Zamindars such as the Raja of Bobbili, who played a leading role.

In the case of sugar industries it was mostly landlords and rich peasants who took lead in establishing the co-operative sugar factories at Etikoppaka and Thummapala in Vizagapatam district and Vuyyuru in Kistna district; while big merchants dominated the sugar mills in the private and joint-stock sectors.

In the formation of chemical, pharmaceutical, ceramic and engineering industries professionals played the pioneering role. About the *Andhra Pharmaceutical Works Ltd.*, Bezwada, it was mentioned that it was formed by "a number of medical men and medical stores people" and its "directors are mostly drawn from the Medical profession with a few directors from the business and legal profession".[23] Its Managing Director was a medical graduate. Likewise, the Managing Director of an engineering firm, *The Industrial Engineers and Merchants Ltd.*, Bezwada was "a foreign returned Mechanical Engineer"[24] and its Governing Director was a retired Principal of an engineering college. The urban middle classes, white collar employees and advocates seemed to have invested mostly in electric supply companies, as well as banking and

[21] Government Order (G. O.) Law (General), 3778, 28th Sep. 1945.

[22] G. O. Development (Dev.) 1332, 10th Sep. 1926; G. O. Dev. 1644, 16th April, 1952.

[23] G. O. Dev. 1613, 7th August, 1942.

[24] G. O. Dev. 1308, 6th May, p. 190.

insurance companies. But the artisans of Andhra did not seem to have fared well; there was only a small cotton spinning mill and a silk factory which belonged to the Devanga/Padmasalis, the traditional caste of weavers. Very few Muslim families (Nawabs and Sultans) also entered into industry.

It may be noted, however, that the category of "merchants" did not consist only of the Arya Vaishyas or Komatis – the traditional community of traders. Rich peasants belonging to the dominant castes of Kamma, Naidu, Kapu, Reddy, Velama and Lingayat who entered into business also became merchants. However, the leading Komati families in Andhra, viz., the Maddi and Majeti families in Guntur, Mothey family in Ellore, and Pyde and Neelam families in Kakinada and Rajahmundry were also prominent industrialists. Likewise, the category of "landlord" consisted of two groups (a) big zamindars like the Rajas of Bobbili, Venkatagiri, Chellapalli, Pithapuram, Mirzapuram, Nuzvid etc. and (b) small landlords who were also called "proprietors of villages" and substantial peasants in the ryotwari region. For example, the Etikoppaka sugar factory was dominated by such small landlords belonging to the (Kshatriya) Raju caste. Among the big landlords the Zamindars of Bobbili, Chellapalli, and Nuzvid played a significant role in industrial entrepreneurship. The Raja of Bobbili was involved in grain and moneylending and later moved into business and industry. He also pioneered the sugar and oil-mills in Vizagapatam district: he was mainly responsible for the formation of three sugar mills and one vegetable oil factory in this district in the 1930s and 1940s. The Nuzvid Zamindari family who owned vast mango gardens took interest in the fruit canning industry, while the Raja of Chellapalli participated in a number of concerns; sugar, chemicals, banking, insurance etc.

The Rajas of Pithapuram and Mirzapuram were involved in cinema industry, and also lent money to fellow zamindars. The Raja of Venkatagiri invested in many enterprises in Madras; and he was the President of Indian Chamber of Commerce in 1945. In terms of caste, the Zamindars in Andhra belonged to the dominant non-brahmin upper castes, Velama, Kamma and Reddi.

The substantial Reddi and Naidu landholders (of ryotwari area) of the ceded districts and Nellore, and the Kammas of Guntur and Kistna districts were also prominent in various agro-industries as well as in mining and tobacco business. Mining in the Rayalaseema region and Nellore was almost the preserve of the rich Reddi landlords. It has been noted: "[…] detailed description of the 146 working mines in Nellore in 1944, clearly shows a pattern – the predominance of the Reddis. As high as 55 per cent of total mining leases was with them. Further, most of the large mining leases were under their control. The next in importance were the Komati Chettis and Chettiars who had secured about 23 per cent of the lease. The rest, mainly Nayudus, Kammas and Muslim [...] even if one looks at the list of major mica exporters (who were also mostly mine-owners) the dominance of Reddis is quite clear".[25]

In fact the first micanite industry in the Madras presidency was started by a Nellore Reddi mica-owner-exporter. A study on Kurnool also noted thus: "The rich farmers also invested in various joint-stock companies. [...] During and after World War II, the opportunities for investment in non-agricultural activities such as mining, transport and lift irrigation schemes were on the rise. Much of the rural surplus flowed into these ventures".[26] The entrepreneurs belonging to these dominant castes also invested their surplus capital in hotels, cinema industry, transport, banking, real estate etc. They also entered into contract business (both public works department and railway) in a big way in the 1940s. Thus we find the names of certain leading Kamma-Naidus as first class contractors: they included families like Devini, Yarlagadda, Yalamanchali, Kavuri, Surapaneni, Vallabhaneni, Gogineni, Kommineni, Chalasani, Kakani. Whereas the Komatis were mainly found, besides industry, in the wholesale business (turnover more than Rs. 2 lakhs per annum).[27]

Therefore, it is clear that industrial enterprises in colonial Andhra, during the period under study were dominated by the entrepreneurs drawn mainly, if not solely from, the twice-born castes (Brahmins, Kshatriya, Rajus and Arya Vaishya Komatis) and the non-brahmin upper castes (Reddis, Kammas, Naidus, Velamas, Lingayats etc). The participation of Brahmins in industrial activity was also significant, as they acquired skills and knowledge in technical and professional education they ventured into industry. Whereas the Komatis were involved in trade and commerce for long and when occasion favoured they diversified their investment. The entrepreneurs belonging to the Kamma, Velama and Raju castes in coastal Andhra and Reddis, Naidus and Mudaliars in the ceded districts were conspicuous by their overwhelming presence on the Board of Directors of many companies. The predominance of entrepreneurs drawn from the dominant land holding castes/communities like the Reddi, Kamma, Naidu and Mudaliar was quite pronounced in certain industries, viz., cotton mills, oil mills, and sugar mills. For instance, the *Chittoor Sugar Cane Growers Association*, which proposed to establish a sugar factory consisted of 10 Reddi and two Naidu landlords.[28] *The Bank of Chittoor Ltd.*, was dominated by landlords of Kamma-Naidu, Reddi and Mudaliar castes.[29] The Kammas, a sizeable and prosperous cultivating caste primarily in the coastal districts were together with the Reddis and Rajus among the economically dominant castes in Andhra.

[25] Keshabananda Das, "Growth and Decline of the Mica Mining Industry in Nellore, 1911–1950," *The Indian Economic and Social History Review* 28, 1991, p. 401.

[26] G. O. Dev. 1927, 16th August 1940; G. O. Dev. 3382, 1st Sep. 1945.

[27] *Commercial Directory of Madras Presidency*, Madras 1952.

[28] G. O. Dev. 5426, 3rd Nov. 1948.

[29] G. O. Dev. 2381, 23rd July, 1946.

The rich Kammas of coastal Andhra were very active in the establishment of many rice mills, sugar factories at Vuyyuru and Tanuku and tobacco trade at Guntur. Although the export trade of tobacco was dominated by the ILTD Company, rich and enterprising Kammas increasingly participated in it. Some of them also became big exporters of tobacco to foreign countries. The Kamma entrepreneurs also took keen interest in establishing other medium scale industries such as tiles and brick factories, fruit canning and ceramics. Interestingly, lower castes (i. e. backward and untouchables) were conspicuous by their absence in industrial entrepreneurship. Hence there seems to be a positive correlation between the caste ranking and representation in entrepreneurial activity. There was also a significant positive relationship between caste ranking on the one hand, and education, income and occupational status on the other. Available evidence indicates that the twice-born castes together with the non-brahmin uppcr castes had educational advantages over other lower backward castes. The literary rates of different communities/castes in Andhra confirm this.

However, this study suggests that the emergence of industrial entrepreneurship in colonial Andhra was certainly conditioned by social as well as economic factors. Accumulation and access to capital, possession of business experience and the opportunity to acquire technical and managerial skills were far more important. Moreover, it should be noted that the prevailing social structure and caste system in colonial Andhra had profound influence in determining who acquires capital and obtains business and technical knowledge. It may also be noted that no single caste or community solely dominated the industry, rather industrial entrepreneurs belonged to several castes – excluding the lower castes. A perusal of the lists of Board of Directors of several companies in Andhra indicates that Komati merchants, Brahmins, Kammas, Naidus, Reddis etc., were the main share holders. Most of them had either landed property and/or previous experience in commercial enterprises. It appears that initial capital accumulation by the entrepreneurs was obtained through profits in commercial agricultural and/or money-lending. The local official like Collectors commented that, many of the Directors of industrial concerns were "men with considerable influence and good financial resources". Local merchants assumed an increasingly important role in industrial investment during the inter-war period; hence more persons of trading background had entered the industry. Merchants, rural rich, qualified professionals, and white collar employees of upper castes were found side by side in many industries in Andhra. In terms of caste background, all of them belonged to the twice-born and Sat-shudra communities.

To conclude, in this paper two inter-related aspects i. e. growth of industries and entrepreneurial response to it is highlighted. The growth of agro-based medium and large industries characterised the evolution of industrialisation in colonial Andhra. It was facilitated by changing government policies and economic conditions. The world economic depression and its effects, to a large extent, influenced entrepreneurial response to industrial development. It was found that diversion of surplus profits from commercial agriculture, rural credit, and trade into industrial investment was mediated by merchants and rural rich communities. In the formation of industrial capital and entrepreneurship in Andhra region, a significant role was played by the increasing participation of agrarian capital and rural rich. Unlike in other parts of India, the traditional merchant communities, viz., Arya Vaishya/Komati did not monopolise investment in the industrial sector. Rather, the capitalist class of Andhra consisted of both the traditional merchants and rich agrarian communities belonging to the dominant peasant castes of Kamma, Naidu, Kapu, Reddi, etc. Thus Bagchi's observation that, "there is little evidence that entrepreneurship in agriculture provided a stepping stone to industry"[30] is not applicable to colonial Andhra. It is also interesting to note that landed gentry, like the big zamindars of Bobbili, Chellapalli etc., did play a notable role in industrial investment. Similarly some of the Brahmin landlords/agraharamdars and professional also participated in industrial enterprises.

Therefore, there was a clear-cut divergence between caste and occupation as far as the formation of entrepreneurship was concerned. The emergence of industrial entrepreneurs with peasant background was also a proof of this. Yet in caste/community terms entrepreneurial activity was confined to and the preserve of the dominant upper castes Raju, like Brahmin, Vaishyas, Kamma, Kapu, Reddi etc. It meant convergence of caste and class status, i. e., the upper echelons of these castes evolved as an industrial class. Possession of landed property, economic wealth/resources, educational and technical qualifications, access to sources of power and patronage did enable them to evolve as capitalist class. Caste/class convergence is also confirmed by the absence of entrepreneurs drawn from the lower Shudra and untouchable castes/communities. In other words, lower caste status, meagre landholding, poor economic position and literacy etc., did not provide an opportunity for social mobility and the rise of entrepreneurs from among them; in spite of the fact that caste system was dynamic and undergoing transformation. In this sense, caste was a crucial determinant in the formation of entrepreneurship in colonial Andhra during the period under study.

30 A. K. Bagchi, *Private Investment in India*, p. 213.

Muslim Societies in British India

Jamal Malik*

1. Introduction

Islàm in South Asia – a region otherwise dominated by Hinduism – occurs in a variety of shapes and tendencies. Besides popular beliefs and worship of saints there are pietistic as well as secular groups.[1] Moreover, the European expansion and especially the rule of the British over the Indian subcontinent had inevitably left its impact. The various manifestations of Islam are expressions of the broad range of aspirations of some 300 million Muslims of this region. The present paper tries to give an overview over the Muslim organisations and institutions that came into existence and flourished during the period of the British-Indian Empire and define their programmatical and political development *vis-à-vis* the policy of the British.

The spread of Islam in South Asia began through Arab traders and legal experts who scarted along the coastal region in the 1st century of the Islamic Chronology. The region, east of Indus (Arabic: *sind*) became known in the politico-geographical sense as *al-Hind*.[2] At first, conversion into Islam was achieved by accretion,[3] but when Muslim troops successfully incorporated the north-western parts of India into the realm of Islam, the Hindus were declared as

* This article has been translated from German into English by Swapna Bhattacharya, who would like to see it as her contribution to the volume in honour of Prof. Rothermund.

1 The assessment of J. S. Trimingham (*The Sufi Orders in Islam*, Oxford 1971), that Indian Islam is basically an Islam of the holy man, could be considered as accepted; cp. A. Schimmel, *Mystische Dimensionen des Islam*, München (2nd ed.) 1992.

2 C. A. Wink, *Al-Hind, The Making of the Indo-Islamic World: Early Medieval India and the Expansion of Islam, Seventh to Eleventh Centuries*, Leiden 1990; K. A. Nizami (ed.), *Politics and Society during the Early Medieval Period*, Delhi 1974.

3 That is, the original cosmology remains structurally unchanged, while new divinities are added; they can be identified with the existing entity of the Pantheon. Compare in this regard the excellent article of R. M. Eaton, "Islamization in late medieval Bengal," in: W. Schluchter (ed.), *Max Webers Sicht des Islam*, Frankfurt/M. 1987, p. 156ff; also A. Roy, *The Syncretistic Tradition in Bengal*, Princeton 1983.

protégés (*ahl-al-dhimma*). Up to the mid-14th century AD, Muslim influence in South Asia established itself solely up to jurisdictional level of the rulers. This indeed has been reported by the Moroccan world traveller Ibn Battuta.[4]

The armies were followed by Islamic mystics (Sufis). Their appearance again has to be seen in the wider context of the mystic order of central Asia and Persia in the 12th century. Swarming out towards the West, and also towards the East, their significance for the Islamic expansion in South Asia cannot be overestimated.[5] Above all, the orders of Chishtī, Qādirī and Naqshbandī (named after their respective founders) persistently exercised their influence, thereby provided the members of the order with a fruitful contact with *al-Hind* through the acquisition and use of local languages. The records they left, though barely edited, are useful in providing detailed information on their early social history. In contrast to court chronicles, the conversation of Sufi masters with the youth and sympathisers provides an exact insight into the length and breadth of contemporary life. Representatives of all classes and religions encountered with each other in the centres (*khanqah*) and shrines to take home advices of their holy masters.[6]

Many Sufis were able to settle down in places along the important caravan routes, where they sometimes built fortifications. Such establishments (*qasbah*s) emerged as commercial-administrative-military bases at the regional levels with dignitaries and Islamic scholars who found their clients there. The officials living in such establishments – Muslims and Hindus alike – got huge tracts of land from the Muslim rulers in recognition of their military, fiscal and scholarly services. These officials lived mainly on the income accruing from such lands. In this way a Muslim aristocracy (*ashrāf* or *shurafā*) appeared which categorically differentiated itself from the "uncivilised" or "Barbarians" (*ajlāf*). Further through such differentiations the idea of Islamic "superiority" took a concrete shape.[7] Mysticism and Islamic studies thus set conditions for integration of such widespread an Islamic kingdom.

4 See S. Conermann, *Die Beschreibung Indiens in der "Rihla" of Ibn Battuta: Aspekte einer herrschaftssoziologischen Einordnung der Delhi-Sultanates unter Muhammad Ibn Tughluq*, Berlin 1993.

5 For spread of mystic order see Trimingham, *Orders*. Also see Schimmel, *Dimensionen*, p. 323ff, 367ff.

6 An overview of source materials is provided by J. Paul: "Hagiographische Texte als historische Quelle," *Saeculum*, 41 (1), 1990, p. 17–43.

7 Shurafā can be divided in different categories: 1. Sayyids, who derive their genealogy from the Prophet Muhammed. 2. The Shaikhs, who are to be understood as descendants of the first four Caliphs and the uncle of Prophet, Abbas. 3. The Pakhtuns and Afghans.

2. The Integrative Rule of Mysticism and Islamic Studies

A tendency to popular piety, mystic order and beliefs rendered *qasbahs* a high degree of integrative, occasionally syncretic culture – besides others – through augmentation. That is why the idea of "unity of being" (*Wahdat al-Wujūd*) developed by the Spaniard Ibn ʿArabī (1165–1240) was more popular here than in the rest of the Islamic world. This ontological monism effaced the borders between the religions – an effacation, which became conditional for the functioning of a Muslim minority. The reason is: if "all is He", then there must be also a Divine, present among the Hinduistic and other non-Islamic beliefs. From the 14th century onwards mystic orders like Chishtī and Qādirī enthusiastically preached their pantheistic ideas.

Lessons of Islamic studies were in the centre in philosophical and legal texts: During the periods of the Sultanate of Delhi (13th to 16th century) and Mughal empire (16th to 19th century), special emphasis was laid on the study of such philosophical and legal texts. This school of studies had its basis born in the Persian-Shiah traditions of the 14th and 15th centuries. Persian became the dominant language. Akbar (ruled 1556–1605) patronised these sciences intensively. In this way, relying on the Islamic traditions, he could adjust himself more flexibly to the local Indian peculiarities and thus legitimise his administrative, fiscal and military reforms. The emphasis on this Islamic tradition not only provoked sharp criticism from the orthodox priesthood, but also caused the outbreak of rebellions. These rebellions could be neutralised occasionally through alliances, military interventions or financial donations, given among others to members of religious orders. In the course of this process it was possible to incorporate large parts of South Asia, such as the kingdoms of the Deccan, into the realm of the king's empire. The representatives of Shiite culture of these regions flushed into the whole of South Asia, especially into regions of present Pakistan, North India and the Deccan.

3. The Weakening of the Centres and Islamic Reforms

The politics of integration demanded further concession in favour of local landowners and tax collectors. From the middle of the 17th century onwards, these personalities were successful in appropriating the rights over land and offices into their own private jurisdiction thereby escaping from control of the centre. They put forward their demand for participation in the administration and for stronger adherence to Islamic principles. One of the founders of this group was Ahmad Sirhindī (1564–1624), a member of the Naqshbandī order. He took the monistic concept of Ibn ʿArabī (unity of being) and gave it a new interpretation by explaining the concept in terms of "unity of view and attestation" (*Wahdat al-Shuhūd*). By doing so, he dictated Ibn ʿArabī a new social role aimed at changing the society. After realising the experience of absolute unity, the Sufi comes back to the world, and tries to bring the degenerated moral order into harmony with the divine order.[8]

Even increasing influence of the Naqshbandī order and orthodox priests must have pressed Aurangzeb to continue with his Islamisation policy,[9] in the course of which especially Hindu-landowners, the Sikhs and the Rajputs, revolted. Thus, the unity of the empire was threatened and on the verge of collapse. This crisis of the Mughal empire in the 18th century posed less an overall decay, as normally asserted, than an actual struggle between entrepreneurs, military personals and politicians for capturing economic and political hegemony. After all, along with it, sciences of arts and cultures blossomed.[10]

The emerging independent princes had usually been high officials in the Mughal administration. They regarded their former fiefs as home provinces within which they introduced widespread reforms in order to establish their sovereignty over land and people. The residence cities were meant to manifest the political power of the new rulers, but at the same time these cities stood in the tradition of the Mughals, mirroring the Central Asian and Persian culture of the Muslim "aristocrats" (*ashrāf*).[11] As such, they attracted scholars who moved into the new capitals in large numbers. The fall of Delhi in 1739 accelerated the exodus from the former capital of the Mughals and strengthened the power of the new princes. In their territories a new integrative identity emerged, through devotional religions (sometimes of Hinduistic and Islamic mixture), the construction of libraries and shrines, the promotion of architecture and literature, and not to forget through the medium of the Urdu language which slowly substituted Persian as a *lingua franca*. Every single principality claimed its own religio-cultural "verity". The turn towards the "unity of being" was a precondition that every single principality could claim its own religio-cultural "unity of being".

8 Cp. Schimmel, *Mystische Dimensionen*, p. 514ff.

9 Islamisation strategy of Aurangzeb was regarded as a proclamation of Jihad against the Marathas, who under the leadership of Shivaji (1630–1680), symbolic figure of the Hindu resistance struggle, and his son Sambhaji (1680–1689), defended the Deccan region.

10 C. A. Bayly, *Rulers, Townsmen and Bazaars. North Indian Society in the Age of British Expansion, 1770–1870,* Delhi 1992; M. Alam, *The Crisis of Empire in Mughal North India*, Delhi 1986; J. R. I. Cole, *Roots of North Indian Shiism in Iran and Iraq. Religion and State in Awadh, 1722–1859*, Berkeley 1988; Roy, *The Syncretistic Tradition*; A. Wink, *Land and Sovereignty in India*, Cambridge 1986; S. Bayly, *Saints, Goddesses and Kings. Muslims and Christians in South Indian Society, 1700–1900*; Cambridge (2nd ed.) 1992; J. S. Grewal, *The Sikhs of the Punjab*, Cambridge 1990; J. Pemble, *The Raj, The Indian Mutiny and the Kingdom of Oudh 1810–1959*, Hassocks 1977; J. Kippen, *The Table of Lucknow. A Cultural Analysis of a Musical Tradition*, Cambridge 1988.

11 Compare F. Robinson, "Perso-Islamic Culture in India from the Seventeenth to the early Twentieth Century," in R. L. Canfield (ed.), *Turco-Persia in Historical Perspective*, New York 1991, p. 104–31.

Islamic teachings, which closely connected South Asia with the rest of the Islamic world, underwent a reform. At the beginning of the 18th century the Shiite cultural centre of Awadh, Lucknow, experienced the change of canonical literature into a pragmatic system under the active initiatives of Sunni scholars of the Qādirī order. These scholars were later known under the name of Farangī Mahallis. Selected parts of highly sophisticated treatises, in major parts on logic, philosophy and law – for the first time, contemporary Indian Muslim scholars were taken into regard as well – were studied in depth. This popular representation of canonical literature became instrumental in providing solutions to problems. Tradition and authoritarian relations remained important as before. This functional character of the canon turned out to be so successful that Shiites and Hindus indiscriminately went over to this teaching, and successfully confessed persons were later placed in different principalities as teaching office-bearers in the administration and the military.

Similar to other contemporary streams, the school of Delhi, which stood in opposition to the Farangī Mahall at Lucknow, received its inspirations from Mecca and Medina, where "traditional studies" (*manqūlāt*, i. e. Quran and Hadith studies) were cultivated. Both Mecca and Medina were cosmopolitan centres of the scholarly world in the 18th century, having a number of branches stretching from Maghreb to Southeast Asia. The spread of their teachings was promoted by way of pilgrimage (*hajj*) and particularly through Sufis belonging to the Naqshbandī order.[12] Shāh Walī Allāh (1703–1762) and Mīr Dard (died 1785) were most reputed personalities of the Delhi school.[13] Their reform was characterised by the recourse to early Islamic scholarship. Independent of each other they developed the concept of "Muhammadan Path" (*Tarīqa Muhammadīya*). This path was considered to be better than individual mysticism: Prophetic piety replaced mystic piety. Man became the focus of the society. Parallely, Urdu flourished in Delhi and dissolved the court culture of Persian origin.[14] Poetry and its institutions – such as literary salons – set the process of this emancipation in motion. Traders, officers, bankers and "scribal groups", who belonged mostly to the Sufi order were equally represented.

12 Indeed the Naqshbandīs from India left an impact on the mystical reform movements of the 18th–19th centuries, cp. M. Gaborieau et al. (eds.), *Naqshbandis. Historical Developments and Present Situation of a Muslim Mystical Order*, Istanbul 1990. For reform movement in the 18th century cp. N. Levtzion/J. O. Voll (eds.), *Eighteenth Century Renewal and Reform in Islam*, Syracuse 1987.

13 Cp. J. M. S. Baljon, *Religion and Thought of Shah Wali Allah Dihlawi, 1703–1762*, Leiden 1986; Schimmel, *Dimensionen*; R. Peters, "Islamischer Fundamentalismus: Glaube, Handeln, Führung," in: Schluchter (ed.), *Max Weber*, p. 217ff. Comparable tendencies of "Sunnatisation" in the lifestyle was existent among Shiites, e. g. the debate between Usulis and Akhbaris.

14 A. Schimmel, *Und Muhammad ist sein Prophet*, Düsseldorf-Köln 1981; idem, *Classical Urdu Literature from the Beginning to Iqbal*, Wiesbaden 1975; U. Rothen-Dubs, *Allahs indischer Garten*, Frauenfeld 1989. Widespread thesis of different Urdu-schools (Delhi-Lucknow) goes into the chauvinistic criticism of the literature of early poets from Delhi; the political and cultural competition between Delhi and the princely states (especially Awadh) squeezed in it. Cp. C. Petievich, *Assembly of Rivals. Delhi, Lucknow and the Urdu Gehazal*, Delhi 1992.

At the same time, it was possible to realise the reform of ideas with the help of local languages: "It is the man who brings the life in the world! The world was His mirror even before there was no human being – still a mirror, incapable to make vision possible."[15]

Other remaining urban scholars went on with adjusting their interpretations of canons to the local and regional environment. Writings on philosophy and logic of a few Farangī Mahallis from Lakhnau rapidly crossed the boundary of India. The historical circumstances of the 18th century suggest that as the standardisation of canons, so also promotion of reformist tradition of sciences, reflect an anthropocentric discourse. The contents of both the schools were critically debated; they represented interest of the new urban and rural élites. As important agents of autonomy, they gained greater authority and thus extended their power zones, finally contributing actively to the economic progress.[16] However, this increasingly awakened the interest of the Europeans who since a considerable period of time, maintained loose contacts with India. Thus, a colonial interest emerged from individual trade.

4. Shaping Muslim Structures in a Colonial Setting

Already in their commercial dealings, the European companies had been depending on local collaborators and suppliers. This dependency even increased when the British started to build up a civil administration in Bengal after the battle of Plassey in 1757.[17] Thus in 1772 British courts were introduced, and various experiments for the best method of collecting revenues led to the Permanent Settlement of 1793 which created a new class of land owners. Incidentally, they were all Hindu, but communal categories became important only later.[18] Since 1800, the local administrative staff was trained in Fort William College in Calcutta. The influence of resident Hindu élites of Bengal (*bhadralok*) society was comparable to the Muslim *ashrāf*. The Hindu *bhadralok* occupied key positions while Muslims failed to avail the new opportunities, partly because of religious consideration (for example prohibition to accept interest out of

15 Thus the famous Urdu-Poet Mir Taqi Mir (1724–1810), cited in Rothen-Dubs, *Garten*, 20. Mir Dard was of the opinion "You create the human beings for the suffering of love – for the obedience you have your angel!" or "Throughout the life I heard Him from away, in my dream I brought Him close to my bosom. Now that I arrived before Him as a mirror, He saw Himself; not I look at Him." Quoted in Schimmel, *Liebe zu dem Einen*, p. 121, 124.

16 Bayly, *Rulers;* D. Washbrook, "Progress and Problems: South Asian Social and Economic History, c. 1720–1860," *Modern Asian Studies* 22, 1988, p. 57–97; idem, "South Asia, the World System, and World Capitalism," *Journal of Asian Studies* 49, 1990, p. 479–508.

17 For the following explanation cp. C. A. Bayly, *Indian Society and the Making of the British Empire*, Cambridge 1990 (2nd ed.); Bayly, *Rulers*, and H. Kulke/D. Rothermund: *A History of India*, New York 1990 (2nd ed.).

18 According to the colonial administrator W. W. Hunter,the *Settlement* was responsible for the downfall of Islam in Bengal. This observation he made in 1871 in his widely quoted book *The Indian Musulmans*.

money lending business). Already by the end of the 18th century this affluence of the Hindus was reflected in the construction of numerous Hindu temples, while the economic competition between the two communities found its expression in the riots breaking out in urban areas. The company wanted to ensure peace by introducing a new administration of justice, with the intention to exploit the indigenous potential for expanding their administrative mechanism. With the help of Indian money and especially Bengal revenues, the EIC not only consolidated its authority over Bengal, but also acquired further territories in northern (for example parts of Awadh), and western India. Allied princes were restricted in their power, being e. g. denied their rights to conclude treaties. This resulted in the *pax Britannica*. But while on the one hand introducing new legislation and jurisdiction concerning taxes and land ownership rights as well as connecting India to the world market on much greater scale, the British tried to link themselves with their Mughal predecessors by preserving the notion of cultural unity. They kept on using the terminology of the Mughal empire – Company Bahadur[19] – and made Persian their administrative language. It was in Calcutta that Urdu prose and especially the Urdu novel was fostered.[20]

5. Islamic Reactions

Reactions on colonial penetration were massive in urban as well as in agricultural sectors. A few took initiatives for restorative orders, others did not. In the urban sector Shāh ʿAbd al-ʿAzīz (1746–1824), a son of Shāh Walī Allāh, formulated his demand for reforms according to the politically dominant colonial public mind. From 1803 onwards local rites were regarded as an expression of decadent, obscure and "traditional" cults, and therefore their disqualifications by the colonial public began to leave its impact on local culture. In his legal recommendations, Shāh ʿAbd al-ʿAzīz condemned the features of folk religion, particularly the Shiite cult of saints. The reformer propagated the learning of English language to facilitate the entry into British service. His proposals could be seen as attempts of integration for the Sunni Muslim community to gain a platform for their action – a platform, which was apparently lost with the advent of colonial power.

Other dignitaries preferred to follow an isolationist position. They rejected any interaction with Europeans and instead took care of groups of urban artisans, among them weavers. This led them to organise in guild-like bodies, and thereby strengthened the Sufi communities, for

19 *Bahādur* was a Mughal honorary title and was awarded for extraordinary social and political achievements.

20 An insight view on social structure of colonised society, and on the world of women and courtesans are to be found in the "first" Urdu-novel *The Courtesans of Lakhnau* written by Mirza Muhammad Hadi Ruswa.

example a branch of Naqshbandī order in Delhi.[21] In the areas where nomad-like peasants resided, numerous religiously legitimised revolts broke out. *Qasbahs*, now serving as retreat places for cultural élites, provided the points of departure for chiliastic insurrections which triggered off resistance against the exploitation by local landowners, traders, entrepreneurs and middlemen.[22]

In the first quarter of the 19th century the descendants of Shāh Walī Allāh founded the order of Mohammadan Path (*Tarīqa Muhammadīya*) in northwestern India. Like in other contemporary "Muhammadan Paths" in parts of Africa, central Asia and the Hijaz, the Indian counterpart propagated the purification of Islam from so-called un-islamic elements. These elements were believed to be present in the holy cult and folk beliefs. Therefore they were mistakenly called *Wahhābīya* by the British who identified them with the Arab puritan movement from the 18th century. This corresponded to the colonial notion of pan-Islamic, militant anti-colonial movements. At first, however, the corporate body of Muslim orders in India called for a fight (*jihād*) against the Sikhs, who had established their power since the defeat of the Mughal empire in the Panjab.[23] Only from the second quarter of the 19th century onward Muslim groups started fighting the colonial masters. Other movements were active in Bengal, on the Malabar coast and in the Panjab.[24]

Many of the Islamic reform movements maintained relations with the Arab peninsula. Their founders were inspired by the spiritual atmosphere prevailing there. But, like the "Padri Movement" in Southeast Asia, these were indigenous movements, based on reform traditions of the 18th century, and originally oriented against the restorative character of the present order. Like Christian missionaries they utilised the printing press and transferred their messages of pure Islam very quickly to the local level through local languages such as Bengali and Urdu. The first Urdu translation of the Koran also appeared in this period. In this way the print media supported the creation of a diversified mutually competing Islamic public, which increasingly became literate and nationalistic.[25] This process of emancipation however conflicted with the

[21] Compare J. Malik, "Islamic Institutions and Infrastructure in Shahjahanabad," in: E. Ehlers/Th. Krafft (eds.): *Shahjahanabad/Old Delhi. Tradition and Colonial Change*, Stuttgart 1993, p. 43–64 (here 54ff). This indicates a connection between artisans, guilds, craftsmen and mystic orders which was widespread in the Orient. Compare F. Taeschner, *Zünfte und Bruderschaften im Islam*, München 1979.

[22] Summarised by K. W. Jones, *Socio-Religious Reform Movements in British India*, Cambridge 1989; also Peters, "Islamic Fundamentalism".

[23] There are indications that they really acted in the interest of the British, to weaken the Sikhs. Indeed, Panjab and Sindh were annexed in 1843 and 1849 respectively.

[24] *Farā'idiyya* movement in Bengal; *Mappila*-Muslims in Kerala (Malabar coast); corresponding activities of the Chishtīs in Panjab.

[25] In this context see F. Robinson, *Separatism among Indian Muslims. The Politics of the United Provinces' Muslims 1860–1923*, Cambridge 1974, p. 77–8; *idem*, "Secularization in Islam," in: Schluchter (ed.): *Max Weber*, p. 256ff, traces back the origin of the emancipating effect in the European influence.

colonial interest. Therefore, the "traditionalisation" of India was to make the colonial penetration easier and prevented self-dynamics.

6. The Traditionalisation of India and the Rebellion of 1857

The sources which highlight the mutual relations between Indians and colonial rulers suggest that in order to "traditionalise" Indian society, the colonial masters utilised the criticism made by the former pietists and contemporary reformers to their own (i. e. Islamic) society, turning it into a full swing attack on the orient. They did this with a clear intention to legitimise their power and to achieve a breakthrough in their concept of "modernization".[26] Thereby they traditionalised large areas of India, which now came to represent the counterpole of the modern colonial zone. This was programmatic and corresponds to the perception of colonial spirit which in vain tried to "modernise"[27] the "traditional elements" in the Indian society, fragmented by castes, religions and ethnic divisions. As the British defined group identities (*communitas*) primarily in terms of religious affiliations (and thereby justified their ethnic policy), "communalistic" thinking was created.[28] Revolts against the colonial rulers in their further steps of privatisation, transit duties, etc., were quelled militarily, and thereby reference was made to the castes and religious affiliations of those who revolted.

A "traditional" India of course needed reforms: The period under Governor General William Bentinck (1774–1839) witnessed cuts in the military and administrative budget, but brought only limited improvements for trade. Social reforms, partly caused by the pressure from the Christian missionaries, and changes in law also played their part. The introduction of the English education system offered Indians the possibility to join the lower ranks of the Indian Civil Service. Simultaneously, in 1837 Persian was replaced by English and Urdu. All that immensely weakened the supreme position of Muslim aristocrats (*ashrāf*), especially in the administration of justice.[29] The lawyer Thomas B. Macaulay (1800–1859) proposed a radical anglic-

[26] I would like to argue that the well-known colonial criticism of the Orient is not a genuine European invention. It was constructed on the basis of India's indigenous oriental criticism and shaped it according to her own convenience. That means the colonial masters were not compulsorily the catalysts for "development" and "modernization", because the catalytic moment was already comprehensible and disposable.

[27] The historiography of the 19th century was well reflected in the colonial conception; see the bibliographical notes in R. S. O'Fahey/B. Radtke, "Neo Sufism Reconsidered," *Der Islam* 70, 1993, especially p. 61ff. Cp. also R. Inden, "Orientalist Constructions of India," *Modern Asian Studies* 20, 1986, p. 401–46.

[28] The conceptualisation of society in terms of ethnic identity and religious affiliation was reproduced in the popular rebellions from the period since 1871. The later nationalists willingly took over this ethnification of society; compare N. G. Barrier (ed.): *The Census in British India: New Perspectives*, New Delhi 1981. For Communalism cp. G. Pandey, *The Construction of Communalism in Colonial India*, Delhi 1990.

[29] Reform movements like *Tarīqa Muhammadīya* and *Farā'idiyya* took up this problem and radicalised it and thus sharpened the animosity between the religious communities.

isation. Above all he was of the opinion that a single shelf in a good European library was worth the whole native literature of India and Arabia. Therefore, he wanted to create a "class of persons, Indian in blood and colour, but English in taste, in perception, in morals and in intellect". This led to a marginalisation of the conventional education systems that lasted up to the contemporary period.

The new colonial culture further demanded social readjustments, likewise new exclusive institutions with particularistic interests carrying similar new values emerged. This gave impetus to existing inner social antagonisms which, in connection with efforts of the British Government to centralise and successively annex further regions of the British Empire in India, led to the outbreak of the 1857 rebellion. The rebellion appeared as a freedom fight or as a mutiny according to the respective point of view. In it a large number of discontented groups joined their forces: Muslim scholars, parts of the bureaucracy of the Mughal empire, notables, entrepreneurs, artisans and farmers. The military was a merely a catalytic agent. Already in 1850 the company tried to win over the Indian soldiers for service in foreign countries and replaced the leaders of the army – Brahmans and Rajputs – by members of other castes. Moreover, their payment had been reduced. The fright of ritual contamination stemming from a new kind of rifle cartridge caused the outbreak among Indian soldiers. The rebellion indeed had a traditional Islamic component and aimed at the restoration of the former order. In the meantime, the British had declared themselves as liberators of the Hindus from the tyranny of Muslim rule.[30] The fear of a renewed Muslim rule supposedly drove many Hindus to the side of the colonial masters; in reality the royalists differed from the rebels only in the aspect that the former profited from the colonial administration and trade, whereas the latter suffered persistently since 1801 from deprivation of their lands. With lack of consistency, inadequate coordination, religious and social contradictions and collaboration on the side of the rebels, the Europeans got the upper hand in 1858 after a long battle.

7. New Muslim Identities under Imperial Premises

Although India had been governed by British commercial entrepreneurs up to 1858, it became really "British" only afterwards. As a result of the "mutiny", the Crown of England (i. e.,

[30] The concept corresponds to that of James Mill, who in his *History of India*, divided Indian history into three periods: Hindu, Muslim and British. This concept was further forwarded by Elliot and Dawson (*The History of India as told by its own Historians, 1867*). Later historians replaced this through the nomenclature: antique, medieval and modern. Further it promoted the idea that communalism or ethnification is the leading character of politics and with that also of History. Later Nationalist writers went on writing on this custom and thus legitimised the communal and separatist politics. Cp. H. Mukhia, *Perspectives on Medieval History*, Delhi 1993.

Queen Victoria) took over the administration of India which was from then on governed by a Viceroy. The British on the one hand adapted their system of governance to the Indian set-up (especially by preserving local traditions and customs),[31] but on the other hand "modernisation" which initially took the shape of "anglisation" as demanded by Macaulay, became the political credo. The extension of the communication system (telegraph line in 1861, opening of the Suez Canal) further strengthened the ties between Great Britain and India. The process of political submission that followed lasted until 1935. It was introduced with the help of but also at the cost of Muslim and Hindu groups who initially hardly managed to enter the colonial administration but became more and more conscious of their communal identity.[32] The new Muslim identities were to a higher or lesser grade influenced by European values. Nevertheless, they found their basis in the cities and in the *qasbah*s of the United Provinces, where they could follow a long cultural and intellectual tradition; they were imprinted by an idea of privileged position of Muslims.[33]

An early variation showed itself in 1867 in the *hanafite* movement at Deoband near Delhi. Their protagonists who recruited themselves to a great deal from the *ashrāf*, kept a certain degree of distance to the colonial regime, although a few found jobs in the civil service. Their aim was to get training in traditional sciences (*manqūlāt*) and to acquire a common platform to safeguard the interests of Sunni scholarship. In doing so they emphasised their affiliation with the Delhi tradition and the "Mohammadan Path". A similar 'reformist' position was taken by the association *Ahl-e Hadīth* (founded in 1864), which went beyond the legal schools and emerging modernism. This group found its social basis among trading communities. Both communities tried to explain the new social realities within the framework of Islamic views (Weltanschauungen) as isolated phenomena; their main receptors therefore were among traditional urban groups of society. The third group to complete Islamic discourse were the hanafitic *Barelwīs* (called after Bareilly, the birthplace of their founder Ahmad Ridā Khān) which were active in the agrarian society of Northern India. While the scripturalists (*Deobandis* and *Ahl-e Hadīth*) tended towards the order of the Naqshbandīs' and Sirhindīs' notion of "unity of display", the *Barelwīs* kept themselves closer to the order of Qādirī and Ibn ʿArabī's notion of "unity of being" thus following the Lucknow school. Both traditions continue their debates until today.

Apart from this discourse "within", a second one emerged "externally". The colonial society, becoming increasingly complex and urban, had fostered intellectual exchange between

31 E. g. they alluded to the central rule by proclaiming Queen Victoria as "Empress of India" in 1876.

32 Cp. B. Anderson, *Imagined Communities: Reflections on the Origin and Spread of Nationalism*, London 1991 (2nd ed.).

33 Compare B. D. Metcalf, "Islamische Reformbewegungen," in: Schluchter (ed.), *Max Weber*, p. 242ff; idem, *Islamic Revival in British India: Deoband, 1860–1900*, Princeton 1982.

foreign and autochthonous cultures. The bilingual intelligentsia that emerged out of this tension oscillated between tradition and modernity. It consisted of government bureaucrats, lawyers and especially intellectuals, who constituted an urban élite that was but seldom regarded as belonging to the scholarly group in the narrow sense but that represented throughout the *ashrāf* culture of the *qasbah*s, where they were possessing land. This group derived its identity from a colonial context and claimed to define modernity and traditionality in an obliging manner: colonial society, advancement, dynamism and development on one side and autochthonous society, stagnation, conservatism and barbarism on the other. Such dichotomies actually were also proclaimed by the British as a programme. This Islamic avant-garde saw itself as the only legitimised group to replace the conventional scholarship and its fora.

One possibility to overcome the tension between modernity and tradition was to be found in the social withdrawal, just like the reformist Deobandis tried. Another possibility was through adjustment with the colonial system. The most influential of these integrational cultural articulation of the Muslim élites from 1876 onwards[34] was the Aligarh Movement, centred round S. Ahmad Khān (1817–1899). He postulated unconditional civil servant-like behaviour, through which alone the self perceived (rather: suggested) Muslim conservatism was to be overcome and protected against the dominant majority of Hindus.[35] Altāf Husain Hālī (1837–1914) has impressively sketched this fear in his elegy "Tidings of Islam" (1879).

As the Aligarh movement could not realise the integration of the Ulamā and mystics, other Muslim forces began to establish a new loyal interest group. Thereby they referred to the reconstruction of the early Islamic era, similar to contemporary reformers in Egypt. They utilised the new printing media in the vernacular language. This increasingly undermined the authority of traditional dignitaries because proper Islamic behaviour was possible without them and was anyway accessible to everyone. However, determining the Islamic discourse, they found themselves in a normative dilemma between tradition and modernity. Behind their quest for reform stood the discussion (which began in the middle of the 19th century) about the canon of the Farangi Mahall from Lucknow, that had become overloaded with logic in the meantime. Therefore, an Indian deputy collector[36] demanded in 1892 to found a "Council of scholars" (*Nadwat*

[34] For the Aligarh-Movement and S. Ahmed Khan's ideas, see D. Lelyveld, *Aligarh's First Generation. Muslim Solidarity in British India*, Princeton 1978; Chr. W. Troll, *S. A. Khan: A Reinterpretation of Muslim Theology*, Oxford 1979; A. Ahmad/G. E. von Grunebaum, *Muslim Self-Statement in India and Pakistan 1857–1968*, Wiesbaden 1970, p. 25ff. The years of 1876–77 were marked by widespread agitations as the higher ranks of the ICS were still inaccessible for (mostly Hindu) Indians. The British therefore encouraged the foundation of the Aligarh Movement and later turned it into Aligarh Muslim University.

[35] The myth of Muslim backwardness goes back to W. W. Hunter, whose information in major part was meant to be applicable to Bengal; but Muslim intellectuals and nationalists used the information as if applicable for the whole country.

[36] This was the highest office in the colonial hierarchy an Indian could reach. The anglicisation had still then a very clear boundary.

al-ʿUlamā),[37] which was called to life in the colonial town of Kanpur and later moved to the old famous scholastic centre Lucknow. The panel intended to find new ways of expressing knowledge, organisation and literature in a new environment and at the same time serve as a stabilising and integrating factor of colonial rule. The influence of the own group within the colonial urban society was to be ensured by political and loyal behaviour. Through legal institutions and a college of their own, social service and missionary activities, voluntary organisations and the publication of a journal, they tried to implement their *Solidaritätstraditionalismus* (appeal to traditional solidarity)[38] and their harmonising efforts, the latter both internally (by the lessening disputes about dogmas and religious differences) and externally by bringing Islam and colonial system closer together. In this attempt, Urdu served as the common language even in the academic discourse.

The *Nadwat al-ʿUlamā* was a fabric of the colonial system. Their inherent aim – the stabilisation of imperial unity – was reflected in the new image of Islam the council members (*nadwis*) created for themselves. Through the reform of "backward" *qasbah*s, the power of the crown was to reach areas yet untouched. For this purpose, however, the council had to take the help of further scholars, especially from the Naqshbandī order, which after a short phase of inner reform and after the Khilafat movement came back to the helm. All these fora accelerated Muslim consciousness and provoked tensions among traditional Islamic and Hindu groups pleading for more political participation.

8. Colonial Reforms and Nationalistic Aspirations

Nationalism as it was prescribed by the British could definitely not admit a democratic process, for the Indian society was ruled by 'remote control'. The anglicisation and growing hanker for participation, especially in the Indian Civil Service, led to further frustration. Indian voices had to articulate their interests from a solid platform. However, none of the old known centres, neither Deoband and Farangī Mahall[39] nor Aligarh and Nadwah, or any of the diverse Hindu organisations, were in the position to serve as a platform. Therefore, the Indian Congress, founded in 1885 by a few economic magnates in Bombay, wanted to take up the task. Scholars

[37] For *Nadwat al-ʿUlamā* compare Metcalf, *Islamic Revival*, p. 335ff; J. Malik, "The Making of a Council: the Nadwat al-ʿUlamā," *Zeitschrift der Deutschen Morgenländischen Gesellschaft* 144, 1994, p. 60–91.

[38] This term has been coined by D. Rothermund, cp. his "Der Traditionalismus als Forschungsgegenstand für Historiker und Orientalisten," *Saeculum* 40, 1989, p. 142–8.

[39] They still yielded a considerable influence over a well-functioning press and an extensive book market. The "Jewels of Paradise" of a Deobandi became a "Knigge" for middle class women and became the most popular reading material in South Asia. Cp. B. D. Metcalf, *Perfecting Women*, Berkeley 1991; *idem*, Islamische Reformbewegungen.

of the powerful Deoband school welcomed the foundation of Congress and the spirit of cooperation between Muslims and Hindus in secular matters. In this regard they proclaimed 1888 a legal recommendation (*fatwā*) in which however the idea of Islamic superiority was maintained:

> If Hindus and Muslims go mutually into an economic transaction which neither harms religion, nor harms Sharia, nor the problem of interest or invalid sale does appear, then the transaction is permissible and legal. But no contact should be held with Sayyid Ahmad Khān[40] and one should go into contacts with Hindus. However, the contact is prohibited if Sharia is passed over, or Muslims are weakened, and Hindus are strengthened.

S. Ahmad Khān (Aligarh Movement), on the contrary rejected Congress with the plea that it was Hindu-favouring. Instead he demanded a representation for Muslims and founded the Muhammadan Anglo Oriental Defence Association in 1893. In doing so, he contributed to the petrification of the confessional tensions.

Hindu nationalism stood diametrically opposite to different fora of Muslim élites. At the demand of the Indians, the British issued the *Council Act* of 1892 which provided a rather limited right of say. The Muslim élites were alarmed since under no circumstances they fought for democratic representation, but rather stood for parity and equality. This intensified the animosity between the representatives of both the religious communities, especially between urban Muslims and Hindu landowners and traders. The *Hindi-Urdu controversy*[41] (around 1900) and the prohibition of cow-slaughtering urged the Muslim crusaders in 1900 to found the Urdu Defence Association and in 1906 the *All-India Muslim League,* while referring seriously to the axiomatic superior position of Islam in India so plausible for them.[42] The colonial masters therefore could legitimately assume that some of the Muslim public continued to seek their support against the Hindu majority, say e. g. the Nadwīs, Aligarhis and the *Muslim League*. Only few traditional Islamic scholars, such as the Deoband school, demanded a peaceful coexistence with Hindus and cooperation with Congress.

40 Deoband attacked the exclusive standpoint of Ahmad Khan since he questioned the superiority of the scholars. For the debate between the Deoband and Aligarh schools cp. Ahmed et al. (eds.), *Self-Statement*, p. 66ff

41 The language Hindi, developed as it emerged at the close of the 19th century is based on the grammar of Urdu. It differs from Urdu in the form of script and degree of sanskritisation; the latter being rich in Arabic and Persian loanwords. The controversy particularly reflected the already existent economic competition between the two religious communities. Cp. K. Dittmer, *Die indischen Muslims und die Hindi-Urdu-Kontroverse in den United Provinces*, Wiesbaden 1972.

42 For a summary cp. F. Shaikh, *Community and Consensus in India: Muslim Representation in Colonial India 1860–1947*, Cambridge 1989. The idea of dynamic Islam and stagnant Hinduism is still quite widespread among the Indian-Muslim dignitaries.

9. Nationalist Demands and the Khilafat Movement

In Bengal, especially in Calcutta, nationalism had become more radical meanwhile, nurtured besides others, by the *bhadralok*. In response, the colonial rulers partitioned Bengal (1905), thereby creating a Muslim majority province consisting of East Bengal and Assam. This gave a snub to radical Hindu nationalists and widened the gap between Hindus and Muslims. When the partition of Bengal was lifted again in 1911, Muslim élites were in a difficult position, as they had to give up their privileges and therefore rethought their loyalty.

The colonial government had in the meantime pursued its communal politics with more vigour. Early in the year 1906, shortly before the *Muslim League* was founded in Dhaka, a delegation of Muslim leaders took the initiative for separate electorates. The constitutional reform of 1909 ("Morley-Minto Reforms") met such wishes and safeguarded Muslim interests through political representation, but continued the policy of *divide and rule*. This ethnification was continued in the Montagu-Chelmsford Reforms (1919), and even the Lucknow Pact (1916), in which Congress and *Muslim League* together demanded the right of self-determination, was built on this separatism. The League was granted a veto right on minority issues.[43] In order to prevent the rise of pan-Indian nationalism, the colonial masters segregated themselves even more and reacted with the drastic measure of continuing martial law after the first World War.[44] The *Rowlatt Act* of 1919 were meant to stop the process of political emancipation.

The fora of Muslim political élites represented neither the interest of the wider population nor that of Muslim scholarship. They remained as before an exclusive circle of entrepreneurs and big landowners, mostly from the United Provinces, turning in centres of Muslim separatism only later. Therefore, the *Muslim League* suffered a severe loss of popularity during the Khilafat-agitation (1915–1924), while it was possible for a few Muslim intellectuals to find an audience among the wide parts of the population. Since the middle of the 19th century a pan-Islamic community feeling had developed, the root being the common colonial experience, forced by a common ideography such as common press and common dress (e. g. fes and beard). All these inspired the Muslim community to think themselves as *one* community. The Ottoman Caliphate became the symbol that brought about a feeling of identity.

The British threat to the Caliph and the parcelling of the Ottoman empire under the Allied power (Treaty of Sèvres 1920) was unacceptable to Muslim scholars, Sufis and intellectuals in

[43] C. H. Philips (ed.), *Select Documents on the History of India and Pakistan, 1858–1947*, London 1972, vol. 4, p. 1–22.

[44] The feeling of insecurity among the colonial rulers and their segregation has been literally elaborated in E. M. Forster's *A Passage to India*, London 1924.

India. Support of the caliphate was combined with anti-British ideology to bring about a Hindu-Muslim *entente*. Deobandis already had established contacts with the Ottoman rulers at the beginning of the 20th century, founding the "Association of Helpers" (*Jamīʿat al-Ansār*) in 1909 for this purpose,[45] and in 1913 the "Association of Servants of Kaba" (*Anjuman-e Khuddām-e Ka'ba*) was founded at Lucknow to support the Caliph. All these efforts finally found their institutional outcome in 1919 as the "Association of Scholars of India" (*Jamīʿat-e ʿUlamā-ye Hind*), initiated by scholars of Deoband and Farangī Mahal, which sided with Congress.[46] In the same year Bombay witnessed the emergence of an *All-India Caliphate Committee*, which started as a purely urban institution, born by intellectuals and big entrepreneurs. Using both existent Sufi and Congress Party infrastructure, the committee successfully approached traditional groups of the society. To foster a common identity, rites, Urdu poetry and journals were equally important. Finally, the Salafite Abū'l Kalām Azad (1888–1958) who had become famous through his widely known journal *al-Hilal* after 1912, announced the founding of a new "Party of God" (*hizb Allāh*). He even agitated for an armed resistance (*jihād*); but as this fight had been initiated from an Islamic territory, the emigration to Afghanistan was considered as one possibility of the anti-colonial struggle in the 1920s.[47]

As for the part Congress played in the Khilafat movement, M. K. Gandhi who had returned from South Africa in 1916, became the most powerful leader.[48] Having proved his abilities as a leader in the civil disobedience campaign, Gandhi managed to win over parts of the Islamic public by way of cooperation with the *ʿUlamā*; in a sense he can be regarded as the last prophet of the Muslims. For some time, the cooperation between Hindus and Muslims in the Khilafat movement counterbalanced the British imperial policy of *divide and rule*, but with increasing radicalism, many Muslims deserted the movement, especially those who were well established in the colonial system such as members of the Muslim League. Other Muslim groups that stayed away from the Khilafat movement were the shiit minority and the Barelwīs, the former for dogmatic reasons, the latter because the movement was dominated by the Deobandis. The abolition of the Ottoman Caliphate in 1924 by Mustafā Kemāl curtailed the vigour of the Khilafat movement. The Hindu-Muslim contradictions blazed up again, all the more since many Muslims felt uncomfortable with Gandhi's hinduistic political propaganda and the grow-

45 G. Minault, *The Khilafat-Movement: Religious Symbolism and Political Mobilization in India*, New York 1982; S. F. D. Ansari, *Sufi Saints and State Power. The Pirs of Sind, 1843–1947*, Cambridge 1992; K. H. Ansari, "Pan Islam and the making of the early Muslim Socialists," *MAS* 20, 1986, p. 509–37.

46 Robinson, *Separatism*; P. Hardy, *The Muslims of British India*, Cambridge 1972.

47 Compare G. Minault, "Urdu Political poetry during the Khilafat Movement," *Modern Asian Studies* 8, 1974, p. 459–71; I. H. Douglas, *Abdul Kalam Azad: An Intellectual and Religious Biography*, eds. G. Minault and Chr. W. Troll, Delhi 1988.

48 Cp. Dietmar Rothermund, *Mahatma Gandhi. Revolutionär der Gewaltlosigkeit*, München/Zürich 1989 (2nd, rev. ed. München 1998); idem, *Mahatma Gandhi. An Essay in Political Biography*, Delhi 1991.

ing influence of the *Hindu Mahasabha* (1922) upon Congress. Leaders of the *Mahasabha* themselves suggested the division of India into Hindu and Muslim territories. The vacuum of solidarity, thus emerged, was filled in by new groups demanding now and then an independent Muslim territory. They clearly indicated the diversity of the Islamic public.

10. Islamic Public Divided

Long before the poet-philosopher Muhammad Iqbāl (1873–1938) formulated his idea of a "consolidated North Western Muslim State"[49] on the occasion of the annual meeting of the *Muslim League* in December 1930, the millenarian *Ahmadīyas* established their power in the Panjab[50] under their charismatic leader Ghulām Ahmad (1835–1908) of Qadian. By declaring himself as Prophet he annoyed the orthodoxy and many intellectuals, even though his heretical ideas – he contradicted the very idea of the Prophet Muhammed – were quite popular. It took some time till with the "Missionary Association" (*Tablīghī Jamāʿat*) another popular movement arose. It was a branch of the Deoband school, and its strategies and demands for moral behaviour were soon taken over by the *Nadwat al-ʿUlamā*. The leader of the "Missionary Association" expressed the quietist character as follows: "The aims of modern political authority and the aims of Islam do not conform. If Islam as a religious system is to make any progress, it must be separated from politics." A similar peaceful association emerged among the Pakhtun tribes of Northwestern India under the leadership of ʿAbd al-Ghaffār Khān (1890–1988). His "Servants of God" (*Khudā-ye Khidmatgār*) – they were also known as "red Shirts" – adopted the methods and teachings of Gandhi and therefore rejected Iqbāl's plan of a "consolidated Northwestern Muslim State".

In 1931, shortly after Iqbāl made his plan public, the scientist 'Ināyat Allāh Khān al-Mashriqī (1888–1963) founded in the Panjab the paramilitary association of the "Humbles" (*Khāksār*). He too did not want to cooperate with the *Muslim League*, scholars and Sufis. Instead, he advocated a totalitarian Islamic government over the Indian Subcontinent, equally distant from democracy and communism. Ideologically and institutionally he leaned towards German national socialism. Although he rejected mystical approaches, he nevertheless used the principles of Sufi orders to win popular support. During the Great Depression al-Mashriqī in a very short

49 Cp. Ahmad et al. (eds.), *Self-Statement*, p. 148ff.

50 For the following cp. Ahmad et al. (eds.), *Self-Statement*, p. 77ff, 130ff, 153ff, 156ff; Y. Friedman, *Prophecy Continuous: Aspects of Ahmadi Religious Thought and Its Medieval Background*, Berkeley 1988; M. A. Haq, *The Faith Movement of Mawlana Muhammad Ilyas*, London 1972, W. C. Smith, *Modern Islam in India. A Social Analysis*, (reprint) Lahore 1969; K. Bahadur: *The Jamaʿat-i-Islami of Pakistan*, Lahore 1983; A: Syed, *Pakistan. Islam, Politics and National Security*, Lahore 1984; P. Hardy, *Partners in Freedom and true Muslims. Political Thought of some Muslim Scholars in British India 1912–1947*, Lund 1971.

time won the support of a large number of urban traders as well as migrants for his associations.

Again in the 1930s Abū al-A'lā al-Maudūdī (1903–1979) from Aurangabad formulated his political ideas about state and government which had a great impact on the Arab world, being absorbed by the Muslim Brethren. Just like the *Jamīʿat-e ʿUlamā-ye Hind*, Maudūdī rejected Iqbāl's plan of a Muslim state. Instead, he started to Islamise the political discourse: Muslims do not represent a nation, but rather a party of God, which appears as an agent of God on earth. For this, he saw the self-purification (as formerly postulated by the pietists) as a prerequisite. Towards the end of the 1930s he was convinced that the creation of a Muslim state was not becoming of a good Muslim, and therefore, the idea itself was incapable of being realised. To realise his idea, Maudūdī founded in 1941 the "Islamic Community" (*Jamāʿat-e Islāmī*) and postulated the sovereignty of God on earth in an universal, ideologically Islamic nation. Since 1947, he tried to materialise this idea of an imagined nation[51] in the constitution of Pakistan to where he along with the greatest part of his community, had emigrated. His "Community" won much influence, especially among young intellectuals and the middle class, in the years that followed.

11. The *Muslim League* and Political Independence

The most prominent Muslim party before independence was the *Muslim League*. It had considerable responsibility for the creation of a sovereign state Pakistan. The longstanding leader of the *Muslim League*, M. A. Jinnah,[52] had established his reputation in 1913 when speaking for the reprivatisation of Islamic foundations. As a supporter of the demand for the right of self-determination for all Indians, he joined the League in the same year while retaining his Congress membership. Due to the increasing influence of the Hindu Mahasabha within Congress Jinnah withdrew himself from the party and dedicated himself fully to the League. His 14 Points,[53] published in 1928, were a reaction to the proposals of the Simon Commission and the Nehru Report (both 1927) which made proposals for the future state of India, but evoking hopes for a separate Muslim territory as well. In Cambridge, Jinnah came into contact with the Pakistan National Movement and its leader Rahmat ʿAlī,[54] who was inspired by Iqbāl's idea of

51 Imagined in the sense of Anderson's *Imagined Communities*.

52 Jinnah, a brilliant lawyer, anglicised and tuned in secular outlook, belonged to a Shiite group (*khoja*) and had married into a Parsi family. The scholars therefore observed him with suspicion; cp. A. Jalal, *The Sole Spokesman: Jinnah, the Muslim League and the Demand for Pakistan*, Cambridge 1985.

53 The 14 Points put forward, among other things, the demand for separate electorates, provincial autonomy, federal system of government, constitution, etc. A separate Muslim state was not yet mentioned.

54 Compare K. K. Aziz, *Rahmat Ali, a Biography*, Lahore 1987.

a separate Muslim territory. Driving it further, he gave a name to it: Pakistan (an acronym of Panjab, Afghanistan, Kashmir, Sindh and Beluchistan) or "Land of the Pure". Although this Muslim state neglected the Muslims in the minority provinces,[55] Jinnah – himself a representative of the Muslim diaspora at Bombay – watched his time. After his return to India, he worked to enforce the League's claim of being the sole representative body of Indian Muslims. Since the end of the 1930s, its slogan was that Muslims would be suppressed in an independent India – a thought that had been created by colonial policy and nurtured in Aligarh.

Initially this idea was alien to the overwhelming majority of Muslim Indians. The League could not win the elections in Panjab and Bengal in 1937, in spite of the fact that she entered into an alliance with other political parties in these Muslim-dominated provinces. She received a little above 20% of the seats reserved for the Muslims. After this debacle, Jinnah vigourously worked towards the creation of a common Muslim identity with political aspirations opposed to those of Congress. In developing the "Two-Nations-Theory", Jinnah finally demanded a separate Muslim state in March 1940. Being adopted by the *Muslim League*, his proposals became later known as the "Pakistan Resolution" although he avoided the word "Pakistan" in it.[56]

The League understood to play a populist tune through journals, religious institutions, symbolism, and terminology, and thereby created the preference of an imagined community of brothers and sisters. Islam is endangered, all Muslims constitute one single community who deserves a nation of its own, was the message it conveyed. This emphasised the affiliation to the Arabic-Persian cultural area, ethnified Islam and petrified the division between Muslims and non-Muslims, no matter whether Hindus or other. By way of an exclusive Muslim territory, the Muslim League promised religious, social and political equality as well as economic benefits to Islamic scholars, Sufis, young intellectuals, entrepreneurs, unemployed and even farmers. The slogan: "*Pākistān kā matlab kiyā lā ilāha illā Allāh*" (What does Pakistan mean? It means no other God than Allah!) corresponded to the expectation of all of them. Of all the social groups the Muslim middle class in Bombay, Calcutta, and especially in the cities and *qasbah*s of the United Provinces responded most to this separatism of Muslim brotherhood. They increasingly felt discriminated by the striving Hindu middle class.

Although the conditions of the Second World War imposed certain constraints upon the nationalist demands, the "Atlantic Charter" of August 1941 inaugurated a new perspective on self-determination of the people. While the League could further prove her strength in the 1946 elections, the colonial rulers had no clear concept of how to proceed. The Cabinet Mission Plan of March 1946 fell back on an offer made during the War (Cripps' Offer, 1942), allowing a

[55] Rahmat Ali therefore coined another Muslim state *Bangistan* (for Bengal) in 1942.

[56] Philips, *Evolution of India and Pakistan*, p. 354–5. As its declarations were quite vague (e. g. the problem of the Muslim minorities remained open), the Resolution has to be regarded rather as a working paper for negotiations with the British and the Congress.

Muslim state within an Indian federation. But, as Congress under the leadership of J. L. Nehru (1889–1964) did not agree to abide the recommendation of the Cabinet Plan after the transfer of power, the League withdrew herself from the plan.[57] As the Viceroy wanted to go ahead with the plan, Jinnah resisted and on the 16th August 1946 summoned for a *Direct Action Day*, the result of which were the horrible riots between Muslims and Hindus in Calcutta. To avoid further worsening of the situation, a plan of partition was worked out hurriedly under the new Viceroy Mountbatten (1900–1979). The plan did not maintain the unity of India, but proposed Muslim majority provinces at the cost of the partition of the Panjab and Bengal. *Divide and rule* changed into *divide and quit*. In August 1947 West and East Pakistan were separated from India. The following migration (of about 18 million people) was accompanied by mass massacre, the wounds of which have not been reconciled. Contemporary literature has dealt with the subject intensively.[58] The princely State of Hyderabad with its majority of Hindus decided to remain independent but was merged forcefully with the Indian Union in 1948. Pakistan in turn supported the "war of independence" by the Muslims in Kashmir, where the India sent her troops in response to a request for help made by the then ruler, Maharaja Hari Singh, and the leader of the National Conference,Sheikh Mohammad Abdullah. The Kashmir conflict led to a number of armed struggles between Pakistan and India, and remains to be one of the most crisis-prone areas of South Asia until now.[59]

57 In this respect the assumption is valid that "it was the Congress that insisted on partition. It was Jinnah who was against Partition." Jalal, *Spokesman*, p. 262. Already in 1943 Jinnah expressed his opinion against a federation; cp. Ahmad et al. (eds.), *Self-Statement*, p. 155.

58 Cp. S. H. Manto in Rothen-Dubs, *Garten*, p. 368ff.

59 Compare M. Pernau-Reifeld, *Verfassung und politische Kultur im Wandel: Der indische Fürstenstaat Hyderabad 1911–48*, Stuttgart 1992; T. N. Madan, "Religious Ideology in a Plural Society: The Muslims and Hindus of Kashmir," *Contributions to Indian Sociology* 6, 1972, p. 106–41.

'The only hope for fallen India' The Gurukul Kangri as an Experiment in National Education (1902–1922)*

Harald Fischer-Tiné

"As education is the mother of character and as the strength or weakness of a person or people lies in the character, it is not illogical to say, that nowadays the fortune of a nation is not decided on the battlefield, but in the schoolroom where the children are educated."[1]

I

One of the most important fields of activity for the socio-religious reform movements that emerged in late 19th century India was education. Not only could they spread their religious ideas through the channel of educational institutions – but schools and universities were also ideal instruments to give a voice to their social and political agenda and helped to disseminate their respective visions of an Indian nation. It is hardly surprising then that educational endeavours were at the core of many influential religious and nationalist projects at the time: The brand of Islamic reform represented by Syed Ahmad Khan for instance was centred around the famous Anglo Muhamaddan College in Aligarh, the Islamic seminary in Deoband was pivotal for Muslim reformers with less modernist ambitions, Tagore's Shantiniketan was a project that caused tremendous stir all-over India, prominent representatives of what was later to be labelled as the Hindu right joined the campaign for the foundation of 'national schools' in Bengal

* The quotation is taken from a fund-raising appeal for the school published in *The Vedic Magazine & Gurukula Samachar* 3 (3), Sept. 1909, p. 64.

1 Indra Vedalankar, first graduate and later headmaster of the Gurukul Kangri, in a speech entitled "The Vedic Guru and his Pupil", delivered on the occasion of the school's 12th anniversary in March 1914 (*The Vedic Magazine & Gurukula Samachar* 7 (9/10), Apr.-May 1914, p. 719–24).

1905–10 and of a Hindu university in the 1910s,[2] and later Gandhi came up with his scheme of *naī tālīm.*[3] Indeed, it has even been argued that the partition of India was in a way anticipated by the strife to establish separate Hindu and a Muslim Universities.[4]

The impact of the above-mentioned institutions and projects on diverse Indian nationalisms has been highlighted by many authors and their histories have been reconstructed and analysed in great detail in the past decades.[5] Strangely enough, the *Gurukul*[6] Kangri, one of the most controversial and radical attempts of making a school to the nucleus of 'national regeneration', has been largely overlooked so far. In 1902 the 'vegetarian wing' of the Punjab Arya Samaj founded the Gurukul in Kangri near the holy city of Hardwar with the avowed aim of "making an experiment in truly national education"[7] which would rekindle the spirit of the "virile civilisation of the ancients", thereby encouraging a complete reconstruction of society and finally allowing India to rise again to "the position of the queen of the civilized world".[8]

That this important facet of the Aryas' work has been hitherto neglected by critical research is astonishing since the Samaj is not only considered to have been the most influential Hindu reform movement in late 19th and early 20th centuries,[9] it is also regarded as an important 'an-

[2] There were numerous other educational projects with a clear nationalistic bias in other parts of India; the Satyabadi schools in Orissa and the Fergusson College in Maharashtra may be mentioned here as examples.

[3] *Naī tālīm*, Urdu for 'new education'; for an outline of Gandhi's educational ideas see K. N. Sen, *Education and the Nation. An Indian Perspective*, Calcutta 1970, p. 163–204.

[4] J. Lütt, *Religion und Politik in Indien. Pandit Malaviyas Vermittlerrolle im politischen Hinduismus des frühen 20. Jahrhunderts*, Heidelberg (unpubl. habilitation thesis) 1976, p. 10.

[5] Cf. G. Minault/D. Lelyveld, "The Campaign for a Muslim University 1898–1920," *Modern Asian Studies* 8 (1) 1974, p. 145–89; Metcalf, B., "The Madrasa at Deoband: A Model for Religious Education in India," *Modern Asian Studies* 12 (1), 1978, p. 111–34; D. Lelyveld, *Aligarh's first Generation. Muslim Solidarity in British India*, Princeton 1978; B. D. Metcalf, *Islamic Revival in British India. Deoband 1860–1900*, Princeton 1982; J. Lütt, "The Movement for the Foundation of the Benares Hindu University," Cultural Dept. of the German Embassy in India (ed.), *German Scholars on India. Contributions to Indian Studies,* vol. 2, Delhi 1974, p. 160–95, and K. Kumar, "Hindu Revivalism and Education in North Central India," in K. N. Panikkar (ed.), *Communalism in India. History Politics and Culture*, New Delhi 1991, p. 173–95. Of course there have been several publications on the educational activities of Gandhi and Tagore but they are mostly concerned with strictly educational and psychological questions while ignoring the political dimension of the problem. Cf. for instance W. Cenkner, *The Hindu Personality in Education. Tagore – Gandhi – Aurobindo,* Delhi 1976. The best example for a such a completely ahistorical approach is M. M. Krischke-Ramaswamy, *Revitalisierende Pädagogik: Konzepte zur kulturellen Erneuerung im Indien des 20. Jahrhunderts*, Göttingen (unpubl. 1977 Ph. D. thesis).

[6] Gurukul literally means 'the line (or family) of the teacher'. It was used to denote the traditional system of educating the sons of brahmins who lived with their teacher's families during their education. For details cf. A. S. Altekar, *Education in Ancient India,* Benares 1934, p. 92–101.

[7] Arya Pratinidhi Sabha, Punjab (ed.), *The Rules and the Scheme of Study of the Gurukula, sanctioned by the Arya Pratinidhi Sabha, Punjab, together with an Introduction by Lala Ralla Ram*, Lahore 1902, p. 8.

[8] *The Vedic Magazine & Gurukula Samachar* 5 (10), 1911, p. 64.

[9] C. Heimsath, *Indian Nationalism and Hindu Social Reform*, Princeton 1964, p. 292.

cestor' of today's Hindu nationalist organisations.[10] Christophe Jaffrelot, for instance, claims that the ideological essence of a militant, overtly political Hinduism had already been in existence albeit "in a latent state" in the Samaj.[11] If the movement did in fact play such a crucial role for the development of Hindu nationalism, one could also expect new insights into the nature of the so-called 'Hindu fundamentalist' ideology by analysing the ideals and values transmitted through this particular type of 'Arya' education.

Notwithstanding this, most of the research on the Arya Samaj – including Kenneth Jones' pioneering work[12] – has concentrated on the politically active so-called 'moderate wing' of the Arya movement. The Gurukul wing has not drawn the same attention[13] since it has often been regarded as 'apolitical' or 'devotional'.[14] My aim in this paper is to show that, first, the Gurukul did indeed have a highly elaborated political agenda and, secondly, in spite of its relative insignificance in terms of sheer numbers of its graduates, the school has had a considerable impact on contemporary Indian nationalist projects.

What, then, did the school actually contribute to the process of nation building? What were the specifically 'national' elements in the Gurukul brand of education and to whom did they appeal? I want to show that it is by applying the model of the 'nation of intent' as developed by Tønesson and Antlöv, that we might best understand the political significance of the vision of an 'Aryan nation' that was inculcated in the brahmacharies[15] through their training in the Gurukul:

> A nation of intent is a vision of a territorial entity, a set of institutions, an ideal type of citizen and an identity profile that a group of 'social engineers' have in mind and try to implement. It will often be an idealistic form shared by a number of people who identify themselves […] with a whole nation whose other members, they hope, will join their vision.[16]

10 The most eloquent elaboration of this theory is found in the well-acclaimed work of the French political scientist Christophe Jaffrelot: *The Hindu Nationalist Movement and Indian Politics 1925 to the 1990ies. Strategies of Identity Building, Implantation and Mobilisation* (*with Special Reference to Central India*), London 1996. A similar view is presented by D. Gold," Organized Hinduisms: From Vedic Truth to Hindu Nation," in: M. Marty/R. S. Appleby (eds.), *Fundamentalism Observed*, Chicago 1991, p. 531–91.

11 Cf. C. Jaffrelot, "The Growth and Development of Hindu Nationalism in the Punjab: From the Arya Samaj to the Hindu Sabha (1875–1910)," *Indo British Review* 21 (1), 1993, p. 3–39, especially p. 29.

12 K. W. Jones, *Arya Dharm. Hindu Consciousness in 19th Century Punjab*, Berkeley 1976. Besides this book Jones has about a dozen articles on the Arya Samaj to his credit.

13 The only exception is Jordens who devotes a few pages to the Gurukul in his biography of the school's founder, Munshiram alias Swami Shraddhananda. J. T. F. Jordens, *Swāmī Shraddhānanda. His Life and Causes*, Delhi et al 1981.

14 Cf. I. Talbot, *Punjab and the Raj*, New Delhi 1988, p. 72f.

15 In allusion to the first stage in a male brahmin's life according to the *varṇāśrama* concept, students in the Gurukul were called brahmacharies; besides, *brahmacarya* (chastity) was the guiding principle of their student's life. Note: I use the spelling common in the English sources instead of the Hindi *brahmacārī*.

16 S. Tønesson/H. Antlöv, "Asia in Theories of Nationalism and National Identity," in: idem (eds.), *Asian Forms of the Nation*, Richmond 1996, p. 1–39, esp. p. 37f. The term 'nation of intent' has been coined with

I argue that the Gurukul students were trained precisely to become such social engineers and to form the core of the proposed nation. In order to verify this assumption, I will concentrate on the activities of the institution in three particular fields which are generally regarded as being crucial for the construction of a national identity: historiography, language policy and homogenisation through the moulding of an ideal citizen and 'inventing' the image of an ideal society. In the specific case of creating a homogenous Hindu society, the overcoming of caste barriers and other 'social evils' played a crucial role. The Gurukul's efforts in regard to these problems will also be discussed. To put these points into perspective, however, it is helpful to start with a brief description of the general educational situation in India at the turn of the 19th century, and to provide a short outline of the history and general features of the Gurukul.

II

a) The state of education in late 19th century India

Towards the end of the 19th century, the shadow of Macaulay's famous 'Minute on Education' was still looming large on the minds of the intelligentsia in India. Although it had never been fully implemented, distrust towards oriental learning and cultural arrogance dominated the educational institutions run either directly by the British or at least "on western lines"[17] by missionaries or private carriers. At the level of primary education, missionaries were much more active than the government and many Hindus feared that an education in a Christian school would finally lead to cultural alienation of their children or was even part of a conspiracy that would lead to a "wholesale conversion to christianity".[18]

On the level of higher education the problems were of a slightly different kind. The curriculum taught in colleges and high schools that prepared students for the university entrance examination was modelled after its British counterpart and had almost nothing to do with the everyday experience of Indian students.[19] Krishna Kumar has explained this circumstance convincingly with the assumption that the main purpose of British educational efforts in India was not the transmission of useful knowledge but rather the production of reliable colonial citizens

slightly different connotations in the late sixties by the Africanist P. Rotberg, "African Nationalism: Concept or Confusion," *Journal of Modern African Studies* 4 (1) 1967, p. 33–46.

17 R. Nathan (ed.), *Progress of Education in India 1897/98 –1901/02*, vol. 1, Calcutta 1904, p. 4.

18 *Singh Sahai*, 12-4-1895; *Selections from the Vernacular Newspapers Published in the Punjab* 1895 (hereafter quoted as *SVNP*), p. 2. Similar statements can be found in countless newspaper articles of the 1880ies and 1890ies all over Northern India.

19 Cf. E. McDonald, "English Education and Social Reform in Late Nineteenth Century Bombay: A Case Study in the Transmission of a Cultural Ideal," *Journal of Asian Studies* 25 (1), 1966, p. 453–70, *passim*.

through moral upliftment and 'character training'.[20] The resulting alienation was catalysed by the fact that higher education was imparted exclusively through the medium of English which was, after all, a foreign language. Moreover, in the 1880s the growing number of graduates could no longer be absorbed by the above-mentioned professions and unemployment became a serious problem.[21] The resulting frustration and discontent made the educational system the target for severe criticism especially by those with nationalist leanings. Some of the defects commonly attributed to the prevailing system were:[22]

(1) The curricula with their stress on the English language, literature and history led to cultural alienation. Worse, the colleges were anti-national because they inculcate contempt for the indigenous culture and uncritical admiration for western culture.
(2) the vernaculars were completely neglected;
(3) physical exercise was not encouraged sufficiently;
(4) Practical and technical education were lacking;
(5) The same was true for moral and religious instruction.

Yet, one basic assumption that the critics shared with the criticised was the tremendous optimism that the right type of education would not only produce morally and physically superior individuals but also solve economic problems and wipe out all 'social evils' and *ergo* contribute to the strengthening of the 'race' or 'nation'.[23] As a consequence, the decades from 1880 to 1930 witnessed quite a few initiatives mostly from socio-religious reform organisations to establish idiosyncratic educational institutions that had to be modern in the sense that they included instruction in natural sciences and English in their scheme of studies and were at the same time 'national', avoiding all the above-mentioned shortcomings of the governmental system and equipping their graduates with a sense of self-respect and pride for their 'national heritage'. It is obvious that in the heterogenous cultural, religious and linguistic landscape of India the ideas of what actually constituted this cultural heritage were as diverse as the different groups that referred to it. It is in this context that we are now going to analyse in some detail the specific conceptions of the Arya Samaj.

20 Cf. Kumar, *Political Agenda of Education. A Study of Colonialist and Nationalist Ideas*, Delhi etc. 1991. See especially p. 23–46.

21 S. C. Ghosh, *The History of Education in Modern India 1757–1986*. Delhi 1995, p. 101f.

22 One of the most influential voices to utter this critique was that of Rabindranath Tagore in his 1892 article *shikhṣār her fer*. cf. *Ibid.*, p. 131f, and U. Dasgupta, "Santiniketan: The School of a Poet," in: M. Hasan (ed.), *Knowledge, Power & Politics. Educational Institutions in India*. Delhi 1998, p. 258–303, p. 264f. See also J. Lütt, "The Movement for the Foundation of the Benares Hindu University," p. 162.

23 Cf. also C. A. Watt, "Education for National Efficiency: Constructive Nationalism in North India 1909–1916," *Modern Asian Studies* 31 (2), 1997, p. 339–74, p. 342.

b) Early Arya efforts in education

The firm belief that education was an individual right for everyone including women and *śūdras* and that it should be made compulsory, had already found expression in the teachings of Swami Dayanand (1824–83). In his *satyārth prakāś* he had devoted one full chapter to this question,[24] where he gave detailed instructions about the nature of the schools he had in mind and the course of studies the brahmacharies ought to follow. Though the founders of the Gurukul and their successors always refer to Dayanand's precepts on educational matters as their guiding principles, interestingly the term Gurukul was never used by him. And indeed, the few educational experiments undertaken by the Swami himself during his lifetime were of a completely different type than the Kangri Gurukul.[25] Nonetheless, there are a few features in his proposed schools that became important for the institution founded in 1902 and are therefore worth being mentioned here.[26]

The first characteristic is the strict observation of *brahmacarya* during the whole period of education, i. e. until the age of 25 for boys and 16 for girls. To prevent the students from the "indulgence in lascivious thoughts", girls' and boys' schools were to be located at a distance of at least three miles from each other. The second point that was implemented was the idea, that education ought not to be merely intellectual but also physical and spiritual. The third essential feature of the scheme was absolute equality of treatment of the students "be they princes or sons of paupers."[27] This provoking statement reoccurred almost literally decades later in the various reports and prospectus of the Gurukul.[28] A last element that became important was the special relationship between teachers and students (*guru-śiṣya sambandh*) that Dayanand laid

[24] D. Sarasvatī, *Satyārth prakāś*, (ed. Sārvdeśik Ārya Pratinidhi Sabhā, Delhi (repr.) 1993 [²Lāhaur 1884], p. 36–75. The formal aspect of initiation to student's life is also touched upon in the same author's *Samskār vidhi*, Naī Dillī (repr.) 1995; see esp. p. 93–113.

[25] Dayanand founded two Sanskrit *pāṭhśālā*s which did not have much in common with the comprehensive reformist scheme of the Kangri school. They were concerned solely with the teaching of *deva vāṇī*, as the religious prestige language was called by the Samajis, and remained largely within the framework of traditional religious education. They were not all too successful either and had to be closed down before long because of the corruption of the teaching staff. Cf. Jordens, *Swāmī Dayānanda Sarasvatī. His Life and Ideas*, Delhi 1978, p. 64ff and Mukhopādhyāy, *Mahārṣi Dayānand kā jīvan carit* (transl. from Bengali into Hindi by Ghāsīrām, repr.), Dillī 2050 VS, p. 195f [¹1933].

[26] For early 20th century accounts on Dayanand's educational views cf. Ram Rattan, "Swami Dayanand as Educationist," in H. B. Sarda (ed.), *Dayananda Commemoration Volume*. Ajmer 1933, p. 129–34. A more recent outline is given in S. P. Chaube, *Recent Educational Philosophies in India*, Agra 1993, p. 20–45. A more detailed but similarly uncritical account can be found in: R. Safaya/D. Bhan, *Educational Philosophy of Swami Dayanand*, Ambala 1977.

[27] Sarasvatī, D., *Satyārth prakāś*, p. 37.

[28] Cf. for instance Arya Pratinidhi Sabha, Punjab (ed.), *The Rules and the Scheme of Study of the Gurukula 1902*, p. 18.

stress upon. According to him and the Gurukul founders, successful education could only be accomplished if every external impact (including that of the children's parents) was strictly excluded.

c) The establishment of the Kangri *Gurukul*

The Dayanand Anglo-Vedic High School,[29] the first serious attempt to turn Dayanand's concept into reality, however, was far less radical than the founder of the Arya Samaj had suggested. The prominent role of English and western sciences and the neglect of Sanskrit and religious education soon provoked harsh criticism by the hardliners within the movement, and after the formal split of the Punjab Arya Samaj in 1893, the 'radicals', led by Lala Munshiram (1857–1926), started an agitation for the foundation of their own educational institution, the Gurukul. The actual fund-raising campaign lasted from 1897 to 1900, but it took another two years to find a proper place near the pilgrimage centre of Hardwar where Munshiram, who was appointed governor, wanted the institution to be situated. The *vidyālay* (high school) section of the Gurukul Kangri was opened in March 1902 with 53 brahmacharies.[30] A college section (*mahāvidyālay*) followed in 1907 and in 1917 there were already 340 students.[31] The teaching staff consisted of c. 15 professors and teachers in the latter year.

The whole course of studies extended over 14 years:[32] ten classes in the high school section and four in the college. The curriculum focussed on Sanskrit and Vedic literature but English and the sciences were also taught from the beginning. Later, additional courses in agriculture and traditional medicine (*āyurveda*) were introduced. All subjects – except for English – were taught through the medium of Hindi. The Gurukul even awarded its own degrees[33] to the brahmacharies who had successfully undergone the final examination, but these degrees were not recognised by the government and the institution voluntarily stayed outside the official system of education. In a pamphlet published in 1911 it was stated that:

29 The D. A.-V. High School was inaugurated in 1886 and followed by a College section three years later. For a detailed analysis of the D. A.-V. movement cf. K. W. Jones, *The Arya Samaj in the Punjab. A Study of Social Reform and Religious Revivalism*, Berkeley (unpubl. Ph. D. thesis) 1966, chs. 3 and 4, and S. K. Gupta, "Dayanand Anglo-Vedic College Movement (1886–1986)," *The Panjab Past and Present* 20 (1) 1986, p. 226–41.

30 Gurukula Vishvavidyalaya Hardwar (ed.), *Prospectus and Rules Regarding Examinations, Admission etc.*, Lahore 1912, p. ix.

31 G. Pāṭhak, *Gurukul Kāṃgṛī kā itihās*, Kāṃgṛī n. d. [c. 1935], p. 32f. Out of the 340 enrolled, 276 studied in the high school (*vidyālay*) and 64 in the college (*mahāvidyālay*) section.

32 Originally 18 years had been envisaged but the Gurukul authorities had to cut down the schedule due to economic constraints.

33 The degree of *vidyālaṃkār* was equivalent to B. A., *vedālaṃkār* was for those who had specialised in Vedic literature, *siddhāntālaṃkār* for philosophy. Later *ayurvedālaṃkār* for traditional medicine, *vidyāvācaspati*, (Ph. D.) and *vidyāmarṭanḍ* (D. Litt.) were introduced.

> Under the present circumstances of our country, a seat of learning that aspires to become a centre of Arya (Hindu) culture and to give the first place to any methods of juvenile training must perforce forego official recognition; for you cannot dovetail into an occidental system [*sic*] a system which is based upon entirely different and in some respects opposite principles. All lovers of the indegenious [*sic*] system cannot therfore [*sic*], but fall back upon the Gurukula as the sole national educational centre of the ancient Aryan-race.[34]

This anti-colonial stance had several consequences that decisively influenced the institution's history: First: it earned the Gurukul both the sympathy of militant nationalists[35] and the suspicion of the government who kept the school under surveillance and closely watched every move of its teachers. Secondly: it kept the scope of the school very limited. Not too many parents were ready to send their boys away for such a long period when all lucrative jobs remained out of reach for them afterwards. As a result, the number of graduates from the college section between 1912 and 1932 rarely exceeded 15 per annum.[36] Most of the students' guardians belonged to the lower urban middle classes and came from a background which would have made it difficult to afford an education in one of the western colleges. Apart from the financial advantages, the decision to have one's son sent to the Gurukul – tuition was free and only a nominal fee for food, shelter, and clothes of Rs 10 was charged[37] – it also brought about a considerable gain in religious prestige since the institution soon became very famous and was respected and even copied by "orthodox" Hindus.[38] The symbolic importance of the Kangri school is also evident by the extraordinarily vivid public debate on the pros and cons of such an institution throughout the 1910s.[39] Moreover, the list of guests and visitors of the Gurukul demonstrates that its significance can hardly be overestimated. Apart from British officials like Lieutenant Governor James Meston and Viceroy Hardinge an considerable number of western politicians

[34] Gurukula Kangri Vishvavidyalaya (ed.), *The Aims Ideals and Needs of the Gurukula Vishvavidyalaya Kangri,* Kangri 1971 VS [1914], p. liif. In 1914 James Meston, the Lieutenant Governor of the United Provinces, had even offered Munshiram to include the Gurukul in the Government's grant-in-aid scheme and to recognise the diploma if the curricula were slightly altered. In spite of the school's critical funding situation, Munshiram refused to cooperate with the British. Cf. I. Vidyāvācaspati, *Amar śahīd svāmī Śraddhānand, mere pitā*, Dillī, n. d. [1953], p. 113f.

[35] *Karmayogi*, 18-1-1910; *SNNUP*, 1910, p. 132.

[36] Cf. Vidyāsāgar Vidyālaṃkār, *Gurukul snātak paricāyikā,* Dillī 1977, p. 1-70. The number of the neophytes was around 30 per annum.

[37] The project was chiefly financed through donations by the Arya public. In 1912 for instance 57.6% of the school's budget was supplied from the various funds and fund-raising delegations. Cf. Munśīrām (ed.), *Gurukul Kāṃgrī kā vṛttānt jismeṃ saṃvat 1966–1967 kā vṛttānt ādhikārī parīkṣā etc.*, Kāṃgṛī 1911, p. 80f.

[38] In 1906 a 'Rishikul', apparently modelled after the Kangri institution, was founded in Hardwar by the Sanatan Dharm Sabha. Cf. Parmanand, *Mahamana Madan Mohan Malviya, A Historical Biography*, vol. 1, Varanasi 1985, p. 243.

[39] Dozens of articles referring to the Gurukul Kangri can be found in the selections of the vernacular newspapers of both the Panjab and the United Provinces.

and intellectuals[40] were attracted by the academy, and leading figures of the national movement like Gandhi, Jawaharlal Nehru, M. M. Malviya, Lala Lajpat Rai, Rajendra Prasad, S. P. Mookerjee, Vinoba Bhave et al. paid a visit to the remote school and gave speeches before the school's staff and students. All of them expressed their admiration for what they saw.[41]

d) The aims of the Gurukul

The general criticism levelled against education on western lines referred to in the introductory section, was fully shared by the adherents of the Gurukul concept. They were convinced that modern education or "slavish imitation of western models" were "extremely unnationalising in [their] effects"[42] and threatened the very existence of the Hindu 'race'.[43] The *gurukul śikṣā praṇālī*[44] was developed to counter this threat; it was a brand of education that was religious in its rhetoric and political in its goals. It was designed to produce a well trained and highly motivated avant-garde that would serve as multiplicators of Arya ideals and were expected to guide the "indifferent, unenthusiasistic, inactive mass of Hinduism"[45] on their way to reform and regeneration, thereby "welding it into one coherent mass".[46] Once the first goal, i. e. the unification of the nation, was achieved, in a second step, the supporters of the Gurukul aspired to the spiritual conquest of the west:[47]

40 The list of Western visitors includes C. F. Andrews, Beatrice and Sidney Webb, later British prime minister Ramsay Macdonald, the American educationist Myron Phelps and the German indologist Otto Strauss, to name just the more illustrious.

41 Cf. Viṣṇudatt Rākeś (ed.), *Dīkṣālok* [*Gurukul Kāṃgṛī viśvavidyālay meṃ pradatt dīkṣānt bhāṣaṇoṃ evaṃ sārasvat vyākhyānoṃ kā saṇgrah*] Haridvār 1997, *passim*.

42 Alakh Dhari, "Essential Elements of Sound Education," *The Vedic Magazine & Gurukula Samachar* 2 (2), 1907, p. 21–6, p. 26.

43 In the early years of the Gurukul-movement, the term 'Hindu' was rejected because of its foreign origin and negative connotations and the word 'Arya' was used instead. However, as it became evident that the "ignorant dharmic brethren" refused to accept the Arya suggestion the Samajis began to employ the word 'Hindu' in the period after 1910–12 to foster solidarity within the community. Cf. for instance *Sadharm Pracārak*, 11. jyeṣṭh 1970, p. 3.

44 *Śikṣā praṇālī* (Hindi): educational system.

45 M. C. Sinha, "Gurukula as a System of Education," *The Vedic Magazine & Gurukula Samachar* 8 (11/12). 1915, p. 1063–83, p. 1070.

46 "The *Round Table* on the Arya Samaj," *The Vedic Magazine & Gurukula Samachar* 7 (5) 1913, p. 400–10, p. 409.

47 The effort towards universal dissemination of their ideologies seems to be a common feature of this type of religious nationalism. Similar ideas can be found found in Swami Vivekananda who tried to spread his political Vedanta in England and America, Bipin Chandra Pal and many others.

> If the Brahmacharies fulfill the fond hopes [...] the day is not far off when captive Ind[ia] will by the force of her Brahmacharya take captive her conqueror and London will become the diffusive centre of Vedic thought.[48]

The national scale, however, definitely had priority and the advocates of the Gurukul system concentrated their efforts accordingly on the strengthening and homogenising the Hindu community. With its emphasis on religious regeneration, the institution was supposed to provide an ideological tonic as well. The spread of '*dharmic* values', would not only help to "deny the seven devils of secularity entrance" in (Hindu) India,[49] it would also prevent the suspected mass conversion to Christianity referred to above.

In the logic of the *ārya dharm* the *gurukul śikṣā praṇālī* was portrayed as being in continuity with the educational system that had prevailed among the Aryans in vedic times and yet at the same time was more scientific, rational and advanced than the latest western pedagogical theories.[50] In this scheme, the Gurukul Kangri played the role of a model institution that was intended to serve as an example for similar schools and universities. The final goal of the Arya efforts was to establish a network of hundreds of Gurukuls all over India and thus completely replace the existing educational system.

After having thus laid down the broad aims and strategies of the Gurukul system, the following section is dedicated to a closer analysis of the actual process of 'welding together the community', the key activities in nation-building as practised in the Kangri school.

III

a) The creation of a national history

The pitiable state of Hindu society and its lack of self confidence and pride was seen as being partly caused by "distorted representations" of Indian history.[51] The rewriting of ancient Indian history with the avowed aim of correcting the mistakes and misrepresentations by western orientalist scholars, therefore, was a crucial point in the programme of the Gurukul movement

48 Ratan Lal: "A Glimpse on Rishi Dayanand's Revived System of Education, The Gurukula," *The Vedic Magazine & Gurukula Samachar* 6 (7), 1911, p. 525–35, p. 535.

49 Ratan Lal, "A Glimpse," p. 534f.

50 See for example Balkrishna, *The Gurukula System of Education and its Critics*, Kangri 1911, p. 6–18, and, Ratan Lal, "A Glimpse," p. 531.

51 This view was shared by a considerable part of the Hindu intelligentsia both within and outside the Arya Samaj. Cf. for example the articles by Lala Hardayal on national education; in *Hindustan*, 15-5-1908, *SNNUP* 1908, p. 318f, *Hindustan*, 23-9-1908, *Ibid.*, p. 591 and *The Vedic Magazine & Gurukula Samachar* 4 (6), Dec. 1910, p. 30–3.

right from the outset.[52] It took seven years after the opening of the school for the project of an alternative historiography to be commenced by Ramdev,[53] then headmaster of the Gurukul. A programmatical article that appeared in the *Vedic Magazine* shortly before the first volume of his comprehensive history of ancient India was published, shows that the perception of the role of history and historiography was not only largely influenced by the well known ideas of a 'national history' prevalent in Europe in the 19th century but was also moulded by the ever recurring theme of being 'uncivilised' and backward compared to the West:

> National History is that golden chain which links the past with the present and the future. It keeps alive in a people the spirit of unity; inspires them with common ideals; infuses in them common interests and common sentiments [...] The nation whose history is alive is never in danger of decay from internal causes. Hence all civilized nations look upon the preservation of history as their sacred and paramount duty.[54]

With these ideals in mind, Ramdev wrote *Bhāratvarṣ kā itihās*. The book became one of the most widely ever circulated publications of the Gurukul and also received considerable attention even outside Arya circles.[55] It was used in the institution as the standard history textbook until the 1970s.[56] As pointed out, the book was considered to be a corrective to Western representations of Indian history, hence its aggressively assertive character throughout. Almost every page contains a quotation from or a reference to the statements of historians and indologists like W. Jones, H. H. Wilson, J. Todd, F. M. Müller, V. A. Smith et al. which are subsequently debunked.[57]

52 In several speeches given in Lahore in January 1900, Munshiram mentioned this point as one of the eight foremost goals of the Gurukul. Cf. G. R. Garg, "The Gurukul Movement of Education," Vedic Path, 53 (4) 1981, p. 52–6, p. 56. It reappears in Ralla Ram's first prospectus for the school written the following year.

53 Ācārya Ramdev (1881–1939) had started his education in the D. A-V. High School in Lahore and joined the Gurukul-wing led by Munshiram around 1899. He held an B. A. degree and refused a job as district school inspector in order to work as a teacher of English, western philosophy and history. He replaced Munshiram as principal in 1917. For further details of his work and biography Cf. Rāmgopāl Vidyālaṃkār, "Ācārya Rāmdev," in: Dharmpāl (ed.), *Ācārya Rāmdev jī ādarṣvād ke jyotistambh. Vyaktitva evam kṛtitva*, Naī Dillī 1991, p. 9–32.

54 "National History," *loc. cit.*, p. 30f.

55 Rāmdev, *Bhāratvarṣ kā Itihās* (*BVKI*), vol. 1, Kāṁgṛī 1910, vol. 2, Kāṁgṛī 1914, vol. 3, Kāṁgṛī 1933; among the admirers of the book were V. D. Savarkar and the Hindi poet Maithili Sharan Gupta who allegedly was inspired by the work to write his famous *mahākāvya*-poem *Bhārat bhāratī*. Cf. Śankar Dev Vidyālaṃkār, "Jñānyogī ācārya Rāmdev jī," in: Dharmpāl, op. cit., p. 51–60, p. 56. Immediately after its publication it was examined by the Department of Criminal Intelligence in order to find out whether it was of a 'seditious character'. But although it was stated that the book "was obviously intended to provoke discontent with the present rather than to give a faithful picture of the past", it was never banned. Cf. NAI, Home Poll – B, Proceedings March 1911, D. C. I.–"Report for Feb. 1911," p. 14f.

56 Personal communication from Dr. Dharmvir Arya, graduate of the Gurukul Kangri and director of the *Ārya Paropkāriṇī Sabhā*, Ajmer; Ajmer 10-12-1996. The fact, that it has been reprinted thrice (the last time in 1996) also gives ample evidence to the fact that it is not regarded as outdated.

57 Specifically all dates given by western historians are shown to be incorrect, thus leading to the conclusion that the Aryan civilisation was the oldest and most developed in the history of mankind.

In the first section the author vigorously refutes the Western assumption that the Aryans had no historiography worth the name and attempts to prove instead that the Vedas and the books of the Rishis (*ārṣ granth*) were important historiographical accounts and not merely fiction.[58] Subsequently he proceeds to divide ancient Indian history according to his main sources into five periods:[59] of the *Brāhmaṇas*, of the *Manusmṛti*, of the *Rāmāyaṇa*, the *Mahābhārata* and the *Śukranītisāra*.[60] In line with Dayanand's interpretation and that of Ramdev's contemporary Harbilas Sarda,[61] he devotes the major part of the second volume to demonstrate that the Aryan culture had strongly influenced all major civilisations of the world including China, Greece, Rome, Africa, and America.[62] Throughout the book, not only the incommensurable glory of the ancient 'Aryan empire' but also its modern and rational outlook are constantly highlighted. All major achievements of modern European history had already been realised in Bhāratvarṣ; for example:

> The king had a House of Parliament built in his Capital. He passed resolutions after consulting the representatives of the people and on the basis of the *vedas* and *dharmaśāstras*. In matters, the representatives [...] could not agree upon, he would decide after consulting the *brāhmaṇ sabhā*. Whoever has only a trifle of historical understanding and reads the evidences given above, will agree with us on the statement, that the government in ancient Bhāratvarṣ was democratic.[63]

According to Ramdev, apart from a democratic form of government far superior to the English system[64] complete with separation of judicial, executive and legislative functions, an advanced system of education had also been part of the magnificent Aryan civilisation.

When it comes to an analysis of the political implications of the Arya brand of nationalist historiography, the question about the attitude towards Islam inevitably arises. Originally, a fourth volume was planned to cover the medieval and modern periods but unfortunately it was never completed and we can only get an idea of the assessment of the so-called Muslim period of Indian History through the preface, where Ramdev describes the general purpose of the book. As one would expect, Indian History is understood exclusively as Hindu-history. The establishment of the Muslim empires is presented as a catastrophe for the glorious Hindu civilisa-

58 *Bhāratvarṣ kā Itihās* (*BVKI*), 1, p. 21–5.

59 According to a view established by Dayanand, the Veda proper was timeless and contained no historical information. The vedic Saṃhitās, therefore, do not figure in the list of sources.

60 The *Śukranītisāra* is an early medieval text on society and policy in the vein of the famous *Arthaśāstra*. It includes contributions of various authors but is ascribed to the mythical sage Śukra. It probably was made available to Ramdev through a critical edition by G. Oppert, which was published in Madras in 1882. I am grateful to Pandit K. P. Aithal for this reference.

61 H. B. Sarda, *Hindu Superiority: an Attempt to Determine the Position of the Hindu Race in the Scale of Nations,* Ajmer 1906.

62 *BVKI* 2, p. 256–362.

63 *BVKI* 1, p. 94. This and all the following translations from Hindi are the present author's.

64 *Ibid.*, p. 95f.

tion which was caused just by treason and the "stupidity and egoism of some of its leaders"[65] and not by the fact that they had been defeated on the battlefield.

Ramdev's magnum opus was not the only contribution of the Gurukul Kangri to the rewriting of Indian history[66] but by far the most comprehensive. For the brahmacharies the book was compulsory reading. Their interpretation of the past was additionally influenced by the so-called *sarasvati yātra*s (educational tours) that took the advanced students to "ancient and historical places"[67] where the relics of former times were explained to them according to the Arya view of history.[68]

Thus, the Gurukul teachers provided their students with an understanding of history that was supposed to give them pride and self esteem. Past defeats and weaknesses were turned into victories by a revisionist construction of the past. The Aryan nation they hoped to build was projected into an ancient golden age, complete with a state that displayed all the features of modernity and was at the same time based on the firm foundations of *dharma*. This historical knowledge, they hoped, would guide their actions in the present, by inspiring them with a sense of "national pride" (*jātīya abhimān*) and making them "proceed even more firmly on their way to progress".[69]

b) The creation of a national language

The question of language had been a cornerstone of the Arya reform scheme ever since the time Svami Dayanand had adopted *āryabhāṣā* – the heavily Sankritised form of Hindi that the Samajis cherished – for his writings and speeches in 1873. As the participation in the Hindi agitation in the U. P. had gained them sympathies in the wider world of Hinduism, it was only natural that the propagation of Hindi as national language would also be a prominent feature of the Gurukul's programme for 'national regeneration'. In fact, the step-motherly treatment accorded to Hindi and Sanskrit in the D. A.-V. College had been one of the causes for the breakaway of the Gurukul faction in 1893.[70] Two decades later, the Gurukul founder Munshiram

65 *Ibid.*, p. 3f.

66 Dharmdatt Vidyālaṃkār, probably a student of Ramdev, wrote a book entitled *Prācīn Bhārat meṃ svarājya*, which was published in 1920. Countless articles published mainly in the *Vedic Magazine* upheld similar views. For a typical example see "The Ancient Glory of a Conquered Race," *The Vedic Magazine & Gurukula Samachar* 10 (9), 1917, p. 679–85.

67 *Gurukul Kāṃgṛī kā vṛttānt jismeṃ saṃvat 1966–1967 kā vṛttānt, ādhikārī parīkṣā etc.*, Kāṃgṛī 1911, p. 9.

68 E. g. during the *sarasvatī yātrā* 1907 the group visited Delhi where Munshiram told his students that the "fanatical and bigotted Muslim conquerors" had not contributed anything noteworthy in the field of architecture and that the Qutb Minar had not been built by a Muslim but by the Hindu hero Prithviraj Chauhan, *The Vedic Magazine & Gurukula Samachar* 1 (8), 1908, p. 488. Cf. also *The Vedic Magazine & Gurukula Samachar* 1 (6), 1907, p. 370, and *The Vedic Magazine & Gurukula Samachar* 1 (9), 1908, p. 567.

69 *BVKI*, p. 4.

70 M. L. Thakur, "Factors leading to the Split of the Arya Samaj in 1893," *Proceedings of the Punjab History Conference, 18th session 1983,* Patiala 1985, p. 225–31, p. 231.

summed up his position on the language question during a programmatic speech held in Bhagalpur on the occasion of the fourth *Hindī sāhitya sammelan*:

> To unite a country without the propagation of a national language [*rāṣṭrabhāṣā*] is as impossible a task as to survive without water. How can the integration of a society progress, if its members possess no means to understand the inner feelings of their fellow members. The political leaders of Bhāratvarṣ have realized by now that the nation cannot be built without a national language. But the opinions still differ when it comes to the question as to which language should be chosen. I am convinced that only *āryabhāṣā* can become the national language.[71]

The Gurukul was to contribute to this propagation in three different ways. The first was that the whole course of instruction over fourteen years including 'modern sciences' like physics (*bhautikī*) and chemistry (*rasāyan*), was conducted in Hindi. For that purpose standard textbooks were translated from English into Hindi[72] and a good deal of textbook literature was originally produced in that language by Gurukul teachers. In the Government system the use of Hindi – like that of other 'vernaculars' – had almost exclusively been restricted to primary and lower secondary education. This emancipation of Hindi from its image of being nothing but 'rustic speech', a language appropriate mostly for private communication, into a medium of higher education, containing countless newly created technical terms, was well-acclaimed even by people from outside the Samaj.[73]

Next to this emancipatory impetus it was also the nature of the type of language used in the Gurukul that was relevant for the national project of the Gurukul spokesmen. The preface of the standard *āryabhāṣā* textbook written exclusively for use in the Gurukul[74] gives us clues as to what ideal Hindi should look like. While explaining why none of the twenty other Hindustani textbooks in use in the Government schools of the United Provinces could be adopted in Kangri, the author remarks:

> All the Hindi textbooks accepted by the Board of Instruction of this province are written in a language that cannot be called Hindi or *āryabhāṣā* […] All Sanskrit words have been banned from this language, ignoring the rule, that without the help of a classical language vernaculars cannot exist. Classical languages only can give life to vernaculars.[75]

71 Munśīrām Jijñāsu, "Maṭṛbhāṣā kā uddhār," in: Bh. Bhāratīya (ed.), *Svāmī Śraddhānand granthāvalī*, vol. 6, Naī Dillī 1987, p. 30–45, p. 34.

72 Govardhan, *Vijñānpraveśikā – rasāyan* was a translation of *Chemistry* by William S. Furneoux; the same author's *Vijñānpraveśikā – bhautikī* was based on the *Physics Primer* by Balfour Stewart.

73 Cf. for instance *The Vedic Magazine & Gurukula Samachar* 6 (8), 1913, p. 654. Even Lord Chelmsford, who visited Kangri in 1916, was impressed by the fact that the science classes in the Gurukul were conducted entirely in Hindi. *The Vedic Magazine & Gurukula Samachar* 10 (11), p. 826.

74 Bh. Gupta, *Ārya bhāṣā pāṭhāvalī*, 2 Vols., Kāṅgrī 1913.

75 *Ibid.*, p. 1f.

The demand that purity (*śuddhtā*), i. e. the use of Sanskritised neologisms often with clear religious connotations for all abstract terms[76] should be the dominant quality of a language propagated as 'national' shows the exclusive character of the proposed nation. Muslims and adherents of all other religions except Hinduism could not but feel alienated by such an idiom. And even the ordinary Hindu population had difficulties in following the Arya brand of Hindi: an undercover agent of the Intelligence Department observes about the speeches given during the annual festival of the school that they "were made in Arya Bhasha, a form of Hindi which few but themselves understand."[77]

The Gurukul served as a testing ground[78] for the planned spread of this artificial idiom over the whole subcontinent since it drew its students also from outside the Hindi speaking areas. An article in the *Saddharm Pracārak*, a Hindi newspaper edited by Munshiram, describes how new students from different regions of the country arrive at the Gurukul and start to quarrel for they have no common language to communicate in and comments:

> This is the disastrous state of affairs in the mutual relationship of the sons of Aryavarta. But only one week in the Gurukul and they are all moulded into a uniform Gurukuli shape. All of them become *āryya bhāṣā* speaking sons of Aryavarta.[79]

However, the propaganda work was not confined to the teaching of Hindi to the brahmacharies in the classes. The fostering of Hindi language and literature was also one the foremost aims of the *sāhitya pariṣad* (literary council) founded in 1908.[80] It was a voluntary forum for teachers and advanced students of the institution. The *pariṣad* met every fortnight to discuss a paper that one of its members had given on a literary or philosophical topic. On special occasions it organised competitions in Hindi poetry writing as well.[81] That the club "produce[d] good and finished writers in Sanscrit [*sic*] and Arya Bhasha"[82] was a desired side-effect for the Gurukul authorities, as graduates who had undergone this additional training would be most useful for the proposed propaganda work.

The wider public was to be reached by the various books published from the Gurukul and by the *ārya bhāṣā sammelan* (Hindi conference) that was held together with the annual festival of the school (*varṣikotsav*). These annual festivals drew up to 90,000 visitors[83] and thus were an

[76] *Ibid.*, p. 6.

[77] Home Dept. Poll. – B, Proceedings May 1912, nos. 14–18, "Weekly Report of the Director of Criminal Intelligence for April 1912," p. 15.

[78] The advocates of the institution used a similar metaphor, depicting the Gurukul as 'laboratory and exhibition' (*prayogśālā aur pradarśini*) of the Arya Samaj. Cf e. g. Indra Viyāvācaspati, Gurukul aur Ārya Samāj'; in: *Śraddhā*, 8 phālguṇ 1977 VS [18-2-1921], p. 3–4, p. 3.

[79] *Saddharm Pracārak*, 27-paus 1970 VS [10-11-1914], p. 11.

[80] *The Vedic Magazine & Gurukula Samachar* 2 (11/12), 1909, p. 111–13.

[81] *The Vedic Magazine & Gurukula Samachar* 13 (3), 1920, p. 183f.

[82] *The Vedic Magazine & Gurukula Samachar* 2 (11/12), 1909, p. 111.

[83] Home Dept. Poll. – B, Proceedings June 1909 Nos. 108–14, "Weekly Report of the Director of Criminal Intelligence for April 1909," p. 9–11.

ideal platform for the Hindi conference that not seldom was attended by famous poets, scholars and intellectuals from outside the Arya world.[84] The main work of the conference consisted of the passing of resolutions for the promotion of Hindi. These usually included the following:

(1) Hindi should be adopted as the national language
(2) The *devanāgrī* script should be used for *all* Indian languages
(3) Libraries and reading rooms supplying books and papers in *āryabhāṣā* should be opened
(4) All national institutions should conduct all their affairs in the national language.[85]

The lively participation of non-Arya writers in these *sammelans* suggests that (in contradistinction to the delicate issues of caste reform, women's upliftment and conversion) the commitment for the cause of Hindi as national language was a sphere of Arya activities where they met with the approval of most other organised Hindu forces. Their work in this field not solely contributed considerably to the development of what was later to become the idiom of Hindu nationalism.[86] The so-called *sarkārī*-Hindi[87] finally adopted by the Congress led government of independent India is also clearly Sanskrit biassed and in fact very close to the ideal of a pure *āryabhāṣā*.

c) The creation of an ideal type of citizen

It has already been hinted at above that the production of the 'perfectly socialised individual' was at the core of the Gurukul's educational mission. In the Arya ideology society was imagined as an organism, whose different limbs had to acknowledge their responsibilities for the whole and fulfill their respective duties. This conception, doubtless, had a basis in various Hindu traditions, where the imagination of society as a body is well known, but it was influenced at least to the same extent by the theories of Herbert Spencer, as the countless quotations from his works in articles and pamphlets published from the Gurukul suggest. The Spencer quote chosen as a motto for the Gurukul newsletter tells much about the self perception of the institution:

> The welfare of society and the justice of its arrangements are at bottom dependent on the characters of its members… there is no political alchemy by which you can get golden conduct out of leaden instincts.[88]

[84] In 1914 for example Madan Mohan Malaviya presided over the meeting.

[85] *The Vedic Magazine & Gurukula Samachar* 10 (11), 1917, p. 824–6. These are the main contents of the four resolutions passed by the *sammelan* in 1917 which is by far the best documented. It seems that the resolutions passed in other years were quite similar. Cf. also Home Dept., Poll. – B, June 1911, Nos. 4–8, "Weekly Report of the Director of Criminal Intelligence for May 1911," p. 5.

[86] See also R. Siṃhā, *Hindī bhāṣā aur sāhitya ko ārya samāj kī den*, Lakhnaū 1966, p. 119–23.

[87] Government-Hindi.

[88] Actually, the editors of the *Gurukula Samachar*, published monthly as an appendix to the widely read *Vedic Magazine*, had chosen two mottos which appeared on the front page of every edition from the end of 1907

The ideal of social responsibility was blended with the colonial postulation of moral and physical superiority through education. The self perception as being weak, degenerated and effeminated was a stereotype in the Hindu reformist discourse in late 19th and early 20th centuries.[89] Hence the final goal of the instruction in the Gurukul was "to breed a nobler race of men [...] who might stand the battle of life with the courage of heroes",[90] and *caritra nirmāṇ* (character building) was among the most important aims of Arya education. As the mere choice of this term suggests, the influence of contemporary British educational concepts was omnipresent. The stress laid on sportsmanship and physical exercise, the revulsion from sexuality and sensual pleasures, the contempt for the "emasculate bookworm", the ideal of selfless service for the community with its underlying anti-individualism,[91] the militarised language[92] were all as much part of the Gurukul as they were for instance of the Boy Scout movement that emerged in Britain a few years after the Gurukul had been inaugurated.[93] All these points found expression in the curriculum as well as in the organisation of the daily routine in the school.

The ties with society were fostered already on the occasion of the initiation ceremony (*vedārambh saṃskār*), through the symbolical act of a begging tour through the nearby Kangri village. This procedure (*bhikṣā*) had a long tradition but as a reversal to the ancient practice where the public supported the sons of brahmins to earn religious merit, it became now a metaphor for the brahmacharies' obligation to pay back for the help received during the time of studies with their commitment to the cause of the upliftment of society as a whole.[94] Like the rigid discipline that prevailed in Kangri, the ideal of self denial (*ātma-tyāg*) in the service of the community propagated by the Gurukul authorities was one of the features that appealed very strongly to the public and brought the school even the admiration of government officials and Muslim

kula Samachar 1 (6), 1907, p. 381.

89 Cf. e. g. K. W. Jones, "The Negative Component of Hindu Consciousness," *Indo British Review* 1, 1991, p. 57–72, J. Rosselli, "The Self-image of Effeteness: Physical Education and Nationalism in Nineteenth Century Bengal," *Past and Present*, 86, 1980, p. 121–48, and M. Sinha, *Colonial Masculinity. The 'manly Englishman' and the Effeminate Bengali in the Late Nineteenth Century*, Delhi (repr.) 1997, esp. p. 1–24 and I. Chowdhury, *The Frail Hero and Virile History. Gender and the Politics of Culture in Colonial Bengal*, Delhi et al. 1998.

90 "The Spiritual Aspect of the Gurukula," *The Vedic Magazine & Gurukula Samachar* 6 (10/11) 1913, p. 863–85, p. 873.

91 Cf. "A Glimpse of Rishi Dayanand's Revived System of Education, the Gurukula," *The Vedic Magazine & Gurukula Samachar* 2 (8), Feb. 1909, p. 1–9.

92 The brahmacharies were often referred to as "soldiers" or "recruits" (cf. for instance *Saddharm Pracārak*, 27. Pauṣ 1970 VS, p. 11) who would leave the institution "better equipped and better armed to meet the foe". *The Vedic Magazine & Gurukula Samachar* 7 (4) Oct. 1913, p. 319.

93 The striking similarities – both in ideology and the stress of physical culture – between the various indigenous Boy Scout Organisations that emerged in British India from the 1910ies onwards and the Gurukul are dealt with exhaustively by C. A. Watt, "Ephebic Patriots or Seditious Sevaks? The Boy Scout Movement in Colonial India, 1908–1921," (unpubl. Conference paper), Cambridge 1998.

94 Cf. Satyaketu Vedālaṃkār, *Ārya Samāj kā itihās*, 7 Vols., Naī Dillī 1987, vol. 3, p. 185.

journalists – needless to mention that both groups were normally not particularly in favour of Arya Samaj activities.[95]

It has already been shown, how the diverse regional identities of the brahmacharies were wiped out in the field of language through the imposition of *āryabhāṣā*. On a different level, the homogenisation was achieved through the adoption of a school uniform: The brahmacharies had to wear yellow *dhotī*s and white *kurtā*s. Shoes or sandals were forbidden and so were caps and umbrellas.[96] Additional clothing items were not allowed. The strict prohibition to keep any personal belongings was another point that added to this equalising tendency.

The moral improvement, the "cultivation of will and spiritual culture" was expected to be realised through leading "a simple and hard life [sic!] and through control in the matters eating drinking and sex"[97] – in short – through the keeping of *brahmacarya*. To effectively implement this concept, the Gurukul authorities had introduced a rigid system of control. Apart from the teachers, the *vidyālay* pupils were supervised by more than a dozen of *adhiṣṭhātā*s (superintendents) that accompanied them every minute of the day apart from the time they were under the control of the teachers during classes. They had to keep track whether they dedicated enough time to their studies, kept their rooms in order, ate with discipline and eschewed "inappropriate thoughts and deeds" during the night.[98] The superintendents were also present on the rare occasions when they were entitled to see their parents or other relatives. Other than that, the students were strictly prohibited to leave the Gurukul or keep in touch with the world outside through writing letters. The isolation was reinforced by the fact that the school was situated in the middle of the jungle about eight kilometres from the outskirts of the city and could only be reached on foot.

The strategy of its implementation might have been radical but the concept of *brahmacarya* understood as "complete control of the lower self" was in fact very close to the Gandhian concept of inner *svarāj*,[99] and indeed the Mahātmā who visited the school several times,[100] not only expressed his admiration for "spirit of self sacrifice" and praised it as "democratic and national institution" but also sent the pupils of his South African Phoenix farm to the school twice and

95 Cf. For example "Al Hadil," 1-5-1908; *SNNUP* 1908, p. 419f.

96 Cf. Munshiram (ed.), *Gurukul Kangri: Biennial Report 1907–08*, Suppl. I, App. B, p. 61. Apart from the homogenising aspect, the adoption of a school uniform suggests that here also British customs were emulated.

97 D. Gajra, "The Metaphysical Basis of Education," *The Vedic Magazine & Gurukula Samachar* 10 (1), 1916, p. 109–25, p. 122f.

98 Cf. Gurukul Kāṃgṛī Viśvavidyālay Haridvār (ed.), *Adhiṣṭhātāoṃ ke karttavya*, Haridvār ²1959 [¹ca 1903], *passim*.

99 Cf. A. J. Parel, (ed.), *M. K. Gandhi, Hind Swaraj and other writings*. Delhi (repr.) 1997, p. liv.

100 For the following see Gandhi's speech "Saccī ṣikṣā," in: Viṣṇudatt Rākeś (ed.), *Dīkṣālok*, p. 36–41.

had them spend several months there. He was especially fascinated by the organisational capacities of the Gurukul leaders and the school's experiments in agriculture and practical teaching.

Notwithstanding this common ground, the understanding of *brahmacarya* as it prevailed in Kangri included one feature that distinguished the Gurukul clearly from the Gandhian stance: its emphasis of physical culture, military virtues and the cult of virility. The Samajis missed no opportunity to emphasise that "exercises and manly games [we]re compulsory" in the Gurukul[101] and that it offered the better alternative to government colleges considered as institutions in which the pupils only underwent lessons "in the grand science of being a book-worm":[102]

> The Gurukul has a claim [...] on Indians [...] who are filled with horror when they look at the bloated and wasted looks of our students who are fathers before they are out of their teens – and whose flabby muscles and hectic glances proclaim the degeneracy of our race – who know that there is a tragic lack of grit, self assertion and virility in our public life and that most of or public workers are incapable of sustained effort and united work.[103]

All these deficiencies were supposed to be removed through two compulsory sports lessons a day which consisted of working with dumb bells, wrestling, swimming etc. in the morning and games (cricket, hockey, football, *kabaḍḍī*) in the evening.[104] In addition, there were regular drill exercises and lessons in fencing and horseback riding. The success of the training was demonstrated on the occasion of the annual festivals where the brahmacharies broke chains and bamboo sticks by sheer physical force and displayed feats of swordsmanship with the result "that the people in thousands were convulsed with commotion and everybody was talking on the wonderful system of physical culture followed in this institution"[105]

The ideal citizen, then, as produced in Kangri was not merely intellectually cultivated and spiritually raised, he was also physically strong. All three fields were interconnected and again subordinated to the underlying ideal of service to the community. Especially the essential role that physical culture and the constant stress of 'manliness and virility' play in the schedule deserves our attention.

d) Towards an ideal society: the problems of caste and child marriages

The vision of a model citizen was of course closely linked with that of a homogenous society functioning on the lines of rationality and efficiency. The proposed reshaping of Hindu society according to these principles was centred around the Arya Samaj interpretation of the *varṇāśra-*

101 V. L. Sharma, A *Handbook of the Arya Samaj*, Allabad ²1912, p. 81.

102 'Educationist' (pseud.): "Physical Education. Its necessity in India," *The Vedic Magazine & Gurukula Samachar* 13 (3), 1920, p. 124–8.

103 Munshiram (ed.), *Gurukul Kangri: Biennial Report 1907–08*, p. viif.

104 Indra Vidyāvācaspati, *Amar śahīd*, p. 61f.

105 *The Leader*, 1-4-1918, p. 5. I am indebted to Carey Watt for making me aware of this particular source.

ma system and was conceived to work on various levels. Dayanand had regarded the *varṇa vyavasthā* as being not based on birth but on *guṇ, karm* and *svabhāv* (abilities, behaviour and nature).[106] The respective *varṇa* was only ascribed to the individual after his education had been completed. The Gurukul was originally thought of as being the institution responsible for the implementation of this meritocratic concept. If everybody, including the children of *śūdras* and outcastes had an equal opportunity to receive the best type of education and thus 'earn' his later position in the society, the basis of untouchability (*chūt chāt*) was destroyed. As untouchability and the division into castes and subcastes was perceived – and not only by the Samaj – as being largely responsible for the 'deplorable state' of Hinduism, its abolition was considered to be of the utmost importance:

> The Hindu race can never acquire the place due to it under the sun as long as it is not welded into one nationality and nationality can never be formed, as long as castes and their iron rules are not broken; but they can never be successfully and willingly broken without the Gurukula system of education.[107]

The egalitarian way of life that should bind together the heterogenous elements of Hindu society and prevent a possible breakaway of the untouchables from the fold of Hinduism was demonstrated in the model institution where brahmin and *śūdra* boys ate at the same table and slept in the same room. That way, the brahmacharies were supposed to develop a sense of mutual responsibility and finally become "perfectly socialised individuals".[108]

The abolition of caste and untouchability was on the agenda of most Hindu reform organisations of the time. Many of them, however, had tried to throw overboard the concept of *varṇa* altogether and had been excommunicated by the authorities of brahmanical Hinduism. In their endeavour to reform the entire Hindu community, the Arya Samajis themselves had experienced more than once that they were rejected by the Hindu majority for being too radical. By sticking to the *varṇa* concept – though in a completely modified manner – and employing religious symbols that were widely accepted, the adherents of the Gurukul-faction hoped to gain "favorable access to old orthodox Hindu heart"[109] and eventually to be able to act as the unifiers of Hinduism.

In a similar way the *āśrama* system was also seen as an ideal instrument to check the presumed decline of the 'Hindu race' without alienating its more traditional members. A revival of the virtue of *brahmacarya* was to solve two of the most virulent problems that – according to the Samaji perception – threatened the existence of the Aryan race. The decreasing number of Hindus, evident from the decennial census carried out by the British, was seen as being mainly

[106] Cf. also Jordens, *Swāmī Dayānanda*, p. 283ff.

[107] M. C. Sinha, "Gurukula as a System of Education," *loc. cit.*, p. 1079.

[108] Balkrishna, *The Gurukula System of Education and its Critics*, Kangri 1911, p. 22.

[109] Sinha, "Gurukula as a System," p. 1078.

caused by three phenomena: conversion, the prohibition of widow remarriage and child marriages which again resulted in infant mortality and a general degradation of the virile power of the offspring. Whereas the former two should be contained by the Arya inventions of *śuddhi* and *niyog*,[110] the latter was to be stopped through the application of *brahmacarya* which would also guarantee the amelioration of the genetic stock of the Hindu 'race'. Since the principle prescribed sixteen and twenty-five as the proper ages of consent for women and men respectively, child marriages would disappear as a natural result once it was generally followed, and "the sad spectacle of prematurely worn out and early dying Indian manhood"[111] could be stopped. This biological argument also included references to the science of eugenics[112] which was popular in Europe at the time.

The Gurukul was regarded by its founders as the only institution that could succeed in making the revised *varṇāśrama* system work and thus solve a whole bundle of problems that resulted from the specific structure of Hindu society.

IV

As we have seen, the effort to establish a 'national' school like the Gurukul Kangri was to some extent a result of the educational situation in late 19th century India. It was particularly the Hindu intelligentsia that felt jeopardised by the onslaught of missionary educational activities

110 For the former concept cf. H. Fischer-Tiné, 'Kindly Elders of the Hindu Biradri: The Arya Samaj's Struggle for Influence and Hindu Muslim Relationships 1875–1926,' in: A. Copley (ed.): *Gurus and their Followers. New Religious Reform Movements in Colonial India*, Delhi 2000, p. 107–27, and C. Clémentin-Ojha, "La śuddhi de l'Arya Samaj ou l'invention d'un rituel de (re)conversion à l'Hindouisme," *Archives de Sciences Sociales des Religions* 87 (3) 1994, p. 99–114; for the Arya reinterpretation of *niyog, a* sanctioned temporary sexual relationship of a widow with one or several men with the sole aim of begetting children see Jordens, *Swami Dayanand*, p. 117f and M. Kishwar, "The Daughters of Aryavarta," *Indian Economic and Social History Review* 23 (2), 1986, p. 151–86.

111 *The Vedic Magazine & Gurukula Samachar* 7 (6), 1913, p. 412.

112 In an article published in the *Vedic Magazine* the concept of *brahmacarya* is linked with pseudo-scientific views in a way that reminds on the racial laws of Nazi-Germany: "[...] it is necessary, that only fit persons should be allowed to marry and take on themselves the responsible duties that pertain to parenthood. It is very essential that they should be of good stock. For parent-hood of the diseased, the insane, the alcoholic [...] is a crime against the future." Cf. "Eugenics: The Ennoblement of Mankind," *The Vedic Magazine & Gurukula Samachar* 4 (12), 1911, p. 1–15. See also Keshav Dev Shastri: "Sexual Hygiene," *The Vedic Magazine & Gurukula Samachar* 15 (4), 1921, p. 192–7 and An Admirer (pseud.), "Swami Dayanand on Conscious Race Culture," *The Vedic Magazine & Gurukula Samachar* 10 (11), 1917 p. 827–33. Before drawing unfair conclusions, it has to be taken into account, that the belief in eugenics was so widespread in Europe at the time that it almost was part of general knowledge. Cf. H. C. Harten, "Pädagogik und Eugenik im 'rassenhygienischen' Diskurs vor 1933," *Paedagogica Historica* 33 (3) 1997, p. 765–800, especially p. 767–84 and M. Thomson, *The Problem of Mental Deficiency. Eugenics, Democracy and Social Policy in Britain c. 1870–1959*, Oxford 1998, especially p. 19–23. For a general discussion of racism in the Indian context see P. Robb, *The Concept of Race in South Asia*, Delhi et al. (Repr.) 1997.

and the cultural alienation through a 'spread of materialism' in western colleges. However, among the many efforts to amalgamate western educational concepts and contents with instruction in (selected and reformulated) parts of the indigenous cultural traditions the Gurukul was unique in its encompassing approach. Few other projects had such a clear cut and comprehensive idea of the nation they wanted to build, and fewer even implemented their ideology so radically. We have shown, that the institution was perceived by its founders not merely as a testing ground for Arya ideals but as the nation *en miniature*. In the logic of the model of the 'nation of intent' the founders of the Gurukul hoped to produce 'social engineers', a *minorité agissante* that would carry their national values to the 'ignorant and passive masses'. In this manner, the school would not only train the élite of the proposed nation, it would also provide all the other features that – in an adoption of western criteria – were regarded as essential for a national community:

> First: a national history which allowed the members of the nation to be proud of their forefathers by retelling the deeds of the ancient Aryan heroes and at the same time to be rational and 'modern' by projecting all the important features of a 19th century European nation state into the Hindu empires of the past. *En passant* it also defined national territory (*āryavarta*) and the relevant canon of national literature (*veda, ārṣ granth*).
>
> Secondly: A 'purified' and modernised national language (*āryabhāṣā*) which would be suitable for the needs of the 20th century together with a national script (*devanāgarī*).
>
> Thirdly: An ideal type of citizen who would be mentally, spiritually and physically equipped to serve society, having internalised quasi religious values such as selflessness, discipline and devotion to the cause of the nation.
>
> Fourthly: A remedy for the 'social evils' which divided and weakened Hindu society, (the reformulated *varṇāśrama vyavasthā*).

When it comes to an assessment of the whole project, two inherent problems of the scheme have to be mentioned, one regarding its relationship to the colonial power and one regarding its effect on non-Hindus. Our study of Gurukuli vision of an ideal citizen has shown that, in spite of their religious and sometimes even aggressively anti-colonial rhetoric, the Gurukul founders tacitly accepted some essential assumptions of their masters, e. g. that education was the cure for all diseases and that the masses of society needed moral and physical upliftment from their paternal well wishers – be they English or Arya. The emphasis placed on discipline and self control is also perfectly in accordance with the British ideal of a 'colonial citizen', and one has to raise the question of whether the whole project indeed brought about an emancipation from the intellectual hegemony of the British.

As to its capacities as a model for national integration, particularly the analysis of the Gurukuli brand of historiography and its language policy can leave no doubt that the nationalist ideology as implemented by the institution not only failed to integrate non-Hindu elements (most importantly the Muslims) but risked contributing actively to tensions between the different communities of British India. It must be stated that, during the time covered by the present study, the Gurukul certainly was not a militant anti-Muslim institution. Nonetheless, it was among the first Hindu institutions that directly linked *body building* with *character building* which was again seen as a prerequisite for *nation building* and employed exclusively Hindu symbols in its vision of national virility. In this respect it paved the way for overtly militant Hindu organisations like the Arya Vir Dal and the RSS. Thus, our assumption that a detailed study of the Gurukul would enhance our knowledge about the role of the Arya Samaj in the emergence of militant Hindu nationalism has been confirmed. All the same, contrary to the widespread assessment that places the Arya Samaj exclusively in this context, we have found some indications that the influence of the school went much further. Especially a study of the impact of the 'Gurukuli values' on the allegedly secular brand of nationalism propagated by the Indian National Congress seems to be a promising project for the future.

Religious Revival, Ethnicity and Nationalism in Southeast Asia

Bernhard Dahm

1. Introducing the Topic and the Region

Among the many contributions to a new and better understanding of the terms "nation", "nationalism" etc. in recent years some were helpful, indeed, to re-interpret developments in my own field of specialisation. I am thinking in particular of Benedict Anderson's description of nations as "imagined communities"[1] and Ernest Gellner's emphasis on the existence of a state as a precondition for nationalism.[2] The term nationalism is therefore used in my paper as a term describing the striving of an articulate élite to bring the two, the "imagined community" and the "politically centralised unit" (as its frame) together. Less attention has been payed in the literature to the "addressees" of nationalism and to the conditions of the people who were supposed to form the future nation. So the question arises: What was there before nationalism? Were the people prepared for the message of the "imaginators"? Or was it nationalism itself which mobilised them for the struggle for independence?

My paper will therefore deal with the proto-nationalist phase rather than with the period when nationalism was spread by a new élite in Southeast Asia. The reason is that the latter, although quite familiar with Western nationalist developments and concepts of nationalism, had obviously difficulties getting the so-called "last wave" (B. Anderson) of nationalism started in a way comparable to former developments in Europe. Out there, in Southeast Asia, the preconditions for a "nation" were only in exceptional cases comparable with the situation in the European world, say, in the second half of the 19th century, when the Germans and Italians were finally able to achieve their nation states.

1 Benedict Anderson, *Imagined Communities. Reflections on the Origin and Spread of Nationalism*, London 1983.

2 Ernest Gellner, *Nations and Nationalism*, Oxford 1983.

Let us, briefly, look at the three criteria which, according to Hobsbawm, allowed people to be firmly classed as a nation in that period. These are 1) historic association with a current state or with a fairly lengthy and recent past, 2) the existence of a long-established cultural élite, possessing a written national history and administrative vernacular and 3) the proven capacity for conquest.[3] In the Southeast Asian setting there would be, at the end of the 19th century, only three countries which would fit into these categories or qualify for that ranking of a nation: Siam or the Kingdom of Thailand, British colonised Burma and French colonised Vietnam. Most of the others, including the vast archipelagos of the Philippines and of the Dutch East Indies, would not, and if, like in the case of central Java, only with significant modifications. There was neither the memory of a common past nor was there a long established cultural élite, thinking in terms of territorial units, which, as indicated above, is the sine qua non prerequisite for a national state.

Nevertheless, in those years nationalists in what was to become the Philippines or Indonesia started to spread nationalist ideas and the wish for independence like their contemporaries did in Burma or in Vietnam, in particular after the Japanese victory over the Russian armada had shown, in 1905, that the West was not invincible. And the leaders found response among the masses, in spite of the absence of the preconditions mentioned above. What was the reason for this? Was it because the illiterate peasants in the villages, or the ethnical groups of distant islands were taken out of their lethargy by the visions of newly imagined communities by some of the leaders in the capitals of the colonies? Or, were the people longing for the restoration of the glory of former kingdoms such as Angkor, Majapahit, Mataram, Banten etc. ? Or, did they respond because of promises of help from outside and the demands for national self-determination from Woodrow Wilson and the Communist International after World War I?

2. Religious Revival as Precondition of Independence-Movements in Southeast Asia

All these factors had, at some later stage, influenced the ideology of the various independence movements, but none of them was responsible for what might be called the awakening of the masses. Visions of new states could not excite local or cultural communities whose major concern was to defend their own identity under the threat of cultural alienation.[4] Glorious king-

[3] See J. E. Hobsbawm, *Nations and Nationalism since 1780. Programme, Myth, Reality*, Cambridge 1990, p. 37f.

[4] On this aspect see my paper "Religious Revival as Reaction to the Threat of Cultural Alienation in Southeast Asia," *Temenos* 32, 1996, p. 37–54.

doms of the past were virtually unknown in the latter part of the 19th century, like "independence" or "national self-determination", the key words of a later phase.

The awakening of the masses was, instead, a consequence of Dutch, Spanish, British or French acts of interference in the period of imperialism. Their deposition of kings and destruction of traditional élites like in Burma and in Vietnam, their enforced opening of formerly secluded and self-reliant villages, their introduction of money economy, capitation tax, of plantation economy and indentured labour in most parts of Southeast Asia led to the downfall of long established crisis-regulating mechanisms, led to misery, to desperation and, of course, to the quest for help. But where could one find help? Traditional service-agencies in the villages, such as mutual help organisations, communal taxation (considering hardships of individuals of the village), family-connections, special patron-client bonds etc. had lost their functions. There was only one source left: the various religious traditions, with their local variations, offering salvational aspects independent of the interference of alien powers. This is where the masses turned to.

Thus, at a time, when the new élites had hardly begun their training for a position in the colonial system and had not yet found the occasion to study Western ideas, which would eventually be decisive for their own imaginations of the future, the masses were already mobilised. Since these peasants, plantation workers, local artisans and so on were not waiting for new concepts of foreign origins, their first protest movements were determined by something intimately known to them like their religions. Most religions promised for a time of crisis a chance for an escape from the present hardships: the help of God, who had promised his rewards for the faithful, the arrival of a messiah, leading the people to a new golden age of plenty, the power of magic and rites in tribal and/or secret societies, depending on the area within Southeast Asia, etc.

This religious revival thus has to be seen as the first phase of the independence movement, leading eventually to the secular movement, which was able to focus all energy on the establishment of a modern state. However, the transition from religious revival to the secular aims of the nationalists was not always a direct route. In a country like Burma with its long tradition of a well functioning state, the transition from the religious revival of Buddhism to secular nationalism was rather smooth. It is undeniable that the beginning of the Burmese independence movement was deeply imbued with a revival of Buddhist values, and so, quite logical, the first organisations used Buddhist names: The Young Men's Buddhist Association (1906) developed gradually into a General Council of Buddhist Associations. The latter's name was changed in

1920 in General Council of Burmese Associations. The initials remained the same, GCBA, but the change of the name indicated the shifting of emphasis in outlook and aims at this time.[5]

Burma, however, shows also the difficulty of the integration of ethnic minorities into a modern state, which, in the past was their adversary rather than their associate. The smooth tradition from religious revival to the acceptance of the concept of a modern state can be observed only in those parts of Burma that were integrated parts of the former kingdoms of Burma. The Arakanese, the Shan, the Kachin, the Karen were and are resisting their integration into the Burmese state even if they are also believers in Buddhism like the Shan.

3. Obstacles for Nationalism Caused by Religious Revival

Burmese developments underline the importance of long integrated or associated historical periods as a precondition for a modern nation. But what then about the tribal societies in most of island Southeast Asia, which constitute the modern states of the Philippines and Indonesia? Here we also had religious revival as reaction against colonial rule, but, in most cases, we do not have the tradition of an organised state. We have instead a multitude of ethnical groups, whose ethnical consciousness did not allow (with a few exceptions) the emergence of centralised kingdoms. Religious revival did not open the gates for nationalist ideas. Ethnicity is closely connected with local religious traditions, and their revival therefore can be regarded as obstacles rather than as push-factors in the direction of national integration. Other obstacles to nationalism caused by religious revival are in my opinion the spread of messianism and the radicalisation of religious groups. Both, messianism and religious fanaticism have political potential, but this potential, like revived ethnicity, can easily thwart the efforts of the new élite with regard to the foundation of a modern nation state.

According to Anthony Smith, the decisive dimensions of an ethnie are a collective name, a common myth of descent, a shared history, a distinct shared culture, an association with a specific territory and a sense of solidarity. These six essentials would qualify an ethnie, if I understand Anthony Smith correctly, for the formation of a modern state.[6]

The problem, however, is, that we have so many ethnies in Southeast Asia having most of the essentials, in Sumatra alone we would find about half a dozen such ethnies: Aceh in the North, the Batak, the coastal Malays, the Minangkabau, the Rejang and the Lebang in the South, not to speak about the many subdivisions, in particular among the Batak with the Karo, the Pak Pak, the Simalungun, the Toba, the Angkola and the Mandailing, all of whom with

[5] On the role of Buddhism in Burmese politics see D. E. Smith, *Religion and Politics in Burma*, Princeton 1965.

[6] See Anthony D. Smith, *The Ethnic Origins of Nations*, Oxford/New York 1986, p. 22ff.

distinct characteristics of their own, but also with the same myth of descent, with a shared culture, the same form of social organisation, and the association with their area of origin, in their case the Toba Lake and its surroundings.

Acehnese, Bataks, Minangs are perhaps the three ethnical groups with the clearest distinctions, and all of them have revived some of their characteristics in the time of their confrontations and clashes with the Dutch colonial power. The Acehnese, a thoroughly Islamised people, were having a pre-colonial state with a sultan as its ruler and a vaguely defined territory, administrated by a feudal aristocracy. They are the only ethnie which has, up to the present day, refused to be fully integrated into the Indonesian Republic. Like the Shan or the Karen in Burma, they are fighting for an independent status or for complete independence. Among all ethnies in Indonesia (with the exception of the later conquered people from Irian Jaya and East Timor) it is only the Acehnese who have developed a nationalism of their own. In contrast, the Minangkabau have been leading the process for Indonesianisation in the archipelago. They, too, are thoroughly Islamised, but they fostered Islamic reformism which proved to be a close ally of the efforts of Minangkabau nationalists during the process of Indonesianisation. They did not have in recent centuries a centralised and hierarchically structured government, with a clearly defined territory of its rule. They had, instead, a great number of self-governing village "states" (*nagari*), a situation which, in a way, reflected the situation in Indonesia at large. This is perhaps one explanation why they did not demand a special status for themselves in the Indonesian republic, another is certainly their openness and their good relations with the nations of the Islamic world. Still, a greater contrast in the framework of nation building in Indonesia as that between the two ethnies, the Acehnese and the Minangkabau in Sumatra, is hardly imaginable.

Sandwiched between the two are the Bataks, who demonstrated a different reaction in response to the imposition of colonial rule. Since they had never accepted Islam in the course of history but had, instead, always maintained a cultural identity of their own *vis-à-vis* their neighbours, the Acehnese in the North and the Minangkabau in the South, it was this Batakness – a mixture of animism, ancestor-cult and some notions of Hinduism – which were revived after the Dutch had begun to interfere with their affairs. This happened at the same time, when German missionaries from the Rheinische Mission had started to convert the Batak people in the early 1860s to Christianity. Therefore, we find already some attempts in their revivalist movements to fight Dutch military superiority by alluding not only to the charisma of their priest-king without government, the *Si Singamangaraja*, but also to the imagined powers of the missionaries.[7]

[7] On this see Masashi Hirosue, *Prophets and Followers in Batak Millenarian Responses to the Colonial Order: Pormalim, Na Siak Bagi and Parhudamdam*, Ph. D. thesis, Australian National University, Canberra 1988.

This shows that the Bataks were rather responsive to possible new sources of help. This awareness about new potentials to defend their identity has always been an asset of the Bataks and has helped them to defend their identity against the Acehnese and the Minangkabau. To foreigners they appeared already in early times as a tightly knit community. William Marsden, writing in 1783, called the Bataks therefore "a nation", as did Raffles, writing some 40 years later. But by the end of the 19th century the term "nation" for the Bataks was dropped in favour of "tribal group", because, as a German traveller related, "they are not a unified people, bound together by common interests and a unified language, they just live next to each other as related tribes."[8]

This observation is born out also by the many subdivisions of the Bataks, mentioned already, and by their unlimited hunger for *harajaon*, that is the drift to dominate, to dominate in their family, in their village, and, if possible, also beyond. The German missionaries, knowing this, opened new avenues for the Bataks' ambitions in creating positions in the organisation of the church and by opening schools.[9] So there was a realistic awareness of the power-relations after the religious-revival movements in the late 19th and the early 20th centuries had led to nothing. They discovered the chances of being part of an independent state, even though the period of religious revival had strengthened the ethnical characteristics and thus deepened the traditional gap between them and their neighbours, rather than narrowed it.

It was unthinkable, therefore, that the three ethnic groups, discussed in this chapter, were willing to accept a new scheme of the Dutch in the 1930ies and to integrate themselves into a future State of Sumatra. The religious revival, caused by the interference of the Dutch in the traditional communities, had strengthened their ethnic identities and had thus prevented, if we look at geography, the gradual evolution of a unified Sumatra. The strengthening of ethnic consciousness – not only in Sumatra but also elsewhere in the archipelago – left no other choice for the new élite of the nationalist period but to think, when imaging new communities, in terms of a greater Indonesia. Thus, the imagination of "Indonesia" was responsive to actual developments rather than creative, and was not only due to the fact that Dutch rule had created a centralised administration in the archipelago – which was simply taken over.

Next to ethnical revivalism religious fanaticism and revived messianism were mentioned as potential obstacles to nationalist aims. Both developments could be noticed in Indonesia already a few years after the impact of the new Dutch policies in the so-called liberal period

[8] References see in Daniel Perret, *La Formation d'un Paysage Ethnique: Bataks et Malais de Sumatra Nord-Est*, Paris 1995, p. 49ff. The German traveller, quoted in Perret, is J. F. von Brenner, *Besuch bei den Kannibalen Sumatras: Erste Durchquerung der unabhängigen Batak-Lande*, Würzburg 1894, quotation p. 170f.

[9] For a good discussion of the christianisation of the Bataks and the response of the missionaries to the Batak-traditions see Lance Castles, *The Political Life of a Sumatran Residency, Tapanuli 1915–1940*, Ph. D. thesis, Yale University, New Haven 1973.

made itself felt in the villages: The lease of land, formerly used by the village population, to foreign entrepreneurs to establish and extend their cash crop-plantations; the introduction of capitation tax, virtually dividing formerly mutually supportive village networks into so and so many heads had the consequences of rapidly spreading pauperisation and individual misery. This in turn gave birth in particular in densely populated Java to movements, leading to preparations of a *jihad* (Holy War) in regions with a predominant Islamic population like in Banten, or to growing unrest and speculations about the imminent arrival of the *Ratu Adil* (messiah) in other parts of Java, where Indian cultural traditions were still more meaningful to the people.

There is no need to present new evidence. Sartono Kartodirdjo has provided a lot of material on both forms of social protest reaction to colonial rule in Java. In his dissertation[10] he analyses the preparation of a holy war by Hajis after their return from Mecca in Banten, a traditionally unruly area of Western Java in the 1880s. In several later studies he discusses the various forms of millenarianism, Messianism, nativism, which, according to him, can be observed at the same time in other parts of Java.[11] Sartono Kartodirdjo interprets these protest movements in the first place as a proof that Javanese society was not as static as it is sometimes depicted in the literature, that Javanese peasants also in the past were ready for change, and that religious expectations provided their social protest with a special dynamic. For me, the decisive point of religious revival on Java is not the "readiness" of the Javanese peasants for change (which can be disputed if we look at the history of messianism up to the Rebellion of Diponegoro, 1825–1830), for me the decisive point of religious revival is its political potential, and its capacity of mass-mobilization. Some time ago I have attempted to categorise the religious revival movements on Java in the late 19th and early 20th centuries. At that occasion I have distinguished[12] between an Islamic Tarekat-Jihad Type on the one hand and a Ratu Adil-Mahdi Type on the other. The former was well organised. New adepts had to swear an oath of obedience to their Master. The association received its strength during the mystical religious sessions (*dikr*), amplified by political agitation against the unbelievers. It was characterised by a growing determination to fight the latter and expel them from the Islamised parts of Javanese soil if this would become necessary. Messianic elements were no essential part of the teachings of the Sheikhs, the essential part was the duty to defend Islam even at the cost of one's own life.

The Ratu-Adil/Mahdi Type of movement was not well organised, if it was organised at all. It depended entirely on rumours and speculations, whether the new "messiah" was accepted by his followers or not, when somebody declared himself to be the chosen one, posing his claim

10 Sartono Kartodirdjo, *The Peasants Revolt of Banten in 1888*, Den Haag 1966.

11 Sartono Kartodirdjo, *Religious Movements of Java in the 19th and 20th Centuries*, Yogyakarta 1970 and id., *Protest Movements in Rural Java*, Singapore 1973.

12 See Bernhard Dahm, *Emanzipationsversuche von kolonialer Herrschaft in Südostasien. Die Philippinen und Indonesien: Ein Vergleich*, Wiesbaden 1974, p. 95ff.

on prophesies from either Islamic or Hindu/Buddhist traditions. There was no need to fight for him, he would reveal his magical qualities and superiority when the decisive hour had come. Formerly, up to Diponegoro and his Java War, the Ratu Adil had been expected to be a descendant of one of the princely houses on Java. However, after the Javanese aristocracy had gained the reputation of being only puppets of the Dutch during the exploitative cultivation-system in the mid 19th century, the messiah was no longer expected to be a prince, he could come from any stratum of society. This explains perhaps the multitude of cases reported in the time roughly from the 1880s to the 1920s.

Both types of the religious revival movements mentioned above, the Tarekat/Jihad- and the Ratu Adil/Mahdi-type, were difficult to handle for the new national élite for obvious reasons: The Tarekat/Jihad-type prepared for a rebellion which could be easily suppressed by the colonial government and providing it, in addition, with the pretext to uproot the movement entirely.

The Ratu Adil/Mahdi-type movement could easily create an atmosphere, as if victory was at hand. People would cheer the leader and his lieutenants up to the moment when he had to prove his magical qualities. If he turned out to be an impostor (and this is, of course, what happened) the whole support would disappear at once, or even turn into animosities for having cheated his followers.

Both tendencies have made themselves felt in the Indonesian independence movement and did hurt the cause of the nationalists. The so-called Communist Rebellion of 1926 was, with regard to Banten, a new version of the rebellion of 1888, described by Sartono Kartodirdjo, prepared and provoked by religious leaders. Banten was the only place on Java from where in 1926 serious resistance was reported. The now available documents proof that it was the concern about the future of Islam and not about the Communist Party, which later had to bear the consequences, which, in turn, led to the actual fights in the area of Tjaringin and Pandeglang. Bantam had another holy war.[13]

Revived messianism, the Ratu Adil/Mahdi-type of movement, helped charismatic leaders such as Tjokroaminoto, Sukarno or later Aidit in their meteoric rise to the top-position in the nationalist or communist movements. But the noisy acclamations were no guarantee for reliable support by the masses in times of crisis, all of the political Ratu Adils were to experience this in Indonesia at one or the other stage of their careers. In the efforts with regard to the creation of a true political or national consciousness, the jihad- and messianic aspects of religious revival were as dubious helpers for the spread of nationalist ideas as were the strengthening of ethnical identities discussed above.

[13] See *Ibid.*, p. 123ff.

4. Religious Revival as a Bridge to Nationalism

At the beginning of our paper we raised the question what was there before the new élite of Southeast Asian countries at the beginning of the 20th century started to spread its nationalist ideas. We now have a clear answer: Practically in all regions of colonised Southeast Asia, and that is, with the exception of Thailand, the whole of Southeast Asia from Burma to Vietnam and from Sumatra to Mindanao we find revivalist movements of a religious or a semi-religious nature, where ever the colonial power had started to directly interfere with the daily life of the rural population. Resistance was particularly severe where the colonial power harshly interfered in government affairs, deposing kings or the cultural or administrative élite like in Burma, Vietnam, or in Aceh and Banten.

Since traditional crisis regulating mechanisms were uprooted or destroyed, people took recourse to their religions. While reviving salvational aspects of the religion, in particular the lower strata of the population, peasants, plantation workers, local artisans were mobilised and even ready to fight for the revived ideals. These were not identical with the concepts and ideas of nationalism which were disseminated by the new élites at about the same time.[14] In most countries it was only after World War I that we can see a confluence of the movements of the masses with the ideals of nationalism, a full generation after the first visible signs of religious revival in the late 1880s.

One can see religious revival therefore as the first phase of the independence-movements and as a bridge to nationalism with its secular aims. For a long period the aims of religious revival and those of nationalism were not identical; the opposite seems to be true: religious revival strengthened cultural and/or ethnical groups which had strong reservations with regard to national solutions. At the begin there was certainly no "*désir d'être ensemble*" (Renan) with other groups, given all the cultural varieties. This desire came only with a new generation, trained in the colonial capitals.[15] They started to build the bridges from the consequences of religious revival to nationalism. Even if there were different revivals in the same religion like in Islam, they could lead, as we have seen, into the direction of nationalism: The Acehnese wanted to have their own Islamic state, the Minangkabau wanted to spread reform-Islam in the whole of Indonesia, thus strengthening the Process of Indonesianisation, another example of bridge-building. The same seems to be true for the Christian groups emerging in various parts

[14] I argued in my paper in Turku (see fn. 4) that religious revival was, next to the wish to survive physically, in the first place an attempt to avoid cultural alienation.

[15] On this see also Anderson, with his comments on "educational pilgrimages" with their "Romes" in the various colonial capitals, *loc. cit.*, p. 127.

of the archipelago: A broader national frame opened better prospects for their new belief as well as for their revived identities and they therefore began to actively support the idea of a greater Indonesia.

What has been exemplified here by mainly referring to developments in Indonesia could also be shown in other parts of Southeast Asia with the necessary modifications. Decisive was the degree of interference of the colonial power in the life rhythm of the rural population. Where this was less, like in Laos, Cambodia, Malaysia, the revivalist movements were also of less importance. Nationalism was here mainly a product of World War II and its aftermath.

Submerging the People? Post-orientalism and the Construction of Communalism*

Michael Roberts

I

In the scholarship on South Asia in recent years one sees a reformative political project which seeks to undermine and challenge its various forms of communalism and nationalism. This scholarship is attempting to unmask the objectified and essentialised ways in which such categories as 'Hindu' and 'Muslim' on the one hand, and 'Tamil' and 'Sinhala' on the other, have been accepted and used in the last century or so. Such usages, it is charged, reify the oppositions, which the categories mark, as age-old, eternal conflicts. This is wrong. It is an ahistorical reading of the present back into the past.

These collective identities, it is claimed, are a product of the British era – with some writers going so far as to suggest that these categories had little or no political meaning in the pre-British periods; while others, more sensibly, add a critical qualifier and speak of "these collective identities *as we know them today*".[1] These arguments, therefore, underline the transformations that took place under the British raj. Particular emphasis is placed on the manner in which British rule implanted a new intellectual framework, what was in effect "an essentialist sociology of knowledge" – now unmasked by a body of scholarship that Rogers labels "post-Orientalist".[2]

* An earlier version of this paper was presented at the annual conference of the Australian Anthropological Society at Albury in September 1996. I thank Tom Ernst, Rohan Bastin and David Baillie for comments on the article. With reference to the Indian world, I have been assisted by the following: Hermann Kulke referred me to N. K. Wagle, Richard Eaton provided a meticulous set of comments on the penultimate draft of this paper; and Dilip Basu, Dipesh Chakrabarty and Gautam Ghosh conveyed information on *nere* and related facets of Bengali history. The views remain mine; and, as the concluding segments will indicate, I pursue a line of interpretation that differs fundamentally from that of Eaton.

1 For pertinent references, see Rogers 1994, Kaviraj 1992, Pandey 1992, and paragraph 8 in this article.

2 John Rogers, "Post-orientalism and the Interpretation of Premodern and Modern Political Identities: the Case of Sri Lanka," *Journal of Asian Studies* 53, 1994, p. 20.

Thus, informed by the vocabulary of Said, Foucault and Benedict Anderson, these post-Orientalist writings have unpacked and displayed "a particular construction of knowledge about Indian society" on the one hand[3] and Sri Lankan society on the other.[4] Two principal forces have been identified among the agents of change. Firstly, Orientalist scholars, whether British and indigenous, who sought to understand and describe the indigenous societies, their customs and their histories. And secondly, the British colonial state and its institutional innovations – such as the census, the gazetteer, the museum and the tourist-cum-pilgrimage site. In the Sri Lankan case the influence of the Theosophists is also highlighted.

Such lines of research have been an attractive path for several South Asian anthropologists: They are able to skip the hard grind of ethnographic work among people in their everyday world; instead they can sit back in their 'cloisters' and decipher – the favoured term here is 'deconstruct' – texts. In the result, one witnesses today a convergence of interests between anthropologists and those historians who have been prepared to combine their empirical investigations with post-modernist deconstructionism. It may be a mark of this convergence that at the meetings of the American Anthropological Association in San Francisco in 1996 space was devoted to an invited session (thus a prestigious one) entitled "Culture at large: Partha Chatterjee meets his interlocutors."

Chatterjee is one of the founder members of the *Subaltern Studies* (SS) collective. It is the criticism of several Indian scholars that, from about the 4th or 5th volume of the *SS* series, the *SS* has begun to diverge from its original foci and to lose its coherence as its expanding body of authors moved in diffuse post-modernist directions.[5] So what we see today in 1996 is *Subaltern Studies* Mach 2.

There is, nevertheless, a strand of intellectual continuity that threads through both phases of the *SS* enterprise. One can gain access to this line of emphasis by focussing on a key text by the *guru* under whose feet the *SS* series was born, namely Ranajit Guha's brilliant *Elementary Aspects of Peasant Insurgency*.[6] This monograph is a people's history, one threaded by a populist Marxism with a Gramscian hue. It is a celebration of the counter-hegemonic capacities of

[3] Gyanendra Pandey, *The Construction of Communalism in Colonial North India*, Delhi 1992, p. 6.

[4] Jonathan Spencer (ed.), *Sri Lanka. History and the Roots of Conflict*, London 1990; P. Jeganathan and Ismail Qadri (eds.), *Unmaking the Nation*, Colombo 1995; David Scott, "Religion in Colonial Civil Society: Buddhism and Modernity in 19th Century Sri Lanka," *The Thatched Patio*, July/August 1994, p. 1–16.; J. Rogers, "Post-Orientalism".

[5] One of the clearest expositions of this view was conveyed to me in conversation by Neeladri Bhattacharya in Delhi in April 1995. I have also benefited from conversations with Nandini Gooptu. Sumit Sarkar, himself a *subalternist* at one stage, has essayed criticisms of the post-modernist trends in *subaltern studies*, mostly in Bengal publications but indirectly in an *EPPW* article (1993). For a telling rejoinder, see Chakrabarty 1995. Paradoxically, perhaps, Chakrabarty's comments on the emotions and aesthetics surrounding personhood and friendships in India (p. 753) have potential parallels with my attention in the latter half of this essay to the revulsions associated with distasteful habits of the communal "other".

[6] Ranajit Guha, *Elementary Aspects of Peasant Insurgency in Colonial India*, Delhi 1983.

the Indian underclasses of the 19th century, understood as peasants for the most part. It illustratively constitutes "the peasantry as a subject of history, endowed with its own distinctive forms of consciousness and ... acting upon the world in its own terms".[7] Therefore, to follow Chatterjee's recent summary, Guha proposes "a paradigmatic form of the peasant consciousness" and isolates "an invariant structural form" – which means that he "has not attempted to give us a history of this consciousness as a movement of self-transformation".[8]

Running alongside Guha's assault on elitist historians through his story of insurgent peasant assaults on those who lorded it over them is another theme: a scathing critique of the British colonial state. The anti-state emphasis has remained a central thread in subsequent *SS* work, whether in its Mach 1 or Mach 2 variants; and perhaps extends beyond the British order to the post-colonial state. It also runs through Gyan Pandey's set of essays assembled under the heading *The Construction of Communalism*.[9] As Nita Kumar observes, "Pandey's is essentially a negative exercise, showing up the negations of the colonial state".[10]

It is an attractive exercise. It caters to the anti-state individualism that is a *habitus* in the corridors of Western academia. It also dovetails neatly with the efflorescence of post-Orientalist writings in the last seven years or so, that is, with the political interventions which I outlined at the outset of this paper. To illustrate this further: "European imperialism," thunders David Ludden, "... invented the religious traditionalism that formed its ideological other in the orient," continuing with the further comment – "Most scholars of India today argue that communal conflict never was caused by the religions of Hinduism and Islam; many agree with Said

[7] Partha Chatterjee, *The Nation and its Fragments*. Princeton 1993, p. 160.

[8] *Ibid.*, p. 164. The richest illustrations of peasant insurgency in Guha's book come from the actions of 'tribal peasants', especially the Santals. Yet Guha uses the term 'tribal peasantry' only on occasions, buried deep in the book (e. g. page 170), and prefers to subsume them within the concept 'peasant'. (Note J. Tharamangalam, "Indian Peasant Uprisings: Myth and Reality," *Journal of Peasant Studies* 13, 1986, p. 116–34, and Dipanka Gupta, "On Altering the Ego in Peasant History: Paradoxes on the Ethnic Option," *Peasant Studies* 13, 1985, p. 5–24).

In his recent review Chatterjee argues that Guha shows how "the cultural apparatus of signs and meanings ... available to a peasant consciousness, far from being narrow and inflexible, is capable of a vast range of transformations to enable it to understand, and to act within, varying contexts, both of subordination and of resistance." Thus, Guha is deemed to have avoided the 'objectivisation' of peasant consciousness through reductions to "its determinate institutional form – tribe, caste, religious denomination, locality, whatever" (Chatterjee, *The Nation and its Fragments*, p. 164). This appears to be a benign reading. Cf. "Which of these two antagonisms – class or communal – prevailed and directed its overall character? The former beyond any doubt." (Guha, *Elementary Aspects*, p. 172) Note, also, Rosalind O'Hanlon's contention that in the figure of the subaltern may lie the idea of the autonomous individual that is so deeply embedded in Western philosophy (Rosalind O'Hanlon, "Recovering the Subject: *Subaltern Studies* and Histories of Resistance in Colonial South Asia," *Modern Asian Studies* 22, 1988, p. 189–224). I would also argue that the insistence on the autonomy of the peasantry by Guha is not sustainable; and contradicts the Marxist framework (in contrast Gyan Prakash, "Post-colonial Criticism and Indian Historiography," *Social Text* 31 (2), 1992, p. 8–19).

[9] Gyanendra Pandey, *The Construction of Communalism in Colonial North India*, Delhi 1992.

[10] Nita Kumar, "Review Essay," *Indian Economic and Social History Review* 29, 1992 p. 230–1.

and Pandey that as a historical and historiographic phenomenon, communalism is a product of orientalism and the colonial state".[11] In similar vein, when Jonathan Spencer introduces a set of essays on Sri Lanka, he argues that "the *roots* of the present understandings of ethnic identity [lie] in Victorian Orientalist scholarship".[12] Again, in what is a more specific and more nuanced study, Chatterjee notes that claims of the Hindutva type "become possible only within the modern forms of historiography, a historiography which is necessarily built around the complex identity of people-nation-state".[13]

There are various shades of emphasis in these post-Orientalist writings on the construction of communalism. It would be facile to pick on those prone to the excessive.[14] I would rather concentrate on certain underlying tendencies that require trimming. That is my project here. But first some caveats. Speaking broadly, I share the hostility evinced by the post-Orientalists to the extreme chauvinist claims of many contemporary nationalist ideologues. I acknowledge the useful insights into the processes of change in the 19th and 20th centuries which their work has generated. I salute their emphasis on the danger of reading the past into the present. What I do question, however, is the conversion of part-truths into whole truths, which, in their totalisations, obscure the capacities (however horrible) of the people we are seeking to depict.

In the first place the construction of communalism thesis is ruptured by a paradox. The intensity of its hostility to the state produces an exaggeration of the power of the British colonial order and a concomitant devaluation of the capabilities of the diverse colonial peoples. Indeed, there is a sense in which this thesis shapes up as a variant of the old modernisation thesis, albeit far removed – and this is an important distinction – from the cold-war politics of that intellectual strand. In making this criticism I do not wish to deny the significance of the transformations under the British – not least the unification of previously disparate polities through the development of road, rail and postal communications and the promotion of a new class of English educated functionaries.[15] The institutionalised practices of the British raj, not

[11] David Ludden, "Introduction. Ayodhya: A Window on the World," in: D. Ludden (ed.), *Contesting the Nation. Religion, Community and the Politics of Democracy in India*, Philadelphia 1996, p. 9, 11.

[12] Jonathan Spencer, "Introduction: the Power of the Past," in: J. Spencer (ed.), *Sri Lanka. History and the Roots of Conflict*, London 1990, p. 4 (emphasis mine).

[13] Partha Chatterjee, "Claims on the Past: the Genealogy of Modern Historiography in Bengal," *Subaltern Studies VIII* (ed. by David Arnold and David Hardiman), Delhi 1994, p. 2.

[14] E. g. Bryan Pfaffenberger, "Introduction: the Sri Lanka Tamils," in: C. Manogaran and B. Pfaffenberger (eds.), *The Sri Lanka Tamils*, Boulder 1994, p. 1–27; M. Roberts, "Nationalism, Past and Present: the Case of Sri Lanka," *Ethnic and Racial Studies* 16, 1993, p. 141–52.

[15] A process highlighted in the older histories and rather taken for granted in some post-Orientalist essays e. g. D. Ludden, "Introduction. Ayodhya," in: Carol Breckenridge and Peter van der Veer (eds.), *Orientalism and the Post-colonial Predicament: Perspectives on South Asia*, Philadelphia 1993.

least that of the law courts,[16] have been of critical importance in moulding contemporary ways of seeing and being.

But such a line of argument should not be permitted to overemphasise the extent of the transformation; and to underestimate the manner in which pre-colonial and pre-capitalist tendencies managed to nestle powerfully amidst the rationalities and contradictions of the new order. An outstanding instance would be the non-market principle which Walter C. Neale has called "land to rule"[17] and G. Obeyesekere "the ideology of status".[18] It is my contention, therefore, that we need to attend to the ways in which indigenous forms of thought and indigenous categories shaped the thinking of the British.[19] I am not alluding, here, only to the notorious brahmanical influence on the British views of caste.[20] I demand that scholars attend to the possibility that indigenous labels distinguishing the various communities provided the foundation for the British categories. That the British gave these a greater systematicity, and located them within an either/or epistemology,[21] thereby endeavouring to have all things cut and dried, is indubitable. But where did the categories come from? What meanings did they carry before, and during, the British ordering? And didn't *some* of the pre-existing labels have a relational precision of difference from an identified Other? Illustratively put, I am asking for answers to specific questions: did, for instance, the stereotype of the Marathas as a martial people which took root among the British develop solely from orientalising procedures and British readings of their initial military confrontations? Or did the Marathas already have this self-image of themselves and insinuate that image into the British cosmos, both unintentionally and intentionally, through life style and rhetoric?

This brings me to my second point: a methodological weakness in the literature. Most of the post-Orientalist scholars, like me, are specialists in 19th and 20th centuries as fields of work.[22] They have limited knowledge of the pre-British period. But a reasonably comprehensive understanding of the cultural apparatus of the various sub-continental regions in the early

16 Rather underplayed in the literature; cf. M. Roberts et al., *People Inbetween*, Ratmalana 1989, p. 57–8.

17 Walter C. Neale, "Land to rule," in: R. E. Frykenberg (ed.), *Land Control and Social Structure in Indian History*, Madison 1969, p. 3–15.

18 Gananath Obeyesekere, *Land Tenure in Village Ceylon*, Cambridge 1967.

19 For instance, note the manner in which the *cakravarti* style of patronage and leadership, conceptualised as the Asokan Persona by the analyst, appears to have informed modern politics in Sri Lanka (M. Roberts, *Exploring Confrontation,* Reading 1994, ch. 2–5).

20 E. g. Nicholas Dirks, "The Invention of Caste: Civil Society in Colonial India," *Social Analysis* 25, 1989, p. 44–8.

21 Cf. M. Roberts, *Exploring Confrontation,* p. 38, 71.

22 For Sri Lanka, important exceptions are H. L. Seneviratne, G. Obeyesekere and J. S. Walters. R. A. L. H. Gunawardana and C. R. de Silva should also be added to the list *now* – but note that Gunawardana's seminal essay on "People of the Lion" was written in the late 1970ies before the proliferation of post-Orientalist literature.

18th century-and-before (and for the Sri Lankan littoral in the early 16th century-and-before), is a prerequisite for our understanding of the transformations which the British instituted. Without such a baseline, or, rather, without a series of regional baselines, one's quests become doubly speculative.

This shortcoming is compounded by yet another methodological weakness in the post-Orientalist literature: the over-reliance on printed texts and a relative neglect of palm-leaf texts, oral sources and visual evidence from painting and sculpture. I am not unaware that Pandey and some of the *subalternists* do attend to such sources on occasions. However, for the issues which I have raised such material can be central; and one can fairly claim that the post-Orientalists have been inattentive to the sedimentation of history in contemporary rituals[23] and the sort of yield which the researches of a Richard Young are extracting from palm-leaf texts.[24] Indeed, Nita Kumar complains that the indigenous sources that Pandey taps are "almost all confined to political ones." This, she says, is because India's "rich English-language holdings of administrative records, periodicals and private papers [encourage scholars to concentrate on] a study of nationalist thought;" and results in the relative neglect of endeavours to refigure what the people's "everyday life and values-in action" may have been like.[25]

In brief, it is my charge that the post-Orientalists underweigh the force of oral exchanges in street, marketplace and family compound. In my speculation these exchanges, in turn, *would have been* embedded, as they are today, in a whole range of practices pertaining to cuisine, bodily inscription, coiffeur, dress and domestic architectural preferences which served to differentiate Muslim *turuks*, Vaishnavaites and Saivites in the Hindi-speaking belt, Muslims, Saktas and Vaishnavaites in the Bengali region; and *Damilas, Yon* (Muslims),and *Sinhalas* in pre-Portuguese Sri Lanka (while operating amidst markers of caste distinction).

It is a standard reasoning among the post-Orientalists that the pre-colonial cultural identities were "not political"; and that the conception of community in those epochs[26] were "fuzzy" –

[23] This is an emphasis which I have gathered from Bruce Kapferer, who drummed this point into my ears over the years, on the foundations provided by his work on *tovil* ceremonies in Sri Lanka. For other illustrations, see G. Obeyesekere, *The Cult of the Goddess Pattini*, Delhi 1987, and note, too, Obeyesekere's use of 20th century folklore for historical reconstruction in his 1989 essay (G. Obeyesekere, "The Myth of Human Sacrifice: History, Story and Debate in a Buddhist Chronicle," *Social Analysis* 25, 1989, p. 78–93).

[24] Richard Young, "The Carpenter-preta: An Eighteenth-century Sinhala Buddhist Folktale About Jesus," *Asian Folklore Studies* 54, 1995, p. 49–68; id., "Imagined Beleaguerment and the Self-representation of Mohottivatte Gunananda," in: M. Roberts (ed.), *Collective Identities Revisited*, vol. 1, Colombo 1997, ch. 6.

[25] Nita Kumar, "Review Essay", p. 230.

[26] The term "epoch" is favoured by the *subalternists*, entering Pandey's writing (*The Construction of Communalism,* p. 15) as well as Kaviraj's (Sudipta Kaviraj, "The Imaginary Institution of India," *Subaltern Studies VII*, ed. by P. Chatterjee and G. Pandey, Delhi 1992, p. 1–39). It would appear to bear a more powerful import than, say, the manner in which I use the terms "era" and "period." It seems that the Foucaultian stress on "rupture" has been merged with both *kalpic* and Marxist strands of thinking.

having no territorial basis, no maps and no enumerated cosmos.[27] This contention is often linked to the argument that, even where Muslim-'Hindu' animosity was displayed in northern India in pre-British times, the sentiments were highly localised in their implications.[28] In this view "sharply-defined identities and animosities across large expanses of space had relatively little chance of development".[29] In some versions the pre-British period appears bathed in the roseate glow of inter-communal harmony and widespread syncretism.[30]

A rethinking is called for. A rethink after investigating the classificatory procedures and everyday practices in the pre-colonial states. These investigations, of course, must also be attentive to the syncretist practices, boundary crossings and pluralisms of that era, while also being alive to the force of caste differentiation. The central contention to be kept in mind here is that the existence of cosmopolitan milieus and vibrant cultural exchanges does not *necessarily* preclude a sharpened understanding of difference.

In making these suggestions I am also arguing that scholars must break free from their near-total reliance on printed texts and explore the possibilities, however fragmentary, provided by a number of visual sources. Such data can be leavened by the clues and possibilities opened up by the traces of historical images in 20th century folklore and ritual practice as well as the pointers provided by 20th century differentiation in domestic architecture, cuisine, dress, bodily demeanour and body inscription. Influenced, here, by Deane Fergie's emphasis on the significance of domestic spatial practices I provide an illustration of the sort of pointers that arise from present-day world of architectural arrangements: Arthur Saniotis found that some Muslims in Nizamudeen *basti* in the city of Delhi had clear preferences regarding the direction of the front of their house and the direction of their squat toilet – the dos and don'ts being governed by the directional location of the *Ka'ba* at Mecca; while my memories from the town of Galle mark the disposition among the Muslims to whitewash their houses in shades of bilious blue, green or pink – a preference that was not in tune with the upper class aesthetic to which I was party and thereby earned disparaging remarks (e. g. in the local argot, "*seeni bola* colours").[31] In sum, then, this article is a clarion call for social historians of pre-British India and Sri Lanka to be armed with the sensibilities of a Pierre Bourdieu and Michel Certeau.

27 Kaviraj "The Imaginary Institution", p. 20–6, n. 3; Pandey, *The Construction of Communalism*, 158–9.

28 This is the thrust of Pandey's seminal work (Pandey, *The Construction of Communalism*, esp. p. 158–9, 198–200). For an express, albeit brief, questioning of this point, see Peter van der Veer, *Religious Nationalism. Hindus and Muslims in India*, Berkeley 1994, p. 92. Also see Shahshi Joshi and Bhagwan Jhoshi, *Struggle for Hegemony in India 1920–47*, vol. 3, New Delhi 1994, p. 347–51, and Sudhir Kakar, *The Colors of Violence*, Chicago 1996, p. 14–20.

29 Tapan Basu et al., *Khaki Shorts and Saffron Flags*, New Delhi 1993, p. 3.

30 To judge from the summary, perhaps overdone, in S. Kakar, *The Colors of Violence*, p. 14–20.

31 Fergie's suggestions were presented at the Anthropology Seminar, University of Adelaide, April 27, 1998. Saniotis is a postgraduate student at the University of Adelaide.

II

> "One thing is certain, no foreign foe be it English, Dutch, French or Kaffir will conquer Lanka. Through the protection of the four gods, the Guardians of its Religion, and the merits of the King, for five thousand years no foe will continue to reside here …"[32]

III

> When collecting visual evidence recently on "communal riots" in contemporary India I was shown a photograph of a few uncapped men, with their hands up, as prisoners of armed members of the provincial constabulary. I sought details from the man who had been behind the camera. Said Praveen Jain: "These are Muslims in Meerut." Said the ignorant outsider: "How do you know they are Muslims?" Answer: "Because of their sarongs" – the style of their sarong, that is, the *lungi* as distinct from the Hindu's *dhoti*. Any North Indian would have known this.
>
> Local knowledge

IV

The two epigrams which I have inserted at this point are intended to highlight and initiate the rethinking that I have called for. Here, I forego the stronger case, the Sinhalese one, where my initial questionings of the post-Orientalist thesis have been bolstered at the ethnographic level by a recent article by Obeyesekere,[33] for the terrain in which my expertise is negligible: namely, the Indian scene evoked in the conversation with Praveen Jain, a photographer attached to one of India's national newspapers. I shall initially qualify and embellish Jain's reading. When he read the men in his frame to be Muslims, I suspect that Jain was guided not only by their *lungis*, but also by their beards and facial features as well as the temporal and spatial field of interaction framing his photographic act. Secondly, let me note, on the basis of casual conversations with those who have lived in northern India, that Hindus today also wear the *lungi* – at

[32] An extract from a letter sent in 1811 from the Kandyan court to the British Governor in Colombo (see encl. in Wilson to Liverpool, 26th February 1812, Col Office 54/42 in Public Record Office).

[33] M. Roberts, "Sri Lanka: Ethnic Conflict and Political Crisis. A Review Article," *Ethnic Studies Report* 6, 1988, p. 44–5 and id. "Nationalism, Past and Present: the Case of Sri Lanka," *Ethnic and Racial Studies* 16, 1993, p. 141–52; G. Obeyesekere, "Buddhism, Nationhood, and Cultural Identity: A Question of Fundamentals," in: M. E. Marty and R. S. Appleby (eds.), *Fundamentalism Comprehended*, Chicago 1995, p. 232–44.

least in some localities. But there can be further nuances: when I asked Prabhu Mohapatra whether Hindus in his home region of Orissa wore the *lungi*, he answered in the affirmative – adding "but they wear it tied from the right side, whereas Muslims tie it from the left."[34]

These are contemporary boundary markers, arguably outcomes of the processes that the post-Orientalists have delineated. But are we sure of this? Did the *turuks*, the Muslims, in the pre-British period wear *dhotis* at all? and conversely did non-Muslims – whom I shall designate "Whatevers"[35] – in some localities wear *lungis* on occasions?

We must add more questions. When Muslims, Vaishnavites and Saivites worshipped at Sufi shrines (at the same moment?),[36] what did the worship mean to each set of adherents? And did Muslims of orthodox persuasions ever visit a 'Hindu' temple?[37] Surely not. And alternatively did the Whatevers, being so syncretistic, enter mosques? Or, more to the point in Muslim-dominated kingdoms, were they permitted to enter mosques?

Again, were 17th century Whatevers not aware that the *turuks* who resided in their midst (i. e. most of them) were invaders by origin? And that these *turuk* Muslims looked down upon them, the Whatevers agglomerated, as '*kāfirs*'? Even the briefest of excursions into pre-British Indian history is sufficient to emphasise hostilities and conflictual moments mingling with ac-

34 My memory may have got the right-left the wrong way round, but that's not the point.

35 This artifice is borrowed from Obeyesekere (Obeyesekere, "Buddhism, Nationhood, and Cultural Identity"). Like the quotation marks bracketing the term 'Hindu', it is an effort to recognise the fact that the category *Hindu* may not have carried the contemporary meaning in medieval and early modern times. Thus, it is claimed that in the 16th and 17th centuries Hindu was used by European and other visitors to India to refer to all natives of India – in the sense "Gentoo" (Frykenberg, "Constructions of Hinduism," p. 524–5). It is presumably this ambiguity that has guided post-Orientalist writings of Pandey, Ludden and others. The work by Alam, Wagle and Talbot referred to later in the text suggests that, whatever its political correctness, the ethnographic foundations for this claim can be questioned. The simple step of consulting *Hobson-Jobson* also indicated that as early as 1290 a Persian writer distinguished between "the *Musalmans* who were *Hindis* (country born)" and the *Hindu*(*s*); while, much later, in 1563 a Portuguese writer differentiated the Moors (*Mosalman*) from the Gentoos (*Indu*).

36 This is one of the most favoured illustrations utilised by those who contend that religious syncretism and pluralism were a marked feature of Indian ways of life and that religious strife was muted in the pre-British era (see Kakar's summary in *The Colors of Violence*, p. 14–20). Much earlier, Paul Brass also attached weight to these alleged commonalities as part of his transactionalist interpretation of the rise of Muslim demands for a separate state in northern India (P. Brass, *Language, Religion and Politics in North India*, Cambridge 1974). Likewise, the literature on Sri Lanka has attempted to combat contemporary nationalist extremisms by stressing the degree of commingling in pre-colonial times (e. g. B. Pfaffenberger, "Introduction ...," p. 2–4; R. A. L. H. Gunawardana, "The People of the Lion: the Sinhala Identity and Ideology in History and Historiography," in: J. Spencer (ed.), *Sri Lanka. History and the Roots of Conflict*, London 1990, p. 65–9; Stanley J. Tambiah, *Buddhism Betrayed?* Chicago 1992, p. 139–70). Tambiah's work provides the most sophisticated and qualified version of this line of reasoning, but is not attentive to oral traditions (e. g. M. Roberts, "A Tale of Resistance: the Story of the Arrival of the Portuguese in Sri Lanka," *Ethnos* 55, 1989, p. 65–82; G. Obeyesekere, "Buddhism, Nationhood, and Cultural Identity ...," p. 237–8). Readers should, therefore, refer to Obeyesekere, "Buddhism, Nationhood, and Cultural Identity" and Roberts, "Nationalism, Past and Present," p. 134–52, for other perspectives.

37 Again, the word 'Hindu' is bracketed by connotation marks to recognise that it may have carried a different connotation, see fn. 35 above.

commodations. Muzaffar Alam has found that in medieval North India the "average literate Muslim believed that Islam and Hinduism belonged to two radically diverse traditions" of an irreconcilable sort.[38] Cynthia Talbot's researches on medieval Andhra led to the conclusion that the "Muslim warriors of Turkic origin who invaded and settled in peninsular India were certainly a separate ethnic group, comprising their own social unit and possessing their own culture" – to the extent that there was "a sharp delineation between Muslim and non-Muslim in discourse".[39] Again, the 16th century Marathi *bhakti* poet Eknath incorporated a polemical debate between a Turk (i. e. *turak*) and a Hindu (*hinduku*), in which the Turak refers to the Hinduku as '*kāfir*', a debate which the poet deploys as a preamble to a reconciliatory move; while an 18th century Muslim poet highlights the mutual hostility to "the doings of the Yavanas" and "the ways of the Maharashtra *dharma*" expressed by the respective camps.[40] While Wagle speaks of "a symbiotic relationship" between the two traditions, he is careful to note that this "does not preclude social tensions"[41] – both comments which cry out for greater elaboration.

A review of the ethnographic material, in all the pertinent regions of India, should extend to valued daily practices of a commensal character on the one hand, and the body, its putative attributes and its manifestations on the other. Sudhir Kakar has recently indicated that those attached to 'Hindu' norms would have been disgusted by the Muslims' eating of beef.[42] To this one can inquire how those nurtured towards the principle of brotherhood through the commensal act of eating rice and other food from the same (large) dish during significant communal gatherings, namely many a Muslim, would have looked upon the commensal restrictions and caste taboos of those who followed Siva and Vishnu. In addition one must explore the possibility that the Muslims of that era have, like some Muslims today, been horrified by the Hindu practice of cremation, an antipathy directed by the belief that the spirits of those so interned could not conceiveably sleep in peace and would haunt the neighbourhood.[43]

This sets the stage for the final and critical question I would direct at those who downplay the force of difference between Muslim and Other during the pre-British period: were the Whatevers not aware that the *turuk* men (that is, those born into the fold as distinct from adults

38 Quoted in Kakar, *The Colors of Violence*, p. 17.

39 Cynthia Talbot, "Inscribing the Other, Inscribing the Self: Hindu-Muslim Identities in Pre-colonial India," *Comparative Studies in Society and History* 37, 1995, p. 720.

40 N. K. Wagle, "Hindu-Muslim Interactions in Medieval Maharashtra," in: G. D. Sontheimer and H. Kulke (eds.), *Hinduism Reconsidered*, Delhi 1991, p. 51.

41 *Ibid.*

42 S. Kakar, *The Colors of Violence*, p. 21–3.

43 Information provided by H. M. Z. Farouque, who indicated that the Sunni Muslims understood their commensal act to be based on the Prophet's practice – the *Sunna* as laid down in the *hadith*; and by Arthur Saniotis, on the basis of his ethnographic researches among the Sufis of Nizamudeen *basti* in Delhi.

and teenagers who had been converted?) were circumcised? Indeed, how can boundaries be fuzzy when one lot (from the dominant gender) are circumcised?

Today, Muslims in the Hindi-speaking regions are subject to the epithet '*katua*' and in West Bengal to the pejorative '*nyära*' or '*nere*', while the demagogues of the RSS-VHP-BJP combine denigrate them from the public platform in similar fashion – using words which were translated as 'foreshortened ones' and 'eunuchs' in Anand Patwardhan's anti-communalist and anti-patriarchal documentary *Father, Son and Holy War* (1994). The question, then, is whether such epithets were occasionally deployed during face-to-face exchanges, either in banter or as abuse,[44] during the pre-British era?

I attend to the latter by raising tentative suggestions regarding the etymological history of the epithet '*nere*' in Bengal – in a preliminary move demanding further investigation by specialists in Bengali history and culture. From casual conversations with Bengali speakers I gather that this pejorative has its disparaging power compounded by the phonetic overlaps with the term "*lere*" or "*lele*," which refers to the male genitalia and gathers further searing power from the description of hairless street dogs as *lere kutta*.[45] The literal meaning of *nere*, however, is "shaven head." The latter meaning, it is said, resulted in its usage in the past to describe Buddhists. The implication in these conversations is that in the distant past *nere* (*lere*) was a disparaging epithet utilised by Bengali-speaking 'Hindus' to refer to Buddhists – possibly assisted by the fact that in late 'medieval' times this more egalitarian religious tradition was favoured by elements drawn from the so-called 'untouchable castes'.[46]

Though Muslim traders were known to the inhabitants of the Bengal delta from the 10th century at the very least, the partial Islamisation of Bengal dates from the late 16th and early 17th centuries. This process was partly a product of the outreach of Mughal power and partly due to the initiative of Muslim holy men who organised the taming of the forest and the extension of cultivation.[47] By the 16th century Buddhism appears to have been long extinct in Bengal, but it would appear that some sediments remained – not least the epithet *nere*. It was feasible for the dominant elements in Bengali society, notably the Saktas and the upper castes, to extend the term to Muslims – especially because many of the converts to Islam in East Bengal were

44 For illustrations of the occasions and contexts when such banter and abuse occur, see my analysis of Sinhala epithets directed at the various colonial rulers and those seen to be their descendants, in "Pejorative phrases: the anti-colonial response and Sinhala perceptions of the self through images of the Burghers" (ch. 1 of M. Roberts et al., *People Inbetween*).

45 Note from Dilip Basu, 26th February 1998.

46 Richard Eaton is convinced that the contemporary Bengali view that the so-called lower castes "provided a disproportionate number of new Muslims converts is another stereotype, and a false one at that" (Letter, 9th September 1997). Basu is equally certain that this claim has validity as a generalisation. Based on analogues elsewhere and for structural reasons I favour the latter opinion.

47 Richard M. Eaton, *The Rise of Islam and the Bengal Frontier, 1204–1760*, Berkeley 1993, p. 226–7 and ch. 7.

believed to have been Buddhists and/or of lower caste.[48] This extension was facilitated because, as expressed in a flash of inspiration by Dilip Basu during one of our dialogues, the "shaven head"/bald head of the Buddhist monk, as outstanding synecdochic marker of the religious Other, could as readily be transferred to the bald head of the Muslim man's penis.[49]

To present such speculative theories on the basis of fragmentary data and popular representations in contemporary times, of course, will offend those attached to political correctness and/or rigid empiricism.[50] But I have learnt over the years to value the sedimentation of history in oral stories and popular traditions. Disparaging epithets are a form of power. Indeed, the wielding of the slur *nere* (or *nyära* or *lere*) in late 20th century Bengal has always been understood by Gautam Ghosh to mean "we upper caste/class Hindus know who you really are: low caste Hindus, even untouchables, you can't fool us with this 'I'm Muslim' crap."[51] Thus, I trust that enough has been said in this explanatory paper to persuade specialists in Indian history in the pre-British period that one must attend to the everyday practices associated with domestic arrangements, the body, coiffeur, cuisine and commensality as well as the force of oral exchanges when charting the history of socio-political differentiation. With resort to such resources printed texts derive a hegemony that is in tune with the modernist world view of the analysts evaluating their weight.

V

Epithets usually require an amenable political arena, whether the institutionalised freedom of speech or the political dominance of those mouthing the epithets or the political weakness of those at the butt-end of the denigration. In Sri Lanka in the mid-late 20th century the minority Muslim community (six to seven per cent) have been teased and abused as 'tip-cut' or '*tun kalai*' by individuals from the other communities. But it is extremely unlikely that any Sri Lankan migrant workers in the Gulf states today would hurl such an epithet at an Omani or a Kuwaiti. They could, however, use such language in the closed circle of their ethnic networks. My point here is obvious: ethnic epithets not only differentiate, they help create a community of 'speakers' – whether those laughing derisively together as the Other is rubbished; or those suffering

48 Note from Gautam Ghosh, 6th February 1998.

49 This suggestion emerged as exclamatory ejaculation ...!!... in the course of a dialogic conversation at a restaurant in Santa Cruz.

50 It is from an empiricist position that Eaton finds several of my suggestions "too speculative" and "too conjectural". On similar ground he inquires "How do you know that these *turuk* men had been circumcized?" (Letter, 9th September 1997). I still don't, but consider it a reasonable speculation.

51 Note, 6th February 1998. Ghosh, it should be noted, presented this as an ethnographic understanding and a perspective to which he was hostile.

the same forms of denigration. It will not be easy for anyone to convince me that such words as *katua, nere* and *tun kalai* are Orientalist inventions. Tip cut, of course, is a product of the range of foreshortened cut and thrust, crisp speech, which the English language provides. But, in my speculation, it has arisen from a field already furrowed out by such terms as *tun kalai* and *katua* more than the earnest researches of Indologists working on Pali and Sanskrit texts or the administrative operations of the British Raj.

Cross-Border Migrations in South Asia and Regional Security

Partha S. Ghosh*

1. Introduction

The history of movements of people from one place to another is as old as the human civilisation. It was as much a natural phenomenon as birds nesting from tree to tree or animals demarcating their territories from place to place. The problem of international migration which we hear so often about nowadays was unheard of then. Even after the creation of the modern nation state in the 18th and 19th centuries with their defined borders people continued to move from one country to another as a matter of course. Since there was hardly any organised protest from the host countries the question of refugees or migrants did not arise.

In the 19th and early 20th centuries millions of Europeans moved to the Americas, Australia, New Zealand and South Africa. Between 1846 and 1890, on an average 377,000 Europeans emigrated per annum. Soon the phenomenon picked up momentum and between 1891 and 1910 it touched 911,000 a year. To be sure between 1846 and 1930, over 50 million people of Europe left their homes to settle outside their continent.[1] The problem of integration of the migrants into the host societies started only when the ethnic questions became politically exploitable and the modern developments made the possibility of social assimilation more difficult. The developmental logic legitimised organised human endeavours to tame nature for the unrestricted exploitation by man which naturally made the conflicts over resources more acute. In such situations scapegoating of "aliens" for one's economic hardships was inevitable. The anti-Japanese sentiments that pervaded the west coast of the United States in the late 19th century, known as the "yellow peril", was one of the examples.

* It is an honour for me to participate in this Festschrift to felicitate Prof. Dietmar Rothermund. It was he who introduced me to South Asian studies by recommending my name for a Humboldt Fellowship in 1984. Ever since I have not looked back and written extensively on South Asian affairs.

1 Paul Kennedy, *Preparing for the Twenty-First Century*, New York 1993, p. 42.

In recent times, South Asia has been one region where the problem of cross-border migrations has been massive. Ever since the partition of the Indian subcontinent in 1947 about 35 million people have been involved in cross-border movements in search of security of life, honour and property, or for protection from religious and other kinds of persecution, or to avoid strives and wars, or for work and food, or by drives towards ethnic, racial, ideological or religious homogenisation.[2] To complicate matters, there have been problems of international terrorism to which is connected the question of drug and gun trafficking. Together, all these movements of people have caused complications for inter-state politics and thwarted regional cooperation. In this paper an attempt has been made to address the issue from the perspective of regional security.

2. The Security Connection

In South Asia the issues of cross-border migrations and regional security have both causational and consequential linkages. But before this inter-meshing is analysed a brief note on the centrality factor of India in South Asian politics would be in order.

From time immemorial India has been an attractive destination for all kinds of people ranging from travellers to looters, warriors to adventurers. Even the Aryans are known to have come from outside. No wonder that the theme caught the imagination of the great Bengali poet Rabindranath Tagore who underlined this unbounded hospitality of India in his celebrated poem "Bharat-Tirtha" (in Bengali, meaning Pilgrimage India). The translation of a stanza from the poem which I have ventured here would read:

No one knows to whose clarion call
Peoples responded and came
In gushing streams
And got merged into the ocean?
Hither came the Aryans, the Barbarians,
The Dravidians, the Chinese, the Sakas,
The Huns, the Pathans, the Mughals
To merge into one body and soul.
Today, doors to the West are open
New ideas are flowing
Incessant givings and receivings

[2] For a brief analysis of the types of migrants and their estimated number, see Partha S. Ghosh, "Population Movements and Interstate Conflicts in South Asia," *Environment and Conflicts Project Occasional Paper* (Center for Security Studies and Conflict Research, Zürich, and Swiss Peace Foundation, Bern), No. 14, September 1995.

Meetings and mixings are on
They will not return
From this supreme ocean of Humanity
That is India.

The phenomenon did not stop ever. Even after the partition it continued although the partition itself was an anathema to the phenomenon. The subsequent second partition which saw the creation of Bangladesh encouraged the process further. The difference between the earlier experience and the post-independence one was that while during the earlier phases the immigrants were from outside the South Asian region[3] the later ones were from within the region with some minor exceptions. Indeed this was to some extent inevitable because the geographical limits of India themselves got truncated with the coming of independence.

In almost all the cases of cross-border migrations India happens to be the common denominator. While this is essentially on account of its geographical location, the ethno-linguistic plurality of India also contributes to it. It would be instructive here to underline the fact that out of the 25 states that constitute the Indian Union 17 have international borders, namely, Arunachal Pradesh, Assam, Bihar, Gujarat, Himachal Pradesh, Jammu and Kashmir, Manipur, Meghalaya, Mizoram, Nagaland, Panjab, Rajasthan, Sikkim, Tamil Nadu, Tripura, Uttar Pra-

Table
Indicators of Regional Hegemony: Leading Country Shares of Regional Aggregates (%)

	South Asia	Middle East		Latin America			Africa		Southeast Asia*		
Aggregates	India	Iran	Egypt	Brazil	Mexico	Argentina	Nigeria	S. Africa	Indonesia	Philippines	Thailand
GNP	79.4	34.7	7.6	35.7	19.4	12.0	16.4	23.0	30.3	21.0	18.4
Population	75.7	30.0	31.7	33.7	18.6	8.2	17.8	7.0	42.5	13.0	12.9
Armed Forces	67.9	22.8	23.7	35.1	7.3	12.3	26.9	5.0	15.6	7.0	13.5
Military expenditures	81.2	40.5	7.0	38.6	17.3	13.5	22.9	32.5	28.4	11.0	10.7
Installed energy	86.7	42.4	27.5	35.0	19.8	16.6	3.4	56.0	10.8	29.7	24.6
World trade (exports and imports)	63.0	28.3	4.8	32.0	13.3	15.0	21.0	19.0	26.1	13.2	12.4

* Vietnam commands 38.5% of the armed forces in the area. In addition to Indonesia, the Philippines, and Thailand, this group includes Malaysia, Vietnam, Myanmar, Cambodia, Laos and Singapore.

Source: Lloyd I. Rudolph and Susanne Hoeber Rudolph, *In Pursuit of Lakshmi: The Political Economy of the Indian State*, Chicago 1987, p. 5.

[3] South Asia here connotes the members of the South Asian Association for Regional Cooperation (SAARC), namely, Bangladesh, Bhutan, India, the Maldives, Nepal, Pakistan and Sri Lanka.

desh, and West Bengal. The states which do not have international borders are only Andhra Pradesh, Goa, Haryana, Karnataka, Kerala, Madhya Pradesh, Maharashtra and Orissa.

Besides the geographical factor there is another reason of assigning primacy to India in our discussion and that is India's power in the South Asian regional balance. India accounts for three-fourths of the region's area, population, GNP, etc. No other region compares in similar fashion where one country has so much of preeminence *vis-à-vis* the other regional constituents (see table).

3. Migration-Foreign Policy Interface

Security is a complex construct. It is no longer viewed narrowly in only military terms. All kinds of threats including environmental, demographic, ecological, economic, etc., have become the parts and parcels of security analysis. According to Ullman:

> A threat to national security is an action or sequence of events that: 1) threatens drastically and even over a relatively brief span of time to degrade the quality of life for inhabitants of a state, or 2) threatens significantly to narrow the range of policy choices available to the government of a state or to private non-governmental entities (persons, groups, corporations) within a state.[4]

For our purposes here the most important point in the above definition is the phrase "a relatively brief span of time". When non-military threats cannot be visualised in terms of a specific time-frame, as for example the depletion of the ozone layer, global climatic changes, population growth, etc., the states cannot respond to them in clear-cut foreign policy terms. But there are aspects of non-military threats which can both be seen as impacting foreseeable national interests as well as requiring identifiable foreign policy responses. The problem of cross-border migrations falls in this domain.

Throughout history migrations and foreign policy have close connections. Of late, these connections seem, to have become more manifest. The reunification of Germany provides the best example. In July and August 1989 there was an exodus of East Germans to Austria through Czechoslovakia and Hungary. It precipitated the opening of East Germany's Western borders leading to massive migration to West Germany. All these led to the collapse of East Germany and its absorption by the West. "It was flight, not an invasion, that ultimately destroyed the East German state."[5]

4 Richard H. Ullman, "Redefining Security," *International Security* 8 (1), 1983, p. 129–53.

5 Myron Weiner, "Security, Stability, and International Migration", *International Security* 17 (3), 1992/93, p. 91.

4. The South Asian Experience

In South Asia there are several instances when the movements of people and foreign policy have found interesting correlationships. The phenomenon does not only give the sending states a potential handle to indulge in espionage and other kinds of covert activities in the host countries, the presence of the immigrants and refugees leads in due course to the politicisation of the issue resulting in ethnic and religious conflicts which vitiate the bilateral and multilateral relations. Drugs, guns and international terrorism coupled with the growing danger of corruption and criminalisation of politics which is the bane in the entire region[6] convert this volatile mix into a witch's brew to which the South Asian nations get sucked in.

In South Asia the host countries generally have exploited the issue of migrations to their political advantage. During the Bangladesh crisis the presence of millions of East Pakistani refugees had not only helped India to launch an international campaign against the military rulers of Pakistan for their failure to respect the human and democratic rights of the East Pakistanis but it also had provided New Delhi with the opportunity of training a section of the refugees to join the anti-Pakistan war on behalf of the Mukti Bahini. India perceived the problem from a demographic angel also. It believed that behind this refugee flow was the calculated design of the Pakistani military to push millions of East Pakistanis, mostly Hindus, to India so as to neutralise the numerical advantage of East Pakistan *vis-à-vis* the western wing.[7]

In the eighties, India once again took advantage of the presence of thousands of Sri Lankan Tamil refugees in Tamil Nadu to impart military training to a section of them so as to enable them to wage a war against the Sri Lankan state.[8] That some of these trained militants eventually became an albatross hung around India's neck which the latter is still struggling to extricate itself from merely underscores the security dimensions of the refugee problem.

Pakistan has a similar experience *vis-à-vis* the Afghan refugees. Their arrival proved to be a boon in disguise to then rulers of Pakistan. Through them Zia ul-Haq bargained with the United States a new lease of his political life besides huge amounts of arms and economic aid. Not before long it resulted in the perilous nexus between the multi-million dollar illegal trade in narcotics and arms on the one hand and the massive corruption in the politico-military-bureaucratic establishment on the other. It not only marred Pakistan's political development se-

6 According to a survey of 54 economies conducted by the Washington-based Transparency International there are 26 countries which are most corrupt in the world of which 10 are in Asia. Of these 10, four are from South Asia, including Bangladesh, India and Pakistan. *Times of India* (New Delhi), 4th October 1996.

7 Weiner, "Security, Stability, and International Migration," p. 123.

8 K. M. de Silva, *Regional Powers and Small State Security: India and Sri Lanka, 1971–90*, Washington D. C. 1995, p. 160–1.

verely, it also dragged Pakistan into the vortex of the inter-ethnic conflicts of Afghanistan from which it would find difficult to rid itself of. The more the Afghan situation would be murky the greater would be Pakistan's problems with its North West Frontier Province which has the same ethnic complexion as the couple of the major warring factions engaged in the Afghan civil war have. These developments inevitably would cast their shadow on the India-Pakistan-Iran relations causing further complications for South Asian regional security.

5. Recent Developments

In recent years India-Pakistan relations have deteriorated by mutual allegations of interference in each others ethnic and subnational conflicts. A significant proportion of the millions of dollars of arms that were pumped into the south-western region after the Afghan war has found its way into the trouble-torn state of Jammu and Kashmir where a "fifth column" is ever present to raise the banner of revolt against the Indian state. The intensification of the civil war in Afghanistan in the aftermath of the Geneva Accord (1988) complicated the scenario. The part played by Pakistan's ISI-trained infiltrators belonging to some Muslim nations, most importantly Afghanistan, added a new dimension of Islamic fundamentalism to Kashmir's politics hitherto largely unknown to the state's composite Hindu-Muslim culture. The danger inherent in the situation was brought into sharp focus in 1995 when the centuries-old shrine of Charar-e-Sharif, revered by both Muslims and Hindus, was burnt in the cross-fire between the militants led by the Sunni Afghan militant leader Mast Gul and the security forces.

The fall of Kabul to the ISI-trained Taliban militia added a new dimension to the insurgency in Kashmir. It was feared by the Indian authorities that emboldened by their success in Afghanistan the Taliban might send their mercenary guerrillas to the Kashmir valley to bolster Islamic fundamentalism there. That the apprehension was not unfounded was proved by the fact that in 1996, of the 476 foreign mercenaries arrested or killed in the valley 136 were Afghan nationals.[9] Indian army officers involved in encounters with the Afghan mercenaries have testified to their brutalities and valour.[10]

The Taliban victory has resulted in some refugee problem for India. Hindu and Sikh settlers in Afghanistan particularly felt threatened and left for India. One of the members of the first group of 80 such refugees that arrived at the Rajasansi airport in Panjab on 17th October 1996 said: "It is not just that we are required to go out in a burqua. The general atmosphere of fear

[9] Government of India, Ministry of Home Affairs, *Annual Report 1996–97*, New Delhi 1997, p. 108.

[10] *Times of India*, 29th September 1996. See also M. K. Narayan, "Changes in Kabul Do Not Augur Well for India," *Asian Age*, New Delhi, 14th October 1996.

and terror that stalks the land has made our lives miserable."[11] For several years now the Indian settlers have felt the situation in Afghanistan inconducive for their continuation there and have left for India. According to one report they are about 30,000 in number.[12]

Pakistan's own ethnic problems are also viewed from similar angles. Zia ul-Haq was reported to have told Rajiv Gandhi in early 1987 that if India desired a declaration from Pakistan to the effect that the latter would not interfere in the internal affairs of India it could come through a package under which the latter should also declare that it had no link with the so-called "Sindhu Desh and Pakhtoonistan".[13] In May 1987, the ruling Muslim League in a Party resolution had reiterated the proposal.[14] Of late there have been allegations that India is actively behind the militancy launched by the MQM (Altaf) that have rocked Karachi.[15]

In the Indo-Nepal relations also a new security dimension has been added. India is suspicious of the operations of the ISI, LTTE, and Kashmiri and Panjabi terrorists on the Nepali soil and fear that at critical moments they could penetrate into India to foment trouble. During the assembly elections and the parliamentary elections held in Jammu and Kashmir in August and October 1996 respectively there were reports in the Indian press that Pakistan was planning to disrupt the polls by sending thousands of trained militants to disrupt the exercises. Indian intelligence reports said that about two thousand such militants were about to cross the Line of Control in J&K to disrupt the assembly elections which made the army boost their defences.[16] The same type of reporting was there on the eve of the parliamentary elections in the state.[17]

During the 1996 general election India sealed the 739 km border between India and Nepal following intelligence reports about ISI designs to create disturbances during the elections.[18] Later, the foreign ministers of India and Nepal agreed to set up a joint working group "to discourage movement of undesirable elements across the border". Both sides reiterated their resolve not to allow any activities on their soil which was "prejudicial to the security of the other."[19]

The reported use of Nepalese soil by the terrorists might eventually complicate India-Nepal relations. As one Nepalese scholar writes:

> This could create unwarranted trouble for Nepal in case such immigration in the guise of common Indian citizen remains unchecked. This migration across the international border which

11 *Times of India*, 18th October 1996.

12 *Ibid.*, 29th September 1996.

13 *Pakistan Affairs*, 40 (1), 1987, p. 1.

14 *Times of India*, 21st May 1987.

15 Ishtiaq Ahmad, "What Altaf Must Realise," *The Nation*, Lahore, 2nd June 1996.

16 *Asian Age*, 10th August 1996.

17 *The Hindu*, New Delhi, 12th October 1996.

18 *Times of India*, 3rd April 1996.

19 *The Hindu*, 15th August 1996.

was not a serious source of conflict previously could then turn out to be a content of inter-state dispute. Incidentally, the intermittent quarrel over the 'people of Indian origin' (which has also become a strong point in reference to the origin of Sadvawana Party in Nepal) could generate unwarranted ethnic turmoils in Nepal (which, in fact, has already encouraged several Jana-Jati groups to build pressure on the government).[20]

With regard to Sri Lanka the recent refugee arrivals in India following the LTTE defeat in Jaffna have also had some security connections. Both India and Sri Lanka have agreed that quite often these movements are sponsored by the LTTE.[21] According to one Tamil Nadu official dealing with the LTTE and other extremists: "This has been the case especially after Canada, Cambodia and the UK became cold towards the LTTE after a recent anti-terrorism conference in Switzerland." The Tigers probably have other reasons too to encourage the people to flee to India. According to C. Chandrahasan, head of the PROTEG, a Chennai-based Sri Lanka Tamil human rights organisation, "so long as the Tigers were administering populated areas like Jaffna they needed the people to show that they were running a liberated zone with all the paraphernalia of a government. But the moment they had to retreat to the Vanni jungles after the Sri Lanka troops recaptured Jaffna, the Tigers had no use for the people. Now they do not mind if people leave for India in droves."[22]

In the eastern flank of the region the insurgencies of all kinds which pose serious security problems to Bangladesh and India have close links with the region's demographic complexion which is under constant pressure from external migrations. The Chinese presence in the neighbourhood used to be viewed with alarm by India in this context in the past. With the relative thawing in Sino-Indian relations the problem is now somewhat palliated but the threat remains potential.

The entire north-east India and the adjoining region are infested with all kinds of ethnic insurgencies in which the cross-border and other types of migrations have a role to play. The Indian government at one point of time had pressurised the Bangladesh government to stop the land settlements in the Chittagong Hill Tracts (CHT) which were resulting in the displacements of the local tribals and their eventual flight to India. The latter has the leverage with Bangladesh because restrictions on trade and river water flows could affect Bangladeshi economy severely.[23] Lately, India's relation with Bangladesh has descended heavily upon the north-east insurgents operating from its soil. As a result, the United Liberation Front of Assam (ULFA)

[20] Dhruva Kumar, "Reconsidering Nepal-India Bilateral Relations," *Contributions to Nepalese Studies* 21 (1), 1994, p. 83.

[21] *The Hindu*, 5th November 1996.

[22] Quoted by P. K. Balachandran, "Lankan Refugees: Tamil Nadu's Cautious and Wary Approach", *Sunday Times*, Colombo, 8th December 1996.

[23] Weiner, "Security, Stability, and International Migration," p. 123.

which had been protecting the Bangladeshi migrants in Assam is now demanding the deportation of the foreigners which means the Bangladeshis.[24]

In respect of the tri-junction between Bangladesh, India and Myanmar there is always a close connection between the cross-border movements of people and international security. When as a result of the Burmese (Myanmar) policy of settling non-Muslims in Arakan many Muslims flocked to Bangladesh as refugees the Bangladesh government threatened to arm them if such settlement policy was not stopped.[25] Similar linkages were noticeable in the Indo-Burmese relations also. In 1994, India and Myanmar entered into agreements aimed at solving border problems. As a result, the Mizoram government forcibly repatriated about 10,000 Chins to Myanmar.[26] But when India welcomed student activists and pro-democracy members and kept them in refugee camps the relations soured with the result that the joint counter-insurgency operations were suspended. Arrested insurgents told the police that some miltary officers of the State Law and Order Restoration Council (SLORC) were extending full support to some underground organisations of Manipur. Besides, all the outfits in the region were sending new recruits to camps in Myanmar for guerrilla training.[27]

6. The Response

Considering the importance of refugee-related security problems of the region some of the South Asian states have entered into bilateral agreements to contain the danger. In the east Bangladesh, Bhutan, India, Myanmar and Thailand have entered into constructive negotiations in this regard. If the so-called Asian super-highway idea is operationalised it would be a big boost to international confidence building in the region.[28]

In April 1992, Bangladesh and Myanmar signed an agreement for the "safe and voluntary" return of refugees. Once the repatriation completed, both the governments "agreed to cooperate for the prevention of illegal border crossings", enhance security on the borders and prevent their territories from being used for terrorism, insurgency, smuggling, gun-running and drug-trafficking. The accord was a significant development in the sense that it made the Burmese to

24 *The Hindu*, 24th April 1997.

25 Weiner, "Security, Stability, and International Migration," p. 122.

26 Gary Rozema, "No Protection for Burma's Refugees," paper presented to the Seminar on Migrants, Refugees and Stateless Persons in South Asia – Need for a Regional Protocol, Kathmandu, 18th–22th November 1996.

27 *The Hindu*, 24th April 1997. Sino-Burmese contacts also worry India. See C. Uday Bhaskar, "Visit to Myanmar," *Journal of Indian Ocean Studies* 2 (1), 1994, p. 64–9.

28 For the details of the Agreement, see *The Hindu*, 10th and 11th March 1997.

accept that the Rohingya issue existed and that they were an integral part of the Burmese society.[29]

Following the signing of the accord repatriation began on 22nd September 1992 and by mid-1995 about 200,000 had returned. The problem of repatriation was, however, compounded by the fact that 18,000 new babies had been born in the camps and every day many births were taking place.[30] Also some of the Islamic fundamentalist groups in Bangladesh, most notably the Jamaat-i-Islami, were fanning a no-return sentiment among the refugees by trying to make them dream of an independent Arakan state. They also toyed with the idea that if these refugees could be settled in the CHT region then they would take care of the Chakma problem to the advantage of Dhaka.[31]

There have also been agreements between Bangladesh and India in respect of the repatriation of tribal refugees. On 9th March 1997, the Bangladesh government and the Chakma refugee leaders in India signed an agreement for the repatriation of the 50,000 refugees sheltered in six camps in Tripura for the last 11 years. The repatriation commenced on 28th March 1997 and by April 1997, 6701 refugees had been repatriated.

To prevent the infiltration of Bangladeshi nationals India has taken up a project for the construction of roads and fences along the India-Bangladesh border in the states of Assam, Meghalaya, Mizoram, Tripura and West Bengal. Until 30th September 1996, 1658.35 km of roads and 629.78 km of fences had been completed out of the approved target of 2,784 km of roads and 896 km of fences. In the western sector, as one of the measures taken for effective policing of the border and for curbing infiltration/exfiltration and insurgent activities it has undertaken fencing/flood-lighting of the vulnerable stretches of the India-Pakistan border in Panjab, Rajasthan and Jammu sectors. A total length of 1171 km of fencing and 1205 km of flood-lighting in the entire vulnerable stretches of Panjab and the Bikaner, Sriganganagar, Jaisalmer and Barmer sectors of Rajasthan was completed by January 1997. The work of border-fencing/flood-lighting covering a length of 312.60 km in Jaisalmer sector of Rajasthan has been taken up in three phases to be completed by December 1999.[32]

29 For details, see Amera Saeed, "Rohingya Refugees in Bangladesh: Their Impact on Regional Stability," *Spotlight on Regional Affairs*, Islamabad, 12 (11), 1993, p. 30–44, mimeo.

30 A 1995 newspaper report showed that 3,000 refugee mothers were expecting babies. *Asian Age*, 27th June 1995.

31 Imtiaz Ahmed, "Refugees and Security: The Experience of Bangladesh," in: S. D. Muni and Lok Raj Baral (eds.), *Refugees and Regional Security in South Asia*, New Delhi 1996, p. 141.

32 Government of India, Ministry of Home Affairs, *Annual Report 1996–97*, p. 11–12, 15.

7. In Perspective

The relevant literature on how to control illegal immigration is generally West-centric. As such, the problem has been viewed primarily from a North-South perspective. Some of the strategies that are being considered in the developed countries in this regard include more trade relations with the immigrant countries, more FDI and ODA directed towards them, and the introduction of the system of temporary worker programme.[33] Yet another strategy that has been worked out, particularly in France, is not to try to totally eliminate the possibility of illegal immigration but to prevent illegal employment which would automatically prohibit illegal immigration.[34]

None of these strategies seem to be effective in the South Asian situation. Barring Bangladeshi and Nepali migrants to India and Indian migrants to Nepal, all the other kinds are not economic refugees. Even for economic refugees in the region the above-mentioned solutions have little efficacy. Both with Bangladesh and Nepal, apart from treaty agreement which allows free entry of Nepalis to India, there already exist wide ranging trade and aid relations. Any effort to further encourage them is fraught with political risk as there is a strong anti-India constituency in Nepal. The same is true to a large extent in respect of Bangladesh, although Indo-Bangladesh trade relations are improving and a water sharing treaty has been signed.

So far as the prevention of illegal work is concerned it may be noted that most of the migrants are employed in unorganised sectors as domestic servants, menial workers or daily wage earners which no law can easily do handle particularly when there is already a serious problem of governance. There are other related problems as well. For example, given the rise in the crime graph the police department of Delhi now insists on the registration of domestic servants with them. As a result, whenever a Nepali servant is caught for some crime a whole lot of other Nepali servants are rounded up causing consternation amongst the local Nepali community.

One Assamese author has given a solution which is worth considering although it has several intractable economic and social implications. According to him:

> India can consider issuing residential and work permit along with traveling and reentry permits for the same period to all the foreigners irrespective of their country of origin after detecting and registering them. These people must be divested of voting rights in the elections to state assembly and parliament but may even be allowed to civic rights in the local level. They may be provided reasonable civic amenities, their rights may be protected by suitable legislations

33 W. R. Bohning, "Helping Migrants to Stay at Home," and Gary P. Freeman, "Can Liberal States Control Unwanted Migration?" *The Annals*, Philadelphia, No. 534, 1994, p. 165–77 and p. 25–7, respectively. See also Doris Meissner, "Managing Migrations," *Foreign Policy*, No. 86, Spring 1992, p. 66–83.

34 Claude-Valentin Marie, "From the Campaign Against Illegal Migration to the Campaign Against Illegal Work," *The Annals*, Philadelphia, No. 534, July 1994, p. 118–32.

and part of their income may be allowed to be repatriated to their families back home. Such a humane, practical and profitable policy will ensure that poor of our neighbouring countries are not uprooted from their hearths and homes and keep their roots intact. In most cases the families will stay back. This will also greatly diminish social tensions in Assam and the North-East.[35]

But what would happen to those who get lost into the Indian crowd after the expiry of the permits? Let alone India, even the United States has not been able to prevent this from happening. In 1990, there were 90 thousand illegal over-stayers in America.[36]

8. Conclusion

One of the paradoxes of the problem associated with the refugees and migrants in South Asia – "teflon citizenship meets symbolic xenophobia"[37] – has been the way in which the political rhetoric of expulsion of unauthorised immigrants has increased in direct proportion to the inability of the states to control the movements. Probably the only solution lies in a regional cooperative approach. The developmental goals of the regional states have to be mutually coordinated which should not only subsume strategies to remove intra-national economic disparities as far as possible but also help develop some sort of participation in an overall security system. The task is daunting but the stakes are too high to be neglected.

35 Dhruba Jyouti Borah, "Social Alienation and Tension in the North-East," paper presented to the symposium on "Focus on North-East" on the occasion of 'The Shillong Times Golden Jubilee Celebration', India International Centre, New Delhi, 18th March 1995.

36 Gary P. Freeman, "Can Liberal States Control Unwanted Migration?" *The Annals*, No. 534, July 1994, p. 23.

37 The phrase has been borrowed from the report (prepared by John Stone) of a workshop organised by the Woodrow Wilson Center Washington, D. C., on "Ethnic Conflict in the Post-Cold War Era: Problems in Advanced Industrial Societies," January 1995, p. 5.

Security Aspects of the Conflict in Sri Lanka

Dagmar Hellmann-Rajanayagam

1. Introduction

Two events prompted me to take up the topic discussed in this paper, one short-term and one long-term. The long-term one is the fact that for over ten years I was a consultant to German courts on questions of Tamil asylum applications, and in some cases also an expert witness. The short-term one was the diplomatic offensive begun by the Sri Lankan government in late 1996 to have the Liberation Tigers of Tamil Eelam (LTTE) declared a terrorist organisation and banned in several western states. Since I have been working on the conflict in Sri Lanka for quite some time, these two factors combined to make me enquire more closely into the implications this conflict might have both for South Asia and internationally. My remarks and conclusions must remain preliminary, tentative, and in some cases speculative since I embarked on the project only a short while ago. Another, more significant reason for this is, however, a quite different one:

In the research undertaken recently in Paris, Delhi and Chennai (Madras) it became obvious to me that a lot of information on precisely this aspect has been and is being gathered, of which very little, however, is in writing. If it is, it is either inaccessible to the normal researcher or so speculative and unsubstantiated that it is of very little academic use. Oral information may be imparted by the authorities concerned more or less freely, but in many cases comes with the proviso: 'off the record' or 'unquotable' or 'quotable without attribution'. Which puts this researcher in the strange case of writing a paper nearly exclusively on 'unattributable' or even 'unquoted' sources, or, an equally dismal prospect, on newspaper reports and clippings which especially in this case are notoriously unreliable.

These difficulties notwithstanding, I have endeavoured in this essay to pull together whatever accessible information on this topic, one might say, 'regardless of its origin' in order to trace out some major lines of development and discussion. As mentioned, these remain tentative and speculative. How convincing and plausible the argument and the conclusion sound in the light of this, remains for the reader to judge.

2. Background

Until a few years ago, the question of the wider security implications of any local or internal conflict in the so-called 'Third World' would either not have been put or been answered very simply: Internal conflicts were proxy wars for the two big Cold War powers, fuelled, if not instigated and kept alive by them. Any security considerations were coloured and informed by this perception.

When the Cold War ended, it was consequently widely expected, that this would spell the end of all kinds of irritating problems as well. Instead, quite the opposite happened; the number of internal conflicts rose sharply, not only in Asia and Africa, but also in Europe. Instead of the breakdown of an outdated and corrupt system and the new flourishing of humankind the world witnessed in horror that the lid had been taken off an explosive and noxious brew of national, ethnical and religious ties, affiliations and claims whose essential characteristic in many cases was their total intolerance towards other such ties and claims. Bosnia-Herzegowina is only one of the most extreme of these cases. After the communist 'glue' was gone not only did a state break up or down into its constituent parts, but these parts often started to destroy each other as well. Historians, especially those of Asia, were not surprised. They had seen it all before, and many had argued long in the proverbial wilderness that internal conflicts had little to do with the differences of two ideological camps, but were *sui generis*. When the cosiness of the Cold War, to borrow Chandran Jeshurun's term,[1] gave way to the uncertainties of the new World (Dis)Order, they saw themselves vindicated, indeed they could have said 'told you so', but the majority refrained. It was clear that the underlying causes for internal conflicts had to be looked for in the situations and conditions of the respective countries themselves instead of outside, and if one wanted to look for solutions, these issues had to be addressed somehow.

The new uncertainties arose precisely over the questions of security and stability. As long as the two superpowers were supposed to rein their clients in, these questions had seemed clear-cut and unambiguous to many observers, but now, that ethnic, linguistic, and other antagonisms surfaced, front lines became jagged and fuzzy, and conflicts in one area could easily destabilise a neighbouring state in various ways.

But the anxiety went deeper. That internal conflicts in one state could impinge on the interests of a neighbour had been realised and occasionally been commented upon earlier, but as

1 Chandran Jeshurun (ed.), *China, India, Japan, and the Security of Southeast Asia*, Singapore 1993.

long as these conflicts remained geographically delimited, this constituted a headache only for the country concerned which had to deal with unrest, refugees and so on. Refugees and rebels filtering into other countries were sometimes considered a nuisance, but rarely a danger. This perspective changed with the refugee trickle turning into a migrant stream, and ethnic and racial animosities rearing their ugly heads in Europe itself. Moreover, internal conflicts, guerilla warfare and rebel movements were now increasingly tied to arms smuggling and the narcotics trade worldwide,[2] activities that concerned many countries and states. Besides, the successor states of the USSR are not only often unstable, but are also known to have access to conventional and nuclear arsenals which could prove extremely dangerous in the future. Many, though certainly not all, of these assumptions have remained just that, and while making good material for a spy thriller, would need to be substantiated to be of use for serious research.

3. Sri Lanka

The security implications of this new state of uncertainty are thus disturbing, but they also seem to vary with the type of internal conflict we look at. Much depends on how broadly or narrowly security and stability are defined, though the tendency is to define them rather broadly nowadays, including not only military security, but political and – increasingly – social stability, law and order, justice, and so on. And sometimes these security threats seem less or rather different from what we imagined them to be. This applies in particular to Sri Lanka, where the government has recently gone on a diplomatic offensive to impress on friendly states the risks and dangers the Tamil guerilla constitutes for regional and international security.

The conflict in Sri Lanka is atypical in that its close observers have always realised that it did not fit neatly into Cold War categories (even though as late as 1987 one German journalist told me very seriously that all these guerilla groups were guided and controlled from Moscow, never mind the fact that the USSR had already in 1984 said that the Tamil cause was reactionary and bourgeois and not to be supported).[3] It was a conflict with a history going back to pre-independence times, termed first linguistic, then ethnic, until it was obvious that none of these categories did really apply. At the time of writing, the LTTE guerilla seems to be losing rather heavily to the Sri Lankan army, though the situation can change at short notice in this case. It was, moreover, a movement with no outside help, if we disregard the training some of the cadres got from the PLO and Libya and the covert support by way of training and material India gave to the militants in the early 1980s. Instead the militants relied to a considerable

[2] W. M. J. Olson, "Small wars", *The Annals of The American Academy of Political and Social Science* 541, 1995, p. 47f, 73f.

[3] Urmila Phadnis, *Ethnicity and Nation-building in South Asia*, New Delhi 1989, p. 228.

tent for their moral and material support on a sizeable Tamil diaspora world-wide and also on the tacit or not so tacit support of Tamils in Tamil Nadu, official or unofficial. This fact has given rise to a number of questions and concerns regarding the implications the conflict might have for South Asian and regional and even international security. The problems here take different form according to the geographical area concerned, but revolve basically around two distinct, but often confused and conflated, issues:

(1) The activities of the militant groups, foremost the LTTE, abroad, including propaganda work, front organisations for arms purchases, smuggling and the narcotics trade;

(2) The overseas Tamil community including expatriates, naturalised citizens, and refugees and their involvement, financially and politically, in supporting the Tamil cause.

These two issues are indeed quite separate, but are consciously or unconsciously very often seen as one. Besides, the Tamil community overseas is likewise often portrayed as an undifferentiated mass of 'refugees' or 'sympathisers' which again tends to give a wrong picture. A number of more or less lurid articles and reports have appeared over the last two to three years in various journals and magazines addressing the alleged international activities of the Tamil militants.[4] At the end of last year, Sri Lanka's Foreign Minister Lakshman Kadirgamar went on a whirlwind tour to Europe, the US and Asia and gave a speech in the UN General Assembly denouncing the Tamil militants as terrorists, emphasising the dangers they constituted not only for Sri Lanka, but also for other countries and asking for a ban on them as a 'terrorist organisation'.[5] This speech was problematical precisely for the reasons cited above and for some additional ones:

(1) Though several definitions of 'terrorist' have proliferated, there does not yet exist a generally accepted and binding definition of 'terrorist' in international law.[6] The same ap-

4 *McKenzie Briefing Notes*, The McKenzie Institute, Toronto, *n. d.* (probably early 1996). The problem with this publication is not only that it is anonymous, but that there is no publication address or name either. *Asia Week*, 26th July 1996, p. 30–8. This article has been translated and reprinted, sometimes without attribution, by a number of European magazines, e. g. *Focus* 31, 1996, *Courier International*, No. 305, 5ème au 11ème Septembre 1996.

5 Address by the Hon. Lakshman Kadirgamar, P. C., M. P., Minister of Foreign Affairs and Chairman of the Delegation of Sri Lanka at the 51st Session of the United Nations General Assembly, New York, 26th September 1996.

6 *The Laws of War. A Comprehensive Collection of Primary Documents on International Laws Governing Armed Conflict*, with an introduction and commentary by W. Michael Reisman and Chris T. Antoniou, New York 1994, p. 293, says this about terrorism: "Terrorism has come to mean the intentional use of violence against civilian and military targets generally *outside of an acknowledged war zone* by private groups or groups that appear to be private but have some measure of covert state sponsorship" (my emphasis). The commentary goes on, however, to emphasise the ambiguous and equivocal understanding of the term and mentions that one of the characteristics of terrorism is the lack of discriminat[ion] between combatants and noncombatants, but, rather, intentionally target[ing of] civilians", *ibid.* Though the compilation quotes some resolutions on terrorism and mentions that it violates international law, it does not give a ratified and legally binding definition, *Ibid.*, p. 294–316.

plies to a number of countries where the Tamil militants are said to be active.[7] Moreover, we all know what has already become a common-place that 'today's terrorist is tomorrow's hero' and 'one country's terrorist is another's freedom fighter'. Among others, the freedom fighters in India provide here an excellent example.

(2) The second, connected, problem concerns the security perspectives of Sri Lanka and other countries. While for the former, the Tamil militants definitely constitute a security threat, a 'clear and present danger', for the rest of South Asia and other regions this security threat is by no means so unequivocal. We shall illustrate this point in more detail with regard to India below. But first let us take a look at the global situation, i. e. in Southeast Asia and Europe.

4. The Activities of the LTTE Overseas

The mentioned reports state that the Tamil militants have a network of commercial and business connections worldwide and particularly in Southeast Asia through which they finance their purchase of arms and supplies. Part of the finance, it is alleged, arises from the international trade in drugs, another from organised crime.[8] KP (Kumaran Pathmanathan) was named as the chief LTTE negotiator for international arms deals.[9] While the LTTE confirm that KP has been their negotiator for business deals and armament purchases in the past, the position has now apparently been handed over to somebody else for obvious reasons.[10] The business connections of the LTTE thus seem well substantiated, the question, however, arises, whether these connections and activities are *per se* dangerous for the country concerned or illegal. The allegation of organised crime arises mainly from the assumption that, since a large part of the LTTE leader- and membership belongs to the fishing caste, and this community has been over the centuries also been known to engage in smuggling between India and Sri Lanka, they have now extended this activity into an international concern at least in Southeast Asia: these reports trace a net of LTTE connections from Burma through Northeast India down the coasts of the Bay of Bengal down to Thailand, Malaysia, and Singapore and up to Sri Lanka and the Coro-

[7] In German law, there is the term 'criminal organisation', on which charge e. g. the Baader-Meinhof-group were prosecuted, but no 'terrorist organisation'. In the UK, similarly, a 'group' cannot be prosecuted under the law, but only persons who have committed criminal or terrorist acts, regardless of their group allegiance.

[8] *McKenzie Briefing Notes*, p. 4–6; *Asia Week*, p. 31.

[9] *Ibid.*, p. 30.

[10] Personal information, April 1997.

mandel coast again,[11] thus making the Bay into an 'LTTE lake'.[12] While it is quite true that in the distant and recent the past fishing communities were indeed also engaged in smuggling between India and Sri Lanka, an activity arising out of the then political situation, it is rather doubtful whether this fact allows one to jump to the conclusion that this has now been transposed onto the international stage. It certainly seems to invest the LTTE with a lot of power and foresight. The McKenzie report goes a step further: it claims that the LTTE grew out of criminal gangs operating in Jaffna and abroad long before the civil war erupted and that it had no interest whatever in the issues at stake![13]

5. Security Risks?

Before looking into the problem of overseas LTTE activities further, we have to face the question just mentioned: In what way do the activities highlighted by the Sri Lankan government actually constitute 'terrorist activities' and moreover a security risk for the particular countries they occur in? To get at the root of this problem, we have to clear away a number of non-issues first.

a) Nonissues

If raising funds in support of a political or social, even radical cause among an ethnic or political diaspora is indeed a 'terrorist activity', then few militant and rebel organisations would be exempt either in the presence or in the past. To name a few: IRA (funded from the US), Israel (funded from the US), PLO (funded from US and Europe), Moro (supported actively by ASEAN countries in the region), ANC (supported from the UK). In very few cases, the mere fact of raising funds has ever led to accusations of illegality or 'terrorism'.

The same applies to the rather sensitive topic of arms acquisition, which in the first place, is very hard to substantiate, and in the second, politically and ethically equivocal. Legal or black-market small arms are hawked around the world to groups of all shades, even while the defence budgets of major powers continue to decrease.[14] The fact that LTTE tries to acquire weapons is neither astonishing nor a 'terrorist activity' as such; it remains to be seen where the connections lead and for whom this constitutes a risk or a threat, which to me, in this case, seems anyway a

[11] *Asia Week*, p. 32.

[12] Personal info Lt.-Gen. K. S. Khajuria, Delhi, 17.5.97. The General who was in charge of intelligence during the IPKF operations in Jaffna, discounted this idea as 'fanciful'.

[13] *McKenzie Briefing Notes*, p. 3.

[14] Olson, *Small Wars*, p. 54, 72; see also p. 67–8.

bit exaggerated. It is, however, hard to see in what way legitimate business enterprises can be termed 'illegal' or 'terrorist' or 'front organisations' merely because they are set up by supporters or even members of a particular grouping and support that grouping morally or materially (e. g. by donations). These activities might be questionable from an ethical and political point of view, but they are not legally prohibited and consequently hard to curb. Nor can they be said to threaten the security of any country but the one the actual conflict is taking place in, and the same would, with qualifications, also apply to arms.

b) Actual Security Threats

This point seems to have been recognised by a number of countries in Southeast Asia with sizeable Tamil minorities who turn a blind eye to being used as transshipment points or conduits for this kind of activities. The LTTE is banned in these countries, but other agencies can be used, not necessarily only Tamils.[15] In Europe, where the LTTE has a recognised presence and is consequently closely watched by the security agencies, this type of activity would be correspondingly more difficult. The fact that these links exist has again given rise to the accusation of 'terrorist sympathisers' against the Tamil diaspora. These are non-issues precisely because they constitute a security threat mainly for Sri Lanka who must then address the problems at source. Having got these non-issues out of the way, we now come to a rather more murky and ambiguous topic, viz. whether any activities of the LTTE abroad do indeed impinge on the security of the host countries. It is here that the issue of the LTTE and that of the refugees are unfortunately fatally linked in the minds of many observers. But let us take a closer look.

Some of the published reports and accounts seem to imply that the security threats emanating from the conflict are only derived from the existence and actions of the Tamil militants, i.e. the LTTE, at home and abroad. By subsuming the totality of the problem under this heading, the question of the role of the Sri Lankan government, that of civilian casualties and refugees and of peripatetic effects of the crisis in general are completely left out of the equation. In other words, our question would have to be in two parts: in what way does the conflict in Sri Lanka *in general* pose a threat to the security and stability of other countries, and does the LTTE in itself pose or aggravate this threat by its actions abroad? We should look at the second question first, since it is easier to answer. Business activities of the LTTE do certainly not constitute a security threat beyond Sri Lanka and maybe India (see below).[16] However, the problems attend-

15 Interview Major-Gen. Afsir Karim, Delhi, 13.5.97.

16 The German *Verfassungsschutzbericht 1995*, p. 219, on 'Sicherheitsgefährdende und extremistische Bestrebungen von Ausländern' has merely a short paragraph on Raiah Sivaneswaran, the leader of the LTTE in Germany that contacts to the outside are limited, but that appeals to raise funds are still going out to the

ing a sizeable presence of refugees in any one country have in this case also been blamed on the LTTE. There have been accusations of extortion, blackmail etc. which portray the refugee community as victims on the one hand and of 'fake refugees' on the other which portray them as perpetrators.[17] Moreover, the LTTE has been linked to the narcotics trade world-wide and to organised crime. The fatal shooting of two LTTE supporters in Paris in 1996 gave rise to speculations about possible rivalry within the group.[18] Outside India and Sri Lanka, the LTTE have been rather circumspect in their actions, and no outright violent or terrorist acts could actually be pinned on them.[19] Whether this would indeed have brought about a world-wide ban, is again another question. When Palestinians started to hi-jack plane loads full of people in the 1970s to draw attention to their plight, this was indeed seen as a terrorist act by the international community, but was not sufficient to ban the PLO throughout.[20]

Instead, accusations of extortion, organised crime, violence and so on in the Tamil community itself proliferated.[21] It is here that we get into deep water. Extortion would be criminal by any definition. In Germany, accusations of extortion surfaced in the late 1980s. There was evidence that these accusations had indeed some substance, i. e. money was squeezed from refugees in Germany by individual LTTE members (or people claiming to be LTTE members). In the UK, people were sometimes heard to grumble to this researcher about 'methods of fund-collecting' and muted complaints could be heard at one stage, not about actual extortion, but rather heavy 'moral armtwisting'. Accusations of violent extortion have led to court cases against Tamils in Switzerland and Canada, though these trials have in one case ended in acquittal and are in the other not yet finished.[22] LTTE of course maintains that all funds contributed are given voluntarily and claims that it does not condone violent and criminal methods of fund-raising, primarily because enough support is given voluntarily. Members who are involved in these activities are demoted or expelled.[23] There is, however, a deeper problem involved here, which can be illustrated by the case of Toronto: over the years, more than 100,000 Tamils have come to and settled in Toronto either professionally or as refugees. These Tamils are by no means all LTTE supporters. Some may be, many are uncommitted, others support or supported

Tamils living there.

17 *McKenzie Briefing Notes*, p. 6–7.

18 Interview Dr. Eric Meyer, Paris, 8.5.1997; *Courrier International*, 13 Décembre 1996, p. 18; The *Sri Lanka Monitor*, October 1996.

19 The United States State Department, *Patterns of Global Terrorism 1994*, while denouncing the actions of the LTTE, mentions explicitly that it has refrained from attacking foreigners and Western tourists.

20 In fact, the PLO had an official representative and spokesman in Germany all these years.

21 *McKenzie Briefing Notes*, p. 3 and *Lanka Outlook*, Jan.-March 1997, p. 8.

22 One of the accused, Murali from Switzerland, has in the meantime been released on bail, the case against the accused in Canada, Suresh, is continuing.

23 Personal information, April 1997.

rival Tamil organisations. They often live in ghetto-like districts and suburbs. Add to this a certain amount of caste or status rivalry and professional jealousy, and you have a potent mixture for crime, extortion, and lawlessness. Consequently, a sort of Tamil gang warfare seems to be going on since quite some time, which does comprise extortion, robbery, violence, narcotics and so on, and for which the McKenzie report, for one, pins the blame on LTTE. The problem seems to be considered serious by all observers.[24] Here, the problem of the LTTE and that of the refugees get nearly inextricably enmeshed, a picture that seems to be fostered by interested agencies.

6. The Tamil Diaspora Abroad

Indeed, what the Sri Lankan government emphasises in its attacks on the LTTE are less the activities of arms purchase and smuggling (except when intercepting and shooting at neutral vessels suspected to have questionable cargo off the Sri Lankan coast).[25] These are not undertakings of the LTTE alone, but are activities engaged in by groups of the most varied hues and political persuasions,[26] and have until now proved intractable to curb.

Sri Lanka concentrates rather, at least on the international stage, on the problems the physical presence of Sri Lankan Tamils overseas constitutes for herself and the respective countries. For a start, it is claimed that all or a major proportion of the Sri Lankan Tamils abroad are 'fake refugees' who have been sent there by the LTTE in order to do their nefarious work and deplete the resources of the host country. It is implied, and *Sri Lanka Outlook* says so openly that Sri Lankan Tamils have no reason to flee the country either for political or economic reasons, and if they do, they do so under duress or on the instigation of criminal elements.[27] Besides, the LTTE members and spokesmen in various European countries, it is claimed, are also 'fake refugees' who got asylum on false pretences and are now abusing not only the welfare system of the receiving country, but information and communications systems as well and now disseminate (mis)information about the nature of the conflict. These reports themselves contain a number of misrepresentations which have to be cleared up. To take again the last problem first:

(1) The LTTE have established liaison and propaganda offices in a number of mainly Western countries, among them the US, Canada, Australia, Germany, France, Switzerland etc., from

24 Personal information, April 1997; *McKenzie Briefing Notes*, p. 4; V. Suryanarayan, *Backgrounder. Sri Lankan Refugees in Tamil Nadu: Humanitarian and Security Dimensions*, unpubl. doc. for Society for Indian Ocean Studies, Madras chapter, n. p., n. d. (April 1997).

25 Though *Lanka Outlook* Jan.-March 1997, p. 11–13 concentrates heavily on this particular aspect.

26 Olson, *Small Wars*, p. 47f; tables p. 56–7, p. 65ff.

27 *Lanka Outlook*, p. 8–10. It should be noted that in this as in other instances, *Lanka Outlook* uses very little original material, but reprints selectively from other papers and journals.

which they conduct mainly very extensive information and propaganda work, in some cases also business activities. LTTE members and supporters are, moreover, working from diverse Information and Research Organisations or under their own name in many western countries quite openly. A number of LTTE spokesmen in Europe came as *bona fide* political refugees at the height of the conflict in the 1980s and were granted asylum by their respective host countries.[28] To imply that these were 'fake' throws doubt on the juridical and legal ability of the host countries' institutions. However, a large part of these spokesmen are not refugees, recognised or otherwise at all, but came to Europe as students, in search of jobs as expatriates or professionals and on regular work permits or student visas in the 1970s and early 1980s. The latter applies particularly to the UK and Australia. Many of them are now naturalised citizens of their host countries.[29] Their integrity and liberty to choose political opinions are thus thrown open to doubt by the mentioned reports. While LTTE members or supporters are under surveillance by the security services in the respective states as a matter of course,[30] and do represent some of the 'usual suspects' in cases of terrorist attacks (together with 'Islamic fundamentalists', IRA, RAF etc.), until now no country has yet seen fit to ban or proscribe the LTTE because of its propaganda or because of any criminal activities.[31] Malcolm Rifkind made it clear during his visit to Sri Lanka,[32] that while individuals can be prosecuted for terrorist acts, an organisation cannot so be prosecuted or banned (example IRA). Moreover, Sri Lanka herself has not yet banned the LTTE. The demand for a ban drew sympathy from a number of governments, but very little in the way of action. Germany has not banned the LTTE either, though the law does furnish a lever for proscribing organisations which work against the constitution or commit violent and terrorist acts (vide Baader-Meinhof). Again, this can only come into force, when the organisation advocates and commits these criminal acts. Up to now, even the US has not banned LTTE, though it has termed it a terrorist organisation. And this leads us to the other problem:

(2) There exists indeed a large, and to a large extent, though not exclusively, Sri Lankan, Tamil diaspora in a number of countries in all continents. There are Tamils in the US, Canada, Australia, UK, France, Germany, Sweden, Switzerland, the Netherlands, South Africa, Mauritius etc., as well as ethnic Tamils in Malaysia and Singapore. Reading the McKenzie report, one is led to the conclusion that all these Tamils are either 'refugees' who have come there to solicit political asylum, or criminals supporting a criminal organisation by

28 This applies to a number of LTTE spokesmen in London and Paris.

29 This applies also to many LTTE supporters in France.

30 See above, n. 16.

31 India will be discussed below.

32 Nanban, 31.8.96.

any means whatever. Apart from casting a slur on millions of doubtlessly hard-working, prosperous and law-abiding citizens of several countries simply because of their ethnic background, and most of whom are anything but 'refugees', economic or otherwise, this sweeping statement is impossible to back up by evidence.

The issue turns, however, primarily on those Tamils who have fled from Sri Lanka to India and Western countries. Refugees can indeed be if not a security threat, so at least a destabilising factor for the receiving country, as was seen in the Bangladesh crisis and in the late 1980s in South India, when large numbers of refugees started flocking to the state of Tamil Nadu.[33] India did perceive this clearly as a threat at least to social peace and took steps to deal with the problem, culminating in the Indo-Lanka accord 1987. The point to emphasise here is that at this time, India did not see the Tamil militants as the major threat, but the crisis in general and especially the way the *Sri Lankan government* handled it. India was not very sympathetic to Sri Lankan president Jayewardene's complaints during his visit in 1984 about the security threat the militants constituted for Sri Lanka, especially as this claim followed shortly after the terrible massacre of 1983.[34]

Other, in particular Western, countries, did not experience the influx of refugees to the extent India had to weather. However enough Tamil refugees seeking political asylum made their way to Europe, North America and Australia from the 1980s onwards to generate concern about the problem there and about possible repercussions at home. Again, it was not primarily the militants who were perceived as threatening, but the crisis in general which led to large numbers of Tamils heading for these countries and acting as a drain on resources. Two ways were devised to deal with this: one – similar to the Indian method – to pressure both sides in the conflict to negotiate an agreement and to take the Sri Lankan government up on its human rights record. The other one was an attempt to limit the numbers of people seeking asylum or refugee status by legal means. With an increasing influx of refugees from East Europe (during the 1980s) and particularly Bosnia (after 1990), the attitude towards them changed and the attendant problems began to loom larger. It was assumed, in many cases no doubt correctly, that many refugees had come on forged documents and were often economic, rather than political, refugees. Both assumptions were to an extent correct. I do not intend to go into the controversy over defining refugees, asylants and the difference between political and economic refugees here, but want to concentrate on the question of refugees coming on forged documents: If people are so desperate that they resort to crime and considerable danger (e. g. crossing to India in rickety boats under heavy gunfire) just in order to escape from a situation considered as intolerable, the claims of the Sri Lankan government that there are no reasons for the Tamils to

33 Cf. V. Suryanarayan, *Backgrounder*, passim.

34 Cf. Manoj Joshi, "On the Razor's Edge: The Liberation Tigers of Tamil Eelam", *Studies in Conflict & Terrorism* 19, 1996, p. 19–42, here: p. 22–3; V. Suryanarayan, *Backgrounder*.

flee ring rather hollow and its demands that they should therefore be expelled or not admitted into the country in the first place sound spurious. If, as Chandrika Kumaratunga herself acknowledges, the Tamils in Sri Lanka do have genuine grievances that have until now not been satisfactorily addressed, then the argument about 'fake refugees' simply does not hold. In themselves the refugees constituted a risk mostly to the dole bills of the respective governments, and that was enough to take action. In Germany, Switzerland, and some Scandinavian countries the rules and regulations about asylum have been tightened considerably, and a number of Tamil refugees have been deported or returned at the borders. The problem goes, however, deeper: As we said, people feel compelled to resort to crime to escape, and that constitutes a golden opportunity for all sorts of unscrupulous and criminal elements to come in: In Colombo, the agents who arrange for labourers and maids to go to the Middle East and Southeast Asia, at the same time forge travel documents for would-be refugees for a high fee.[35] If we talk about organised crime, it is here that it is most pertinent. A nexus of criminal activity did grow around and in the wake of the refugee movement. Both in Sri Lanka and abroad we have evidence of forging and trafficking syndicates, trading not only in Tamil refugees, but also in illegal labour, Sinhalese and Indian as well.[36] In this regard, the crisis in Sri Lanka has indeed turned out to be a potential security risk or at least destabilising for a number of other countries. Criminal elements, forgers etc., saw the desperation of the refugees as an excellent way to make money by exploiting their plight and blackmailing them into illegal acts.[37] And here we have a clear link to the narcotics trade. In Italy and in France trials about ten years ago unearthed a number of Sri Lankan Tamils employed as couriers or conduits for the drug trade.[38] Most of the accused were convicted, but are now largely at liberty again. And most of them were refugees, who had been pressured into acting as middlemen either out of financial straits or because of blackmail. A proven link to the LTTE remains, however, tenuous. There is no clear proof of *direct* LTTE involvement,[39] though all kinds of rumours and speculations are circulating freely. For what it is worth, the LTTE has always staunchly denied any involvement in this trade, whenever Tamil drug couriers have, been caught in airports all over the world since 1986. The question then would be, who are they? In many cases they may be would-be refugees forced into acting as couriers by agents against the receipt of forged documents and free passage (see above). Also, it cannot be excluded that members of other Tamil groups now forced out of the seats and

[35] Cf. Interview Dr. Eric Meyer, Paris 8.5.1997; V. Suryanarayan, *Backgrounder*, p. 14–15.

[36] On Christmas day 1996, a ship with illegal immigrants from Sri Lanka, India and some other countries sank off the coast of Italy, and nearly all of the passengers drowned. *Sri Lanka Monitor*, December 1996. A similar incident happened on 18.1.1997 off Lampedusa Island, Sicily, when a boat trying to land 82 refugees, was intercepted by Italian police. *Sri Lanka Monitor*, January 1997.

[37] Cf. also *Sri Lanka Monitor*, October 1996 and February 1997.

[38] Interview Prof. Muthiappanathan, Paris, 9.5.1997; cf. *The Sunday Times*, 30.8.1987.

[39] *Asia Week*, p. 38.

sources of power, engage in this trade to supplement their income. It thus seems clear that a Tamil connection does exist, but it would be somewhat simplistic to assume that the LTTE is solely responsible. In the absence of access to official documents these can neither be repudiated nor confirmed.

7. The Case of India

One country, however, did ban the LTTE because it perceived a definite danger to its interests. This was of course India who after Rajiv Gandhi's assassination on 21st May 1991 proscribed the LTTE, its supporters and any agitation or support in favour of it under the TADA (Terrorist Activities Detection Act). Until then, Tamil militant groups had been active in South India rather openly and with more or less impunity. There have traditionally been strong cultural links between Sri Lanka and South India, especially Tamil Nadu. If we agree that extortion, organised crime, violence and terrorist acts in the *host* countries to further their aims at home would constitute a security risk by the LTTE for the host country, then India seems to have been rather sanguine about this until 1991. Let us examine the evidence. There are some instances: in 1982, Prabhakaran and his rival Uma Maheswaran had an armed showdown in classical Western-movie style in the populated Pondy Bazar in Madras' fashionable district of T-Nagar. The population, though sympathetic to the cause of the militants, did not in the least like this, and the government insisted both leave the country. This did not prevent LTTE members (and Prabhakaran) from returning to Tamil Nadu after 1983 and working from Madras until 1986. When the Thimpu talks 1985 failed, India or better, Tamil Nadu security agencies, i. e. the DGP Mohan Das,[40] decided to crack down more decisively on the militants. Nearly all their weapons stored in the state were confiscated, their training camps closed down and some guerilla leaders, including Prabhakaran, were put under house arrest on 8th Nov. 1986.[41] The action, however, rebounded on the police. It was stated by the state government under MGR that it was done without his authorisation, and that the leaders be released and their weapons restored.[42] The DGP resigned over the affair. Prabhakaran nevertheless, decided to leave India and only returned in 1987. In the late 1980s, the feelings of the Tamil population in the state were torn between admiration for the resolve of the militants and complaints about the growing 'gun-culture' there. The latter was caused, it was said, by the presence of a number of militant groups who carried on their arguments with the help of guns and in the streets of Madras and

40 Personal information former DGP K. Mohan Das, Chennai, 23.5.1997. cf. Dagmar Hellmann-Rajanayagam, *The Tigers – Armed Struggle for Identity*, Heidelberg 1994, p. 104.

41 *India Today*, 15.12.1986, p. 33.

42 *India Today,* 15.12.1986, p. 33; Interview former DGP K. Mohan Das 23.5.97.

intimidated the population.[43] The security forces took steps to curb this, but stopped short of banning or expelling LTTE and other organisations until 1991. The LTTE, a recent publication claims, were a law unto themselves.[44] Not even the assassination of EPRLF leader Padmanabha and twelve of his followers in Tamil Nadu in 1990 led to a ban. To sum up, India did not hesitate to act decisively when she judged either the Sri Lankan crisis in general or the militants in particular a security threat, but this has always been tied to specific situations and has been liable to considerable changes over the years. Only recently has this policy been questioned by some authors who, however, argue from the hindsight of Gandhi's assassination, that a vast terrorist network exists in India including the LTTE, ULFA, ISI and beyond, which all cooperate to destabilise India.[45]

However, throughout the 1980s India was in a bind where the conflict in Sri Lanka was concerned. The repressive regime of the Sri Lankan government towards the Tamils did not leave those in Tamil Nadu unmoved. The state had, after all, a tradition of opposition to the Indian Union.[46] India could, therefore, not openly advocate secession, because that might have undesirable repercussions in Tamil Nadu, but could not afford to overlook the problem either, for the same reason. Rajiv Gandhi tried the, in his view, second-best option: to pressure both sides into an agreement underwritten by India, an option which eventually cost him his life.

After 21st May 1991, the LTTE was proscribed *in toto*. The charge was that of the LTTE being involved in illegal and criminal acts, that endangered Indian security at the highest level. Since then, it has been hounded by the security forces in Tamil Nadu with a zeal sometimes amounting to paranoia. This was evident during the crack-down on refugees in 1992–93 when the 'persuade and repatriate'-rule was interpreted very 'creatively' by the authorities on the order of an extremely insecure and apprehensive Jayalalitha government who had to disguise and deny its earlier close links to the organisation. Eventually, this led to protests by the UNHCR commissioner in Madras, and the practice was stopped.[47] Though in Tamil Nadu in general, a clear distinction was drawn between the LTTE and refugees (though few doubted the implication of the LTTE in the assassination), the government was obviously unable to draw this distinction and equated refugees with the LTTE. In the process, they were denied access to educational facilities and dry rations, unless registered in the camps, and NGOs were forbidden

43 Cf. *Indian Express*, 2.1.1986, *The Statesman*, 1.1.1986; *The Hindu*, 3.1.1986; *Vīravāṅkai*, March-Apr. 1986, p. 3.

44 Maj.-Gen. Afsir Karim (AVSM retd.), *Transnational Terrorism. The Danger in the South*, Lancer Paper 5, New Delhi 1993, p. 28–9.

45 *Ibid*., p. 16 and passim.

46 Cf. Dagmar Hellmann-Rajanayagam, *Tamil – Sprache als politisches Symbol*, Stuttgart 1984.

47 V. Suryanarayan, *Backgrounder*, p. 24; Interview with Sunil Bahadur Thapa, UNHCR Officer-in-Charge Chennai, 22.5.97.

access to the camps and at one point even operating in Tamil Nadu.[48] A particularly virulent crackdown occurred within the context of the International Tamil Conference in Thanjavur in Jan. 1995, when not only were all Sri Lankan refugees in the district either rounded up and sent away or confined to the camps, but Sri Lankan citizens were not even admitted to participate in the proceedings (in spite of having registered and paid their fees). On top of that, six Sri Lankan scholars were taken into custody around midnight on the 1st January (the famous 'midnight knock') and deported a few days later.[49] The buck for the responsibility of these measures is still being passed between the centre, the state government, and the security authorities. NGOs and refugee self-help organisations made strenuous efforts to discount the link between the LTTE and themselves, pointing out that most of the current refugees had come after 1990, when the IPKF had withdrawn from Sri Lanka and the LTTE were in control.[50] But this serves to show that sympathies not only for the LTTE, but to some extent also for the Sri Lankan refugees, had dropped since 1991. If one wants to be cynical one could say, the prevalent feeling was, we support your cause and give you sanctuary, but assassinating our prime ministers goes too far. We can do that ourselves, thank you. The hysteria seems to have lessened considerably after the change of government 1996, and the access of the refugees to educational facilities, dry rations etc. has been restored. Police circles acknowledge that this is by far the better policy in order to curb law and order problems, since it facilitates the integration of the refugees into the population.[51] About 8000 new refugees did arrive in India until December 1996 (about half of them former refugees who had returned to Sri Lanka after 1995[52]), who were checked and sent to different refugee camps by the Tamil Nadu authorities, after it was established that they were not LTTE members.[53] India continues to take measures designed to curb or prevent the entry of LTTE cadres into the country, e. g. heavy screening of Sri Lankan Tamil visa applications, but these are fairly low-key actions. However, though the suspicions of the refugee camps being riddled with LTTE cadres (a patently ridiculous notion, since what they could do in the tightly controlled and supervised camps is anybody's guess) have receded, a recent seminar on refugees and security problems in Madras still shows an underlying concern with the general and particular law and order situation. The LTTE is still seen as a threat: In February, some people, a Sri Lankan Tamil, some LTTE supporters, an Indian doctor and Australian citizen, were arrested in a flat in Madras for planning to smuggle medicine to LTTE

48 V. Suryanarayan, *Backgrounder*, p. 20–1; Interview Mr. S. C. Chandrahasan, Co-ordinator for India, Pro TEG and Treasurer, OfEER, Chennai, 23.5.97.

49 For a detailed description see *Frontline*, 31.1.1995.

50 Interview Mr. S. C. Chandrahasan, 23.5.97 and Dr. Nirmala Chandrahasan, Attorney-at-Law, Chennai, 21. 5. 97.

51 Personal information from Police sources in Chennai, 22.5.97.

52 Interview Sunil Thapa, 22.5.97.

53 *Sri Lanka Monitor*, December 1996.

members injured in Jaffna.[54] Shortly afterwards, the editor of a Tamil magazine was arrested for verbally supporting the LTTE cause.[55] All arrested are now out on bail. But the case shows the lengths to which the TADA can be taken: as I mentioned to one of my conversation partners in the police: the fact that we are sitting here and discussing the problem, might be construed as subversive, to which he agreed that it was plainly ridiculous, but unfortunately true.[56] This leaves the question, if not the refugees, how much of a threat is the LTTE to Tamil Nadu and to India in general? Here, as we saw, opinions differ markedly. Sources in Madras stated, that undoubtedly smuggling of fuel, medicines and other daily needs was still going on off the coast of Tamil Nadu in spite of close surveillance of the coastline to Sri Lanka. Beyond this, however, the LTTE is no longer perceived as an acute security threat which would have to be countered by decisive action. Any more decisive and integrated activities besides these business contacts, are denied by the authorities in Madras.[57] This would also be the attitude of the Indian government, which under the Gujral doctrine of asymmetry assigns very low priority to the Sri Lankan problem,[58] if not closing its eyes altogether. This is in distinct contrast to some other sources in the military and security who to be sure do not perceive an immediate threat but harbour the idea of a national and international network of the LTTE and other 'terrorist' links worldwide, all out to destabilise India. The mentioned short monograph by Afsir Karim is an example.[59] His conclusions sound far-fetched and are not substantiated by referenced sources, however, he did work with the IPKF and was the co-author of a book on the failure of the IPKF in Sri Lanka.[60] He sees this cooperation of the LTTE with other outfits not so much in ideological as in business and organisational terms, since he, too, is at a loss to explain why the LTTE would want to plunge India into chaos. When he talks about the potentially disturbing effects and intentions of the LTTE in Tamil Nadu, he sees an actual problem from the wrong angle: it is not the LTTE that tries to create Tamil nationalism and secessionism in Tamil Nadu, which has existed there long before. The LTTE could, however, feed into this dormant nationalism and awaken it to crisis point. And exactly at this point the LTTE becomes less an actual threat in Tamil Nadu than a convenient political stick to beat one's opponents with.[61] This applies the more so, since a possible link between the LTTE and other agencies in India where the Rajiv Gandhi assassination is concerned have not been finally discounted. The trial of 41

54 *The Sun*, 23rd Feb. 1997; *The Hindu* 8.2.1997.

55 *Sri Lanka Monitor*, February 1997; *Tamil Times*, March 1997, p. 3f.

56 Personal information from Police sources in Chennai, 22.5.1997.

57 *Ibid.*

58 Interview Commodore Jasjit Singh, Director, IDSA, Delhi, 15.5.97; Interview Col. Parvinder Singh, Military Attaché, High Commission of India, Kuala Lumpur, March 1997.

59 Karim, *Transnational Terrorism.*

60 Major Shankar Bhaduri and General Afsir Karim, *The Sri Lankan Crisis*, Lancer Paper I, New Delhi 1990.

61 Interview Mr. Chandrahasan, Chennai, 23.5.97.

accused drags on and is expected to 'finally' finish within six months. At the same time, the Jain Commission continues to sit and to listen to all kinds of lurid claims and accusations regarding the murder. This has, however, now become more an inner-Indian affair, washing political dirty linen in public, than an indictment of the LTTE. The activities of the LTTE in India as well as in other countries are at the time of writing seen as rather low-key.

8. Conclusion

What emerges out of this rather blurred and tentative picture is that the conflict in Sri Lanka can indeed be said to impinge on security concerns in the wider region and internationally, albeit in rather diffuse and intangible ways. The one country that did see both the crisis in Sri Lanka in general and the LTTE in particular as a definite threat to her security was India, and she has not only taken a number of steps to curb it, but also considers herself successful.

In other countries the only security threat of any magnitude is that of a break-down of law and order among large numbers of refugees or Tamil immigrants. This has so far happened in a rather limited area of Toronto. This state of affairs definitely counts as a security risk for the city of Toronto, but it is obviously not only the LTTE which is involved here, but a number of other organisations and gangs. A ban on LTTE would therefore hardly defuse the situation. This and the foregoing Indian example are chosen to point out that the security risks arising out of the conflict in Sri Lanka often take a different form and shape from the expected ones. In addition, it has to be kept in mind that, whereas the LTTE is still a militant guerilla outfit and will fashion its actions towards this end, some of the rival Tamil groups, a few of whom are nowadays allied with the Sri Lankan government, have to all intents and purposes descended into mere criminal organisations indulging in their own brands of lawlessness abroad.[62] An example for this was the failed coup in the Maldives in 1988 which was masterminded by PLOT mercenaries.[63]

In other countries this threat does not exist. Moreover, even if the LTTE is active abroad, it merits mentioning, that it has never attacked foreigners in Sri Lanka or outside, has never engaged in spectacular terrorist acts abroad.[64] The lawlessness in Sri Lanka and the breakdown of an ordered life has brought along with the stream of refugees quite a number of criminal elements gaining a windfall alongside ordinary people who are often forced into crime just to be

62 It is sometimes claimed that the murder of Perinbanathan and Gajendran in Paris was carried out by members of a rival militant or rival LTTE (Mahathaiya) organisation. Interview Prof. Muthiappanathan, Paris, 9.5.97.

63 Joshi, "On the Razor's Edge," fn. p. 42. Joshi does not mention that it was PLOT that masterminded that manoeuvre, but implies that it was the LTTE.

64 Cf. n. 19 above.

able to leave the country and survive. The presence of these elements does constitute a threat to law and order in the host countries, and steps are taken by the authorities to curb these. Incidentally, the latest instance of trafficking in humans was a plane-load with 173 Sri Lankan Tamils, dumped onto Schiphol Airport in Amsterdam by Turkmenistan Airlines illegally, i. e. without flight and landing permission in the middle of February 1997.[65] Though organised human trafficking was suspected by the authorities, the Tamils were not – as would have been possible under Dutch law – deported within 24 hours. They were taken to refugee camps and their applications for asylum will be investigated. The threat from these Tamil sources looks, however, at least to this researcher, far less serious than e. g. the Russian mafia in Germany or even some types of suspected Vietnamese triads. . The point is, that none of these – traders in human flesh, Russian mafia or triads – can be immediately linked to political ideology or activity, they are purely criminal outfits. Though some western countries do label the LTTE a terrorist organisation, at the same time it is clear that their members overseas are not the Tamils who constitute a security threat. Most of them are indeed almost painfully law-abiding. The security threat comes from quite another direction. And this threat cannot be eliminated by ad-hoc measures in the host countries, but has to await a solution at source, i. e. an end to the conflict in Sri Lanka itself. To assume that banning the LTTE in the US and Europe could in any way take care of this problem is rather simplistic, and the implication that all criminal activities in which Tamils are involved or suspected to be involved are masterminded by the LTTE, does invest this group with quite an inordinate amount of power. Some of the links to the refugees and to the Tamil diaspora cannot be discounted, e. g. in the business sector or arms trade,[66] but the LTTE does not make any effort to deny these, claiming that political, financial or moral support is not illegal in itself. In these two fields, LTTE is, moreover, not the only player. A ban would simply criminalize and drive underground a group which up to now operates fairly openly and on whom tabs can be kept, and would therefore probably do more damage than good. Only a resolution of the conflict in Sri Lanka itself would encourage and enable the refugees to return to their home country. At the moment, this solution seems unfortunately, to recede further and further into the future (or the past).

[65] *Süddeutsche Zeitung*, 19.2.97.

[66] Cf. Olson, *Small Wars*, p. 60–1.

Nationality Problems and Political Parties of Pakistan: The National Awami Party (NAP) and its Successors

Inayatullah Baloch

iIs Pakistan a nation-state or a multinational country? This ideological debate has taken the lives of millions since the creation of Pakistan. This paper is an attempt to focus on the policies and strategies of the National Awami Party (NAP) and its successor organizations concerning ethnic problems in Pakistan.

Pakistan's nationality problems remain unsolved. There are only two alternatives in dealing with them – either fierce state repression which conjures up further resistance and bloodshed or a skilful federal diplomacy which defuses militancy by means of greater autonomy and self determination.

The state of Pakistan claims a single nation in Pakistan. The very concept of nationality, federalism and regional autonomy did not fit with the ideological foundations of this state. Pakistan was supposed to be a nation state according to the two nations theory propounded by the founder of Pakistan, M. A. Jinnah. Raising the question whether it was not in fact a multinational state, was considered to be treason. Millions of Bengalis, Baluch, Pakhtuns and Sindhis died because of this unresolved conflict which also led to foreign intervention and several military coups.

The National Awami Party (NAP) and its successor organisations regard Pakistan as a multinational and multiethnic state, each of whose nationalities has had a distinct history of its own which often included its own state formation.[1] The advocates of multinationality view the regions to the West of the Indus as parts of the Middle East and Central Asia. They regard Sind as separate entity, the home of South Asia's oldest culture, cut off from India by the Thar desert and the Rann of Kachh, whereas the Panjab is considered to be a part of the North Indian plains.

[1] See the following works on the state formation: Inayatullah Baloch, *The Problem of Greater Baluchistan: A Study of Baluch Nationalism*,Stuttgart,1977; Feroz Ahmad, *Sindhi National Question*, New York, n. d.; Abdur Rahman Pazhawak, *Pakhtunistan*, New York, 1960.

1. The Foundation and Ideology of the National Awami Party

The NAP was the first political organisation with a Leftist ideology which emerged at the national level in Pakistan. It wis founded in 1957 by the leaders of various groups such as the Red Shirts led by Abdul Ghaffar Khan, the "Frontier Gandhi", the Ostman Gal led by Prince Karim (of Kalat) and Mir Bizenjo, a spokesman for an independent Baluchistan. There were also representatives of the Sind Hari Committee, a wing of the All-India Communist Party led by Hyder Bakhsh Jatoi, the Sind Muhaz led by the Sindhi Nationalist leader G. M. Syed, the Azad Pakistan Party, a union of Panjabi nationalists and communists led by Mian Iftakharuddin in the Panjab, and in East Pakistan the leftist faction of the Awami League led by Maulana Bhashani and the Ganatantri Dal (Democratic Party) led by Mahmud Ali. The main objectives of the NAP were: Reorganisation of the federal provinces on linguistic, cultural, historical and geographic basis along the lines of the Soviet model of nationalities, the dissolution of the West Pakistan "One Unit" province, socialism, secularism, nonalignment and democracy.[2] Despite its radical programme the NAP was not a Marxist party. Many of its leaders such as Ghaffar Khan, Samad Achakzai, Bhashani, Prince Karim, and Bizenjo were not Marxists, but social democrats influenced by Atatürk, King Amanullah, Gandhi and Nehru. Its initial thrust was the demand for regional autonomy and an independent foreign policy.

In 1957, the NAP with the help of several other political parties succeeded in getting a bill passed by the West Pakistan Assembly which provided for the dissolution of the "One Unit". This democratic victory was resisted by the civil and military elite and thus led to the military take-over, the abrogation of the constitution of 1956 and military action against the autonomists in Baluchistan.[3] Since the democratic success of the NAP had been subverted in this way, the radicals and Marxist hardliners in the party gained more influence, they aligned themselves with the Soviet Union. In practice the NAP was not all a party of the working class, it was dominated by leaders with a feudal or tribal background who had no intention of establishing a socialist state, but for tactical reasons they aligned themselves with the Soviet Union so as to combat the pro-Western power elite in Pakistan. However, by moving to the left and giving more scope to radical leaders after 1960, the NAP was able to penetrate Marxist movements among students, peasants and workers. In the martial law period (1958-1962) the NAP was not allowed to function, but NAP continued to work underground in the rural areas of Sind, Baluchistan, the NWFP and East Pakistan (now Bangladesh). During this period of under-

[2] Inayatullah Baloch, "Baluch Question in Pakistan and Right of Self-Determination", in: W. P. Zingel (ed.), *Pakistan in its Fourth Decade*, Hamburg 1983, p. 201–22.

[3] NAP's *Constitution and Program*, Lahore n. d.

ground activities, the NAP was mainly controlled by socialists and radical elements, who had links with Indian or Afghan communists or nationalists. A group of NAP leaders went to Syria and Iraq to get help from Arab national communists. Whether all these activities were actually part of the party's general policy or not remains an enigma.[4] The Pakistan power elite took note of the presence of the NAP leaders in Kabul, Delhi and Baghdad and denounced them as agents of foreign powers bent on disintegrating Pakistan. Many leaders and workers of the party were apprehended in Pakistan and imprisoned without trial.

2. The Ideological Split of the NAP in 1967

The radicalisation of the NAP in the period of underground activities was bound to lead to tensions between a more "socialist" wing of the party and one which stressed the old demands for democracy and autonomy. The Sino-Soviet split provided a paradigm for the articulation of this conflict and in 1967 the NAP broke apart, the radical wing being supposedly Pro-Peking and the other Pro-Moscow. Bhashani wanted to organise the peasants of East Pakistan for a revolutionary struggle and became identified with Peking, Wali Khan, the son of the "Frontier Gandhi", Ghaffar Khan, continued the campaign for a reorganisation of Pakistan on the Soviet model of nationality and was considered to be Pro-Moscow. However, there were representatives of the opposite wing in each camp. Prof. Muzaffar Ahmed led the Pro-Moscow elements in East Pakistan and the General Secretary of the NAP, Afzal Bangash, opposed Wali Khan in West Pakistan, and was identified with Peking. He held against Wali Khan that he was promoting Pakhtun chauvinism and neglecting the importance of class struggle. Bangash then founded a militant peasant organisation. This split weakened the NAP in NWFP. In Baluchistan and Sind such splits were avoided. This was partly due to a more accommodating attitude of the party leadership. In Baluchistan Sher Mohammad Marri, a close confidant to the NAP leader Nawab Khair Bakhsh Marri, formed a militant organisation of nomads and peasants which followed the path of armed socialism.[5] Whereas Wali Khan expelled Bangash from the party, Nawab Marri and Bizenjo, who led the NAP in Baluchistan put up with Sher Mohammad Marri's radical ventures. It seems that this party pledged to the advocacy of the regional autonomy also permitted a great deal of autonomy to its regional branches.

[4] Interview with Mr. A. Barakzai (Baluch), one of the leaders of the Baluchistan Democratic Party based in Syria and Iraq in 1960ies and 1970ies. The Interview was held in London.

[5] Sher Mohd. Marri founded the "Mazlum Party" in 1947 against the Sardari System in Baluchistan. In the 1960ies, the party was reorganized with the help of the NAP. The Mazlum Party published the montly "*Chingari*"(flame) in Baluchi and Urdu.

3. The NAP and the Elections of 1970

In March 1969, President Ayub Khan handed over power to General Yahya Khan who announced that election would be held in October 1970. He also dissolved the "One Unit" and restored the earlier provinces inherited from British rule. This was an important concession to the NAP, whose pro-Moscow wing welcomed it and did not press for any further redrawing of provincial boundaries. The pro-Peking wing on the other hand was no longer interested in democracy and boycotted the elections. The result of the elections did not contribute to interest aggregation and national unity, on the contrary three parties with distinct regional strongholds emerged from this contest: The Awami League controlling East Pakistan, the Pakistan People's Party of Zulfikar Ȧli Bhutto with its stronghold in the Panjab and Sind, and the NAP (pro-Moscow) in the NWFP and Baluchistan. Only Bhutto's party advocated federalism with a strong central government, the other two wanted a loose federation with a great measure of autonomy for the provinces. Secularism and socialism which had been highlighted by the NAP at an earlier stage were no longer a major issue. This was also due to the fact that the NAP did not have a majority in the NWFP and had to depend on an alliance with the Jamiat-ul-Ulama-i-Islam (JUI), an orthodox religious party which opposed the concept of the nation state, but also had no use for secularism and socialism. In Baluchistan the NAP was in a better position. It had obtained 45 per cent of the votes and had a comfortable majority as far as the seats in the provincial assembly were concerned. The "unholy alliance" of the NAP with the JUI frustrated many leftists in the party. In Baluchistan the NAP government led by Mengal could pursue a policy of social and economic reforms unencumbered by such an alliance, but the reforms introduced there greatly alarmed the central government at Islamabad.[6] External factors were also of major importance. Mohammad Daud's coup in Afghanistan constituted a serious threat to Pakistan, because Daud was known to be an ardent supporter of the claim for an independent Pakhtunistan. He could also be expected to back the NAP in its stand against Islamabad. Bhutto's government forestalled such eventualities by outlawing the NAP and sending the military into the recalcitrant border provinces. This practically meant a move back to square one: the NAP was once more faced with a similar situation as in 1958 when Ayub Khan had forced it to go underground.

[6] Inayatullah Baloch, "Baluch Question ...," p. 204–5, as well as by the same author, "Afghanistan, Pashtunistan, Baluchistan," *German Foreign Affairs* 31, 3rd Quarter 1980, p. 283–301.

4. The NAP and Language Policy

The language issue has been hotly contested ever since Pakistan was founded. East Pakistan insisted on Bengali and did not want to accept Urdu, whereas Jinnah asserted in Dhaka in 1948 when discussing the Bengali demands, that only Urdu could be the national language of Pakistan. Actually only about seven per cent of the population of Pakistan spoke Urdu as their native tongue, the rest spoke different other languages though some of these other people were able to use Urdu as a link language just like English. The NAP had therefore supported Urdu as a link language which should replace English, but had also demanded for the autonomous development of the major regional languages, e. g. Baluchi, Bengali, Panjabi, Sindhi etc. Whereas Bengali was belatedly accepted as an alternate official language, no such concessions were made to other linguistic regions. In 1972 when the NAP governments were formed in Baluchistan and the NWFP, they endorsed Urdu as official language and thereby alienated those party members who hoped for a greater emphasis on the respective regional languages.[7] Probably the NAP governments being aware of their precarious position *vis-à-vis* the central government did not want to highlight which had been a major cause of the secession of Bangladesh. A decision against Urdu would have immediately raised the scare of secession. Moreover, the "Unholy Alliance" with the JUI mentioned above, must have acted as a check on the NAP language claims as the JUI could be expected to defend Urdu.

5. The NAP Policy and the Provincial Boundaries and International Frontiers

Closely related to the language issue was the problem of the redrawing of provincial boundaries. Pakistan as well as India had inherited boundaries drawn by British rulers. In India they were redrawn so as to create linguistic provinces, but in Pakistan all central governments refused to do that. When the NAP came into power in Baluchistan in 1972, the chief minister, Sardar Mengal, suggested that the northern Pakhtun areas of Baluchistan should be transferred to the NWFP whereas Baluch areas in Sind and Panjab (i.e. Dera Ghazi Khan and Jacobabad) should be attached to Baluchistan.[8] The ruling elite of the NAP in the NWFP failed to grant the right of self determination to its non-Pakhtun population which forms more than 30 per cent of the population of that province. On the other hand, it claimed parts of northern Panjab without

[7] *Ibid.* "Baluch Question," p. 204.

[8] Sardar Ataullah Mengal's statement in the daily *Dawn*, Karachi, 30th June 1972.

taking into consideration the factors of ethnicity, language etc. It seems that the NAP leaders never gave any serious thought to the rights of minorities and the principle of self-determination and just raised claims which suited their own interests. And even these they did not really state with great vigour, perhaps they were staked only because of their nuisance value or so as to serve as political bargain counters.

The NAP leaders have also been silent or vague as far as the western frontier of Pakistan is concerned, the only exception being Ghaffar Khan who openly rejected the Durand line as an imperialist frontier dividing the Pakhtuns of Pakistan and Afghanistan. He has been supported in this stand by various rulers of Afghanistan, who advocated the merger of Pakhtun areas (sometimes including Baluch territories) with Afghanistan or an independent Pakhtunistan. The NAP leaders of Baluchistan have rejected Afghan claims on Baluchistan.[9] On the other hand, Gul Khan Nasir, the NAP's General Secretary in Baluchistan and theoretician of his party has staked the claim that the frontier between Persia (Iran) and Baluchistan should be denounced as the result of an imperialist plot to divide Baluch territories.[10]

There were certain contradictions in the NAP policy due to the divergent interests of ethnic groups represented in the party. Thus the NAP highlighted the nationality question as far as Iran was concerned – because of the Baluch interests involved there – but it failed to do so with regard to Afghanistan. Ghaffar Khan in his speeches in Kabul had even explicitly supported the Afghan concept of a nation state.[11] This fitted in with his vision of Pakhtunistan, but was bound to be resented by the Baluch and other ethnic minorities in Afghanistan and its sympathisers in the NAP. The Indo-Pakistan frontier on the other hand has never been of interest to the NAP leadership.

The vague position of the NAP (and its successors) with regard to Pakistan's western frontier has encouraged the Soviet Union, India and Iraq to support the Afghan policy concerning the Pakhtun and Baluch territories. This support has also sometimes been used so as to put pressure on Pakistan to cut its links with the Western powers.

6. The NAP and the Pakistani Judiciary

Successive governments of Pakistan have accused the NAP of being against the state and working for foreign powers (e. g. India, Afghanistan, Iraq and the Soviet Union) wishing to disinte-

9 Baloch, "Afghanistan, Pashtunistan, Baluchistan," p. 283–301. For further study cf. Pazhwak, *Pakhtunistan* (see fn. 1), I. Baloch, *Afghan Jirga: A Documentary Study of the Red Shirts*, Islamabad 1976 and Mir Ghaus Bakhsh Bizenjo's statement in the daily *Morning News*, Karachi, 4th October 1972.

10 Interview with Mir Gul Khan Nasir in Quetta, 1978.

11 Abdul Ghaffar Khan, *My Life and Struggle*, New Delhi/Kabul, n. d., p. 216–48.

grate Pakistan. Consequently the NAP leaders have been charged with sedition and tried by the higher courts. The first instance was the trial of the NAP president Ghaffar Khan in 1956. In his statement Ghaffar Khan argued that he had been against the division of India, because he was convinced that Muslims would gain more in a united socialist federal India in which nationalities had full autonomy. On the other hand he also referred to his first speech in the Constituent Assembly of Pakistan in 1947 when he had pledged loyalty to Pakistan. He pleaded before the High Court, Lahore that he stood for the abolition of the "One Unit" and that he wanted that more respect should be shown for ethnic sentiments. He concluded that he and his associates were freedom fighters, true Muslims and patriotic Pakistanis.[12] The court acquitted him,[13] and perhaps this discouraged the government from using the courts against the NAP in subsequent years. Thus Ayub Khan and Yahya Khan accused the NAP of anti-state activities and the party was banned in 1971, but none of its leaders to face a court of law.

In February 1975 when Bhutto banned the NAP once more, he sought the approval of the Supreme Court for his action under the Political Parties Act. He charged that the NAP and its leaders had never accepted Pakistan and its ideology and had promoted the theory of the self-determination of nationalities. This was interpreted as a rejection of the two nations theory and the preparation for a secession of the western provinces. It was also stated that the NAP had received financial help from Afghanistan and had engineered an insurgency in Baluchistan and terrorism in the NWFP. In March 1975, the working committee of the NAP met in Islamabad. Several of its most important leaders (Wali Khan, Khair Bakhsh Marri, Bizenjo, Ataullah Mengal and Jam Saqi) could not attend as they were imprisoned. In its resolution the working committee stated that all charges against the party were false and malicious and were aimed at the liquidation of the party and all other democratic forces. The committee denied that it followed the nationality doctrine; it stressed the difference between that theory and a mere claim for more autonomy and for linguistic and cultural rights of the federal units. It affirmed its loyalty to Islam and to Pakistan.

Subsequently, the top NAP leaders who could not attend the meeting were requested to attend to record their statements. Amongst these statements those of Wali Khan, Bizenjo, Nawab Marri and Jam Saqi are most interesting with regard to their views on nationality. Wali Khan and Bizenjo claimed that they believed in a Pakistani nation composed of four nationalities with distinct languages and cultures. They claimed that they saw non contradiction between the concept of one nation and different nationalities. Marri said he believed in Pakistani patriotism and that he regarded Pakistan as a multinational state in which nationalities not only have

12 A copy of Ghaffar Khan's statement was supplied to the author by his son-in-law, Mr. Yahya Jan in 1975 in Peshawar. See also Farigh Bukhari, *Bacha Khan*, Peshawar 1957, p. 296–317.

13 *Pakistan versus Abdul Ghaffar Khan* in West Pakistan High Court, *Pakistan Legal Decisions*, Lahore 1976, p. 148–95.

their distinct languages and cultures, but also their own statehood. Jam Saqi viewed Pakistani nationalism as political nationalism and argued for the Soviet model of nationality. The statements of these leaders were definitely in conflict with each other. The party did not succeed in clearing its position before the court and decided to boycott the court proceedings. By the end of 1975, the Supreme Court confirmed the action taken by the Bhutto regime. It banned the NAP declaring that the concept of nationality was definitely incompatible with the concept of a Muslim nation state.[14] It also charged the NAP with having been involved in a conspiracy with Afghanistan to disintegrate the federation. In 1976 a special tribunal was established by the central government to try the NAP leaders under the Treason and Anti-National Activities Acts.[15] This tribunal was abolished by General Zial ul-Haq when he overthrew Bhutto and released the NAP leaders.[16]

7. The Successors of the NAP[17]

In 1978, Zia released the NAP leaders from prison but did not lift the ban which made the party an unlawful organization. The former leaders of the NAP were no 1onger interested in the party's revival due to their differences on ideology and strategy. Sardar Mengal and Nawab Marri lost hope of gaining their national rights within Pakistan. They went into exile aiming to achieve the liberation of Baluchistan through armed struggle. The remaining leaders of the NAP founded various successor organisations. Today there exist many leftist political organisations which rose from the ashes of the NAP. The following are the most important:

(1) The Baluchistan National Movement (BNM): It stands for socialism, national rights and the right of self-determination as well as the abolition of the Sardari Nizam (tribal-feudal system). It draws its support from lower middle class, students, and working class people (fishermen, peasants, and mine workers). It has also some influence among tribesmen.

14 *Pakistan versus Abdul Wali Khan*, the president of the NAP in the Supreme Court, 1975, *Pakistan Legal Decisions*, Lahore 1976, p. 57–195, as well as see the written statements of the NAP's prominent leaders in *Aur Biyan Apna* (our statement), Lahore 1976.

15 Weekly *Al-Fatah*, Karachi, 9th–16th July 1976, p. 9–16.

16 Mushtaq Raj, *Zindah Wali-wa-Zindah Masih se Mulaqat* (Urdu), Lahore 1976. It provides interesting information on the proceedings of the NAP's case.

17 Monthly *Pakistan Forum*, Karachi, May 1979, p. 8–12; *The Juhd* (published by the Baluch Students Organization), Quetta, Sept. 1989, p. 2–9.; Unpublished *Declaration of the Sindh, Baluch, Pashtoon Front*, issued on 18th April 1985, p. 1–4; Tahir Bizenjo, *Baluchistan*, 1989, (it represents the views of the PNP on the national question, as well as criticism on the BNM and Sardar Mengal); Nawab Akbar Bugti, *Let the people decide*, in the weekly *Viewpoint*, Lahore, 19th March 1992. For further information see the files of the monthly, *Azad Baluchistan*, London, published by the BLO and the *Jabal*, published in Baluchi/English by the BPLF (Baluch People's Liberation Front).

(2) The Baluchistan National Party (BNP): It has been founded by the members of tribal élite who took part in the armed struggle against Islamabad. It advocates a confederal system in Pakistan. It commands a great influence among tribesmen and has considerable following in middle classes. The BNP is headed by Sardar Alaullah Mengal, the first elected Chief Minister of Baluchistan in 1972–74.

(3) Jamhuri Watan Party (JWP): It is led by a tribal chieftain, Nawab Akbar Khan Bugti. Its social base is confined to tribal areas of Baluchistan. It has considerable influence in non-Baluch ethnic groups.

(4) The Baloch Students Organisation (BSO), vanguard of the Baluch nationalism, is a powerful pressure group. Its total membership has been estimated 25,000. It was a great supporter of the BPLF and the Afghan Saur Revolution. At present, it supports the BNM. During the military rule of Zia ul-Haq, many of its members were imprisoned, hanged or forced to go in exile. It stands for socialism and the right of self-determination, including separatism.

(5) The Awami National Party (ANP): It is led by Abdul Wali Khan, son of the "Frontier Gandhi" and the former president of the NAP. He commands a great respect in India and had enjoyed significant influence on the foreign policy of (pre-Islamic) Afghanistan, especially on the political status of the Durand Line, the Pak-Afghan frontier. The social base of the ANP is limited to the Pakhtun rural areas. Its influence has declined due to its support of revolutionary Afghanistan and Islamic revivalism, as well as due to the greater representation of Pakhtuns in the power structure of Pakistan.

(6) Another major organisation of the Pakhtuns is the Pashtun Khaw Milli Awami Party (PKMAP), a child of the former Pashtun Khwa National Awami Party (PKNAP). These organisations were founded by Mahmud Khan Achakzai and his father, the late Samad Khan Akhakzai, a founder of the NAP. The PKMAP accuses the defunct NAP for ignoring the interests of the Pakhtuns of northern Baluchistan. It draws its support from lower middle class students and labourers. Its main rival are the religious political organisations such as the Jamiat-ul-Ulama-i-Islam (JUI), an ally of the Taliban of Afghanistan. Its main demand has been the separation of the Pakhtun areas from Baluchistan and their merger into the NWFP, a majority Pakhtun region.

It would be interesting to mention that there are some rightist political organisations of settlers from India in Sindh. They have been demanding the "nationality" status for their groups. Their demand has been opposed by the leftist as well as by rightist political parties on the pretext that migration does not create a nationality.[18] In their view Pakistan's ethnic diver-

[18] *Dawn*, Karachi, 3rd Sept. 1995; *Pakistan Progressive*, New York, Dec. 1980, p. 69–72; Inayatullah Baloch, "The Soviet Nationality Policy and Afghanistan," paper presented at the 9th European Conference on Modern South Asian Studies, Heidelberg, 9th–12th July 1986.

sity can only be defined in terms of the five historical "nationalities" Panjabis, Pakhtuns, Seraikis, Sindhis and Baluch.

Since 1998, the successor organisations of the NAP have formed an alliance called the "Pakistan Oppressed Nations Movement" (PONM). The PONM has a single agenda programme aimed for a complete autonomy of the provinces and the re-demarcation of the provincial frontiers. It favours only three subjects for the federation, such as defence, foreign affairs and currency.

The PONM has also been joined by nationalist organisations of Sindh and the Southern region of Panjab, namely the Sindh National Front, headed by Mumtaz Ali Bhutto and the Seraiki Muhaz under the leadership of Taj Langah. The PONM demands the creation of a new Seraiki province in southern Panjab. These organisations draw their support from students, the middle class, peasants and big landlords (*wanderas*).

8. Nationality and Elections

Since 1970, Pakistan has had five elections based on an adult franchise In these elections, the nationality issue has been a crucial one. In the election of 1970, ethnic political parties won in three provinces out of the five, as well as a majority in the National Assembly. The military rulers refused to transfer power to majority ethnic political parties, which resulted in the disintegration of Pakistan in 1971. In the period after Zia ul-Haq, Pakistan has had four elections in which the successors of the NAP campaigned on the question of nationality, including the right of self-determination.

In Baluchistan, the advocates of nationality doctrine secured 47.8 per cent of the votes in 1988, while in 1970 they got 45.1. In the election of 1990, they received 51.74 per cent. In the NWFP the ANP and the nationalist Ulama secured 29.80 per cent in 1988, whereas in 1990 they got 34.93. It is important to mention that a non-1eftist ethnic organisation, the Muhajir/Mutahida Quami Muhaz (MQM), secured 25 per cent in 1988 and 27.0 in 1990. Election results of 1997 in Pakistan suggest that despite the state's opposition, the nationality issue remains on the political agenda of Pakistan.[19]

The following are the major unresolved issues which continue to destabilise Pakistan:

(1) Self-determination and provincial autonomy,
(2) Re-demarcation of provincial boundaries on ethnic and cultural lines,

[19] Monthly *Herald*, Karachi (Election's special issue) Nov.–Dec. 1990; Andrew Wilder, "Changing Patterns of Punjab Politics in Pakistan," *Asian Survey*, April 1995; *The News International*, London/Islamabad, 5th February 1997.

(3) The inter-provincial migration and control of illegal settlement of foreigners,

(4) Allocation of natural resources such as water and minerals. This is the most contested field between the provinces and between the nationalities.

9. Conclusions

It is difficult to predict how Pakistan's nationality problems will be solved and how long Pakistan will continue its quest for identity. However, it is certain that nationality problems will continue to destabilise the country. It seems to me that a change in the attitude of Pakistan's power élite is necessary regarding the concept of the nation state. We have to remember that the ideological controversy on the subject of one nation versus nationalities in multiethnic states like Pakistan is due to a misperception of our concepts of the nation state and of nationalism. The anti-imperialist struggle should not be confused with nationalism, or the post-colonial state with the concept of the nation.

The idea of a nation state is alien to the pre-colonial history of Southwest and Central Asia. In their history, tribes and ethnic groups played a major role shaping political systems. Therefore, it will be suggested that it is the concept of the nation state and not that of nationality or ethnicity which has created confusion, bitterness and tension, and has alienated the minority ethnic groups from the state (of Pakistan), forcing them to seek a solution in separatism.

The international frontiers and administrative boundaries in Southwest Asia are a constant source of conflict between states and ethnic groups. Moreover, these frontiers have hindered the economic and cultural development of Southwest Asian nations. The frontier system is a product of European Colonialism and is arbitrary, illogical and artificial. Therefore, these boundaries and demarcation lines are no longer desirable. Durable stability can be realised by recognising various identities in multinational states as well as promoting the idea of a confederation, which will enable divided ethnic groups to reunite and promote stability in Southwest and Central Asia.

Democracy, Party System and Civil Society in India

Subrata Kumar Mitra

1. Introduction

Political parties have been described as "creatures of modern and modernising political systems", symbols of "economic modernity", "a measure of identification with the nation-state as distinct from parochial groupings" and, most vitally, as intermediaries between state and society in their capacity as agents of articulation and aggregation of interests. In view of their diversity, the states of Asia provide a vast space in which to analyse the origin, growth and demise of political parties. Considering that political parties are often seen as typically western political institutions, their role in facilitating the interaction of the modern state and traditional society, particularly in the context of post-colonial states, extends the scope of the comparative analysis of party systems.

With the stability of multi-party democracy as its main focus, the paper has two objectives. In the first place, it seeks to answer the puzzle as to how political parties, which are products of the politics and social history of Europe in the 19th century, have become a part of the political process in India though the country has not been subject to the same historical process, such as rapid industrialisation and urbanisation preceding the extension of suffrage. In answer to this puzzle, the paper presents an analysis of the political conditions under colonial rule that facilitated the growth of political parties as intermediaries between British colonial rule and Indian society, the transformation of the party system in India after independence from a one-dominant-party system where Congress played a hegemonial role to a multi-party system, and, the interweaving character of partisanship and social cleavages which has facilitated the integration of parties into the political culture and process. In the second place, drawing on the opinions of supporters of India's main political parties on a range of issues that present the modern state and traditional society in conflict, the paper seeks to underline the contribution of political parties into the creation of a tolerant and plural society in India.

The case study of India is intended to contribute to the analysis of a general theme, namely, political parties and civil society in Asia. Though they are conveniently grouped together in terms of a common geography, the political systems of Asia contain tremendous diversity of size, depth of colonial rule, education, affluence, ethnic diversity, models of development and integration with the international market economy, and finally, the political role of the military. In view of its pivotal position between state and society, the party system provides a useful focus for this analysis. For the same reason, the legitimacy and stability of the party system is vulnerable to the challenges from other agents of social change, particularly those which are able to draw more effectively on national culture and traditions. Multi-party democracy has been relatively more successful in India than in the majority of post-colonial societies. However, underneath the generally effective structure of multi-party democracy there are areas of vulnerability that need to be examined in a theoretical and comparative perspective. The collapse of Indian democracy in 1975–77 and its numerous formal and informal replications at the regional level show the importance of looking at the vulnerability of multi-party democracy in India as part of a general explanation of its success in the first place.

2. Transformation of the Party System, Social Change and Civil Society in India[1]

a) The Problem Stated

How secure is the future of multi-party democracy and civil society[2] in India? The question first gained currency in the 1950ies when India, following independence from British colonial rule, was rocked by separatist movements based on language, region and religion. The issue has come to the fore from time to time. It gained salience in 1975 when the declaration of a national Emergency severely restricted democratic freedoms and political parties. More recently, in 1992 when a four hundred year old mosque in the North Indian city of Ayodhya was torn down by a Hindu mob, the ability of a democratic India to sustain a civil society, committed to a public sphere and free communication for all sections of her citizens,[3] came for national and

[1] The public opinion data used in this paper were collected by the Data Unit of the Centre for the Study of Developing Societies, Delhi, in a survey of a sample of 10,000 individuals, representing the adult population of India, conducted in May-June 1996.

[2] For a range of concrete meanings of this concept and their critics, see Jean Cohen and Andrew Arato, *Civil Society and Political Theory*, Cambridge (Mass.) 1992. For further debates see John Keane (ed.), *Civil Society and the State*, London 1988; Gordon White, “Civil Society and Democratization, I: Clearing the Analytical Ground,” *Democratization* 1 (3), 1994, and, “Civil Society and Democratization, II: Two Case-Studies,” *Democratization* 2 (2), 1995, 56–84.

[3] Some of the values that constitute the basis of civil society in India such as equal citizenship, rights of participation, occupation and association, freedom of worship and practice, movement and residence are defined in

international scrutiny once again. Has India of the 1990s, a more prosperous and powerful country than at independence, also become a less secure and less agreeable place for her religious and ethnic minorities? Have democratic freedoms and civic rights been lost to aggressive cultural nationalism, itself, paradoxically a consequence of the blossoming of majoritarian democracy?

These questions, asked in the specific context of India, are part of a larger debate on civil society and the politics of transition in post-colonial and post-revolutionary societies. In the ideal type form, at the start of the process of transition, the state in these societies represents an alien presence, sustained by a colonial power, or, an élite that originates from within the society but espouses values alien to local culture. The quantitative question here is to ask to what extent conditions that bridge the ideological gap between the state and society are present at a given point of time. Along with social movements and the market, a competitive party system, singled out here for detailed analysis, constitutes three major distinct but complementary agencies through which post-colonial and post-revolutionary societies move in the direction of a civil society.[4]

Though the problematic relationship of multi-party democracy and civil society[5] is posed in the specific context of India in this paper, its ubiquitous presence can be seen in rich, western, industrialised, stable democracies as well as in non-western societies with fledgling democracies, where a largely agrarian population is making its uncertain way with the help of institutions that are often alien to the local political culture. The party system, which provides the crucial link between the social process and the policy-makers, is usually the first to register the emergence of issues affecting the interests of large social groups or questioning the values that underpin the political system. The rise of extreme right movements in the recent politics of western stable democracies, suffering from recession, rising unemployment and violent crime, and the growth of political parties which are committed to restricting the public sphere at least

the Preamble and Article 19 of the Constitution of India. The empirical research agenda on civil society in India consists of the measurement of these rights and their perception at the level of the mass public.

4 Considering the fact that the concept of civil society originated from western historical experience, its application to contexts with different historical trajectories and social characteristics can be problematic. It is important to conceptualise the formation of civil society in quantitative terms so as to avoid the possible incursions into cultural relativism. Otherwise, the scientific question tends to get mired in a polemical debate on national values or in a vague search for the true meaning of democracy. Such debates make sense in the context of a philosophical analysis of cultural relativism or of methods of political mobilization but not in a comparative and empirical analysis of the formation of civil society. For further discussion of this point, see Gordon White, Jude Howell and Shang Xiaoyuan, *In Search of Civil Society: Market Reform and Social Change in Contemporary China*, Oxford 1996, p. 1–6.

5 This can be seen as a collective goods problem. The problem arises from the fact that parties, locked in competition as they are for increasing their share of the vote, must cater to the political needs of the electorate. On the other hand, by individually committing themselves to political and racial intolerance, they might contribute to the demise of those political and civil liberties that make party competition possible in the first place.

for sections of the population who are different in colour or religion are examples of the problematic relationship of multi-party democracy and civil society from the contemporary west.[6] In non-western societies where long standing commitments to the public sphere on the part of citizens, a history of popular struggle for those values and the legal and material basis of protest are not available, the emergence of issues threatening the public sphere can quickly take a fatal turn, leading to the collapse of the constitution altogether, with ominous implications for the threatened social groups, the political system and multi-party democracy.[7]

India offers an interesting case study for the problematic relationship of multi-party democracy and civil society. Its rather unusual combination of constitutional commitment to multi-party democracy and social and economic conditions of poor, post-colonial, non-western societies provides a broad and diverse backdrop. The challenges to the integrative ability of the party system emerging from rapid political mobilization of a diverse population living in vastly different worlds, further divided by language, religion, caste and region have been enormous. In response, the party system has transformed itself radically, and democracy, with the minimum civil liberties that make it meaningful, despite one near-collapse, has survived. The paper intends to analyse the reasons for this resilience and its further implications both for India and for the functioning of multi-party democracy and civil society in post-colonial countries in general.

b) Some Empirical Context

After five decades of experimentation with multi-party democracy and social change, India continues to offer reasons for hope, but still with a lingering sense of doubt. The former arise from the record of achievements since independence.[8] Regular, relatively free and fair elections

6 The political crisis being faced by the centre-right government in France which intends to restrict immigration is an example of both the nature of the crisis as well as of the ability and willingness of citizen groups to engage in political protest in order to defend the threatened public sphere. The problem of political parties in general and the left in particular arises from the fact that public opinion is divided, with an articulate section of French intellectuals expressing their commitment to the Rights of Man which form part of the legacy of the French Revolution while two thirds of the people saying that "there are too many Arabs" in France. The *Economist*, 1st–7th March, p. 32. For a detailed case-study of the rise of the extreme right in France, see Pierre Brechon and Subrata Mitra, "The National Front in France: The Emergence of an Extreme Right Protest Movement," *Comparative Politics*, October 1992, p. 63–82.

7 The difficulty of providing the conditions for political dialogue hindered the functioning of mulitiparty democracy in Pakistan, eventually leading to the Liberation War and the creation of Bangladesh, and, currently plagues the political process in Sri Lanka.

8 "A deeply divided society with, supposedly, a mainly majoritarian type of democracy, India nevertheless has been able to maintain its democratic system." Arendt Lijphart, "The Puzzle of Indian Democracy: A Consociational Interpretation," *American Political Science Review* 90 (2), 1996, p. 258. Lijphart describes the institutionalisation of a sophisticated system of powersharing as the main cause for success in maintaining democratic institutions.

have been held for the office of the President and to legislatures at national and regional levels from 1952 onwards. Participation in these elections has been respectable, in comparison to the United States if not to continental Europe. Parties in power have changed at the centre and in the regional States frequently as a result of elections. Compared to the situation at independence, a significantly higher level of welfare and food security has been achieved. These and other achievements[9] should normally place India among the stable multi-party democracies of the world. But doubts persist because India's record as a stable, multi-party democracy is not positive in its entirety.[10]

Ethnic conflict and communal violence which place informal but effective restrictions on free political participation and dialogue are routinely reported in the media in India and abroad. A rough calculation would put the number of Indians living under informal army rule at forty million people.[11] Even at the national level, democracy all but collapsed in 1975 when Indira Gandhi imposed the Emergency Rule.[12] Democracy did bounce back at the central level in 1977 but then, the resort to the curtailment of democracy through the declaration of direct central rule at the regional level has continued unabated. Even in normal times, a number of preventive detention laws, created over the past years to check terrorism, have restricted civil liberties.[13]

To the extent that multi-party democracy and civil society are effectively present, India, along with a few other poor, non-western societies as Barbados, Botswana, Costa Rica, Ja-

9 Both inflation and explosive population growth have been tamed. And now, with the liberalisation of India's economy, international business confidence in India is higher than ever. For a detailed discussion of some of these indicators, see Subrata Mitra, "India," in: Gabriel Almond and G. Bingham Powell (eds.), *Comparative Politics Today*, New York 1996 (6th ed.).

10 Myron Weiner (*Indian Paradox: Essays in Indian Politics*, New Delhi 1989, p. 9) describes the existence of high levels of political violence and India's ability to maintain a democratic process as a 'puzzling contradiction'. The contradictory aspect of this phenomenon can be partly explained as a fallacy of aggregation because political violence in India is not uniformly distributed across regions. Those that are most afflicted by political insurgency such as Panjab, Kashmir, Nagaland, Assam, Manipur and Mizoram are also precisely the regions where multi-party democracy has been less successful. This is cushioned by the other regions which are both comparatively free of this form of extreme political violence and enjoy stable, multi-party democracy. Weiner's point still stands because even the regions afflicted by insurgency are not terminally lost to democracy. Following the successful assembly elections of 1996 and 1997, Kashmir and Panjab have gone back to popular multi-party rule.

11 For the specification of the concept of 'informal army rule' and the discussion of the reasons for the absence of an explicit role of the military in India's high politics, see Stephen Cohen, in: Atul Kohli (ed.), *India's Democracy: An Analysis of Changing State-Society Relations*, Princeton 1988.

12 The Constitution of India provides for temporary suspension of popular rule in the centre as well as in the States in extreme cases when lawful government is no longer possible. On the basis of the authoritarian spell of 1975–77, Powell classifies India, along with Sri Lanka, Jamaica and Turkey under "major suspension of democracy". See G. Bingham Powell, *Contemporary Democracies: Participation, Stability and Violence*, Cambridge (Mass.) 1982, p. 169.

13 The draconian anti-terrorist laws such as TADA and other forms of preventive detention have become a source of restriction on civil liberties.

maica, Malta, Mauritius and Papua New Guinea appears as a counter-examples against widely held beliefs that link stable democracies with high levels of social and economic development.[14] Ensconced within the first puzzle is a second one: how does a poor society with no democratic tradition of its own manage to maintain not only democratic institutions, but a competitive, *multi-party* democracy as well, successfully warding off the challenges of non-party, plebiscitary democracy, and, strong executive leadership based on popular authoritarianism, deemed by many non-western societies as a more appropriate form of government?

We need to dwell briefly on a methodological issue before embarking on empirical analysis. Even after five decades of independence and democratic government in a federal set up, politics in India still faces a methodological problem of cross-cultural comparability with modern, industrial, liberal, stable democracies.[15] In contrast to the political culture of western democracies, India comes across either as organic or as morally anomic. Whether it is seen in a well-meaning way – or with fear and distrust[16] – the Indian mind is seen as incapable of individual rationality, indispensable for sustaining the complex political institutions of democracy. Even when political behaviour in India is seen in terms of individual calculations of interest, the very perceptions and preferences of individuals are seen as reflections of the interests of the family, caste and tribe.[17] Since the articulation and aggregation of *individual* interests are the crucial determinants of the existence and effectiveness of competing parties and elections, these pre-suppositions about India's political culture explain the unreality and unreliability attributed to elections and multi-party democracy in India. Western audiences sometimes find it difficult to think of Indians as skilful political actors, with goals and strategies, and enough information about their political opponents as they manoeuvre their way through the murky world of politics.

The paper is based on data from general elections to the Lok Sabha (the lower house of the Indian Parliament which is responsible for key legislation and executive accountability) and

14 Robert Dahl, *Democracy and its Critics*, New Haven 1989, p 253.

15 Outside the narrow circle of North American political scientists, India continues to be the subject of a *methodenstreit*. Though Arendt Lijphart's seminal "The Puzzle of Indian Democracy: A Consociational Interpretation," *American Political Science Review* 90 (2), 1996 makes no mention of the difficulty of cross-cultural comparison, understanding India in terms of individual interests continues to be a problem for western mass publics where India remains the quintessential example of 'otherness'. Samuel P. Huntington's *The Clash of Civilizations and the Remaking of World Order*, New York 1996, discussed, reviewed and translated around the world is a recent example of the idiosyncratic description of India (and other non-western societies) in terms of civilisations rather than political systems.

16 We can call it the 'Little Buddha' syndrome after the film of the same name. This attitude to India has a historical genealogy in European Orientalist constructions of India, vigorously questioned by Ronald Inden's *Imagining India*, Oxford 1990.

17 For a succinct analysis of a political culture dominated by 'amoral familism' see Banfield's classic study of Southern Italy. Edward Banfield, *The Moral Basis of a Backward Society*, New York 1958.

two national surveys.[18] The main assumptions that underpin the behaviour of parties and electors in India are not any different from those typically made about voters in stable democracies.[19] They suggest that the peasant, like the businessman, is also an expected utility maximiser and responds to changes in the institutional context which underpins their daily lives. Electoral information, just like political participation, are political resources. The leaders of political parties as well as electors are engaged in purposive action,[20] and the sum of their choices constitutes the primary explanation both for the evolution of multi-party democracy in India as well as its occasional collapse.

3. Competitive Elections and Evolution of the Party System in India

The party system and elections in India are based on single member constituencies, first-past-the-post-system of plurality voting and a bicameral legislature at the centre. The leader of the majority party or coalition in the lower house forms the government. The President of the Republic normally plays the ceremonial role of a formal head of the state. With minor differences, these rules resemble the British system of parliamentary democracy. However, the British party system is the product of the great economic and social changes that rocked society and state in 19th century Europe and produced the political basis for the extension of franchise.[21] India did not go through a similar historical experience. The familiar sequence of the early stirring of the industrial revolution, the radical changes in agriculture, migration and the evolution of the working class movement for the extension of suffrage did not occur in India prior to the institutionalisation of universal adult franchise and a competitive party system. Hence the puzzle: why did multi-party democracy appear in India and how do her people cope with western style political parties and elections?

Part of the explanation of this puzzle lies in the history of political developments in India during the last six decades prior to independence in 1947. A brief perusal of the interaction of

18 The survey was conducted through face-to-face interviews during May-June, 1996, in the aftermath of the eleventh Parliamentary Elections. A representative sample of about 10,000 adults was interviewed by trained investigators from the Centre for the Study of Developing Societies, Delhi. The 1971 survey, conducted by the same institute, was based on a sample of 5500 persons.

19 These assumptions are consistent with those made by Anthony Downs in his *An Economic Theory of Democracy*, New York 1957. See, Chapter 2 "Party Motivation and the Function of Government in Society" for the basic models on electoral choice and partisan behaviour. For a discussion of the basic assumptions of individual expected utility maximisation, see William Riker and Peter Ordeshook, *An Introduction to Positive Political Theory*, Englewood Cliffs 1973.

20 The sociological concept of purposive action expresses the technical concept of expected utility maximisation in a more general way as the basis of rational behaviour.

21 See Joseph LaPalombara and Myron Weiner, "The Origin and Development of Political Parties," in: La Palombara and Weiner (eds.), *Political Parties and Political Development*, Princeton 1966.

the British Raj and Indian resistance to it during this crucial period reveals that conditions for the emergence of political parties were steadily growing. Partly under the impact of Utilitarianism but mostly as a matter of expediency, the British had started experimenting with limited self-rule in issues of minor importance such as municipal administration by the 1880s. This formed part of the British strategy of ruling India with the help of Indian intermediaries, in this case, selected by a very restricted electorate of urban, rich and loyal subjects. The Indian National Congress was set up in 1885 by Sir Alan Octavian Hume, a retired British Civil servant, in order to present Indian interests to the British Crown in a systematic and organised manner. It soon became the leading voice of the Indian middle classes, constantly clamouring for more jobs under the colonial government and for greater political participation. The successive acts of the British Parliament in 1909, 1919, 1935 extended the franchise and brought increasingly greater number of Indians into the scope of party politics based on restricted participation.

The process was not as effortlessly incremental nor linear as it may sound. Periods of extension of franchise and cooperation between colonial rulers and elected representatives were interspersed with ruthless suppression and imprisonment of Indian leaders. The Congress Party itself was often divided in its opinion between collaboration with colonial rule with the hope of greater concessions, and, radical resistance to it on the agenda of independence. Gandhi brought these two strands together in his strategy of non-violent non-cooperation and built a powerful mass movement that united the peasantry and the national bourgeoisie under the banner of the Congress Party. By the 1930s however the national movement was split once again, this time on the issue of religion. The majority of Muslims, under the leadership of the Muslim League, had started agitating for an independent homeland for the Muslims of the subcontinent. As a result, when independence finally arrived in 1947, British India was partitioned into India and Pakistan. Congress Party under Nehru inherited power in a smaller but politically and religiously more homogeneous country, with their links to the constituents intact. This was not the case in Pakistan where the Muslim League, victorious at last, took power, but only at the cost of abandoning its political hinterland in Northern India which blighted the growth of a competitive party system in Pakistan.

This brief historical background partly explains the relative ease with which India developed electoral democracy and a competitive party system in contrast with Pakistan. Universal adult franchise was introduced in 1952, and both the non-democratic left and non-democratic right were authorised to compete equally with the centre and moderate left and right for political power through elections.[22] At independence, the electorate consisted of large numbers of

[22] Participating in the first general elections after independence were the Communist Party of India which only three years earlier had rose in a violent peasant revolution against the nascent Indian state, as well as the Hindu right-wing party Jan Sangh which had been banned after the assassination of Mahatma Gandhi by a member of the Rashtriya Svayamsevak Sangh, a Hindu extremist group. This bold gamble on the part of

voters who had not experienced direct British rule and were stepping out of feudalism straight into popular democracy. Hindus, still recovering from the trauma of partition, were being asked to become citizens of a secular state which did not recognise any religion as its official religion. Millions of poor marginal, land hungry peasantry radicalised through communist agitations and, unorganised manual labourers and unionised industrial workers were all being asked to repose their faith in multi-party democracy as the most effective method of social change. What should have followed is described by several specialists. One of the most cited is Selig Harrison, whose *India: The Most Dangerous Decades* spelt out a future of communal conflict, disharmony and balkanisation.[23] Huntington's *Political Order in Changing Societies* predicted structural discontinuity in the face of popular mobilization.[24] State theorists like Gunnar Myrdal in his *Asian Drama* came up with the formulation of the 'soft state', based on popular consent which would necessarily be lacking in the authority with which to tackle basic problems of structural change.[25] Weaving all these strands into a unified and comparative theory, Barrington Moore, in his *Social Origins of Dictatorship and Democracy*, predicted a state of peaceful paralysis for India in the years following independence.[26]

But, as the record shows, elections have been held regularly (see Table 1). Major policy initiatives have been taken by governments. Parties have alternated in power as a result of elections. On all aggregate indicators of participation, as the data show, India has kept up steady progress. The level of electoral participation has steadily gone up, reaching the levels of continental European voting in some parts of the country. Participation in elections has been widely spread across all social strata, and, in urban areas as well as villages. The level of participation of women, former untouchables, tribals does not lag far behind that of the national average.

The literature on civic culture informs us that the presence of substantial numbers of citizens as opposed to parochials is necessary in order to sustain the kind of electoral and party competition depicted above.[27] Elections and party competition in India, in view of her politically active castes, tribes and ethnic and religious conflict, appears problematic. The answer to

Jawaharlal Nehru appears to have paid rich dividends, by encouraging attitudes favourable to multi-party democracy within these extremist groups.

23 Selig Harrison's *India: The Most Dangerous Decades*, Princeton 1960, was one of the earliest to warn the dangers of disintegration in India.

24 Samuel P. Huntington, *Political Order in Changing Societies*, Yale 1968, reflects the strong commitment to orderly change, if need be at the cost of political coercion, characteristic of the modernisation approach.

25 Gunnar Myrdal, *Asian Drama: An Inquiry into the Poverty of Nations*, 3 Vols., New York 1968.

26 Barrington Moore, *Social Origins of Dictatorship and Democracy: Lord and Peasant in the Making of the Modern World*, Boston 1966.

27 See "The Intellectual History of the Civic Culture Concept" in Gabriel Almond and Sidney Verba (eds.), *The Civic Culture Revisited*, London 1989. On issue dimensions and political parties, see Arendt Lijphart, *Democracies: Patterns of Majoritarian and Consensus Government in Twenty-one Countries*, New Haven 1984, p. 130.

this apparent contradiction lies in the fact that elections and party competition in India have played a double role. Rather than inhibiting the growth of party competition, social conflict, which has got interwoven with political conflict, helps deepen political partisanship. As beneficiaries of the process of political reform introduced by the British towards the end of colonial rule, elections with limited franchise facilitated political transition by acting as the institutional context in which power was transferred by the British rulers to elected Indian leaders. After independence, the same process accelerated the pace of social change, leading to a second phase of political change when the social class and generation that was identified with the freedom movement was replaced by younger leaders, many of whom came from upward mobile, newly enfranchised, lower social classes.[28]

Table 1
Election Data, Indian Parliamentary Elections, 1952–1996

Year	Seats	Candidates	Polling Stations	Electorate (In Millions)	Vote Polled (In Millions)	Turnout (%)
1952	489	1874	132,560	173.2	79.1	45.7
1957	494	1519	220,478	193.7	92.4	47.7
1962	494	1985	238,355	217.7	120.6	55.4
1967	520	2369	267,555	250.6	153.6	61.3
1971	518	2784	342,944	274.1	151.6	55.3
1977	542	2439	373,908	321.2	194.3	60.5
1980	542	4629	434,442	363.9	207.4	57.0
1984	542	5493	479,214	400.1	256.5	64.1
1989	543	6158	579,810	498.1	308.3	61.9
1991	537	8953	594,797	501.0	256.0	51.1
1996	543	13952	767,462	592.6	343.3	55.8

Source: Data Unit, CSDS, Delhi

This transition from social hierarchy to egalitarianism has neither been uniform all over India nor has the progression been linear. But, seen overall, and in comparison to the situation at the period immediately after independence, it is possible to discern a radical difference in the

[28] The issue has been debated by a number of authors. See in particular, Lloyd and Susanne Rudolph, *The Modernity of Tradition*, Chicago 1967; Francine Frankel and M. S. A. Rao (eds.), *Dominance and State Power in Modern India*, 2 Vols., Delhi 1989/90 and Rajni Kothari, *Politics in India*, London 1994. For detailed analysis of the electoral process, see Subrata Mitra and James Chiriyankandath (eds.), *Electoral Politics in India: A Changing Landscape*, New Delhi 1992; D. L. Sheth (ed.), *Citizens and Politics: Aspects of Competitive Politics in India*, New Delhi 1975, is an excellent source for the political sociology of the electoral process. Robert Hardgrave and Stanley Kochanek, *India: Government and Politics in a Developing Nation*, Fort Worth 1993, is a very good source for manifestos and background information. See especially chapter 6, "Parties and Politics".

level of political consciousness of the electorate.[29] A move in this direction had already started under colonial rule through two basic processes, namely, partial enfranchisement of the electorate, and, the identification of specific groups for special representation such as the Scheduled Castes and Scheduled Tribes, and 'minorities' under communal award. Towards the last years of the British Raj, as the competition between the Indian National Congress and the Muslim League was transforming the political geography of North India, the potential to generate power through group formation gave rise to new groups and political parties such as the Justice party in South India.[30] These processes set an important precedent for the acceleration of the pace of political mobilization after independence.

The introduction of universal adult franchise and extension of the right to vote to social groups devoid of any political influence gave them a new political resource. The right to vote by secret ballot, exercised at a polling booth conveniently located in the village created an environment which was helpful for political participation. The right to vote in secrecy, and without coercion, thanks to the presence of specially recruited election officers, acted as a direct challenge to social dominance, posed by newly lower castes and minorities who felt empowered thanks to the value of the vote. Since the literature of modernisation warns against the disorder that follows rapid expansion of participation in traditional societies,[31] the question that we need to raise here is why did the social pyramid not break chaotically?

We learn from the Indian case that while the pace of social change has been accelerated through social reform legislation, recruitment of new social élites into the political arena and the political mobilization through electoral participation, their overall impact on the stability of the political system has been moderated by the existence of political intermediaries and parties at the regional and local levels. The process has been described by Lloyd and Susanne Rudolph as the transformation of social relations based on dominance of lower social castes by those at

[29] This theme has given rise to a vast literature on the *jajmani* system and its steady transformation through the effects of economic change, social reform and political mobilization. The traditional *jajmani* system describes a system of social relations in terms of the reciprocal bonds of obligation through which social groups owning land are tied to other social groups on the basis of status, occupations and power. Politically, the social bonds of *jajmani* lead to a 'pyramid' of dominance. Politically, the small group of social élites cumulate power, status and wealth, which makes it possible for them to dominate the many others devoid of these resources. Once again, since the bond that thus binds the élite and the non-élite is deeply ingrained, the social pyramid looks like a natural rather than a political construction. Empowered by the principle of universal adult franchise, the relatively powerless bottom of the pyramid quickly learns how to pool their collective voting strength and use it as a political resource. See Francine Frankel and M. S. A. Rao (eds.), *Dominance and State Power in Modern India* for regional variations on this main theme.

[30] See Eugene Irschick, *Politics and Social Conflict in South India*, Berkeley 1969 and *Dialogue and History: Constructing South India, 1795–1895*, Delhi 1994 for the contrast between northern and southern India in terms of politics and social change.

[31] Huntington, *Political Order in Changing Societies*, p. 55 warns about the potential for political decay when participation expands faster than institutionalisation.

the upper levels of social hierarchy into *differential* and horizontal relations.[32] Typically, as the marginal social groups discovered the negotiable value of the vote during the early years after independence, they became avid players in the political arena at the local and regional levels. Established *jajmani* systems – reciprocal social bonds based on the exchange of service and occupational specialisation – broke down to create new groupings. Finally, caste associations, based on horizontal social and economic interests emerged as links between parties and the society.[33] These processes that facilitate social and political mobility and multi-party competition have taken the form of federalism, consociationalism and élite policy initiatives.[34] This has created a useful room to manoeuvre in the middle in the hands of national, regional and local élites.[35]

These innovations have been possible in India because of three factors. First, the Gandhian legacy which gave the first formal shape to the two-track strategy that combines institutional politics such as voting, lobbying and other forms of participation based on party politics and protest movements, undertaken as a rational device to complement the former. Politics after independence gave formal acknowledgement to this development.[36] The second factor is the ability of the national and regional élites to transfer knowledge from one arena to another.[37] The

[32] Vertical mobilization refers to political linkages that draw on and reinforce social and economic dominance. Horizontal mobilization takes place when people situated at the same social and economic level get together to use their combined political strength to improve their situation. Differential mobilization refers to coalitions that cut across social strata (Lloyd and Susanne Rudolph, *The Modernity of Tradition: Political Development in India*).

[33] For the formulation of these ideas in terms of an analytical framework on elections and social change in India based on a model of electoral norms and organisational structures corresponding to them, see Subrata Mitra, "Caste, democracy and the Politics of Community Formation in India," in: Mary Searle-Chatterjee and Ursula Sharma (eds.), *Contextualising Caste: Post-Dumontian Approaches*, Blackwell/The Sociological Review 1994, p. 49–72.

[34] See Arendt Lijphart, "The Puzzle of India's Democracy," *American Political Science Review* 1996, for a discussion of the efficacy of federalism and consociationalism in promoting democracy and social change. A comparative analysis of élite policy initiatives in six Indian States is part of my current DFG project on 'Order and Anarchy in India after Independence'.

[35] For an application of this concept as a framework for the discussion of political participation in India, see Subrata Mitra, "Room to Maneuver in the Middle: Local Elites, Political Action and the State in India," *World Politics* 43 (3), 1991.

[36] For a discussion of this point based on an analysis of local élites in India, see Subrata Mitra, *Power, Protest, Participation: Local Elites and the Politics of Development in India*, London 1992.

[37] *Panchayatiraj*, a traditional political institution rejuvenated and recast as the basic foundation stone of democracy at the local level, first developed in western India and then transported with great success to the communist-ruled State of West Bengal, is a good example. See the chapter on "Institutional Innovation: The Politicized Panchayats" in Atul Kohli, *State and Poverty in India*, Cambridge 1990, p. 108–16 for a discussion of the efficacy of West Bengal's communist regime in making use of the *panchayati* system in promoting order and welfare.

third was the availability of the 'Congress system' and the élite consensus that defined it during the formative years after independence.[38]

a) The Evolution of the Party System Since Independence

A competitive party system provides the crucial backdrop to the political articulation of competing interests. As such, it is an important indicator of a functioning civil society. Party competition creates the political space in which social groups come together in order to engage in competition for the allocation of scarce public resources and for the assertion of their collective identity and values on the public space. A non-competitive party system denotes the existence of social closure, a restricted public sphere, and, of élite values and interests that are above politics. The absence of a party system altogether denotes the absence of an effective and enduring basis of a dialogue and transaction between social interests and the state.

The party system of contemporary India is the result of the six decades of growth under British rule prior to independence, which has been considerably reinforced with the political mobilization of all sections of society. It is a fairly complex system which specialists of comparative party systems find hard to characterise because of the continuous and influential presence of the Congress Party in the national political arena, the emergence of a powerful Hindu nationalist movement, the world's longest elected communist government at the regional level and the occasional lapse into authoritarian rule. The picture becomes much clearer if we divide the post-independence period into one of the 'one-dominant-party system' period (1952–1977) presented in Table 2 and its transformation into a multi-party system (1977–1996), presented in Table 3 below.

i) First Party System, 1952–1977

The Indian National Congress, successor to the anti-colonial Freedom Movement, was the ruling party during this period both at the centre and in India's States except Kerala which was briefly ruled by the Communists in the 1950s. Though parties of the left and right routinely took part in elections which were by and large both free and fair, the fragmented character of the opposition and the combination of the first past the post system of voting in single member constituencies systematically resulted in a Congress majority in the legislature. This hegemonic position of Congress has caused this period to be described as the period of one-party domi-

[38] The concept is discussed at length below. The two most useful references to its functioning are, Rajni Kothari, "The Congress 'System' in India," *Asian Survey* 4 (12), 1964, and Rajni Kothari, "The Congress System Revisited: A Decennial Review," *Asian Survey* 14 (12), 1974.

nance.[39] The main ideological doctrines of the Congress Party such as secularism, democratic socialism and non-alignment constituted the main parameters of the policy process during this period. The opposition parties were present as active players in the Parliament and in national politics but their role was confined to influencing policy from the sidelines of the institutional process rather than making policy and alternating with Congress in the wielding of ministerial office.

Table 2
Summary of Lok Sabha Elections, 1952–1971
(Seats and Per Cent of Vote)

Party	1952		1957		1962		1967		1971	
INC (1)	364	45.0%	371	47.8%	361	44.7%	283	40.8%	352	43.7%
BJS/BJP	3	3.1%	4	5.9%	14	6.4%	35	9.4%	22	7.4%
JP/JD	–		–		–		–		–	
CPM	–		–		–		19	4.4%	25	5.1%
CPI	26	5.4%	29	8.9%	29	9.9%	23	5.0%	23	4.7%
BKD/LD/SJP	–		–		–		–		1	
INC (2)	–		–		–		–		16	10.4%
Soc.	21	16.4%	19	10.4%	18	9.5%	36	8.0%	5	3.4%
Swatantra	–		–		18	7.9%	44	8.7%	8	3.1%
Regional Parties	14		20		20		32		42	
Independents	38	15.9%	42	19.4%	20	11.1%	35	13.7%	14	8.4%
Others	23		9		14		13		11	
TOTAL	489		494		494		520		518	

Source: Subrata Mitra and James Chiriyankandath (eds.), *Electoral Politics in India – A Changing Landscape*, New Delhi 1992, p. 269–70

Abbr. BJS – Bharatiya Jana Sangh; BJP – Bharatiya Janata Party; BKD – Bharatiya Kranti Dal; CPI – Communist Party of India; CPM – Communist Party of India (Marxist); INC (1) – Indian National Congress (–1967), Congress (Requisionist) (1971), Congress (Indira) (1980–); INC (2) – Congress (Organisation), Congress (Urs) (1980), Congress (Socialist) (1984–); JD – Janata Dal; JP – Janata Party; LD – Lok Dal; SJP – Samajwadi Janata Party

Note: The 'Socialist' category includes the Socialist Party, the Kisan Mazdoor Praja Party, the Praja Socialist Party, and the Samyukta Socialist Party

The challenge to the dominance of the Congress Party had already become clear in the fourth general election of 1967 when the first coalitions of the left and right took place at the

[39] The literature on the Congress Party is enormous. See Subrata Mitra, "Party Organization and Policy Making in a Changing Environment: The Indian National Congress," in: Kay Lawson (ed.), *How Political Parties Work: Perspectives from Within*, Westport 1994; Mike Shepperdson and Colin Simmons (eds.), *The Indian National Congress and the Political Economy of India, 1885–1985*, London1988; Richard Sisson and Stanley Wolpert (eds.), *Congress and Indian Nationalism: The Pre-independence Phase*, Berkeley 1988; Ram Joshi and R. K. Hebsur (eds.), *Congress in Indian Politics: A Centenary Perspective*, Bombay 1987; Meenakshi Jain, *The Congress Party, 1967–1977: The Role of Caste in Indian Politics*, Delhi 1991.

regional level, leading to the breakdown of the dominance of the Congress Party in several States. These opposition coalitions were successful in some States like in Kerala and West Bengal and became the basis of the beginning of a multi-party system, with Congress alternating with other political parties and coalitions very much like a normal political party. At the national level, however, the Congress Party continued to rule, albeit with a reduced majority. The situation changed radically after the split of the Congress Party in 1969 into the Congress

Table 3
Summary of Lok Sabha Elections, 1977–1996
(Seats and Per Cent of Vote)

Party	1977	1980	1984	1989	1991	1996
INC (1)	154 34.5%	353 42.7%	415 48.1%	197 39.5%	227 37.6%	136 28.1%
BJS/BJP	–	–	2 7.4%	85 11.4%	119 19.9%	160 23.5%
JP/JD	298 43.0%	31 19.0%	10 6.7%	143 17.8%	56 10.8%	43
CPM	22 4.3%	36 6.1%	22 5.7%	33 6.5%	35	33
CPI	7 2.8%	11 2.6%	6 2.7%	12 2.6%	13	12
BKD/LD/SJP	–	41 9.4%	3 5.6%	–	5	17
INC (2)	–	13 5.3%	5 1.6%	1 0.3%	1	4
Soc.	–	–	–	–		
Swatantra	–	–	–	–		
Regional parties	36	27	65	30	42	86
Independents	9 5.5%	9 6.4%	5 8.1%	12 5.2%	1	
Others	16	8	9	16	11	
TOTAL	542	529	542	529	511	543

Source: Subrata Mitra and James Chiriyankandath, eds., Electoral Politics in India – A Changing Landscape (New Delhi: Segment Books; 1992), p. 269–70

Abbr.: BJS – Bharatiya Jana Sangh; BJP – Bharatiya Janata Party; BKD – Bharatiya Kranti Dal; CPI – Communist Party of India; CPM – Communist Party of India (Marxist); INC (1) – Indian National Congress (–1967), Congress (Requisionist) (1971), Congress (Indira) (1980–); INC (2) – Congress (Organisation), Congress (Urs) (1980), Congress (Socialist) (1984–); JD – Janata Dal; JP – Janata Party; LD – Lok Dal; SJP – Samajwadi Janata Party

Note: The 'Socialist' category includes the Socialist Party, the Kisan Mazdoor Praja Party, the Praja Socialist Party, and the Samyukta Socialist Party

(Requisionist) and the Congress (Organisation). The faction led by Indira Gandhi, referred to as Congress (R), brought about radical changes in the programme of the centrist Congress Party. A number of new, left leaning policies like the nationalisation of banks, abolition of the special privileges of Indian princes and closer ties with communists were reinforced with a more forceful populist leadership style. These policies brought the party great electoral success in 1971 but led to the corrosion of its organisational links with the electorate.

In retrospect, the period 1967–77 can be thought of as a period of transition from one-party dominance to multi-party democracy. The setback suffered by the Congress Party in the election of 1967 demonstrated the vulnerability of the centrist Congress to broad electoral coalitions of the left and the right. After its initial setback, however, Congress, under Indira Gandhi's forceful leadership, turned its new policy of radical, populist leadership its main asset. Its initial success in the 1971 election was further reinforced in the assembly elections of 1972 when Indira Gandhi transformed India's successful intervention in the Liberation War in East Pakistan leading to the birth of Bangladesh into the electoral platform of the Congress Party. However, the radical rhetoric rebounded on the party when a number of interest groups including industrial workers, railway employees and students started political agitations. The culmination of this period of unrest was the authoritarian interlude of 1975–1977.

The period of national Emergency was imposed by the President at the advice of the Prime Minister under article 352 of the constitution in June 1975 as a temporary measure against rising lawlessness. The conditions that facilitate the functioning of party competition such as free assembly, participation, freedom of in/formation and movement were drastically curtailed. General Elections were postponed and the term of the Parliament was extended. Though the regime of Indira Gandhi claimed that the Emergency was brought about to ward off grave threats to the unity and integrity of India, it was more likely a response to the challenges to her rule. Elections were announced in 1977 when the regime got the impression that because of a significant increase in law and order, food supply and general prosperity, the election would lead to a victory for the Congress Party. However, as Table 3 shows, that was far from the case. The Congress Party was punished by the electorate for the authoritarian excesses of the Emergency in terms of a net fall in the percentage vote for Congress from 43.7% to 34.5%. But, even more important was the drastic decline in the number of seats, from 352 to 154, reducing it to a minority in the Lok Sabha for the first time in the post-independence history of India.

ii) The Second Party System, 1977–1997

The general elections of 1977 ushered in a new period in Indian politics. Since then, Indian politics has entered a period of broad based coalitions forming part of an unstable multi-party-system. Table 3 presents the evolution of the second party system during this period. During the second party system, India has witnessed a situation where relatively stable multi-party systems at the regional level find themselves within an unstable multi-party system at the national level. The gap between Congress and the vote share of the largest non-Congress party or coalition has steadily narrowed following the election of 1984, which, in view of the sympathy wave in favour of the Congress, led by Rajiv Gandhi following the assassination of Indira Gandhi, has been thought of as a deviant election, temporarily obscuring the secular decline of the Congress (see Figure 1).

Though governments have been relatively short-lived during this period, rather like the Fourth Republic of France, governmental instability has coexisted with policy stability. When new cabinets are constituted with the same ministers, or, ministers committed to the same policies, policy stability is maintained in spite of governmental change. Some macro level evidence of continuity can be seen in Narasimha Rao's minority government which lasted its full term and Deve Gowda's government, in spite of its coalitional character and minority status, has continued past policies, successfully undertaking elections in Kashmir, Uttar Pradesh, Panjab;

Figure 1

% of Votes of the Congress Relative to the Largest non-Congress Party or Coalition

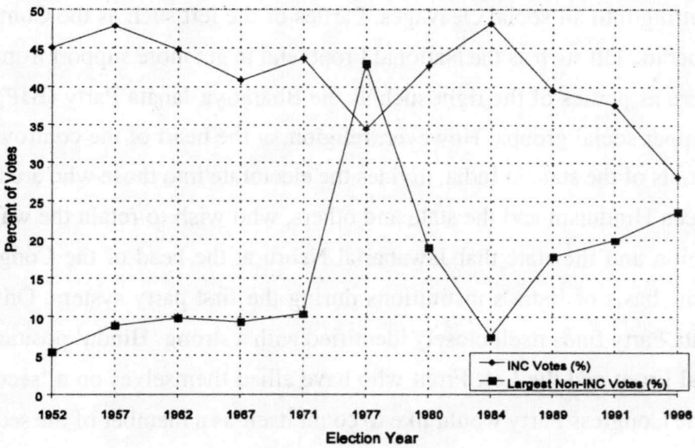

*Largest Non-INC parties (votes):	
1952	CPI
1957	CPI
1962	CPI
1967	BJS/BJP
1971	INC (2)
1977	JP/JD
1980	JP/JD
1984	BJS/BJP
1989	JP/JD
1991	BJS/BJP
1996	BJS/BJP

mediating in regional conflicts; maintaining a forceful Indian position on the CTBT issue; keeping the pace on reservations, women, liberalisation.

4. Competitive Elections and Interest Articulation

So far we have seen how the Indian party system originated under British rule as part of deliberate policy to rule India effectively and cheaply through indigenous intermediaries whose character gradually changed in keeping with the pace of rising political consciousness. This core was greatly reinforced after independence when social change and political conflict got interwoven within the fabric of a democratic state. The ultimate expression of the plural character of Indian society was a multi-party system. The issue that we need to address now is what keeps the party system socially anchored and reasonably stable.

i) Political Parties and Social Cleavages

A stable multi-party democracy is based on an effective linkage between social cleavages and political parties. The nature of the party system typically follows the complexity of social cleavages. Political systems with the first past the post system where social class constitutes the main cleavage tend to develop two party systems. Those with other cleavages such as religion, language and region in addition to social class produce more complex, multi-party systems. India's multi-party system, as we shall see below in Table 4, exhibits the effects of multiple cleavages. The Congress party, occupying the ideological centre of Indian politics, continues to be a catch-all party,[40] cutting into all social cleavages. Parties of the left such as the Communists and the social democratic left such as the National Front tend to get more support from the lower social classes where as parties of the right such as the Bharatiya Janata Party (BJP) get more support from the upper social groups. However, religion, at the heart of the controversy about the secular credentials of the state in India, divides the electorate into those who are for a closer relationship between Hinduism and the state and others, who wish to retain the wall of separation between religion and the state that Jawaharlal Nehru at the head of the Congress Party had drawn on as the basis of India's institutions during the first party system. On this issue, the Bharatiya Janata Party finds itself closely identified with a strong 'Hindu' position as compared to the National Front and the Left Front who have allied themselves on a 'secular' agenda. One faction of the Congress Party would like to count itself as a member of the secular front, but, keeping to its centrist character, the Party itself tends to be ambiguous on the issue. Some of these observations would be illustrated below with reference to particular political parties.

The 1996 elections to the Lok Sabha produced the best results for the Bharatiya Janata Party, considered to be the main symbol of Hindu nationalism, in recent electoral history. The cross-tabulations with socio-demographic groups (see Table 4) reveal the strong support it enjoys among the more educated, urban, affluent and younger voters. However, its vote remains confined to particular regions of India. Moreover, within these regions, the party is identified with particular sub-populations. Thus, while on the one hand, the BJP has the most efficient vote to seat ratio, as the recent Uttar Pradesh elections demonstrate, it might have already exploited the support among its 'natural' clientele to saturation. Unless it changes its positioning radically, it would have great difficulties in making further progress.

In spite of a net fall in votes cast in its favour, the Congress Party appears to have retained the broadly dispersed character of its social base. The image of Congress as a 'coalition of mi-

[40] See Otto Kirchheimer, "The Transformation of the Western European Party Systems," in: LaPalombara and Weiner (eds.), *Political Parties and Political Development*; Princeton 1966, p. 177–200.

norities' lingers on. Its support among Muslims is about eight percentages above its national average. Similarly, its support among Scheduled Castes and Tribes is also higher than its national average. It is important to remember that these were the traditional support bases for the INC. The 1996 data confirm the heterogeneous social base of the Congress Party but also demonstrates, as we will see later, the presence of other contenders (National Front for the Muslim vote and the BSP for the Scheduled Caste vote) for support from these groups and their increasing ability to lure support away from Congress. It should also be noted that support for Congress is proportionately low among the educated and the young which represent the mirror opposite of the Bharatiya Janata Party.

Table 4
Social Bases Of Political Parties in India

	INC+	BJP+	NF	LF	BSP
All India Average	27.4	24.8	10.0	7.5	3.4
Rural	28.1	22.7	10.6	8.8	3.8
Urban	25.2	32.0	8.3	3.5	2.0
Men	27.4	26.7	10.7	7.4	3.6
Women	27.6	23.0	9.2	7.6	3.1
Hindu	26.1	28.7	8.3	7.4	3.7
Muslim	35.1	3.1	24.5	9.9	1.2
Christian	42.9	3.7	1.8	6.2	–
Sikh	18.1	14.2	16.5	2.4	5.5
Scheduled Castes	31.6	14.4	5.9	11.2	11.6
Scheduled Tribes	40.1	20.3	5.9	6.7	0.9
OBCs	21.8	23.1	16.2	5.8	2.3
Upper Castes	27.2	33.2	7.0	8.2	0.5
Illiterates	28.8	21.1	12.2	6.6	4.9
Up To Primary	27.8	22.5	9.6	9.1	3.2
Middle School	29.0	25.0	8.4	8.5	2.3
Higher Secondary	25.5	31.3	7.9	7.7	1.6
College +	20.6	37.1	6.0	6.2	0.9
Up To 25 Years	25.9	27.0	9.8	6.9	3.8
26–35 Years	26.9	25.5	9.7	7.6	3.5
36–45 Years	28.5	25.0	9.7	8.3	2.9
46–55 Years	27.0	23.2	10.2	8.5	3.4
56 Years Or More	29.9	21.5	10.8	6.4	2.8

Note: Parties here represent pre-poll alliances, i. e. INC+ (INC + AIDMK), BJP+ (BJP + Samata Party + Shiv Sena + Haryana Vikas Party), NF (JD + Samajvadi Party) and LF (CPI +CPM + RSP + FBL).

The National Front, drawing on the legacy of the previous Lok Dals and still led by some of their leaders, gets more support in rural India than from the urban voter. Its rural character is further reinforced by its strong showing among the Backward Classes where its support is sixty percentage higher than its national average. At 24.5%, its support among Muslims is outstanding by the standards of its national support of 10%. The survey data also cast a shade of doubt on the characterisation of the National Front as a party of peasant proprietors and the upwardly mobile and more affluent sections of the rural population. This is seen in the more than average support for the National Front among the illiterates. Significantly, its support among Scheduled Castes (5.9%) and Scheduled Tribes (5.9%) is much below its national average.

The Left Front appears as a 'rural' party, with its support confined to 3.5% of the urban population compared to 8.8% among the rural voters. This is explained by the regionally localised character of the left movement, which, from its beginnings in the urban electorate, has moved to the countryside, as the example of West Bengal shows. Its support is marginally higher at both extremes of the social scale, with more than average support among the Scheduled castes and upper castes. The picture appears to resemble that of the Congress Party. But unlike the Congress, the Left Front draws less support among the illiterate. Its main support comes from low/middle educated and middle-aged people.

The Bahujan Samaj Party – the Joker in the pack of Indian politics today – is very much the party of the Scheduled Castes (11.6% compared to the national average of 3.4%), illiterates (4.9%) and rural rather than urban. Its strong support among the poorest part of the Indian population is further reinforced by data on education of which the level is negatively related to support for the party. The picture resembles a mirror opposite to that of the profile of the Bharatiya Janata Party.

ii) Broadly based sense of political efficacy

Established patterns of party-cleavage linkages would be meaningful only if individuals who constitute those social cleavages perceive political parties as efficient instruments for the articulation of their interests. The survey data, as we can see from Table 5, provide adequate evidence that such a sense of efficacy is present in large sections of the Indian electorate.

The question "*Do you think your vote has effect on how things are run in this country, or, do you think your vote makes no difference?*" was asked to measure voters' sense of efficacy in their vote. A majority of people believe that their vote has an effect on the political state of affairs in the country. The percentage of such people has gone up from about 48% in 1971 to about 60% in 1996. Interestingly, though it is very much a minority phenomenon, the number of those who do not believe that their vote has any effect has also gone up, from 16% in 1971 to 21% in 1996. Over the past twenty-five years, there has been a steady growth in consciousness of the efficacy of vote as well a sense of relative inefficacy. As a consequence, the percentage of those who could not answer this question one way or another has gone down from 35% in 1971 to 19% in 1996.

Table 5
Effectiveness of Vote

	1971	1996
Has Effect	48.3	59.4
Makes No Difference	16.2	21.3
Don't Know	35.2	18.9
Vote Has Effect (%)		
Illiterate		47
Scheduled Tribes		48
Older (> 56 years)		52
Hindu		58
All		59
Scheduled Castes		60
Muslim		61
Young		61
Urban		64
Men		66
College and Above		79

Like participation in different electoral activities, here too, we find that the lower social orders have lesser confidence in their votes. The women and the older people also belong more or less to this group. The highly efficacious groups are the well educated, Christians and people from higher income groups. It is important to note here that even at its lowest, the sense of efficacy is still respectably high. Even among the illiterate, close to half hold their vote as efficacious. The Scheduled Castes and the Muslims as a group are not far too behind, indicating thereby, their above the average sense of political efficacy. Most important for us, among 'partisans', i. e., those who say that they have voted for one of the major parties, the figure for "vote has effect" is higher than the national average.[41]

iii) Political Legitimacy

If the existence of a sense of efficacy at the micro-level is a necessary condition for the effectiveness of a multi-party system then the perception of the system of competing parties and elections as legitimate constitutes a sufficient condition. The larger implications for the relationship between efficacy and legitimacy should be clear by now: an efficacious electorate which does not hold the party system as legitimate would look for other institutions to articulate and aggregate their interests. Worldwide comparison makes it quickly obvious that candidates for selection as representatives of popular interest against the background of a failing party system are indeed many. Political parties are one of the main agencies available to people to articulate and aggregate their demands; censor errant officials; and, seek to influence public policy. But they are not the only ones. The same arguments have been made for the justification of military intervention, for the political role of the church, *mullahs, sadhus, bhikkhus,* students and all manners of left radicals.

[41] The figures are as follows: Left Front voters 67.9%, National Front 62.2%, BJP 61.4%, Congress 59.4%, Bahujan Samaj Party, 55.8%. This shows both the close relationship between partisanship and efficacy as well as the widely dispersed nature of the sense of efficacy across the whole ideological spectrum of political parties.

The survey asked two main questions to measure legitimacy of the system of parties and elections. The first question "*How much in your opinion do political parties help to make government pay attention to the people – good deal, somewhat or not much?*" provides answer to the usefulness of parties. (Table 6) In 1996 as well as in 1971, only a minority of the people was prepared to describe the instrumentality of political parties in positive terms. It is important, however, to make the point that the positive evaluation of parties has grown relatively, from about 32% to over 42%. Opinion is more sharply polarised now, which is why the "don't know" category has shrunk from 41% to 30%.

Table 6
Usefulness of Political Parties (1971–1996)

	1971	1996
Good Deal	10.9	9.5
Somewhat	21.6	33.0
Not Much	25.7	27.3
Don't Know	41.1	29.8

The question "*How much in your opinion do political parties help to make government pay attention to the people – good deal, somewhat or not much?*" provides answer to worthwileness of parties.

The second question, a more direct measurement of system legitimacy, asked "*Suppose there were no parties or assemblies and elections were not held – do you think that the government in this country can be run better?*" The responses show how much significance people attach to the system which provides basis for their direct participation in it. (Table 7)

Table 7
Better Government Without Parties, Assemblies and Elections?

	1971	1996
Yes	14.2	11.4
No	43.4	68.8
Can't Say Or Don't Know	41.5	19.8
Government Not Better Without Parties, Assemblies and Elections (%)		
Illiterate		61
Older (> 56 years)		63
Hindu		68
All		69
Young (< 25 years)		71
Muslim		72
College and Above		74

When asked to conjecture on a situation where no elections are available, asked deliberately in a manner that highlights the absence of elections rather than their presence, Indians overwhelmingly reject a future without parties and elections. An impressively large 70% of the sample disagrees with the proposition that the country could be run better without elections. Significantly, this percentage has gone up from the relative low of 43% in 1971 to 69% in 1996. In retrospect, the high voting for Indira Gandhi's Congress in the 1971 election did not have the backing of deep trust in the institution of elections which, perhaps, facilitated the imposition of authoritarian rule in a matter of years following the electoral victory of her party. Perhaps, as a lasting legacy, particularly in view of the high trust we see in the 1996 data, a repetition of the 1975–77 type of emergency regime is less likely today. The confidence that the voter exudes in the process of voting is the consequence of the successful removal of Indira Gandhi's Congress from power in the parliamentary election of 1977.

The young (71%), the educated (74%) and the urban people constituting the group called 'opinion-makers' have come out overwhelmingly in favour of sustaining the system. More importantly, they are also joined, at least on this indicator, by Muslims (72.4%) and Christians (72.5%), but interestingly, not by Sikhs, who, at 63%, are 6% lower than the national average. The positive evaluation of the political system based on parties and elections by the better informed and the minority Muslims reinforces the picture of steady empowerment of the electorate through participation in electoral politics. Against this background the less than average support that elections and party politics receive from Sikhs can perhaps be understood in terms of the failure of the system based on parties and elections long years of political unrest in Panjab which led to one of the longest stretches of direct rule from the centre.

iv) Cross-cutting Value Conflict and Partisan Competition

The demolition of the Babri Masjid at Ayodhya on 6th December 1992 was one of the most important landmarks of Indian politics after independence. The world media and the Indian press have consistently focussed on it as a key issue in Indian politics and a key indicator of civil society in India. The interesting point to note here is that contrary to speculations in the media, Indian opinion is neither as homogeneous nor as hostile to Muslims as one is led to believe. Of all those who express an opinion on it, 64% do not believe that the demolition was justified.

Babri Mosque in Ayodhya has been used as the bone of contention by religious extremists on both sides for ages but what happened on 6th December 1992 rocked the nation. The Mosque was demolished by the *Karsevaks* – activists – of the Vishwa Hindu Parishad and the Bajrang Dal, supposedly with the connivance of the BJP which headed the State Government at that time. Many places in the country witnessed the worst communal riots of their kind; people got divided, albeit temporarily; and, the BJP was isolated by almost all the political parties of the country.

The question "*Some people say that the demolition was justified while others say it was not justified. What would you say, was it justified or not justified?*" elicited the following responses.

Table 8
Partisan Response to the Demolition of the Babri Mosque

	Congress	BJP	NF	Left Front	BSP	Total
Unjustified	42.6	25.4	47.9	54.8	27.3	37.9
Cannot Say / Don't Know	8.1	11.4	7.7	8.8	20.1	10.1
Justified	16.4	40.5	24.5	8.9	27.6	22.8
Inapplicable	33.0	22.7	20.0	27.5	25.1	29.1

Demolition of Babri Masjid Not Justified (%)	
Hindus	32
Scheduled Castes	33
Rural	34
OBCs	37
All	38
Upper Castes	49
Urban	50
College and Above	59
Muslim	86

Interest in the data on the attitudes towards the destruction of the Babri Mosque arises from the fact that in view of the expectations aroused by the spectre of Hindu fundamentalism, not the least by Huntington's imagery about the clash of civilisations, one would expect an internally undifferentiated phalanx of Hindus (and Muslims) taking radically opposite stances. However, when the Indian electors (an overwhelming majority of whom are Hindus) were asked to pass a judgement whether they considered the demolition justified or unjustified, they have largely condemned the act as unjustified. When we take only those who are willing to express an opinion, as high as 62.5% of all Indians took the position that the demolition of Babri Mosque was unjustified. 97.9% of Muslims have found the act unjustified. Similarly, the opinionated people from all sections of the society have more or less condemned the demolition. For example, 66.2% of urban, 67.5% of graduates and above and 63.8% of Hindu upper castes have found the act unjustified.

Similarly, on the issue of Kashmir, at 33.3% the largest category of people are for a resolution of the issue by negotiation, a percentage which goes up to 74.5% when we consider only the opinion of those who are either for suppression of militancy or for a political solution.

People's response to an emotive issue like Kashmir does not show any communal bias in it. Giving credence to their secular values, the vast majority of Indian electors have rejected the option of suppressing the agitation by any means. Of the opinion holders, as many as 75.6% have suggested that the problem of Kashmir cannot be solved by using suppressive measures but by negotiations only. It receives support from almost all relevant segments of the society, be they urban, young, educated, rich or belonging to minority communities.

Question: "*People's opinions are divided on the issue of the Kashmir problem – some people say that government should suppress the agitation by any means, while others say that this problem should be resolved by negotiations. What would you say, should the agitation be suppressed, or resolved by negotiation?*" Responses to this question are quite revealing.

The same positive attitude of religious and regional reconciliation within India is also reflected in attitudes towards Pakistan. Those who suggest that India should make more efforts to

Table 9
Partisan Opinion on Resolution of Kashmir Problem

	Congress	BJP	NF	Left Front	BSP	Total
Negotiation	33.1	34.9	31.9	32.8	25.4	33.3
Cannot Say / Don't Know	35.6	27.9	34.3	30.0	30.1	34.1
Should be suppressed	9.9	17.5	11.6	4.9	14.4	11.2
Not heard of Kashmir	21.4	19.7	23.2	32.3	30.1	21.4

Kashmir Problem Should Be Solved by Negotiation (%)	
Hindus	32
All	33
Young (<25 Years)	38
Muslim	45
Urban	59
College and Above	62

develop friendly relations with Pakistan outnumber those who suggest the opposite or do not have an opinion on the issue. If we consider only those who are either for friendly relations or its opposite, then the percentage of those in favour of friendly relations goes up to 72%.

People's views on Indo-Pak relations are positively in favour of negotiation. The people of India by and large want that the government should make more efforts to develop friendly relations with Pakistan. Not only that 71.2% of the opinion holders support the development of friendly relations, but the people who matter in building a national opinion have come forward to lend more support than the non-opinionated sections of the society. For example, urban dwellers (74.7%), people pursuing high ranking occupations (72.4%) well-educated (72.9%), the rich (71.5%) and the upper caste (70.7%) have agreed to the proposition that India should make more efforts to develop friendly relations with Pakistan. The Muslims, the worst sufferers from the hostility between the two governments, have supported this view point almost unanimously: almost 90% of them want friendly relations with Pakistan, compared to 44.4% for the sample as a whole.

The question "*India should make more efforts to develop friendly relations with Pakistan. Do you agree or disagree?*" is summarised in Table 10.

The issue of a common personal law for all Indians is one of the most important issues facing the country today. In this context, it is interesting to note here that a significant percentage of Indians are willing to concede to each community the right to retain its own personal law in the areas of marriage and property rights.

The issue of uniform Civil Code reflects the tensions regarding the undissolved issue of identity and nationhood in India. Proponents of an exclusive definition of nation in India plead for a uniform law on all aspects of life. This position, very strongly propagated by the BJP gets far less support than the more inclusive view of nationalism in India. An impressive 44.5% of the total sample or 60% of the opinion holders say that every community should be allowed to have its own laws to govern marriage and property rights. Against this, only 30.1% say the opposite and the rest, that is 25% fail to express any opinion on it. It is true that the Muslims

Table 10
India Should Develop Friendly Relations with Pakistan

	Congress	BJP	NF	Left Front	BSP	Total
Disagree	17.1	23.3	11.7	17.8	12.5	17.5
Don't Know / No Opinion	37.2	34.7	37.1	37.2	37.3	38.0
Agree	45.6	41.9	51.2	44.9	50.2	44.4

Develop Friendly Relations with Pakistan (%)	
Scheduled Tribes	34
Scheduled Castes	39
Hindu	41
All	44
Upper Castes	54
Urban	59
College And Above	68
Muslim	72

have lent greater support (66.9%) to the idea of having or continuing with separate Civil Code, but the fact that their stand is also supported by the majority community makes a strong case for continuing with present law. However, this has a caveat to it, that is like "Muslim Personal Law", other communities would also like to enjoy autonomy, at least on governing their marriage and property rights.

In order to measure attitudes towards Personal Law, the survey asked: "*Every community should be allowed to have its own laws to govern marriage and property rights. Do you agree or disagree?*"

Judging from the above, there is considerable support within the electorate for a civil society in India. Of course there is greater sensitivity within Muslims for their own community to have the right to define the scope of their social institutions similar to other minority communities, also concerned about their Personal Law. However, this position is supported by a considerable section within the majority community as well as across the broad spectrum of India's political parties, including the supporters of the Hindu Nationalist Bharatiya Janata Party.

5. The 'Grey Area' of Multi-party Democracy in India

So far, we have concentrated on the hypotheses that explore the basis of the functioning of multi-party democracy in India and found reasonable evidence for its acceptance by the main actors in Indian politics. Is this however an act of faith, an unconditional commitment, or, a limited commitment, conditional on performance? The question arises from the fact that Indira Gandhi, the unrepentant author of the 1975 Emergency, was actually brought back with popular acclaim in 1980 when the Janata Party, who were the heroes of the anti-Emergency movement, failed to deliver stable, efficient and honest governance. In this section we shall explore the reasons for the residual doubts about the stability of multi-party democracy in India. Once again, India is not alone. In historical and comparative perspective, the collapse of an established party system is known to have occurred when an established party system fails to accom-

Table 11
Separate Civil Code for Every Community

	Congress	BJP	NF	Left Front	BSP	Total
Disagree	29.6	36.3	28.6	22.0	30.0	30.1
Don't Know / No Opinion	24.3	23.3	29.1	18.3	25.1	25.4
Agree	46.1	40.4	42.2	59.7	44.8	44.5
Support for Separate Civil Code (%)						
Hindu	41					
All	45					
Sikh	51					
Christian	53					
Muslim	67					

modate the interests of an emerging social group, or, fails to aggregate the interests of groups who are articulate and assertive about their demands.[42]

a) High Trust in Institutions but Distrust of Actors

The presumed collapse of India's institutions has been the staple of academic[43] and journalistic discourse on Indian politics[44] since the early 1980ies. The deinstitutionalisation prognosis was greatly reinforced by the destruction of the Babri mosque in 1992 and gets prominent mention at every outbreak of communal violence. As such, it is important to examine the level of trust and confidence that the people of India have in her major institutions and in the people responsible for running them. When asked: "*How much trust/confidence do you have in different institutions of India?*" the results are highly positive for institutions but more negative for those who are responsible for running those institutions. (Table 12)

Table 12
Evaluation of Different Institutions and Actors

	Great Deal	Somewhat	Not At All
Election Commission	46.2	31.0	21.2
Judiciary	41.5	34.3	23.4
Local Government	39.3	37.5	22.5
State Government	37.5	34.6	18.3
Central Government	35.3	42.6	21.3
Elected Representatives	19.8	40.5	39.0
Political Parties	17.4	43.5	38.5
Government Officials	17.1	40.5	41.8

In order of positive evaluation, the Election Commission, which, under the high profile leadership of Mr Seshan made elections much more orderly than before, gets the best score of 46% of great deal of

[42] The main question asked to measure this phenomenon in the survey was "*Would you say that persons we elect by voting generally care about what people like you think, or that they don't care?*". As astoundingly high 63.1% say that the elected representatives do not care. The larger implications of this would be discussed below at length.

[43] See in particular Atul Kohli, *Democracy and Discontent: India's Growing Crisis of Governability*, Cambridge 1990, and Bhabani Sen Gupta, *India: Problems of Governance*, New Delhi 1996.

[44] See M. J. Akbar, *Riot after Riot: Reports on Caste and Communal Violence in India*, Delhi 1988 (2nd ed. 1991).

confidence and 31% of somewhat confidence. The Judiciary, again the beneficiary of the high profile public interest litigation and prosecutions leading to the exposure of financial misdemeanour of politicians at the highest level, comes next in the order of positive evaluation. Local government, which, since the democratic decentralisation under the initiative of the Balwantrai Mehta Committee of 1957 has steadily spread all over India, gets a positive evaluation from three quarters of the population. Next in order come the State and central governments of India. There is a precipitous fall however when it comes to elected representatives and political parties, for both of which the negative evaluation exceeds the 'great deal' score. Government officials do no better and the police do the worst.

The question "*How much trust/confidence do you have in different institutions of India?*" was asked and the responses are presented in Table 12.

b) High Efficacy in the Context of Low Institutional Legitimacy

A situation where individual voters are articulate about their identity and interests but do not have a great deal of confidence in elected representatives and civil servants responsible for the implementation of policy does not augur well for the effectiveness and stability of multi-party democracy. To recall the theoretical insights of the civic culture and participation research of earlier years, a stable democracy would require reasonably high performance on both dimensions whereas a situation where low efficacy and low legitimacy is the rule, one can have little reason to expect a functioning multi-party democracy. In a context of high legitimacy and low efficacy one can expect an authoritarian regime with limited participation. The fourth case, where personal efficacy overtakes system legitimacy opens up the field for intervention from outside the party system from potential challengers to multi-party democracy such protest movements, the church, students, army – in fact any organised group with the means to convince the masses that they can deliver better results.

The negative evaluation of government officials and the police on the one hand and the plethora of corruption and other scandals involving political leaders on the other explain the uncertain feeling many Indians have about their own political system. While more research is necessary to pin down the causes for limited opposition to Indira Gandhi's Emergency at its height, and the triumphant return of Indira Gandhi's popular authoritarianism in 1980 shortly after the electoral humiliation of 1977 under the slogan "vote for the government that works" indicates the scope that forceful and undemocratic leaders have in order to play a role in India's electoral politics. In order to test the strength of association of efficacy and legitimacy, these two variables were cross-tabulated. The results are presented in Table 13.

We learn from the cross-tabulation of efficacy and legitimacy that the overall relationship between the two is positive though the strength of association is rather low. This helps provide

Table 13
Cross-Tabulation of Efficacy and Legitimacy (%)

	Legitimacy			
Efficacy	Low	Medium	High	Total
Low	37 (22) n=5.4%	56 (13) n=8.3%	7 (10) n=1.1%	100
Medium	25 (62) n=15.4%	67 (65) n=41.5%	8 (43) n=4.8%	100
High	17 (16) n=4.0%	61 (22) n=14.3%	22 (47) n=5.2%	100
Total	100	100	100	

Key: First entry in each cell refers to the row percentage, the second, to the column percentage and the third to the percentage of cases in each cell.
Kendall's τ_b .17, N= 9589

the necessary and sufficient conditions for the existence of a multi-party democracy in India. The 'centre' is occupied by a large group of people, constituting 41.5% of the population who are moderately efficacious and hold the system to be moderately legitimate. The main sources of challenge to the stability of the system comes from those at the bottom left corner of the matrix – namely, the 4% who are highly efficacious but for whom system legitimacy is at its lowest, 15.4% who are moderately efficacious but hold system legitimacy to be low and 14.3% who are highly efficacious but hold system legitimacy to be only moderate. But, balancing these about 38% are about 14% of Indian population, occupying the top right corner of the matrix where legitimacy overtakes efficacy. Once again, while greater research is needed to identify the various social groups in terms of their location in the matrix, we have some interesting evidence here which provides new insights into both the stability of multi-party democracy in India as well as to the sources of its vulnerability.

6. Conclusion

As a part of their efforts to achieve a quick transition to democracy, many post-colonial and post-revolutionary societies have taken recourse to the legalisation of the market process, voluntary associations or political parties. Unfortunately, only too often these attempts have unleashed pent up political demands from social groups long suppressed by alien rulers or politically oppressive regimes, leading to great amounts of ethnic strife and political disorder. These failed attempts show that political mobilization may be a necessary but not a sufficient condition for a functioning civil society. The results presented in this paper show that the growth of a competitive party system and the existence of inter-party consensus on key issues affecting civil liberties are crucial facilitating conditions for a civil society. The party system, in turn, is effective and seen as legitimate only in so far as it succeeds in getting itself accepted by social groups as an effective means for the articulation and aggregation of demands, failing which, a politically mobilised people has every incentive to turn to other agencies like the army, the clergy, radical groups of the left or the right and last but not the least, to mob violence, none of which has a proven record of an abiding commitment to civil society.

From electoral data and results of opinion surveys, multi-party democracy appears to have struck root in India. This is seen particularly from the linkage of partisanship and social cleavages, a broadly based sense of political efficacy and legitimacy, and, cross-cutting value conflicts and partisanship. And yet, some doubts about the stability of multi-party democracy linger on, reinforced by such events as the national Emergency of 1975–77, the destruction of the Babri Mosque in 1992, continuing communal conflict and tension and the sub-national movement in Kashmir. The danger to multi-party democracy from these issues is muted because, as we have seen in the survey data, opinions within India's political parties as well as social groups on these crucial issues is divided, with a substantial percentage of supporters within each major political party, as well as across major social groups in general, coming up with responses that provide a commitment to civil society in India.

Indian data also provides useful insights into a possible solution to the essential tension between majoritarian democracy and civil society in multi-ethnic societies. Parekh formulates these challenges as "... the range of permissible diversity, how to accommodate differences without losing [its] social cohesion, how to reconcile the apparently conflicting demands of equality of treatment and recognition of cultural differences, and how to create a spirit of common citizenship among [its] culturally diverse members."[45] By opting for an inter-party consensus on tolerant pluralism, India's voters have shown themselves capable of avoiding the extremes of both a naive advocacy of national values as well as a mechanical insistence on an essentialised, universal human rights as the basis of civil society in India. This pragmatic pluralism, the policy of live and let live, and above all, the ability of India's social groups to put themselves in the position of other communities, and to devise the rules of communal accommodation as the basis of the creation of a public space for a common citizenship provides a contrasting picture to the 'Clash of Civilisations' and to the gladiatorial positions that Huntington attributes to members of different religions in divided societies.

The local and regional breakdowns of democracy is not unusual in many post-colonial and post-revolutionary countries. The issue is, why do they not become cumulative or terminal in

[45] Bhikhu Parekh, "Cultural Diversity and Liberal Democracy," in: David Beethan (ed.), *Defining and Measuring Democracy*, London 1994, p. 199.

India? As we have already seen from the survey data, there is a significant number of individuals who feel themselves to be efficacious but do not accord a great measure of legitimacy to the institutions of the state, nor to political parties as the most effective instrument for the implementation of the popular will provides some insights into these grey areas of Indian democracy. Pending further investigation, it can be suggested that the breakdown of democracy is a manifestation of attempts by political actors to bring pressure on the system. As long as the system responds, either through policy change or by the change in the rules of the game, the process of democratic politics bounces back. Research on the potential for a responsive political system to gain strength from protest movements and the ability of the Indian political process to accommodate 'rational protest' as a complement to institutional participation provides an additional explanation to the resilience of multi-party democracy and civil society in India.[46]

Speculation about the future of democracy and civil society in India is further complicated by the continued presence of the Congress Party at centre stage. The existence of a large, catch-all political party can be a source of some structural instability because, fragmentation of other parties is crucial to its own power and, the formation of unstable multi-party coalitions is its preferred strategy. Though the Congress Party, compared to its vote and seat share of the first party system (1952–1975) has experienced a net decline, it continues to be an important factor in Indian politics. The return of Congress as a catch-all party at least in some parts of India cannot be excluded. We can look forward to a certain period of instability of the party coalitions but not of a kind that affects the legitimacy of the system or the stability and effectiveness of policy-making.[47]

Finally, while the democratic character of the Indian political system has probably acquired the requisite resilience to withstand challenges from non-democratic ideologies of the left and the right, and has actually transformed these anti-system movements into legitimate partners in government, the future of political parties as the preferred mode of democratic government is not so secure. There is the impatience of the newly enfranchised electors who do not think highly of elected party politicians, visible evidence of corruption in high quarters within the political parties and the Gandhian nostalgia for a non-party, decentralised, direct democracy, based on village *panchayats*. Some of these ideas that were written into the constitution have gradually found their way into law, political institutions and practice. These potential conflict between the principles of partyless direct democracy and party based parliamentary democracy did not matter very much during the early years after independence when the first independence

[46] See Alan Marsh, *Protest and Political Consciousness*, Beverley Hills 1977; Max Kaase, *Political Ideology, Dissatisfaction and Protest*, Mannheim 1972; Subrata Mitra, *Power, Protest, Participation: Local Elites and the Politics of Development in India*, London 1992, for applications of these theoretical conjectures.

[47] The Fourth Republic of France, contemporary Italy, Israel and Japan provide interesting points of comparison.

generation presided over by Jawaharlal Nehru was in charge. India could have her consensus based, accommodating Congress System which linked it to the tradition of united struggle against the British and the Gandhian legacy of non-partisan character of the village community, and, the Nehruvian commitment to party based parliamentary democracy. As if in recognition of the British and the implicit faith in the British constitutional practice, the Indian constitution provided for no guaranteed role nor dedicated state finance for political parties.[48] As we have seen from the record of India's short-lived Emergency in the centre and countless replications of it at the regional level, Nehru's successors have taken greater liberties with the internal restraints on authoritarianism that is built into the informal, customary basis of British parliamentary practice.

It follows from the above that India's multi-party democracy will continue to have a grey area surrounding it, not so much on its democratic institutions and practices as on the stability of the party system on which it is based. If the present regime, based on multi-party democracy, fails to deliver the goods, it is certainly possible for an authoritarian populist to seize the opportunity and raise the banner of non-party democracy as the most effective instrument of the popular will and cultural nationalism as the legitimising device of its power. In order to improve the odds against such a possibility, it will probably not a bad thing for India to take a leaf out of the German book of rules and add a suitable amendment to the Indian Representation of the People Act, reinforcing the necessity of political parties.

48 There is a representation of people act, but no legal provision equivalent to the *Deutsche Parteienrecht* which could strengthen intra-party democracy by ensuring the holding of internal elections, accounting of party funds and most important, by public subsidies to political parties.

The Presidential System as a Mirage or Constitutional Nightmare in South Asia

Dieter Conrad

Images of strong presidential power as a kind of panacea to the evils of unstable government and the "soft state" have ever haunted the political discourse in South Asian post-colonial states. This phenomenon seems complementary to the self-evident legitimacy attributed to the constitutional system inherited from the British colonial patron: parliamentary democracy of the Westminster type. Arguments for an alternative, conveniently labelled Presidential type of government, nevertheless keep recurring. Their general background is the widespread inclination to identify effective and dependable government with concentration of power in a chief executive figure. Given this common predisposition, however, the advocacy of a powerful presidency has taken two broadly distinguishable forms.

1. The Role of the President

a) The President as Guardian of the Constitution

This model would imply a dual, or graduated role of the President. While in normal times he would leave the actual government to political forces functioning, e. g., under a system of parliamentary democracy, he retained, for extraordinary cases, sovereign prerogatives as a sort of reserve power in situations where the constitution or the state itself appeared to be in peril. Naturally he would thus become, even before actual emergency, the focus of power in the state. Perceptions of this kind are clearly influenced by the legacy of colonial history and the partial and conditional devolution of government responsibilities to representative, "parliamentary" bodies – who remained, as it were, in the role of probationers while the colonial executive (Governor-General and Governors with their "special powers") retained responsibility of last resort for the vital interests and stability of the state (i. e. the imperial interest). But this model could also draw support from a less suspect example, namely the German Weimar Constitution of 1919 with its strong Presidential power constructed as a counterpoise to Parliamentary government.[1]

b) The President as Actual and Solely Responsible Chief Executive

This is what is usually referred to as Presidential system. Its main attraction is that the President governs without the fetters of parliamentary accountability and enjoys a secure tenure within his fixed term of office. The designation "Presidential System" borrows some respectability from the example of the Presidential system under the Constitution of the USA. But in the South Asian reality the American system of checks and balances and the separation of powers are regularly dispensed with. "Presidential System" thus has become an euphemistic term for executive dictatorship.

2. The Colonial Legacy: Dominion Constitutions of India and Pakistan

India and Pakistan started on their way into independence with an identical constitutional framework, namely the Indian Independence Act, 1947 setting up each state as a Dominion with a provisional Constitution which was an adapted version of the Government of India Act, 1935. Under this provisional constitution the executive power of the Federation was to be exercised by a Governor-General who like in other Dominions was to officiate as the representative of the Crown.[2] The Act also provided for "a council of ministers, to aid and advise the Governor-General in the exercise of his functions",[3] but there was no provision indicating that the Governor-General was to be bound by the council's advice. This was left to constitutional convention and was in no way intimated or referred to in the express legal text; on the other hand there was an express provision debarring the Courts from inquiring into the existence or contents of advice.[4] In purely legal terms, therefore, the Governor-General was all-powerful. Limitations imposed on the exercise of his powers by the conventions of cabinet government were only to be implied.

[1] For the influence of the model of the Weimar constitutional presidency on the members of the Indian Constituent Assembly see, e. g., K. M. Munshi, *The President Under the Indian Constitution*, Bombay 1963 p. 16ff. The unhappy experience with the Presidential emergency powers in the final crisis of the Weimar Republic does not appear to have been reflected in the deliberations.

[2] Indian Independence Act, 1947 Sec. 5; Pakistan (Provisional Constitution) Order, 1947 Sec. 7.

[3] Pakistan (Provisional Constitution) Order Sec. 9.

[4] Ibid. Sec. 10 cl. 4.

One could perhaps conclude that under a true construction of the Act these conventions were invariably to be followed, since all the former exceptions, namely the special powers of the Governor-General (exercising, in certain matters, individual judgement or discretion independently of ministerial advice) had been removed from the Act.[5] But the question remains why no positive indication of the binding nature of ministerial advice was given. Express provisions to this effect were not unknown in Commonwealth constitutional practice. Sec. 13 of the British North America Act, 1867, e. g., read: "The Provisions of this Act referring to the Governor-General in Council shall be construed as referring to the Governor-General acting by and with the Advice of the Queen's Council for Canada." A similar provision could be found in Sec. 63 Constitution Act of the Commonwealth of Australia, 1900,[6] and a comprehensive and explicit formula had been inserted only a year before in the Ceylon (Constitution) Order in Council, 1946.[7] The omission of any such formula in the provisional constitutions of India and Pakistan may perhaps be traced to the provision made in the Indian Independence Act for the eventual appointment of the same person to serve as Governor-General for both Dominions.[8] Jinnah had, for that eventuality, proposed a clause expressly absolving the Governor-General from the conventional duty to follow advice. The reason for this was the possibility of conflicting advice tendered by the two Dominion ministries. Congress, significantly, had even then objected to such a clause.[9]

It is not clear, why the deliberate lacuna was still retained in both Dominion constitutions after the idea of a common Governor-General had been dropped. Whatever the reasons the resulting ambivalence may serve to explain the remarkable historical fact that under this identical framework the two countries experienced directly opposite developments: while India from the beginning practised the Constitution strictly as a Parliamentary system under the conventions of Westminster, in Pakistan the same constitutional provisions served to introduce a kind of Presidential rule.

The root causes for this contrasting development are often seen in the initial choice of position made by the two principal political leaders on either side: Jinnah's decision to become the first Governor-General of the new state Pakistan, while in India Jawahrlal Nehru opted for the office of Prime Minister. This choice, it is said, predetermined the subsequent constitutional

5 India (resp. Pakistan) Provisional Constitution Order, 1947 Sec. 3 (2).

6 "The provisions of this Constitution referring to the Governor-General in Council shall be construed as referring to the Governor-General acting with the advice of the Federal Executive Council."

7 Sec. 4 (2): "All powers, authorities and functions vested in His Majesty or the Governor-General shall... be exercised as far as may be in accordance with the constitutional conventions applicable to the exercise of similar powers, authorities and functions in the United Kingdom by His Majesty."

8 Indian Independence Act, 1947 Sec. 5 *Proviso*.

9 A. Jalal, "Inheriting the Raj: Jinnah and the Governor-Generalship Issue," *Modern Asian Studies* 19,1985, p. 29–53, with references to *Transfer of Power*, vol. 11 (1982) on the drafting of the Indian Independence Bill.

development, placing the focus of power in the Head of State (Governor or later, President) in Pakistan, in the Prime Minister in India.

In particular, Jinnah's decision is often criticised as paving the way for Pakistan's subsequent Presidential or authoritarian regimes. Part of this criticism may go back to Mountbatten's initial disappointment and hurt vanity about the failure of his original plan to play a mediating role as common Governor-General for the two Dominions.[10] Jinnah, however, had good and rational grounds for his option under the circumstances: generally, Muslim League politicians distrusted the impartiality of Mountbatten – and they can hardly be blamed for this in view of what has since transpired about the very personal and intimate relationship between Nehru and Lord and Lady Mountbatten. In any case the independence of the new state of Pakistan would be more clearly marked, if it was represented by its own Governor-General. Finally what perhaps weighed most with the constitutional lawyer Jinnah were the enormous interim powers granted to the Governor-General by Sec. 9 of the Indian Independence Act: this included powers to adapt and change the Constitution and regulate the monetary system by Order, up to 31st March, 1948.[11]

Taking all in all it appears that Jinnah's decision to become Governor-General must be related to the very precarious situation of the newly founded state and his own exceptional role in creating that state and guiding its initial development. In this context his position must be understood as an interim and exceptional arrangement due to the exigencies of the situation and his towering personal authority, rather than as setting a constitutional precedent. This sense of his exceptional and charismatic role is reflected in his provocative remark to Mountbatten, reversing the traditional order of constitutional convention: "in my position it is I who will give the advice and others will act on it."[12]

Be that as it may the example set by Jinnah's initial choice could hardly have sufficed to inaugurate a tradition, since Jinnah died already a year later, on 11 September 1948. His successor Nazimuddin was a much weaker figure, and with Liaquat Ali Khan staying on as Prime Minister the balance of power could be expected to gravitate, like in India, to the Prime Minister's office. It was only after Liaquat's assassination in 1951 that a definite turn towards an authoritarian set up occurred.

10 Mountbatten's irritation clearly appears in his Personal Report No. 11 of 5th July 1947 where he accuses Jinnah of "suffering from megalomania in its worst form." (*Transfer of Power*, ed. N. Mansergh/P. Moon, vol. 11, London 1982, p. 893ff. Even less restrained his remarks in the later interviews (1971 to 1973) with L. Collins and D. Lapierre in *Mountbatten and the Partition of India*, Delhi 1982, p. 47ff.

11 A careful and balanced analysis of Jinnah's options in Khalid bin Sayeed, *Pakistan. The Formative Phase 1857–1948*, 2nd ed. Karachi 1978, p. 223ff.

12 Mountbatten, Personal Report, p. 162. Jinnah was reacting to a suggestion by Mountbatten, that he had chosen the wrong thing since if he went as a Constitutional Governor-General his powers would be restricted and he would be bound to act on the advice of his Prime Minister, while as Prime Minister he really could "run Pakistan".

3. Developments under the Indian Constitution

As compared with Jinnah, Nehru was able to play a quite different role not least because he lived and was in power much longer. Nevertheless for Nehru also an active effort was required in order to fend off Presidential aspirations and to establish a firm tradition of parliamentary government. In the early years when he had to contend with a rivalling conservative group within Congress, attempts to use the Presidential power as a check on parliamentary leadership were very much in the cards. Again it is to be noted that the Indian Constitution, as originally enacted, had retained the strange lacuna from the Provisional Constitution, omitting any express indication that ministerial advice was to be binding on the President. For a person uninitiated in the subtleties of British constitutional tradition the original Indian Constitution would read like a presidential one, since all executive action is expressed in the name of the President and the limitations imposed through the preponderance of the ministry are nowhere mentioned.[13] This silence of the constitutional text was deliberate. It was studiously defended during the deliberations of the Constituent Assembly against the doubts and queries raised by several members including, notably, the future President Rajendra Prasad. The policy of avoiding any reference to the convention appeared most conspicuously when the President's Instrument of Instructions provided in the Draft Constitution as a sort of conventional code of conduct was removed at the very last moment, in October 1949. Such an Instrument of Instructions had been recommended by B. R. Ambedkar as a substitute for a provision on the binding force of conventions. When in a surprise move it was dropped no explanation was offered, apart from an "assurance" given by the same B. R. Ambedkar during the debate that there was "not the slightest doubt" that a President by disregarding ministerial advice would commit a violation of the Constitution and would be liable to impeachment.[14] Quite on the contrary some not so slight

13 For illustration see, e. g.: "Art. 53 *Executive Power of the Union*. – (1) The Executive power of the Union shall be vested in the President and shall be exercised by him either directly or through officers subordinate to him in accordance with this Constitution. (2) Without prejudice to the generality of the foregoing provision, the supreme command of the Defence Forces of the Union shall be vested in the President and the exercise thereof shall be regulated by law. "… Art. 111. *Assent to Bills*. – When a Bill has been passed by the Houses of Parliament, it shall be presented to the President, and the President shall declare either that he assents to the Bill, or that he withholds assent therefrom … Art. 352. *Proclamation of Emergency*. – (1) If the President is satisfied that a grave emergency exists whereby the security of India or of any part of the territory thereof is threatened, whether by war or external aggression or internal disturbance, he may, by proclamation, make a declaration to that effect…."

14 For a detailed and thoughtful account of the whole issue see Granville Austin, *The Indian Constitution: Cornerstone of a Nation*, Oxford 1966, p. 132ff. Extensive quotations from the *Constituent Assembly Debates*, in particular Ambedkar's attempts to answer the doubts raised by Rajendra Prasad, may be found in the concurring opinion by J. Krishna Iyer, in *Shamser Singh v. State of Punjab*, AIR 1974 SC 2192, at 2212ff.

doubts remain as to whether the ambiguity of the final text may not have been due to a deliberate strategy by a certain group with the object of keeping the President's position fluid and future options open.

The political test was not slow to follow. In the year following the inauguration of the Constitution the first Union President, Rajendra Prasad, in a letter to the Prime Minister Nehru indicated his claim to exercise his individual judgement in the matter of assenting to the proposed Hindu Code Bill and possibly, of withholding Presidential assent against ministerial advice. Prasad's argumentation – the full text of which has by now become available[15] – is not without logic or force. Prasad objected to the Hindu Code Bill because it would effect fundamental changes in Hindu society – notably through the proposed abolition of the Mitakshara joint family – and as a radical reform measure would be highly discriminatory being confined to one religious community. But the decisive argument was that the Constituent Assembly had been elected for the special purpose of framing the Constitution and while carrying on as provisional legislature till the first Parliament was elected had no authority to pass fundamental reform legislation of the kind contemplated. Prasad argued that by the conventions of British parliamentary government such fundamental measures could not be undertaken without obtaining an express mandate from the electorate at a general election. He thus pleaded the latter convention as a countervailing consideration against the convention that the President is bound to act on ministerial advice.

Nehru reacted strongly against such suggestions. He immediately sought and obtained legal advice from two leading constitutionalists: M. C. Setalvad, the Attorney-General and A. K. Ayyar. Both jurists unequivocally took the position that the President is in all matters required to act with the aid and advice of the Council of Ministers and, in particular, has no appellate authority over the Cabinet when giving his assent to Bills. An open conflict could be avoided at that juncture, since the Hindu Code Bill was not passed by the provisional legislature and lapsed upon its dissolution. After the first general elections the new Parliament did not again take up the comprehensive Bill but passed four separate Acts on Hindu Law reform covering much of the same ground but leaving out the controversial question of the Mitakshara joint family. The four Acts, now colloquially termed Hindu Code, received Presidential assent without apparent difficulty. If the critical issue had been, as it were, circumvented rather than squarely settled, the firm position taken by the Prime Minister had set a constitutional precedent against discretionary Presidential powers.[16]

[15] Note dated 14-9-1951, published in R. L. Handa, *Rajendra Prasad. Twelve Years of Triumph and Despair*, New Delhi 1978, App. 2, p. 217ff. The discussion in Austin, *Indian Constitution*, p. 140f., could only be based on a conjectural "reconstruction" from the replies by Ayyar and Setalvad and hence does not do full justice to Prasad's arguments.

[16] For a detailed account of the episode see Austin, *Indian Constitution*, p. 140ff.

Even so attempts have from time to time been repeated to vindicate an independent role of the President *vis-à-vis* the Council of Ministers, as a general protector or guardian of the Constitution.[17] The main arguments have been: that the Constitution has entrusted the President with the task of keeping the constitutional balance between the Union and States; this is concluded from the mode of his election by an electoral college consisting of the members of States Legislatures as well as of the Union Parliament. Secondly, his duty "to preserve, protect and defend the Constitution" is expressly spelt out in the Presidential oath of office prescribed by Art. 60 of the Constitution. Thirdly, it was argued that in cases where under the Constitution the President had to act on his "satisfaction" or after "consultation" with named functionaries other than the Ministers, the Constitution envisaged exercise of his own personal judgement rather than "blind" adherence to ministerial advice. This seemingly limited argument was in fact the most consequential one. The provisions requiring Presidential "satisfaction" pertain to the core area of Constitutional balance. They comprise the decision to proclaim a national Emergency (Art. 352),[18] to proclaim President's rule in a State (Art. 356) and to issue Ordinances during Parliamentary recess (Art. 123, 213). An independent role of the President in these areas would indeed have invested him with functions as a Protector of constitutional government. There is something to be said for such powers if they are used as a kind of brake against questionable advice tendered by a Prime Minister, rather than as rights of independent initiative. Some of the arguments advocating then, in the 60ies, such a function for the President as a check on arbitrary exercise of the Emergency power by a Prime Minister[19] from hindsight have acquired a prophetic ring after what happened in 1975.

On the legal side, however, the debate was closed in 1974 by a decision of the Indian Supreme Court firmly laying down that the President was invariably to act on advice in the exercise of his functions. Expressions such as being "satisfied" or "after consultation" referred to satisfaction or consultation with the responsible cabinet in the first instance, and did not create an area of Presidential discretion *vis-à-vis* the ministerial advice.[20] Interestingly, even after this judicial clarification and in a position of all but uncontested power during Emergency rule the then Prime Minister Indira Gandhi took care to finally close the lacuna left by the Constitution makers. By Constitutional amendment the article dealing with ministerial advice was supplemented by a clause stipulating that the President "shall, in the exercise of his functions, act in

17 See in particular K. M. Munshi, *The President under the Indian Constitution*, Bombay 1963, and K. Subba Rao, *Some Constitutional Problems. Sir Chimanlal Setalvad Law Lectures*, Bombay 1970, p. 244ff. The views of both these authors are deserving of attention, Munshi having been an influential member of the Constituent Assembly, Subba Rao being a former Chief Justice of India and Presidential candidate in 1969.

18 See quotation n. 12 *supra*.

19 See Subba Rao, *Constitutional Problems*, p. 298ff.

20 *Shamser Singh v. State of Punjab*, AIR 1974 SC 2192.

accordance with such advice."[21] The corresponding provision for the Governor (Art. 163) was not supplemented in this way – evidently such a clause might have strengthened the authority of State governments *vis-à-vis* Union influence through the Governor. In the circumstances of 1976 change as well as non-change are indicative of a clear determination to make the Prime Minister the undisputed centre of power.

Before this decision was arrived at, however, other options had apparently been explored albeit in a somewhat obscure and devious manner. Demands for a fundamental change in the Indian Constitution had been raised at the Congress Party Session in Kama Gata Maru Nagar in December 1975. In early 1976 an anonymous document "appeared", as it were, from nowhere and attracted public attention.[22] The identity of its author has not till today come to light, neither has it ever appeared in print. In the prevailing atmosphere of repression, distrust and apprehension, however, it was ascribed to sources close to the Prime Minister,[23] if not to the Prime Minister herself. In this memorandum a complete overhauling of the Indian Constitution and a switch-over to a Presidential system was urged. A president was to be elected for a fixed term by popular vote. During his term of office he was to enjoy untrammelled powers surpassing even the powers of the USA President. Ministers were to be responsible to the President, not to Parliament. But the President was also to have supervisory powers over the judiciary, presiding over a "Superior Council of the Judiciary" with powers to interpret the Constitution, determine the validity of legislation and remove or dismiss any judge. The President was – a scurrilous detail – even to have the power to punish for his own contempt, i. e. he was to have power summarily to punish offences affecting his self-perceived dignity. Furthermore, legislative restrictions on fundamental rights were to be facilitated, preventive detention laws were to be tightened and many things more – all this with the end "to ensure the unobstructed working of the executive" and, needless to say, "in the interest of the people".

The scheme seems to have met with a lukewarm response and some outright opposition in Congress circles. It was never officially owned and, after a while, silently dropped. Plans for a more moderate "overhauling" of the Constitution were then pursued through the Swaran Singh Committee, leading to the 42nd Amendment in the fall of 1976. Mrs. Gandhi later publicly disclaimed any intention of introducing a Presidential system in India. Nevertheless one may speculate about the reasons, why the debate was first started, then abandoned.[24] Perhaps the

21 Art. 74 (1) as amended by Constitution (Forty-second Amendment) Act, 1976, sec. 13.

22 On this episode and the document see R. Dhavan, *The Amendment. Conspiracy or Revolution*, Allahabad 1978, p. 40ff, with extensive quotations. Cf. also Kuldip Nayar, *The Judgement*, New Delhi 1977, p. 115.

23 According to K. Nayar, *The Judgement*, p. 115, it originated with B. K. Nehru, then Indian High Commissioner in London, and was later elaborated by Rajni Patel.

24 In the conclusion of R. Dhavan, *The Amendment*, p. 43: "Mrs. Gandhi had clearly been thinking about the presidential system and, perhaps, reading literature on it. But, equally, she may have decided, at some stage, that the presidential system could not be introduced in India."

proposal had only been a kite flown in order to probe public reactions. There was also some uncertainty about the position of the Supreme Court which had, since the Fundamental Rights case in 1973, claimed and exercised the power to strike down amendments changing the "basic structure" of the Constitution. A veto position had been built up which it was difficult to calculate in advance. But there had also occurred an ominous precedent in a friendly neighbouring country. Early in 1975 Sheikh Mujibur Rahman, the leader of the movement for Bangladesh and Prime Minister of the new state, had brought about an abrupt change in the Bangladesh Constitution, replacing its original parliamentary system by a so-called presidential system through a constitutional amendment, and assuming the office of President under the new dispensation.[25] In this case as in many others "presidential system" was nothing but window-dressing for autocracy, since all fetters on Presidential powers had been removed through a one-party system, enforced party discipline in Parliament and removal of judicial independence. Whether this system ever stood a chance of improving the desperate situation of Bangladesh nobody can tell.[26] Half a year after its introduction Sheikh Mujib was assassinated by a group of military officers with the tacit backing of some members of his own party and government. Possibly by assuming sole and unfettered responsibility for the political fate of his state Mujib had at the same time singled himself out as the principal target for vendetta and violent change. Since then the constitutional history of Bangladesh has seen a slow, step by step return to the original parliamentary system and the restoration of the Constitution of 1972. This has finally been achieved by the 12th Amendment in 1991.[27]

Perhaps the tragic and sanguinary end of Mujib's Presidential autocracy was a timely warning and saved India from similar experiments. Reflecting, however, on the two options apparently considered in the emergency year 1976 it appears that there is a common denominator in the desire to exclude all possible checks and constitutional fetters impeding reckless use of executive power. The "Presidential system" outlined in the anonymous memorandum of 1976 clearly was to serve that purpose. If such a Presidential system was impracticable or unpalatable in India, the alternative pursued was to make the Prime Minister's power as absolute as possible. This was to some extent achieved by the 42nd amendment. What was shunned in both alternatives was the acceptance of a constitutional balance, of government powerful within the framework of institutional constraints. The abrupt shift from Presidential autocracy to an all-powerful Prime Ministership had been attempted before in Pakistan: by Bhutto's Constitution of 1973. It is to that country's experience that we now turn our attention.

25 Constitution (Fourth Amendment) Act, 1975 (passed on 25-1-1975).

26 For a discussion and balanced appraisal of Mujib's "second revolution" see Moudud Ahmed, *Bangladesh: Era of Sheikh Mujibur Rahman*, Wiesbaden 1984, p. 231ff.

27 Constitution (Twelfth Amendment) Act, 1991.

4. Pakistan's Experience with Presidential Power

Since 1951 Pakistan had seen a steady drift towards authoritarian government by the head of state and the bureaucracy. After the assassination of Liaquat Ali Khan the Governor-General Nazimuddin "stepped down" to become the Prime Minister. In his stead a bureaucrat from the financial service, Ghulam Muhammad, became the new Governor-General. With him the "establishment", a combination of bureaucracy and the military, took power. Two years later the Governor-General was in a position to dismiss the Prime Minister though the latter had an undisputed majority in the Constituent Assembly. The fact that the Assembly was unable or unwilling to counteract this brazen violation of the conventions of responsible government is indicative of the weakness of the party system and, in particular, the Muslim League organisation. This, perhaps, was the most crucial difference to the Indian Parliamentary situation with the well-trained machinery of the Congress Party.

The authoritarian drift in Pakistan's development is sometimes attributed to Islamic tendencies which increasingly made themselves felt during the deliberations of the Constituent Assembly. Undoubtedly traditionalist concepts of Islamic government for obvious historical reasons generally presuppose a monarchical leader (*Amir, Khalif* or *Imam*) while the role of an assembly is customarily restricted to a consultative function (*shura*). Consequently in the debate of the Ulama Board convened to advise the Constituent Assembly the question of the personal qualifications of the Head of an Islamic State played a dominating, from the perspective of the modern state, disproportionate role.

But with the ruling group such problems remained peripheral. Ideas of a different order had a major influence which is often overlooked: namely, legal concepts drawn from the British monarchical and colonial tradition and still reigning in the minds of the colonial bureaucratic élite. This appeared clearly in the constitutional crisis of 1954. A year after Nazimuddin's dismissal the Constituent Assembly had made a belated attempt to redress the constitutional balance, by passing a constitutional amendment which *int. al.* expressly enacted the conventions of the Parliamentary system including the binding nature of ministerial advice tendered to the Governor-General.[28] This exercise in constitutional propriety provoked a drastic reaction by the Governor-General: after securing the support of the army chief he dissolved the Constituent Assembly. The rather unprecedented arrogation of overriding powers was explained in his Proclamation thus:[29]

[28] Government of India (Fifth Amendment) Act, 1954 (passed on 21-9-1954).

[29] Governor-General's Proclamation dated 24th October 1954.

The Governor-General having considered the political crisis with which the country is faced, has with deep regret come to the conclusion that the constitutional machinery has broken down. ...[30]

This is a well-known formula originally used to characterise the situation justifying Governor's or Governor-General's Rule under the Government of India Act, 1935. Such powers had been deleted from the Provisional Constitution in 1947. A year later they had been re-introduced in Pakistan by Jinnah, but only as applied to the Provinces.[31] No corresponding power for the centre had been re-introduced on which the Governor-General could have relied. Nevertheless, the Federal Court later justified the dissolution as legal.[32] Obviously this could not be done either under the Indian Independence Act which had no provision for a dissolution, or under the adapted Government of India Act (i. e. *Provisional Constitution*) from which the power of dissolution had been removed in 1947.[33] Therefore, recourse was had to the unwritten English doctrine of Crown prerogative. The influence of English legal advisors at the time was very strong. To name only the most prominent: Sir Ivor Jennings who later published a book on the constitutional crisis,[34] Sir Edward Snelson (Law Secretary in the Government of Pakistan), Diplock Q. C. appearing for the Federation in the dissolution cases.[35] The English doctrine invoked is this:

In ceded or conquered colonies the Crown may make constitutional provision by *Order-in-Council*. In the classic case of Campbell v. Hall,[36] this power had been limited to situations where representative institutions had not been granted. But following later remarks by the Privy Council[37] the principle could be extended to situations where representative assemblies had been dissolved *or become illegal*. This was based on a doctrine that there can never be a *lacuna* in a Constitution under the Crown: "If all else fails the Queen (i. e.: the Governor-General) *is the constitution*, for every power that is not vested in somebody else must be vested in her."[38]

The notion that in the absence of a Parliament – howsoever that absence has been contrived – the Head of the State regains full sovereign powers under prerogative, and may even make provisional constitutional arrangements by *Order*, has survived the transition from Dominion status to an independent republic. Under the Constitution of the Islamic Republic of Pakistan,

30 Proclamation dated 24th October 1954.

31 Pakistan Provisional Constitution (Third Amendment) Order, 1948 (10th July 1948).

32 Reference by H. E. the Governor-General, PLD 1955 -FC 435.

33 Pakistan (Provisional Constitution) Order, 1947, Schedule.

34 Sir Ivor Jennings, *Constitutional Problems in Pakistan*, Cambridge 1957.

35 Apart from the *Reference* case already cited, two previous cases belonging to this group are: *Federation of Pakistan v. Moulvi Tamizuddin Khan*, PLD 1955 FC 240 and *Usif Patel v. The Crown*, PLD 1955 FC 387.

36 K. B. 1774, 98 E. R. 1045.

37 *Sammut v. Strickland*, (P. C. 1938) 1938 A-C- 678: "... while the legislative institutions continue to exist ..."

38 Jennings, *Constitutional Problems*, p. 72.

1956, there could hardly be a claim to Crown prerogative anymore. Yet in 1958 the country witnessed the extra-ordinary spectacle that the President felt free to abrogate the new Constitution – the very Constitution to which he owed his position – yet still to remain President and to make provision, in that capacity, for a new constitutional set-up by a *Laws (Continuance in Force) Order.*[39] As an explanation of this legal miracle we again have the testimony of the (British) Law Secretary to the Govt. of Pakistan, Sir Edward Snelson, to the effect that the legal advisors interpreted the cases of 1954/55 to mean that the residual sovereign power lay with the Head of State.[40] The Head of State was thus interpreted to be some sort of supra-constitutional figure with an overall responsibility for the country transcending all constitutional limitations.[41] We may see in this the contours of the President as Guardian of the State: standing forth from the background in times of distress and intervening in order to "save" the polity if not necessarily the Constitution. The appropriate metaphor for this kind of guardianship would perhaps be the wolf posing as the watchdog.

President Mirza's coup was soon superseded by Ayub Khan's coup forcing Mirza unceremoniously to quit his office and leave the country. Ayub Khan proclaimed himself President and later introduced a Presidential Constitution according to his predilections. It is interesting, however, to note that the Constitution Commission appointed by the President in 1960 and reporting in 1961 also came out with a recommendation for a Presidential system.[42] The report makes strange reading. After analysing the many cases of executive interference with the Parliamentary process, and after glossing over the failure even once to hold general elections under the Constitution the authors still arrive at the conclusion that under the conditions of instability prevailing in Pakistan's political life and party system it is the executive to whom the *salus publica* is to be entrusted, and that there is more safety in a Presidential system. The ceaseless official propaganda attributing all the maladies of Pakistan's political life to the machinations of irresponsible party politicians evidently has had some effect. The report takes care, though, to explain that the recommendation is for a system on American lines, i. e. with a system of checks and balances and a strong independent Parliament.

The recommendation for Presidential system was the one recommendation in the Report which Ayub Khan accepted. This was logical as his original ideas did not contemplate a system of political parties at all – without which a Parliamentary system cannot function. Other recommendations like separation of powers and a strong independent Parliament as a balance to Pres-

39 Laws (Continuance in Force) Order, 1958j, President's Order (Post-Proclamation) No. 1 of 1958.

40 *Sir Edward Snelson v. Judges of the High Court of West Pakistan*, PLD 1961 SC 237, at 248.

41 Interview of Iskander Mirza with A. H. Ispahani in London, 23rd September 1967, partly published in *Dawn Overseas* 21.3.1981 p. 7. "I decided to take action. There were two courses open to me: Either to suspend the constitution or to abrogate it." The obvious alternative that he had to uphold the Constitution under his oath of office apparently did not occur to him.

42 *Report of the Constitution Commission, Pakistan. 1961*, Karachi (Manager of Publications) 1962, p. 19ff.

idential powers were not among Ayub's priorities. Accordingly in his Constitution of 1962 he introduced not anything resembling the American system but his own brand of a Presidential system – with a weak parliament composed of "Basic Democrats" and little checks and balances. From 1965 onwards he ruled with Emergency Powers.

After Ayub Khan's downfall in 1969 and the abrogation of his constitution a presidential system of sorts was continued, with the army commander and Chief Martial Law Administrator General Yahya Khan appointing himself as the new President.[43] He presided over the break-up of his country in the civil war of 1971. Certain elements in this tragedy may be traced to the long spell of presidential autocracy which had stifled the political process in the preceding decade. There was a lack of public political debate, of direct and open negotiation and, consequently, of party leaders experienced in the art of political compromise. Instead there was criminalization of unwelcome political demands, such as the Bengalis' demand for autonomy, there were separate and confidential talks with select politicians behind closed doors, in Larkana or in Dhaka, surprise decisions sprung on the public, like the postponement of the National Assembly session in Dhaka, finally there was the role of an anonymous military junta calling the shots from behind the scene. The result was an atmosphere of unpredictability, deadly distrust and suspicion which in itself was an impediment to reliable, negotiated solutions. A more devastating critique of the illusions of stability and security expected from a "presidential system" can hardly be imagined.

5. Search for New Solutions in Pakistan

After the disastrous events of 1971 Bhutto took over at first in the paradoxical role of a civilian President under authority of Martial Law ("Awami Martial Law"). But he attempted a new departure in the Constitution which was drafted under his guidance. It enacted a complete shift of emphasis from the Head of State to the Prime Minister who was to become the new centre of power. It was an attempt to introduce a Parliamentary system of Government, after the legitimacy of the Presidential regimes had been discredited. The President now was conceived as a constitutional figure head. Care was taken to insert a provision making ministerial advice binding (Art. 48). Art. 58 gave a right to the Prime Minister to demand a dissolution; no independent rights of dissolution was reserved to the President.

It is a revealing observation, nevertheless, that in spite of this new approach Bhutto remained hesitant to deliver himself to the Parliamentary system in its full consequences and risk. In summer 1972, during the deliberations on the new Constitution he provoked a crisis by

[43] Proclamation of Martial Law dated 25-3-1969 and Provisional Constitution Order, 1969 Sec. 3 (2).

publicly musing about the "luxurious" Westminster model, and by referring to other European Constitutions – a clear hint to the relevance of De Gaulle's Presidential Constitution of 1958. This led to the resignation of his Law Minister, M. A. Kasuri, under protest.[44] In the Constitution then an attempt was made to fortify the position of the Prime Minister beyond all proportion: not only was the "constructive no-confidence vote" borrowed from the German Basic Law, but for 15 years a vote of no-confidence was to be passed with ⅔ majority only. Under public pressure this was reduced to a provision that for 10 years votes against the P. M. would not be counted if the majority of the party voted in his favour. The parliamentary system was moulded in a way as to introduce a dictatorship by the Prime Minister. Soon the typical moves indicative of the dictatorial temperament were to follow: attempts to undermine judicial independence and to manipulate the higher judiciary;[45] this is comparable to Mrs. Gandhi's hostile attitude against the higher judiciary, the manipulation of appointments and transfers, the attempts to create a "committed" judiciary etc.

Finally there are reports from reliable sources that in spite of all his quasi-dictatorial powers Bhutto was still hankering after a Presidential system and that the rigging of the elections in 1977 provoking the fatal crisis of his regime was motivated by his desire to win a two-thirds majority in the National Assembly by all means, in order to be able to change the Constitution.[46] If so, the craze for Presidential powers would have been a major cause of his undoing.

We need not consider details of the "Presidential system" of Zia ul-Haq, i. e. his rule under Martial Law from 1977 to 1985. But the changes introduced into the Constitution by him bring us to the threshold of today's events. When he restored constitutional government by the "Revival of the Constitution Order, 1985"[47] (note again the use of the concept of a Presidential Order as creating constitutional law), he tried to shift the power balance back from the Prime Minister to the President, by incorporating various discretionary powers. In Art. 58 the right of the Prime Minister to demand a dissolution was now juxtaposed with an independent power of the President to

> "dissolve the National Assembly *in his discretion* where, *in his opinion* … (b) an appeal to the electorate is necessary."[48]

This provision would have given the President an uncontrolled power of interfering with the functioning of Parliament and a responsible ministry, at any time and for any motive. It

[44] On this episode *cf.* Hamid Khan, *Eighth Amendment. Constitutional and Political Crisis in Pakistan*, 2nd ed., Lahore 1955, p. 8–9.

[45] Constitution (Fourth Amendment) Act, 1975 and Constitution (Fifth Amendment) Act, 1976.

[46] Khalid B. Sayeed, *Politics in Pakistan. The Nature and Direction of Change*, New York 1980, p. 106 (Information by Leslie Wolf-Phillips, who had been contacted as an advisor by Bhutto).

[47] P. O. 14 of 1985, dated 2-2-1985.

[48] Art. 58 (2) (b) as amended by P. O. 14/1985 (italics supplied).

would have completely undermined the position of the Prime Minister as originally intended in the Constitution. Not surprisingly, it was in the centre of the negotiations between the newly elected Assembly and the President and – still at that time – Chief Martial Law Administrator, involving the *ex post* validation of Martial Law and constitutional reforms through the 8th Amendment.[49] The National Assembly eventually was able to extract a substantial concession by inserting the following qualification in Art. 58:

> (the President may dissolve the National Assembly in his discretion where, in his opinion) …
> "(b) *a situation has arisen in which the Government of the Federation cannot be carried on in accordance with the provisions of the Constitution and* an appeal to the electorate is necessary."[50]

This is the well-known old formula from Governor's rule. It might have introduced an interesting compromise between Presidential and Parliamentary system, a constitutional balance reserving to the President a power of last resort to step in in case of a system crisis. The old problem, of course, would recur: how to prevent that the crisis would originate with the President himself, that the "Guardian" would not use his power to protect the Constitution but to instrumentalise it, as he so often had done, for his own political purposes?

This very issue had been a subject of a famous debate in Germany, in the years of the final crisis of the Weimar Republic. At that juncture, one prominent constitutional writer, Carl Schmitt, put forth the proposition that the President, rather than the Supreme Court (*Reichsgericht*), was the true "Guardian of the Constitution", since by his emergency powers and command over the armed forces he would be best in a position to take speedy and effective remedial action. Schmitt was confronted by his colleague Hans Kelsen with the argument that this really was a rehash of 19th century monarchist ideology as expounded in Benjamin Constant's doctrine that the monarch was a *pouvoir neutre* and could play the role of a disinterested arbiter between contending political forces. If it was felt necessary, argued Kelsen, to have a specific functionary watching over the constitutionality of the acts of constitutional organs, it was elementary that this function could not be entrusted to one of the organs which fell to be controlled and which had actual power to subvert the Constitution.[51] These observations can be amply illustrated with instances from Pakistan's constitutional history. Far from being a neutral power, the President has regularly either played his own political game or, where his own position was not sufficiently strong, he has been used as an agent by other powers, notably the Military. The danger that the extraordinary power under Art. 58 (2) (b) would again be misused

49 Constitution (Eighth Amendment) Act, 1985. See generally Hamid Khan, *Eighth Amendment*, p. 43.

50 The inserted passage has been italicised by me.

51 Carl Schmitt, *Der Hüter der Verfassung*, Tübingen 1931; Hans Kelsen, "Wer soll der Hüter der Verfassung sein?" *Die Justiz* (Berlin) 6, 1931, p. 5ff.

to thwarting the political process could only be averted by an active role of the Courts clearly marking out the constitutional limits of the Presidential power.

A hopeful beginning in this direction was indeed made in 1988 in the case of *Federation v. Mhd. Saifullah Khan*.[52] This case dealt with President Zia's last act of dissolving his own Parliament in 1988, but was decided after the death of Zia in an air crash. Perhaps this fact helped the Court to muster courage and strike down the Presidential dissolution order. It was held that Art. 58 (2) b contemplates a "break down of constitutional machinery" – a total blockade of government, not just bad government or violation of certain constitutional provisions. This strict criterion had not been met by the four grounds mentioned in the Presidential Order, namely: corruption in Parliament, breakdown of law and order in Sindh, lack of progress in Islamisation, public morality deteriorating to an unprecedented level. It was obvious that to accept vague allegations like a Presidential assessment of a decline in public morals as a ground for dissolution would have deprived the constitutional limitation of all practical meaning.

Had the Court stuck to that position, it could have restricted Presidential intervention to cases of manifest necessity and could thereby have ensured an equilibrium of political powers. But already the next case – dissolution in 1990 and dismissal of the government of Benazir Bhutto – saw an obvious involvement of military and bureaucratic interests in the familiar conspiratorial style. Regrettably, in this situation the High Courts and later the Supreme Court saw fit to beat a retreat. Now it was held that a complete breakdown of constitutional machinery was not necessary, but that it was sufficient to establish "extensive, continued and pervasive failure to observe not one but numerous provisions of the Constitution, creating the impression that the country is governed not so much by the Constitution but by methods extra-constitutional."[53]

This was in direct contradiction to the holding in Saifullah's case without, however, overruling it. It endorsed the habit of the President to have prepared long lists of misdeeds, voluminous and often propagandistic indictments of the government, in order to justify an order of dissolution. But the next exercise of this kind, the dismissal of Nawaz Sharif's government in 1993, led to a reassertion of judicial power: the Court returned to the strict rationale of Saifullah's case, struck down the Presidential Order and, for the first time, re-installed the National Assembly and Government.[54]

Relying on this ruling Benazir Bhutto felt confident in 1996 that the Supreme Court would again strike down the dissolution order by the President.[55] But one could witness a rather

52 PLD 1989 SC 166 (1988).

53 *Khawaja Ahmad Tariq Rahim v. Federation*, PLD 1992 SC 646.

54 *Nawaz Sharif v. President*, PLD 1993 SC 473.

55 President Leghari dissolved the National Assembly by an Order dated 5-11-1996, *Dawn* (Karachi) 5-11-1996, p. 1.

strange behaviour of the Court: dragging on the decision of this urgent case by all sorts of dilatory proceedings – until 5 days before the scheduled elections. Apart from these dilatory tactics the Court reverted to the rule in Ahmad Tariq Rahim's case, holding that extensive, continued and pervasive failure to observe not one but many provisions of the Constitution is enough, and that a complete breakdown of constitutional machinery is not necessary to justify a Presidential dissolution order.[56]

By this decision the contours of the Presidential power had again been blurred so as to create a situation of profound uncertainty for every incumbent of the office of Prime Minister. The Court in the event had at its disposal two interpretations directly contradicting each other so as to be able to strike down or uphold a dissolution order at its convenience. This was a result which should have been avoided at any cost, since it inevitably made the courts appear as players in the political game of other powers. It destroyed their guardian role together with the guardian role of the President.

Be that as it may, after the elections of February 1997 had produced a two-thirds majority of the new government in Parliament both houses by a swift move on April 1, 1997 passed, with near unanimity, a Constitutional Amendment abolishing the Presidential power of extraordinary dissolution.[57] One might say that the last vestiges of a Presidential system have thereby been removed in Pakistan. Pakistan thus has joined the mainstream of constitutional development in the South Asian subcontinent which is everywhere leading to Parliamentary systems. This would apply to Bangladesh after the 12th Amendment, and to Nepal, after the revolution of 1990 reduced the once formidable almost sovereign position of the Monarch to the role of a constitutional Head of State bound by the Constitution to act in accordance with ministerial advice.[58] Sri Lanka is a particularly instructive case. After the inherited Constitution of the Westminster type[59] this country experimented with an almost dictatorial position of Prime Minister and National State Assembly in the Constitution of 1972[60] and, again, with a system of executive Presidency patterned somewhat after the French model in the Constitution of

[56] Only the Short Order of this judgement was available at the time of writing. *Mohtarma Benazir Bhutto v. President of Pakistan*, 1997 *Supreme Court Monthly Review* 353 (29-1-1997).

[57] Constitution (Thirteenth Amendment) Act, 1997 (received assent on 3rd April 1997). The voting balance was 190 votes to none in the 217 member National Assembly, 79 to none of the 87 Senate members.

[58] Constitution of the Kingdom of Nepal, 2047 (= 1990), Art. 35: "*Executive Power*:
(1) The executive power of the Kingdom of Nepal shall, pursuant to this Constitution and other laws, be vested in His Majesty and the Council of Ministers.
(2) The powers of His Majesty, under this Constitution, except those which are specifically mentioned as to be exercised exclusively by Him or at His discretion or on the recommendation of any institution or official, shall be exercised by and with the advice and consent of the Council of Ministers. Such advice and consent shall be submitted through the Prime Minister."

[59] Ceylon (Constitution) Order in Council, 1946 as amended by Ceylon Independence Order in Council, p. 194–7.

[60] Constitution of the Republic of Sri Lanka (Ceylon).

1978.[61] Under either of these systems what took place was a strong centralisation of executive power, while the Constitution of 1972 as well as of 1978 lacked effective balancing institutions, notably a fully developed judicial review by the independent higher courts.[62] Sri Lanka also, if the plans for constitutional reform materialise, is going to return to parliamentary democracy of the Westminster type.[63] It seems that the parliamentary system, after many unhappy experiences in various countries, has become the hallmark of constitutional legitimacy. The bad name which presidential system meanwhile has acquired in the popular perception is graphically illustrated by a statement of a Pakistani politician during the recent constitutional crisis: there is "no threat to democracy in the country and presidential form of government or [*sic*] martial law will not be imposed" (Sahibzada Munir Khan, Senior Vice President of the Sindh Muslim League).[64]

Nevertheless one might also regret that the chances of a reasonable balance held out by the compromise formula of the 8th amendment in Pakistan went lost by the reckless actions of the Presidents and the vacillating position taken by the courts. To find such a balance is a task remaining on the constitutional agenda. The accumulation of power with the Prime Minister eclipsing all constitutional limitations is not a satisfactory answer to the problems of institutional stability and may lead, as a kind of mirror-image, to similar abuses as an autocratic Presidential system. This can be studied in the constitutional history of Sri Lanka, and it is a distinct danger arising in the present situation in Pakistan. The history of Art. 58 and its interpretation tends to show that the grant of extraordinary powers of intervention to a President is likely to lead to abuse which the courts will not, in fact, be able to stop. It has always, in the case of the Weimar Republic as well as in Pakistan, eventually led to military influence on vital decisions affecting the polity. There is, perhaps, one saving feature in the parliamentary system according to the British tradition as inherited on the subcontinent. The bifurcation of the executive between the Head of State and the Prime Minister, the inbuilt necessity of a dialogue between the two, as presupposed in the conventions of cabinet government, may leave a possibility, however tenuous, for a President to informally assert himself and exercise a moderating influence. This could be recently observed in India when for the first time the objections of the President against rash ministerial advice seem to have prevented the imposition of President's rule in a dubious case. The President, to be sure, would hardly have had even that measure of influence

61 The Constitution of the Democratic Socialist Republic of Sri Lanka (certified on 31st August, 1978).

62 Radhika Coomaraswamy, "Let Fools Contest: Parliamentary Democracy vs. the Presidential System – a Realist Approach," in: *Lanka Guardian* 15-10-1992, p. 6ff.

63 See Select Committee's Report on Constitutional Reform, presented to Parliament on 24.10.1997, Art. 60 (1): "The President shall always, except on the appointment of the Prime Minister and as otherwise required by the Constitution, act on the advice of the Prime Minister, or such other Minister to whom the Prime Minister may have given authority to advise the President on any particular function assigned to that Minister."

64 *Dawn* (Karachi), 19-11-1997.

but for the presence of a strong independent judiciary which in recent times has begun to scrutinise and even strike down unwarranted proclamations of President's rule.[65]

[65] *S. R. Bommai v. Union of India*, AIR 1994 SC 1918 relying, interestingly, on the Pakistan case of *Federation v. Mhd. Saifullah Khan* cited *supra* n. 52.